Nong Khai

Loei

Udon Thani

Mukdahan

Khon Kaen

NORTHEAST
THAILAND

Ubon
Ratchathani

Khorat

Chanthaburi

THAILAND

KHORAT PLATEAU
Pages 258–271

MEKONG RIVER VALLEY
Pages 272–293

WESTERN SEABOARD
Pages 314–331

EASTERN SEABOARD
Pages 302–313

BANGKOK
Pages 66–145

0 kilometers 100

0 miles   100

tani

Narathiwat

EYEWITNESS TRAVEL GUIDES

THAILAND

EYEWITNESS TRAVEL GUIDES

THAILAND

LONDON, NEW YORK,
MELBOURNE, MUNICH AND DELHI
www.dk.com

PROJECT EDITOR Rosalyn Thiro
ART EDITORS Ian Midson, David Rowley
EDITORS Jonathan Cox, Marcus Hardy, Tim Hollis,
Lesley McCave, Sean O'Connor
US EDITORS Mary Sutherland, Michael Wise
DESIGNERS Susan Blackburn, Des Hemsley,
Tim Mann, Malcolm Parchment, Adrian Waite
MAP CO-ORDINATORS Emily Green, David Pugh
RESEARCHER Warangkana Nibhatsukit

CONTRIBUTORS
Philip Cornwel-Smith, Andrew Forbes, Tim Forsyth,
Rachel Harrison, David Henley, John Hoskin, Gavin Pattison,
Jonathan Rigg, Sarah Rooney, Ken Scott

PHOTOGRAPHERS
Philip Blenkinsop, Stuart Isett, Kim Sayer, Michael Spencer

ILLUSTRATORS
Stephen Conlin, Gary Cross, Richard Draper,
Roger Hutchins, Chris Orr & Assocs, John Woodcock

Reproduced by Colourscan (Singapore)
Printed and bound by South China Printing Co. Ltd., China

First American Edition, 1997

Reprinted with revisions 1999, 2000, 2001, 2002, 2004, 2006

07 08 09 10 9 8 7 6 5 4 3 2 1

Published in the United States by
DK Publishing, Inc., 375 Hudson Street,
New York, New York 10014

ISSN 1542-1554
ISBN-13: 978-0-7566-0174-4

Transliteration of Thai words in this book mostly follows the General
System recommended by the Thai Royal Institute, but visitors will
encounter many variant spellings in Thailand.

THROUGHOUT THIS BOOK, FLOORS ARE REFERRED TO IN ACCORDANCE WITH
EUROPEAN USAGE, I.E. THE "FIRST FLOOR" IS ONE FLOOR UP.

**The information in every
DK Eyewitness Guide is checked regularly.**
Every effort has been made to ensure that this book is as up-to-date
as possible at the time of going to press. Some details, however,
such as telephone numbers, opening hours, prices, gallery hanging
arrangements and travel information are liable to change. The
publishers cannot accept responsibility for any consequences arising
from the use of this book, nor for any material on third party websites,
and cannot guarantee that any website address in this book will be
a suitable source of travel information. We value the views and
suggestions of our readers very highly.
Please write to: Publisher, DK Eyewitness Travel Guides,
Dorling Kindersley, 80 Strand, London WC2R 0RL, Great Britain.

CONTENTS

Lakshman and Sita, characters
from the Ramakien

Cho fas, Wat Pan Tao in Chiang Mai

◁ The *chedis* of Wat Chong Klang reflected in the tranquil waters of Chong Kham Lake, Mae Hong Son

Hat Maenam, a beach on Ko Samui in the Gulf of Thailand

Carved pumpkin

The Khmer shrine at Phimai

HOW TO USE THIS GUIDE

THIS GUIDE helps you get the most from your vacation in Thailand. It provides detailed practical information and expert recommendations. *Introducing Thailand* maps the country and sets it in its historical and cultural context. The five regional chapters, plus *Bangkok*, describe important sights, using maps, pictures, and illustrations. Features cover topics from architecture and crafts to wildlife and sports. Hotel and restaurant recommendations are found in *Travelers' Needs*. The *Survival Guide* has information on everything from transportation to personal safety.

BANGKOK

The center of Bangkok has been divided into five sightseeing areas. Each has its own chapter, which opens with a list of the sights described. The *Farther Afield* section covers the best sights outside the center. All sights are numbered and plotted on an area map. The information for each sight follows the map's numerical order, making sights easy to locate within the chapter.

A locator map shows where you are in relation to other areas of the city center.

All pages relating to Bangkok have red thumb tabs.

Sights at a Glance lists the chapter's sights by category: Wats and Palaces; Museums and Monuments; Parks and Districts; Markets and Notable Roads.

1 Area Map
For easy reference, the sights are numbered and located on a map. Sights in the city center are also marked on the Street Finder *on pages 138–45.*

2 Street-by-Street Map
This gives a bird's-eye view of the key areas in each chapter.

Stars indicate the sights that no visitor should miss.

A suggested route for a walk is shown in red.

3 Detailed Information
The sights in Bangkok are described individually. Addresses, telephone numbers, opening hours, and other practical information are also provided. The key to the symbols used is on the back flap of the book.

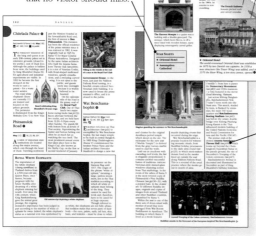

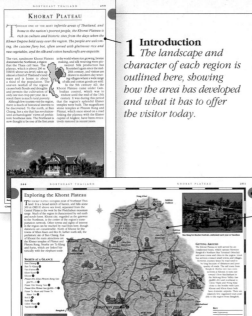

1 Introduction
The landscape and character of each region is outlined here, showing how the area has developed and what it has to offer the visitor today.

THAILAND AREA BY AREA
Apart from Bangkok, Thailand has been divided into ten regions, each of which has a separate chapter. The most interesting towns and places to visit have been numbered on a *Pictorial Map*.

Each area of Thailand can be identified quickly by its color coding, shown on the inside front cover.

2 Pictorial Map
This shows the main road network and gives an illustrated overview of the whole region. All entries are numbered, and there are also useful tips on getting around the region by car, train, and other forms of transportation.

3 Detailed Information
All the important towns and other places to visit are described individually. They are listed in order, following the numbering on the Pictorial Map. *Within each entry, there is detailed information on important buildings and other sights.*

Story boxes explore related topics.

For all the top sights, a Visitors' Checklist provides the practical information you need to plan your visit.

4 Thailand's Top Sights
These are given one or more full pages. Three-dimensional illustrations reveal the layouts and interiors of historic monuments. Interesting town and city centers are given street-by-street maps, featuring individual sights.

INTRODUCING THAILAND

Putting Thailand on the Map

THAILAND is located at the heart of Southeast Asia, between the Indian Ocean and the South China Sea. The country covers 513,000 sq km (198,000 sq miles) and has a population of 60 million, the majority of whom are concentrated in the fertile Central Plains and in the capital, Bangkok. The verdant North is mainly mountainous, and towering ranges run along the long western border with Burma. In contrast, the Northeast is a flat, poor, arid region. Much of the eastern border with Laos is defined by the Mekong River. Further south are the hills of northern Cambodia. Thailand's Southern peninsula is where many of the best beaches and islands are found.

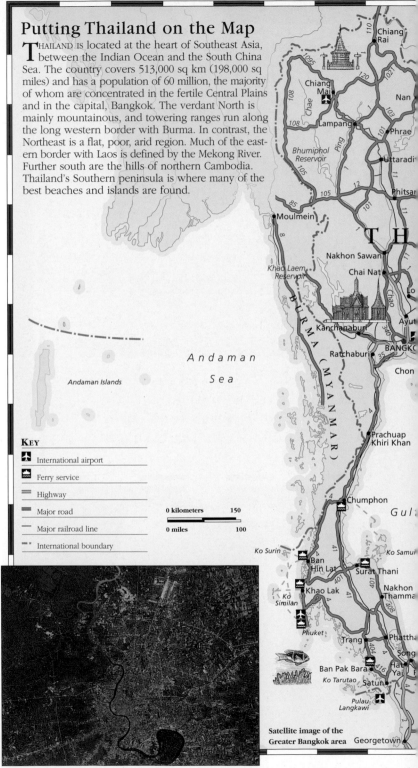

Chiang Rai

Chiang Mai

Nan

Lampang

Phrae

Uttaradit

Bhumiphol Reservoir

Phitsar

Moulmein

T H

Nakhon Sawan

Khao Laem Reservoir

Chai Nat

Lo

Kanchanaburi

Ayut

BIRMA (MYANMAR)

Ratchaburi

BANGK

Chon

Andaman Sea

Andaman Islands

Prachuap Khiri Khan

KEY

✈ International airport

⛴ Ferry service

━━ Highway

━━ Major road

─── Major railroad line

─ ∙ ─ International boundary

Chumphon

Gul

0 kilometers 150

0 miles 100

Ko Surin

Ban Hin Lat

Ko Samui

Surat Thani

Khao Lak

Nakhon Thamma

Ko Similan

Phuket

Trang

Phattha

Song

Ban Pak Bara

Ko Tarutao

Hat Yai

Satun

Pulau Langkawi

Satellite image of the Greater Bangkok area Georgetown

◁ **Spectacular limestone cliffs and turquoise waters characteristic of the Phi Phi islands in the Andaman Sea**

Satellite image of Southeast Asia

SOUTH
China
Sea

SOUTHEAST ASIA

CHINA

SOUTH
KOREA

JAPAN

NEPAL   BHUTAN

BANGLA-
DESH

TAIWAN

INDIA

BURMA   LAOS

THAILAND

Bangkok

VIETNAM

CAMBODIA

PHILIPPINES

SRI
LANKA

BRUNEI

MALAYSIA

SINGAPORE

INDONESIA

PAPUA
NEW
GUINEA

AUSTRALIA

Northern Thailand

AN EXTENSIVE ROAD NETWORK covers most of the North, North-east, and Central Plains of Thailand. Air-conditioned buses run between many of the major towns, and local buses are plentiful. Only in isolated border areas are road links unreliable. The railroad system connects Bangkok to the Central Plains and Chiang Mai, and most main towns in the North-east. Bangkok and Chiang Mai have international airports, and many major towns are served by domestic flights.

KEY TO AREAS

- Northwest Heartland
- Far North
- North Central Plains
- South Central Plains
- Khorat Plateau
- Mekong River Valley
- Bangkok

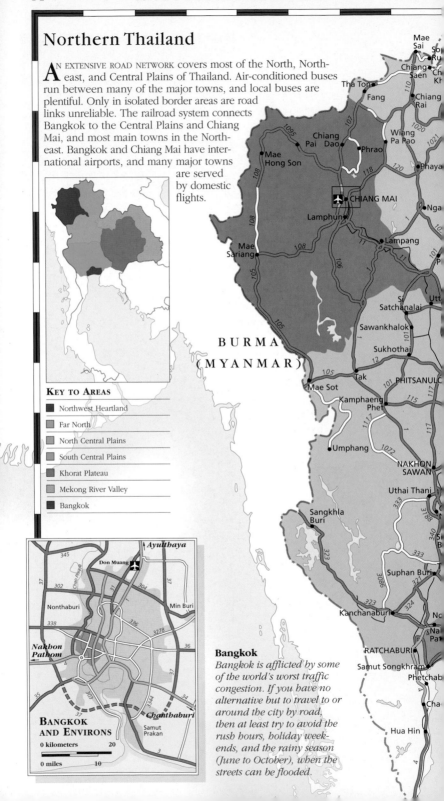

BURMA
(MYANMAR)

BANGKOK AND ENVIRONS

0 kilometers   20

0 miles   10

Bangkok
Bangkok is afflicted by some of the world's worst traffic congestion. If you have no alternative but to travel to or around the city by road, then at least try to avoid the rush hours, holiday week-ends, and the rainy season (June to October), when the streets can be flooded.

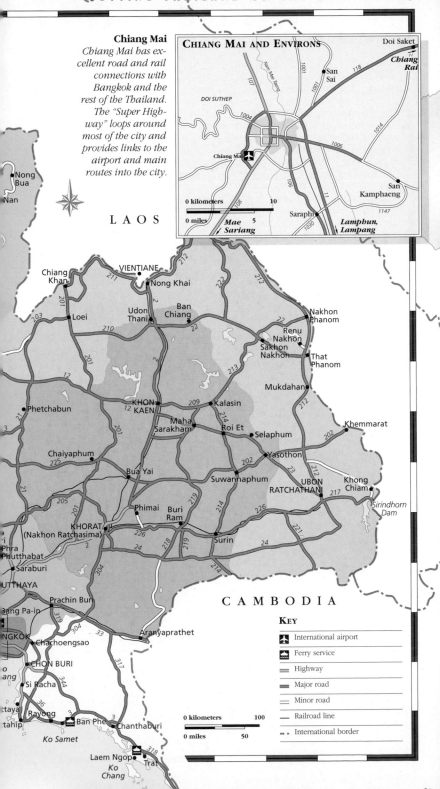

Chiang Mai

Chiang Mai has excellent road and rail connections with Bangkok and the rest of the Thailand. The "Super Highway" loops around most of the city and provides links to the airport and main routes into the city.

CHIANG MAI AND ENVIRONS

Doi Saket

Chiang Rai

San Sai

DOI SUTHEP

Nam Mae Taeng

107

1001

118

1004

Chiang Mai

1091

1014

1006

San Kamphaeng

106

108

11

1147

Saraphi

0 kilometers 10

0 miles 5

Mae Sariang

Lamphun, Lampang

LAOS

Nong Bua

Nan

Chiang Khan

VIENTIANE

211

212

Nong Khai

201

222

212

Loei

203

Udon Thani

Ban Chiang

210

22

Nakhon Phanom

Renu Nakhon

22

Sakhon Nakhon

That Phanom

213

Mukdahan

12

KHON KAEN

209

Kalasin

212

Phetchabun

201

12

Maha Sarakham

214

Roi Et

Selaphum

Khemmarat

3

21

Chaiyaphum

225

201

202

202

Yasothon

23

Bua Yai

Suwannaphum

212

UBON RATCHATHANI

Khong Chiam

217

21

205

201

Phimai

219

Buri Ram

214

226

221

Sirindhorn Dam

KHORAT (Nakhon Ratchasima)

226

Surin

24

221

i

Phra Phutthabat

2

304

219

214

Saraburi

UTTHAYA

CAMBODIA

Bang Pa-in

Prachin Buri

319

304

33

Aranyaprathet

NGKOK

Chachoengsao

ang

CHON BURI

317

Si Racha

344

ttaya

36

Rayong

3

Ban Phe

3

Chanthaburi

tahip

Ko Samet

318

Laem Ngop

Trat

Ko Chang

KEY

	International airport
	Ferry service
	Highway
	Major road
	Minor road
	Railroad line
	International border

0 kilometers 100

0 miles 50

Southern Thailand

THAILAND'S LONG COASTLINE, fine beaches, and idyllic offshore islands are a major attraction for visitors to the Gulf of Thailand and the South. Good-quality roads stretch from the Cambodian border in the east to the Malaysian border in the south and along the western Andaman Sea coast. Air-conditioned buses operate regularly between the main towns. There is one north-south railroad line from Bangkok that passes through, or has connections with, most of the towns on the Gulf of Thailand. The Eastern Seaboard has good road connections with Bangkok, but the railroad line terminates at Sattahip. Ferry services from ports to the main islands are frequent, and it is possible to buy tickets in Bangkok that combine train, bus, and ferry trips. Ko Samui and many towns have regional airports, and Phuket is served by international flights.

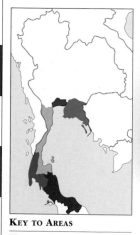

KEY TO AREAS

■	Eastern Seaboard
■	Bangkok
■	Western Seaboard
■	Upper Andaman Coast
■	Deep South

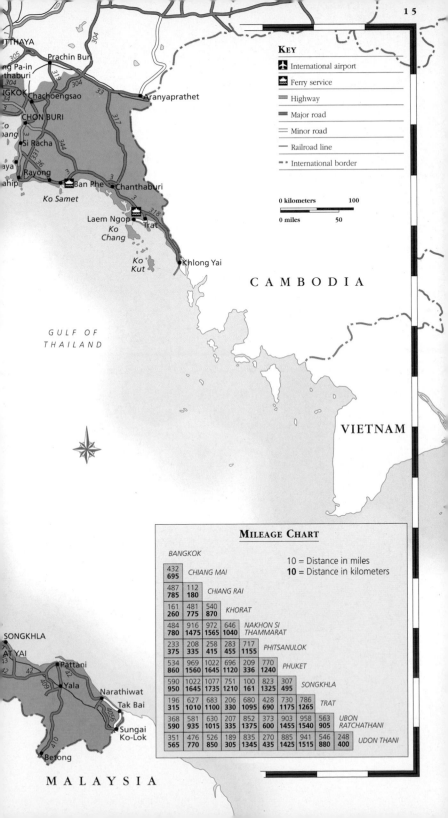

TTHAYA

Prachin Bun

ng Pa-in
thaburi
304
34
IGKOK
Chachoengsao
Aranyaprathet

CHON BURI

o
ang
Si Racha

aya
Rayong
ahip
Ban Phe
Chanthaburi

Ko Samet

Laem Ngop
Trat
*Ko
Chang*

*Ko
Kut*
Khlong Yai

*GULF OF
THAILAND*

C A M B O D I A

VIETNAM

KEY

✈	International airport
⛴	Ferry service
▬	Highway
═	Major road
═	Minor road
─	Railroad line
▬·▬	International border

0 kilometers   100

0 miles   50

SONGKHLA
AT YAI

Pattani

Yala

Narathiwat
Tak Bai

Sungai
Ko-Lok

Betong

M A L A Y S I A

MILEAGE CHART

10 = Distance in miles
10 = Distance in kilometers

BANGKOK										
432 **695**	*CHIANG MAI*									
487 **785**	112 **180**	*CHIANG RAI*								
161 **260**	481 **775**	540 **870**	*KHORAT*							
484 **780**	916 **1475**	972 **1565**	646 **1040**	*NAKHON SI THAMMARAT*						
233 **375**	208 **335**	258 **415**	283 **455**	717 **1155**	*PHITSANULOK*					
534 **860**	969 **1560**	1022 **1645**	696 **1120**	209 **336**	770 **1240**	*PHUKET*				
590 **950**	1022 **1645**	1077 **1735**	751 **1210**	100 **161**	823 **1325**	307 **495**	*SONGKHLA*			
196 **315**	627 **1010**	683 **1100**	206 **330**	680 **1095**	428 **690**	730 **1175**	786 **1265**	*TRAT*		
368 **590**	581 **935**	630 **1015**	207 **335**	852 **1375**	373 **600**	903 **1455**	958 **1540**	563 **905**	*UBON RATCHATHANI*	
351 **565**	476 **770**	526 **850**	189 **305**	835 **1345**	270 **435**	885 **1425**	941 **1515**	546 **880**	248 **400**	*UDON THANI*

A PORTRAIT OF THAILAND

SET WITHIN A LUSH, TROPICAL LANDSCAPE, *Thailand is a theater of cultural and sensual contrasts for the visitor. The long, rich heritage and abundant natural resources of this proud Buddhist nation jostle for space within the dynamism of a country undergoing economic boom and bust. In turns zestful and tranquil, resplendent and subtle, Thailand is always compelling.*

Thailand is located in a fertile monsoon belt midway between India and China, the two civilizations that have molded Southeast Asia. But the Thais have long delighted in their distinctive culture. For instance, though the Tai (rather than Thai) ethnic group probably originated in Southern China sometime in the first millennium AD, their tonal language is quite unlike any form of Chinese. Moreover, the elegant Thai script, though derived from that of ancient Southern India, is distinct.

Tuk-tuk

Today, Thailand is a member of the Association of Southeast Asian Nations (ASEAN), though Thais still take pride in a long tradition of independence. Unlike all her immediate neighbors, Burma (Myanmar), Laos, Cambodia, and Malaysia, the country never fell to a European colonial power. More fundamentally, though, the Thai sense of identity is allied with Theravada Buddhism and the monarchy. Both have been dignified institutions since the Sukhothai period (13th–14th century), an era when the first real Thai kingdom flourished. Indeed, the colors of the modern Thai flag *(thong trai rong)* symbolize the nation (red), the three forces of Buddhism (white), and the monarchy (blue).

Colorful *korlae* fishing boats in the clear waters of Southern Thailand

◁ Young men parading in Old Sukhothai for the annual Loy Krathong Festival

Today, the great majority of Thailand's 60 million inhabitants regard themselves as Thai. Hill tribes are the most obvious ethnic minority groups, but it is the Chinese who form the largest (and most integrated) group. The various peoples live relatively peaceably nowadays, though in 1939, in a wave of nationalism encouraged by Prime Minister Phibun Songkram, the country's name was changed from Siam to Prathet Thai (Thailand), or "land of the Thai people."

Downtown Bangkok, a rapidly modernizing, expanding area of the city

The country is divided into four main regions, and there are many subtle differences between the peoples and dialects of the Central Plains, North, Northeast, and South. Each region also has its own topographical identity. The North is an area of forested mountains, where hill-tribe minorities coexist with mainstream society. In the South, the narrow Kra Peninsula presents a 2,500-km (1,500-mile) coastline with a hilly interior of rainforests and rubber plantations. Malay-Muslim culture is a major influence here.

Between these two extremes are the Central Plains, the cradle of Thai civilization and a fertile, rice-growing region. Near the mouth of the Chao Phraya River, the capital, Bangkok, sprawls ever farther each year. Though its 200-year-old palatial splendor can still be discerned, the city is among the world's most congested and polluted. Different again is Northeast Thailand (also widely known as Isan), the poorest part of the country occupying the Khorat Plateau, its eastern border with Laos defined by the Mekong River. In this semiarid region traditional farming communities, many of them Thai-Lao, eke out a subsistence living.

ECONOMIC DEVELOPMENT

Rice and other agricultural crops were long the mainstays of the Thai economy, and farming is still regarded with great respect by Thais. From the mid-1980s, however, a concerted export drive, backed by an attractive climate for foreign investment, triggered an unprecedented economic boom. For several years Thailand enjoyed double-digit growth and was known as one of Asia's "tiger" economies. Economic growth came to an abrupt halt however, in a chain of events that began in May 1997 with financial speculation against the Thai *baht*. Flotation of the *baht* in July

Fisherman on the Mekong, the river defining Northeast Thailand's border

Noodle vendor at Damnoen Saduak Floating Market, a colorful and popular sight near Bangkok

pushed the economies of various Asian countries, including Thailand, Indonesia, and South Korea, into a state of crisis. By the end of 1997 even the mighty Japanese economy was suffering.

While Thai politicians denounced each other and blamed everyone from bankers to city-dwellers, the people of Thailand immediately suffered, with large-scale redundancies, pay cuts, and repossessions.

Tourism is one of the few Thai industries to have survived the economic crisis intact, and it continues to be the country's single largest foreign exchange earner. 1998 was declared "Amazing Thailand Year" by the Tourism Authority of Thailand (TAT). The number of tourists is already more than six million each year, and is likely to increase with the more favorable exchange rate of the *baht* to foreign currencies. Bangkok, Chiang Mai, and the beach resorts attract the vast majority of visitors, and have deluxe hotels ranking among the world's best.

Transport infrastructure remains a weak point, resulting in Bangkok's notorious traffic chaos. Commerce and communications are concentrated in Bangkok, with a population of seven million and rising, while the rest of the country remains largely rural.

Raw materials top the country's list of imports, and the leading exports include garments, electrical goods, mechanical equipment, seafood products, gems, and jewelry.

The environment has taken many blows in the last 50 years, during which forest cover has declined from 70 percent of the land to less than 20 percent. Many animal species have lost their habitats and been hunted almost to extinction. On the positive side, conservation awareness is increasing, and measures are being taken to preserve what remains of the nation's rich natural bounty.

Muslim Thai in Southern Thailand

SOCIETY AND POLITICS

In spite of the pressures of change, Thai society is relatively stable. The concept of the extended family is important in Thailand, as in other parts of Asia. Children live with their parents, often until marriage and living alone is rare. Elders are always accorded respect within families and in society.

Elephant in Bangkok, surprisingly not a rare sight

There is no caste system, but the social hierarchy, topped by the monarchy, is quite rigid. Social standing is dictated mainly by wealth and family connections. Women have less standing than men, despite playing a major role in the economy, mainly as laborers and white-collar workers.

Seated Buddha image, one of thousands in Thailand

Hierarchy permeates daily life in many ways. The traditional greeting, the *wai*, in which the hands are brought together near the chin, is always initiated by the inferior, and the height of the *wai* reflects the social gap between the parties. If the gap is extreme, inferiors may approach their superiors on their knees. Other rules of etiquette, such as never raising the voice, transcend class. Despite such rules that they apply to themselves, Thais are renowned for their tolerance of other cultures and friendliness to visitors. Offense is taken only if there is any perceived disrespect to the king or Buddhism.

There is no criticism of the king in Thailand's press. Constitutional since 1932, the monarchy is revered almost as much as when kings were *chakravatin,* or "king of kings." Kingship and

religion are inextricably linked in Thailand. The present monarch, King Bhumibol Adulyadej (Rama IX), served as a monk in his youth and presides over some major religious ceremonies. He is the longest-reigning living monarch in the world, having ascended to the throne in 1946, and has won widespread respect for his devotion to welfare and environmental projects throughout Thailand. The monkhood *(sangha),* some 250,000 strong, plays a crucial social role. Most teenage boys become novice monks for a while, which is seen as fortuitous for their families, especially their mothers, as well as a rite of passage.

Garland of jasmine, a ubiquitous sight

Some enter the monkhood properly later in life and may choose its austere precepts for life. Monks conduct numerous Buddhist rites, ranging from festivals to everyday blessings and other social events. In rural areas, they traditionally play an important role as teachers, a profession that in Thailand is perhaps held higher in regard than anywhere else in the world.

In contrast, politicians are held in far less respect, and the Thai press makes no hesitation in criticizing the running of the country. Parliamentary politics are plagued by old-style patronage and privilege and are still threatened by military coups: there have been 19, mostly peaceful,

Lisu women and children during the Thai New Year, in April

Monks chanting in Pali, the language of Theravada Buddhism

images and murals, and decorative arts, such as woodcarving, stucco relief, gilt, lacquer, colored glass mosaic, and mother-of-pearl inlay, are all used to striking effect.

The literary tradition of Thailand is confined mostly to classic tales, the most important of which is the Ramakien, an ancient moral epic with its origins in the Indian Ramayana. Such sagas provided the narrative content for the once-thriving performing arts, best preserved today in highly stylized classical dance-drama called *khon* and *lakhon*. Thailand's most notable literary figure is the 19th-century poet Sunthorn Phu.

coups or attempted coups since 1932. A mass prodemocracy demonstration in 1992 ended in bloodshed when the army opened fire. A great tragedy, the event did at least succeed in raising public awareness and securing a broader base for democratic reform.

THAI CULTURE AND ARTS

Thailand's classical arts have developed almost exclusively (and anonymously) in the service of Theravada Buddhism. Accordingly, the best showcase is the *wat*, where traditional architecture, typified by sweeping, multitiered roofs, countless Buddha

Lakhon dancers at a Buddhist shrine

Avant-garde and neo-traditionalist painting is booming, while the film industry thrives on a diet of comedies, thrillers, and period dramas. One very popular novel, *The Four Reigns* (1953), was written by former Prime Minister Kukrit Pramoj. A few films, such as *Luk Isan* (1978), set in the Northeast, and a number of books tackle social issues.

On the sports front, Thailand's world-renowned, unique style of kick boxing draws big crowds, while other traditional pastimes range from *takraw,* a game not unlike volleyball, but using the feet, to kite-flying. Numerous colorful festivals, many linked to both Buddhism and the changing seasons, are celebrated with exuberance. Whatever the activity, Thais believe that life should be *sanuk* – "fun." *Sanuk* can be found in all things, from eating – something for which Thais have a passion – to simply going for a stroll with friends.

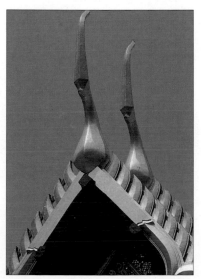

Cho fas, or roof finials, at the Grand Palace, Bangkok

Monsoon Country

Thailand's pre-eminent crop

THE RICE CYCLE, upon which the Thais have long believed their health, wealth, and happiness depends, is governed by the advance and retreat of the monsoon rains. As most people in the kingdom define themselves as *chao na,* rice farmers, the monsoon could be said to govern the cycle of life. This analogy is seen clearly in many Thai beliefs and practices. The rice goddess must be honored before cultivation if the crop is to be bountiful. The rice grain contains a spirit *(kwan)* and is planted in the rainy season to become "pregnant." The Thai word for irrigation *(chon prathan)* translates as "gift of water."

The Central Plains *of Thailand enjoy good conditions for wet rice cultivation. The flat paddies become flooded in the rainy season.*

Bundles of rice seedlings ready for transplanting

Transplanting takes place in the rainy season, when the heavy clay soil is saturated.

A "calling for rains" Buddha image – a standing posture with both arms pointing to the earth – is found in some Northern wats. The rice crop depends on rain.

Songkran, *or Thai New Year, in April, is a water festival marking the imminent end of the cool, dry season. People celebrate by pouring or throwing water over each other.*

MONSOON SEASONS

"Monsoon" comes from the Arabic *mawsim* (season). It refers to South Asia's seasonal winds (not heavy rain). In Thailand, the southwest monsoon is the rainy season; the northeast monsoon is dry, called the cool season; and between these periods is the hot season.

The southwest monsoon *comes from the Indian Ocean with rain-laden clouds, from about June to October. Most days there are downpours, though Thailand's east coast is fairly dry.*

Flooding in Bangkok at the end of the rainy season

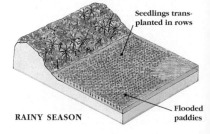

Seedlings transplanted in rows

RAINY SEASON

Flooded paddies

Machinery *has replaced animals on many farms, reflecting the increasing mechanization of the Thai farming industry. However, plowing and cultivating the land is still hard work.*

The main harvest *for lowland wet rice cultivation takes place in the middle of the cool season. Entire families and villages labor in the fields at this busy time, cutting off the golden stalks with sickles.*

Water channel
between fields

Seedlings need to
be semisubmerged

Threshing *is usually undertaken in the rice fields by the same laborers who have harvested the crop. The stalks are beaten to separate the grain from the chaff. The grain is then dried in the sun.*

TRANSPLANTING

Since most varieties of rice can only propagate in flood conditions, rice seedlings may initially be nurtured in nursery fields, where irrigation can be carefully managed and monitored. Later these seedlings will be transplanted into flooded paddies.

The northeast monsoon *from central Asia usually blows from November to March, bringing relatively cool, dry conditions to Thailand, though rains often affect the east coast.*

Between the two monsoons *the land heats up, creating an area of low pressure above it. Eventually the high pressure over the Indian Ocean moves inland, and the monsoon cycle begins again.*

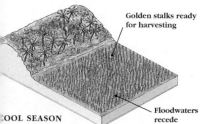

Golden stalks ready
for harvesting

Floodwaters
recede

OOL SEASON

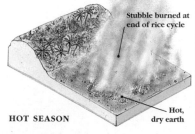

Stubble burned at
end of rice cycle

Hot,
dry earth

HOT SEASON

The Landscape and Wildlife of Thailand

THAILAND STRETCHES from south of the tropic of Cancer to about 1,000 km (620 miles) north of the equator; its tropical climate is affected by two monsoons *(see pp22–3)*. Varied topography and a gentle climate have led to a rich diversity of flora and fauna. Limestone hills in the North are clad in dense tropical forest. Open forest is more usual in the Northeast and Central Plains while the South and Gulf have superb coastlines and pockets of rainforest. Many habitats are threatened by industry and tourism; deforestation is rife, and some animal species face extinction *(see p209)*. As a result, many national parks have been established. The first, Khao Yai *(see pp174–5)*, opened in 1962.

Green parakeet

Coconut palms on the island of Ko Samui in the Gulf of Thailand

MONTANE TROPICAL FOREST
This type of forest is made up mostly of broadleaf evergreens and some deciduous trees such as laurel, oak, and chestnut. Mosses, ferns, and epiphytic orchids, growing on other plants, are common.

Atlas moths are the world's largest species. The female is larger than the male.

Serow, a type of antelope, are becoming increasingly rare in the hills of Northern Thailand.

Palm civets are nocturnal. They are found in tropical forests, but may also live near humans and eat cultivated fruit.

OPEN FOREST
The most common trees in the open forest, also called savanna forest, are dipterocarps, a family of trees native to Southeast Asia. The ground around them is often carpeted by coarse scrub.

Sambar, Thailand's largest deer, can be seen on the Central Plains and in the Northeast.

Capped gibbons are found mainly on the southern edge of Northeast Thailand. They are extremely agile.

Wild boars have been heavily hunted in the past. They feed mainly on grass.

THAI FLOWERS

The diversity of Thailand's flowers reflects its range of natural habitats. Most famous of all are its orchids; there are some 1,300 different varieties. Unfortunately, illegal collection has led to their growing rarity in the wild. Other flowers are used as spices and for medicinal purposes.

The mallow flower, a relative of the hibiscus, is common throughout Southeast Asia.

Lotus lilies' seed pods and stems are edible. Other lilies are grown for ornament only.

Mountain pitcher plants are insectivorous. Their prey falls into the "pitcher" where the plant's juices slowly dissolve it.

Orchids (see p210) *come mainly from Northern Thailand; they are prized for their beauty.*

WETLANDS

Freshwater swamp forests have been decimated by farming, though some survive in the South. River basins and man-made lakes and ponds can be found all over Thailand.

Dusky leaf-monkeys are found in the Thai-Malay peninsula. Three other species of leaf-monkey also live in Thailand.

Painted storks migrate to Thailand's swamps to breed. During this time the pigment in their faces turns pink.

Purple swamp hens are common. Long-toed feet allow them to walk on floating vegetation.

COASTAL FOREST

The seeds of trees such as pines and Indian almond are transported on sea currents; thus ribbons of coastal forest are found all over Southeast Asia. Thailand's coastal forests are now threatened by farming and tourism.

Green turtles are the only herbivorous sea turtles; they feed on sea grass and algae and are nocturnal.

Lizards are common in island forests. Most eat insects, though some species eat mice and small birds.

Crested wood partridges are found in the South, in areas of coastal, lowland forest.

Thai Buddhism

A<small>T LEAST</small> 90 percent of Thais practice Theravada Buddhism. This was first brought to the region from India around the 3rd century BC and is based on the ancient Pali canon of the Buddha's teachings (Tripitaka). However, Thai practice incorporates many Hindu, Tantric, and Mahayana Buddhist influences. The worship of Buddha images, for instance, is a Mahayana Buddhist practice. Animist beliefs in spirits

Monk with Thai flags

and the magical and in astrology are also widespread. Thais believe that Buddhism is one of three forces that give their kingdom its strength, the other two being the monarchy and nationhood. Religious rituals color daily life, especially in the form of merit-making *(see p125)*.

King Bhumibol, like many kings before him, spent time as a monk. For Thais, this act reinforces the notion that Buddhism and the monarchy are unified powers.

Siddhartha sets out to attain Enlightenment.

Most Thai males *are ordained as monks at adolescence – a major rite of passage. They usually spend at least a few months as monks, earning merit for themselves and their families. Few Thai women become nuns.*

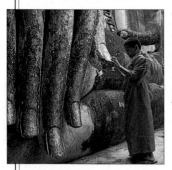

Applying gold leaf *to Buddha images is a popular act of merit-making. Books of gold leaf can be readily purchased at temples, and the thin leaves are applied in profusion on Buddha images, wat decoration, and murals.*

STORY OF THE BUDDHA

The Buddha was born Prince Siddhartha Gautama in India in the 6th century BC. He gave up his riches to seek Enlightenment, and later taught the way to *nirvana*. Statues of the Buddha *(see p163)* and murals depicting his previous ten lives *(jatakas)* abound in Thailand.

The family *is held in high regard in Thailand. A senior monk will be asked by the family for his blessing at child-naming ceremonies, weddings, to bless a new house or car, or simply after a donation to the wat has been made. Children are taught the simple moral codes of Buddhism from an early age.*

Walking meditation is practiced by most monks. Here, the most senior monk leads the line walking around the temple clockwise. Meditation on the nature of existence is a major way in which Buddhists progress toward Enlightenment – "Buddha" literally means "One who is Enlightened."

Vishnu, with four arms, is one of the three principal Hindu gods.

Thai folding book painting, c.1900

A ring of jasmine symbolizes the beauty of the Buddha's teachings and, as it perishes, the impermanence of all life. Vendors offer wreaths of jasmine to be hung in cars and shrines.

Heavenly beings *(devas)* bear the Prince through the air.

Cremation ceremonies are sober but not morbid; they are a rite of passage from this life to the next. The scale of the pyre reflects the status of the deceased. Chulalongkorn's funeral (see pp62–3) was one of the grandest.

Incantations in the ancient Pali script

Ritualistic tattooing is an ancient Hindu-Buddhist custom. Such tattoos are believed to act as powerful talismans against bad forces.

THE BASIC TENETS OF BUDDHISM

Buddhist cosmology encompasses many states of being and heavenly realms. Buddhists believe in perpetual reincarnation, whereby each life is influenced by the actions and deeds of the previous one. This underlying philosophy of cause and effect, known as *karma*, is symbolized by the "wheel of law." Enlightenment *(nirvana)* is the only state that will end the cycle of rebirth. To reach this, Buddhists try to develop morality, meditation, and then wisdom (the "three pillars"). Following certain codes of behavior in each life, including the basic principles of tolerance and nonviolence, assists in this aim.

The "wheel of law" on the Thai flag of Buddhism

The Wat Complex

A WAT IS A COLLECTION OF BUILDINGS within an enclosure serving dual purposes: Buddhist monastery, temple, and community center. There are about 30,000 *wats* in Thailand. Their construction is often funded by wealthy patrons – contributing to a *wat* is a good way to make merit *(see p125)*. Each period of Thai history has seen modifications to *wat* architecture, and the exact layout and style of buildings vary considerably. However, the basic layout of most *wats* follows set principles, as do the functions of different buildings.

A mondop *is a square-based structure topped with either a spire, as pictured here with the* mondop *at Wat Phra Kaeo (see pp76–9), or a cruciform roof. The edifice contains an object of worship or sacred texts.*

A Bodhi tree is found in many *wats*. According to Buddhist lore, the Buddha sat beneath one as he attempted to attain enlightenment *(see pp26–7).*

A wall or cloister *may enclose the main part of the temple (known as the* phutthawat). *A cloister sometimes houses a row of Buddha images, and murals may be painted on its walls.*

Monks' living quarters and dormitories are in a separate compound known as the *sanghawat*.

The *sala kanparien* is a small meeting hall, sometimes the venue for lectures on the holy scriptures.

Minor *salas* (halls) act as meeting places for pilgrims.

Ornamental pond

The *ho trai*, *or library, is used to house holy scriptures. A comparatively rare feature of* wat *complexes, they come in an assortment of shapes and sizes; this one at Wat Paknam in Bangkok is typical of a* ho trai *in a city* wat. *A* ho trai *in the countryside may have a high base, or be surrounded by water to minimize damage from insects.*

IMPORTANT WATS

Wats whose names begin with Rat-, Racha- or Maha- have been founded by royalty, or contain highly revered objects (with names often prefaced by "Phra"). There are about 180 important *wats* in Thailand. The *bot* and *wihan* are grand affairs, and there are a number of minor *salas*, as well as extensive monks' quarters. Lesser *wats* have fewer buildings and sometimes no *wihan*.

A chedi *is a solid structure encasing a relic of the Buddha, such as a hair or fragment of bone, or the ashes of a king.* Wat *complexes are often built expressly to surround a sacred* chedi.

The wihan, *an assembly hall, is very similar to but usually larger than a* bot *and not demarcated by* bai semas. *There may be several* wihans. *This one at Wat Rachabophit (see p87) is, like several in Bangkok, an eclectic mix of architectural styles.*

Buddha images in the cloister help mark the divide between the profane, outer world and the inner, sacred *wat*.

The cho fa, *which means "tassle of air" is the most recognizably Thai architectural detail. Its shape is thought to derive from a highly stylized* garuda, *a fierce bird featured in Hindu mythology.*

Bai semas, sacred boundary stones, are used to demarcate the consecrated ground of the *bot*.

Entrance to *wat*

The bot *(or* ubosot) *is the ordination hall reserved mainly for monks. It looks like a* wihan *but is surrounded by* bai semas. *The bot usually faces east and often houses the* wat's *main Buddha, as seen here at Wat Suthat (see pp86–7), Bangkok.*

Ho rakangs *or bell towers are used to toll the hour and summon monks to prayer. This one at Wat Rakhang (see p121) is a comparatively large, ornate structure.*

Religious Architecture

THAILAND'S RELIGIOUS SITES span more than 11 centuries. The materials used to build them invariably determine how much of each site can be seen today. Hindu-Buddhist Khmer temples were built of stone and, where restored, are fairly complete. Generally, all that is left of the *wihans* and *bots (see pp28–9)* of the Buddhist temples at Sukhothai and Ayutthaya are foundations and stone pillars, though some stone structures such as *chedis* and *mondops* are still standing. There are many fine examples of later Lanna and Rattanakosin Buddhist temples.

Gilded pediment of *wihan,*
Wat Saket *(see p83)*

KHMER (9TH TO 13TH CENTURIES)

Stone temple complexes, or *prasats*, in Northeast Thailand were built by the Khmers *(see pp254–5)*. Most have staircases or bridges lined with stone *nagas* (serpents) leading to a central sanctuary which is usually decorated with carved stone reliefs depicting Hindu myths and topped by a *prang* (tower). The two most important Khmer sites in Thailand are Prasat Hin Khao Phnom Rung *(pp270–71)* and Prasat Hin Phimai *(see pp266–7)*.

Khmer *prangs* symbolized Mount Meru, the mythical abode of the gods.

Lintels and pediments over the entrances depict Hindu and Buddhist deities.

The inner chamber of the *prang* housed either a *lingam* *(see p255)* or a Buddha image.

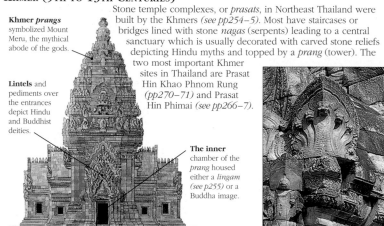

Central sanctuary of Prasat Hin Khao Phnom Rung

Naga **antefix on the** *prang* **of**
Prasat Hin Khao Phnom Rung

SUKHOTHAI (MID-13TH TO 15TH CENTURIES)

The cities of Sukhothai *(see pp184–7)* and Si Satchanalai *(see pp188–90)* witnessed the most radical architectural leap in Thai history. Amid sacred Khmer ruins, King Si Intharathit *(see p54)* and his successors built *wihans* and *bots* to house Buddha images. *Chedis*, modeled on Sri Lankan bell-shaped reliquary towers *(see p188)*, were added. Vast new temple complexes, such as Wat Mahathat *(see pp186–7)*, sometimes incorporated a unique development, the lotus-bud *chedi*.

Central lotus-bud *chedi*

Small *chedis* surround the main one.

Niches (foreground) once housed stucco Buddhas.

Some *chedi* (background) show Khmer influence.

A frieze of walking monks is carved around the base.

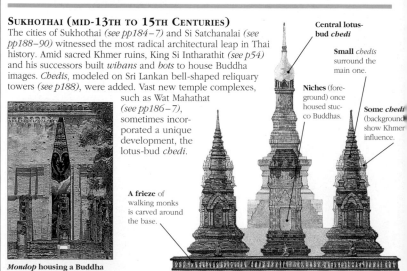

Mondop **housing a Buddha image at Wat Si Chum** *(see p185)*

Six (illustrated) of the nine *chedis* **at the heart of Wat Mahathat**

AYUTTHAYA (MID-14TH TO LATE 18TH CENTURIES)

The architects of Ayutthaya (see pp166–71) looked to the past, subtly modifying such features as Khmer *prangs* and Sri Lankan-style *chedis*. Temple buildings were ornate structures, with elaborate *hang hong* and door and window pediments. Few *bots* or *wihans* survived the Burmese sack of 1767 (see p56); one exception is Wat Na Phra Men (see p170).

Carved Buddhas sit in the niches of the *prang*.

The ringed spire of the *chedi* tapers to a fine point.

This *chedi* has an entrance to the relic chamber.

Surviving Ayutthayan *wihan* of Wat Na Phra Men

Sri Lankan-style *chedi* of Wat Phra Si Sanphct (see pp168–9)

Bullet-shaped *prang* of Wat Ratchaburana (see p166)

LANNA (MID-13TH TO 19TH CENTURIES)

Religious buildings during the Lanna period in the North (see pp58–9) were inspired first by Dvaravati architecture (see pp52–3), then later by Sukhothai, Indian, and Sri Lankan styles. Lanna's golden age was in the 14th–15th centuries. Unfortunately, few buildings remain from this period. Later 18th–19th-century *wats*, seen in such towns as Chiang Mai (see pp214–17), often feature intricate woodcarving, gilded *hang hong*, and murals.

Square-based *chedi* of Wat Chiang Man, Chiang Mai

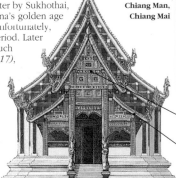

Intricately carved and gilded gables

Low, sweeping roofline

Hang hong, Wat Pan Tao, Chiang Mai

Lanna *wihan* of Wat Phra Sing, Chiang Mai

RATTANAKOSIN (LATE 18TH CENTURY TO PRESENT)

After the devastation of Ayutthaya the Thais attempted to recreate their lost past. The first *bots* and *wihans* built in the new capital, Bangkok, were similar to Ayutthayan structures; the most notable examples can be seen at Wat Phra Kaeo (see pp78–9). Later temple buildings were grander and more elaborate. In the 19th century buildings such as Wat Bencha-mabophit (see pp102–3) and Wat Rachabophit (see p87) were built incorporating Western elements. The Rattanakosin style is also known as the Bangkok style.

Gilded *hang hong* and detailing set off the green, red, and orange of the roof tiles.

Eight *bai semas* (boundary stones) encircle the *bot*.

Western-style stained-glass window, Wat Benchamabophit

Early Rattanakosin *bot*, Wat Suthat (pp86–7)

Traditional Thai Houses

TRADITIONAL THAI HOUSES are well adapted to the tropical climate. Many are raised on stilts to protect from flooding. A steeply slanting roof helps to channel rainwater off the house, and natural materials such as hardwoods, bamboo, and dried leaves help keep the building cool. The design also reflects spiritual beliefs. The innermost room is believed to be the abode of the spirits of family ancestors, and this is usually used as the sleeping quarters. Traditional Thai houses are most often seen in rural areas, though grand versions may be found in cities.

Plantation house, Northern Thailand

NORTHERN HOUSES

Northern Thailand can be relatively cool. As a result, the windows of Northern houses are smaller than those in the rest of the country. The kitchen and living areas are often joined together, which makes good use of the available heat. Outer walls are commonly built to slope outward, toward the roof, for strength. In more rural areas of Northern Thailand some houses have thatched roofs.

Decorative *kalae*, a traditional feature of Northern houses

Traditional Northern houses, constructed from teak

Typically *the whole structure of a Northern house is raised on pillars. An open balcony running along the front of the house is common, as are plain or decorative* kalae.

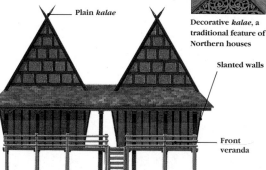

Plain *kalae*

Slanted walls

Front veranda

CENTRAL PLAINS HOUSES

In the hot Central Plains, a large, centrally situated veranda is the dominant feature of many traditional houses and acts for much of the year as an outside living area. Some houses in the Central Plains have covered verandas running along the sides of the main structure. Sometimes, a communal veranda will have several houses clustered around it. A relatively recent addition to houses found in the Central Plains is wood-paneled walls.

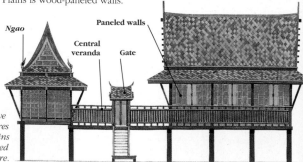

Ngao

Paneled walls

Central veranda

Gate

Wood-paneled gable

The gables *often have decorative features called* ngaos, *the origins of which can be traced to Khmer architecture.*

HOUSES ON WATER

River houses can be found in the Central Plains. The *khlongs* of early Bangkok *(see p123)* had many floating shop-houses. Such houses are very practical in areas prone to seasonal flooding. Houses can either be anchored to posts above the water line, or built on bamboo rafts so that during flood conditions they are able to float on the rising waters.

Thatched roof

Loosely fitted floorboards

Anchor post

Floating houses, Sangkhla Buri *(see p158)*

Houses *close to the river's edge are often anchored on posts. Floorboards are loosely fitted so that they move with the water beneath them.*

ROYAL HOUSES

Royal houses and mansions are typically a mixture of Thai temple and house styles and Western architecture. The main structural material of such buildings is usually teak, which gives them their distinctive rich, red color. Windows and doors usually have ornate frames and pediments, which are themselves sometimes decorated in gilt bronze.

— *Cho fa*   **Teakwood roof tiles**

Window pediment, Prince of Lampang's Palace *(see p133)*

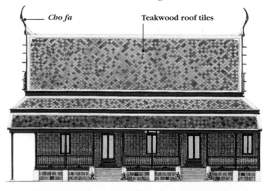

The Red House *at the National Museum (see pp84–5) is a typical royal house. As its name reflects, it is built entirely of teak and, like a temple, has cho fas.*

SPIRIT HOUSES

Spirit houses can be found on the grounds of many Thai homes. They are small structures, usually elevated on a pole, and house the spiritual guardian of the property. Resembling both dolls' houses and bird-tables, they come in a wide collection of styles: sometimes simple replicas of the houses to which they belong, at other times elaborate models of religious buildings. Spirit houses are erected to placate the spirits of the land, traditionally before the construction of the main building begins. They are then adorned daily with incense, flowers, and food to further mollify the spirits. Spirit worship predates Theravada Buddhism *(see pp26–7)*, but the flexibility of Thai religion means that worship of the Buddha and spirits is a normal part of daily life.

Decorated spirit house

The Art of Thai Food

Elaborately carved melon

THAI FOOD IS JUSTIFIABLY renowned for its quality and diversity – and for being as much a feast for the eyes as for the stomach. The simplest of dishes is often served with a carved carrot flower or a scallion tassel; a full-blown Royal Thai meal in a high-class restaurant may be accompanied by spectacular virtuoso fruit and vegetable sculptures. The cooking and presentation techniques of Thai cuisine are so respected that Bangkok's celebrated cooking schools attract pupils from all over the world. For the majority of Thais, eating is an informal, social activity. Whether it is an important family occasion, such as a wedding, an impromptu outdoor garden party, or a colorful festival, food will play a central role. Many restaurants serving Northern *khantoke* dinners may be aimed at tourists, but the principle of communal sharing of food is genuinely Thai.

The pre-rice planting festival *in Northern Thailand, like many Thai festivals, involves the preparation and consumption of a wide variety of food.*

White radish petals around a papaya heart

Royal Thai cuisine *is based on the dishes that at one time were served only at the Thai court. It is characterized by complex cooking methods and elaborate decoration. Royal Thai cooking also often uses ingredients that are (or were) expensive, such as ice for chilled dishes.*

Papaya has a firm texture and is a popular fruit to carve.

Cucumber carved into leaves

Radish

FRUIT AND VEGETABLE CARVING

Few visitors to Thailand fail to be impressed by the exquisitely carved fruit and vegetables that accompany many dishes in restaurants. Scallions are transformed into tassels and chrysanthemums; carrots and chilies become flowers; and tomatoes are magically turned into roses. The practice was once the preserve of the women of the royal court. Today, most Thais know the basic carving skills, but few have the dexterity and application needed to master the more advanced techniques. Skilled practitioners, capable of producing astonishingly elaborate creations, are highly esteemed.

Khantoke *is a traditional way of eating in Northern Thailand. Guests sit on raised platforms around a circular table and share a selection of typical Northern dishes served with sticky rice.*

Demonstrating the art of vegetable carving

Cooking schools provide trainee chefs and interested amateurs with a grounding in Thai cooking techniques, although most chefs learn their trade over a period of years in a restaurant kitchen. The most famous schools are in Bangkok (see p446).

Thai pumpkin

Carrot

Pumpkin

Beets, expensive in Thailand, are sometimes replaced by dyed carrots.

Miang kham, *a snack dish of ginger, coconut, lemons, red onions, dried shrimps, peanuts, and a syrup sauce, is presented here with a typical Thai attention to detail. The idea that food should look as good as it tastes applies to simple as well as elaborate dishes.*

Rice is endowed with spiritual significance in Thailand (see pp22–3) as well as being the central pillar of the country's cuisine. Here, Brahmins present offerings of rice in a Bangkok temple.

Luk chub *are utterly exquisite sweetmeats made to resemble tiny vegetables. Because few people possess the skills to make them, they are quite expensive, but well worth trying nonetheless.*

Cucumber petals

A **communal meal** *is the subject of this 19th-century temple mural. Although the Thais are inveterate snackers, sitting down for a full meal is still an important social event. Weddings and funerals are never without food and drink for all guests to enjoy. Eating out of doors, in a pavilion or a garden, is a popular way of dining in Thailand and is known as* suan ahan. *On Sundays many* wats *host a large communal meal.*

The Ramakien

THE RAMAKIEN, the Thai version of the Indian Ramayana, is an allegory of the triumph of good over
evil. The hero, Rama, is a paragon of virtue – the ideal
king. The villain, the demon king Tosakan, is a tragic
character of great dignity. This epic tale is thought to
have become established after the Thais occupied
Angkor in the 15th century. It has been an inspiration
for painting and classical drama. All the Chakri kings
have taken Rama as one of their names, and the old
capital of Ayutthaya *(see
pp166–71)* was named
after Ayodhya, a fictional
kingdom in the story.

Hun krabok (rod puppets), in a
scene from the Ramakien

Monkey armies accom-
pany Rama to Longka.

Buildings and chariots
are painted in Thai style
even though the story is set
in India and Sri Lanka.

*Rama is a skilled archer, as
this bas-relief marble panel at
Wat Pho (see pp88–9) shows.
Rama wins Sita's hand by
stringing a bow that no other
suitor is even able to lift.*

THE STORY

Rama, the heir to the throne of Ayodhya, is sent into
exile for 14 years, through the intrigues of his stepmother.
His wife, Sita, and brother Lakshman go with him deep
into the forest. Tosakan, the demon king of Longka (Sri
Lanka), abducts Sita and carries her off to his island kingdom in the hope of marrying her. The brothers pursue
him. Hanuman, the white monkey god, volunteers his
services. Together they win the alliance of two monkey
kings, Sukrip and Chompupan, each with a powerful
army. They march south to the coast opposite Longka.
The monkey armies build a road of stone through the
sea and lay siege to Longka. Many victorious battles are
waged against Tosakan's demon armies. Finally, when
all his champions have been defeated, Tosakan fights
Rama and is killed. Rama then crowns his ally, Piphek
(Tosakan's banished brother), as King of Longka and
returns with Sita to resume his reign in Ayodhya.

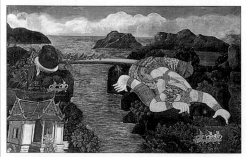

Mural at Wat Phra Kaeo: Hanuman using his tail as a bridge

*Many demons were overcome by
Rama during his forest exile. Some
recognized his divine nature. As
they died, his blessings released them
from the punishment of being reincarnated as demons in the next life.*

**Nang yai
shadow plays**
(see p373), *based
on the Ramakien,
were first docu-
mented in the
15th century.
Today this art
form is rarely
performed in
Thailand but can
still be seen in
Cambodia.*

In this view, the sea is narrowed
to allow both countries in the tale
to be seen.

Rama in the chariot
rides high above his
followers, as befits a king.

THE MAIN CHARACTERS

Hundreds of characters are
featured in the many episodes
of the epic Ramakien. However, the central thread of the
drama is carried by the five
most important figures, who
are described below.

Rama, *often
depicted with a
deep green
face, is an
incarnation of
the god Vishnu.
Rama's purpose is
to defeat the
demon race
whose power
threatens the
gods.*

Sita, *the daughter of
Tosakan's consort and
incarnation of the god-
dess Lakshmi, remains
loyal to Rama while
held captive by the
evil Tosakan.*

Lakshman,
*Rama's loyal
younger brother, is
often shown in gold.
He accompanies
Rama into exile
in the forest.*

Hanuman, *the white
monkey, son of the
wind god, is
totally devot-
ed to Rama,
but still finds
time to seduce
beautiful
women.*

RAMAKIEN MURALS AT WAT PHRA KAEO

The Ramakien is beautifully depicted through a series of
178 colorful murals, dating from the late 18th century, at
Wat Phra Kaeo *(see pp76–9)*. In this scene Hanuman
displays his supernatural powers to assist Rama in
rescuing Sita by building a stone causeway across the sea.

**Hanuman finds
Sita** *imprisoned
by the wicked king
of Longka,
Tosakan. He
gives her
Rama's ring
and tells her
she will soon
be rescued.*

Tosakan (meaning "ten
necks"), *the demon
king of Longka, has
multiple heads
and arms. In
the Indian
version of the
Ramayana he is
called Ravanna.*

Thai Theater and Music

Classical Thai dancer

THE TWO PRINCIPAL FORMS of classical Thai drama are *khon* and *lakhon*. *Khon* was first performed in the royal court in the 15th century, with story lines taken from the Ramakien *(see pp36–7)*. The more graceful *lakhon*, which also features elements from the *jataka* tales *(see p26)*, was originally performed inside the palace, but moved outside at a later date. Both *khon* and *lakhon* involve slow, highly stylized, angular dance movements set to the music of a *piphat* ensemble.

Students learn gestures by imitating their teacher. Training begins at an early age (when limbs are still supple) and includes a sequence of moves known as the Alphabet of Dancing (mae bot).

Graceful gestures typify classical Thai drama. Here, weapons are raised to attack the enemy.

Lavish costumes, made of heavy brocade and adorned with jewelry, are modeled on traditional court garments.

White mask of Hanuman (see p37)

Ganesh, the elephant god

Khon *masks*, decorated with gold and jewelry, are treated as sacred objects with supernatural powers.

Khon *and* lakhon *performances* are often staged at outdoor shrines. Dancers are hired to perform to the resident god by supplicants whose wishes have been granted.

A KHON PERFORMANCE

In *khon* drama, demons and monkeys wear masks, while human heroes and celestial beings sport crowns. As the story is told mainly through gestures, *khon* can be enjoyed by non-Thais. Visitors today are most likely to see performances at restaurants catering to tourists.

INSTRUMENTS OF CLASSICAL THAI MUSIC

A *mahori* ensemble shown in a mural

Thailand's classical music originated in the Sukhothai era. The basic melody is set by the composer, but, as no notation is used, each musician varies the tune and adopts the character of the instrument, like actors in a play. A tuned percussion ensemble, or *piphat*, accompanies theater performances and boxing matches *(see p40)*. A *mahori* ensemble includes stringed instruments.

Ranat **(xylophones)**

The keys of a flat xylophone produce a different tone from those of a curved one.

Likay, *by far the most popular type of dance-drama, is a satirical form of* khon *and* lakhon. *The actors wear gaudy costumes and the plot derives from ancient tales laced with improvised jokes and puns.*

Khon *and* **lakhon** *troupes, employed by the royal palace until the early 20th century, are now based at Bangkok's Fine Arts Department.*

Finger extensions, *emphasizing the graceful curves of a dancer's hands, are seen in* lakhon *perfomances and in "nail dances" of the North.*

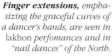

This mural *at Wat Benchamabophit, Bangkok, depicts a scene from a khon performance. In it, Erawan, the elephant mount of Indra, descends from heaven.*

Natural-looking makeup enhances the features of characters who do not wear masks. This replaces a heavy white paint that was traditionally worn.

Hun krabok *puppets, rodded marionettes, are operated by hidden threads pulled from under the costume.* Hun krabok *performances are very rare today.*

Khong wong lek (small gong circle)

Chake ("crocodile")

The hollowed hardwood body is inlaid with ivory.

Small gongs are struck by the player to give the tune's basic melody.

The strings of a *chake* are plucked. It accompanies fiddles and flutes in a string ensemble.

A piphat mon ensemble, including a vertical gong circle, plays at funerals.

Thai Boxing

THAI BOXING *(muay thai)*, Thailand's unique national sport, is gaining popularity worldwide. It was first documented in 1411, but probably evolved from an earlier form of armed combat, *krabi-krabong*. *Muay thai* is highly ritualistic – many techniques are inspired by battle stories from the Ramakien *(see pp36–7)*. The country's first famous boxer was Nai Khanom Dtom, who in 1774 defeated ten Burmese fighters. Due to a high injury rate, the sport was banned in the 1920s. In 1937 it was revived with rules for protecting fighters.

Nai Khanom Dtom

In the stadium, *the audience becomes excited, shouting encouragement to the boxers. Thais bet furiously, often staking large sums on their favorite fighter. Bouts between famous boxers can be sold out well in advance.*

This manuscript, *which dates from the early 20th century, depicts a fight between two Thai boxers.*

Training gear varies in style from camp to camp.

Phone Kingphet *was the first world champion Thai boxer. He trained in the cool climate of Phu Kradung National Park (see pp276–7) in preparation for his numerous bouts abroad.*

Feet are kept bare in training sessions, though ankle covers may be worn for protection during a match.

A ringside **piphat band** *is an essential element of a Thai boxing match. During the opening ceremony, the music is soft in tone; when the fighting begins it switches to a more upbeat "fight melody." As the action becomes more frenzied, the music increases in tempo, adding tension to the match.*

TYPES OF MOVES

Points are awarded for each blow to the opponent. The groin is not a valid target, and biting and head-butting are not allowed. A match may end with a spectacular knockout.

The jumping downward strike elbow is a physically demanding move. It gives the boxer an excellent vantage point over his opponent.

Amulets (see p74), *worn around one or both biceps during the match, are believed to offer protection to the boxer while fighting. They consist of a piece of cord that usually contains a Buddha image or an herb that is thought to be lucky.*

WHERE TO SEE THAI BOXING

Matches are held at Ratchadamnoen Stadium (p443) every Mon, Wed, Thu & Sun. Lumphini Stadium (p443) has matches on Tue, Fri & Sat. For other towns, check sites. Several TV channels now televise Thai Boxing.

Fists are bound with cloth for protection during training. Before 1937, glass-impregnated hemp was often used, to injure the opponent.

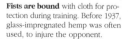

The **wai kru**, *a ritual bow, is the first part of the ram muay, a gesture of respect to the trainer (kru) and the spirit of boxing. In honor of their training camp, boxers often take its name as their surname.*

Before the match, *the boxer performs a slow, solemn dance* (ram muay). *The exact movements differ according to the boxer's camp, but usually involve sweeping arm motions, which are said to draw the power of earth, air, fire, and water into the body.*

THAI BOXING VERSUS WESTERN BOXING

Thai boxing, or "kick boxing," exerts parts of the body not used in Western boxing, such as the feet and elbows. Thai boxing matches are also faster paced, and are thus limited to five rounds of three minutes, each separated by a short break. Professional boxers, who may start the rigorous training as young as six, often retire by 25. Several Thai boxers have won Western boxing titles.

Kicks are common *in Thai boxing. A high kick to the neck, as shown here, may knock out a rival. A push kick, in which one boxer pushes the sole of his foot into the face of the other, is regarded as a great insult to the opponent.*

Knee hooks *can be devastating. To perform a "rising knee," aimed at either the head or body, the boxer pushes down his rival's head, bringing his knee up to hit it.*

Elbows deliver *fierce blows to the face, and, like knee strikes, are often decisive in matches. An elbow strike is more powerful than a punch, the weakest blow.*

Festivals in Thailand

THAI FESTIVALS are rarely solemn occasions, and few countries celebrate them with so much fun and color. Annual rites and festivities, marking religious devotion or the passage of seasons, have long been an integral part of Thai life. A 13th-century inscription reads: "Whoever wants to make merry, does so; whoever wants to laugh, does so." This still applies today, with dozens of festivities taking place each month. The main festivals, such as Songkran, are celebrated nationwide, with the most exuberant activities taking place in Bangkok and other major cities. Each region has its own unique festivals, too. Many festival dates change each year, as they follow the lunar calendar.

Phi Ta Khon, held in Dan Sai and Loei

Decorated oxen, paraded for Bangkok's Royal Plowing Ceremony

BANGKOK

SONGKRAN, the Thai New Year, is celebrated nationally from April 12th–14th *(see p44)*. In Bangkok, festivities take place at Sanam Luang, where a revered Buddha image is bathed as part of the merit-making rituals. Over the years, the festival has become a boisterous affair involving water throwing when few people escape getting soaked.

Visakha Bucha *(see p45)*, in May, marks the birth, Enlightenment and death of the Buddha, all said to have occurred on the same day of the year. It is celebrated with candlelight processions around important temples.

The Royal Plowing Ceremony is held at Sanam Luang at the start of the rice-planting season in May *(see p44)*. The display features oxen plowing and Brahmin priests sowing rice seeds. The oxen predict the coming year's harvest by selecting one of several types of food offered to them.

The Golden Mount Fair *(see p46)* is in November. With its carnival, performers, and candlelight processions, this is Thailand's best temple fair.

December's Trooping of the Colors in the Royal Plaza is the best of many nationwide celebrations marking King Bhumibol's birthday *(see p47)*.

CENTRAL PLAINS

EVERY MARCH, pilgrims flock to the Temple of the Holy Footprint near Saraburi for the elaborate Phra Phutthabat Fair *(see p44)*, which has theater and folk music performances.

Full-moon night in November is the occasion for Loy Krathong. It is celebrated throughout the country, but magically amid the ruins of Old Sukhothai *(see p185)*, where it is said to have originated. The festival is held in honor of Mae Kongkha, the goddess of waterways, and takes place by rivers, lakes, and ponds. Small, lotus-shaped vessels carrying offerings for Mae Kongkha are floated to take away the sins of the past year and to bring good luck for the future.

Khwae River Bridge Week (late November/early December), held at Kanchanaburi, marks the building of the infamous bridge with historical displays and a dramatic sound and light show.

NORTHERN THAILAND

BO SANG, which is famous for its hand-painted umbrellas, holds an Umbrella Fair every January. Umbrella painting competitions, umbrella exhibitions, parades, and a "Miss Bo Sang" beauty contest are part of the festival.

Northern Thailand shows off its beautiful blooms to full effect during Chiang Mai's Festival of Flowers in February, when parades of lavish floral floats fill the town with color. Events include floral exhibitions, handicraft sales, and a beauty pageant.

Mae Hong Son comes alive during its Poi Sang Long Festival, held in late March

Painting umbrellas for the Umbrella Festival in Bo Sang

Young Buddhist novices at the Poi Sang Long Festival in Mae Hong Son

or early April. The highlight of this Buddhist festival is a mass ordination ceremony for Shan boys. Wearing sumptuous costumes, the novices parade through the town before exchanging their finery for simple monks' robes in a symbolic gesture of renouncing worldly goods.

NORTHEAST THAILAND

NORTHEAST THAILAND is renowned for its unique festivals. In May, the town of Yasothon hosts the Bun Bang Fai (Rocket Festival), perhaps the most thrilling of Thailand's regional celebrations. This two-day event, accompanied by much high-spirited revelry, is staged to ensure plentiful rains during the coming rice-planting season. On the first day there is a parade of carnival floats, as well as carnivals, music, and folk dancing. The next day, huge, home-made rockets are set off.

Dan Sai and Loei, both in Loei province, are known for their Phi Ta Khon Festival (see p279), held in June. Celebrations begin with a parade, where locals dressed as ghosts follow a Buddha image through the streets of town to make Buddhist merit and call for rain.

Ubon Ratchathani has a Candle Festival in July, its own version of the nationally celebrated "beginning of the rains retreat," or Khao Phansa (see p45). As part of the celebrations, huge, intricately carved beeswax candles are exhibited on floats in the town before being presented to temples, where they burn throughout the rainy season.

The national holiday of "end of the rains retreat," or Ok Phansa, is celebrated in particular style at Nakhon Phanom in October with the Illuminated Boat Procession. Intricately fashioned model boats carrying single candles are set adrift on the Mekong River at nightfall.

GULF OF THAILAND

MODERN-STYLE merrymaking is found at Pattaya, which hosts the week-long Pattaya Festival in April. Floral float parades, beauty contests, and fireworks displays feature amid a nonstop carnival atmosphere. One of Thailand's most colorful water festivals is the Receiving of the Lotus Festival, which is celebrated in late October at Bang Phli, just south of Bangkok. Here, Ok Phansa is marked by a ceremony in which a locally revered Buddha image is showered with thousands of lotus buds while it is paraded by barge along Khlong Samrong, the local canal. Lively crowds, thronging the canal banks, throw flowers until only the image's head remains visible above the mounting floral offerings. Other events include boat races, boxing matches fought on poles placed across the canal, and likay theater shows.

Displays of self-mortification, part of the Vegetarian Festival, Phuket

SOUTHERN THAILAND

TRADITIONAL Southern culture gets an airing at the week-long Narathiwat Fair (last week of September). This features races between brightly painted traditional korlae fishing boats (see p378), as well as dove-cooing contests and performances of Southern music and dance.

For sheer spectacle, it is hard to beat Phuket's Vegetarian Festival (late September/ early October, see p350). This nine-day festival, marking the start of Taoist Lent, is celebrated by people of Chinese ancestry. During the festival followers eat only vegetarian food and take part in acts of self-mortification, such as piercing the body with skewers, with no apparent harm.

Mud-covered revelers at Dan Sai, Northeast Thailand

THAILAND THROUGH THE YEAR

THE THAI YEAR revolves around the monsoon seasons – which dictate the year's farming activities – and the religious calendar. Most religious festivals are Buddhist, and often observed on significant days of the lunar cycle, such as full moon. Festivals may also mark a seasonal change, such as the end of the rains, or a related agricultural event, such as the beginning of the planting season. The three seasons – wet, cool, and hot – are

Celebration of Loy Krathong, Sukhothai

produced by the Southwest and Northeast monsoons (see pp22–3). At the start of the wet season farmers plant rice seedlings. The rice-growing period is the traditional time for boys to enter the monkhood for a few weeks. In the cool season the drier weather ripens the crop, which is gathered before the hot season. Village life then slows down. During most weeks a festival is held somewhere in the country, especially in the cool season.

HOT SEASON

HIGH TEMPERATURES combined with high humidity make this an uncomfortable time, April being especially hot. With the fields empty and rivers running low, the landscape appears faded and spent in the bright sunshine. Considering the heat, it is not surprising that Thailand's traditional New Year, Songkran, is celebrated with water.

MARCH

ASEAN Barred Ground Dove Fair (first week), Yala. Dove-singing contest that attracts bird lovers from as far away as Cambodia, Malaysia, Singapore, and Indonesia.
Phra Phutthabat Fair (first or second week), Saraburi. Celebration of the annual pilgrimage to the Temple of the Holy Footprint (see p162).

Temple of the Holy Footprint during the Phra Phutthabat Fair

Water throwing during Songkran celebrations in Chiang Mai

Phra That Chaw Hae Fair (third week). A colourful procession of townspeople, all dressed in traditional Lanna attire, carry robes to cover the chedi.
Poi Sang Long Festival (late Mar/early Apr), Mae Hong Son. Mass ordination of 15- and 16-year-old-boys, who dress up as princes in memory of the Buddha's origins.

APRIL

Chakri Day (Apr 6). Commemorates Rama I founding the Chakri Dynasty. The Royal Pantheon – which displays statues of former kings – in Wat Phra Kaeo's grounds, Bangkok, is open to the public on this day only.
Songkran (Apr 12–14/15). Traditional Thai New Year. Celebrated nationwide, but Chiang Mai has the reputation for the most fun (see p226).

Pattaya Festival (mid-Apr). Features a week of food and floral floats, beauty contests, and a huge fireworks display.
Phnom Rung Fair (Apr full moon). Daytime procession and a nighttime sound and light show at Prasat Hin Khao Phnom Rung (see pp270–1).

MAY

Coronation Day (May 5). Ceremony to mark the crowning of King Bhumibol.
Royal Plowing Ceremony (early May), Bangkok. Observes the official start of the rice-planting season with an elaborate royal rite at Bangkok's Sanam Luang.
Bun Bang Fai (Rocket) Festival (second week), Northeast Thailand. Homemade rockets are fired to ensure plentiful rains amid a carnival atmosphere. Celebrated exuberantly at Yasothon (see p264).

AVERAGE DAILY HOURS OF SUNSHINE

Hours: 10, 8, 6, 4, 2, 0
Jan Feb Mar Apr May Jun Jul Aug Sep Oct Nov Dec

Sunshine Chart
Even during the rainy season, most days have some sunshine. The tropical sun can be very fierce, and adequate precautions against sunburn and sunstroke should be taken. Sun screen, a sun hat, and sunglasses are highly recommended. Drinking plenty of water reduces the risk of dehydration.

Visakha Bucha celebrations at Wat Benchamabophit, Bangkok

Visakha Bucha *(May full moon)*. Most important date on the Buddhist calendar. Celebrates the birth, Enlightenment, and death of the Buddha. Sermons and candle-lit processions at temples.

RAINY SEASON

THE RURAL SCENE comes alive with the advent of the annual rains, which soften the soil ready for plowing. Once the rice has been planted, there is a lull in farming activity. This coincides with the annual three-month Buddhist Rains Retreat, the period when young men traditionally enter the monkhood for a brief period. This is something that young Thai men should do at least once in their lives. The rainy season is a good time to observe the ordination ceremonies held throughout Thailand, which blend high-spirited festivities with deep religious feelings.

JUNE

Phi Ta Khon Festival
(mid/late Jun), Loei. An event unique to the Dan Sai district of Loei province, comprising masked players reenacting the legend of Prince Vessandon, the Buddha's penultimate incarnation *(see p279)*.

JULY

Asanha Bucha *(Jul full moon)*. Second of the year's three major Buddhist festivals. Commemorates the anniversary of the Lord Buddha's first sermon to his first five disciples.
Khao Phansa *(Jul full moon)*. Marks the start of the three-month Buddhist Rains Retreat (which is also referred to as Buddhist Lent), when monks remain in their temples to devote themselves to study and meditation. Young men are ordained for short periods.

Candle Festival *(Jul full moon)*, Ubon Ratchathani. Unique festival held in the Northeast to mark the beginning of Khao Phansa. Features parades of carved candles (made by villagers from all over the province) displayed on floats and later presented to temples throughout the city. Some candles are several meters tall *(see pp292–3)*.

AUGUST

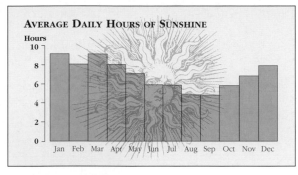

Her Majesty the Queen's Birthday *(Aug 12)*. Buildings and streets are lavishly decorated in honor of Queen Sirikit's birthday. The most elaborate decorations can be seen in Bangkok, especially along Ratchadamnoen Avenue and around the Grand Palace, where the streets and government offices are exuberantly adorned with colored lights.

Young man in ordination robes

Parade of candles at the Ubon Ratchathani Candle Festival

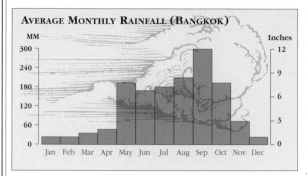

AVERAGE MONTHLY RAINFALL (BANGKOK)

MM   Inches

300   12

240   9

180   6

120   3

60

0   0

Jan Feb Mar Apr May Jun Jul Aug Sep Oct Nov Dec

Rainfall Chart
Thailand's rainfall is not evenly distributed. The southern peninsula has the highest, some 2,400 mm (95 inches) annually; the north and central regions receive 1,300 mm (51 inches). In many places, torrential rain falls almost daily during the rainy season, usually from June to October.

SEPTEMBER

Food and Fruits Fair *(first week)*, Nakhon Pathom. Held at Thailand's largest Buddhist temple, Phra Pathom Chedi. Cooking, folk theater, and floral floats.
Phichit Boat Races *(Sep)*, Nan. This annual regatta takes place on the Nan river as part of the Nan Provincial Fair and feature traditional low-slung boats.
Narathiwat Fair *(last week)*. A good opportunity to experience Southern culture.

Mangoes on display at Nakhon Pathom

OCTOBER

Vegetarian Festival *(early Oct)*. Trang and Phuket provinces *(see p350)*. Self-mortification rituals following abstinence from meat.
Chulalongkorn Day *(Oct 23)*, Bangkok. Commemorates the death of Rama V (King Chulalongkorn). Floral

tributes are placed by the King's equestrian statue by the Royal Plaza in Bangkok.
Receiving of the Lotus Festival *(late Oct)*, Bang Phli *(see p43)*. The end of the rains celebrated by pouring lotus buds over a locally revered Budda image.
Ok Phansa *(Oct full moon)*. Nationwide celebration of the Lord Buddha's reappearance on Earth after a season spent preaching in heaven. Marks the end of the Buddhist Rains Retreat.
Krathin *(begins Oct full moon)*. One-month period during which monks are presented with new robes.
Nan Boat Races *(late Oct)*. Festive regatta *(see p245)*.
Illuminated Boat Procession *(Oct full moon)*, Nakhon Phanom. Boats with candles and offerings set afloat down the Mekong River. Entertainments provided in the town *(see p286)*.

COOL SEASON

AFTER THE RAINS, the skies clear and the air cools to a comfortable warmth. The countryside looks its best, lush and green from the rains, with full rivers and waterfalls. In general this is the best time to visit Thailand, especially during the coolest months of December and January. Numerous festivals, to celebrate of the end of the rains, afford a period of relaxation before rural activity climaxes with the rice harvest in December and January.

NOVEMBER

Golden Mount Fair *(first week)*, Bangkok. Thailand's largest temple fair, held at the foot of the Golden Mount.
Elephant Roundup *(third week)*, Surin. Annual spectacle honoring the many and varied roles played by the elephant in Thailand's development *(see p268)*. More than 150 elephants take part in displays of forestry skills and a mock battle.
Khwae River Bridge Week *(late Nov/early Dec)*, Kanchanaburi. Commemorates the construction of the bridge by POWs and slave labor.
Loy Krathong *(Nov full moon)*. One of Thailand's best-loved national festivals. Pays homage to the goddess of rivers and waterways, Mae Khongkha. In the evening, people gather at rivers, lakes, and ponds to float *krathongs*. Sukhothai is the best place to watch this festival *(see p185)*.

Colorful spectacle of the boat races at Nan in Northern Thailand

AVERAGE MONTHLY TEMPERATURE (BANGKOK)

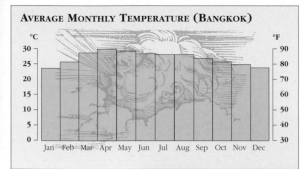

°C / °F chart with months Jan Feb Mar Apr May Jun Jul Aug Sep Oct Nov Dec

Temperature Chart
For visitors from temperate climes, Thailand is hot and humid throughout the year, especially in the South. It is uncomfortably so during April and May, pleasantly so in November and December. Though it is less humid in Northern Thailand, it can be chilly at night during the coolest months.

DECEMBER

Trooping of the Colors
(Dec 3), Royal Plaza, Bangkok. A very impressive ceremony that offers a vivid picture of regal pageantry. It is presided over by the king and queen and features members of the elite Royal Guards, arrayed in bright dress uniform. The guardsmen swear allegiance to the king and march past members of the royal family.
His Majesty the King's Birthday *(Dec 5)*. Government and private buildings throughout the country are elaborately decorated, and the area around the Grand Palace is illuminated. In the evening, crowds gather around Sanam Luang for celebrations. This occasion shows the deep respect Thais have for their king.

Soldiers in dress uniform for the Trooping of the Colors in Bangkok

JANUARY

Chinese New Year *(Jan/Feb)*. Not an official holiday, but this three-day festival is widely observed by the large number of Thais of Chinese origin.
Umbrella Fair *(mid-Jan)*, Bo Sang, Chiang Mai province. Celebrates traditional paper and wood umbrella making *(see p218)*.
Don Chedi Memorial Fair *(late Jan)*, Suphan Buri province. Marks the victory of King Naresuan of Ayutthaya over the Burmese. The highlight of the events is an elephant-back duel.

FEBRUARY

Festival of Flowers *(first week)*, Chiang Mai. Beautiful blooms of the north displayed on floral float parades.
Kite Flying Season *(Feb–Apr)*, Sanam Luang, Bangkok. Colorful displays and kite flying contests.

Makha Bucha *(Feb full moon)*. Third of the year's major Buddhist festivals. Merit-making and candlelit processions at temples.

PUBLIC HOLIDAYS

Western New Year's Day (Jan 1)
Makha Bucha (Feb or Mar full moon)
Chakri Day (Apr 6)
Thai New Year – Songkran (Apr 13-15)
Labour Day (May 1)
Coronation Day (May 5)
Royal Plowing Ceremony (early May)
Visakha Bucha Day (May full moon)
Asanha Bucha and Khao Phansa (Jul full moon)
Queen's Birthday (Aug 12)
Chulalongkorn Day (Oct 23)
King's Birthday (Dec 5)
Constitution Day (Dec 10)
Western New Year's Eve (Dec 31)

Wat Phra Kaeo on the King's Birthday

THE HISTORY OF THAILAND

THE HISTORY OF THAILAND is that of an area of Southeast Asia, rather than of a single nation, and over the centuries numerous peoples have made their home in this region. The most recent were the Tai of Southern China, who migrated south in the first millennium AD, and from whom most Thais today are descended.

Prehistoric Thailand was once regarded as a cultural backwater. In the Northeast of the country, however, archaeologists recently uncovered the earliest evidence of agriculture and metallurgy in Southeast Asia. Also among the finds were ceramic pots, some dating as far back as 3000 BC, that display a high level of artistic skill.

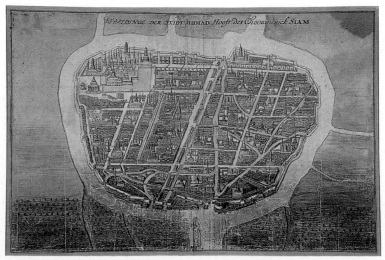

Votive tablet from Ayutthaya

The earliest known powers in the region were the Dvaravati Kingdom (6th–11th centuries AD), the Sumatran-based Srivijaya Empire (7th–13th centuries), and the Khmer Empire (9th–13th centuries) based at Angkor *(see p254)*, all of which were heavily influenced by Indian culture and religion.

The Lanna Kingdom in the North and the Sukhothai Kingdom, which imported Theravada Buddhism to Thailand, in the Central Plains grew in power from around the 12th century. Today, Thai schoolchildren are taught that Sukhothai marks the beginning of their history. Of all its kings, Ramkamhaeng (1279–98) stands out: part heroic myth, part historical figure.

Sukhothai was conquered by the Kingdom of Ayutthaya – also Tai – in the 14th century. At its height Ayutthaya controlled most of what is now Thailand, and the city of Ayutthaya saw the arrival of the first Europeans. The city was destroyed by the Burmese in 1767. Subsequently, a new city, Krung Thep (Bangkok), was built farther south, on the Chao Phraya River, and the Chakri dynasty founded. In the 19th century Kings Mongkut and Chulalongkorn modernized Thailand. During this period, Thailand resisted colonization by France and Britain.

A revolution in 1932 ended absolute monarchy, and in 1939 Phibun Songkram, formerly a soldier in the Thai army, changed the country's name from Siam to Thailand. There have been a number of coups since then, and a cycle of economic boom and bust in the 1980s and '90s, but Thailand remains relatively stable in comparison to neighboring countries.

Dutch map of the city of Ayutthaya, probably drawn in the 17th century

◁ **Chakri period painted screen, dating from the late 18th century**

Prehistoric Thailand

Jewelry from Ban Chiang

HUNTER-GATHERERS were already established in the area of modern-day Thailand by around 40,000 BC. They lived in semi-permanent settlements and made tools from wood and stone. Ancient seed husks found in caves in Northern Thailand have led to speculation that agriculture began to develop around 9000 BC. Rice was being cultivated around 3000 BC. Subsequently, in the area of Ban Chiang, elaborate pottery and bronze work began to be produced. This Bronze Age culture is believed by some historians to be the earliest in the world.

PREHISTORIC SITES

Ban Kao Tripod
This three-legged, terracotta pot was made by Neolithic artisans around 2000 BC. It was found at Ban Kao (see p160) in the Central Plains.

The flared rim and slightly more complex geometric pattern on this black and white, cord-incised pot were new stylistic features.

Bronze Axe Head
The earliest bronze artifacts found at Ban Chiang are thought to date from about 3000 BC. This ax head is from around 2000 BC.

Molded shoulders

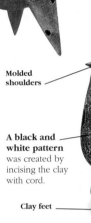

A black and white pattern was created by incising the clay with cord.

Clay feet

3000–2000 BC

c.1600

Clay Molds
Clay molds confirm that bronze objects were cast at Ban Chiang and not imported from elsewhere.

BAN CHIANG POTTERY
Pots found at Ban Chiang *(see p262)* date from 3000 BC to AD 200. Until their discovery in 1966, this area of Southeast Asia was thought to have produced little of cultural merit in prehistoric times. These, and other finds, show that the indigenous peoples were capable of producing sophisticated, beautiful works of art.

TIMELINE

40,000 BC Hunter-gatherers in area of modern-day Thailand

Bronze spearhead

2000–1500 BC Bronze artifacts created at Ban Chiang

1000 BC Cave and cliff paintings at Pha Taem *(p288)*

6000 BC First pottery created by inhabitants of Spirit Cave

3000 BC Domestication of animals (pigs, dogs, chickens, and cattle)

50,000 BC	5000 BC	4000 BC	3000 BC	2000 BC

3500 BC Rice chaff left in Banyan Valley Cave – beginning of rice cultivation

2000 BC Clay and bronze pots created at Ban Kao

1000 BC Bronze animals cast at Don Tha Phet

9000–7000 BC Seed and plant husks left in caves in Northern Thailand may indicate the beginnings of agriculture

3000 BC Elaborate cord-marked pottery manufactured at Ban Chiang

Iron Age Rooster
A find of bronze and iron artifacts at Don Tha Phet, near Kanchanaburi (see p160), includes this iron rooster from about 1000 BC.

Cave Painting
These paintings at Pha Taem date from around 1000 BC. The artists were probably descended from the early inhabitants of Ban Chiang.

Paint rather than cord is used to create a complex geometric pattern.

WHERE TO SEE PRE-HISTORIC THAILAND

At Ban Chiang *(see p262)* visitors can see burial sites and artifacts housed in the Ban Chiang National Museum. More Ban Chiang artifacts can be seen in the Bangkok National Museum *(pp84–5)*. At Ban Kao *(p160)* there are burial sites and a museum, and cave paintings can be seen at Pha Taem *(p288)* and Phu Phrabat Historical Park *(p285)*.

***Burial sites** at Ban Chiang were filled with pots that were placed around the dead.*

Narrow stand

300 BC–AD 1

300 BC–AD 200

Rust-colored geometric designs were painted on a beige ground.

Bronze Bracelets
As well as practical objects, the craftsmen of Ban Chiang were skilled at making elaborate jewelry. These bracelets probably date from the height of Ban Chiang's Bronze Age, around 300–200 BC.

---

500 BC Bronzeware created at Ban Na Di

1st–6th centuries AD Indianized Kingdom of Funan exerts strong cultural influence on the area around the Central Plains

Limestone sculpture of Vishnu (4th century AD)

AD 1	100	AD 200	300	AD 400

1st century AD Indian merchants begin to arrive in the Thai peninsula *(see pp336–7)*

Ban Chiang pot (300 BC–AD 200)

3rd–5th centuries Kingdom of Dan Sun in South flourishes and trades with Indian merchants

The First States

F ROM THE FIRST FEW CENTURIES BC Hindu and Buddhist missionaries from India and Sri Lanka came to Southeast Asia. Over the next millennium distinctly Indianized kingdoms emerged. The Dvaravati Kingdom (6th–11th centuries) flourished in what is now the heart of Thailand; the Srivijaya Empire of Sumatra (7th–13th centuries) was strong in the peninsula (see pp336–7); while the Khmer Empire (9th–13th centuries) expanded from Cambodia (see pp254–5). The Tai, from southern China, migrated to the area from the 11th century onward.

Srivijayan votive tablet

KHMER EMPIRE IN AD 960

☐ Extent of Khmer Empire

Flying Buddha (8th–9th centuries)
This Dvaravati sculpture shows the Buddha on the back of Panaspati, a strange beast that comprises Nandin the bull, Shiva's mount, and a garuda (a mythical bird).

Vishnu, asleep on the back of the naga, dreams of a new universe.

Stone Relief
Dvaravati craftsmen were renowned for their stonework. They excelled at bas-reliefs such as this one, at Wat Suthat (see p86), which depicts Buddhist and Hindu figures.

Dvaravati Deities
Dvaravati bas-reliefs, found in a cave near Saraburi, central Thailand, depict Brahma, Vishnu, the Buddha, and flying figures.

The naga (serpent) bearing Vishnu represents the Milky Sea of Eternity.

TIMELINE

Early 6th century Mon people establish Dvaravati culture. They have already inherited Buddhism from Indian missionaries

7th century Srivijaya civilization expands from Sumatra

8th century Tai people inhabit the upland valleys of Laos, northern Vietnam, and southern China

Dvaravati coin

| 500 | 600 | 700 | 800 |

Dvaravati stucco head

AD 661 Haripunchai said to be founded at Lamphun, Northern Thailand (see p219), by Buddhist holymen

7th century Chamadevi of Lop Buri becomes Queen of the Dvaravati Kingdom

9th century Khmer Empire founded at Angkor

Devaraja
This Khmer bas-relief, one of many found at Angkor Wat (see pp254–5), shows the god-king, or devaraja, *King Suryavarman II (1113–50).*

Terra-cotta Lion *(8th-century)*
Dvaravati figures, such as this lion from Phetchaburi (see pp318–19), were influenced by earlier Gupta art from India.

The Creator,
Brahma, sitting on a lotus blossom springing from Vishnu's stomach, has the task of realizing Vishnu's dream of creating a new universe.

WHERE TO SEE THE FIRST STATES

Dvaravati, Srivijayan, and Khmer artifacts can be seen at the Bangkok National Museum *(see pp84–5)* as well as at other regional national museums. Two Dvaravati-style *chedis* can be seen at Wat Chama Thewi in Lamphun *(p219)*. Phra Boromathat Chaiya *(p323)* is the best-surviving example of a Srivijayan temple. Khmer sites in Thailand include Prasat Hin Phimai *(pp266–7)* and Prasat Hin Khao Phnom Rung *(pp270–71)*.

***Prasat Hin Phimai** was built mostly during the reign of Suryavarman I in the 11th century.*

Srivijayan Buddha
This Buddha image, one of the most notable of the Srivijaya period, was found in Chaiya (see p323), an ancient city in peninsular Thailand.

KHMER LINTEL
The Khmers built temples throughout their vast empire, many of which are in present-day Northeast Thailand. Intricate stone carvings are a striking feature of the monuments – the characters depicted *(see p37)* are mainly Hindu, though some are Mahayana Buddhist. This lintel, from Prasat Hin Khao Phnom Rung *(see pp270–71)*, depicts a Hindu creation myth.

11th–13th centuries Lop Buri incorporated into Khmer Empire as a significant provincial capital	**1001–1002** Reign of Udayadit-yavarman, who invades Haripunchai (Lamphun) following an assault on Lop Buri	**1229–43** Reign of Indravarman II **1115–55** Lop Buri tries to assert its independence from Khmer control	
900	**1000**	**1100**	**1200**
10th–12th centuries Srivijaya becomes involved in ruinous wars with Chola state in India	**11th–12th centuries** Population of Tai people increases in areas of present-day Thailand, then under Khmer control	**1113–50** Reign of Suryavarman II *Lop Buri Buddha*	**1181–1220** Reign of Jayavarman VII, the most powerful and innovative of the Khmer kings

The Kingdom of Sukhothai

Sukhothai coin

Sukhothai was the first notable kingdom of the Tai people, centered around the city of Sukhothai (see pp184–7) in the Central Plains. The Khmers referred to the Tai as *Siam*, a name that came to be used for this and subsequent Tai kingdoms. Theravada Buddhism achieved new expression during the Sukhothai period, in innovative architecture and images of the Buddha finely cast in bronze. Sukhothai was made powerful by its most illustrious ruler, Ramkamhaeng, but by 1320 was only a local power again.

SUKHOTHAI IN 1300
☐ *Sukhothai Kingdom*

Potteries and other industries were located north of the city.

Minor *wats* on low hills

Wat Chang Lom, the symbolic power center

Ramkamhaeng (c.1279–98)
This modern relief depicts Ramkamhaeng, Sukhothai's most illustrious ruler. He extended the kingdom and negotiated treaties with neighboring states.

Inscription No. 1 (1292)
Ramkamhaeng is credited with inventing the Thai alphabet and using it to record the history of Sukhothai on this stone.

Rice fields and houses

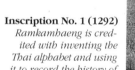

Roof Decoration
Ceramics were used to adorn buildings. This one is from the 14th century.

RECONSTRUCTION OF SI SATCHANALAI

Sukhothai's twin city, Si Satchanalai *(see pp188–90)* was the classic Thai *muang* or city-state. Within the walls was the symbolic power center of the crown prince. Beyond were the life-giving waters of the Yom River, rice fields, homes, and potteries, all within a ring of forested mountains, the outer limits of the *muang*.

TIMELINE

King Ramkamhaeng

c.1240s Si Intharathit is first known king of Sukhothai	**c.1279** Ramkamhaeng is made king; during his reign Sukhothai becomes a large kingdom	**1287** Ramkamhaeng forges alliance with states of Lanna *(see pp58–9)* and Phayao
1240	**1260**	**1280**
	c.1270–79 Reign of Ban Muang; Sukhothai remains merely a local power	**1283** According to legend, Ramkamhaeng modifies Sri Lankan script to create Thai alphabet
		1294 Ramkamhaeng campaigns in the south, near Phetchaburi

Slate Engraving
This 14th-century engraving shows the Buddha being reincarnated as a horse. It is one of a series discovered at Wat Si Chum (see p185) at Sukhothai.

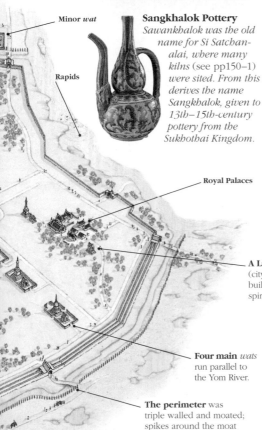

Minor *wat*

Rapids

Sangkhalok Pottery
Sawankhalok was the old name for Si Satchanalai, where many kilns (see pp150–1) were sited. From this derives the name Sangkhalok, given to 13th–15th-century pottery from the Sukhothai Kingdom.

WHERE TO SEE THE SUKHOTHAI KINGDOM

The main sites are Sukhothai itself (*see pp184–7*), Si Satchanalai (*pp188–90*), and Kamphaeng Phet (*pp182–3*). Artifacts are housed in the Bangkok National Museum (*pp84–5*), the Ramkamhaeng National Museum (*pp184–5*), the Sawankha Woranayok National Museum (*p190*), and the Kamphaeng Phet National Museum (*see p182*).

Wat Sa Si (see p185) *is just one of dozens of wats at Sukhothai Historical Park.*

Royal Palaces

A Lak Muang
(city pillar) was built to appease the spirits of the land.

Walking Buddha
New, sophisticated techniques for casting bronze produced this classic 14th-century Walking Buddha image.

Four main *wats* run parallel to the Yom River.

The perimeter was triple walled and moated; spikes around the moat deterred war elephants.

1298 Ramkamhaeng dies

End of 13th century Sukhothai first called Siam by Chinese

14th–15th-century Sangkhalok bowl

1346–7 Reign of Ngua Nam Thom

| 1300 | 1320 | 1340 |

1298–1346 Reign of Lo Thai, who succeeds Ramkamhaeng. Empire begins to unravel

14th–15th-century Sukhothai stoneware

1321 Tak, formerly part of Sukhothai, falls under Lanna control; Sukhothai is now a small kingdom, one of many competing states

1347–1368 Reign of Maha Thammaracha I

The Kingdom of Ayutthaya

AYUTTHAYA SUPPLANTED SUKHOTHAI as the most powerful kingdom in Siam in the mid-14th century and by 1438 had incorporated it into its empire. By the mid-16th century Ayutthaya controlled the entire Central Plains area and at its height held sway over much of what is now Thailand. The Ayutthaya period saw military, legal, and administrative reforms and a flowering of the arts, as well as diplomatic and trade links with the West *(see pp152–3)*. Its end came after years of conflict with Burma, when in 1767 the capital was sacked.

Ayutthayan Buddha

AYUTTHAYA IN 1540

☐ *Kingdom of Ayutthaya*

Ayutthayan Frescoes
Few frescoes have survived. These, from the 15th century, are from Wat Ratchaburana in Ayutthaya (see pp166–71).

Gold Elephant
The Ayutthayans were masters at working gold. This elephant, studded with gems and crafted to look as though it is paying homage, was discovered in Wat Ratchaburana.

Votive Tablets
Clay and terra-cotta tablets from the Ayutthaya period often show the Buddha resplendent beneath a naga (serpent).

Ornate, stylized carvings

A huge oar at the stern helped steer the boat.

Gold lacquer was used to decorate the barges.

RECONSTRUCTION OF A ROYAL BARGE

When foreigners *(farangs)* first came to Ayutthaya, they often met the sight of grand royal barges. This illustration is based on French engravings in some of the first accounts of the opulent city of Ayutthaya to reach the West.

TIMELINE OF THE AYUTTHAYA KINGDOM

1351 Ayutthaya is established and Ramathibodi I becomes king

1409–24 Reign of Intharacha

1448–88 Reign of Borommatrailokanat, who introduces far reaching administrative and legal reforms

1350	1400	1450	1500

1388–95 Ramesuan captures Chiang Mai in Lanna *(pp58–9)*

1424–48 Borommaracha II conquers Angkor

1491–1529 Reign of Ramathibodi II

1507–15 Ayutthaya at war with Lanna

Ayutthayan coin

Gilded Lacquer Cabinet
The craftsmen of Ayutthaya were adept at working wood. The doors of this cabinet are inlaid with gold; the pattern is of trees. Other such cabinets depict scenes from the jataka *or Westerners.*

WHERE TO SEE AYUTTHAYA

The city of Ayutthaya in the South Central Plains has some of the most spectacular ruins in Thailand *(see pp166– 71).* Ayutthayan artifacts are housed in the Chao Sam Phraya National Museum *(p168)* and in the Bangkok National Museum *(pp84–5).*

Wat Chai Watthanaram, *built by King Prasat Thong in 1630.*

Door Panel from Ayutthaya
This 17th–18th-century wood panel once formed part of the door of a temple. It was discovered in Wat Huntra in Ayutthaya.

Carving of the king

Royal insignia

The oarsmen would chant barge songs to keep paddling in time.

Deva Figure
Carved "angels," such as this 18th-century figure, were used in religious ceremonies.

1585–7 Naresuan defeats Burmese twice

Ayutthayan soldier

1593 Naresuan defeats Burmese at Battle of Nong Sarai *(pp58–9)*

1555 Naresuan is born

1660 Narai tries to take Chiang Mai and Lampang in Lanna from Burmese rule, but is repelled by a Burmese army

1685 First French mission in Ayutthaya

1766 Burmese forces, after taking Chiang Mai, besiege Ayutthaya

| 1550 | 1600 | 1650 | 1700 | 1750 |

1608 Siam sends its first diplomatic mission to Europe

1662 Narai invades Burma

1564 Burmese invade the kingdom of Ayutthaya

1569–90 Ayutthaya under Burmese rule

1688 Narai's death leads to "revolution" in Ayutthaya

King Narai

1767 Ayutthaya sacked, capital moves to Thon Buri

Lanna and Burmese Kingdoms

THE NORTHERN KINGDOM of Lanna was established at the same time as Sukhothai and endured for 600 years. Its first ruler, Mengrai, extended Lanna rule into Burma, and the reigns of Ku Na and Tilok saw a golden age. Wars with Burma and Ayutthaya in the 16th and 17th centuries, however, led to decline. Ayutthaya had driven the Burmese **Lanna** out of Lanna once before, but in 1615 the Burmese **urn** took back the Lanna capital, Chiang Mai, for almost a century. In the late 18th century, newly allied Siamese and Lanna forces drove the Burmese out. Lanna remained autonomous into the 19th century.

LANNA IN 1540

☐ *Lanna Kingdom*

Golden Door
Decorated with gold leaf, this temple door is at Wat Phra That Lampang Luang (see pp224–5), one of the oldest Lanna structures in Thailand.

Naresuan, on his elephant, engages the Burmese crown prince.

Ayutthayan soldiers, in traditional helmets, rally round Naresuan.

Lanna Elephant
This bronze elephant, from the 16th century, was used as a pedestal upon which Buddhist merit offerings were presented.

Bronze Buddha
Buddha images such as this one from the 14th–15th century are regarded as the pinnacle of classical Lanna art. After the Burmese took the north, this style of Lanna art declined.

BATTLE OF NONG SARAI (1593)

The Burmese attempted to control all of Siam, and, in 1564, invaded Ayutthaya. This 19th-century painting shows the Battle of Nong Sarai, when Naresuan (1590–1605) defeated the Burmese crown prince and Ayutthaya gained independence. In 1598 Ayutthaya drove Burma from the north, but in the 17th century the Burmese retook it.

TIMELINE OF LANNA AND BURMESE KINGDOMS

1259–1317 Reign of Mengrai; northern principalities unified

1289 Mengrai extends Lanna control into Burma

1292 Chiang Mai founded

1355–85 Reign of Ku Na leads to period of stability

1441–82 Reign of Tilok

1442–3 Ayutthaya sends an army against Lanna

1250	1300	1350	1400	1450	1500

1281 Mengrai conquers Haripunchai *(p219)*

1262 Chiang Rai *(pp240–1)* founded

1369 Ku Na invites a Sukhothai monk, a follower of Sri Lankan Buddhism *(p188)*, to establish a monastery in Chiang Mai

King Mengrai

1456–7 Lanna and Ayutthaya are engaged in a protracted war for control of the upper Central Plains

Model Wihan

Models of wihans are common throughout Thailand. This Lanna one, from the 18th–19th century, cast in bronze, has a high base, an exaggerated version of the bases found on many Lanna temple buidings.

WHERE TO SEE LANNA AND BURMESE THAILAND

Lanna artifacts can be seen in national museums at Chiang Mai, Lamphun *(see p219)*, and Bangkok. Chiang Mai *(pp214–17)*, Chiang Khong *(p239)*, Lamphun, and Lampang *(p226)* all have buildings that date from the Lanna period. Mae Hong Son *(pp206–7)* and Phrae *(pp248–9)* have buildings showing Burmese influence.

The **ho trai** *(scripture library) of Wat Phra Sing, Chiang Mai, is one of the most notable late Lanna structures in Thailand.*

Burmese Dancer

This temple mural of a Burmese dancing girl is from Chiang Mai (see pp214–17). A number of wats in the North bear similar indications of Burmese occupation.

Burmese soldiers wear simple bandanas around their heads.

Lanna Coin

During the 18th and 19th centuries, bronze rings were used as coinage in the Lanna Kingdom.

Lanna Wood Carvings

The pediment of the 19th-century wihan at Wat Pan Tao (see p215) is typical of the elaborate work produced by Lanna wood carvers.

1558 Burmese take Chiang Mai for the first time

1590 Ayutthaya establishes independence from Burma at Battle of Nong Sarai

1660 Narai of Ayutthaya attempts to wrest control of North from Burmese but is repulsed

19th-century Lanna box

1550	1600	1650	1700	1750	1800

1615 Burma regains control over Lanna

1598 Naresuan of Ayutthaya expels Burma from the North, though this is short-lived

15th–17th-century Lanna Buddha

1727 General Thip proclaims himself king of Lampang after defeating Burmese

1776 Taksin of Thon Buri and Kawila of Lampang reconquer Chiang Mai

The Early Chakri Dynasty

Court dress, c.1850

Aᴛᴇʀ ᴛʜᴇ sᴀᴄᴋ ᴏꜰ ᴀyᴜᴛᴛʜᴀyᴀ, Taksin, an army general, established a new capital at Thon Buri, on the west bank of the Chao Phraya opposite what would later become Bangkok. He became king in 1768, and in ten years Siam was a regional power again. However, he became increasingly despotic and, in 1782, was ousted by the military commander Chao Phraya Chakri, who was later pronounced King Rama I. Chakri's descendant, King Mongkut (Rama IV), modernized Siam, opening it up to foreign trade and influence.

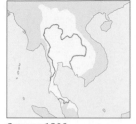

Sɪᴀᴍ ɪɴ 1809

☐ *Siamese territories*

Chakri Kings
The reigns of Ramas I, II, and III signaled an era of stable monarchical rule. Rama II was a literary man, while Rama III was a great merchant.

Kblongs are an important means of transportation

Chakri Throne
The Busabok Mala Maha Piman Throne was built in the reign of Rama I for important occasions. It is in the Grand Palace (see pp76–81).

The Grand Palace *(see pp76–81)* was founded in the late 18th century; by the mid-19th century it is already vast.

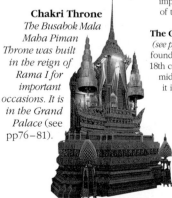

Sir John Bowring
The Bowring Treaty (1855) allowed the British free trade. Later, Siam forged similar treaties with other colonial powers, thus avoiding annexation.

Tɪᴍᴇʟɪɴᴇ

1768 Taksin begins to re-establish Siamese Empire

Ramakien mural

1800 Burmese finally expelled from Siam

1797 Rama I "writes" Ramakien *(see pp36–7)*

1813 Siam withdraws from Cambodia leaving Vietnam as dominant power

| 1770 | 1780 | 1790 | 1800 | 1810 |

1782 Rama I overthrows an increasingly despotic Taksin; relocates capital

1783 Wat Phra Kaeo begun

1785 Massive Burmese invasion repulsed

1805 Rama I appoints a committee of judges to reform Siamese law

1808–24 Reign of Rama II

Thai Etiquette *(1855)*
In mid-19th century Siam, prostrating oneself before a superior was common. It was officially abolished by Rama V (see pp62–3).

Where to See Early Chakri Thailand

Almost all the best examples of architecture from the early Chakri – or Rattanakosin *(see p31)* – period can be seen in Bangkok. The earliest Chakri building is the *bot* of Wat Phra Kaeo *(p76)*. Other examples include the *bot* of Wat Suthat *(pp86–7)*, the *wihan* of Wat Suthat, Wat Pho *(pp88–9)*, and Phra Nakhon Khiri in Phetchaburi *(see p320)*.

Wat Suthat, built in the early 19th century by Rama I, is the site of Bangkok's tallest wihan.

Mongkut *(1851–68)*
Before coming to the throne Mongkut, pictured here with his favorite wife, traveled widely, meeting many Westerners.

Thon Buri, on the western bank of the Chao Phraya, is still just a small town.

Early Bangkok (Krung Thep)

The Siamese capital was moved from Thon Buri to the east of the river in 1782 as a defense against the Burmese. Its official 43-syllable name matches the majesterial plans that Rama I had for his new city: the first two words, "Krung Thep," mean "city of angels." This mural from 1864 shows the temples and river houses of early Bangkok.

King Mongkut Mural
In this mural King Mongkut is in his palace observing an eclipse through a telescope, his subjects below him.

1824–1851 Reign of Rama III

Chakri coin

1840s Siam dominant in Cambodia

1855 Signing of the Bowring Treaty

1820	1830	1840	1850	1860

1826 Limited trade agreement, Burney Treaty, signed

1830s Siam goes to war in Cambodia, to defend Buddhism against the Vietnamese

1827 Vientiane is sacked by Siamese army

Rama IV (1851)

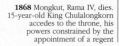

1868 Mongkut, Rama IV, dies. 15-year-old King Chulalongkorn accedes to the throne, his powers constrained by the appointment of a regent

Reign of King Chulalongkorn

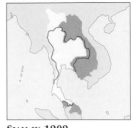

PERHAPS THE GREATEST KING of the Chakri dynasty, Chulalongkorn (1868–1910) carried on the modernization of Siam that his father, Mongkut, had started. Financial reforms were made, the government restructured, and slavery abolished. Reform angered older ministers, the "conservatives" *(hua boran)*, and led to the Front Palace Crisis of 1875. This was also a time when Britain and France were consolidating their positions in Southeast Asia.

Rama V in Western garb

Chulalongkorn's policies and diplomacy kept the colonial powers at bay, though parts of Burma, Laos, Cambodia, and the Malay states were ceded to them.

SIAM IN 1909

☐ *Siamese territories*

▨ *Ceded territories*

Rama V

Chulalongkorn (Rama V) came to the throne, under the guidance of a regent, at the age of 15. He had received an excellent Thai and Western education and was well qualified for the task of reforming Siam.

Soldiers attending the cremation wore colonial uniforms.

Drummers wore traditional Thai headdresses.

Life on the Khlongs
At the end of the 19th century, and into the 20th, Bangkok was known as the "Venice of the East" (see p123).

Classical Dancers at Court
Many Siamese traditions, among them classical dance, remained unchanged. Scenes such as this were often recorded with the aid of new technology – photography.

TIMELINE

1874 Chulalongkorn (Rama V) introduces a series of reforms that anger the "conservatives" or *hua boran*

1874 Thai High Commissioner sent to govern Lanna

1875 Front Palace Crisis – the "conservatives" demonstrate their anger. Chulalongkorn has to tone down some of his reforms

Tile detail, Wat Rachabophit

1887 Prince Devawongse attends the celebrations, in London, of Queen Victoria's 50th year; the prince studies European government with a view to reform in Siam

1885 Enlightened Prince Devawongse made Foreign Minister

1888 New administrative system, centralizing power, is introduced

1870	1875	1880	1885

Franco-Siamese Crisis

In an attempt to consolidate her hold over Indochina, in 1893 France asserted sovereignty over Siamese-controlled Laos. This cartoon shows a French "wolf" hungrily assessing a Siamese "lamb."

Chulalongkorn's body was cremated in this funeral tower.

CREMATION OF CHULALONGKORN

Chulalongkorn's cremation, held in Bangkok in 1910, was a grand state affair. As a great reformer, he was idealized by his subjects, and even today the people of Thailand commemorate his death on Chulalongkorn Day *(see p46)*.

(see p46)

WHERE TO SEE LATE CHAKRI THAILAND

During the latter part of the 19th century there was little change in the basic style of religious buildings. Chulalongkorn, however, left his mark on some buildings in Bangkok. Wat Benchamabophit *(see pp102–3)* employs an eclectic mixture of Chinese, Italian, and Khmer styles, while Wat Rachabophit *(p85)* displays traditional Thai and Western motifs.

(see pp102–3) ... (p85)

***At Wat Rachabopit**, Rama V had the interior decorated in Italianate-Thai style.*

Modern Developments
Chulalongkorn promoted many new ideas; cars appeared in Bangkok at the beginning of the 20th century.

1893 French take control of Laos; leads to Franco-Siamese Crisis

French gunboat

1910 Chulalongkorn dies. His son Vajiravudh (Rama VI) comes to throne

1907 Cambodia ceded to the French

| 1895 | 1900 | 1905 | 1910 |

1892 ministries are created to ... Siam

1893 Paknam Incident – French gunboats sail up the Chao Phraya River

1905 After years of gradual reform, slavery is finally abolished

1909 Siamese sovereignty over the Malayan states of Kelantan, Perlis, Terengganu, and Kedah ceded to the British

Modern Thailand

Modern Thai flag

In 1932 SIAM became a constitutional monarchy. Under Prime Minister Phibun Songkram, the 1930s saw rising nationalism: the country was renamed Prathet Thai (Thailand) and sided with Japan against the Allies in World War II. By contrast, during the Vietnam War in the 1970s, fear of Communism led Thailand to help the US. A number of military coups have since hindered democratization. Economic growth accelerated during the 1980s, but in 1997 the Thai *baht* faced heavy speculation leading to an economic crisis.

ASEAN IN 2000

☐ *Association of SE Asian Nations*

King Vajiravudh
Chulalongkorn's son Vajiravudh (1910–25) clashed with his father's senior advisors. To build a following of his own he created the elite corps, the Wild Tigers, in 1911.

Democracy Monument
A meeting place during prodemocracy rallies, this monument was built in 1939 to mark the revolution of 1932. The last major demonstration held here was in 1992.

Ayutthaya-style barge

MODERN BANGKOK

With an official population of five million in the late 1990s (unofficially it could be closer to ten million), Bangkok is one of the most frenetic, congested, and polluted cities in the world. It is also a colorful city where old traditions are still important. The 1982 Bangkok Bicentennial and celebrations of Bhumibol's 50th year as King in 1996 (shown here), featured splendid royal barges.

TIMELINE

1911 Wild Tigers, an elite paramilitary corps, formed

1934–8 Increasing power struggle between Phibun Songkram and Pridi Phanomyong

1935 Prajadhipok abdicates, Ananda Mahidol becomes king

1940 Thais invade Laos and Cambodia after fall of France to Germany

1959 Sarit Thanarat becom Prime Minister in coup; ushers era of modern developm known as *samai patta*

1946 Phibun resigns; Pridi Phanomyong forms governmen

1920	1930	1940	1950

1917 Siam sends a small force of men to fight on the side of the Allies in WW I

Phibun Songkram

1925 Prajadhipok becomes king

1932 Revolution; Siam made a constitutional monarchy

1938 Phibun Songkram becomes Prime Minister

1939 Phibun renames Siam

1946 Mahidol killed; Bhumibol made king

1941 Phibun capitulates to Japan; Pridi Phanomyong organizes underground resistance

Traffic Congestion

As modern Bangkok has grown, so too has the problem of traffic congestion. Lack of proper road planning means that the city's streets are constantly gridlocked.

King Bhumibol

Against a backdrop of unstable politics, the revered King Bhumibol (Rama IX) has represented virtue and stability. Through his authority, the military coup and bloody demonstrations of 1992 were ended.

WHERE TO SEE MODERN THAILAND

Apart from palaces and *wats*, most 20th-century architecture in Thailand, particularly in Bangkok, tends to be very dull and functional. However, some of the many new buildings of the 1980s and 90s are worth a look if only for their sheer outrageousness (*see p117*). Modern resort hotels sometimes incorporate traditional touches.

The Robot Building, *in downtown Bangkok, was designed by Sumet Jumsai in the mid-1980s.*

Luxury hotel on the west bank of the Chao Phraya

Shop-houses

Oarsmen in traditional navy attire

Tourism

Although the 2004 tsunami was a terrible disaster Thailand's huge tourism industry (12 million visitors in 2004) was not badly affected.

	US fighter plane	**1973–6** Turbulent democratic government; student demonstrations	**1980s** CPT a spent force; Thailand enters a period of rapid economic growth	**1988** Fully democratic elections	**2004** December 26, west coast of Southern Thailand hit by a tsunami – some 5,300 deaths
				1997 Thai economy collapses	
1960	1970	1980		1990	2000
1964 US military aircraft operate from Thai soil as Vietnam War escalates	**1967** Thailand becomes founder member of the Association of Southeast Asian Nations (ASEAN)	**1976** Massacre of students at Thammasat University brings huge support for the CPT (*see p278*)		**1992** Massacre of pro-democracy demonstrators in Bangkok followed by democratic elections	

King Bhumibol

BANGKOK

Introducing Bangkok

Thailand's capital city, straddling the great Chao Phraya River, 20 km (12 miles) upstream from the Gulf of Thailand, is an exuberant, exhilarating, infuriating metropolis of seven million people. Founded by Rama I in 1782, this relatively young city is known to Thais as Krung Thep ("city of angels"), a shortened form of a full name in excess of 150 letters. Bangkok may be a lesson in the dangers of uncontrolled urban expansion, but it is also one of the world's most exciting cities. Its lively nightlife and markets, shops and restaurants, and magnificent wats, museums, palaces, and parks, have something for everyone.

Guard statue at Wat Arun

The National Museum (see pp84–5) *contains a wealth of treasures, such as this 7th–8th-century head of the Buddha.*

The Grand Palace and Wat Phra Kaeo complex (see pp76–81) *is Bangkok's premier tourist attraction. The sacred Emerald Buddha, or Phra Kaeo, is housed in one of many splendid buildings.*

THON BURI
(see pp118–125)

OLD CITY
(see pp72–89)

CHAO PHRAYA

Wat Pho (see pp88–9) *is one of the oldest temples in the capital, dating originally from the 16th century. It is also a famous center for traditional medicine and contains the much respected Institute of Massage.*

Wat Arun (see pp120–21), *otherwise known as the Temple of Dawn, is one of Bangkok's best known landmarks. Its Khmer-influenced prangs are encrusted with thousands of pieces of broken porcelain.*

◁ Intricately decorated *prangs* of the Grand Palace and Wat Phra Kaeo embellishing Bangkok's skyline

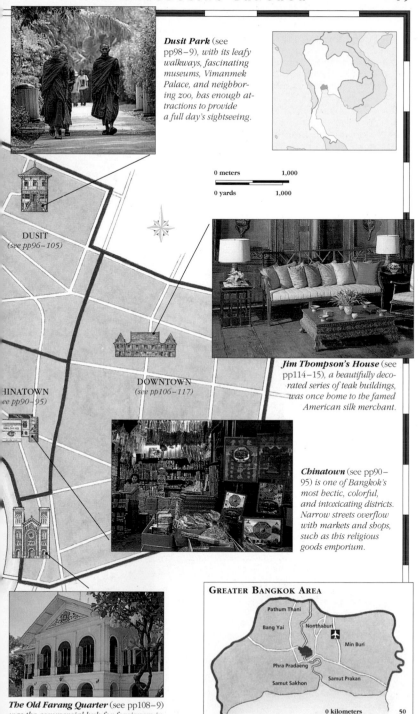

Dusit Park (see pp98–9), *with its leafy walkways, fascinating museums, Vimanmek Palace, and neighboring zoo, has enough attractions to provide a full day's sightseeing.*

0 meters 1,000

0 yards 1,000

DUSIT
(see pp96–105)

HINATOWN
ee pp90–95)

DOWNTOWN
(see pp106–117)

Jim Thompson's House (see pp114–15), *a beautifully decorated series of teak buildings, was once home to the famed American silk merchant.*

Chinatown (see pp90–95) *is one of Bangkok's most hectic, colorful, and intoxicating districts. Narrow streets overflow with markets and shops, such as this religious goods emporium.*

GREATER BANGKOK AREA

Pathum Thani

Bang Yai Nonthaburi

Min Buri

Phra Pradaeng

Samut Sakhon Samut Prakan

0 kilometers 50

0 miles 25

The Old Farang Quarter (see pp108–9) *was the commercial hub for foreigners in the 19th century. Some colonial buildings, such as the Portuguese Embassy, survive.*

A River View of Bangkok

A typical Chao Phraya barge, transporting goods along the river

T HE TWO GREAT RIVERS of the North, the Ping and the Nan, join at Nakhon Sawan in the Central Plains to form the Chao Phraya ("river of kings"), Thailand's most important waterway. This vital transportation link drains some of the country's most fertile rice-growing land. The stretch shown here is actually a canal, built in the 16th century as a shortcut at a point where the Chao Phraya took a huge meander along what is now Khlong Bangkok Noi and Khlong Bangkok Yai. Along this busy "royal mile" you can catch glimpses of the Grand Palace, temples, and colonial build-ings, and experience a flavor of old Bangkok's colorful riverfront.

To Phrapin-klao Bridge

The Buddhaisawan Chapel in the National Museum (see pp84–5) *is home to the Phra Buddha Sing, one of the most venerated Buddha images in Thailand after the Emerald Buddha. Elsewhere in the museum is a fabulous collection of arts and crafts from every period of Thai history. Exhibits include Buddha images, weapons, and pottery.*

RIVERBOATS ON THE CHAO PHRAYA

The Chao Phraya is a major transportation artery, for both goods and people. Hefty rice barges, tiny boats laden with fruit and vegetables, and a variety of ferry services continually ply the river. No visitor to Bangkok should miss seeing the city from the water, and jumping on the Chao Phraya Express is one of the easiest and cheapest ways to do so. The stops are indicated on the Street Finder (maps 1–2, 5–6). There are also cross-river ferries from almost every river pier, as well as countless long-tail boats that operate as buses or can be specially chartered to explore the city's *khlongs*.

Long-tail boat on the Chao Phraya

Wat Rakhang (see p121) *is a little visited but rewarding temple contain-ing fine murals painted in the 1920s.*

| 0 meters | 200 |
| 0 yards | 200 |

Wat Phra Kaeo (see pp76–9) contains one of Thailand's most sacred Buddha images, the Emerald Buddha. The temple and palace complex is a superb collection of buildings with lavish decorative details.

Sanam Luang, ("field of kings"), the venue for national ceremonies, is one of Bangkok's few open spaces.

LOCATOR MAP

☐ *See Street Finder maps 1, 5*

Wat Pho (see pp88–9), the city's oldest temple, dates from the 17th century. It is famed for its school of massage, as well as for fine details such as this painting of a Chinese soldier.

To Memorial Bridge →

From the roof of the Shangri-La Hotel in the Old Farang Quarter (see pp108–9), there is an excellent view of the Chao Phraya River.

Wat Arun (see pp122–23) is covered in pieces of broken porcelain. This Buddha image is outside the main bot.

OLD CITY

As THE SPIRITUAL and historical heart of Bangkok, the Old City is dense with temples and shrines. Known as Rattanakosin, this was the center of the new capital Rama I founded in 1782 *(see pp60–61)*. Remnants of a defensive wall can be seen between the Golden Mount and Wat Rachanadda. Some of Thailand's finest Rattanakosin period architecture is within the Old City. The foremost example is the Grand Palace, within which is Wat Phra Kaeo, home of the country's most venerated image, the Emerald Buddha. South of here is Wat Pho, one of the city's oldest temples, while to the north lies Sanam Luang ("field of kings"), the site of royal ceremonies. Alongside Sanam Luang, the National Museum contains Southeast Asia's most impressive artifacts. Two Buddhist universities in temples nearby: Wat Mahathat and Wat Bowonniwet. The latter is famed for its murals combining Western and traditional Thai styles.

Buddha images, ready for transit

SIGHTS AT A GLANCE

Wats

Grand Palace and
Wat Phra Kaeo pp76–81 **1**
Wat Bowonniwet **5**
Wat Mahathat **2**
Wat Pho pp88–9 **14**
Wat Rachabophit **12**
Wat Rachanadda **7**

Wat Rachapradit **13**
Wat Saket and the Golden Mount **8**
Wat Suthat and the Giant Swing **11**

Museums and Galleries

National Gallery **4**
National Museum pp84–5 **3**

Notable Roads and Districts

Bamrung Muang Road **10**
Monk's Bowl Village **9**

Monuments

Democracy Monument **6**

0 meters 500

0 yards 500

GETTING THERE

If you are staying near the river, the easiest way to get to the Old City is by ferry. The Chao Phraya Express piers of Chang and Maharaj are best for the Grand Palace while Tien and Rachinee are close to Wat Pho. Many buses go to the Old City.

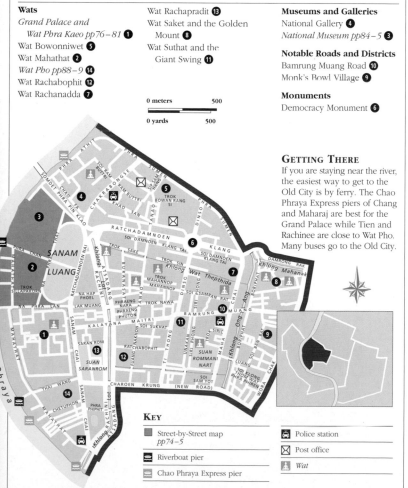

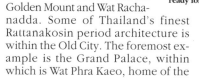

KEY

▪ Street-by-Street map *pp74–5*	🚓 Police station
🚢 Riverboat pier	⊠ Post office
🚢 Chao Phraya Express pier	🛕 *Wat*

◁ **The elaborately decorated roof of the Aphonphimok Pavilion, Grand Palace**

Street-by-Street: Around Sanam Luang

สนามหลวง

A monument in Sanam Luang

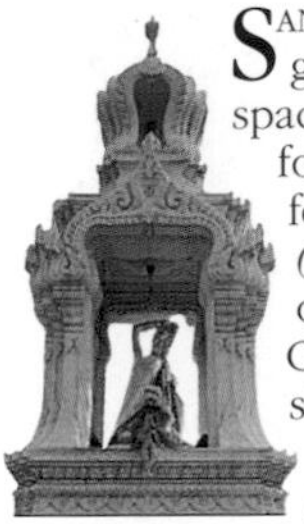

SANAM LUANG ("field of kings" or "royal ground") is one of the few sizeable open spaces in Bangkok. It is the traditional site for royal cremations, the annual kite flying festival, and the Royal Plowing Ceremony *(see p44)*. Spiritually speaking, this area is one of the luckiest in the city, with the Grand Palace, the Lak Muang (City Pillar) shrine, and the Amulet Market bordering Sanam Luang. Neighboring streets overflow with salesmen hawking lotions, potions, and amulets for luck, love, or protection from evil spirits. Astrologers gather to chart your stars or read your palm. Notable sights include Wat Mahathat, Thailand's most revered center of Buddhist studies, and the National Museum, which charts Thailand's fascinating history.

DUSIT
THON BURI
OLD CITY
CHINATOWN

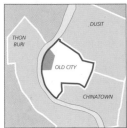

Locator Map
See Street Finder map 1

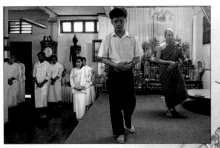

Wat Mahathat
Meditation classes are held at the Buddhist university within this temple's compound. Dating from the 18th century, the wat *is more notable for its bustling atmosphere than its buildings* ❷

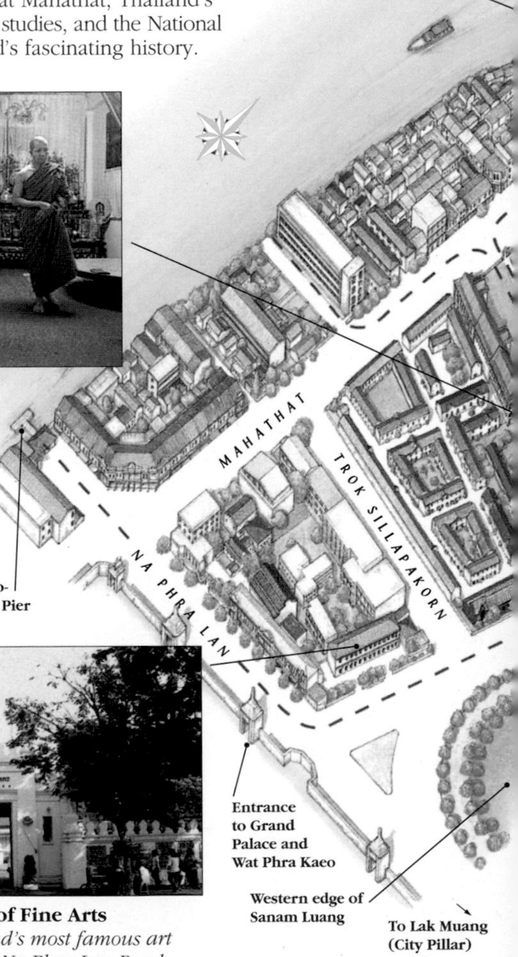

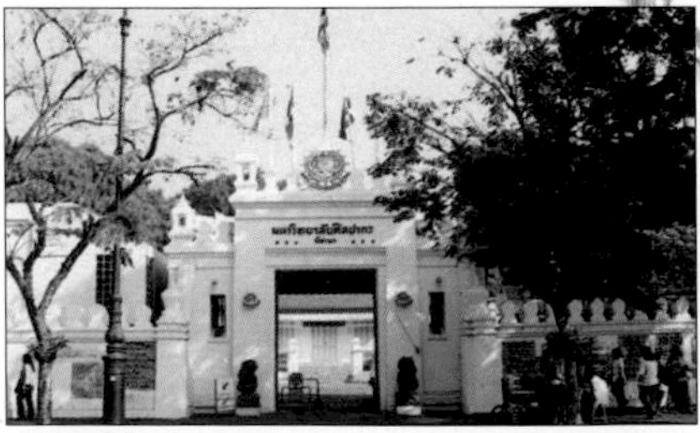

Phra Chan Pier
MAHATHAT
TROK SILLAPAKORN
NA PHRA LAN
0 meters 500
0 yards 500
Tha Chang Chao-Phraya Express Pier
Entrance to Grand Palace and Wat Phra Kaeo
Western edge of Sanam Luang
To Lak Muang (City Pillar)

Silpakorn University of Fine Arts
The entrance to Thailand's most famous art school can be found on Na Phra Lan Road. The university regularly puts on excellent art shows in its exhibition hall. See the signs outside the entrance for details and opening times.

Key

- - - - Suggested route

AMULETS

The Thais are a highly superstitious people – those who do not wear some form of protective or lucky amulet are firmly in a minority. Amulets come in myriad forms and are sold in specialty markets, often near spiritually auspicious sites. Although many are religious in nature – such as tiny Buddha images and copies of sacred statues – others are designed for more practical purposes, such as model phalluses to ensure sexual potency. Amulets are such a big business that there are even magazines dedicated to them.

A selection of charms sold at stalls around Sanam Luang

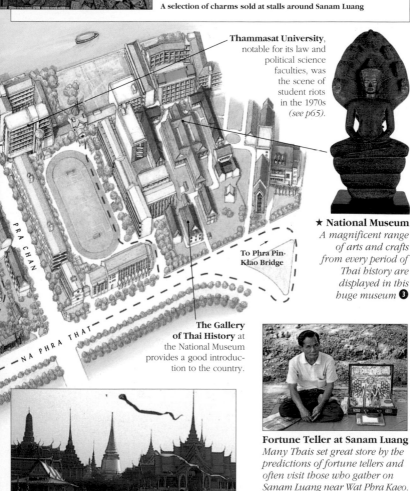

Thammasat University, notable for its law and political science faculties, was the scene of student riots in the 1970s *(see p65).*

★ **National Museum**
A magnificent range of arts and crafts from every period of Thai history are displayed in this huge museum ❸

To Phra Pin-Klao Bridge

PRA CHAN

NA PHRA THAT

The Gallery of Thai History at the National Museum provides a good introduction to the country.

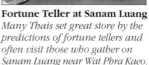

Fortune Teller at Sanam Luang
Many Thais set great store by the predictions of fortune tellers and often visit those who gather on Sanam Luang near Wat Phra Kaeo.

★ **Kite Flying at Sanam Luang**
King Chulalongkorn (1868–1910) was an avid kite flyer and permitted Sanam Luang to be used for the sport. Fiercely contested kite fights can often be witnessed here between February and April.

STAR SIGHTS
★ **National Museum**
★ **Kite Flying at Sanam Luang**

Grand Palace and Wat Phra Kaeo ❶

พระบรมมหาราชวังและวัดพระแก้ว

Detail on Phra Mondop Library

Cᴏɴꜱᴛʀᴜᴄᴛɪᴏɴ ᴏꜰ this remarkable site began in 1782, to mark the founding of the new capital and provide a resting place for the sacred Emerald Buddha (Phra Kaeo) and a residence for the king. Surrounded by walls stretching for 1,900 m (2,080 yards), the complex was once a self-sufficient city within a city. The Royal Family now lives in Dusit, but Wat Phra Kaeo is still Thailand's holiest temple – visitors must cover their knees and heels before entering.

Wat Phra Kaeo's skyline, as seen from Sanam Luang

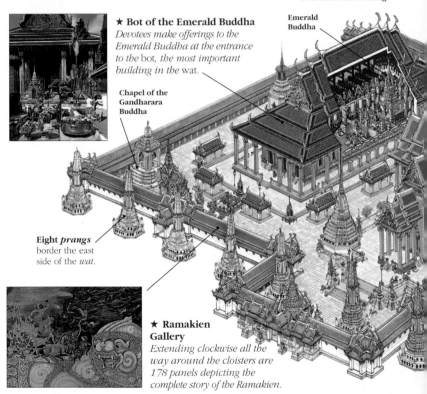

★ Bot of the Emerald Buddha
Devotees make offerings to the Emerald Buddha at the entrance to the bot, *the most important building in the* wat.

Emerald Buddha

Chapel of the Gandharara Buddha

Eight *prangs* border the east side of the *wat*.

★ Ramakien Gallery
Extending clockwise all the way around the cloisters are 178 panels depicting the complete story of the Ramakien.

TIMELINE

		1750		1800		1850		1900		1950	

1783 Work begins on Wat Phra Kaeo, Dusit Throne Hall, and Phra Maha Monthien

1855 New buildings epitomize fusion of Eastern and Western styles

1925 Rama VII chooses to live in the less formal Chitrlada Palace at Dusit. Grand Palace reserved for special occasions

1782 Official founding of new capital

1809 Rama II introduces Chinese details

1840s Women's quarter laid out as a city within a city

1880 Chulalongkorn, the last king to make major additions, involves 26 half-brothers in renovation of Wat Phra Kaeo

1932 Chakri Dynasty's 150th year celebrated at palace

1982 Renovation of the complex

Decorative Gilt Figures

Encircling the exterior of the bot *are 112* garudas *(mythical beasts that are half-man, half-bird). They are shown holding* nagas *(serpents) and are typical of the* wat's *dazzling decorative details.*

VISITORS' CHECKLIST

Na Phra Lan Rd. **Map** 1 C5.
🚌 *1, 3, 25, 33, 39, 53.* 🚤
Chang, Tien. ⏰ *8:30am–3:30pm daily.* 🔵 *ceremonies.* 🎟 *includes Vimanmek Palace.* 📷 *in* bot.
📷 W *www.palaces.thai.net*

Apsonsi

A mythical creature (half-woman, half-lion), Apsonsi is one of the beautiful gilded figures on the upper terrace of Wat Phra Kaeo.

Phra Mondop (library)

The Phra Si Rattana Chedi contains a piece of the Buddha's breastbone.

Upper Terrace

Ho Phra Nak (royal mausoleum)

Wihan Yot

WAT PHRA KAEO

Wat Phra Kaeo (shown here) is a sub-complex within the greater Grand Palace complex. The temple is Thailand's holiest shrine, but unlike other Thai *wats*, has no resident monks.

The Ho Phra Monthien Tham is the auxiliary library.

The Royal Pantheon

GRAND PALACE AND WAT PHRA KAEO

1 Entrance
2 Wat Phra Kaeo complex
3 Dusit Throne Hall
4 Aphonphimok Pavilion
5 Chakri Throne Hall
6 Inner Palace
7 Phra Maha Monthien Buildings
8 Siwalai Gardens
9 Rama IV Chapel
10 Boromphiman Mansion
11 Audience Chamber

KEY

⬜	Wat Phra Kaeo complex
⬜	Buildings
⬜	Lawns

STAR FEATURES

★ **Bot of the Emerald Buddha**

★ **Ramakien Gallery**

Exploring Wat Phra Kaeo

Guard outside *chedi*

WHEN RAMA I ESTABLISHED the new capital of Bangkok in 1782 his ambition was to construct a royal temple along the lines of the grand chapels of previous capital cities. Symbolizing the simultaneous founding of the Chakri dynasty, this temple was to surpass its larger Sukhothai and Ayutthaya predecessors in the splendor of its design and decoration. The result of his vision was Wat Phra Kaeo, or Temple of the Emerald Buddha (officially known as Wat Phra Si Rattana Sasadaram), so called because the *bot* houses the Emerald Buddha image, brought here from Wat Arun *(see pp120–1)* in 1785.

The Emerald Buddha crowning the ornate gilded altar inside the *bot*

THE BOT AND PERIPHERAL BUILDINGS

THE MOST SACRED building within the palace complex, the *bot* of Wat Phra Kaeo was erected to house what is still the most revered image of the Buddha in Thailand: the Emerald Buddha.

The exterior doors and windows of the *bot* are inlaid with delicate mother-of-pearl designs. Along the marble base supporting the structure runs a series of gilt bronze *garudas* (half bird, half human). The staircase of the main entrance is guarded by Cambodian-style stone lions, or *singhas*.

Inside, the surprisingly small image of the Emerald Buddha sits in a glass case high above a golden altar. Carved from a single piece of jade (not emerald), it is 66 cm (26 in) tall and has a lap span of 48 cm (19 in). The Buddha has been attributed to the late Lanna School of the 15th century. It is dressed in one of three costumes: a crown and jewelry for the summer season; a golden shawl in winter; and a gilded monastic robe and headdress in the rainy season. The reigning monarch or a prince appointed by him presides over each changing of the Buddha's attire in a deeply symbolic ceremony.

Inside the *bot* are murals from the reign of Rama III (1824–51). They depict the classic subjects of Thai mural painting, namely the Traiphum (Buddhist cosmology), the Buddha's victory over Mara (the god of death), and scenes from the previous lives of the Buddha – the *jatakas*. Around the temple are 12 open-sided *salas* (small pavilions) built as contemplative shelters.

Southeast of the *bot* is the 19th-century **Chapel of the Gandharara Buddha**. The bronze image of the Buddha calling the rains housed here is used in the Royal Plowing Ceremony in May *(see p42)*. The bell in the nearby belfry is rung only on special occasions such as New Year's Day.

THE UPPER TERRACE

OF THE FOUR structures on this elevated terrace, the **Phra Si Rattana Chedi**, at the western end, is the most striking. It was built by King Mongkut (Rama IV) to enshrine a piece of the Buddha's breastbone. The golden tiles decorating the exterior were later added by King Chulalongkorn (Rama V).

The adjacent **Phra Mondop**, used as a library, was built by Rama I as a hall to house Buddhist scriptures. Although the Library is closed to the public, the exterior is splendid in itself. The Javanese Buddha images on the four outer corners are copies of early 9th-century originals, which are now in the museum near the entrance

Gold Angel Guardians decorating the wall of the Phra Mondop

Mural depicting a scene from the Ramakien in the Ramakien Gallery

THE PRANGS, YAKSHAS, AND RAMAKIEN GALLERY

SURROUNDING the temple complex is the cloisterlike Ramakien Gallery, decorated with lavishly painted and meticulously restored murals. This is Thailand's most extensive depiction of the ancient legend of the Ramakien (see pp36–7). The 178 panels were originally painted in the late 18th century, but damage from humidity means that frequent renovation is necessary. The murals are divided by marble pillars inscribed with verses relating the story, which begins opposite Wihan Yot and proceeds in a clockwise direction.

Guarding each gateway to the gallery is a pair of *yakshas* (demons). Placed here during the reign of Rama II, they are said to protect the Emerald Buddha from evil spirits. Each one represents a different character from the Ramakien myth: the green one, for example, symbolizes Tosakan, or the demon king.

The eight different-colored *prangs* on the edge of the temple complex are intricately decorated with Chinese porcelain. They represent the eight elements of the Buddhist religion, including the Buddha, the Dharma (law), the *sangha* (monkhood), and the *bhiksunis* (female Buddhists).

to the palace complex. Outside the building are memorials to all the kings of the present Chakri dynasty, and bronze elephant statues representing the royal white elephants (see p102) from the first five reigns of the dynasty (see pp60–1).

To the north of the *mondop* is a model of Angkor Wat in northwest Cambodia (see pp254–5). The model was commissioned by Rama IV to show his people the scale and gracious splendor of 12th-century Khmer architecture – Cambodia during his reign being under Thai rule.

The **Royal Pantheon** houses life-size statues of the Chakri kings. Rama IV had intended the hall to hold the Emerald Buddha, but decided that it was too small. The pantheon is open to the public only on Chakri Day (see p44).

THE NORTHERN TERRACE

HO PHRA NAK was originally constructed by Rama I in the late 18th century to enshrine the Nak (literally, alloy of gold, silver, and copper) Buddha image that had been rescued from Ayutthaya. Rama III, however, demolished the original hall, preferring to build the present brick and mortar structure to house the ashes of

minor members of the royal family. The Nak Buddha was moved into the neighboring **Wihan Yot**, which is shaped like a Greek cross and decorated with Chinese porcelain.

Also on the Northern Terrace is the **Ho Phra Monthien Tham**, or Auxiliary Library, built by the brother of Rama I. The door panels, inlaid with mother-of-pearl, were salvaged from Ayutthaya's Wat Borom Buddharam. Inside, Buddhist scriptures are stored in fine cabinets.

Ramakien figure outside *chedi*

THE LEGEND OF THE EMERALD BUDDHA

In 1434 lightning struck the *chedi* of Wat Phra Kaeo in Chiang Rai in Northern Thailand (see pp240–1), revealing a simple stucco image. The abbot of the temple kept it in his residence until the flaking plaster exposed a jadeite image beneath. Upon learning of the discovery, the king of Chiang Mai sent an army of elephants to bring the image to him. The elephant bearing the Emerald Buddha, however, refused to take the road to Chiang Mai, and, treating this as an auspicious sign, the entourage re-routed to Lampang. The image was moved several more times over the next century, then was taken to Wat Pha Kaew in Laos (see pp284–5) in 1552. It was not until General Chakri (later Rama I) captured Vientiane in 1778 that the Emerald Buddha was returned to Thailand. It was kept in Wat Arun (see pp120–1) for 15 years, before a grand river procession brought it to its current resting place on March 5, 1785.

The small Emerald Buddha inside the *bot*

Exploring the Grand Palace

BUILT AT THE SAME TIME as Wat Phra Kaeo, the Grand Palace was the king's official residence from 1782 to 1946, although King Chulalongkorn (Rama V) was the last monarch to live here. Today, the royal family resides at Chitrlada Palace *(see p102)*. Throughout the palace's history, many structures have been altered. Within the complex there are a few functioning government buildings, such as the Ministry of Finance, but most others are unused. Important ceremonies are still held in the Dusit Throne Hall and the Amarin Winichai Hall.

Decorative demon guardian

DUSIT THRONE HALL

THIS CROSS-SHAPED throne hall was originally built in 1784 as a reproduction of one of Ayutthaya's grandest buildings, Sanphet Maha Prasat *(see pp168–9)*. Five years later the hall was struck by lightning and rebuilt on a smaller scale. Crowned with a sumptuously decorated tiered spire, it is one of the finest examples of early Rattanakosin architecture *(see p31)*. Inside is a masterpiece of Thai art: the original Rama I teak throne, inlaid with mother-of-pearl. In the south wing is a window in the form of a throne. The hall is used for the annual Coronation Day celebrations *(see p44)*.

APHONPHIMOK PAVILION

KING MONGKUT (Rama IV) built this small wooden structure as a royal changing room for when he was giving audiences at the Dusit Throne Hall. The king would be carried on a palanquin to the pavilion's shoulder-high first step. Inside the building he would change into the appropriate apparel for the occasion. The pavilion's simple structure, complemented by its elaborate decoration, makes it a building of perfect proportions: indeed, it is considered a glory of Thai architecture. It inspired Rama V so much so that he had a replica built at Bang Pa-in *(see p171)*.

CHAKRI THRONE HALL

ALSO KNOWN AS the Grand Palace Throne Hall, Chakri Maha Prasat was built in Neo-Classical style by the British architect John Chinitz. Rama V commissioned the building in 1882 to mark the centenary of the Chakri dynasty, a fact reflected in the theme of the sumptuous decoration. The structure was originally intended to have a domed roof, but the royal court decided that, in the interest of maintaining aesthetic harmony with the surrounding buildings, a Thai-style roof would be more appropriate.

Housed on the top floor of the Central Hall are the ashes of royal monarchs, and the first floor functions as the main audience hall where the King receives ambassadors and entertains foreign monarchs.

Behind the Niello Throne in the Chakri Throne Room is the emblem of the Chakri dynasty: a discus and trident. The paintings in the room depict diplomatic missions, including Queen Victoria welcoming Rama IV's ambassador in London. The East Wing is used as a reception room for royal guests. The long hall connecting the Central Hall with this wing is lined with portraits of the Chakri dynasty. In the West Wing is the queen's personal reception room. Portraits of the principal queens of Rama IV, Rama V, and Rama VII decorate the hall between the Central Hall and this wing.

Elephant statue by Chakri Throne Hall

PHRA MAHA MONTHIEN BUILDINGS

THIS CLUSTER of connected buildings, located to the east of the Chakri Throne Hall, is the "Grand Residence" of the palace complex.

The focal point of the 18th-century **Amarin Winichai Hall**, the northernmost building of the group, is Rama I's boat-shaped Busabok Mala Throne. When an audience was present, two curtains hid the throne as the king ascended, and, with an elaborate fanfare, the curtains were drawn back to reveal the king wearing a loose, golden gown and seeming to float on the prowlike part of the throne. In the 19th century two British ambassadors were received in such manner here;

Exterior of the Dusit Throne Hall, with its elegant multitiered spire

Lavish decor of the connecting hall of the Chakri Throne Hall's West Wing

John Crawfurd by Rama II and Sir John Bowring by Rama IV. The hall is now used for some state ceremonies.

Connected to the hall by a gateway through which only the king, queen, and royal children may walk is the **Phaisan Thaksin Hall**. This was used by Rama I as a private hall when dining with family, friends, and members of the royal court. In 1809 a Borom Rachaphisek Ceremony was performed in this hall to mark the coronation of the new king, Rama II. On the high altar is the Phra Siam Thewathirat, a highly venerated guardian figure, placed here by Rama IV.

The third building is the **Chakraphat Phiman Hall**. It served as a residence for the first three Chakri kings. It is still the custom for a newly crowned king to spend a night here as part of his coronation.

INNER PALACE

BEHIND A GATEWAY to the left of the Chakri Throne Hall is the entrance to the Inner Palace, which is closed to the public. Until the time of Rama VII, the palace was inhabited solely by women of the royal family: principal wives, minor wives, and daughters. Apart from sons, who had to leave the palace on reaching puberty, the king was the only male allowed to live within its walls.

The palace functioned as a small city, with its own government and laws, complete with prison cells. Under the strict guidance of a formidable "Directress of the Inside," a small army of uniformed officers policed the area.

Rama III renovated the overcrowded and precarious wooden structures, and, in the late 19th century, Rama V built small, fantastical Victorian style palaces here for his favorite consorts. Because his successor, Rama VI, had only one wife, the complex was left virtually empty, and it eventually fell into disrepair.

One of the palace buildings that continues to function is the finishing school for the daughters of high-society Thai families. The girls are taught flower weaving, royal cuisine, and social etiquette.

SIWALAI GARDENS

THESE BEAUTIFUL gardens, which are often closed for state functions, lie east of the Inner Palace and contain the **Phra Buddha Ratana Sathan**, a personal chapel built by Rama IV. The pavilion is covered in gray marble and decorated with white and blue glass mosaics. The marble *bai sema* (boundary stones) are inlaid with the insignia of Rama V, who placed the stones here, Rama II, who had the gardens laid out, and Rama IV.

The Neo-Classical **Borom-phiman Mansion** in the gardens was built by Rama V as a residence for the Crown Prince (later King Rama VI). The building served as a temporary residence for several kings: Rama VII, Rama VIII, and Rama IX (King Bhumibol). Today it is used as a guest house for visiting dignitaries.

AUDIENCE CHAMBER

VISIBLE FROM OUTSIDE the palace walls, this chamber – Phra Thinang Sutthaisawan Prasat – is located between Thewaphithak and Sakchaisit gates. It was built by Rama I as a place to grant an audience during royal ceremonies and to watch the training of his elephants. Rama III strengthened the wooden structure with brick, and decorative features were added later. These include the crowning spire and ornamental cast-iron motifs.

Mosaic-decorated Phra Buddha Ratana Sathan in the Siwalai Gardens

Entrance to the Buddhist University at Wat Mahathat

Wat Mahathat ②

วัดมหาธาตุ

3 Maharaj Rd. **Map** 1 C5.
0-2221-5999. AC: 203, 506.
Chang Maharaj. daily.

THIS IS A LARGE, busy temple complex, interesting more for its atmosphere than for its architecture. Dating from the 1700s, the *wihan* and *bot* were both rebuilt between 1844 and 1851. The *mondop*, which gives the temple its name – "temple of the great relic" – has a cruciform roof, a feature rarely found in Bangkok.

The *wat* is the national center for the Mahanikai monastic sect, and it holds one of Bangkok's two Buddhist universities (meditation classes are offered here at 7am, 1pm, and 6pm in Section Five, near the monks' quarters). There is also a traditional herbal medicine market, and, on weekends, numerous stalls selling a wide range of goods.

National Museum ③

พิพิธภัณฑ์สถานแห่งชาติ

See pp84–5.

National Gallery ④

หอศิลป์แห่งชาติ

4 Chao Fa Rd. **Map** 2 D4. 0-2282-2639. AC: 506. Phra Athit. 9am–4pm Wed–Sun. public hols.

THAILAND'S MAIN art gallery, housed in the old mint building, was established in 1977. It concentrates on modern Thai and international art. Initially the gallery suffered from lack of funds, but in 1989 new wings were added. The high-ceilinged, spacious halls now attract exhibitions from all over Asia. Temporary shows of prominent Asian artists are often better than many of the permanent exhibits. Modern art can also be found at the Visual Dhamma Gallery *(see p132)*. Check the *Bangkok Post* for details.

Modern sculpture at the National Gallery

Wat Bowonniwet ⑤

วัดบวรนิเวศน์

248 Phra Sumen Rd. **Map** 2 E4.
0-2281-2831. 12, 15, 56; AC: 511 (Express). 8am–5pm daily.

HIDDEN IN QUIET, tree-filled grounds, this mid-19th-century temple was constructed by Rama III. The style bears his trademark Chinese influence. A central gilded *chedi* is flanked by two symmetrical chapels, the most interesting of which is next to Phra Sumen Road. The interior murals are attributed to monk-painter Khrua In Khong, who is famous for the introduction of Western perspective into Thai temple murals. As court painter to King Mongkut (Rama IV) he was exposed to Western ideas and adapted these to a Thai setting. The result was a series of murals that on first glance look wholly Western, but that portray the same Buddhist allegories found in traditional Thai murals. For instance, a physician healing a blind man can be interpreted as the illuminating power of Buddhism. The images are all the more remarkable for the fact that Khrua In Khong never traveled to the West. The main Buddha image, Phra Buddha Chinasara, is one of the best examples from the Sukhothai period.

King Mongkut served as abbot here during his 27 years in the monkhood and founded the strict Tammayut sect of Buddhism, for which the temple is now the headquarters. Since Mongkut, many Thai kings have served their monkhoods at the *wat*, including the current monarch, King Bhumibol (Rama IX). The temple also houses Thailand's second Buddhist university. Across the road from the temple is a Buddhist bookstore that sells English-language publications.

Mid-19th-century, Western-style mural at Wat Bowonniwet

Democracy Monument ❻

อนุสาวรีย์ประชาธิปไตย

Ratchadamnoen Klang. **Map** 2 E4.
🚌 *AC: 503, 509, 511.* ⭕ *daily.*

A FOCAL POINT during pro-democracy demonstrations, this monument (built 1939) commemorates the revolution of 1932 *(see p64)*. Each feature symbolizes the date of the establishment of Thailand's constitutional monarchy, on June 24, 1932.

The four wing towers are each 24 m (79 ft) high. The 75 cannons indicate the year 2475 of the Buddhist Era (1932), and the pedestal, containing a copy of the constitution, is 3 m (10 ft) high, referring to the third month of the Thai calendar (June).

The structure was designed by Silpa Bhirasi, an Italian sculptor who took a Thai name and citizenship.

Central edifice of Democracy Monument (1939)

Wat Rachanadda ❼

วัดราชนัดดา

Maha Chai Rd. **Map** 2 E4. 🚌 *2, 44, 59; AC: 79, 503, 511.* ⭕ *9am–4pm daily.*

T HE MOST interesting feature at Wat Rachanadda (also often spelt Ratchanaddaram) is the metal monastery. Originally conceived as a *chedi* to complement the temple, it evolved into an elaborate meditation chamber

One of hundreds of meditation cells at Wat Rachanat

modeled on a 3rd-century BC Sri Lankan temple (the original is now ruined). Passages dissect each level, running north to south and east to west. The meditation cells are at each intersection.

In the temple's courtyard is Bangkok's best amulet market. Tourists may face disapproval if they attempt to take talismans home as souvenirs. Across the road, behind the old city walls, is the Doves' Village, where singing doves are sold for competitions.

Wat Saket and the Golden Mount ❽

วัดสระเกศและภูเขาทอง

Chakkaphatdi Phong Rd. **Map** 2 F5. 🚌 *8, 15, 37, 47, 49; AC: 38, 543.* ⭕ *7:30am–5:30pm daily.* 📷 📹 *Golden Mount Fair (Nov).*

B UILT BY Rama I in the late 18th century, Wat Saket is one of the oldest temples in Bangkok. Visitors come to climb the artificial hill topped with a golden tower within the grounds. Rama III built the first Golden Mount, but the soft soil led to its collapse. King Chulalongkorn (Rama V) provided the necessary technology to create the 76-m (250-ft) high representation of the mythical Mount Meru seen today. It is believed to house relics of the Buddha presented to Rama V by the Viceroy of India. A circular staircase lined with strange

monuments and tombs leads to the top, where there is a small sanctuary. The wonderful panoramic view from the gallery takes in the Grand Palace, Wat Pho, and Wat Arun. The octagonal building opposite, Mahakan Fort, is one of 14 original watch-towers of the city walls.

Until the 1960s the Golden Mount was one of the highest points in Bangkok. Today, it still forms a prominent landmark, although it is dwarfed by skyscrapers *(see p117)*.

During the 19th century the grounds of Wat Saket served a macabre function as a crematorium. The bodies of the poor were sometimes left for vultures and dogs. By contrast, a fair with dancing and a candle procession is now held on the grounds in November.

The Golden Mount, a distinctive Bangkok landmark

National Museum ❸

พิพิธภัณฑสถานแห่งชาติ

Colorful Bencharong drums

T HE NATIONAL MUSEUM has one of the largest and most comprehensive collections in Southeast Asia and provides an excellent introduction to the arts, crafts, and history of Thailand. Two of the museum buildings, the 18th-century Wang Na Palace and Buddhaisawan Chapel, are works of art in themselves. The chapel contains the venerated Phra Buddha Sihing image and the palace an eclectic selection of artifacts from ancient weaponry to shadow puppets. The two wings of the museum are devoted mainly to art and sculpture. Other attractions include galleries of history and prehistory and the Royal Funeral Chariots Gallery. The labeling of the collection is not always helpful, so taking one of the frequent, free guided tours is highly recommended.

Doors of Throne Hall
These beautifully decorated black and gold lacquered doors to the Wang Na Palace date from the 19th century and show a strong Chinese influence.

Phra Buddha Sihing
The history of this image, one of Thailand's holiest after the Emerald Buddha, is shrouded in legend. It probably dates from the 13th century and was brought here from Chiang Mai by Rama I in 1787.

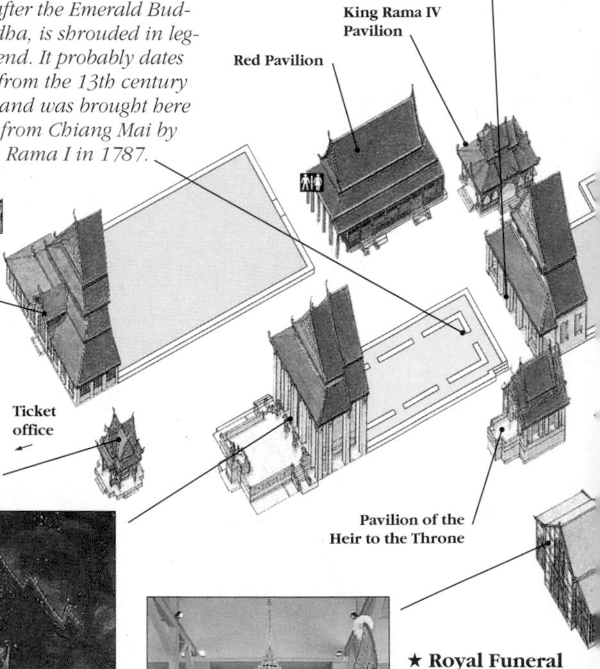

King Rama IV Pavilion

Red Pavilion

The Gallery of Thai History houses the 13th-century Ramkamhaeng Stone. This is thought to be inscribed with the earliest extant example of the Thai script.

Ticket office

King Vajiravudh Pavilion

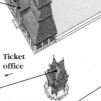

Pavilion of the Heir to the Throne

★ **Buddhaisawan Chapel**
Built in 1787, this beautiful building is decorated with some of the best Rattanakosin period murals in Thailand.

★ **Royal Funeral Chariots Gallery**
Several lavishly decorated, gilded teak chariots used in royal funeral processions can be seen in this gallery, including Racharot Noi, built in 1795.

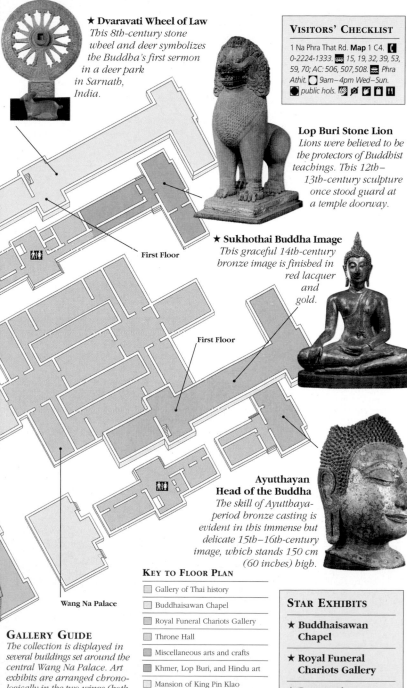

★ Dvaravati Wheel of Law
This 8th-century stone wheel and deer symbolizes the Buddha's first sermon in a deer park in Sarnath, India.

VISITORS' CHECKLIST

1 Na Phra That Rd. **Map** 1 C4. 0-2224-1333. 15, 19, 32, 39, 53, 59, 70; AC: 506, 507, 508. Phra Athit. 9am–4pm Wed–Sun. public hols.

Lop Buri Stone Lion
Lions were believed to be the protectors of Buddhist teachings. This 12th–13th-century sculpture once stood guard at a temple doorway.

First Floor

★ Sukhothai Buddha Image
This graceful 14th-century bronze image is finished in red lacquer and gold.

First Floor

Ayutthayan Head of the Buddha
The skill of Ayutthaya-period bronze casting is evident in this immense but delicate 15th–16th-century image, which stands 150 cm (60 inches) high.

Wang Na Palace

KEY TO FLOOR PLAN

- Gallery of Thai history
- Buddhaisawan Chapel
- Royal Funeral Chariots Gallery
- Throne Hall
- Miscellaneous arts and crafts
- Khmer, Lop Buri, and Hindu art
- Mansion of King Pin Klao
- Dvaravati, Srivijayan and Lop Buri art, Gallery of Ban Chiang and Javanese Sculpture
- Lanna, Sukhothai, Ayutthayan, and Rattanakosin art

STAR EXHIBITS

★ **Buddhaisawan Chapel**

★ **Royal Funeral Chariots Gallery**

★ **Dvaravati Wheel of Law**

★ **Sukhothai Buddha Image**

GALLERY GUIDE
The collection is displayed in several buildings set around the central Wang Na Palace. Art exhibits are arranged chronologically in the two wings (both of which have upper and lower levels), starting from the left (south) wing. The ticket office, near the entrance on Na Phra That Road, sells guide books.

Monk's bowl being heated to blacken and finish the surface

Monk's Bowl Village (Ban Bat) 9

บ้านบาตร

Bamrung Muang Rd, Soi Ban Bat.
Map 2 F5. ▦ AC: 508.

Mᴏɴᴋs' ʙᴏᴡʟs were first used 2,500 years ago and are still widely used today in Buddhist countries for early morning alms-gathering (see p125). Such bowls have been made at Monk's Bowl Village in Bangkok since the late 18th century. The village once stretched as far as Wat Saket (see p83), but modern developments have reduced the village to just four homes and a cluster of small workshops. This area may be hard to find amid the maze of sois, but the bowls are sold at Wat Suthat.

The process of bowl making is time consuming and requires eight pieces of metal, representing the eight spokes of the wheel of Dharma. The first strip is beaten into a circular form to make the rim. Three pieces are then beaten to create a cross-shaped skeleton. Four triangular pieces complete the sides. After being welded in a kiln, the bowl is shaped, filed smooth, and fired again to give an enamel-like surface. About 20 bowls are produced daily in the village.

At the center of the maze of alleyways next to the small village hall is an unusual and intriguing shrine, constructed from old Chinese cylinder bellows, that is dedicated to the "Holy Teacher and Ancestor."

Bamrung Muang Road 10

ถนนบำรุงเมือง

Map 2 F5. ▦ AC: 508.

Bᴀᴍʀᴜɴɢ ᴍᴜᴀɴɢ, like Charoen Krung (see p110), was an elephant trail until the 20th century, when it became one of Thailand's first paved roads. The stretch between Maha Chai Road and the Giant Swing provides an enlightening peek into the thriving business behind the Buddhist practice of merit-making. Along here the road is lined with shops selling religious paraphernalia: monks' robes, votive candles, and Buddha images of all shapes and sizes, many rather incongruously packaged in cellophane. Monks shop here for temple essentials; other people buy offerings and shrines for the home. Although the religious objects look enticing

Plastic-wrapped Buddha image

to tourists, they are not intended as souvenirs: images of the Buddha cannot be taken out of the country without an export license (see p451).

Wat Suthat and the Giant Swing 11

วัดสุทัศน์และเสาชิงช้า

Bamrung Muang Rd. **Map** 2 E5. ▦ 10, 12, 19, 35, 42, 56, 96. ◯ 8:30am–4pm daily (wihan Sat & Sun only).

Tʜᴇʀᴇ ᴀʀᴇ sᴇᴠᴇʀᴀʟ superlatives for Wat Suthat, a temple that was begun by Rama I in 1807 and completed by Rama III. Its wihan is the largest in Bangkok. The art and architecture beautifully exemplify Rattanakosin style (see p31). Its central Buddha, at 8 m (26 ft) high, is one of the largest surviving Sukhothai bronzes. This image was moved from Wat Mahathat in Sukhothai (see pp54–5) to Bangkok by Rama I. The

View through the immense portal of the wihan at Wat Suthat

murals in the immense *wihan* are some of the most celebrated in Thailand. Amazingly intricate, they depict the Traiphum (Buddhist cosmology) and were restored in the 1980s. The teak doors to the *wihan* are also noteworthy, carved in five delicate layers and standing 5.5 m (18 ft) high. (One made by Rama II is now in the National Museum.) The cloister around the outside of the *wihan* is lined with 156 golden Buddha images.

In the square in front of Wat Suthat is a red-painted, lofty frame. The structure, known as the Giant Swing, is the remains of a swing used for a Brahmin ceremony, dedicated to the god Shiva, that used to be performed in the presence of royalty.

Wat Rachabophit ⓬

วัดราชบพิธ

Fuang Nakhon Rd. **Map** 2 D5. 📞 *0-2222-3930.* 🚌 *2, 60; AC: 501, 502, 512.* 🚢 *Thien.* ◻ *5am–8pm daily.*

THE CIRCULAR FORM of Wat Rachabophit is a successful architectural blend of East and West. Construction of the temple began under King Chulalongkorn (Rama V) in 1869 and continued for over 20 years. The whole complex is splendidly decorated with porcelain tiles, which were made to order in China. The focal point is the central, Sri Lankan-style, gilded *chedi,* whose full height from the terrace is 43 m (140 ft).

Inside the *wat* are four Buddha images, each facing one of the cardinal points.

Rows of tiny carved figures on eaves of the *bot* at Wat Rachapradit

Leading off from the circular gallery are the *bot* to the north, the *wihan* to the south, and two lesser *wihans* to the east and west: an unusual layout for a Thai *wat.*

East-West flourishes permeate the entire complex. The 10 door panels and 28 window panels of the *bot* are decorated with typically Thai mother-of-pearl inlay that illustrates the insignia of five royal orders. The moldings over the door depict King Chulalongkorn's seal. The carved, painted guards on the doors are distinctively *farang* (European), and the interior is decorated in an incongruous Italian Renaissance style.

Accessible through the temple grounds (parallel to Khlong Lot) is a fascinating royal cemetery rarely explored by visitors. The monuments to members of King Chulalongkorn's family are an eccentric mix of Khmer, Thai, and European styles.

"Farang," Wat Rachabophit

Wat Rachapradit ⓭

วัดราชประดิษฐ์

Saran Rom Rd. **Map** 2 D5. 📞 *0-2223-8215.* 🚌 *AC: 501, 502, 512.* 🚢 *Thien.* ◻ *5am–10pm daily.*

LOCATED IN THE northeast corner of the former Saranrom Palace gardens (now the Ministry of Foreign Affairs), this charming, peaceful temple is rarely visited by tourists. It was built in the mid-19th century by King Mongkut (Rama IV) and his East-meets-West taste in architecture is apparent in the choice of building materials. The main *wihan,* for instance, is covered in forbidding gray marble. The interior murals were painted in the late-19th century and depict the festivals of the Thai lunar calendar. Among other scenes are some extravagant preparations for the Giant Swing ceremony, people celebrating the annual Loy Krathong water festival, and an image of King Mongkut observing an eclipse of the moon *(see p61).*

Striking carvings adorn the doors, eaves, and gables of the temple. Other notable edifices in the grounds of the *wat* include graceful pavilions, Khmer-style *prangs,* and a gray marble *chedi.* Near to Wat Rachapradit, next to Khlong Lot, is a small gilded boar, a shrine to Queen Saowapha Phongsi (King Chulalongkorn's consort), who was born in the year of the pig.

THE SWING IN ACTION

Sao Ching Cha, the "Giant Swing" at Wat Suthat, was built in 1784 by Rama I. During ceremonies – Brahmin in origin – teams of four would swing in 180 degree arcs up to 25 m (82 ft) high. One participant would try to bite off a sack of gold hung from tall poles. The event, linked to the god Shiva swinging in the heavens, caused many deaths and was abolished in 1935.

Young Brahmins performing on Sao Ching Cha

Wat Pho ⑭
วัดโพธิ์

O FFICIALLY KNOWN AS Wat Phra Chetuphon, Wat Pho is not only Bangkok's oldest and largest temple but also Thailand's foremost center for public education. Unlike the Grand Palace (see pp 76–81), it has a lively and lived-in dilapidated grandeur. In the 1780s Rama I rebuilt the original 16th-century temple on this site and enlarged the complex. In 1832 Rama III built the Chapel of the Reclining Buddha, housing the stunning image, and turned the temple into a place of learning. Today Wat Pho is a traditional medicine center, of which the famous Institute of Massage is a part. Nearby on Chetuphon Road is the temple mon-astery, home to some 300 monks.

Farang guard

Wihan
The western wihan *is one of four around the main* bot.

★ Medicine Pavilion
Embedded in the inner walls of this pavilion are stone plaques showing massage points. The pavilion is now a souvenir shop.

★ Reclining Buddha
The 46-m (150-ft) long, gilded plas-ter and brick image fills the whole wihan.

Small buildings
at this end of the *wat* are reserved for children.

Feet of the Reclining Buddha
The striking, intricate mother-of-pearl images on the soles of the feet of the Reclining Buddha represent the 108 lakshanas, which are the auspicious signs of the true Buddha.

The Phra Si Sanphet Chedi
encases the remains of a sacred Buddha image

Bodhi Tree
It is said that this grew from a cutting of the tr under which the Buddl meditated in India.

Ceramic Decoration
This porcelain design is on the Phra Si Sanphet Chedi.

Institute of Massage

VISITORS' CHECKLIST

Sanam Chai Rd. **Map** 5 C1. 0-2225-5910. AC: 25, 32, 44, 60, 508. Thien Chang, Rachinee. 9am–5pm daily. Institute of Massage 0-2221-2974. 8:30am–5pm daily.

Main Bot
Wat Pho's bot houses a bronze meditating Buddha image salvaged from Ayutthaya by Rama I's brother. Scenes from the Ramakien (see pp36–7) *are carved into the outer base and inner doors.*

Miniature Mountains
This tiny stone mountain by the southern wihan is one of several within the complex. The statues of naked hermits are posed in the different positions of healing massage.

Visitors' entrance

Farang **guards**
stand at the compound's inner gates. These huge stone statues with big noses, beards, and top hats are caricatures of Westerners.

TRADITIONAL MASSAGE

Since the 1960s Wat Pho has run the most respected massage school in the city. Traditional Thai massage *(nuat paen boran)* supposedly dates from the time of the Buddha and is related to Chinese acupuncture and Indian yoga. The highly trained masseurs at the *wat* specialize in pulling and stretching the limbs and torso to relieve various ailments ranging from general tension to viruses. Visitors can experience a massage or learn the art through a 10- or 15-day course in Thai or English.

Braving a traditional Thai massage at Wat Pho

STAR FEATURES

★ **Reclining Buddha**

★ **Medicine Pavilion**

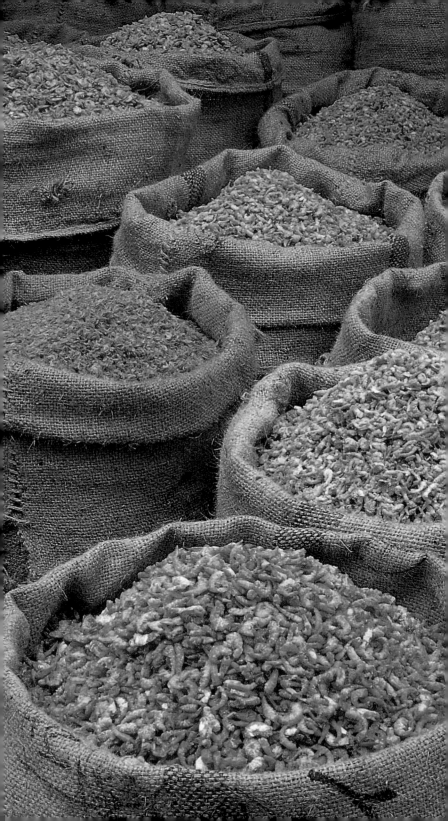

CHINATOWN

Modern painting of a Chinatown street vendor

ANGKOK'S CHINESE residents originally lived in the area where the Old City is today. When Rama I decided to move his capital across the river in 1782, the entire community was relocated. Since then the district around Yaowarat and Sampeng roads has been the focus of Chinese life in the city, although now it is also home to a small Indian community. Once the financial center of Bangkok, Chinatown remains a thriving, bustling, noisy area. Between the two great traffic-choked thoroughfares of Yaowarat Road and Charoen Krung Road lies a maze of narrow alleyways

packed with market stalls. The most accessible are the wholesale fabric market of Sampeng Lane and the diverse offerings of the vendors along Soi Isara Nuphap. Other major markets in Chinatown include Pak Khlong, Nakorn Kasem, and Phahurat. Near to Hua Lamphong Station is Wat Traimit with its splendid interior and huge gold Buddha image. The area is peppered with Chinese shrines, many of which combine elements of Confucianism, Taoism, Mahayana Buddhism, and animism. Old Chinese noodle shops patronized by mahjong-playing, undershirt-clad men make interesting snack spots.

SIGHTS AT A GLANCE

Wats
Wat Traimit ④

Markets
Nakorn Kasem ③
Pak Khlong Market ①
Phahurat Market ②

Historic Buildings
Hua Lamphong Station ⑤

0 meters 500

0 yards 500

GETTING THERE
Chinatown is easily accessible from the Chao Phraya Express Ratchawong pier, by bus along Charoen Krung Road, or train to Hua Lamphong station.

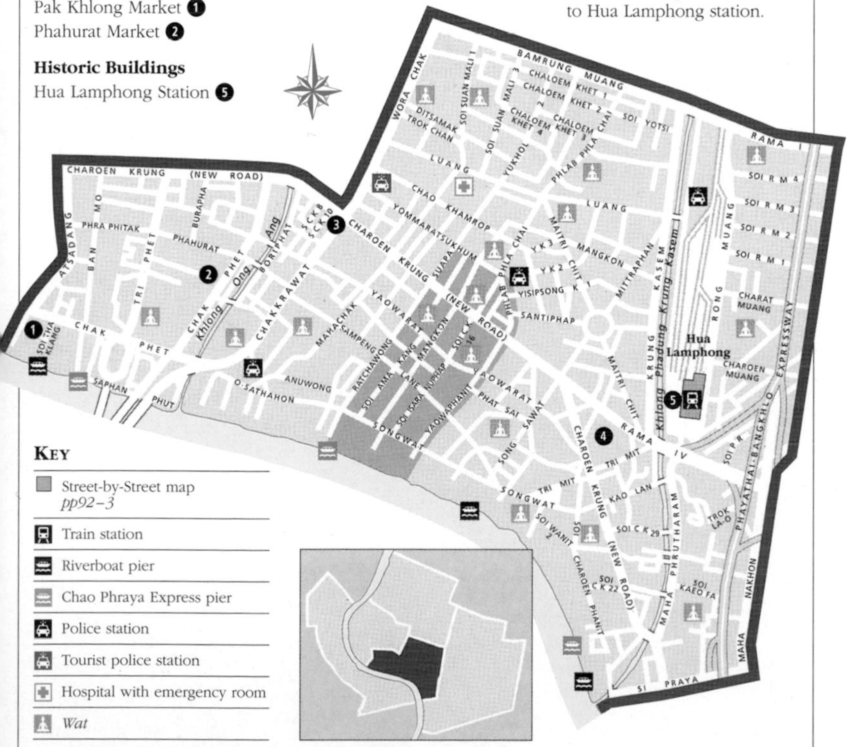

KEY

▨	Street-by-Street map *pp92–3*
🚉	Train station
🚢	Riverboat pier
🚤	Chao Phraya Express pier
🚔	Police station
🚔	Tourist police station
✚	Hospital with emergency room
🛕	*Wat*

◁ **Bags of dried shrimp in one of Chinatown's numerous, pungent markets**

Street-by-Street: Central Chinatown

เยาวราช

THIS AREA IS CHINATOWN at its most atmospheric, with its vibrant colors, pungent smells, overwhelming cacophony, and frenetic bustle. A cross-section of the district can be experienced by walking up Soi Isara Nuphap from Ratchawong pier. After Songwat Road, with its old wooden buildings, the street is lined with wholesale spice shops. Past the fabric market of Sampeng Lane, the sidewalk is crowded with fresh and preserved foods. Once over Yaowarat Road, with its countless gold shops and Chinese herbal medicine stores, snack stalls predominate before giving way, after crossing traffic-choked Charoen Krung Road, to sellers of Chinese religious paraphernalia.

Khanom dao – a soy sweet

Kao Market
Fresh produce, such as mushrooms, is sold at Kao ("old" Market, which has been here since the late 18th century.

Tang To Kang Gold Shop
This antique water filter is displayed at Tang To Kang, a seven-story structure built as Chinatown's central Gold Exchange in the late 19th century.

To Sampeng Market

Sanchao Kuan Oo
People who hope for luck in gambling leave offerings of vegetables in front of a gilded horse's head in this temple.

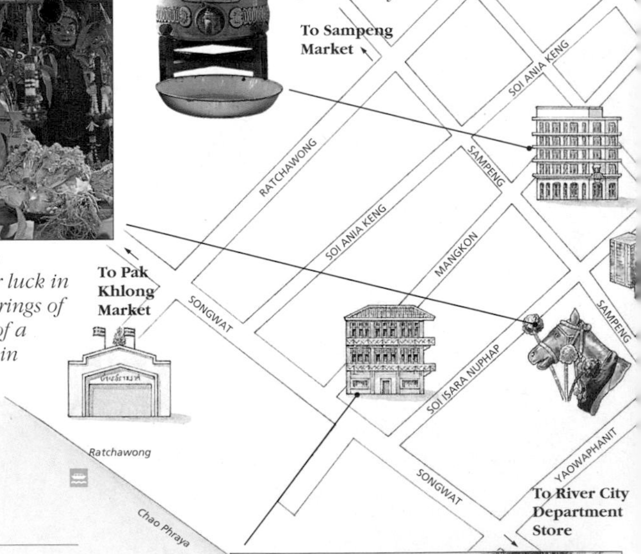

To Pak Khlong Market

To Sampeng Market

To River City Department Store

```
0 meters        100
0 yards         100
```

KEY

🛳 Chao Phraya Express pier

RATCHAWONG
YAOWARAT
SOI ANIA KENG
SAMPENG
RATCHAWONG
SOI ANIA KENG
MANGKON
SAMPENG
SONGWAT
SOI ISARA NUPHAP
YAOWAPHANIT
SONGWAT
Ratchawong
Chao Phraya

Songwat Road
Despite the trucks transporting goods to the busy pier at Ratchawong, the old houses and commercial buildings along Songwat Road give a flavor of Chinatown as it was in the 19th century. This old wooden warehouse stands opposite Soi Thanam San Chao.

★ Leng Noi Yee
This Buddhist shrine combines elements of Confucianism and Taoism, attracting a wide range of devotees. The main chamber contains several gilded Buddha images.

LOCATOR MAP
See Street Finder map 6

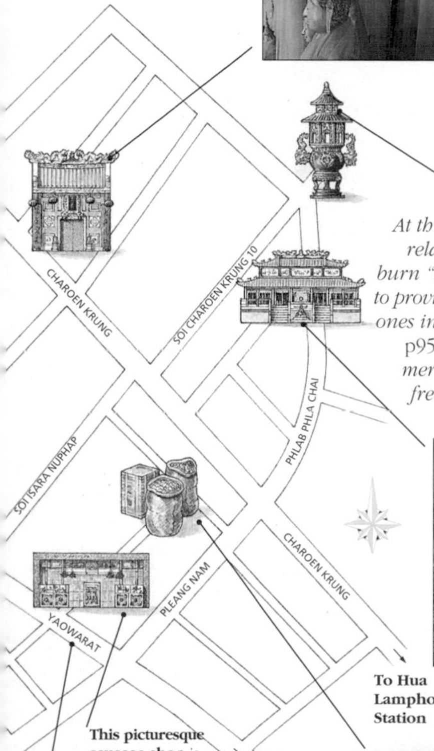

Sanchao Dtai Hong Kong
At this popular temple relatives of the dead burn "hell's banknotes" to provide for their loved ones in the afterlife (see p95). Devotees make merit by buying and freeing caged birds.

Li Thi Miew
This atmospheric temple within a courtyard is topped by fierce dragons. Inside, incense smoke swirls around statues of Taoist deities.

To Hua
Lamphong
Station

This picturesque sausage shop is said to date from the 19th century.

To Wat
Traimit

Mai Market
Mai ("new") Market can't boast the pedigree of Kao Market, but it is still a good source of everyday and unusual items like snake parts for Chinese medicine.

★ Yaowarat Road
One of Chinatown's main traffic arteries, this bustling road is packed with gold shops, herbal sellers, cafés, and restaurants.

STAR SIGHTS

★ Leng Noi Yee

★ Yaowarat Road

Vendor selling a wide range of chilies, Pak Khlong Market

Pak Khlong Market **❶**

ตลาดปากคลอง

Maharaj Rd. **Map** 5 C2. 🚌 *AC: 501, 512* 🚢 *Rachinee, Pak Khlong.* ☐ *daily.*

OPEN 24 HOURS A DAY, Pak Khlong Market provides the city with fresh flowers and vegetables. Known for offering the best array of flowers in Thailand, it is a one-stop florist's dream. Deliveries arrive from 1am and by dawn the display has roses, orchids, lotus, jasmine, and Dutch tulips. The widest variety of blooms can be seen at 9am. Visitors can buy bouquets or floral basket arrangements.

Phahurat Market **❷**

ตลาดพาหุรัด

Phahurat Rd. **Map** 6 D1. 🚌 *6, 37, 82, 88; AC: 3, 82.*

THIS PREDOMINANTLY Indian market offers all the tastes, sights, and smells of Bombay. The main bazaar, which spills out around Phahurat and Chak Phet roads, specializes in fabrics. Downstairs, cloth merchants sell anything from tablecloths to wedding saris. The dimly lit upstairs section is devoted to traditional Indian accessories such as sandals and ornate jewelry.

In the surrounding streets are many delicious "hole-in-the-wall" Indian restaurants and samosa stalls. Off Chak Phet Road is Siri Guru Singh Sabha, a traditional Sikh temple.

Nakorn Kasem **❸**

นครเกษม

Charoen Krung Rd. **Map** 6 E1. 🚌 *AC: 501, 507.*

POPULARLY KNOWN AS Thieves' Market because stolen goods were allegedly once sold here, Nakorn Kasem has discarded its illicit past and now has a miscellaneous collection of shops selling metal wares, musical instruments, and a wide range of ornaments.

Nearby is Saphan Han Market, a covered market along both sides of Khlong Ong Ang. Its specialty is electrical goods. The area is filled with smells wafting from nearby noodle stalls.

Wat Traimit **❹**

วัดไตรมิตร

Tri Mit Rd. **Map** 6 F2. 🚌 *1, 4, 11, 25, 53, 73; AC: 501, 507.* ☐ *9am–5pm daily.*

ALSO CALLED the Temple of the Golden Buddha, Wat Traimit is houses the world's largest solid gold Buddha. The gleaming 4-m (13-ft) high 13th-century Sukhothai image is made of 18-carat gold and weighs five tons.

The Buddha was discovered by accident in 1955. While extending the port of Bangkok, workers for the East Asiatic Company unearthed what appeared to be a plain stucco Buddha. The image was kept at Wat Traimit under a makeshift shelter for 20 years until a crane dropped it while moving it to a more permanent shelter. The plaster cracked, revealing the gold Buddha beneath. The statue had probably been encased in stucco to hide it from Burmese ransackers – a common practice during the Ayutthaya period (*see pp56–7*).

Local Chinese residents come here to worship the Golden Buddha and to make merit by rubbing gold leaf on the temple's smaller Buddha images.

Wat Traimit, which houses the revered Golden Buddha image

Hua Lampong Station **❺**

สถานีหัวลำโพง

Rama IV Rd. **Map** 7 A2. ☎ *0-2223-7010.* 🚌 *4, 21, 25, 29, 34, 40, 48, 109; AC: 501, 507, 529.*

KING CHULALONGKORN (Rama V), a great champion of modernization, was the instigator of rail travel in Thailand. The first railroad line, begun in 1891, was a private line from Paknam to Hua Lampong. Today, the historic station is Bangkok's main rail junction. From here, trains leave for the North, Northeast, the Central Plains, and the South. The city's other station, Bangkok Noi, serves only the South.

The Chinese in Thailand

THE FIRST CHINESE IMMIGRANTS arrived in Thailand as merchants in the 12th century. During the late 18th and early 19th centuries, following years of war in Thailand *(see p60),* Chinese immigration was encouraged in order to help rebuild the economy. The subsequent integration of the Chinese into Thai society was so successful that by the mid-19th century half of Bangkok's population was of pure or mixed Chinese blood. There have been periods of anti-Chinese feeling and immigration restrictions, but the Chinese still dominate Thailand's commercial sector. Chinese traditions and beliefs remain strong in their communities.

Warrior on the roof of a temple in Chinatown

Leng Noi Yee Temple *in Bangkok is an important Mahayana Buddhist shrine that also incorporates elements of Taoism and Confucianism. The temple, with its glazed ceramic gables topped by Chinese dragons, is the focal point of the annual Vegetarian Festival* (see p43).

"Hell's banknotes" *are a form of* kong tek – *paper replicas of real objects, burned to provide for the dead during their next life.*

Intricate Chinese designs feature on many utensils, such as these pan covers.

Fresh vegetables are essential to many Chinese dishes.

CHINESE SHOP-HOUSES
Shop-houses are a common feature of Chinatown. The family lives on the first floor while the ground floor is devoted to the family business, whether it is a small workshop or a store selling, for example, food or household goods.

Chinese opera, *performed by traveling troupes, features a dramatic mixture of martial arts, acrobatics, singing, and dance.*

Dim sum, *literally "touch the heart," can be sampled in many of the area's Chinese restaurants. The bite-size snacks include shrimp toast and pork dumplings.*

Sign painting *is not just a decorative art form. These good luck messages, written in gold, are said to ward off evil and sickness. They are displayed in great numbers during the Chinese New Year.*

DUSIT

Detail from gates in Dusit Park

DUSIT IS THE CENTER of Thai officialdom and an oasis of relative calm in a chaotic city. Tree-lined avenues, *khlongs*, old buildings, and the low skyline have all been preserved here. King Chulalongkorn laid out the district along European lines, with grand vistas, broad boulevards, and a geometric road grid surrounding his palaces. A century later is still the royal quarter. Ratchadamnoen Avenue ("royal way") leads up to Vimanmek Mansion and the royal museums in

Dusit Park. Nearby is the royal "marble" temple of Wat Benchamabophit and Chitrlada Palace, the King and Queen's residence. Political power is also concentrated in Dusit. The National Assembly, Government House, several ministries, and the Prime Minister's house are located here. By contrast, horse racing at the Royal Turf Club, *muay thai* boxing at Ratchadamnoen Stadium, and animal encounters at the landscaped Dusit Zoo provide popular public entertainment.

SIGHTS AT A GLANCE

Wats and Churches
Dusit's Christian Churches **2**
Wat Benchamabophit **10**
Wat Indrawihan **4**

Museums
SUPPORT Museum **6**
Vimanmek Mansion **5**

Notable Roads
Phitsanulok Road **9**
Ratchadamnoen Avenue **11**

Landmark Buildings
Chitrlada Palace **8**

Markets
Thewet Flower Market **3**

Parks and Zoos
Dusit Park
pp98–9 **1**
Dusit Zoo **7**

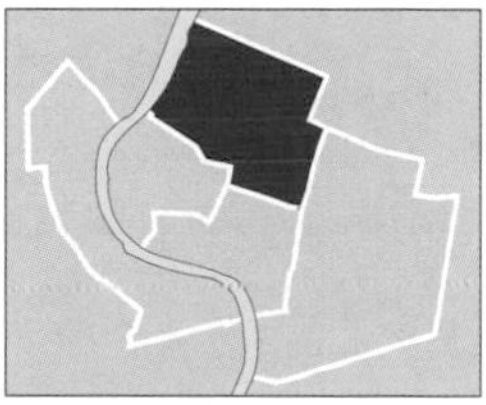

GETTING THERE
The Chao Phraya Express calls at Wat Sam Phraya, Wisut Kasat, and Thewet piers. The latter is the most convenient stop for the majority of Dusit's sights. The area is well served by buses, particularly along Ratchadamnoen Avenue and Dusit's other main arteries.

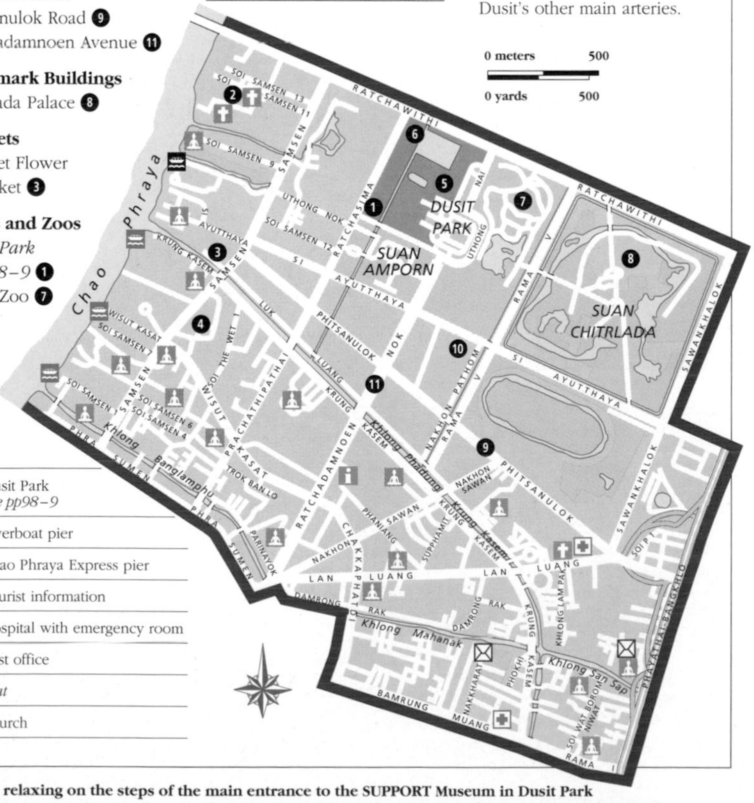

0 meters 500
0 yards 500

KEY

- Dusit Park *See pp98–9*
- Riverboat pier
- Chao Phraya Express pier
- Tourist information
- Hospital with emergency room
- Post office
- *Wat*
- Church

◁ **Nuns relaxing on the steps of the main entrance to the SUPPORT Museum in Dusit Park**

Dusit Park ❶

แผนผังสวนดุสิต

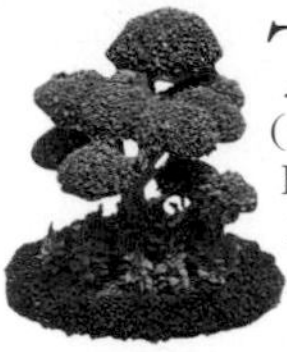

Topiary at Vimanmek

T HIS MAGNIFICENT PARK is the major attraction of the Dusit area. King Chulalongkorn (1868–1910), the first Thai sovereign to visit Europe, was determined to Westernize Bangkok, and the manicured gardens, genteel architecture, and teak mansions in Dusit Park all bear testimony to his efforts. Highlights include Vimanmek Mansion – the world's largest golden teak building – and the graceful Abhisek Dusit Throne Hall, which houses the SUPPORT Museum of traditional arts and crafts. A visit to the park and the neighboring zoo (*see p101*) can easily occupy a whole day.

LOCATOR MAP
See Street Finder maps 2, 3

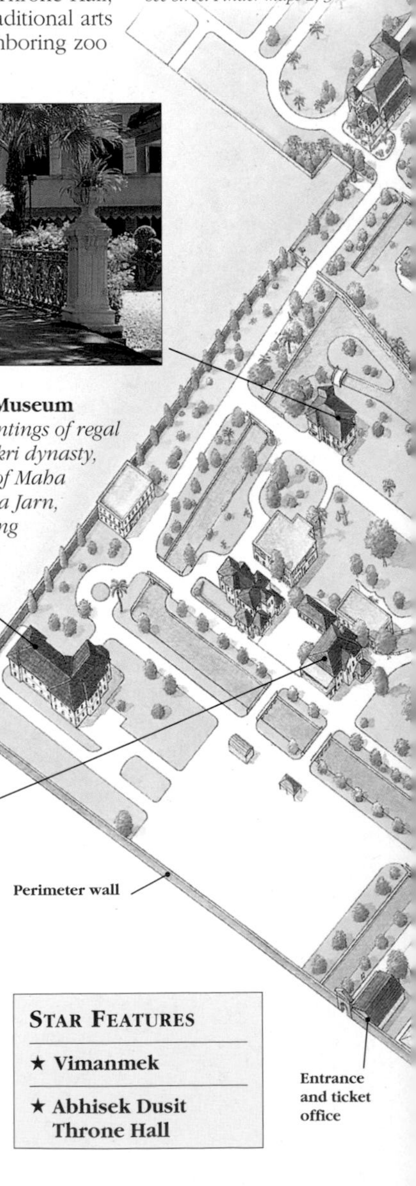

King Bhumibol's Photographic Museums

Most of the photographs in these museums were taken by King Bhumibol, an avid photographer. The royal family features in many.

Rank and Portrait Museum

Photographs and paintings of regal figures from the Chakri dynasty, such as this portrait of Maha Uparaja Bovornvijaya Jarn, the deputy king to King Rama V, can be seen in this museum.

Perimeter wall

Ancient Cloth and Silk Museum

This small collection includes the robes of King Rama IV and King Rama V. There are also desplays of the different types of Thai silk from all over Thailand.

STAR FEATURES

★ **Vimanmek**

★ **Abhisek Dusit Throne Hall**

Entrance and ticket office

★ **Abhisek Dusit Throne Hall**
This hall (see p101) is a fancifully ornamented white edifice. The major attraction inside is the SUPPORT Museum, with its collection of traditional, crafted artifacts, such as works using the exquisitely colored wings of jewel beetles.

VISITORS' CHECKLIST

Map 2 F1. 🍴 *0-2280-5928.* 🚌 *56, 70; AC: 70, 510, 515.* **Vimanmek Mansion** ◯ *9:30am–3:15 pm daily (tickets sold till 3pm).* 📷 *compulsory.* **SUPPORT Museum** ◯ *9:30am–3:15pm daily.* **All other buildings** ◯ *9am–4pm daily.* 🔴 *for occasional royal ceremonies.* 🎫 *Royal Mansion ticket (valid for 30 days) includes admission to Dusit Park and to all buildings.* 🚫 *inside all buildings.*

Canal

Bridge

Lakeside Pavilion
An elegant pavilion behind Vimanmek Palace affords a pleasant view across the lake to some particularly fine traditional Thai teak houses. The farther bank is, however, closed to visitors.

★ **Vimanmek Mansion**
More like a Victorian mansion than a Thai palace, this three-storied, golden teak structure (see pp100–1) was built using wooden pegs instead of nails. The palace is full of intriguing artifacts.

Old Clock Museum

Royal Carriage Museum
This museum contains the royal family's collection of unusual and interesting vehicles. Inside, there are two long stables lined with antique cars and ceremonial carriages.

Royal Ceremonial Photographic Museum

0 meters	50
0 yards	50

Dusit's Christian Churches ②

โบสถ์คุสิตควิสเตียน

Map 2 E1. 3, 9, 30, 53; AC: 506; MB: 8, 10.

B Y THE BANK of the Chao Phraya River, just south of Ratchawithi Road, is a small group of Christian churches.

The first of these, **St. Francis Xavier Church**, is near Krung Thon Bridge. Built in the early 1850s, it is notable for the statue of the saint atop its triple-arched portico frontage. Among its congregation are members of the local Vietnamese Catholic community, who settled here in 1934.

Just south is the smaller **Church of the Immaculate Conception**. It was built in 1837 by French missionaries on a site previously occupied by a Portuguese church.

Behind it is an even earlier church constructed in 1674, during King Narai's reign *(see pp56–7)*, by Father Louis Laneau for the early Portuguese community. Their descendants, and those of some Cambodian refugees who settled here in the late 17th century, still live in the parish. They take part in religious festivals here, hence the church's nickname, the Cambodian Church. It now houses the **Wat Mae Phrae Museum** (no set opening times), which contains a statue of the Virgin Mary, venerated in an annual ceremony held in October.

Porticoed entrance of St. Francis Xavier Church

Modern mural of a reclining Buddha, Wat Indrawihan

Thewet Flower Market ③

ตลาดดอกไม้เทเวศน์

Krung Kasem Rd. **Map** 2 E2. AC: 506. **National Library** Samsen Rd. 0-2281-5212. 9:30am–7:30pm daily.

O NE OF BANGKOK'S premier plant and garden markets flanks both sides of Khlong Phadung Krung Kasem, west of Samsen Road. It stocks an enormous range of goods, including ornamental garden pots, orchids, trees, and pond bases. Although Thewet Market is not as extensive as Chatuchak Market *(see p131)*, its prices are generally lower. It is a pleasant place to browse, even if you buy nothing.

Around the corner is the **National Library**, which contains a large collection of books in Thai and English. A number of Thai paintings hang in the lobby. The exterior incorporates several traditional Thai architectural touches *(see pp30–31)*, as do many government offices in the area.

Wat Indrawihan ④

วัดอินทรวิหาร

Wisut Kasat Rd. **Map** 2 E3. 3, 53; AC: 506. daily.

Y OU CANNOT MISS the reason for Wat Indrawihan's fame: an impressive 32-m (105-ft) standing Buddha. The statue was commissioned in the mid-19th century by King Mongkut (Rama IV) to enshrine a relic of the Buddha from Sri Lanka. (Relics such as fragments of bone and hair are housed in countless Buddhist monuments worldwide.)

While admittedly not the most beautiful of Buddha images because of its rather flattened features, it stands out attractively against the sky. Its enormous toes make a bizarre altar for the many offerings presented, including garlands of flowers.

Ornamental garden pots at Thewet Flower Market

Inside the *bot* of Wat In (a popular abbreviation for the temple) are hundreds of Bencharong (five-color) funerary urns. Traditional-style, modern murals can also be seen inside the *bot*. In another, smaller building, "lucky" water is sold in plastic bags.

Vimanmek Mansion ⑤

พระที่นั่งวิมานเมฆ

Ratchawithi Rd. **Map** 2 F1. 0-2280-5928. 56, 70; AC: 70, 510, 515. 9:30am–3:15pm daily. 1–6 Jan. (free for Grand Palace ticket holders). inside. compulsory.

C ONSTRUCTED ENTIRELY without nails, the world's largest golden teak building was reassembled on this site in 1901, after being moved from its original location on Ko Sichang *(see pp306–7)*. It soon became a favored retreat of King Chulalongkorn

(Rama V) and his family and concubines while they were waiting for nearby Chitrlada Palace *(see p102)* to be completed. Apart from the king, the mansion was for women only. After closing in 1935 and falling into disrepair, this "celestial residence" was magnificently restored in 1982 at the request of Queen Sirikit for Bangkok's bicentennial celebrations *(see pp64–5)*.

The guided tour takes in 30 of the 81 rooms via circuitous corridors. Highlights include the audience chambers, the music room, sweeping staircases, and the king's apartments, which are contained within an octagonal tower. The palace was the first building in Thailand to have electricity and an indoor bathroom; an early light bulb and a showerhead are two of the items on display.

Treasures from the Rattanakosin era include porcelain, furniture, betel-nut sets, the first Thai alphabet typewriter, hunting trophies, and royal photographs. King Chulalongkorn was known for his taste in Western-style design, and the palace, with its verandas and high ceilings, has the appearance of a Victorian mansion.

Although the tour allows little time inside, visitors can walk around outside or sit in a lakeside porch, where Thai dancing *(see pp38–9)* and disquieting monkey acrobatics are staged twice daily.

Vimanmek Mansion, the summer residence of Rama V

Domed ceiling of the Ananta Samakom Throne Hall

SUPPORT Museum ⑥

พิพิธภัณฑ์ศิลปาชีพ

Ratchawithi Rd. **Map** 2 F1.
☎ 0-2628-6300. 🚌 AC: 510, 515.
⏰ 9:30am–3:15pm daily. 📷

HOUSED IN the Abhisek Dusit Throne Hall beside Vimanmek Palace (and included on the same ticket), the SUPPORT Museum is a showcase for traditional crafts that have been saved from decline by Queen Sirikit, founder of the Promotion of Supplementary Occupations and Related Techniques (SUPPORT). One such craft is *yan lipao* weaving, which originated in Nakhon Si Thammarat *(see pp368–9)*. The fine reed used in *yan lipao* lends itself to intricate patterns, its sheen giving the end product a luster.

Crafts on display include nielloware, rattan, bamboo, celadon, lacquerware, and an art form that uses the iridescent green-blue wings of jewel beetles. Some of the designs were created by members of the royal family. One of the training centers for SUPPORT is at the Bang Sai Folk Arts and Crafts Center near Bang Pa-in *(see p171)*. South Abhisek Dusit is another throne hall, **Ananta Samakorn**. Dating from

Black bear in Dusit Zoo

1912, this ornate, Italianate building once housed the parliament. Today it is used for royal receptions and private functions. Its spectacular interior is open to the public only on Children's Day, the second Saturday in January.

Dusit Zoo ⑦

สวนสัตว์ดุสิต (เขาดิน)

Rama V & Ratchawithi rds. **Map** 3 A2.
☎ 0-2281-2000. 🚌 AC: 510, 515.
⏰ 8am–6pm daily. 📷

FORMING A GREEN wedge between Dusit Park and Chitrlada Palace are the lush gardens of Dusit Zoo. One of Asia's better zoos, it has reasonable space for birds and large mammals such as tigers, bears, elephants, and hippos, although some of the other enclosures are much more confining. There are also elephant rides and several animal-feeding shows. The grounds were originally the private botanical gardens of Rama V, and some varieties of tropical flora are still cultivated here. The lawns, lakes, and wooded glades are ideal for relaxing strolls. Other pursuits include eating at a café, or simply watching Thai families enjoying a day out.

Chitrlada Palace ❽

พระตำหนักจิตรลดา

Ratchawithi & Rama V rds. **Map** 3 B2.
🚌 18, 28; AC: 510. ◐ to public.

T HE PERMANENT RESIDENCE of
the king and queen is an
early 20th-century palace set in
extensive grounds (closed to
the public), east of Dusit Zoo.
Although the palace is hidden
from view, the buildings used
by King Bhumibol (Rama IX)
for agricultural and industrial
experiments are visible. In
1993 he became the first
monarch in the
world to earn a
patent – for a waste
water aerator.
The royal white
elephants (there
are currently 11)
are trained and
housed on the
palace grounds.

**Board celebrating King
Bhumibol's 50-year reign**

The perimeter
is illuminated from the King's
Birthday (Dec 5) to New Year.

Phitsanulok Road ❾

ถนนพิษณุโลก

Map 2 E2. 🚌 16, 23, 201, 505.

A NUMBER OF important state
institutions are located
along this major avenue,
which cuts through the heart
of Dusit. Traveling northwest
past the Mission Hospital at
the Sawankhalok Road end,
the first of interest is **Ban
Phitsanulok**. This mansion
has been the official residence
of the prime minister since it
was restored in 1982. It was
originally built in 1925 by
Rama VI for Major General
Phraya Aniruttheva. Designed
by the same Italian architects
who built the Ananta Samakorn Throne Hall *(see p101)*,
it is a riot of Venetian Gothic,
with floral-shaped mullioned
windows, spindly crenella-
tions, and a sweeping curved
wing. It is not open to the
public, and guests
rarely stay overnight
because it is widely
believed to be
haunted.
On the opposite
side of the road is
the grassy oval of
the **Royal Turf
Club**, one of Thai-
land's two major
horse-racing tracks *(see p113)*.
Races alternate between the
two tracks, and are held here
from 12:30 – 6:30pm every
other Sunday. The stands fill
with bettors from all levels of
Thai society. Experiencing the
banter and furious betting can
often be as much fun as
watching the race itself. The
most prominent annual event
that takes place here is the
King's Cup, also known as
the Derby Cup, on the first or
second weekend of January.

**Filling in the results at the end
of a race at the Royal Turf Club**

Government House, to the
west, just past the Nakhon
Pathom Road turning, is a
fanciful, cream-colored Neo-
Venetian style building. It is
now used to house the prime
minister's office, and it is
closed to the public.

Wat Benchama-bophit ❿

วัดเบญจมบพิตร

69 Rama V Rd. **Map** 3 A3.
☎ 0-2282-7413. 🚌 3, 16, 23, 505.
🕐 8:30am–5:30pm daily. 📷

E UROPEAN INFLUENCE on Thai
architecture *(see p31)* is
exemplified by Wat Benchamabophit, the last major temple
to be built in central Bangkok.
In 1899 King Chulalongkorn
(Rama V) commissioned his
brother Prince Naris and the
Italian architect Hercules
Manfredi to design a new *bot*

ROYAL WHITE ELEPHANTS

The importance of
the white elephant
(chang samkhan) in
Thailand derives from
a 2,500-year-old tale.
Queen Maya, once
barren, became
pregnant with the
future Buddha after
dreaming of a white
elephant entering her
womb. Ever since the
13th century, when
King Ramkamhaeng
gave the animal great
prestige, the reigning

Old manuscript depicting a white elephant

its presence on the
Siamese flag until
1917. The origin of
the phrase "white el-
ephant," meaning a
large, useless invest-
ment, lies in the Thai
tradition according to
which all white el-
ephants must belong
to the king. They
cannot be used for
work and, therefore,
have to be cared for
at huge expense.
Though referred to

monarch's importance has been judged in
part according to the number of white elephants he owns. Indeed, the white elephant's
status as a national icon was symbolized by
as white, the elephants are not fully albino.
But tradition states that seven parts of their
body – the eyes, palate, nails, tail hair, skin,
hairs, and testicles – must be close to white.

Singhas guarding the entrance to Wat Benchamabophit

Ratchadamnoen Avenue ⑪

ถนนราชดำเนิน

Map 1 D4. 🚌 *15, 33, 39, 70, 159, 201; AC: 511, 503, 157, 170, 183.*

PLANNED BY King Mongkut (Rama IV) in the style of a European boulevard, this thoroughfare has three parts.

The first section, Ratchadamnoen Nai ("inner"), starts at Lak Muang and skirts **Sanam Luang** *(see pp74–5),* before veering east at the Royal Hotel as Ratchadamnoen Klang ("middle"). From here it passes the **Democracy Monument** *(see p83)* and 1930s mansions – a vista featured in the movie *Good Morning, Vietnam.*

Just across Khlong Banglamphu, Ratchadamnoen Nok ("outer") turns north into the Dusit area. This stretch, shaded by trees, is flanked by ministries, the main TAT headquarters and **Ratchadamnoen Boxing Stadium** *(see p41).* Just before the ornate double bridge over Khlong Phadung Krung Kasem is the Thai-influenced modern building of the United Nations Economic and Social Commission for Asia and the Pacific (ESCAP).

The avenue ends at the domed **Ananta Samakorn Throne Hall** *(see p101),* which looms up beyond the Chulalongkorn Equestrian Statue in the parade ground, the site of December's Trooping of the Colors ceremony *(see p47).*

Ratchadamnoen Avenue is decorated and illuminated in December as part of King Bhumibol's birthday festivities.

and cloister for the original Ayutthaya-period temple which stood on the site. The nickname for the new *wat* ("Marble Temple") is derived from the gray Carrara marble used to clad the walls.

Laid out in cruciform with cascading roof levels, the *bot* is elegantly proportioned. It contains another successful fusion of traditions: intricate Victorian-style stained-glass windows depicting scenes from Thai mythology. In the room of the ashes of Rama V is the most revered copy of Phitsanulok's Phra Buddha Chinarat *(see pp150–51),* with a pointed halo. In the cloister are 53 different Buddha images, originals and copies of images from around Thailand and other Buddhist countries, assembled by Rama V.

Within the *wat* is one of the three sets of doors inlaid with mother-of-pearl that were salvaged from Wat Borom Buddharam in Ayutthaya. The building in which Rama V lived as a monk features

murals depicting events that occurred during his reign.

Wat Benchamabophit is a popular location for witnessing monastic rituals, from Buddhist holiday processions to the daily alms round *(see p125),* in which merit-makers donate food to the monks lined up outside the *wat* along Nakhon Pathom Road. This is a reversal of the usual practice where the monks go out in search of alms.

Annual Trooping of the Colors ceremony, Ratchadamnoen Avenue

Buddhist monks in the forecourt of the European-inspired Wat Benchamabophit ▷

DOWNTOWN

THE CENTER OF Bangkok's vast and continually expanding downtown is the area spanning Silom and Ploen Chit roads. The business district originated in the 19th century in the Old Farang Quarter of Charoen Krung Road, where charming colonial buildings have been conserved around the Oriental Hotel. The concrete canyon of Silom is the preserve of business people by day, but after dark its northern end is the heart of city nightlife. Farther north, showcase stores line Ploen Chit and Rama I roads while the stalls of Silom Road and Siam Square provide cheaper shopping. Amid the tower blocks, Lumphini Park provides green relief, and a few traditional Thai buildings remain, such as Jim Thompson's House and Suan Pakkad Palace.

SIGHTS AT A GLANCE

Wats, Shrines, and Churches
Assumption Cathedral ❷
Erawan Shrine ⓬
Maha Uma Devi Temple ❺
Wat Pathum Wanaram ⓭

Museums and Libraries
Jim Thompson's House pp116–17 ⓯
Neilson-Hays Library ❻
Suan Pakkad Palace ⓱

Notable Roads and Districts
Charoen Krung (New) Road ❸
Patpong ❼
Pratunam ⓰
Siam Square ⓮
Silom Road ❹

Parks and Sports Grounds
Lumphini Park ❾
Royal Bangkok Sports Club ⓫

Historic Buildings
Chulalongkorn University ❿
Oriental Hotel ❶

Zoos
Snake Farm ❽

GETTING THERE
Many buses run along the main roads. The Chao Phraya Express stops at Si Phraya, Wat Muang Khae, and Oriental piers. Avoid any heavy traffic jams by taking the Skytrain.

KEY

▨	Street-by-Street map pp108–9
Ⓜ	Subway
▣	Skytrain station
▤	Riverboat pier
▤	Chao Phraya Express pier
▣	Police station
▣	Tourist police station
✚	Hospital with emergency room
⊠	Post office
🛕	Wat
✝	Church

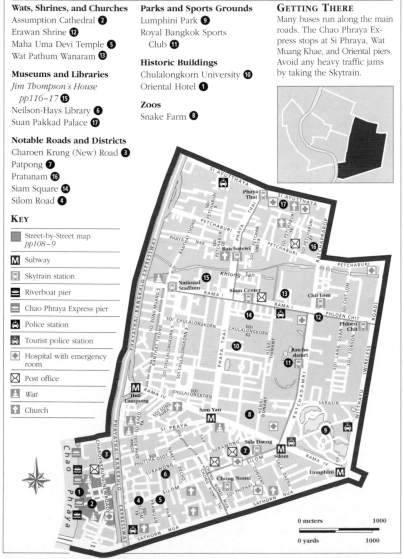

Street-by-Street: Old Farang Quarter

ย่านที่อยู่ของฝรั่งสมัยก่อน (ย่านเจริญกรุง)

Emblem on gate of French Embassy

Tнis area was Bangkok's original port and foreign commercial district in the 19th century. In 1820 Portugal was granted land in Bangkok, which resulted in the construction of the Portuguese Embassy. Embassies of other countries, such as France, soon followed. These outside influences created an amalgam of Western and Eastern architectural styles. Charoen Krung (New) Road, the first road in Thailand to be paved, cuts through the Old Farang Quarter and is home to gem traders, tailors, and antique dealers. The elegant Assumption Cathedral faces Bangkok's only European-style square. The Quarter's back streets are surprisingly quiet and contain some attractive wooden houses.

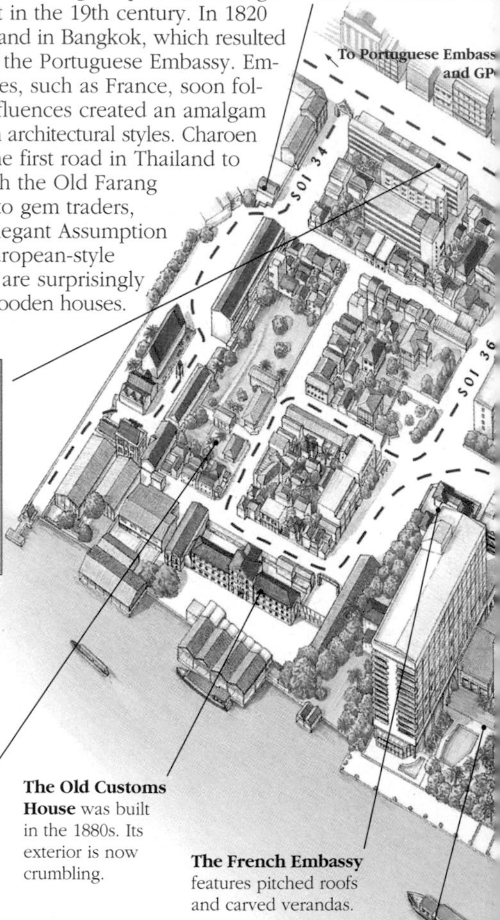

Harmonique restaurant is one of a row of Chinese shophouses built around 190

To Portuguese Embass and GP

SOI 34

SOI 36

The Rare Stone Museum is a tiny shop/museum selling rocks and fossils. Geological oddities – such as dinosaur droppings and tektites (glassy meteorites) from Northeast Thailand – can be seen here.

The Haroon Mosque is a quaint stucco building with a Muslim graveyard. The mosque, which faces Mecca, is off a street lined with wooden houses, many displaying extravagantly carved grilles.

The Old Customs House was built in the 1880s. Its exterior is now crumbling.

The French Embassy features pitched roofs and carved verandas.

STAR SIGHTS

★ Oriental Hotel

★ Assumption Cathedral

★ Oriental Hotel

The world-renowned Oriental Hotel was established in 1876 by two Danish sea captains. In 1958 a new structure (the Tower Wing) was added, and in 1976 the River Wing, a ten-story annex, opened ❶

The China House, one of Bangkok's most expensive restaurants, is in a building dating from the reign of King Vajiravudh *(see p63)*. The structure next door, the Commercial Co. of Siam, was erected in the same era. It is built of wood and masonry and has been converted into offices.

LOCATOR MAP
See Street Finder map 6

★ **Assumption Cathedral**
This elegantly decorated cathedral was built in 1910. The cathedral's Rococo interior features a high, vaulted ceiling and a striking marble altar from France ❷

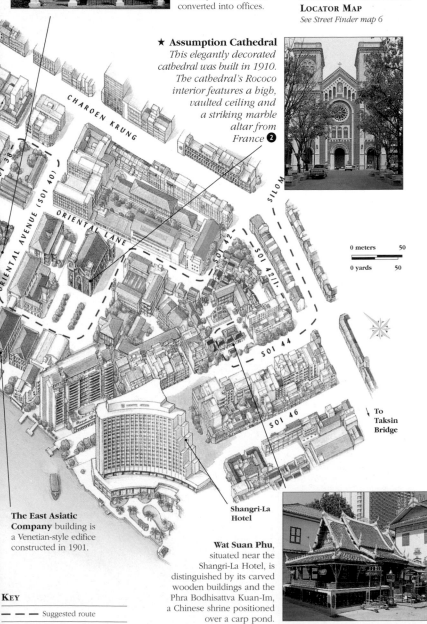

0 meters   50
0 yards   50

To Taksin Bridge

Shangri-La Hotel

The East Asiatic Company building is a Venetian-style edifice constructed in 1901.

Wat Suan Phu, situated near the Shangri-La Hotel, is distinguished by its carved wooden buildings and the Phra Bodhisattva Kuan-Im, a Chinese shrine positioned over a carp pond.

KEY

– – – Suggested route

**Neo-Classical façade of the Authors'
Wing of the Oriental Hotel**

Oriental Hotel ❶

โรงแรมโอเรียนเต็ล

Oriental Ave, off Charoen Krung Rd.
Map 6 F4. **(** 0-2659-9000.
🚌 35, 75. 🛥 Oriental.

R EPEATEDLY VOTED the world's
best hotel for its service
and attention to detail, the
Oriental was Thailand's first
large hotel. It was established
in 1876 and completely rebuilt in 1887. New wings have
since been added. The hotel
owes much of its charm to
the Armenian Sarkies brothers, creators of the luxurious
Raffles Hotel in Singapore.
The Oriental's status, lavish
decor, and spectacular setting
on the banks of the Chao
Phraya River account for its
elevated prices.

The hotel's original, white-
shuttered wing contains the
renowned Authors' Suites.
Somerset Maugham was one
such author who stayed here
in the 1920s. Recovering from
a bout of malaria, he wrote of
the "dust and heat and noise
and whiteness and more dust"
of Bangkok, though his perception of the city was to
change once he was able to
explore the *wats* and *khlongs.*

Classic, English-style high
tea is served in the Authors'
Lounge of the hotel, a riot of
potted plants and fan-backed
wicker chairs. A teak barge
shuttles back and forth to the
Sala Rim Naam on the opposite bank, one of the Oriental's
eight highly acclaimed restau-

rants *(see p414). Khon* performances *(see pp38–9)* are
staged here as guests dine.
The hotel runs a respected
school of Thai cookery.

Assumption
Cathedral ❷

วัดอัสสัมชัญ

Oriental Lane, off Charoen Krung Rd.
Map 6 F4. 🚌 35, 75. 🛆 daily.

T HIS ROMANESQUE-STYLE brick
edifice was built in 1910
on the site of an earlier cathedral. Its rose window is
flanked by twin squat towers.
The richly ornamented, Rococo
interior is dominated by a lofty, barrel-arched blue ceiling
patterned with gold starbursts.

The cathedral faces a traffic-
free, tree-shaded piazza, the
site of several other Western-
style buildings. These include
the modern Assumption Col-
lege, the Neo-Classical Catholic Mission, and the Renaiss-
ance-style Catholic Center,
which backs onto the river.

Charoen Krung
(New) Road ❸

ถนนเจริญกรุง

Map 6 F2. 🚌 1; AC: 504.

S KIRTING THE Chao Phraya
River – from Wat Pho
through Chinatown and on to
Yannawa – Charoen Krung, or
New Road (as it is often also
called) is one of Bangkok's
oldest thoroughfares.

Linking the Customs House
and many trading companies,
the road was once the center
of Bangkok's European community. At their insistence it
became Thailand's first paved
highway. Still home to the gem
and antique trades, today the
road is choked with traffic
pollution and noise, but side
streets, lined with trees and old
wooden buildings, can be blissfully serene. Along the road is
the imposing **General Post
Office**, whose brown stone
façade is adorned with reliefs
of *garudas* (mythical beasts,
half bird, half human). In

Decorative wooden bells inside the spacious lobby of the Oriental Hotel

front is a statue of King Chula-longkorn. The coin and stamp stalls (open Sundays) outside the post office and the **Bangrak Market** (open daily), selling clothing and fruit, give the area vibrancy.

Silom Road ❹
ถนนสีลม

Map 7 A4. ▦ *AC: 177, 504, 514, 532, 544.* Ⓜ *Silom.* ▤ *Saladaeng (skytrain).*

THE COMMERCIAL HEART of Bangkok, Silom Road is becoming a polluted canyon of skyscrapers, shopping malls, and elevated railway lines. Just a few decades ago the area consisted of orchards flanking a canal. One feature that remains unchanged is the many thousands of barn swallows that nest here from October to March.

Towards the river end of the road, and also on parallel Surawong Road, are several gem and silk shops. Near Patpong *(see p112)* is the Dusit Thani Hotel that overlooks Lumphini Park and the bustle of the local nightlife. Close by is Convent Road, taking its name from the **Carmelite Convent**, and also home to the Gothic-style **Anglican Christ Church**, built in 1904.

Street vendor pushing his cart

Maha Uma Devi Temple ❺
วัดศรีมหาอุมาเทวี

Corner of Silom and Pan rds. **Map** 7 B4. ▦ *AC: 76, 502, 504.* ◐ *7am – 6pm.* 🎎 *Deepavali (Nov).*

TAMILS FOUNDED this colorful Hindu temple during the 1860s. They were part of an influx of Indians who decided to move to Bangkok when India was handed over to the British Crown in 1858.

The main temple building is topped by a gold-plated copper dome above a 6-m (20-ft) high façade depicting various Hindu gods. Always buzzing with activity, and often with

Multicolored deities on the roof of Maha Uma Devi Temple

live Indian music, the temple is also the focus for Deepavali (Festival of Lights) celebrations in November. An oil-lamp ritual is held most days at noon, and on Fridays at 11:30am there is a *prasada* (vegetarian ceremony), in which blessed food is distributed to devotees.

Although some Thais might call the temple Wat Khaek ("Indians' temple"), a common cultural heritage means that many local Thais and Chinese also regularly worship here. The Hindu deities Shiva and Ganesh feature in Thai Buddhism, and Hindus regard the Buddha as one of the incarnations of Vishnu.

Neilson-Hays Library ❻
ห้องสมุดเนลสันเฮยส์

195 Surawong Rd. **Map** 7 B4. 🕿 *0-223-1731.* ▦ *16, 93.* ◐ *9:30am–4pm Tue–Sun.*

HOUSED WITHIN an elegant building beside the British Club is the Neilson-Hays Library. Its 20,000 volumes form one of Southeast Asia's finest English-language collections.

The library was built in 1921 in honor of Jennie Neilson-Hays, who was the mainstay of the Bangkok Library Association between 1895 and 1920. The internal domed rotunda is used as a modern art gallery.

WESTERN WRITERS IN BANGKOK

Western impressions of Thailand were for a long time heavily influenced by just one author – Anna Leonowens. An English teacher at the court of King Mongkut (Rama IV), Leonowens wrote the book that inspired the musical *The King and I.* However, the portrayal of the king as a comic figure stirred up anger in the country, and the book is now regarded as an unreliable historical source. Less controversially, Joseph Conrad wrote about his journey up the Chao Phraya in *The Shadow Line,* and Somerset Maugham described his impressions of Thailand in *The Gentleman in the Parlour.* These are just two of the Western authors commemorated by suites at the Oriental Hotel. Others include Noël Coward, Gore Vidal, Graham Greene, and Barbara Cartland. The Oriental has also ventured into other literary projects: it is the site for the annual prize-giving ceremony of the SEAWrite Award, established in 1969 to promote contact between writers in Southeast Asian countries.

Joseph Conrad in 1904

Entrance to Patpong, as seen in daytime from Silom Road

Patpong ❼

พัฒน์พงษ์

Silom Rd, Patpong 1 and 2. **Map** 7 C3.
🚌 AC: 76, 177, 504, 514. Ⓜ Silom.
🚉 Saladaeng (skytrain).

T HE PRIVATE STREETS of Patpong 1 and 2, named after
the one-time owner, Chinese
millionaire Khun Patpongpanit,
comprise what is probably the
world's most notorious red
light district. In the 1960s the
area was the home of Bangkok's entertainment scene – the
go-go bars sprang up to sat-
isfy airline crews and US GIs
on leave during the Vietnam
War. Since the 1970s, the sex
shows have been sustained

mainly through tourist patronage. A less visible homosexual
scene exists in adjacent Silom
Soi 6, while Soi Taniya's host-
ess bars are frequented
mainly by Japanese clients.

The tourist police department monitors Patpong, and
the area is surprisingly safe. A
night market, with stalls selling souvenirs and original and
fake fashions, gives the area a
thin veneer of respectability.
A bookstore in the center of
Patpong is one of Southeast
Asia's major outlets for books
on feminism and exploitation.
Many visitors come to Patpong
out of curiosity rather than to
indulge in the flesh trade: most
leave feeling disturbed.

Snake Farm ❽

สวนงู

Rama IV Rd. **Map** 7 C3. 📞 0-2252-
0161. 🚌 AC: 50, 507. Ⓜ Silom.
🚉 Saladaeng (skytrain).
🕐 8:30am–4:30pm Mon–Fri,
8:30am–noon Sat, Sun & public hols
(shows at 10:30am, 2pm). 🎟 📷

T HE QUEEN SAOWAPHA Snake
Farm is run by the Thai
Red Cross. It makes snakebite
serums and informs the public about local snakes. Unlike
the tourist-oriented farms, the
emphasis is on education.
Demonstrations of venom
milking take place twice daily
(once daily on weekends), pre-
ceded by an explanatory slide
show. Handlers open a snake's
mouth and pierce the cellophane lid of a glass jar with its
fangs. The milky venom then
squirts harmlessly into the jar.

Cobra before milking, Snake Farm

SEX WORKERS AND THEIR CLIENTS IN THAILAND

Historically, prostitution in Thailand was
reinforced by the institution of polygamy. Both
are now illegal, but the use of prostitutes by
Thai men is still widespread. Every town has
at least one massage parlor. The glitzy broth-
els of Patpong and such towns as Pattaya
and Hat Yai may form the foreign perception
of the Thai sex industry, but they are a relatively recent development, dating from the
presence of US servicemen in Thailand during
the Vietnam War. Some estimates put the number of sex workers as high as two million, but

a more realistic figure is 250,000, one fifth
of whom are male. The majority of prostitutes
work for Thai clients, but a few service the
many tourists who come for so-called "sex
holidays." Increasingly, concern about exploitation, pedophilia, AIDS, and sex tourism are
being voiced around the world, and countries
such as Sweden now prosecute their nationals
caught paying for sex with children abroad.

Many prostitutes come from the poorest
regions of Thailand or neighboring countries
such as Burma. The income, and a somewhat
fatalistic attitude, can outweigh any social disapproval they may face. But some do not
become involved in the industry willingly,
and cases of beatings and imprisonment are
not uncommon. Health problems, stigma,
lack of skills, and death from AIDS (*see p458*)
spell grim prospects for all sex workers.
Despite a government campaign and the work
of programs by charities such as Empower,
AIDS statistics for the mid-1990s estimate the
number of prostitutes infected at 14 percent
for the whole country, and up to 70 percent
for provinces such as Chiang Rai.

Gaudy nightclub sign in central Bangkok

Perfecting the art of tai chi chuan early one morning in Lumphini Park

Lumphini Park ❾
สวนลุมพินี

Map 8 D3. 🚌 *14; AC: 50, 507.*
Ⓜ *Silom.* 🚊 *Saladaeng (skytrain).*
🕐 *5:30am–9pm daily.*

NAMED AFTER the Buddha's birthplace in Nepal, Bangkok's principal greenbelt sprawls around two boating lakes. Dominating the Silom Road corner of the park is a statue of Rama VI.

The best time to visit is early morning, when it is used by Thais for jogging and Chinese for practicing the rhythmic movements of tai chi chuan. The superstitious can be seen consuming fresh snake blood and bile to keep ill health at bay, purchased from stalls along the park's northern edge. The park is a relaxing place to stroll and observe elderly Chinese playing chess, and impromptu games of *takraw* (a type of volleyball in which the hands may not be used).

Chulalongkorn University ❿
มหาวิทยาลัยจุฬาลงกรณ์

Phya Thai Rd. **Map** 7 C3. 🚌 *16, 40, 47, 50; AC: 501; MB: 1.* **Imaging Tech Museum** 🕿 *0-2218-5580.* 🕐 *10:30 am–3:30pm Mon–Fri.* 🖼 **Art Gallery** 🕿 *0-2218-2961.* 🕐 *daily.* ● *public hols.* **Museum of Ecology** 🕿 *0-2218-5442.* 🕐 *8:30am–4:30pm Mon–Fri.*

DEDICATED TO THE modern-minded king who founded it, this is Thailand's oldest,

richest, and most prestigious university. Chulalongkorn's central gardens, between the busy Phya Thai and Henri Dunant roads, are the site of several attractive buildings and a pond that is often used during the festival of Loy Krathong *(see p46)*.

The **Imaging Technology Museum**, to the south of the lake, features hands-on photographic displays, including a room where you can develop and print your own film, and exhibitions of high-quality photography from Thailand and other countries. Nearby are an auditorium, used mainly for classical concerts, a contemporary **Art Gallery**, which stages various temporary exhibitions, and a **Museum of Ecology**.

Royal Bangkok Sports Club ⓫
ราชกรีฑาสโมสร

Henry Dunant Rd. **Map** 8 D2.
🚌 *16, 21; AC: 141.* 🕿 *0-2255-1420.*
🕐 *9am–6pm alternate Sundays for races only.* 🖼

CONSIDERED TO BE Thailand's most exclusive social institution, the RBSC has a waiting list to prove it. It offers a wide range of sports to its members – including rugby, soccer, and field hockey – who form some of the top Thai teams in these sports. Nonmembers may enter to watch horse races at the club, one of Thailand's two principal race courses; the other is the Royal Turf Club on Phitsanulok Road *(see p102)*.

Gambling is virtually a national institution in Thailand, and the RBSC gives Bangkokians the perfect opportunity to indulge in one of their favorite pastimes. On race days, thousands of bettors from all social classes flock to the track. As the start of the race draws near, betting becomes increasingly furious, and huge electronic screens keep track of the odds on each horse and the total money wagered. Visitors are welcome to join in, and should watch the screens for clues as to which horse to bet on, although they may have to ask for help to fill out one of the Thai-language betting slips.

Horses on the home stretch, Royal Bangkok Sports Club

The Siam Center, Rama I Road, one of Thailand's first shopping malls

Erawan Shrine ⑫

พระพรหมเอราวัณ

Ratchadamri Rd. **Map** 8 D1. ∎ *AC: 501, 504, 505.* ∎ *Rachadamri or Siam (skytrain).*

DRIVERS CAN BE SEEN taking their hands off the steering wheel to *wai* (a gesture of respect) as they pass the Erawan Shrine, such is the widespread faith in the luck that this landmark brings. The construction of the original Erawan Hotel in the 1950s, on the site now occupied by the Grand Hyatt Erawan Hotel, was plagued by a series of mishaps. In order to counteract the bad spirits believed to be causing the problems, this shrine dedicated to Indra and his elephant mount, Erawan, was erected in front of the hotel. Ever since, the somewhat gaudy monument has been decked

Dancers in traditional Thai costume performing at the Erawan Shrine

with garlands, carved wooden elephants, and other offerings in the hope of, or thanks for, good fortune. By the shrine are women in traditional costume. Anyone wishing to express gratitude at the shrine for recent good fortune can pay the dancers a substantial fee, and they will do a thank you dance around it. Near the shrine, and along Phloen Chit and Sukhumvit roads, are several of Bangkok's most upscale shopping complexes *(see p431)*, including Sogo, Siam Center, World Trade Center, Gay Sorn Plaza, Amarin Plaza, and Le Meridien.

Wat Pathum Wanaram ⑬

วัดปทุมวนาราม

Rama I Rd. **Map** 8 D1. ∎ *AC: 25, 501, 508.* ∎ *Siam (skytrain).* ◯ *7am–6pm daily.*

THE MAIN REASON for visiting this temple is to see Phra Meru Mas, a reconstruction of the crematorium of the late Princess Mother. Following her cremation at Sanam Luang *(see pp74–5)* in March 1996, her remains were transferred to these grounds in an elaborate procession. The crematorium is a rare example of ancient craftmanship, featuring ornate stencils and lacquered sculptures. It represents Mount Meru, the heavenly abode of the gods.

Siam Square ⑭

สยามสแควร์

Rama I Rd. **Map** 7 C1. ∎ *AC: 25, 501, 508.* ∎ *Siam (skytrain).*

STREET SHOPPING is fast disappearing in Bangkok as shopping malls proliferate. The principal exception to this phenomenon is the network of *sois* (alleys) collectively known as Siam Square, between Chulalongkorn University *(see p113)* and the Siam Center.

The square is packed with independent shops and stalls selling, in particular, music, books, accessories, and clothing – much of it by enterprising young Thai designers.

Rama I Road, on one side of the square, is the showcase for Thailand's movie industry. Three grand theaters – the Scala, the Lido, and the Siam – are located here. On the western edge of the square, on Phaya Thai Road, is the **Mah Boon Krong Center**, which houses a department store and various shops and stalls. Beyond it is the **National Stadium**, Thailand's main arena for major soccer and other sports events. However, the future of the entire district looks uncertain: it is feared that the land may be redeveloped when its lease expires.

Movie poster on Rama I Road

Jim Thompson's House ⑮

บ้านจิมทอมป์สัน

See pp116–17.

Pratunam ⑯

ประตูน้ำ

Map 4 E5. ∎ *12; AC: 504.*

ALTHOUGH IT IS off the beaten tourist track, Pratunam district is worth a brief visit. The lively and colorful **Pratunam Market** is a vast maze of stalls, stores, and workshops, trading mostly in everyday goods such as fresh produce and clothing. Just west of the market is the

Bargain-price clothing for sale at Pratunam Market

Modernist **Baiyoke Tower**, which reigned briefly as the tallest building in Bangkok from 1987 until 1995. Despite evidence of settling in the surrounding ground, permission was granted for construction of the adjacent **Baiyoke Tower II**, which will have twice as many stories (90).

Suan Pakkad Palace ⑰

วังสวนผักกาด

352 Si Ayutthaya Rd. **Map** 4 D4. [0-2245-4934. ▥ AC: 201, 513. ▣ Phayathai (skytrain). ◯ 9am–4pm daily. ◩ Ⓦ www.suanpakkad.com

THIS PALACE, a group of five traditional teak houses, was originally the home of Prince and Princess Chumbhot. The houses were assembled in the 1950s within a lush garden landscaped out of a cabbage patch – *suan pakkad* in Thai – that gives the palace its name. Each building has been converted into a museum, and together they house an impressive private collection of art and artifacts that once belonged to the royal couple.

The eclectic assortment ranges from Khmer sculpture, betel-nut sets, and pieces of antique lacquered furniture, to Thai musical instruments and exquisite shells and crystals. More important, perhaps, is the first-class collection of whorl-patterned red and white Bronze Age pottery, excavated from tombs at Ban Chiang *(see p262)* in Northeast Thailand.

The highlight for most visitors, though, is the Lacquer Pavilion, which was built from two exquisite temple buildings retrieved by Prince Chumbhot from Ayutthaya province.

Immaculately crafted, charmingly detailed black and gold lacquered murals inside each edifice depict scenes from the Buddha's life and the Ramakien *(see pp36–7)*. They also portray ordinary Thai life from just before the fall of Ayutthaya in 1767 *(see pp56–7)*. These murals are some of the only ones to survive from the Ayutthaya period. Scenes include foreign traders exchanging goods, graphic battle scenes, everyday market scenes, as well as gruesome depictions of hell.

Elegant façade of the Lacquer Pavilion at Suan Pakkad Palace

BANGKOK'S MODERN ARCHITECTURE

Away from Bangkok's many *wats* and palaces, an apparently endless mass of dull concrete towers, monotonous rows of shop-houses and gaudy mock-classical edifices give this vast city the overall impression of a sprawling urban jungle rather than the Oriental splendor visitors might expect.

Nonetheless, there are a small number of modern buildings within the city that were designed by visionary architects. Postmodern architecture of an international standard is particularly noticeable along Sathorn Tai and Silom roads. Other interesting buildings include the Thai Airways headquarters and the triple-towered "Elephant Building."

One of Bangkok's most progressive design companies is Plan Architecture, responsible for a number of striking buildings in the city, in-

Baiyoke Towers I and II in downtown Bangkok

cluding the Baiyoke Towers I and II, the bullet-shaped Vanit Building II on Soi Chidlom, and the amazingly narrow Thai Wah II Tower on Sathorn Tai Road. Thailand's most famous, and perhaps most witty, modern landmark is probably the Bank of Asia's head office on Sathorn Tai Road. Dr. Sumet Jumsai's innovative, bizarre design has earned it the nickname the "Robot Building" *(see p65)*.

Perhaps the two most sophisticated examples of Thai Modernism, both of which are hotels, were designed by Westerners. The roof of the Siam Inter-Continental was designed to resemble a traditional "Mongkut" crown, and the gardens of the elegant Sukhothai evoke the serene waterscape of the old capital of the same name *(see pp184–7)*.

Jim Thompson's House ⑮

บ้านจิมทอมป์สัน

Khmer *singha* in the garden

Oₙₑ ₒf ₜₕₑ ₑₛₜ-ₚᵣₑₛₑᵣᵥₑd traditional Thai houses in Bangkok and finest museums in the country is the former home of Jim Thompson. The entrepreneurial American revived the art of Thai silk weaving *(see pp256–7)* following its demise during World War II. His house stands in a flower-filled garden across from the ancient silk weavers' quarter of Ban Khrua. In 1959 Thompson dismantled six teak houses in Ban Khrua and Ayutthaya province and reassembled them here in an unconventional layout. Thompson was an avid collector of antiquities and artworks from all over Southeast Asia. His distinguished array, which spans 14 centuries, is attractively displayed, and left much as it was when he mysteriously disappeared in 1967. Unlike many other domestic museums, this feels like a lived-in home.

Master Bedroom
Fine 19th-century paintings of the jataka tales line the walls of this room.

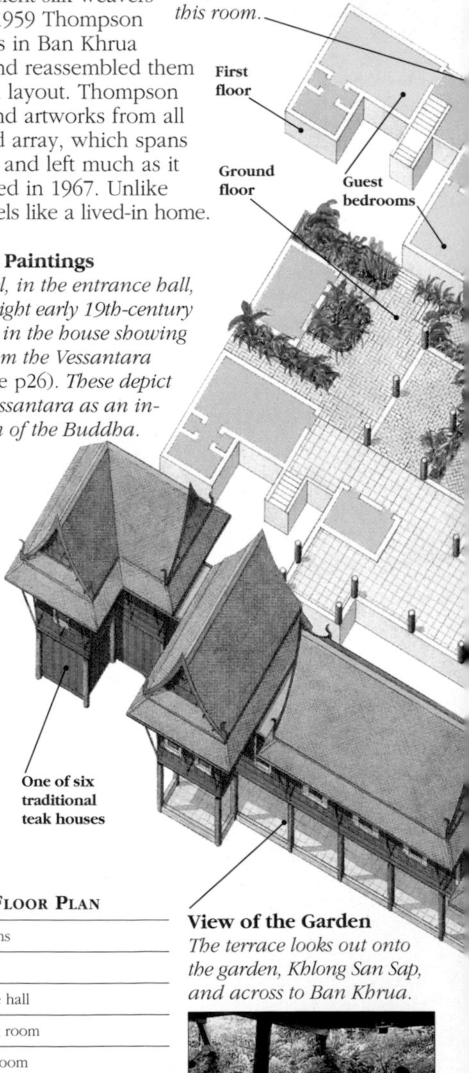

First floor

Ground floor

Guest bedrooms

★ **Jataka Paintings**
This panel, in the entrance hall, is one of eight early 19th-century paintings in the house showing scenes from the Vessantara jataka (see p26). *These depict Prince Vessantara as an incarnation of the Buddha.*

★ **Burmese Carvings**
This wooden figure of an animist Nat spirit is among Thompson's extensive collection of Burmese images. When Buddhism developed in Burma it incorporated the preexisting worship of Nat spirits.

One of six traditional teak houses

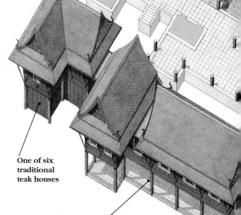

KEY TO FLOOR PLAN

- ☐ Bedrooms
- ☐ Study
- ☐ Entrance hall
- ☐ Drawing room
- ☐ Dining room
- ☐ Secure room
- ☐ Bencharong room
- ☐ Silk Pavilion
- ☐ Other exhibition space

View of the Garden
The terrace looks out onto the garden, Khlong San Sap, and across to Ban Khrua.

STAR EXHIBITS

★ **Jataka Paintings**

★ **Burmese Carvings**

★ **Dvaravati Torso of the Buddha**

Drawing Room
Situated on the right is a 13th-century U Thong sandstone head of the Buddha, while the 18th-century carved wooden figures in the alcoves are of Burmese spirits.

VISITORS' CHECKLIST

6 Soi Kasemsan 2, Rama I Rd. **Map** 3 C5. 📞 0-2216-7368. 🚌 15, 48, 204; AC: 508. 🚊 National Stadium (skytrain). 🕐 9am–5pm daily. 📷 🚫 📷 compulsory. 📷 🍴

The ***khlong*** (canal) was once used by silk weavers, who dried threads of silk on poles along the banks.

Porcelain Chamberpot
This cat, made of Chinese porcelain, is in the guest bedroom.

Dining Room
Beautiful blue and white Ming porcelain adorns the walls of this room.

★ Dvaravati Torso of the Buddha
This torso, made of limestone, is in the garden. Dating from the early Dvaravati period (6th century), it is said to be one of the oldest surviving Buddha images in Southeast Asia.

Spirit house with offerings

WHO WAS JIM THOMPSON?

An architect by profession, Thailand's most famous American came here in 1945 as the Bangkok head of the Office of Strategic Services (OSS), a forerunner of the CIA. In 1948 he founded the Thai Silk Company Ltd, turning the ailing industry into a thriving business once again. Thompson became a social celebrity in Bangkok and finally achieved mythical status following his disappearance on Easter Sunday 1967 while walking in the Cameron Highlands in Malaysia. Explanations for his vanishing include falling from a path or having a heart attack to more sinister suggestions of CIA involvement.

Jim Thompson inspecting Thai silk in 1964

ntrance

The teak houses, the oldest dating from 1800, were erected with some walls reversed so that exterior carvings now face the interior.

THON BURI

KNOWN ORIGINALLY AS Ban Kok ("village of the wild plum"), Thon Buri was the capital of Thailand for 15 years between 1767 and 1782. When Rama I moved his capital across the river its original name followed, and though Thais refer to the capital as Krung Thep, it remains known as Bangkok to foreigners. Thon Buri wasn't linked by bridge to Bangkok until 1932 and was officially incorporated into the city only in 1971. Today this area preserves a dis-

Chinese statue at Wat Arun

tinct identity, offering a sleepier version of Bangkok proper. The best way to explore Thon Buri is by boat. Meandering down the intricate network of canals, the visitor sees scenes of river life – stilt houses, small temples, mansions, and floating shops. On Khlong Bangkok Noi is the Royal Barge Museum with its lavishly decorated boats. Farther south there are some interesting riverside *wats* along the Chao Phraya River, the most prominent and famous of which is Wat Arun.

SIGHTS AT A GLANCE

0 meters 500

0 yards 500

Wats and Churches
Church of Santa Cruz ⑦
Wat Arun pp122–23 ⑤
Wat Kalayanimit ⑥
Wat Prayun ⑧
Wat Rakhang ④
Wat Suwannaram ①

Museums
Museums at the Siriraj Hospital ③
Royal Barge Museum ②

Monuments
Taksin Monument ⑨

KEY
🚢	Riverboat pier
🚢	Chao Phraya Express pier
🚓	Police station
✉	Post office
✚	Hospital with emergency room
卍	*Wat*
☾	Mosque

GETTING THERE

Cross-river ferries operate from all the Chao Phraya piers. The Chao Phraya Express has two stops on the Thon Buri side: Thon Buri Railroad Station and Phrannok. Buses and taxis reach Thon Buri via Taksin, Memorial, Phra Pok Klao, and Phra Pin Klao bridges.

◁ **Detail of the elaborate ceramic decoration, made up of thousands of pieces of broken porcelain, on Wat Arun**

Buddha in classic *bhumisparsa mudra* posture, Wat Suwannaram

Wat Suwannaram ❶

วัดสุวรรณาราม

Charan Sanit Wong Rd, Khlong
Bangkok Noi. **Map** 1 A3. 🚤 *hire a
long-tail from any pier.* 🔓 *daily.*

WAT SUWANNARAM was
constructed by Rama I
on the foundations of a temple dating from the Ayutthaya
era. It was renovated by Rama
III and finally completed in
1831. The temple complex
provides a graceful example
of early Rattanakosin architecture *(see p31)*, in which a
few traces of the Ayutthaya
style still linger. The well-
restored murals of the main
wihan, some of the best of the
early 19th century, are attributed to two renowned painters
of the third reign, Luang Vichit
Chetsada and Krua Khonpae.

Western perspective had
not permeated Thai mural
painting at the time: scenes
are depicted as aerial views
with figures shown at the
same size whether they are in
the foreground or background.
On the side panels are depictions of the last ten tales of
the *jataka* (the Buddha's
previous lives). On the south
wall are the Buddhist cosmological kingdoms, and the
entrance wall is dominated by
a lively scene of the Buddha's
victory over Mara. Notice the
hairstyles of the third reign
(1824–51): the
heads of both
sexes are shav-
en to leave a
small patch of
hair at the top.
Also, look for a
Christian cross
on a hermit's hut, evidence
that missionaries were active
in Thailand at the time.

Royal Barge Museum ❷

พิพิธภัณฑ์เรือพระที่นั่ง

Khlong Bangkok Noi. **Map** 1 B3.
📞 0-2424-0004. 🚌 7, 9,19.
🚤 *hire a long-tail from Chang pier.*
🔓 *9am–5pm daily.* 🚫 📷

HOUSED WITHIN a huge
warehouse-like structure
is a collection of Thailand's
most ostentatious boats, the
royal barges. Paintings of fabulous Ayutthayan barges *(see
pp56–7)* engaged in battles
and stately processions,
together with archive photographs of royal barge ceremonies in Bangkok over the last
150 years, have provided
some of the most splendid
visions of Thailand presented
to the world via postcards and
tourist brochures. Nowadays,
though, the
vessels are
rarely seen
cruising the Chao
Phraya River, since they
have been housed at the
museum since 1967. The
barges are reproductions
of some built 200 years ago
by Rama I, who had copied
Ayutthayan originals.

**Hongsa, on prow of
the king's barge**

In 1981 most of the royal
barges underwent an expensive face-lift. They came out in
all their gilded glory during the
1982 Bangkok Bicentennial
celebrations *(see p64)*, for the
King's 60th birthday in 1987,
and for the Golden Jubilee
of his reign on November 7, 1996.
For such auspicious occasions
more than 50 barges sail in a
lengthy procession down the
Chao Phraya. Most of the 2,000
oarsmen – dressed in traditional uniforms – are sea
cadets, a fitting crew for boats
that were once the naval fleet.

The vessel in the center of
the museum, Supphanahongsa
("golden swan"), is the most
important royal barge. Made
from a single piece of teak, it
is over 50 m (165 ft) long and
weighs 15 tons. In action it
requires a highly trained crew
of 64. The mythical, swanlike
bird Hongsa rears up from its
prow. Anantanagaraj, a barge
bearing a multiheaded *naga*
and a Buddha image, is reserved for conveying monks'

Superbly detailed 19th-century mural at Wat Suwannaram

Ferocious figurehead on a gun barge built in the reign of Rama I

robes. Narai Song Suban Rama IX is the first new barge to be built during the present king's reign. It is 44 m (145 ft) long and can carry 50 people.

Museums at the Siriraj Hospital ❸

พิพิธภัณฑ์โรงพยาบาลศิริราช

Arun Amarin Rd. **Map** 1 B4. 0-2419-7000 (Forensic), 0-2419-8523 (Congdon). 81, 91. *Phrannok and Wanglang.* 8:30am–4pm Mon–Fri. public hols.

TEN MEDICAL MUSEUMS are located at this hospital, of which the **Museum of Forensic Medicine** is the best known. It houses gruesome objects, such as the preserved figure of Si-oui, a

man who suffocated and ate seven children. Thai parents often threaten naughty children with his ghost. In the **Congdon Museum of Anatomy** are still-born Siamese twins. Such twins are so-named because the famous Chan and In, who toured the world in the mid-19th century, were from Siam, as Thailand was then known.

Wat Rakhang ❹

วัดระฆัง

Soi Wat Rakhang. **Map** 1 B5. 57, 83. *Chang to Wat Rakhang.* daily.

WAT RAKHANG was the last major temple to be constructed by Rama I in the early 19th century. The fine murals in the main *wihan,*

which were painted between 1922 and 1923 by a monk Phra Wanawatwichit, include recognizable scenes of Bangkok. Though the capital has changed much since then, the Grand Palace, which stands just across the river from Wat Rakhang, is easy to identify. In the murals, the palace is shown in the middle of an imaginary attack. There is also an elaborate depiction of a royal barge procession.

The raised wooden library *(ho trai)* of Wat Rakhang, in the west of the compound, was used as a residence by Rama I before he became king. The building's eave supports, delicately carved bookcases, and gold and black doors are period masterpieces. Inside the library are murals depicting scenes from the Ramakien and a portrait of Rama I.

Wooden façade of the raised library at Wat Rakhang

LIVING ON WATER: THE ERA OF THE THAI KHLONGS

Ayutthaya and Bangkok, both on the flood plain of the Chao Phraya River, were cities that grew along countless little canals and streams known as *khlongs*. Bangkok was once a floating city. In the 1840s all but about ten percent of its population of 400,000 lived on the *khlongs*. Houses built on rafts could be moored wherever there was space *(see p33)*.

Stilt houses lining the banks of the *khlongs* provided a somewhat more stable habitat. Although roads now cover most of Bangkok's eastern waterways, many still exist in Thon

Buri, where life still largely revolves around the *khlongs*. Children splashing in the water are a common sight, and early each morning water-borne vendors cruise up and down,

Bangkok in the 1890s, before the age of roads and land-based dwellings

selling everything from Chinese pastries and coffee to fruit, vegetables, and cooking utensils. The favored *khlong* vessel today is the long-tailed power-boat – one was memorably commandeered by Roger Moore as James Bond in the movie *The Man with the Golden Gun*. Visitors can easily charter their own from Chang pier to explore the Thon Buri *khlongs*.

Wat Arun ❺

วัดอรุณ

Ceramic flower on main *prang*

WAT ARUN, named after Aruna, the Indian god of dawn, is a striking Bangkok landmark. It owes its name to the legend that, in October 1767, King Taksin arrived here at sunrise from the sacked capital, Ayutthaya. He soon enlarged the tiny temple that stood on the site into a Royal Chapel to house the Emerald Buddha *(see pp78–9)*. Rama I and Rama II were responsible for the size of the current temple: the main *prang* is 79 m (260 ft) high and the circumference of its base is 234 m (768 ft). In the 19th century King Mongkut (Rama IV) added the ornamentation created with broken pieces of porcelain. The monument's style, deriving mainly from Khmer architecture *(see pp254–5)*, is unique in Thailand.

Multicolored Tiers
Rows of demons, decorated with pieces of porcelain, line the exterior of the main prang.

CENTRAL MONUMENT OF WAT ARUN

The monument's design symbolizes Hindu-Buddhist cosmology. The central *prang* (tower) is the mythical Mount Meru, and its ornamental tiers are worlds within worlds. The layout of four minor *prangs* around a central one is a symbolic mandala shape.

★ River View of Temple
This popular image of Wat Arun, as seen from the Chao Phraya, appears on the ten-baht coin and in the Tourism Authority of Thailand (TAT) logo.

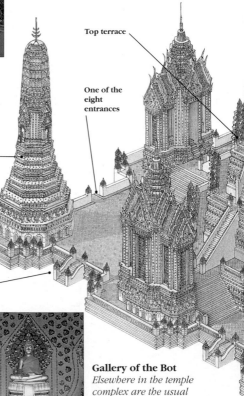

Top terrace

One of the eight entrances

Minor *prangs* at each corner of the *wat*

Chinese Guards
These figures, at the entrances to the terrace, complement the Chinese-style porcelain decorating the prangs.

Gallery of the Bot
Elsewhere in the temple complex are the usual buildings found in a wat. *This image of the Buddha in the main* bot *sits above the ashes of devotees.*

STAR FEATURES

★ **Ceramic Details**

★ **River View of Temple**

Indra's weapon, the *vajra* or thunderbolt, at the crest

SYMBOLIC LEVELS

The Devaphum (top) is the peak of Mount Meru, rising above four subsidiary peaks. It denotes six heavens within seven realms of happiness.

The Tavatimsa Heaven (central section), where all desires are fulfilled, is guarded at the four cardinal points by the Hindu god Indra.

The Traiphum (base) represents 31 realms of existence across the three worlds (Desire, Form, and Formless) of the Buddhist universe.

Stairs on the Central Prang
The steep steps represent the difficulties of reaching higher levels of existence. Visitors can climb halfway up when restoration work allows.

Small Cove
On the second level of the central prang *are many small coves, inside which are* kinnari, *mythological creatures, half bird, half human.*

Decoration of the Four Minor Prangs
Inside the niches of each minor prang *are statues of Nayu, the god of wind, on horseback.*

Mondops at the cardinal points

★ Ceramic Details
Much of the colorful porcelain used to decorate the prangs was donated by local people. The flowers depicted are said to evoke the vegetation of Mount Meru, home of the gods.

Wat Kalayanimit ❻
วัดกัลยาณิมิตร

Soi Wat Kanlaya. **Map** 5 B2. 🚌 *2, 8;
AC: 2 to Pak Klong Talad, then cross
the river by ferry at the pier.*
⬜ *8:30am–4:30pm daily.*

THIS DILAPIDATED temple
complex is one of the five
temples built in Bangkok by
Rama III (1824–51). Rama
liked Chinese design, as can
be seen from the statuary dotted around the courtyard
(brought to Thailand as ballast
on empty rice barges returning
from China) and the Chinese-
style polygonal *chedi.*

The complex's immense
wihan contains a large sitting
Buddha image. In the temple
grounds is the biggest bronze
bell in Thailand.

Near the *wat*, on the other
side of Khlong Bangkok Yai,
is **Wichai Prasit Fortress**,
built to guard the river approach to Thon Buri when
Ayutthaya was the dominant
city in Thailand *(see pp56 – 7).*

**Thailand's biggest bronze bell, in
the bell tower of Wat Kalayanimit**

Church of Santa Cruz ❼
วัดซางตาครู้ส

Soi Kudi Chin. **Map** 5 C2. 🚌 *2, 8 to
Pak Klong Talad then cross the river
by ferry at the pier, or express boat to
Saphan Phut pier.* ⬜ *6am and 7pm
Sun (for Mass).* 🚫 *inside the church.*

THIS PASTEL YELLOW church is
one of the most prominent
reminders of the community of

Newly released turtles feeding on fruit in the pond at Wat Prayun

Portuguese merchants and missionaries who lived here in the
mid-19th century. The church
was built in the late 18th
century, when Thon Buri was
the capital of Thailand *(see
pp60–61).* It was rebuilt by
Bishop Pallegoix in 1834, and
again in 1913. The church is
known in Thai as Wat Kuti
Chin ("Chinese monastic residence"), from the Chinese
influences in its architecture.

Although only a few houses
of Portuguese origin remain
in the muddle of alleyways
surrounding the temple, the
Portuguese legacy can still be
seen in the private Catholic
shrines that are tucked away
among Thai shop-houses.

Wat Prayun ❽
วัดประยุร

Pratchatipok Rd. **Map** 5 C2. 🚌 *6,
43, or express boat to Saphan Phut
pier.* ⬜ *7am – 4:30pm daily.*

THE UNUSUAL artificial hill at
the entrance to this temple
was created on a whim of
Rama III. While reading by
candlelight, the king observed
the interesting wax
formation of the
melting candle. He
then asked one of
his courtiers, Prayun
Bunnag, to create a
hill in the same
shape. The hill is
dotted with bizarre
shrines, miniature
chedis, prangs, grot-
toes, and tiny temples, but is
perhaps most memorable for
its ornamental pond, filled

with hundreds of turtles.
Devotees buy the turtles nearby and then release them into
the pond. This act of setting
free confined creatures (more
commonly releasing caged
birds) is a way of gaining
merit for future lives.

The temple *bot,* although in
a state of disrepair, has doors
and window shutters decorated
with mother-of-pearl. The large
chedi has a circular cloister
surmounted by smaller *chedis.*

Taksin Monument ❾
อนุสาวรีย์พระเจ้าตากสิน

Pratchathipok Rd. **Map** 5 C4.
🚌 *21, 40, 43, 82.*

LOCATED ON THE busy Wong-
wian Yai traffic circle, this
20th-century equestrian statue
commemorates King Taksin
(ruled 1767–82), who moved
the capital to Thon Buri after
the destruction of Ayutthaya
by the Burmese in 1767.

In 1950 the commission to
design the monument was giv-
en to Professor Silpa Bhirasri,
the Italian "father" of Thai

**Detail of King Taksin
monument**

modern art who
took a Thai name
and citizenship.
The striking statue
took three years
to complete and
was finally un-
veiled in 1954.
Each year, on
December 28 –
the anniversary of
King Taksin's Coronation –
many Thais come to pay
homage at the statue.

Popular Buddhist Rituals

THE ACT OF MERIT-MAKING is an essential part of religious life in Thailand (see pp26–7). Practiced both by monks and lay people, it reflects an awareness that good deeds lead to good outcomes, such as happiness, either in this life or the next (as a more fortunate rebirth). To accumulate merit is a way of taking responsibility for one's own *karma* (destiny). Becoming a monk, even for a short period, or sponsoring the ordina-

Child offering a lotus bud

tion of a monk, is the highest form of making merit, and a devout Buddhist monk adheres to strict rules in his daily life. In some rituals – such as the alms round – the lives of monks and lay people interact. Other everyday habits of ordinary people focus on the local temple: the shared act of decorating a Buddhist shrine strengthens community ties. Devout lay people, meanwhile, may meditate and worship at a private shrine in their own home.

Meditation *purifies the mind and clears it of distractions. It is practiced regularly by all monks and some lay people.*

The daily alms round (bintabat) *takes place shortly after dawn, when monks leave their temples to search for their daily meal. Giving food to monks is a popular way for lay people to earn merit and practice generosity (the act of* dana). *Monks are permitted to eat only food that has been offered to them, and they must consume it before noon.*

Shaving the head *is a ritual for monks on the day of the full moon. This mural shows a novice being shaved for ordination.*

Pavilion at Wat Phra Kaeo

Gold leaf *put on the Buddha image honors his teachings.*

Offerings for the Buddha are usually symbolic. Lotus buds represent the purity of the Buddha's thoughts.

Incense sticks, in groups of three, symbolize the Buddha, the *dharma* (teachings), and the *sangha* (monkhood). Candles stand for the light of understanding.

VISITS TO THE WAT
Many lay people in Thailand go to their local *wat* at least once a week. Typically they make offerings to an image of the Buddha, listen to the monks chanting and to a *dharma* talk, and receive blessings. Food is prepared to offer to the monks and as a communal meal. The local community often funds building or restoration projects.

FARTHER AFIELD

MANY INTERESTING SIGHTS lie outside central Bangkok. Extending eastward is Sukhumvit Road, with a plethora of shops, restaurants, small galleries, and museums. Shopaholics will also not want to miss the superb Chatuchak Market or the spectacle of Damnoen Saduak Floating Market, west of the city. To the south and east are a clutch of theme and amusement parks, including the Erawan Museum and the Ancient City, a tranquil park with replicas of Thai monuments. At the

Thai classical dancer

Crocodile Farm reptile wrestling is the major attraction, and Safari World offers further wildlife encounters. Culture lovers will enjoy the art and antiques in the Prasart Museum. Pleasant day trips include the green suburb of Nonthaburi and, to the west, the relaxed provincial towns of Ratchaburi and Nakhon Pathom. The latter is the site of the world's tallest Buddhist monument, Phra Pathom Chedi. Another popular excursion is west to the Thai culture shows and elephant rides at the Rose Garden.

SIGHTS AT A GLANCE

Towns
Nakhon Pathom ❹
Nonthaburi ❺
Ratchaburi ❶

Museums and Cultural Theme Parks
Ancient City ⑪
Erawan Museum ⑬
Prasart Museum ⑩
Rose Garden ❸

Notable Roads
Sukhumvit Road ❼

Swimming Pools
Siam Park ❾

Markets
Chatuchak Market ❻
Damnoen Saduak Floating Market ❷

Zoos
Crocodile Farm ⑫
Safari World ❽

GETTING THERE
Many tour companies offer day trips to popular sights such as the Rose Garden, Safari World and Ancient City. Local bus routes also serve most sights.

KEY

▨	Main sightseeing area
▫	Built-up area
✈	Airport
═	Highway
─	Major road
▪▪	Road under construction
═	Minor road

20 km = 12 miles

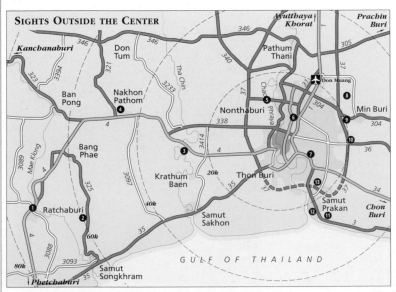

SIGHTS OUTSIDE THE CENTER

Palm-shaded Wat Mahathat, the main sight at Ratchaburi

Ratchaburi **❶**
ราชบุรี

Ratchaburi province. 🏛 *195,977.*
🚌 🚆 **ℹ** *TAT, Phetchaburi (0-3247-1005).*

ORIGINALLY AN estuarial port at the mouth of the Klong River, Ratchaburi is now 30 km (19 miles) from the ocean. During the Ayutthaya period *(see pp56–7)* the town was sacked twice, in 1765 and 1767, by invading Burmese armies en route to besiege the capital city of Ayutthaya.

Nowadays, Ratchaburi makes a pleasant place to stop on the way to Kanchanaburi and the Western Seaboard. Some visitors stay overnight if visiting Damnoen Saduak Floating Market the next morning.

The town has few sights, but Wat Mahathat is worth a visit. Its *prang*, allegedly modeled on the main *prang* at Angkor Wat *(see pp254–5)*, dates from the 15th century, although the temple complex may have been founded as early as the 8th or 9th century. Inside the *prang* are traces of murals from the 15th century, and partially restored stucco work.

Artifacts in the **Ratchaburi National Museum** include archaeological finds such as fine Khmer sculptures and stucco decorations excavated from Muang Khu Bua, a Dvaravati site south of Ratchaburi.

🏛 Ratchaburi National Museum
Woradej Rd. **📞** *0-3232-1513.*
🕐 *9am–4pm Wed–Sun.* ● *public hols.* 🈵

ENVIRONS: The caves of Khao Ngu, 6 km (4 miles) northwest of Ratchaburi on Highway 3087, contain some early Dvaravati art. The splendid reliefs of Buddha images found in Tham Rusi and Tham Fa Tho are probably of greatest interest. Aggressive macaques congregate in the area surrounding the caves.

Damnoen Saduak Floating Market **❷**
ตลาดน้ำดำเนินสะดวก

2 km (1 mile) W of Damnoen Saduak, Ratchaburi province. 🚌 🚆 🚐 *or join tour from Bangkok.* 🕐 *4am–11am daily.* **ℹ** *TAT, Phetchaburi (0-3247-1005).*

IN CONTRAST TO the numerous floating markets in Bangkok that are now organized solely for the benefit of tourists, this is a fairly unspoiled example.

Located near Damnoen Saduak – 100 km (62 miles) southwest of Bangkok – the market is a labyrinth of narrow *khlongs* (canals). The small wooden boats are paddled mainly by female traders, some of whom are dressed in traditional blue farmers' shirts – *mo hom* – and conical straw hats. The fresh produce, including fruit, vegetables, and spices, comes straight from the farm. For the benefit of the tourists, some boats sell souvenir straw hats and refreshments.

The floating market actually consists of three markets. The largest, **Ton Khem**, is on Khlong Damnoen Saduak. On the parallel *khlong* is **Hia Kui**, where structures anchored to the banks function as warehouses selling souvenirs to large tour groups. To the south, on a smaller *khlong*, is **Khun Phitak**, the least crowded market.

The best way of getting around the three markets is by boat: trips can be taken along the *khlongs* or to see nearby coconut plantations. The best time to arrive is between 7am and 9am, when the Floating Market is in full swing.

Trading Thai-style at the bustling Damnoen Saduak Floating Market

Thai Fruits and Vegetables

THAILAND'S CLIMATE and soil conditions are conducive to the cultivation of a huge variety of fruits and vegetables throughout the year. Well known tropical fruits, including papaya, watermelon, mango, and pineapple, are unmistakable, but the orchards and farms of Thailand also offer a wealth of produce that may be less familiar to many visitors. Among the not-to-be-missed treats are the mangosteen, the grapefruitlike pomelo, the much-prized durian, and the sweet-fleshed, hairy rambutan. Thai fruits are sold sliced as snacks by street vendors everywhere, and the full range of fresh produce can be seen at most markets.

Bright red, fresh rambutans

Longans *have a transparent, succulent flesh around a smooth pit.*

Mangoes *can be eaten unripe and sour (green) or ripe and sweet (yellow).*

Mangosteens *are the king of Thai fruit. Their tasty flesh has a melt-in-the-mouth texture.*

Durians *are a favorite with Thais. The pungent smell and flavor are an acquired taste.*

Guavas, *crisp and sour fruits, are best enjoyed with a sweet chili dip or as a refreshing juice.*

Jackfruits, *similar in appearance to durians, only larger, have a sticky flesh with a tangy flavor.*

Gourds

Pea eggplant

Baby tomatoes

Eggplant

Thai vegetables *include several types of* makhua *(the tomato and eggplant family). Gourds and eggplant are frequently used in curries.*

Scallions

Cilantro

Chilies

Thai cuisine *makes liberal use of chilies, galingle, tamarind, and lemon grass to flavor dishes, balancing spiciness with coconut milk and sugar. Cilantro and scallions are popular garnishes.*

The peaceful, immaculately maintained Rose Garden

Rose Garden ❸

สวนสามพราน

Off Hwy 4, 32 km (20 miles) W of Bangkok. ☎ *0-3432-2772, 0-2295-3261.* 🚌 *M: 15; AC: to Nakom Pathom or Suphan Buri, or join tour from Bangkok.* ⏰ *6am–6pm daily (show at 2:45pm).* 🎫

THIS WELL MANICURED garden, west of Bangkok, is part of the Rose Garden Country Resort. Although you can play tennis or golf and swim here, the chief attraction for visitors is the daily show of culture. Packed into the one-hour show are traditional Thai dancing *(see pp38–9)*, ancient sword fighting, a Thai wedding, the ordination of a monk *(see p26)*, and Thai boxing *(see pp40–1)*. The model Thai village within the grounds is a showcase for fruit-carving, basket weaving, and other crafts.

ENVIRONS: Just north of the Rose Garden is the **Samphran Elephant Ground and Zoo**, featuring crocodile wrestling and elephant rides. Farther west, on the way to Nakhon Pathom, the **Thai Human Imagery Museum** has fiberglass statues of notable figures in Thai history, including the Chakri kings *(see pp60–61)* and some renowned monks.

🔗 **Samphran Elephant Ground and Zoo**
☎ *0-2284-1873.* ⏰ *daily.* 🎫
🔗 **Thai Human Imagery Museum**
Pinklao-Nakhonchaisri Hwy, km 31.
☎ *0-3433-2607.* ⏰ *8am–6pm Sat & Sun, 9am–5:30pm Mon–Fri.* 🎫

Nakhon Pathom ❹

นครปฐม

Nakhon Pathom province. 🏛 *167,500.* 🚉 🚌 ℹ️ *TAT, Bangkok (0-2694-1222), TAT, Kanchanaburi (0-3451-1200).* ⏰ *daily.* 🎏 *Phra Pathom Chedi Fair (Nov); Food and Fruit Fair (Sep 1-7).*

SOME 67 KM (42 MILES) to the west of Bangkok, Nakhon Pathom was a major center of the Dvaravati Kingdom, which thrived from the 6th to the 11th centuries AD *(see pp52–3)*.

The highlight of the town is the **Phra Pathom Chedi**, on Phetkasem Highway. This huge monument, housing a large standing Buddha image, is one of the most important places of pilgrimage in Thailand. The original *stupa* (a non-Thai *chedi*) on this site is thought to have been built sometime between the 2nd century BC and the 5th century AD. It commemorated the first Buddhist missionaries in Thailand, allegedly sent here from India in the 3rd century BC. The building fell into decay in the 11th century and was not restored until the early 19th century when King Mongkut had the old shrine encased in a *chedi*. The spire was completed by King Chulalongkorn. The *chedi*, dominates the town and at 120 m (395 ft) in height is the tallest Buddhist monument in the world.

Southeast of the *chedi* is the **Phra Pathom Chedi National Museum**, which has a fascinating collection of locally excavated pieces from the Dvaravati period, including stone Wheels of the Law *23 els* from Chedi Chula Prathon, a 7th–8th century monument east of town.

West of the *chedi* is the early 20th-century **Sanam Chan Palace**. Parts of the palace are open to the public, and the peaceful grounds are a good place from which to view the palace's unusual mix of architectural styles.

🔗 **Phra Pathom Chedi National Museum**
Khwa Phra Rd. ☎ *0-3427-0300.*
⏰ *Wed–Sun.* ⏰ *public hols.* 🎫
🔗 **Sanam Chan Palace**
Off Phetkasem Hwy. **Palace & Grounds** ⏰ *daily.* 🎫

Nakhon Pathom's *chedi*, the world's tallest Buddhist monument

Nonthaburi pier, as seen from the Chao Phraya River

Nonthaburi **❺**

นนทบุรี

Nonthaburi province. 🏛 46,500.
🚉 🚌 ⛴ 🛈 *TAT, Bangkok (0-2694-1222); TAT, Ayutthaya (0-3524-6076).*
🍴 daily. 🍈 Fruit Fair (Apr–Jun)

APPROXIMATELY 10 km (6 miles) north of Bangkok, Nonthaburi offers a relaxing slice of provincial life. The town is best reached by riverboat from one of Bangkok's express piers. The journey takes 50 minutes and offers several interesting sights, the first of which is the Royal Boat House near Wat Sam Phraya pier, where some of the royal barges are kept. Others are housed at the Royal Barge Museum in Thon Buri *(see pp120–21)*. Past the Krung Thon Bridge is a small community of rice barges on the east bank, and shortly before Nonthaburi pier is **Wat Khian**, a temple that is half-submerged in the river.

Nonthaburi has a pleasant, provincial atmosphere that contrasts with the chaos and pollution of the capital just down the river. The town is particularly well known for the quality of its durian fruit *(see p129)* – reflected in the unusual decoration of the lamp-posts on the promenade. You may find the famously smelly fruit for sale in Nonthaburi's colorful, lively market by the side of the river. A round-trip boat ride from Nonthaburi

Door of *bot*, Wat
Chalerm Phrakiet

along Khlong Om will take you on a slow-paced journey through durian plantations and past riverside houses. The tiny river island of **Ko Kret**, accessible only by boat, is home to a community of craftsmen, who are famous for their distinctive style of pottery. Another worthwhile excursion from Nonthaburi is the river journey to **Wat Chalerm Phrakiet**, on the west bank of the Chao Phraya. The *wat* occupies the site of a 17th-century fortress, built by Rama III in the 19th century for his mother. A particularly striking feature is the intricate detailing, including porcelain tile-work, on the doors, gables, and window frames of the *bot*. Behind is a *chedi*, added by Rama IV. The grounds have Chinese-style wooden statues, including one of Santa Claus.

Chatuchak Market **❻**

ตลาดจตุจักร

Chatuchak district. 🚇 *AC: 38, 502, 503, 509, 510, 512, 517, 518, 521, 523.*
🛈 *TAT, Bangkok (0-2694-1222).*
🕐 *7am–6pm Sat & Sun.*

THAILAND'S BIGGEST MARKET is staged each weekend in a northern suburb of Bangkok, between the Northern Bus Terminal and Bangsu Railroad Station. The market moved to this location in 1982 because it had outgrown its original site on Sanam Luang *(see pp74–5)*. Now it is a chaotic collection of over 6,000 stalls, which together occupy the space of over five football fields. It is always full of throngs of eager shoppers, many of whom spend a whole day browsing among the merchandise displays.

The huge variety of goods for sale ranges from fresh seafood to antiques, and from Siamese fighting fish to second-hand jeans. The plant section offers a good introduction to Thai flora, while the food stalls display every conceivable ingredient of Thai food, fresh from the farm or the sea. The antique and hill-tribe sections sell a good selection of artifacts and textiles, both fake and genuine, from all over Thailand and neighboring countries.

The market has been referred to as the "wildlife supermarket of the world," due to some endangered species, such as leaf monkeys, being illegally sold here. Thankfully, such trade is now declining.

Traditional Thai wooden figures for sale at Chatuchak Market

Sukhumvit Road 7
ถนนสุขุมวิท

Phra Khanong district. 🚉 🚌 *AC: 38, 501, 508, 511, 513.*

Hotels, restaurants, and offices lining Sukhumvit Road

THIS ROAD BEGINS at the eastern end of Bangkok's downtown and continues all the way to the Cambodian border in Trat province *(see p313)*. In Bangkok it is the main thoroughfare of an expanding business quarter popular with foreigners.

Though it is a long way from Bangkok's best-known sights, the area has numerous good quality, moderately priced hotels and restaurants, and a few attractions of its own.

Foremost of these is the **Siam Society**, which was founded in the early 1900s (by a group of Thais and foreign residents under the patronage of Rama VI) to research, rediscover, and preserve Thai culture. Within the grounds are two traditional teakwood Northern Thai houses that comprise the country's only genuine ethnological museum. The Kamthieng House, a farm dwelling, was transported piece by piece in the 1960s to Bangkok from the bank of the Ping River, near Chiang Mai. The Sangaroon House is a later addition donated by the architect Sangaroon Ratagasikorn who – inspired by the utilitarian beauty of rural

Sculpture at the Queen's Park

utensils – amassed a sizeable collection. It is a good example of Central Plains style *(see p32)*. Also on the grounds is a reference library on Thai culture, open to visitors. The *Journal of the Siam Society* is one of Asia's most respected publications on art history, culture, and society.

Next to the Eastern Bus Terminal, the **Bangkok Planetarium**, with its hands-on exhibitions, may be of interest to those who have time to spare while waiting for a bus.

The **Queen's Park** is easily found between sois 22 and 24, while the larger **King's Royal Park** is farther out toward Samut Prakan. With its botanical gardens and area for water sports, this park is one of Bangkok's most pleasant oases. The park also has an exhibition on the king's life.

🏠 **Siam Society**
131 Soi Asoke, Sukhumvit Rd, Soi 21.
📞 *0-2661-6470.* ⬤ *Mon–Sat.*
🏠 **Bangkok Planetarium**
928 Sukhumvit Rd.
📞 *0-2392-5951.* ⬤ *Tue–Sun.*
⬤ *public hols.* 📷
♣ **Queen's Park**
By Soi 22, Sukhumvit Rd.
⬤ *daily.*
♣ **King's Royal Park**
Soi Udomsuk, Sukhumvit Rd, Soi 103.
📞 *0-2328-1385.*
⬤ *daily.* 📷

A mock-up of a traditional sleeping area in the Kamthieng House

Safari World 8
ซาฟารีเวิลด์

99 Ramindra Road, Minburi district.
📞 *0-2518-1000.* 🚌 *60, 71 & AC: 501 to Fashion Island Center, then songthaew .* ⬤ *9am–5pm daily.* 📷

THIS CAR-SAFARI PARK offers eight different natural habitats over a 5-km (3-mile) drive. Among the animals on view are tigers, elephants, giraffes, lions, and zebras, and rare species such as white pandas. A marine park features dolphin shows. Other entertainment includes elephant and orangutan shows, and a bird park.

Siam Park 9
สวนสยาม

101 Mu 4 Sukha Phiban 2 Rd, Minburi district. 📞 *0-2919-7200-1.* 🚌 *AC: 519.* ⬤ *10am–6pm Mon–Fri, 9am–7pm Sat, Sun & public hols.* 📷

SIAM PARK, a water and amusement center, is a great place to cool off from the heat of the Thai sun. Its attractions include huge waterslides, a gentle whirlpool, and an artificial lake. Water permeates Thai culture in many ways, not least at Songkran (New Year), when everyone gets soaked on the streets *(see p44, p226)*.

The facilities are well maintained, and there are restaurants and lifeguards. There is also an amusement park with rickety fairground rides and a small zoo. As Bangkok families descend upon the park in numbers at the weekend, it's best to visit during the week.

Prasart Museum ⑩
พิพิธภัณฑ์ปราสาท

9 Soi Krungthepkretha 4a, Bang Kapi
district. 📞 *0-2379-3607.*
🚌 *M: 10.* ⭘ *Tue–Sun.* 📷 🚫 📹
compulsory (book in advance).

T HE PRIVATELY OWNED Prasart
Museum is known to
relatively few tourists and
Bangkokians, but the journey
out to this elegant museum,
set in landscaped tropical
gardens, will be worthwhile
for anyone who loves Thai
art. The collector, Prasart
Vongsakul, started to acquire
Thai antiques in 1965 when
he was only 12 years old.

**Ornate interior of Lanna Pavilion
at the Prasart Museum**

Ancient City ⑪
เมืองโบราณ

Sukhumvit Rd, Bangpu, Samut Prakan
province. 📞 *0-2323-9253.*
🚌 *AC: 511 to the end of the line,
then take the 36 mini bus.*
⭘ *8am–5pm daily.* 📷

M UANG BORAN, or "Ancient
City," is an outdoor
cultural theme park financed
and created in the early 1970s
by the art-loving philanthrop-
ic owner of Thailand's largest
Mercedes-Benz dealership.
The park makes a surprisingly worthwhile visit. The peaceful grounds, shaped roughly
like Thailand itself, display
numerous replicas of
important monuments in
Thailand as well as actual
buildings and sculptures that
have been restored to their
former grandeur. Replicas are
one third real size.

All the Thai art periods are
represented, including a few
mythical and literary ones
such as at the Garden of Phra
Aphaimani, inspired by a 19th-
century verse play *(see p308).*
Some of the buildings, for example the Sanphet Prasat Palace, which once stood near
Wat Phra Si Sanphet in Ayutthaya *(see pp168–9),* are re-
constructions of monuments
destroyed centuries ago in
battle and so provide the only
testaments to past glories.

Crocodile Farm ⑫
ฟาร์มจระเข้

Old Sukhumvit Highway, Samut Prakan
province. 📞 *0-2703-4891.* 🚌 *AC:
511 to Samut Prakan, then
songthaew, or join tour from
Bangkok.* ⭘ *8am–5pm daily.* 📷

T HE LARGEST of Thailand's
crocodile farms and sup-
posedly the largest in the
world, this breeding park/zoo
is home to some 30,000
reptiles. Fresh- and saltwater
species are included, ranging
from South American caimans
to crocodiles from the Nile.
In the breeding section you
can see crocodiles hatching
and in various stages of
growth. You can also see them
transformed into handbags
and key rings in the souvenir
shop. Wrestling shows are
held regularly, and feeding
time happens at 4:30–5:30pm.
A visit to the crocodile farm is
popularly combined with a
day trip to the Ancient City.

**Wrestling, the most spectacular
show at the Crocodile Farm**

Erawan Museum ⑬
พิพิธภัณฑ์ช้างเอราวัณ

Sukhumvit Road, Samut Prakan
province. 📞 *0-2380-0305.* 🚌 *25,
142, 365; AC: 102, 507, 511, 536.*
⭘ *8am–6pm daily.* 📷

A MONUMENTAL three-headed
bronze elephant stands
astride the Erawan Museum,
making it visible for miles
around. Inside is a large
collection of ancient religious
objects, including a number
of priceless Buddha statues.
The exterior of the lower
story of the building is
decorated with tiny pink
enamel tiles in the style of
Thai Benjaron ceramics. An
elaborate double staircase,
which takes you up inside the
body of the elephant, dominates the upper levels. There is
also an elevator that travels
up one of the hind legs.
Outside, the tranquil gardens
contain ponds and fountains
in a variety of styles.

Reconstruction of the Prince of Lampang's Palace, Ancient City

BANGKOK STREET FINDER

INDING YOUR WAY around Bangkok can be a challenge. The lack of standard transliterations for Thai words means that the street names listed here will not always match those seen on street signs. Additionally, some streets are known by more than one name – for example, Charoen Krung Road is New Road and Wireless Road is Witthayu Road. Most major roads (*thanons*) have numerous numbered (and sometimes named) *sois* and *troks* (minor roads and lanes) leading from them. Odd numbered *sois* usually lead off one side of a road, even numbers off the other. Be warned that there can be considerable distances between *sois* – for instance, *sois* 6 and 36 off Phetchaburi Road are more than 3 km (2 miles) apart. Major sights, markets, and ferry piers are also listed in this gazetteer.

The quickest way to get around Bangkok for humans and canines

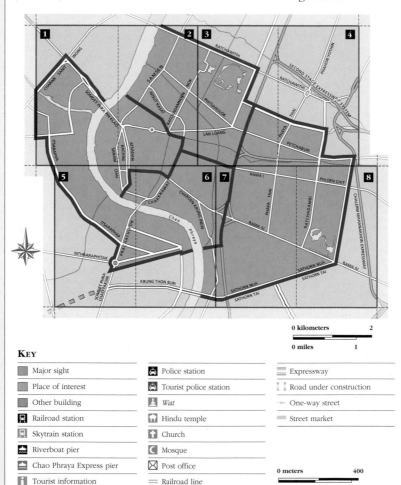

KEY

▦ Major sight	🚓 Police station	▦ Expressway
▦ Place of interest	🚓 Tourist police station	⁞ ⁞ Road under construction
▦ Other building	🛐 *Wat*	→ One-way street
🚉 Railroad station	🛕 Hindu temple	▬ Street market
🚉 Skytrain station	✝ Church	
⛴ Riverboat pier	☪ Mosque	
⛴ Chao Phraya Express pier	⊠ Post office	
🛈 Tourist information	══ Railroad line	**0 meters** 400
✚ Hospital with emergency room	═ Skytrain route	**0 yards** 400

Scale for Street Finder pages

0 kilometers 2
0 miles 1

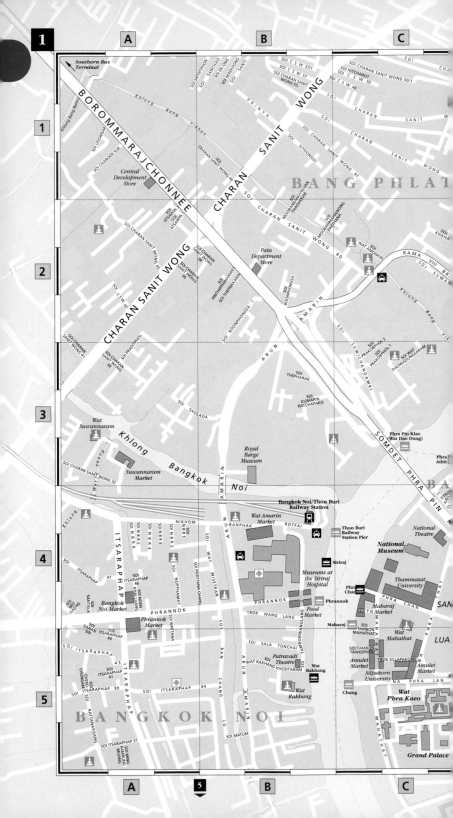

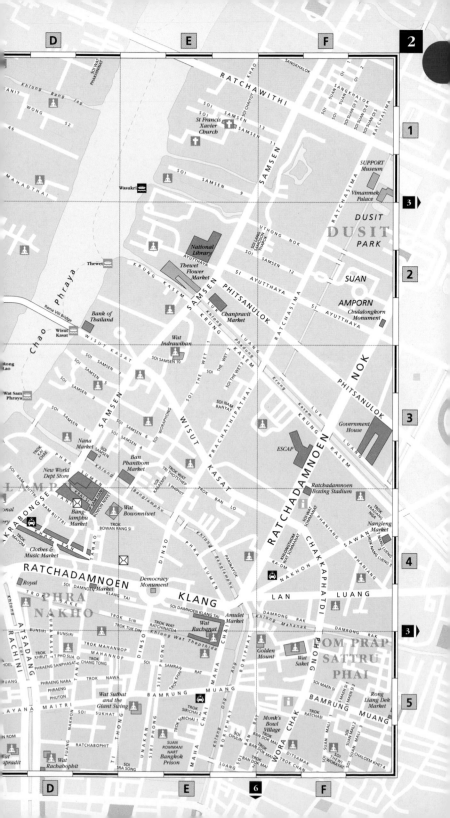

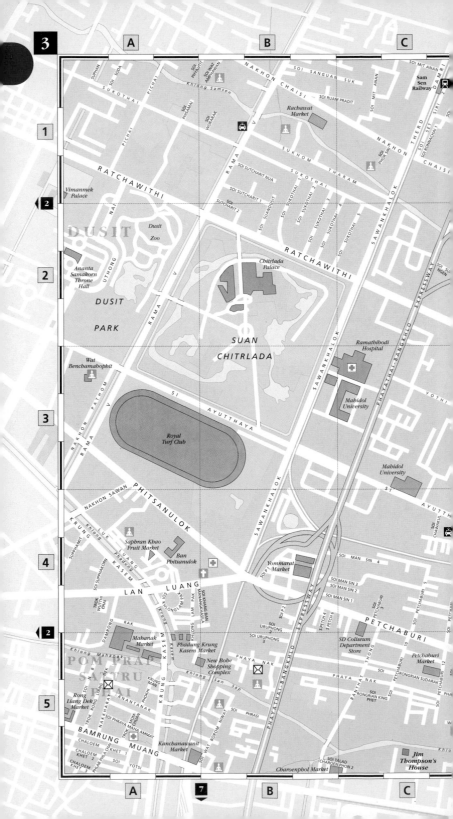

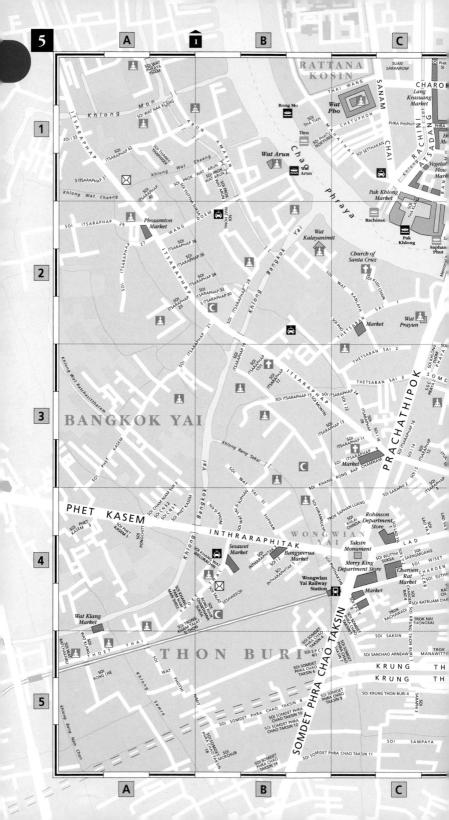

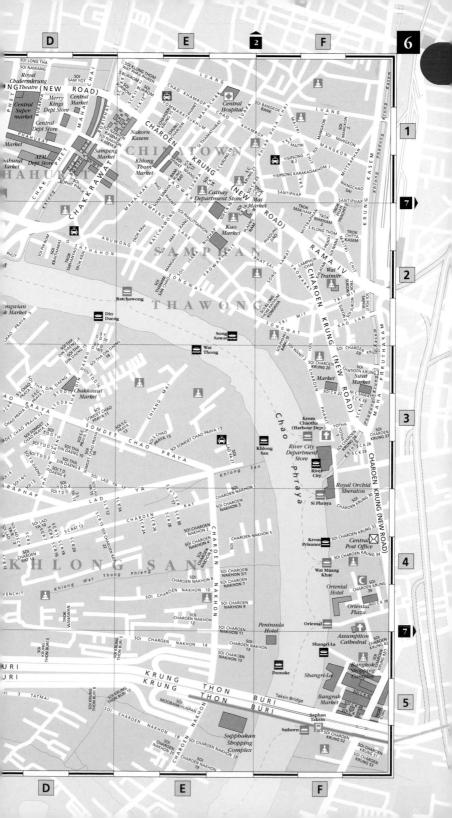

THE CENTRAL PLAINS

Introducing the Central Plains

Si Satchanalai
Chalieng
Historical P

THE FERTILE PLAINS stretching northward from Bangkok are the nation's rice basket and the historic heartland of the Tai people. Here lie the impressive ruined cities of the old Sukhothai *(see pp54–5)* and Ayutthaya kingdoms *(see pp58–9)*. Today this is the country's most wealthy and densely populated region, with fast-expanding towns surrounded by fields of sugar cane and rice. In the forested hills that border the Central Plains are national parks with spectacular waterfalls and a wide range of wildlife, providing a pleasant scenic contrast.

Si Satchanalai-Chalieng Historical Park
(see pp188–90) *encompasses the ruins of one of the most important Sukhothai cities, as well as the remains of an earlier Khmer settlement.*

Kamphaeng Phet

Kamphaeng Phet (see pp182–3) *contains a wealth of Sukhothai-era monuments and ruins and, within the old city walls, a fine museum displaying ceramics such as this 15th-century pot.*

SOUTH
CENTRAL
PLAINS
(see pp154–175)

Kanchanaburi

Kanchanaburi (see pp160–61) *is near the site of the infamous bridge built over the Khwae Yai River during World War II. A museum and cemetery in the town provide a moving testament to the Asian laborers and Allied troops who died.*

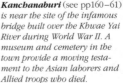

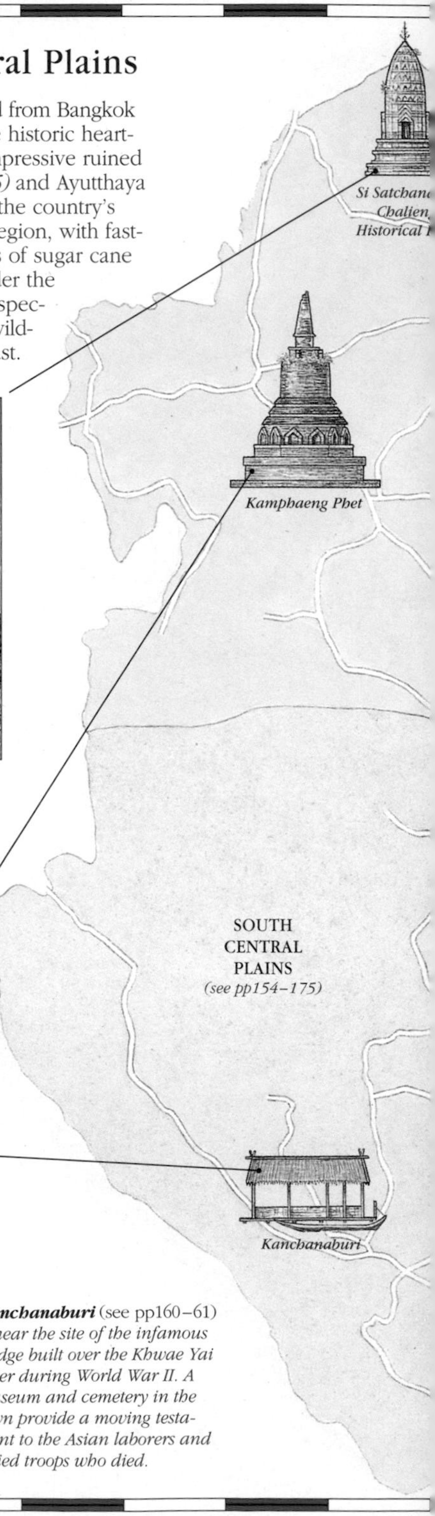

◁ **The remains of a *bot*, featuring a huge, seated Buddha image, Wat Mahathat, Sukhothai**

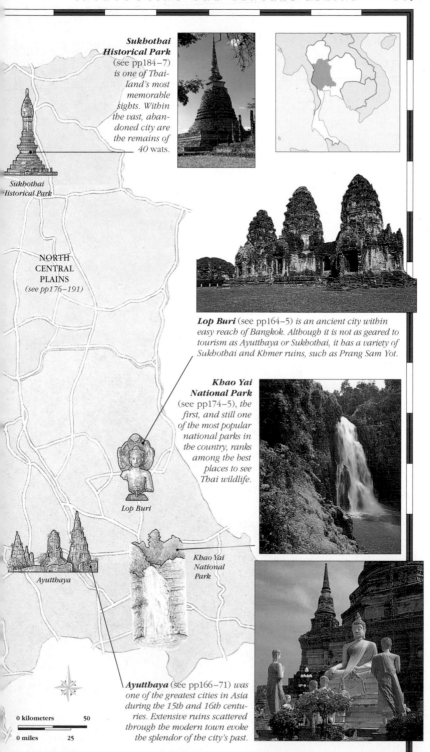

Sukhothai Historical Park (see pp184–7) is one of Thailand's most memorable sights. Within the vast, abandoned city are the remains of 40 wats.

Sukhothai Historical Park

NORTH CENTRAL PLAINS (see pp176–191)

Lop Buri (see pp164–5) is an ancient city within easy reach of Bangkok. Although it is not as geared to tourism as Ayutthaya or Sukhothai, it has a variety of Sukhothai and Khmer ruins, such as Prang Sam Yot.

Khao Yai National Park (see pp174–5), the first, and still one of the most popular national parks in the country, ranks among the best places to see Thai wildlife.

Lop Buri

Ayutthaya

Khao Yai National Park

Ayutthaya (see pp166–71) was one of the greatest cities in Asia during the 15th and 16th centuries. Extensive ruins scattered through the modern town evoke the splendor of the city's past.

0 kilometers   50

0 miles   25

Sukhothai Art

THE PROLIFIC ARTISANS of the Sukhothai School (late 13th–15th centuries) adapted stylistic elements from Sri Lanka, Burma, and other neighboring countries to produce some of Thailand's finest works of art. Numerous Buddha images of immense beauty and fluidity were cast in bronze. The "Walking" Buddha – a posture that is otherwise rare in Buddhist art – is perhaps the best-known artistic achievement of the period. The Sangkhalok *(see p190)* ceramics industry also flourished, and its fine wares, including pale blue-green celadons, were exported all over Asia until the middle of the 16th century.

The Walking Buddha posture possibly represents the Buddha's descent from Tavatimsa Heaven after he had visited his mother.

Bronze replaced stone as the preferred material for Buddha images during the Sukhothai period. It allowed a far more delicate detailing of the Buddha's hair and facial features.

PHITSANULOK BUDDHA
Located in Wat Phra Si Rattana Mahathat in Phitsanulok, this 14th-century Buddha image, known properly as Phra Phuttha Chinarat, is one of the most revered in all of Thailand, second only to the Emerald Buddha in Bangkok. Cast in bronze and later gilded, the serene figure is a supreme example of late Sukhothai art.

This bronze Vishnu, a Hindu god, is in the classic Sukhothai style. Brahmin priests, who presided over some court ceremonies, probably ordered figures like this to be made.

Wedge-shaped joints

The flame like "halo" around Phra Phuttha Chinarat, ending in *naga* heads, is unique.

Fingers all of the same length

Sukhothai bai semas (boundary stones, see p29) were fashioned from slate into leaf shapes. This one, at Wat Sorasak in Sukhothai, is inscribed with details of a land grant.

Monochrome ceramic gable decorations, such as this one from Wat Phra Phai Luang, Sukhothai, are a typical architectural flourish from the period.

Ceramic finials, found on many roofs, were sometimes fashioned as dragons. Such decorations show a fusion of Khmer and Chinese styles.

Sangkhalok ware, such as this delightful, brown monochrome elephant, are often well preserved. Fine pieces like this were produced from the mid-14th century onward, when exports boomed.

King Vajiravudh (1910–25) was highly active in the early archaeological work at Sukhothai: he was a totally untrained but enthusiastic excavator.

Tightly curled hair drawn into flamelike finial

Arched nose and eyebrows

Fish-and-flower motifs, painted beneath the glaze, were popular for bowls and plates. Such items were exported as far afield as Japan.

Gently smiling mouth

Figurines sometimes feature a bulge by the mouth, which may depict the chewing of fermented tea. Female figures are common, often carrying babies.

Diaphanous robes

Pouring vessels, known as kendis, *were sometimes zoomorphic, like this earthenware piece in the shape of a duck.*

THE BAN KO NOI KILNS

The remains of 200 brick kilns were excavated at Ban Ko Noi *(see p189)* near Si Satchanalai in 1980–87. Some contain the pots that were being fired when the kilns were abandoned. There are also a number of kiln sites at Sukhothai.

Entrance

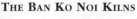

Chimney

Foreigners in Ayutthaya

THROUGHOUT THE 16TH AND 17TH centuries Ayutthaya was one of the most important trading centers in Asia, attracting not only merchants but also missionaries, adventurers, and mercenaries from around the world. Portuguese visitors arriving in the 16th century found a riverine city of canals and magnificent flotillas of barges. They brought firearms to trade and military advisers to help Ayutthaya against the Burmese. The Dutch and English followed in the 17th century and established trading ware-houses. The Japanese came to buy animal hides, while French Jesuits and Persians competed for religious converts. Some foreigners, including Constantine Phaulkon, sought political influence.

St. Joseph's Church (see p170) *stands south of Ayutthaya's main island. Originally built during the reign of King Narai (1656– 88) by French missionaries, it has been restored many times since.*

European illustration of a Siamese official

Royal Palace

Lacquerware *was a specialty of Ayutthaya. Like other as-pects of life in the city, the decorative arts reflected the influence of foreigners or* farangs. *These doors depict farang traders.*

MAP OF AYUTTHAYA
The involvement of Europeans in Siamese affairs led to the publication of several maps of Ayutthaya. This French map, probably an 18th-century copy of one drawn in the 17th century, shows the location of the French, Portuguese, and Siamese quarters. The European spelling of Ayutthaya at that time was Iudia.

Siamese quarter   **Chao Phraya River**

The first French to *arrive in Ayutthaya, in 1662, were Jesuit mission-aries. In 1681 the French asked permission for a full diplomatic mission to visit the city. It arrived in 1685, headed by the envoy from Louis XIV, Chevalier de Chaumont. A Siamese envoy later returned with him to France. This painting shows him being received at court by the Sun King, Louis XIV.*

French Jesuit missionaries *came to Ayutthaya to convert King Narai to Catholicism. They failed in this but encouraged him to cultivate an interest in astronomy. This illustration shows him watching a lunar eclipse in 1685. Following the Jesuits' tutelage he watched a partial solar eclipse in 1688. Narai favored the Jesuits and gave them land to build churches and schools.*

Chilies *were first imported from South America by the Portuguese, who established a trading treaty with the Siamese in 1516. They quickly grew in popularity, and today chilies are an essential ingredient in numerous Thai dishes.*

Siamese quarter

Chinese quarter

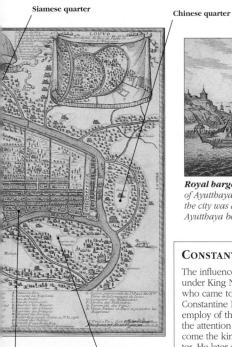

French quarter **Portuguese quarter**

Royal barges *and other boats crowded the waterways of Ayutthaya. Often the first sight that greeted visitors to the city was a convoy of royal barges. As a result, Ayutthaya became known as the "Venice of the East."*

The VOC *(Dutch East India Company) first visited Ayutthaya in 1604. A trading warehouse was set up in 1634, but by the 1670s trade had declined. The warehouse in Ayutthaya was later destroyed by the Burmese.*

CONSTANTINE PHAULKON

The influence of foreigners in Ayutthaya was greatest under King Narai (1656–88). Most notorious of those who came to Ayutthaya was the Greek adventurer Constantine Phaulkon, who arrived in 1678 in the employ of the English East India Company. Attracting the attention of Narai, he quickly moved on to become the king's personal confidant and chief minister. He later advised Narai against Dutch and English interests in Ayutthaya. The French, meanwhile, were allowed to station 600 soldiers in the kingdom. Amid much political wrangling in court, Narai was viewed as cultivating strong ties with Louis XIV, whose ambition was to convert him and Siam to Catholicism, and some people feared a French takeover. When Narai died in 1688 all ties with Westerners were cut, and Phaulkon was executed.

Constantine Phaulkon, prostrate before the Siamese king, Narai

SOUTH CENTRAL PLAINS

F OR CENTURIES, *the broad flood plain of the Chao Phraya, which bisects the South Central Plains north to south, has been Thailand's rice basket as well as its most densely populated region. The river remains a vital link between the country's cultural heartland and its present-day capital, Bangkok. The old capital of Ayutthaya, upstream from Bangkok, is the region's most popular sight.*

Ayutthaya was one of the greatest mercantile centers in Asia during the 14th–18th centuries. Its fabulous temples and palaces, built around the confluence of the Chao Phraya, Lop Buri, and Pasak Rivers, were regarded with wonder by foreigners. In 1767 it was sacked by the Burmese, and the capital was forced to move downstream to Bangkok. The remains of monuments from the earlier period stand among more modern buidings and each day attract hundreds of visitors on round-trips from Bangkok.

Kanchanaburi, to the west of Bangkok, is another popular day trip from the capital. During World War II the Japanese built a railroad from here to the Three Pagodas Pass near Burma, along an old Burmese invasion route. Little of the railroad was ever used, but at Kanchanaburi visitors can see poignant reminders of this grueling episode, when thousands of Asian laborers and Allied POWs died. Despite these and other noteworthy sights, the region still has relatively few tourist facilities. Towns such as Lop Buri – an old Khmer outpost with several Khmer *prangs* – and the pilgrimage site of Phra Phutthabat are unknown to the majority of tourists. There is some accommodation in the Khwae Noi River Valley, along the route to the Three Pagodas Pass. This region is surrounded by a vast expanse of forest and grassland, including two wildlife sanctuaries and the Erawan, Sai Yok, and Chaloem Rattanakosin national parks. At the eastern edge of the South Central Plains, Khao Yai, the oldest national park, is the best place in Thailand to see wild elephants and many other animals.

The bridge over the Khwae Yai River at Kanchanaburi, a poignant reminder of World War II

◁ Wat Mahathat, built in 1384, one of the largest temples at the ancient site of Ayutthaya

Exploring the South Central Plains

THE CHAO PHRAYA RIVER BASIN is fertile terrain, perfect for rice production. It is no coincidence that the kingdoms of Lop Buri and, later, Ayutthaya, the capital of which is the main sight of the region, were founded here. East of the wide plain, Khao Yai is the country's oldest and most accessible national park. Kanchanaburi, in the west, is the site of the notorious Death Railroad of World War II. From there, a road winds up to the Three Pagodas Pass on the Burmese border, passing near numerous national parks and wildlife sanctuaries.

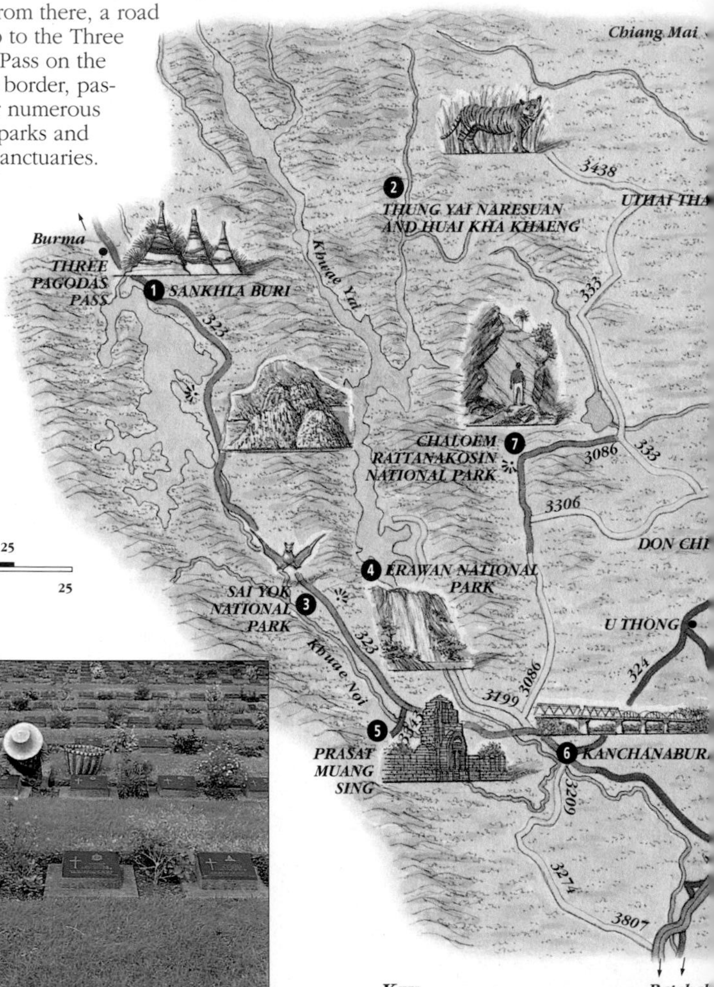

Chiang Mai

3438

2 THUNG YAI NARESUAN AND HUAI KHA KHAENG

UTHAI THA

Burma

THREE PAGODAS PASS

1 SANKHLA BURI

Khwae Yai

333

323

7

CHALOEM RATTANAKOSIN NATIONAL PARK

3086

333

3306

DON CHI

0 kilometers 25

0 miles   25

SAI YOK NATIONAL PARK

3

4 ERAWAN NATIONAL PARK

U THONG

Khwae Noi

323

324

3086

3199

5

PRASAT MUANG SING

6 KANCHANABURI

3209

3274

3807

Ratchat

Phetcha

KEY

Memorial stones at POW cemetery, Kanchanaburi

▬	Expressway
▬	Major road
▬	Minor road
▬	Scenic route
═	River
☆	Vista

GETTING AROUND

Many hotels in Bangkok arrange day tours of Ayutthaya and Kanchanaburi. Boat tours up the Chao Phraya River, from Bangkok to Ayutthaya via Bang Pa-in, are also popular. Roads from Bangkok fan out across the region, providing fast and easy access by bus or car, though leaving Bangkok itself is time consuming. Kanchanaburi, Ayutthaya, and Lop Buri can be all reached by rail.

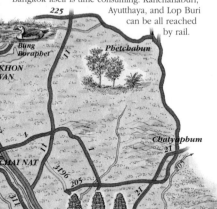

Buddhas at Wat Yai Chai Mongkhon, Ayutthaya

SEE ALSO

- *Where to Stay* pp391–2
- *Where to Eat* pp415–16

Chanthara Phisan Hall, on grounds of King Narai's Palace, Lop Buri

On the way to market, Three Pagodas Pass

Sangkhla Buri ❶

สังขละบุรี

Kanchanaburi province. 👥 *36,000.*
🚌 *from Kanchanaburi.* 🛈 *TAT,*
Kanchanaburi (0-3451-1200). 🛒 *daily.*

I N THE CENTER of Sangkhla
Buri is a market where,
among other things, you can
buy Burmese curries and
samosas, as well as books
written in the Mon language.

However, the main attrac-
tion of this isolated trading
town, which is populated by
Mon and Karen tribespeople
(*see p196*) as well as Thais,
is its serene lakeside location.
The lake is actually a large
reservoir, formed by the dam-
ming of the Khwae Noi River
farther downstream. Some-
times, late in the dry season,

the drowned remains of
old villages and forests
can be seen sticking up
out of the calm surface
of the lake's waters.

The north shore of the
lake is overlooked by the
unusual *chedi* of
Wat Wangwiwekaram.
In the covered gallery
beside it a daily market
sells goods, including
lungis (sarongs) and
simple woodcarvings
from Burma, Indonesia,
and elsewhere. Visitors
can reach the *wat* on foot
by crossing a wooden
bridge that spans the
wide, shallow inlet of the
lake. A large settlement,
consisting predominantly
of Mon tribespeople, has
grown up in close proximity
to the *wat*. An interesting
daily market is held here in
the early morning.

ENVIRONS: At the **Three
Pagodas Pass**, 23 km (14
miles) northwest of Sangkhla
Buri, right on the Burmese border, are situated three small,
physically unimpressive, whitewashed *chedis*. For centuries
this pass, which is less than
300 m (985 ft) above sea
level, was used as an invasion
route. During World War II,
the Burma-Siam Railroad (*see
pp160–61*) passed through
here, and the route the track
took can still be seen beside
the Burmese border. Nowa-
days, the pass is a quiet trading
(and smuggling) route between
the Indian Ocean to the west

and mainland Southeast Asia.
Visitors to this region are
usually permitted to cross the
border on a one-day visa (*see
p451*) to the Burmese town of
Pyathonzu. However, visitors
should note that the relations
between Thailand and Burma
are often uneasy, at times
verging on the hostile, and
mean that this situation is
prone to change at any time.

Thung Yai
Naresuan and Huai
Kha Khaeng ❷

เขตรักษาพันธุ์สัตว์ป่าห้วยขาแข้ง

Kanchanaburi, Tak and Uthai Thani
provinces. 🛈 *TAT, Tak (0-5551-4341);
Kanchanaburi (0-3451-1200); Forestry
Dept (0-2562-0760).* 🚌 *from Kanchanaburi.* 📷 @ *tatkan@tat.or.th &
tattak@tat.or.th*

T HESE TWO HUGE, adjacent
wildlife sanctuaries, covering 6,220 sq km (2,400 sq
miles) and surrounded by a
further 6,000 sq km (2,320 sq
miles) of protected forest,
form one of the most important conservation areas in
Southeast Asia. They are
listed jointly as a UNESCO
World Heritage Site and are
home to some of Thailand's
largest remaining wild elephant
herds, as well as several endangered carnivores, such as
tigers, clouded leopards, and
Malaysian sun bears. The
enormous gaur, a species of
wild cattle, and the country's
last wild buffalo herds also

Herd of wild buffalo, native to Thung Yai Naresuan and Huai Kha Khaeng wildlife sanctuaries

Tourist accommodations in the tranquil Sai Yok National Park

live within the sanctuary. Rare species of gibbon can also be seen. At Huai Kha Khaeng there is a nature trail, but neither wildlife sanctuary is geared up for large numbers of visitors – permission for large parties to enter the parks can be obtained from Bangkok Forestry Department.

Sai Yok National Park ❸
อุทยานแห่งชาติไทรโยค

Kanchanaburi province. Park HQ off Hwy 323, 100 km (62 miles) NW of Kanchanaburi. 🛈 *TAT, Kanachanaburi (0-3451-1200); Forestry Dept (0-2562-0760 or www.dnp.go.th for bungalow bookings).* 🚃 🚌 *from Kanchanaburi.* 🖼

SAI YOK was the site of a large Japanese army barracks and POW labor camp during World War II. The 500-sq km (190-sq mile) national park was established in 1980 and today is renowned for its tranquil river scenery and the impressive Sai Yok Yai waterfall, which tumbles into the Khwae Noi River near to the park headquarters.

Accommodation is available in park bungalows or on pleasant houseboats, and boats can be chartered – at some expense – to some nearby caves. The caves are home to the 3-cm (1-inch) long Kitti's hog-nosed bat, considered by some to be the world's smallest mammal, and which was discovered in 1973 by Thai naturalist Kitti Thonglongya.

ENVIRONS: The Burma-Thailand Railroad Memorial Trail, south of Sai Yok, pays tribute to prisoners who died during the excavation of the Konyu railroad cut. Near to the cut, which was given the name "Hellfire Pass" by the many prisoners of war who labored through the night by torchlight, was the "Pack of Cards Bridge." This rickety 300-m (985-ft) long, 25-m (82-ft) high structure was built at perilous speed with green timber and, as a result, heavy loss of life – the structure collapsed three times during its construction.

The trail, set up with funding from the Australian government, winds up to Konyu cutting through a bamboo grove. The railroad track has long since been removed.

Plaque in memory of POWs, Hellfire Pass

Erawan National Park ❹
อุทยานแห่งชาติเอราวัณ

Kanchanaburi province. Park HQ off Hwy 3199, 65 km (40 miles) NW of Kanchanaburi. 🛈 *TAT, Kanchanaburi (0-3451-1200); Forestry Dept (0-2562-0760 or www.dnp.go.th for bungalow bookings).* 🚌 *from Kanchanaburi.* 🖼

IN THE LUSH FOREST of the 550-sq km (210-sq mile) Erawan National Park, the nearest park to Kanchanaburi, are the stunningly beautiful **Erawan falls**, which drop through a series of cascades and shady rock pools. While park rangers still find occasional tiger prints, visitors are more likely to see pig-tailed and rhesus macaques, and some 80 bird species. The Visitors' Center offers a slide show about the park, and there is a pleasant, 2-km (1-mile) hiking trail which climbs up beside the falls. This is one of Thailand's most popular national parks, and at weekends and holidays it gets very crowded. The large limestone cavern of Tham Wang Badan, situated on the west side of the park, contains many colorful stalactites and stalagmites.

ENVIRONS: The Huai Khamin falls, which are in nearby **Si Nakharin National Park**, do not receive as many visitors as the Erawan falls but, are nonetheless quite impressive. Visitors can make boat trips onto the Si Nakharin reservoir, either from the Kradan pier or from Si Sawat, a small market town situated on the eastern shore of the reservoir.

🏕 Si Nakharin National Park
108 km (67 miles) N of Kanchanaburi. ◻ *daily.* 🖼

The Erawan falls, named after the Hindu god Indra's elephant mount

Central sanctuary of Prasat Muang Sing near Kanchanaburi

Prasat Muang Sing ❺
ปราสาทเมืองสิงห์

Off Hwy 323, 43 km (27 miles) W of Kanchanaburi, Kanchanaburi province.
ℹ TAT, Kanchanaburi (0-3451-1200).
🚌 from Kanchanaburi to Tha Kilen, then songthaew. 🄾 daily. 🄼

THE RUINS of Muang Sing beside the Khwae Noi River date from around the 13th century and mark the westernmost point of expansion of the Khmer Empire (see pp254–5). Earthen ramparts surround an inner wall of laterite that forms a rough rectangle about 1 sq km (245 acres). Near the center of this are the ruins of the Buddhist sanctuary, Prasat Muang Sing. Like most Khmer temples it faces east, in alignment with the city of Angkor.

Although the Muang Sing temple complex looks Khmer, some art historians believe it was actually built by local artisans in imitation of the occupying Khmers – the sanctuary, for example, lacks the stylistic details that are normally associated with Khmer sites. It was probably built after the reign of Jayavarman VII (1181–1220) as the Khmer Empire began to decline and its power in this region was fading. A museum at the site displays artifacts excavated here.

ENVIRONS: Southeast of Muang Sing is Ban Kao, a prehistoric settlement discovered in the 1940s by Dutch archaeologist van Heekeren, a prisoner on the Burma-Siam Railroad. The **Ban Kao Museum** houses stone tools and ornaments.

🏠 **Ban Kao Museum**
35 km (22 miles) W of Kanchanaburi.
🄾 8am–4:30pm Wed–Sat. 🄼

Kanchanaburi ❻
กาญจนบุรี

Kanchanaburi province. 🏯 108,000.
🚉 🚌 ℹ TAT, Saeng Chuto Rd, Kanchanaburi (0-3451-1200).
🄳 daily. 🄼 Khwae River Bridge Week (Nov/Dec).

THOUGH SURROUNDED by beautiful limestone hills and vast expanses of sugar cane, Kanchanaburi is best known for its associations with the infamous Burma-Siam Railroad. Constructed in 1942–3 it crosses over the Khwae Yai River just to the north of Kanchanaburi town center. At the small station beside the bridge are a number of steam locomotives dating from the period. There is also a memorial to those who died during the war, which was erected by the Japanese administration in 1944. Today, 77 km (47 miles) of the railroad remain, and the trip along it from Kanchanaburi to Nam Tok is one of the most interesting in Thailand. The **Thailand-Burma Railroad Center** is a small museum charting the history of this railroad. The

Sign, Kanchanaburi station

building of the railroad cost the lives of more than 100,000 Asian laborers and 12,000 Allied prisoners of war. The **Kanchanaburi War Cemetery**, contains the graves of almost 7,000 mostly British and Australian prisoners and is one of two war cemeteries in the town. It is immaculately maintained by the Commonwealth War Graves Commission.

The smaller of the two cemeteries, **Chong Kai Cemetery**, contains 1,740 graves and lies on the north bank of the Khwae Noi River, a short ferry ride from the center of town. Nearby is **Wat Tham Khao Pun**, overlooking the river and the Burma-Siam Railroad, which at this point heads south toward Ban Kao and Prasat Muang Sing. In the grounds of the *wat* complex a network of narrow passages leads through a cave system filled with Buddha images.

In the **JEATH War Museum**, housed in Wat Chai Chumphon, visitors can see three replicas of the bamboo huts used to house prisoners of war in the camps that sprang up along the Burma-Siam Railroad during the war. The huts display paintings, sketches, and photographs of life in the camps and along the railroad line. JEATH is an acronym for Japan, England, Australia and America, Thailand, and Holland, some of the countries whose nationals worked on the railroad. Many survivors

Steel bridge over the Khwae Yai River, Kanchanaburi

and victims' relatives visit Kanchanaburi each year.

Accommodations here include riverside raft houses.

⚑ Kanchanaburi War Cemetery
Saeng Chuto Rd. ◯ *daily.*

⚑ Chong Kai Cemetery
Ban Kao Rd. ◯ *daily.*

⚑ JEATH War Museum
Wisuttharangsi Rd. ◯ *daily.* 🖳

⚑ Thailand-Burma Railroad Center
73 Jaokunneu Rd. ◯ *daily.* 🖳

Farmers cultivating crops in the hills around Kanchanaburi

Chaloem Rattanakosin National Park ❼
อุทยานแห่งชาติเฉลิมรัตนโกสินทร์

Kanchanaburi province. Park HQ off Hwy 3086, 97 km (60 miles) NE of Kanchanaburi. 🛈 *TAT (0-3451-1200); Forestry Dept (0-2562-0760 or www.dnp.go.th for bungalow bookings).* 🚌 *from Kanchanaburi to Nong Preu, then songthaew.* ◯ *daily.* 🖳

THIS BEAUTIFUL and isolated national park is one of Thailand's smallest, at just 59 sq km (23 sq miles). The main trail runs beside a stream which passes through a cavern, Tham Than Lot Noi, to emerge in a thickly forested, steep-sided ravine. The path continues for 2,500 m (8,200 ft), climbing steeply beside the Trai Trung falls to Tham Than Lot Yai, a limestone sinkhole, and a small Buddhist shrine. On weekday mornings you may find that you are the only visitor in this delightful spot.

THE BRIDGE OVER THE KHWAE YAI RIVER AND THE BURMA-SIAM RAILROAD

The first railroad bridge over the Khwae Yai River, near Kanchanaburi, was built of wood, using Allied and Asian slave labor. In 1943 it was abandoned for an iron bridge, which was repeatedly bombed and damaged by the US Army Air Force from late 1944 on. In 1945, after only a short period in service, the bridge was put out of commission. After the war this infamous river crossing was immortalized in David Lean's movie, *The Bridge on the River Kwai* (1957).

The bridge was part of an immense project, the 414-km (255-mile) Burma-Siam Railroad, conceived by the Japanese after the Allies blockaded sea routes in 1942. It ran from Nong Pladuk, 50 km (30 miles) southeast of Kanchanaburi, to Thanbyuzayat near the coast in Burma. Built under appalling conditions, it operated for only two years. Around 60,000 Allied prisoners of war and 300,000 Asian laborers were forced to work 18-hour shifts on its construction, with many losing their lives to cholera, malaria, malnutrition, and most tragically to maltreatment. It is said that one man died for each tie laid. One reason for the brutal regime was that the Japanese followed a samurai code. They despised the disgrace of surrender and treated the

Painting by prisoner of war in the JEATH War Museum, Kanchanaburi

Allied prisoners of war as if they had forfeited all human rights. The present-day bridge at Kanchanaburi was rebuilt, as part of Japanese war reparations, with two girders from the Japan Bridge Company of Osaka. It has now become a place of pilgrimage for veterans. Kanchanaburi has two cemeteries and a museum, the latter, in particular, presenting a moving evocation of this harrowing episode of World War II history.

Prisoners of war on the wooden bridge over the Khwae Yai River (c.1942–3)

The beautifully tended Chong Kai Cemetery, Kanchanaburi

The Chinese shrine of San Chao Pho, Suphan Buri

Suphan Buri ⓼

สุพรรณบุรี

Suphan Buri province. 👥 *111,000.*
🚍 🚌 ℹ️ *TAT, Ayutthaya (0-3524-*
6077). 🎊 *Don Chedi Fair (Jan 25).*

Like many large towns in this region, Suphan Buri came to prominence with the rise of Ayutthaya in the 14th century. The attractive art and architecture of the town are known to few tourists.

Near the center of town is the beautiful *prang* of Wat Phra Si Rattana Mahathat, restored in the Ayutthaya period and again in the 20th century. At Wat Pa Lelai, on the edge of Suphan Buri, is a Buddha image from the Dvaravati period *(see pp52–3)*. To the east is San Chao Pho Lak Muang, a Chinese shrine. Wat Phra Rup, on the other side of the Suphan Buri River, houses a reclining Buddha image and a carved wooden Footprint of the Buddha. The *bot* of nearby Wat Pratu San contains striking 19th-century murals of the Buddha's life.

Environs: The large white monument of **Don Chedi**, 31 km (20 miles) from Suphan Buri, marks the site of the battle of Nong Sarai, between the Burmese and Thai forces led by King Naresuan *(see p58)*. The **U Thong National Museum** houses 6th–11th-century Dvaravati artifacts, excavated nearby, and Khmer art.

🏛️ **U Thong National Museum**
7 km (4 miles) SW of Suphan Buri.
🔲 *Wed–Sun.* 🎫

Ang Thong ⓽

อ่างทอง

Ang Thong province. 👥 *41,600.* 🚍
ℹ️ *TAT, Ayutthaya (0-3524-6077).*
🚌 *daily.*

This small town is a useful base from which travelers who are interested in Thai images of the Buddha can visit three little known but rewarding sites nearby. To the south of Ang Thong, **Wat Pa Mok** houses a reclining Buddha image from the 15th century. **Wat Khun In Pramun** is to the northwest. In its grounds is a huge reclining Buddha image, about 50 m (165 ft) long, dating from the Ayutthaya period.

At **Wat Chaiyo Wora Wihan**, to the north of Ang Thong, a *wihan* houses a third enormous, seated image of the Buddha from the Rattanakosin period, called the Phra Maha Phuttha Phim.

Wat Pha Mok, which houses a 15th-century Buddha, near Ang Thong

Lop Buri ⓾

ลพบุรี

See pp164–5.

Phra Phutthabat ⓫

พระพุทธบาท

Saraburi province. ℹ️ *TAT, Ayutthaya (0-3524-6077).* 🚌 *from Saraburi, then samlor.* 🔲 *7am–6pm daily.*
🎊 *Phra Phutthabat Fair (Mar).*

In the early 17th century, King Song Tham of Ayutthaya sent a group of monks to Sri Lanka to pay homage to a revered Footprint of the Buddha. (According to legend, these Footprints actually show where the Lord Buddha walked upon the Earth.) The monks were surprised to be told by the Sri Lankans that, according to scriptures, there was a footprint in Thailand. Song Tham, on hearing this, ordered a search for the footprint. It was found by a hunter pursuing a wounded deer – the animal vanished into the undergrowth only to re-emerge healed. On closer inspection, the hunter found a water-filled pool shaped like a footprint. He drank from it and was miraculously cured of a skin disease. The king, on learning of this, had a temple built on the site, which subsequently became one of the most sacred places of worship in Thailand.

Bell, Phra Phutthabat

Today, the 1.5-m (5-ft) long Footprint, Phra Phutthabat, lies in an ornate *mondop*, restored in the late 18th century after the earlier buildings were destroyed by the Burmese in 1765. A museum here displays offerings by pilgrims, who flock to the sight each year. Phra Phutthabat is also the name of the small town here.

Environs: At **Phra Phutthachai** ("Buddha's shadow"), about 40 km (25 miles) southeast of Phra Phutthabat, a faint Buddha image, probably painted by a hermit, can be seen on a cliff face. Pilgrims often visit this site on the journey to Phra Phutthabat.

Gestures of the Buddha

BUDDHA IMAGES throughout Thailand for the most part follow strict rules laid down in the 3rd century AD. There are four basic postures: standing, sitting, walking, and reclining; the first three are associated with daily activities of the Buddha, the last with the Buddha's final moments on earth as he achieved *nirvana*. These postures can be combined with hand and feet positions to create a variety of attitudes *(mudras)*, that represent key Buddhist themes. King Rama III (1824–51) drew up a list of 40 attitudes to be used by sculptors, but many of these are rare. Most images in Thailand represent a dozen or so attitudes, the seated image in *bhumisparsa mudra* occurring most frequently.

Exposition (vitarkha mudra) *symbolizes the first public discourse given by the Buddha, to five ascetics in a deer park in India. On this Sukhothai-era image, the thumb and forefinger form a circle – the "turning of the wheel of law"* (see p27).

TOUCHING THE EARTH
Bhumisparsa is the most common mudra. It symbolizes an important episode in the Buddha's life when he sat in meditation under a Bodhi tree in Bodh Gaya, India, refusing to move until he attained Enlightenment. While his enemy, Mara, offered temptations such as nubile maidens and feasts, the Buddha touched the ground to attract the attention of the Earth goddess, so that she could see his resistance. Just after this he achieved Enlightenment.

Right hand pointing to the Earth

Left hand resting in lap

Legs in lotus position

Meditation (dhyana mudra) *is signified with a sitting posture, shown by this modern Buddha image from Southern Thailand. Both hands are positioned palms up, the right over the left, as still practiced by meditating Buddhists.*

Reassurance (abhaya mudra) *symbolizes the Buddha's offer of protection to his followers. The raised right hand is also representative of an episode in which the Buddha settled a heated dispute over water.*

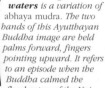

Restraining the waters is a variation of abhaya mudra. *The two hands of this Ayutthayan Buddha image are held palms forward, fingers pointing upward. It refers to an episode when the Buddha calmed the floodwaters of the Nairanjana, a tributary of the Ganges in northern India.*

Reclining Buddhas, such as this one at Ayutthaya, usually represent the point of parinirvana *or ultimate* nirvana.

Street-by-Street: Lop Buri 🔟

ลพบุรี

ONE OF THAILAND'S oldest cities, Lop Buri was known as Lavo in the Dvaravati period *(see pp52–3)* and subsequently became an important outpost of the Khmer Empire *(see pp254–5)*. The Khmer *prang* on the grounds of Wat Phra Si Rattana Mahathat, and those of Prang Sam Yot, date from this time. With the decline of the Khmer Empire and the rise of the Sukhothai Kingdom *(see pp54–5)*, Lop Buri struggled to retain its independence, until, in the 14th century, it was linked by marriage to the emerging state of Ayutthaya *(see pp58–9)*. It reached its political peak in the 17th century when the Ayutthayan King Narai (1656–88) preferred to stay at Lop Buri rather than his official palace at Ayutthaya. Today, the thriving modern town of Lop Buri lies to the east of the old city.

Wat Sao Thong Thong
The wihan at this wat was modified by King Narai so the buildng could be used as a Christian chapel – he replaced Thai windows with Western-style Gothic designs.

The market sells vegetables and other foodstuffs.

★ King Narai's Palace
Abandoned after Narai's death, parts of the palace, including the Chanthara Phisan Hall, were later restored by King Mongkut (see p61).

★ Samdej Phra Narai National Museum
This museum is housed in the partially restored, colonial-style Phiman Mongkut Hall of King Narai's Palace. It has a superb collection of Lop Buri Buddha images, and collections of Dvaravati, Khmer, and Ayutthayan art.

STAR SIGHTS

- ★ King Narai's Palace
- ★ Samdej Phra Narai National Museum
- ★ Wat Phra Si Rattana Mahathat
- ★ Prang Sam Yot

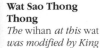

KEY

---- Suggested route

Phaulkon Residence

This house was built by King Narai for his favored minister, the Greek Constantine Phaulkon. Phaulkon encouraged Narai to forge close ties with the French, often excluding other foreigners, though his motive was perhaps to aid Louis XIV's attempt to convert Narai to Christianity. When this came to light it alarmed the Ayutthayan court and Phaulkon was executed (see p153).

VISITORS' CHECKLIST

Lop Buri province. 🏯 *165,000.*
🚉 *Na Phra Kan Rd.*
🚌 *Phra Narai Maharat Rd.*
ℹ️ *TAT, Phra Yam Chamkat Rd.*
(0-3642-2768). 🚪 *daily.*
🎎 *King Narai Festival (Feb).*
Somdej Phra Narai National Museum 📞 *0-3641-1458.* 🕐
Wed–Sun. ⬤ *public hols.* 📷
King Narai's Palace 🕐 *daily.*
📷 **Wat Phra Si Rattana Mahathat** 🕐 *daily.* 📷 🅿 **Phaulkon Residence** 🕐 *daily.* 📷

Prang Khaek

This Hindu shrine has three brick towers. It is believed by some to date as far back as the 8th century.

WICHAYEN

RATCHADAMNOEN

PHRA YAM CHAMKAT

NA WAT

To train station

★ Prang Sam Yot

The Lop Buri style was a variation by local artisans, of already established Khmer art and architecture; this shrine is archetypal. The three prangs were originally consecrated as a Hindu shrine; Buddha images were added later to two of them.

★ Wat Phra Si Rattana Mahathat

This wat complex encloses ruins from two distinct eras. At its center is a 12th-century, Khmer prang, decorated with finely detailed stucco work. The site also includes Ayutthayan chedis and a wihan added by King Narai.

0 meters   75

0 yards   75

Ayutthaya ⑫

พระนครศรีอยุธยา

T HE CITY OF AYUTTHAYA was founded around 1350 by Ramathibodi I (1351–69), who came here to escape an outbreak of smallpox at Lop Buri. By the early 15th century Ayutthaya had become a major power. Sukhothai *(see pp54–5)* fell to Ayutthaya in 1438. Western traders arrived in the early 16th century *(see pp152–3),* and evidence of Ayutthaya's splendor comes from their accounts. In the early 18th century, after years of war, decline set in, and in 1767 the Burmese sacked the city. Today, the ruins stand among the modern buildings of the provincial town.

Ayutthayan bracelet

Stucco and brick *singhas* around the main *chedi* of Wat Thammikarat

🔼 Wat Phra Mahathat

วัดมหาธาตุ

Corner of Chi Kun Rd and Naresuan Rd. ⬤ *daily.* 📷

Wat Phra Mahathat is one of the largest and most important *wat* complexes in Ayutthaya. It was almost certainly founded in the late 14th century by King Borommaracha I (1370–88). Other buildings were subsequently added by his successor, Ramesuan (1388–95).

European-style Pisai Sayalak Tower, behind the Chan Kasem Palace

🔼 Wat Ratchaburana

วัดราชบูรณะ

Cheekun Rd. ⬤ *daily.* 📷

Across the road from Wat Mahathat is Wat Ratchaburana, its *prang* now restored. It was built in the early 15th century by King Borommaracha II (1424–48) on the cremation site of his two brothers, who died in a power struggle. Both of them had wanted to succeed their father, Intharacha I (1409–24), to the throne. Rob-

bers looted the crypt in 1957 and escaped with a huge cache of gold artifacts, only a few of which were recovered. A steep, narrow staircase now descends to the crypt where visitors can see the faded remains of Ayutthayan frescoes *(see p56).*

🔼 Chan Kasem Palace

วังจันทรเกษม

Uthong Rd, opposite the night market. ⬤ *Wed–Sun.* 📷

In the northeast corner of the main island stands the Chan Kasem Palace or Wang Na. It was built in 1577 by the illustrious Naresuan, the son of King Maha Thammaracha (1569–90), before he became king. When Naresuan came to the throne in 1590, the palace became his permanent residence. The buildings seen today, however, date from the reign of King Mongkut (1851–68), as the palace was razed by the Burmese in 1767. It houses a large collection of Buddha images and historical artifacts. Behind the Chan Kasem Palace is the **Pisai Sayalak Tower**, once used as an astronomical observatory by King Mongkut.

🔼 Wat Thammikarat

วัดธรรมิกราช

Uthong Rd. ⬤ *daily.* 📷

At this picturesque site are the dilapidated remains of a large, early Ayutthayan, octagonal *chedi* surrounded by stucco and brick lions, or *singhas*. Beside the *chedi* is the ruin of a *wihan*, slowly succumbing to weeds and trees. A beautiful U Thong Buddha head recovered from here is now in the Chao Sam Phraya National Museum *(see p168).*

🔼 Wang Luang

วังหลวง

Uthong Rd. ⬤ *daily.* 📷

To the west of Wat Thammikarat is Wang Luang, the northern extension of the royal palace built by King Borommatrailokanat (1448–88) in the mid-15th century. Successive monarchs added a number of pavilions and halls. Wang Luang was razed by the Burmese in 1767. The best preserved of the buildings of the former royal palace is the **Trimuk Pavilion**. It was built during the reign of King Chulalongkorn (1868–1910) on the site of earlier foundations.

19th-century Trimuk Pavilion, on the grounds of Wang Luang

🛕 Wat Phra Si Sanphet
See pp168–9.

🛕 Wihan Phra Mongkhon Bophit
วิหารพระมงคลบพิตร

Si Sanphet Rd. ⬤ daily. 🎫
This *wat* contains one of Thailand's largest bronze Buddha images. Now gilded, it probably dates from the late 15th century, though it has undergone numerous restorations. In 1767 Burmese invaders destroyed much of the *wihan* and damaged the image's head and right hand. The image was left open to the sky until the 1950s, when the *wihan* was rebuilt.

🛕 Wat Phra Ram
วัดพระราม

Si Sanphet Rd. ⬤ daily. 🎫
A chronicle relates that Wat Phra Ram was built in 1369 on the cremation site of King Ramathibodi (1351–69) by his son, Ramesuan. The elegant

prang visible today, however, is the result of later renovation by King Borommatrailokanat (1448–88). The *prang* is decorated with *garudas, nagas,* and walking Buddha images. Surrounding it are *wihans* and a *bot.* The *wat* casts beautiful reflections in nearby lily ponds.

15th-century, corncob-shaped *prang* at Wat Phra Ram

VISITORS' CHECKLIST

Phra Nakhon Si Ayutthaya province. 🕌 60,900. 🚉 *Off Bang Ain Rd.* 🚌 *Naresuan Rd.* 🚤 ℹ️ *TAT, Si Sanphet Rd, Ayutthaya (0-3524-6078).* ⬤ *daily.*

🛕 Wat Lokaya Sutharam
วัดโลกยสุธาราม

W of main island. ⬤ daily. 🎫
This *wat* is the site of a 42-m (140-ft) long, whitewashed reclining Buddha image. Large Buddha images such as this do not always depict the Buddha's death, but sometimes, as in this instance, an occasion when the Buddha grew 100 times in size to confront the demon Rahu. The image now lies in the open air, the original *wihan,* having been destroyed by the Burmese; 24 octagonal pillars are all that remain of this *wihan.* The *wat* also houses the ruins of a *bot* and *chedis.*

AYUTTHAYA TOWN CENTER

KEY

🚉 Railroad station
🚌 Bus station
🚤 Riverboat pier
ℹ️ Tourist information
🛕 Wat

0 meters   250
0 yards   250

⬛ Chao Sam Phraya National Museum

พิพิธภัณฑ์เจ้าสามพระยา

Intersection of Rotchana Rd and Si Sanphet Rd. ⬤ *Wed–Sun.* 🎫

Among the exhibits at this museum is a small collection of magnificent gold artifacts, including a jewel-encrusted sword, gold slippers, and jewelry. Dis-covered in the crypt of Wat Ratchaburana's central *prang* when it was looted in 1957, they

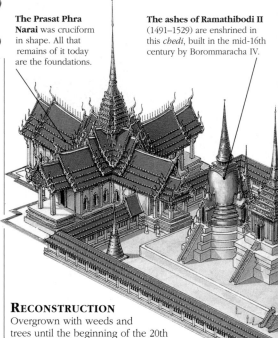

Deity on wooden door-panel

are among the few items from the *wat* to have survived the sack of Ayutthaya by the Burmese *(see pp58–9).* Other artifacts exhibited in the museum in-clude bronze Buddha images and wooden door panels from *wats* around Ayutthaya.

⬛ Ayutthaya Historical Study Center

ศูนย์ศึกษาประวัติศาสตร์อยุธยา

Rotchana. ⬤ *daily.* 🎫

This study center houses inter-esting audiovisual displays depicting Ayutthaya's history and trading relations. There is also a reconstructed model of Wat Phra Si Sanphet. Another part of the study center stands in what was the Japanese quarter at the time when Ayutthaya was at the height of its power.

⬛ Wat Suwan Dararam

วัดสุวรรณดาราราม

Near Pomphet. ⬤ *daily.*

This temple was completely destroyed by the Burmese but later rebuilt by Rama I (1782–1809). The *ubosot* is usually locked, but it is worth request-ing the key to see the murals commissioned by Rama VII (1925–35), depicting scenes from the time of King Nare-suan. Among them is a mural of the Battle of Nong Sarai, which was fought against the Burmese in 1593 *(see p58).*

Nearby is a section of the old city defenses, Phom Phet, which were a strategically important lookout post over the Chao Phraya River.

Wat Phra Si Sanphet

วัดพระศรีสรรเพชญ์

FOUNDED BY KING BOROMMATRAILOKANAT during the 15th century as a state temple, Wat Phra Si Sanphet was later added to by his son, Ramathibodi II, who built two *chedis* to house the relics of his father and brother. The third *chedi* was built by Borommaracha IV to house the remains of Ramathibodi II. The site was extended by subsequent rulers until the Burmese sack of 1767 *(see pp58–9).* Partially renovated in the 20th century, many of its treasures are now kept in museums.

The Prasat Phra Narai was cruciform in shape. All that remains of it today are the foundations.

The ashes of Ramathibodi II (1491–1529) are enshrined in this *chedi*, built in the mid-16th century by Borommaracha IV.

RECONSTRUCTION

Overgrown with weeds and trees until the beginning of the 20th century, Wat Phra Si Sanphet is still a ruin, albeit partially restored. This artist's impression gives an idea of its glory before it was sacked.

Drawing of Chedis
Lying empty after it was sacked by the Burmese, Ayutthaya became the focus of scholarly interest. Henri Mouhot, who drew this image, was one of many late 19th-century vis-itors. Wat Phra Si Sanphet has been under the pro-tection of the Thai Fine Arts Department since 1927.

Wooden Door
This door was probably once situated at the entrance to Wihan Phra Si Sanphet and dates from the reign of Ramathibodi II. A collection of such doors is displayed in the Chao Sam Phraya Museum.

Three Chedis
Apart from the ashes of kings, caskets of precious Buddha images and royal regalia were buried in the chedis' central chambers.

The ashes of Borommaracha III (1463–88), the brother of Ramathibodi II, are buried in this *chedi*.

Entrance to Chedi
The entrance chamber to the chedi *is a scaled-down version of a Khmer* mandapa *(entrance chamber to a Khmer sanctuary). Ayutthayan builders modified many older architectural features, such as Khmer* prangs *and Sri Lankan bell-shaped* chedis.

The ashes of Borommatrailokanat (1448–88) are buried in this *chedi*, the only one to survive the Burmese sack. The other two had to be restored.

Stairway leading to entrance of hollow *chedi*

A Footprint of the Lord Buddha was housed in this elegant, spired *mondop*.

Wihan Phra Si Sanphet
The main wihan – *the entrance to the* wat – *once housed the principal Buddha image of Phra Si Sanphet.*

Exploring Ayutthaya: the Outer Sites

Buddha, Wat Na Phra Men

THE CENTRAL ISLAND of Ayutthaya stands at the confluence of the Chao Phraya, Lop Buri, and Pasak Rivers. The town's most imposing sites are to be found on the central island. However, a short *samlor* ride by bridge over any of the rivers, which more or less encircle it, will bring you to many more sites of interest. Wat Na Phra Men is one of Ayutthaya's most beautiful *wats*, and St. Joseph's Church offers a glimpse of Ayutthaya's connections with Western trading powers *(see pp152–3)* during the city's heyday. The main part of modern Ayutthaya sprawls to the east of the island, over the Pasak River and beyond.

A roundup of wild elephants at the elephant kraal (1890)

�␣ Wat Na Phra Men
วัดหน้าพระเมรุ

Opp Royal Palace, nr Muang Canal. **℄** 0-3525-2163. ◯ *daily.* 🏷
Across a bridge to the north of the main island is Wat Na Phra Men, one of the most beautiful of Ayutthaya's mon- asteries, and one of the few to survive the Burmese sacking of the city in 1767 *(see p56)*. Thought to date from the reign of Intharacha II (1488–91), it was restored during the reign of King Borommakot (1733–58), and again in the mid-19th century. In the *wihan* is a Dvaravati seated Buddha image, Phra Kanthararat, that was moved here from Nakhon Pathom in the mid-16th century. The murals covering the *wihan* walls have now almost com- pletely disappeared. Its doors are from the early 19th century. In the adjacent *bot* is a gilded Buddha image, probably from the reign of King Prasat Thong (1629–56).

🏯 Elephant Kraal
พระที่นั่งเพนียด

NW on Hwy 309. ◯ *daily.* 🏷
Farther to the north is the elephant kraal. It is thought that the original structure, built by King Yot Fa (1547–8), stood within the confines of the old city wall. The present kraal, built later, was in use well into the 19th century – wild elephants would be driven here for training as pack animals or war mounts for senior officers. In the middle of the stockade is a shrine where the elephant guardian is thought to live.

⚯ Wat Phu Khao Thong
วัดภูเขาทอง

2 km (1 mile) NW on Hwy 309. ◯ *daily.* 🏷
To the west, the original *chedi* of Phu Khao Thong was con- structed by King Bayinnaung of Burma to celebrate his cap- ture of Ayutthaya in 1569. Ad- ditions were made in 1744–5 by the Thai King Borommakot.

⚯ Wat Chai Watthanaram
วัดไชยวัฒนาราม

W bank of Chao Phraya River, SW of main island. ◯ *daily.* 🏷
This *wat* was built by King Prasat Thong in 1630. The central *prang* is surrounded by eight smaller ones, decor- ated with stucco reliefs depict- ing images such as the Buddha preaching to his mother in the Tavatimsa Heaven. All the *prangs* have been restored.

⛪ St. Joseph's Church
โบสถ์เซนต์โยเซฟ

SW of main island on the Chao Phraya River. ◯ *daily.*
St. Joseph's, overlooking the Chao Phraya River, has been the site of Catholic worship for over 300 years. The original 17th-century structure was destroyed by the Burmese in 1767. The present church was built during the 19th century.

⚯ Wat Phutthaisawan
วัดพุทไธศวรรย์

S of main island. ◯ *daily.* 🏷
East from St. Joseph's is Wat Phutthaisawan, also located on the river bank. It has a restored 14th-century *prang* surrounded by a cloister filled with Buddha images.

⚯ Wat Kuti Dao
วัดกุฎีดาว

E of railway station. ◯ *daily.* 🏷
This *wat* originally dated from the early Ayutthaya period, but the ruins here today are of an 18th-century renovation by King Phumintharacha. The *chedi* is flanked by a *wihan* and a *bot* with distinctive arched windows and doors.

Bell-shaped *chedi*, part of the ruined Wat Kuti Dao

Reclining Buddha in a ruined *wihan* at Wat Yai Chai Mongkhon

🔲 Wat Pradu Songtham

วัดประตูทรงธรรม

N of railroad station, E of main island.
🔲 *daily.*

Inside the *wihan* of Wat Pradu
Songtham are the remains of
murals dating from the early
Rattanakosin period *(see p31).*
These recount the life of the
Buddha and also show images
of daily life, including one of a
performance of the Ramakien
at a fair. Outside is a bell tower
topped by a small *chedi* from
the late Ayutthaya period.

🔲 Wat Maheyong

วัดมเหยงค์

E of main island. 🔲 *daily.*

The partially reconstructed
ruins of Wat Maheyong date
from the reign of King
Borommaracha II (1424–48).
The principal, bell-shaped
chedi shows a clear stylistic
link with earlier Sukhothai
chedis, while all around the
rectangular base are the
remnants of stucco elephants.
Other *chedis* at this site also
show Sukhothai influence.

🔲 Wat Yai Chai Mongkhon

วัดใหญ่ไชยมงคล

E of main island. 🔲 *daily.* 🖼️

The *chedi* here, one of the
largest in Ayutthaya, was built
by King Naresuan (1590–1605)
to celebrate his victory over the
Burmese at Nong Sarai in 1593
(see pp58–9). Flanking steps
up to the *chedi* are two *mondops* housing seated Buddha
images. On the northeast side
of the *wat* is a ruined *wihan*
containing a reclining Buddha.

🔲 Wat Phanan Choeng

วัดพนัญเชิง

S of main island. 🔲 *daily.*

This *wat* has been renovated
over the years and houses
the large, 14th-century, seated
image of Phra Chao Phanan
Choeng. The *wihan* was built
in the mid-19th century.

🔲 Ban Yipun

บ้านญี่ปุ่น

S of main island.

🔲 *daily.*

Once the site of a 17th-century
Japanese settlement, today a
museum here displays exhibits that explain Ayutthaya's
foreign relations at the time.

Bang Pa-in ⑬

บางปะอิน

Phra Nakhon Si Ayutthaya province.
🏠 59,000. 🚌 🚐 🚤 🛈 *TAT,
Ayutthaya (0-3524-6078).* 🛶 *daily.*

VISITORS to Bang Pa-in stop
off, for the most part, just
to visit **Bang Pa-in Palace**,
whose exuberant 19th-cen-
tury buildings stand in stark
contrast to nearby Ayutthaya.
It is thought that a royal palace
was first built at Bang Pa-in by
King Prasat Thong (1629–56),
to mark the birth of his son
and successor, King Narai.
With the defeat of Ayutthaya
by the Burmese in 1767 the
site fell into ruin; the present
buildings date from the reigns
of Mongkut (1851–68) and
Chulalongkorn (1868–1910).

The beautiful pavilion, Phra
Thinang Aisawan Thipha-at
("divine seat of personal free-
dom"), at the center of an ornamental lake, was built for
Chulalongkorn in 1876, together with the Phra Thinang
Warophat Phiman ("excellent

and shining abode"), to the
left. Behind are the terra-cotta-
and white-striped lookout
tower, Ho Withun Thasana,
built by Chulalongkorn in
1881, and the Chinese-style
mansion, Phra Thinang Wehat
Chamrun, built as a gift for
him by an association of

Chinese merchants in 1889.
Visitors can cross a canal by
cable car to Wat Niwet Tham
Prawat, which was built by
Chulalongkorn in 1877–8.

🔲 Bang Pa-in Palace

พระราชวังบางปะอิน

Bang Pa-in district. 🔲 *daily.* 🖼️

The Phra Thinang Aisawan Thipha-at pavilion, Bang Pa-in Palace

Monks looking out over the ornamental lake of the Phra Thinang Aisawan Thipha-at pavilion, Bang Pa-in ▷

Khao Yai National Park ⑭

อุทยานแห่งชาติเขาใหญ่

Begonia flower

W HEN IT WAS ESTABLISHED in 1962, Khao Yai was Thailand's sole national park. Today there are well over 100 parks, but this one still remains popular. Sprawling over 2,000 sq km (770 sq miles), the park encompasses a wide variety of habitats, including submontane evergreen forests and grasslands. There are also several mountains of around 1,000 m (3,300 ft), including Khao Khieo, south of the park headquarters. Wildlife is abundant and includes many endangered mammals such as elephants, gibbons, tigers, leopards, and Malaysian sun bears, as well as more than 300 bird species. Visitors to the park are advised to hire a guide for trips to more remote areas.

White-Handed Gibbon
These tailless apes use their long arms to move swiftly and agilely through the trees.

Endangered Species
Khao Yai is home to a few of the 500 or so tigers left in Thailand. These noble animals can be found surprisingly close to the park's headquarters; visitors should treat them with respect.

Siamese Fireback Pheasant
Thailand's national bird, this pheasant spends its days on the ground where it feeds on small insects, seeds, and fruit. It roosts in the trees at night.

Deciduous forest grows in the park's low-lying areas.

Haeo Suwat Waterfall
Located along the upper reaches of the Lam Takhong River, this waterfall is one of many dotted around Khao Yai. From March to May each year many varieties of orchids can be seen flowering around the waterfall. Elephants have been known to drown while crossing near waterfalls when the rains are very heavy.

Submontane Evergreen Forest
This type of forest often contains deciduous trees such as chestnuts. It grows at Khao Yai's highest altitudes, 1,000 m (3,300 ft) to 1,351 m (4,450 ft) above sea level.

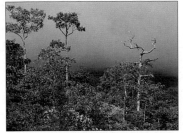

Visitors' Checklist

Khorat, Nakhon Nayok, Saraburi and Prachin Buri provinces. Park HQ off Hwy 1, NE of Bangkok. *TAT, Khorat (0-4421-3666); Forestry Dept (0-2562-0760 or www.dnp.go.th for bungalow bookings).* *Pak Chong, then bus or* songthaew. *during heavy rainfall.*

KHORAT
AK CHONG
Khao Kamphaeng 974 m (3,196 ft)
Khao Wong 146 m (479 ft)
PRACHIN BURI

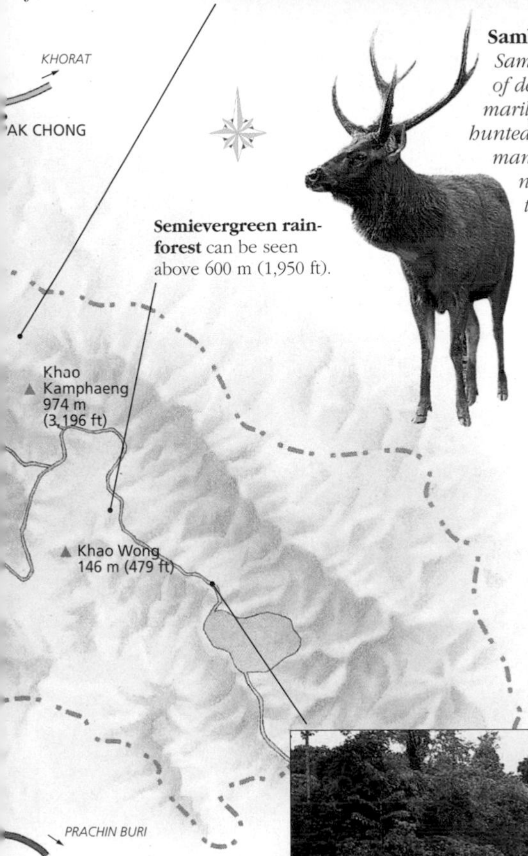

Sambar Stag
Sambar are the largest species of deer in Thailand and are primarily forest dwellers. Though hunted by tigers and leopards, humans are its main predator. It is now common only in well-protected conservation areas.

Semievergreen rainforest can be seen above 600 m (1,950 ft).

Earthball Fungus
This parasitic fungus is found in humid evergreen forests all over Southeast Asia. Unlike many parasites, its presence actually encourages the growth of its host.

0 kilometers 10
0 miles 10

Key

- Expressway
- Major road
- Minor road
- Park border
- Park headquarters
- Camping and bungalows
- Vista

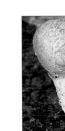

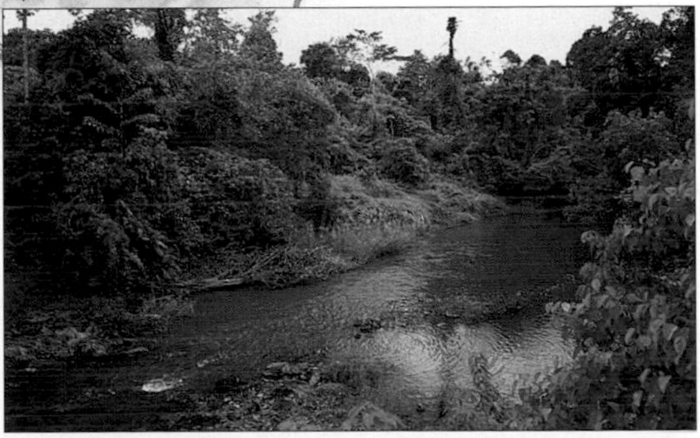

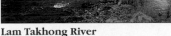

Lam Takhong River
Rainfall in Khao Yai National Park is usually in excess of 3,000 mm (120 inches) per year. Streams swollen by the rains flow off forested slopes forming rivers, among them the Lam Takhong River. Wildlife living around this river includes kingfishers, cormorants, elephants, and macaques.

North Central Plains

THE FARTHER NORTH *the visitor travels through the Central Plains the more sparsely populated the countryside becomes – the landscape here is typified by gentle, rolling hills and rice farms. There are few interesting modern cities in this region. Its major attractions are ancient city ruins, relics of an illustrious past when competing princedoms and city-states fought each other for land and power.*

Visitors to Thailand traveling north from Bangkok tend not to stop off in the North Central Plains, but instead press on to the major destination of Thailand's second city, Chiang Mai. However, some of the most fascinating ruins in Southeast Asia are found here.

In the 13th century, during the reign of King Ramkamhaeng *(see p54)*, one city, Sukhothai, came to dominate the region to such an extent that its influence was felt far beyond Thailand's present borders. But its power was shortlived, and by the mid-14th century the region was once more a collection of fiefdoms. The ruins the kingdom left behind at Sukhothai, and at its satellite cities of Kamphaeng Phet and Si Satchanalai, still inspire wonder. Recently they have been extensively restored and turned into well-managed historical parks.

Other places of interest in the region include the prosperous trading center Phitsanulok, which is at the heart of a transportation network connecting the region to Bangkok and the north. This, and other towns, support a local rice-farming economy.

The hillier areas, in the west and northeast of the region, are the setting for a number of national parks and wildlife sanctuaries. These provide a much needed refuge for endangered plant and animal species *(see pp24–5)* whose habitats are threatened by the impact of illegal logging and the widespread loss of land to agriculture.

Around Mae Sot the influence of Burma is felt; the town is characterized by Burmese architecture, and a common sight is Karen and Shan tribespeople and Burmese who cross the border at this point to trade.

Farmer raking unhusked rice, a typical rural scene in the North Central Plains

◁ Reclining and sitting Buddha images at Wat Phra Kaeo, Kamphaeng Phet

Exploring the North Central Plains

THIS PART OF THE COUNTRY acts as a bridge between the crowded heartland of modern Thailand to the immediate south, and the rolling hills of the North. The region has no big cities, and the majority of tourists do no more than overnight in small, provincial towns near the magnificent ruins of ancient Sukhothai, the first Thai capital. Predominantly, this is rice-farming country, flanked to the east, north, and west by hills. National parks in some of the hilly areas help protect endangered flora and fauna. Magnificent forest scenery and spectacular waterfalls can be found along the western border with Burma, around Mae Sot and remote Umphang. Here, a hint of Burma spills across the border in the shape of Karen and Shan tribespeople and Burmese architecture, goods, and food.

Lampang
Chiang Mai

SI SATCHANA

SI SATCHANAL
CHALIEI
HISTORICAL PAI
tt

Bhumibol
Reservoir

SUKHOTH
HISTORIC
PAI

12

TAKSIN
MAHARAT
NATIONAL
PARK

105

2 TAK

105

1 MAE SOT

LAN SANG
NATIONAL
PARK

Ping

1

KAMPHAENG HET

5

1090

1117

Moi

1090

KHLONG LAN NATIONAL PARK 4

UMPHANG 3

MAE WONG
NATIONAL
PARK

UMPHANG
WILDLIFE
SANCTUARY

1072

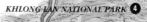

**Buddha under *naga* at Wat
Chumphon Khiri, Mae Sot**

SEE ALSO

- *Where to Stay* pp392–3
- *Where to Eat* pp416–17

KEY

▬	Major road
▬	Minor road
▬	Scenic route
▬	River
✻	Vista

Wat Traphang Thong, a monastery surrounded by a lotus-filled pond at Sukhothai Historical Park

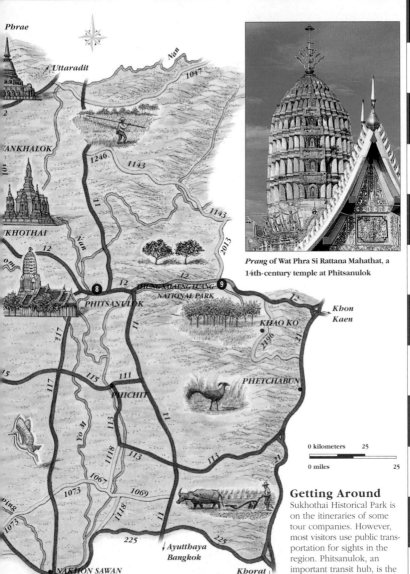

Prang of Wat Phra Si Rattana Mahathat, a
14th-century temple at Phitsanulok

0 kilometers   25

0 miles   25

Getting Around

Sukhothai Historical Park is
on the itineraries of some
tour companies. However,
most visitors use public transportation for sights in the
region. Phitsanulok, an
important transit hub, is the
only major town in the
region served by the regular
train service connecting
Bangkok to the North. It also
has a small airport, as do Mae
Sot and Sukhothai. Highway
1 passes through Kamphaeng
Phet and Tak. Local buses
run to all towns, and a network of main roads connects
nearly all the sights. Only
Umphang remains isolated,
at the end of a spectacular,
winding road from Mae Sot.

SIGHTS AT A GLANCE

Kamphaeng Phet **5**
Khlong Lan National Park **4**
Mae Sot **1**
Phitsanulok **8**
*Si Satchanalai-Chalieng
Historical Park pp188–90* **7**

*Sukhothai Historical
Park pp184–7* **6**
Tak **2**
Thung Salaeng Luang
National Park **9**
Umphang **3**

Wat Chumphon Khiri, Mae Sot, Tak province

Mae Sot ❶

แม่สอด

Tak province. 🏯 70,000. ✈ 🚌
ℹ TAT, Tak (0-5551-4341). 🚌 daily.
@ tattak@north.shane.net

IN THE mid-19th century Burmese and Shan merchants, crossing the Moei River from Burma in the west, helped to establish Mae Sot as a prosperous market town. In more recent years, trade in Burmese hardwoods and gemstones, both legal and smuggled, has brought considerable wealth to this small town. Today Mae Sot retains the feel of a frontier town and makes a relaxing stopover for travelers. Gem traders, usually ethnic Chinese, can often be seen huddled on Mae Sot's pavements, negotiating with buyers from Bangkok and other parts of Thailand. Because of its location and trading history, Mae Sot has a distinct Burmese flavor, evident in architecture and market goods.

Trilingual shop signs can be seen on the streets, Burmese-language publications are sold in shops, and Burmese people wearing traditional sarongs (lungis) can be seen walking along the streets. During the morning food market – one of Thailand's most picturesque and colorful – Karen and Burmese traders haggle with Thais and Indians.

North of the market is **Wat Chumphon Khiri**, which has a magnificent Burmese *chedi* decorated with golden mosaic tiles. On the southeast side of town is the Muslim quarter; at its center is the small **Nurul Islam Mosque**.

Dotted around the town are a number of other temples that have both Karen and Shan characteristics.

ENVIRONS: Some 3 km (2 miles) west of Mae Sot is **Wat Thai Watthanaram**. In the rear courtyard is a huge, Burmese-style, reclining Buddha image built in 1993 and a gallery of 28 seated Buddha images. A further 1 km (1,100 yards) beyond Wat Thai Watthanaram, a bridge over the Moei River links Mae Sot to the Burmese border town of Myawadi. Clustered around the foot of the bridge is a market selling an odd mix of Thai, Burmese, Indonesian, and Chinese goods.

Southeast of Mae Sot are the **Pha Charoen falls**, a very popular spot for picnicking and swimming.

Monks in the grounds of Wat Bot Mani Sibunruang, Tak

Tak ❷

ตาก

Tak province. 🏯 78,000. ✈ 🚌
ℹ TAT, Taksin Rd, Tak (0-5551-4341).
🚌 daily.

DURING MUCH of the 13th century, Tak was a western outpost of the Sukhothai Kingdom. After the death of King Ramkamhaeng and the

Reclining, Burmese-style Buddha in the courtyard of Wat Thai Watthanaram, near Mae Sot

One of many waterfalls in the Umphang Wildlife Sanctuary

subsequent collapse of the Sukhothai Empire *(see pp54–5)*, the town came under the influence of the Lanna Kingdom *(see pp58–9)* to the north. Today Tak sprawls along the left bank of the Ping River, and much of the Lanna influence can still be seen in the teak houses hidden away in quiet lanes at the southern end of town. The houses here date from the late 19th and early 20th centuries.

Wat Bot Mani Sibunruang also shows Northern influences with its finely decorated, Lanna-style *bot* and a small *sala* containing a much revered Buddha image called Luang Pho Phutthamon.

Nearby is a statue of King Taksin, a former governor of Tak, who, after the sacking of Ayutthaya by the Burmese in 1767, established a new capital at Thon Buri, now part of Bangkok *(see pp60–1)*.

ENVIRONS: The 105-sq km (40-sq mile) **Lan Sang National Park** has tracks leading to several beautiful waterfalls. These are best visited during or soon after the rainy season *(see pp22–3)*; at other times of year there is little water. To the north of Lan Sang National Park is the **Taksin Maharat National Park**, the highlight of which is a steeply descending trail to the huge *ton krabak yai*, or big krabak tree, which is some 50 m (165 ft) tall, and

has a girth of 16 m (50 ft). The park offers bird-watching opportunities, boasting a variety of species including the tiger shrike and forest wagtail. Also in the park are the nine-tiered Mae Ya Pa falls.

🏞 Lan Sang National Park
20 km (12 miles) W of Tak, off Hwy 105. 🌐
🏞 Taksin Maharat National Park
15 km (9 miles) W of Tak, off Hwy 105. ℹ *Forestry Dept (0-2562-0760).* 🌐

Umphang ❸
อุ้มผาง

Tak province. 🏘 *23,000.* 🚌 *Mae Sot, then songthaew.* ℹ *TAT, Tak (0-5551-4341).* 📅 *daily.*

ART OF UMPHANG'S charm lies in the journey, as the road from Mae Sot is one of Thailand's most scenic. The village – its population consisting largely of Karen tribespeople – is surrounded by the lush forests of **Umphang Wildlife Sanctuary**, rich in bird life and small mammals. In recent years Umphang has become popular for rafting, hiking, and elephant treks, but its isolation has kept most of the tourist hordes away. Here too are many cascades and rapids (including one of the country's highest waterfalls, **Thi Lo Su**), caves, and Karen settlements. Several agencies in Umphang or Mae Sot can arrange treks. Visitors should avoid school vacations, when this region is crowded and accommodations scarce.

🏞 Umphang Wildlife Sanctuary
150 km (93 miles) S of Mae Sot on Hwy 1090. ℹ *Forestry Dept (0-2562-0760).* 🌐

THAILAND-BURMA BORDER REFUGEES

Scattered along Thailand's western border are more than 30 refugee camps, where about 100,000 Karen and other ethnic groups shelter from the totalitarian regime in Burma (Myanmar). The Karen tribespeople, who have long occupied an area straddling Burma and Thailand, are Burma's largest ethnic minority. The British were supposed to grant the Karen an autonomous homeland within Burma after World War II, but this did not happen. Following pro-democracy demonstrations in Burma in 1988, and the subsequent crack down, opposition MPs and ethnic minorities fled east to refugee villages. It is in such villages that the Karen organize their struggle for an independent state. The Burmese army sporadically ventures into Thailand, attacking and shelling Karen settlements. The Thai government does not openly condemn Burma, and the Thai army does not usually intervene on behalf of the Karen.

Boy soldiers in the rebel army of the Karen tribespeople

Waterfall in Khlong Lan National Park, Kamphaeng Phet province

Khlong Lan National Park ❹
อุทยานแห่งชาติคลองลาน

Kamphaeng Phet province. Park HQ 6 km (4 miles) off Hwy 1117, S of Kamphaeng Phet. **ℹ** *TAT, Tak (0-5551-4341); Forestry Dept (0-2562-0760 inc bungalow bookings).* **🚌** *from Kamphaeng Phet to Klonglan, then songthaew.* **🖥** *www.dnp.go.th*

Tʜɪs 300-sq ᴋᴍ (116-sq mile) national park was formed in 1982. Formerly, the area was controlled by Communist insurgents, and inhabited by a number of hill tribes. Initially, the tribes lived within the park but were later relocated because they were regarded as a threat to the wildlife, which includes gaur, tiger, and the Asiatic black bear.

The highlight of the park is the Khlong Lan waterfall, which is easily accessible from the park headquarters. It falls 95 m (310 ft) into a pool ideal for a refreshing swim. At the foot of the road leading up to the waterfall is a small market selling Hmong handicrafts – a government rehabilitation scheme for the hill tribes relocated from the park.

The adjacent **Mae Wong National Park** is good for hiking and bird-watching, and there are some facilities for visitors. Until the late 1980s it was populated by Hmong, who have also been relocated. Park staff confirm that the number of birds and mammals is steadily increasing. An old road running through the center of the park is now overgrown, but it does make a good hiking trail. Simple accommodations in bungalows are available near the park headquarters.

🦌 Mae Wong National Park
Park HQ SW of Kamphaeng Phet, off Hwy 1117. **ℹ** *Forestry Dept (0-2562-0760, inc bungalow bookings).* **🖥** *www.dnp.go.th*

Kamphaeng Phet ❺
กำแพงเพชร

Kamphaeng Phet province. **👥** *164,000.* **🚉** **ℹ** *TAT, Tak (0-5551-4341).* **🏠** *daily.* **🎉** *Nop Phra-Len Plang (Feb), Kluay Khai Muang Kamphaeng (Sep).*

Tʜᴇʀᴇ ʜᴀs ʙᴇᴇɴ a settlement at this site on the banks of the Ping River since the 11th century, when a northern prince, fleeing a Burmese attack in the area of present-day Fang *(see p232)*, brought his followers here. The community initially survived as an outpost of the Khmer Empire *(see p52)* and, during the 13th century, as part of the Sukhothai Kingdom.

On the east bank lie the impressive remains of the **Old City**, dating from the early 15th century, and which once formed part of a satellite city to the mighty Sukhothai *(see pp184–7)*. Located within its walls is the **Kamphaeng Phet National Museum**. In this collection are several fine 16th-century bronzes of Hindu deities, including a standing image of Shiva and torsos of Vishnu and Lakshmi. There are also stucco and terra-cotta fragments from Kamphaeng Phet's many ruins.

The Old City walls also enclose two important ruins from the late Sukhothai period. Close to the National Museum, **Wat Phra Kaeo** is the Old City's largest site, containing the ruins of several *wihans*, a

Renovated stone elephant at Wat Phra Kaeo, Kamphaeng Phet

Kamphaeng Phet National Museum and surrounding gardens

bot at the eastern end, a *chedi* from the late Sukhothai period, and the laterite cores of a number of Buddha images. At the western end of the site are three more partly restored Buddha images. Neighboring **Wat Phra That** has a fine late Sukhothai, octagonal-based *chedi*. One admission charge covers all ruins in the Old City.

The modern town of Kamphaeng Phet, for the most part, sprawls to the south of the Old City. It mostly comprises commercial buildings, though it also has a riverside park and a few traditional wooden houses, as well as some tourist-oriented facilities.

A *samlor* ride northwest of the Old City are the **Aranyik Ruins**, the area of many forest *wats* once used by a meditational order called the Forest Dwelling Sect. Built during the 14th–16th centuries, the sheer number of ruins at Aranyik attest to the popularity of the sect, which achieved prominence in Thailand during the Sukhothai era. With the assistance of UNESCO, parts of the site have now been restored and landscaped.

The *wihan* at Wat Phra Non, near the entrance, once contained a large reclining Buddha, but this is so badly damaged as to be almost indiscernible. Nevertheless, a number of laterite columns from the *wihan* are still standing. On each side of the *mondop* at Wat Phra Si Iriyabot are images of the Buddha in different postures, though all are damaged. The standing

Buddha on the west side has been partially restored. In the ruined *bot* of Wat Sing (found in the northern part of the Aranyik site) is the laterite core of a Buddha image.

Most impressive of the Aranyik *wats* is **Wat Chang Rop**, consisting mostly of the remains of a very large, square-based *chedi*, flanked by the forequarters of some elephants in laterite. On a few of these, the original stucco decoration has been restored. However, little of the Sri Lankan-style bell-shaped *chedi* is still standing. Among two dozen or so other sites dotted around Aranyik, many of them

scarcely visible in thick undergrowth, Wat Awat Yai is one of the few now cleared of vegetation.

In the modern part of town, other monuments, such as the Sukhothai brick *chedi* of **Wat Kalothai**, can be seen tucked away in quiet lanes. Many such sites have now fallen into considerable disrepair, but their sheer quantity is an indication of the importance of Kamphaeng Phet during the Sukhothai and Ayutthaya periods.

West of the city, the large, white, Burmese-style *chedi* of **Wat Phra Boromathat** was built in the late 19th century on the site of three 13th–14th-century *chedis*, the earliest of which was constructed by King Si Intharathit of Sukhothai (c.1240–70) to house some relics of the Lord Buddha. Also to the west are the laterite walls of **Thung Setthi Fort**, which once protected this side of the city.

🏛 **Kamphaeng Phet National Museum**
Old City, behind Wat Phra Kaeo.
⏱ *Wed–Sun.*
⬤ *public hols.* ♿
🏛 **Aranyik Ruins**
NW of Old City. ⏱ *daily.* ♿
🏰 **Thung Setthi Fort**
Off Hwy 1, W of town. ⏱ *daily.*

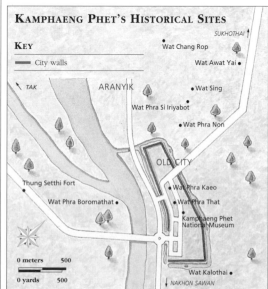

KAMPHAENG PHET'S HISTORICAL SITES

SUKHOTHAI ↑

KEY

▬ City walls

Wat Chang Rop

Wat Awat Yai

↖ *TAK*

ARANYIK

Wat Sing

Wat Phra Si Iriyabot

Wat Phra Non

OLD CITY

Thung Setthi Fort

Wat Phra Kaeo

Wat Phra That

Wat Phra Boromathat

Kamphaeng Phet National Museum

0 meters 500

0 yards 500

Wat Kalothai

↓ *NAKHON SAWAN*

Sukhothai Historical Park ❻

อุทยานประวัติศาสตร์สุโขทัย

Buddha, Wat Traphang Ngoen

THE UNESCO WORLD HERITAGE site of Old Sukhothai lies to the west of the modern town. It is a potent reminder of the ancient Sukhothai Kingdom, which arose in the early 13th century from what had been a distant outpost of the Khmer Empire. Under the leadership of the Tai warrior King Ramkamhaeng, the city came to dominate the Central Plains *(see pp54–5)*. The abandoned city that can be seen today is the best preserved and most popular sight in Central Thailand. On-going restoration has revealed the amazing symmetry of its layout and offers the visitor a remarkable insight into a time when Thai art and culture reached its apex.

Exploring Sukhothai Historical Park

The site of Old Sukhothai has around 40 temple complexes spread over an area of about 70 sq km (28 sq miles). At its center is the walled Royal City, protected by moats and ramparts. Many of the most important ruins are within this inner compound. The layout of Old Sukhothai, as with many major Thai cities *(muangs)*, follows fixed principles: a large, central *wat* complex surrounded concentrically by walls, river, rice fields, and, beyond, forested mountains. Another example of this, on a smaller scale, is Si Satchanalai *(see pp54–5)*.

One way to see the ruins of the Royal City is by bicycle: shops beside the old east gate rent them by the day for a small fee. A quick test ride is advised as some are in poor condition, and an early start is recommended to avoid the midday heat.

The Royal City

Entering from the east, the first *wat* within the city walls is Wat Traphang Thong, which is situated on an islet in a small lotus-filled lake. The Sri Lankan-style *chedi* dates from the mid-14th century, and a small *mondop* beside it enshrines a stone Footprint of the Buddha, still worshipped by resident monks.

The **Ramkamhaeng National Museum** houses photographs, taken around

Khmer-style, laterite *prangs*, part of Wat Si Sawai

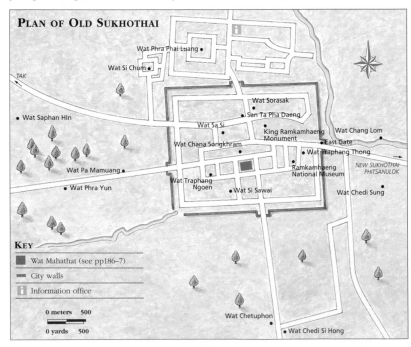

PLAN OF OLD SUKHOTHAI

TAK

Wat Phra Phai Luang
Wat Si Chum
Wat Sorasak
San Ta Pha Daeng
Wat Saphan Hin
Wat Sa Si
King Ramkamhaeng Monument
Wat Chang Lom
East Gate
Wat Chana Songkhram
Wat Traphang Thong
Wat Pa Mamuang
Ramkamhaeng National Museum
NEW SUKHOTHAI PHITSANULOK
Wat Phra Yun
Wat Traphang Ngoen
Wat Si Sawai
Wat Chedi Sung

KEY

- Wat Mahathat (see pp186–7)
- City walls
- ℹ Information office

0 meters 500
0 yards 500

Wat Chetuphon
Wat Chedi Si Hong

Façade of the Ramkamhaeng National Museum

VISITORS' CHECKLIST

13 km (8 miles) W of New
Sukhothai, Sukhothai province.
TAT, Phitsanulok (0-5525-2743).
New Sukhothai, then
songthaew. *6am–9pm daily
(tickets sold until 6pm).*
tatphlok@tat.or.th *Loy
Krathong and Candle Festival
(Nov).* **Ramkamhaeng National
Museum** *8:30am– 4.30pm
daily.* *Ticket (valid for 30
days) includes admission to other
historical parks in Sukhothai.*

1900–1920, of Sukhothai's
ruins prior to renovation and
a large collection of artifacts.
At the heart of the moated
city is **Wat Mahathat** *(see
pp186–7),* the most important
wat complex in Sukhothai.

Nearby, Wat Takuan has a
restored, Sri Lankan bell-
shaped *chedi.* Several Buddha
images found in the vault of
the *chedi* are thought to date
from the early Sukhothai
period, though they remain
something of a mystery.

To the southwest, at Wat Si
Sawai, are three 12th–14th-
century Khmer-style *prangs,*
thought to predate the Tai
takeover of the city.

The *bot* of Wat Traphang
Ngoen, mentioned in Ramkamhaeng's famous Inscription
No. 1 *(see p54),* lies in an
artificial rectangular lake.

Copper Buddha images and
Chinese pottery were recovered from Wat Sa Si, also at
the center of an artificial lake.
These are now in the Ram-
kamhaeng National Museum.

Nearby, Wat Chana Song-
khram has a restored, squat
Sri Lankan-style *chedi.* A
smaller *chedi* here dates
from the Ayutthaya period.

To the north of Wat Mahathat
is the modern **King Ramkamhaeng Monument.** Beyond
lies San Ta Pha Daeng, a
12th-century Khmer shrine
that once housed sandstone
Hindu icons, now in the Ramkamhaeng National Museum.

Wat Sorasak, a small, brick,
bell-shaped *chedi,* dates from
the early 15th century. The
square base is supported by
24 stucco elephants.

East of the Royal City

Wat Chang Lom, a bell-shaped
chedi similar to one at Si Satchanalai *(see p190),* has 36 brick
and stucco elephants around
its base. It represents mythical
Mount Meru, supported by
elephants. Beyond is Wat
Chedi Sung, a beautiful *chedi*
with a high, square base typical of the late Sukhothai era.

North of the Royal City

Wat Phra Phai Luang, a Khmer-
style complex, is thought to
be part of the original mid-
13th century settlement, built
when this region was part of
the Khmer Empire. Only one
of the three laterite *prangs,*

decorated with stucco fragments, is extant. Nearby, the
mondop of Wat Si Chum has
an immense seated Buddha
peering through an opening.

**Reconstructed stucco elephant
heads at Wat Sorasak**

LOY KRATHONG AT SUKHOTHAI

Loy Krathong *(see p46)* occurs at the November full moon to
mark the end of the rainy season and the main rice harvest.
The festival has its origins in the Hindu tradition of thanking
the water god for the rains. *Krathongs,* bowls fashioned out
of banana leaves holding lighted candles, are floated on water
after dark. Though celebrated all over Thailand, the most
exuberant festivities take place at Old Sukhothai. Nowadays,
the festival includes folk dancing and sound-and-light shows.

Loy Krathong festivities at the Sukhothai Historical Park

Wat Mahathat

วัดมหาธาตุ

WAT MAHATHAT was the spiritual center of the Sukhothai Kingdom. The central *chedi* was founded by Si Intharathit (c.1240–70), first king of Sukhothai, and rebuilt in the 1340s by Lue Thai (1298–1346) to house relics of the Buddha. Buildings were added to the complex by successive kings: by the time it was abandoned in the 16th century it had some 200 *chedis* as well as numerous *wihans* and *mondops*.

Arch on central *chedi*

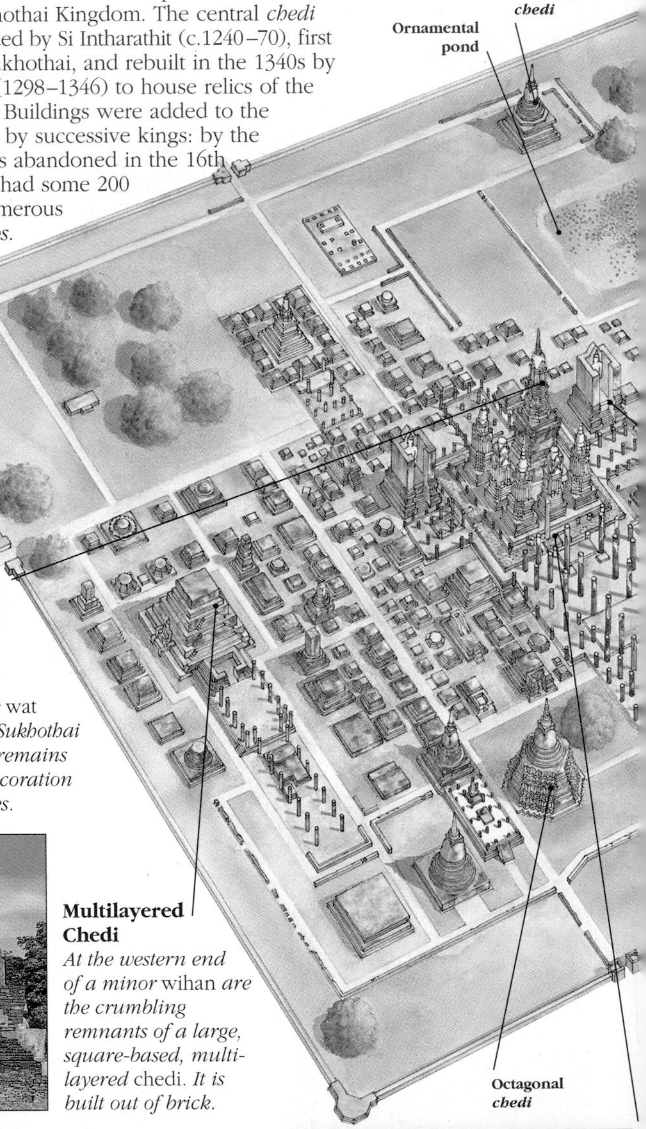

Bell-shaped *chedi*

Ornamental pond

★ Lotus-Bud Chedi

At the epicenter of the wat complex is this classic Sukhothai lotus-bud chedi. The remains of beautiful stucco decoration can be seen in patches.

Multilayered Chedi

At the western end of a minor wihan *are the crumbling remnants of a large, square-based, multi-layered chedi. It is built out of brick.*

Octagonal *chedi*

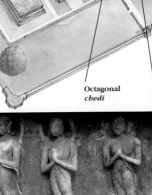

STAR FEATURES

★ **Frieze of Walking Monks**

★ **Lotus-Bud Chedi**

★ **Phra Attharot Buddha Images**

★ Frieze of Walking Monks

A stone frieze runs around the square base of the central group of chedis. It depicts monks processing around the shrine – a ritual called pradaksina.

Remains of Bot
To the north of the central chedi *are the remains of a* bot, *with a large, seated Buddha. Like all major Buddha images in Thailand, it faces east.*

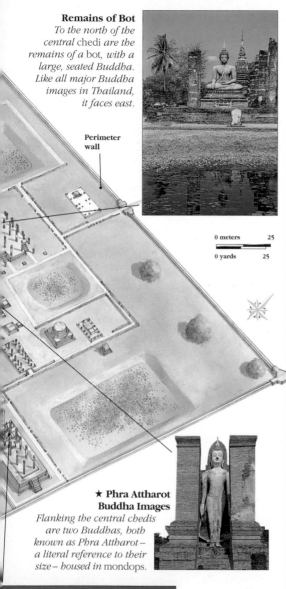

Perimeter wall

0 meters 25

0 yards 25

★ Phra Attharot Buddha Images
Flanking the central chedis *are two Buddhas, both known as Phra Attharot – a literal reference to their size – housed in* mondops.

Remains of Wihan
Aligned on an east-west axis with the central group of chedis *is the main* wihan. *The only remains today are columns that once supported a roof and a seated Buddha image.*

Exploring the Outer Sights
Along a low ridge of hills, around 3.5 km (2 miles) west of the ramparted royal city is another string of ruins that form part of the Sukhothai Historical Park. Most important of these is **Wat Saphan Hin**, where a 12.5-m (41-ft) high Buddha image, Phra Attharot, similar to the Buddha images of the same name at Wat Mahathat, stands on a low summit. There is another large image, similar to Phra Attharot, at Wat Phra Yun, though the head and hands are missing.

Closer to the west city wall is Wat Pa Mamuang, of archeological importance for the inscriptions discovered here relating to King Lo Thai.

To the south are the ruins of Wat Chetuphon, where a *mondop* contains the remains of four Buddha images in varying postures *(see p163)*; two are in good condition, but of the other two, one is missing below the waist and the other has virtually disappeared. At Wat Chedi Si Hong, the base of the laterite brick *chedi* is lined with stucco elephants, interspersed with divinities.

Beyond the southern edge of the Historical Park loom the hills of **Ramkamhaeng National Park**. Covering 342 sq km (133 sq mile), this is home to serow, gaur, and wild pig.

⚡ Ramkamhaeng National Park
S of Sukhothai off Hwy 101.
ℍ *Forestry Dept (0-2562-0760 inc bungalow bookings).*

Farmer cultivating rice in the fields surrounding Sukhothai

Si Satchanalai-Chalieng Historical Park ❼

อุทยานประวัติศาสตร์ศรีสัชนาลัย-ชะเลียง

D URING THE 13TH CENTURY, the Sukhothai Kingdom con-solidated its power in the Central Plains by building a number of satellite cities. The most important of these was Si Satchanalai. Today, its ruins lie on the right bank of the Yom River, 7 km (4 miles) south of modern Si Satchanalai. One of the best examples of a Thai *muang (see pp54–5)*, it was laid out along fixed cosmological lines – temple complexes lay at its heart, surrounded by city walls, rivers, and forest. It is considered by many historians to be the apogee of Thai city planning. The nearby ruins of Chalieng are thought to be an earlier Khmer settlement, an outpost of that empire dating from the time of Jaya-varman VII (1181–1220). At the height of the Sukhothai Kingdom, Si Satchanalai was twinned with the city of Sukhothai. A royal road, the Phra Ruang, linked the two.

Laterite columns and central *chedi* at Wat Nang Phaya

The central, lotus-bud *chedi* of Wat Chedi Chet Thaeo

The Main Wats

At the heart of the moated city a huge Sri Lankan-style, bell-shaped *chedi* forms the center-piece of **Wat Chang Lom** *(see p190)*. To the south is **Wat Chedi Chet Thaeo**, around whose central lotus-bud *chedi* are many smaller ones in different styles, some contain-ing stucco Buddha images. One of these *chedis* is a smaller version of the famous lotus-bud *chedi* at Wat Mahathat at Sukhothai *(see pp186–7)*.

At **Wat Nang Phaya**, the *wihan* is decorated with fine stucco reliefs from the Ayutthaya period, especially on the exterior. There is also a Sri Lankan-style, 15th–16th-century *chedi*. The *wihan's* grille-like windows here are

Exploring the Park

The ruins of Si Satchanalai are not as grandiose as those of Sukhothai but are in some ways more interesting. They have not been as extensively restored, and fewer tourists visit the site. The ruins evoke a once powerful city that, although not a seat of gov-ernment of the Sukhothai Kingdom, was the city of the deputy king and an important commercial center in the 14th and 15th centuries. Its most important trade was in ceram-ics *(see pp150–1)*, for which it was renowned all over Southeast Asia and China.

Today, the ruins at Si Satchanalai cover an area of roughly 45 sq km (18 sq miles) and are surrounded by a moat 12 m (40 ft) wide. A good way to tour the site is by bicycle; there is a bicycle rental store located halfway between Si Satchanalai and Chalieng. Visitors can also ride around the ruined city

on the back of an elephant. An information center located in front of the Ram Narong Gate houses a small exhibition of artifacts found at the site and photographs of Si Satch-analai's many monuments.

SRI LANKAN INFLUENCE

During the Sukhothai period, Theravada Buddhism, which had developed independently in Sri Lanka, arrived in Thai-land. With it came Sri Lankan, bell-shaped *chedis*, reliquary towers symbolizing the ring-ing out of the teachings of the Buddha. The three-tiered base symbolizes hell, earth, and heaven; rings on the spire represent the 33 levels of heaven. A second layer of symbolism designates the base as the Buddha's folded robes, the *stupa* as his alms bowl and the spire as his staff. The entire *chedi* also symbolizes Mount Meru.

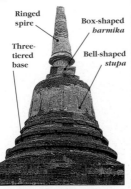

Ringed spire

Box-shaped *harmika*

Three-tiered base

Bell-shaped *stupa*

Sri Lankan-style *chedi* of Wat Suwan Khiri, overlooking Si Satchanalai

also characteristic of Ayutthaya, and less complete examples of this style can be seen elsewhere around the park. Nearby stands Wat Lak Muang, a small, Khmer-style shrine built as the city foundation shrine.

Minor Wats

On a low, wooded hill north of Wat Chang Lom stands Wat Khao Phnom Phloeng, once the site of ritual cremations. Also among the ruins are a seated Buddha, a *chedi*, and a number of columns that once supported a *wihan* roof.

On a hill top, farther west, all that remains of Wat Suwan Khiri is a single *chedi*, though there are great views from here of the rest of the city.

Beyond the City Walls

Farther west, on a mountain outside the city walls, is a row of ruined monasteries reached by a shady path. At the top of the path is the large, ruined *chedi* of Wat Khao Yai Bon.

There are many other minor ruins scattered inside and outside the moated site, and while some have been restored, others comprise little more than the base of a *wihan* or *chedi*. The *mondop* of Wat Hua Khon, for example, once contained seven stuccoed standing Buddha images; today only three are still plainly identifiable. North of the old Tao Mo Gate is Wat Kuti Rai.

There are two rectangular *mondops* here, both built entirely from laterite. Their pediments retain holes for beams, suggesting that they were once linked to other buildings. Inside one *mondop* is a seated Buddha image.

To the north are the kiln sites of Ban Pa Yuang and Ban Noi, where some of the finest Sangkhalok ceramics were produced. A sign of the times is that villagers nearby sell modern replicas to supplement their farming incomes.

Chalieng

Situated 1 km (1,090 yds) to the southeast is the settlement of Chalieng, predating the city of Si Satchanalai and in all likelihood built by the Khmers (*see pp254–5*) as a staging post for travelers. Some of the ruins that can be seen today date from later.

The laterite shrine of **Wat Chao Chan** was built in the Bayon style as a Mahayana Buddhist structure. The *wihan* and *mondop*, now ruins, were added later and reflect a move toward Theravada Buddhism.

Surrounded on three sides by a tight bend of the Yom River, the most important of the Chalieng sites is **Wat Phra Si Rattana Mahathat**, the buildings of which reflect a range of architectural styles from Sukhothai to Ayutthayan. The original Sukhothai lotus-

VISITORS' CHECKLIST

67 km (41 miles) N of New Sukhothai, Sukhothai province. ℹ *Information Center (0-5561-1179) or TAT, Phitsanulok (0-5525-2743).* 🚌 *from New Sukhothai to Si Satchanalai, then samlor.* ◷ *8:30am–4:30pm daily.* 📷 📄

Ancient kiln site, north of the walled city at Ban Pa Yuang

bud *chedi* was built over with a huge Khmer-influenced, Ayutthayan *prang*, one of the finest structures of its type in Thailand. Nearby, a seated Buddha, sheltered under the head of a *naga*, sits inside a half *chedi*. Also close by are remains of stucco reliefs of walking Buddhas, said to be some of the very finest examples of Sukhothai sculpture.

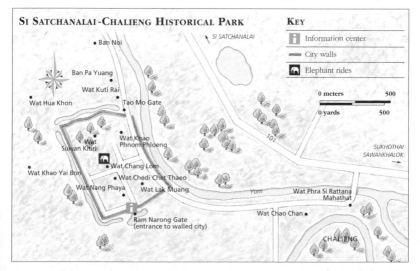

SI SATCHANALAI-CHALIENG HISTORICAL PARK

SI SATCHANALAI

- Ban Noi
- Ban Pa Yuang
- Wat Kuti Rai
- Wat Hua Khon
- Tao Mo Gate
- Wat Suwan Khiri
- Wat Khao Phnom Phloeng
- Wat Khao Yai Bon
- Wat Chang Lom
- Wat Chedi Chet Thaeo
- Wat Nang Phaya
- Wat Lak Muang
- Ram Narong Gate (entrance to walled city)
- Yom
- Wat Phra Si Rattana Mahathat
- Wat Chao Chan
- CHALIENG
- SUKHOTHAI SAWANKHALOK
- 101

KEY

- ℹ Information center
- ▬ City walls
- 🐘 Elephant rides

0 meters   500
0 yards   500

Wat Chang Lom
วัดช้างล้อม

BUILT IN THE REIGN of Ramkamhaeng, this monument is thought to be the first Sri Lankan-style *chedi* of the Sukhothai Kingdom. The style was later copied throughout Si Satchanalai and Sukhothai.

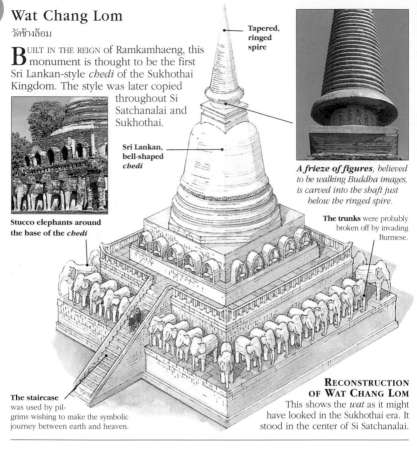

Tapered, ringed spire

Sri Lankan, bell-shaped *chedi*

Stucco elephants around the base of the *chedi*

A frieze of figures, believed to be walking Buddha images, is carved into the shaft just below the ringed spire.

The trunks were probably broken off by invading Burmese.

The staircase was used by pilgrims wishing to make the symbolic journey between earth and heaven.

RECONSTRUCTION OF WAT CHANG LOM
This shows the *wat* as it might have looked in the Sukhothai era. It stood in the center of Si Satchanalai.

Exploring Sawankhalok

With the introduction of new firing techniques by Chinese potters, the kilns around Si Satchanalai and Sukhothai became some of the most important producers of ceramics in Southeast Asia. At their most prolific, during the 14th–16th centuries, as the Sukhothai Kingdom came under the control of the Kingdom of Ayutthaya, it is thought that over 200 potteries lined the banks of the Yom River. They produced a variety of pottery termed Sangkhalok – a derivation of Sawankhalok, the name that was given to Si Satchanalai during the period of Ayutthaya's rule in the region. Today the name applies only to the small town of Sawankhalok, where the **Sawankha Woranayok National Museum** is located. This houses an expansive selection of Sangkhalok ceramics *(see pp150–1)*, which includes plates, storage jars, bowls, temple roof tiles, figures used in religious ceremonies, and everyday statues that may have been **Sangkhalok pottery** toys. A large number of the ceramics on display were salvaged from ships wrecked in the Gulf of Thailand on their way to trade with India, China, the Philippines, and Indonesia. The museum also contains a collection of religious sculptures taken from Sawankhalok's nearby Wat Sawankharam – many were donated to the *wat* by the villagers who unearthed them.

Exploring Si Satchanalai National Park

Founded in 1981, this park covers an area of 213 sq km (82 sq miles). Dotted around the park are the Tad Dao, Tad Duen, Huai Sai, and Huai Pa Cho waterfalls. The Tara Wasan and Kang Khao caves are also worth visiting. The park is good for bird-watching with more than 70 species recorded. Few large mammals inhabit the park, but there may be a small number of wild elephants living here.

🏠 **Sawankha Woranayok National Museum**
Sawankhalok, 17 km (11 miles) S of Si Satchanalai. ◯ *Wed–Sun.* 🖼

🌿 **Si Satchanalai National Park**
N of Si Satchanalai-Chalieng Historical Park, off Hwy 101, (0-2562-0760 or www.dnp.go.th for bungalow bookings). ◯ *daily.* 🖼

Green and ocher roof tiles at Wat Phra Si Rattana Mahathat, Phitsanulok

Phitsanulok ❽

พิษณุโลก

Phitsanulok province. 🏙 183,000.
☒ 🚌 🚉 🚇 TAT, 209/7–8
Borommatrailokanat Rd, Phitsanulok
(0-5525-2743). 🛒 Wed, Sat.
🎎 Phra Buddha Chinarat (Jan/Feb),
Phitsanulok Boat Races (Oct).

MANY VISITORS pass through this town since it is an important transport hub, connecting Bangkok and the Central Plains to Northern Thailand.

There has been a settlement here from as early as the mid-14th century, when **Wat Phra Si Rattana Mahathat** was built on the bank of the Nan River. Initially, this *wat* complex, also called Wat Yai, probably housed a Sukhothai lotus-bud *chedi*, which was later replaced by the tall Ayutthayan *prang* that can be seen today. It was built by the Ayutthayan king Borommatrailokanat (1448–88), who ruled from Phitsanulok after 1463 in order to wage a military campaign against the Kingdom of Lanna *(see pp58–9)*. The golden tiles on the antefixes of the *wat* were added during a later renovation by King Chulalongkorn (1868–1910).

Inside the west *wihan* is the revered Buddha image Phra Buddha Chinarat *(see pp150–1)*, made of gilded bronze and dating from the 14th century. It attracts pilgrims from all over Thailand, and, consequently, a small industry of religious paraphernalia has

grown up around it. In the gallery outside the *prang* are dozens of Buddha images. Across the road, in the *bot* of **Wat Ratchaburana**, are some faded 19th-century murals, depicting scenes from the Ramakien *(see pp36–7)*.

Sergeant Major Thawee's Folk Museum houses a collection of rural folk crafts – wood and bamboo animal traps, farm tools, and basketry. Across the street is the affiliated **Buddha Foundry**, where visitors can watch bronze Buddha images being forged.

The Phra Buddha Chinarat image

ENVIRONS: Five km (3 miles) south of Phitsanulok is the Ayutthayan, laterite *prang* of **Wat Chulamani**. It was built in Khmer style by King Borommatrailokanat in 1464, a year after he moved his capital from Ayutthaya to Phitsanulok. He was ordained as a monk here in 1465 after abdicating

in favor of his son. Eight months later he returned to the throne and, until his death in 1488, continued to rule Ayutthaya from Phitsanulok.

🏠 **Sergeant Major Thawee's Folk Museum**
26/43 Wisuth Kasat Rd. 📞 0-5521-2749. 🕐 Tue–Sun. 📷
Buddha Foundry 🕐 Mon–Sat.

Thung Salaeng Luang National Park ❾

อุทยานแห่งชาติทุ่งแสลงหลวง

Phitsanulok province, Park HQ off Hwy 12, 80 km (50 miles) E of Phitsanulok. 🚉 TAT, Phitsanulok (0-5525-2743); Forestry Dept (0-2562-0760 or www.dnp.go.th for bungalow bookings). 🚌 from Phitsanulok to Nakhon Thai, then songthaew. 📷

WITH ITS OPEN FIELDS interspersed with forest, this 1,262 sq km (487 sq mile) park offers good hiking and bird-watching. Barking deer can also be seen, and elephants are sometimes found at the salt licks. The cascades of Kaeng Sopha lie 9 km (6 miles) from the park headquarters. Farther west, along the main highway, are the Poi falls and smaller Kaeng Song rapids.

ENVIRONS: At **Khao Kho**, to the east, is a rehabilitation project for the Hmong, displaced through involvement in anti-Communist fighting in the 1970s–80s. The King takes great interest in the program and has a palace nearby.

The thinly forested Thung Salaeng Luang National Park

NORTHERN
THAILAND

Introducing Northern Thailand

NORTHERN THAILAND, home of the ancient Lanna kingdom *(see pp58–9)*, offers a great diversity of activities. The old Lanna capitals of Chiang Mai and Chiang Rai are filled with ancient monuments and museums, and markets selling the distinctive local textiles and handicrafts. Smaller towns, such as Nan and Lamphun, offer a more low-key charm. Away from the main settlements, the scenery of Northern Thailand is stupendous: mountains, forests (some of them teak), rice fields set in verdant valleys and several spectacular national parks. The more adventurous visitor can join a trek to remote villages inhabited by hill tribes where elements of lifestyle have changed little in hundreds of years.

Mae Hong Son *(see pp206–7), a rapidly developing tourist center, is particularly popular with budget travelers. The town's main attraction is its beautiful mountain setting.*

Mae Hong Son

Chiang Mai *(see pp214–17) is justly famed for its 300 temples, fine shopping, distinctive Northern cuisine, and (despite its size) relaxed pace of life.*

Chiang Mai

NORTHWEST HEARTLAND *(see pp202–227)*

Lampang

Doi Inthanon National Park

Doi Inthanon National Park (see pp220–21) *incorporates the highest mountain in Thailand. Visitors come for the stunning scenery, including several waterfalls, and rich wildlife.*

Lampang *(see pp224–7) is a thriving town which hosts colorful festivals. It contains a number of important wats and a museum of Lanna artifacts.*

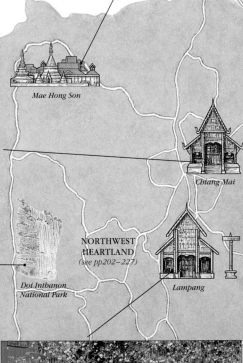

◁ **The Elephant Training Center, southeast of the town of Chiang Dao**

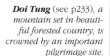

Doi Tung (see p233), *a mountain set in beautiful forested country, is crowned by an important pilgrimage site.*

Doi Tung

Chiang Rai

FAR NORTH
(see pp228–249)

Chiang Rai (see pp240–41) *has long dwelled in the shadow of nearby Chiang Mai, but is now rapidly developing into a significant tourist center in its own right. Its monuments may not be as numerous as those of Chiang Mai, but the city is an excellent source of hill-tribe handicrafts and a major starting point for trekkers.*

Nan

0 kilometers   50

0 miles   25

Nan (see pp244–5) *is a wealthy, sleepy town with several quirky wats, a good museum, and a spectacular mountain setting. Every October the Nan River is filled with colorful canoes taking part in the Lanna boat races.*

The Hill Tribes of Thailand

Ceremonial mask

THERE ARE SIX MAIN GROUPS of hill dwellers living in Northern Thailand: the Akha, Hmong, Lisu, Karen, Lahu, and Mien. These seminomadic peoples, some 500,000 in total, began to arrive here at the end of the 19th century, pushed out of their native Tibet, Burma, and China by civil war and political pressures. Though widely referred to as hill tribes, this label is rather general as each group has its own heritage, clothing, language, religion, and culture. However, the future of the hill tribes is uncertain. Traditionally, most use the slash-and-burn method (swiddening) to grow crops, abandoning land once it is exhausted. But competing pressures on land are drawing them into the Thai market economy. Some are also becoming dependent on tourist handouts.

This 1890s portrait is of Lahu women. Most hill tribes still wear traditional dress, though Western clothing is widely available.

Bamboo sections are pounded rhythmically to honor leaders during the Swing Ceremony.

Young Lisu women and girls wear black turbans adorned with multicolored threads, mainly for important celebrations such as New Year. Silver jewelry, sewn onto their clothes, is a display of the family's wealth.

This Hmong house has been accidentally destroyed by fire. To improve living conditions and economic opportunities, and to stop swiddening, the government aims to integrate hill tribes into the Thai way of life.

FESTIVALS AND GATHERINGS
Colorful ceremonies mark rites of passage such as birth, death, and marriage. Here, the Akha gather for a festival.

New Year is the most important date in the Lisu calendar. A tree is planted in front of each house in the village. A shaman and a priest then perform a ritual to cleanse the village of the past year's bad elements, while young people dance around the trees.

In the past, some hill tribes earned extra income from opium production. They are now encouraged to grow "new" crops such as cabbage.

Akha houses are characterized by a large porch connected to a square living area with a stove. They are usually constructed on high ground near the tribe's rice fields.

Akha people strive to maintain a traditional way of life, the "Akha Way." This is proving more difficult as fertile land disappears and animal numbers are depleted. Here, a villager carries out the vital chore of collecting wood.

An ornate headdress, decorated with silver or, increasingly, aluminum, is worn by Akha women.

A sash, weighed down with coins and beads, distinguishes women from girls.

While many Lahu women no longer wear traditional dress on a daily basis, they still weave distinctive shoulder bags (yam) *from brightly colored fabrics.*

Mien clothing *is particularly distinctive. Women embroider colorful patterns onto black or indigo cloth and stitch red pompons onto caps worn by children.*

Karen typically build houses in lowland valleys, cultivating by crop rotation rather than slash-and-burn. They are the largest and least nomadic tribe.

SPIRITUAL BELIEFS

Many hill-tribe beliefs and practices are based on animism. Villages often have two religious leaders: a priest, who performs rituals and communes with the local guardian spirit, and a shaman, who has the power to consult directly with the spirit world. Rituals influence most decisions in a village, including where it is sited. But as tribes are drawn into modern life, traditional practices and medicine are coming under threat.

Mien tools used during shamanistic ceremonies

Northern Arts and Crafts

Pale green celadon bowl

NORTHERN THAILAND IS FAMOUS for its handicrafts. The high quality of crafts produced today, such as wooden carvings, silverware, fabrics, ceramics, silk, and lacquerware, reflects centuries of Northern Thai, or Lanna, expertise. The region's ethnic minorities and hill tribes *(see pp196–7)* also produce distinctive embroidery, paintings, and silverware. Chiang Mai *(see pp214–17)* is the main crafts center, while villages such as Bo Sang and San Kamphaeng *(see pp218–19)* specialize in particular crafts. In factory-shops, visitors can watch crafts being made. Antiques and excellent copies are sold in outlets in Chiang Mai. Though teak logging has been strictly controlled in Thailand since 1989, wooden crafts produced from imported teak are still widely sold.

Ornate Akba *headdresses feature silver coins and hollow baubles that are expertly crafted by the men of the hill tribe.*

Animal figures*, intricately carved from wood (in many cases teak), often feature in Northern wats. Such wooden crafts are still produced throughout the North, despite the ban on unregulated teak logging.*

Northern lacquerwork *typically consists of a red lacquer-coated wood or bamboo base decorated with a yellow pattern. This is a 19th- or 20th-century box.*

Curved legs were designed to fit over the back of the elephant, near its head.

ROYAL HOWDAH

Before the advent of the car, elephants were used for transportation in Thailand. People sat in howdahs, or elephant chairs, on the elephants' backs. Howdahs stood some 1.5 m (5 ft) high, and their decoration revealed their passengers' status. The most basic form consisted of a seat with raised sides. Howdahs used for transporting royalty and aristocrats, such as this one from Northern Thailand, featured ornate wood carving and usually had a roof.

Umbrellas are the main craft items *produced in Bo Sang. They are made of lacquered paper, stretched over a bamboo frame, then painted with traditional motifs such as elephants.*

Betel sets consist of several containers used to hold the ingredients for betel-chewing (a popular activity in Southeast Asia) – betel leaf, limestone ash, and the narcotic areca palm fruit. A gold set was a sign of status.

Wooden roof brackets, seen on religious buildings, are for decoration rather than support. They often depict nagas (serpents) and other animals.

A roof made from lacquered woven bamboo offered shelter from the heat.

Silver ceremonial jewelry is worn for village festivals and other important occasions. While hill tribes still use old silver, melted down from Indian and Burmese coins, many Thai silversmiths in Chiang Mai nowadays rely on imported silver of a lower quality.

Handles were used for support during bumpy rides. Royal elephant seats were more comfortable than ordinary ones.

In Thailand even everyday items are decorated, such as this wooden clapper, which is painted with a flower motif. A clapper is traditionally worn by water buffalo so they can be located if they stray.

Delicately fashioned wood carving featured only on elephant chairs used by affluent members of society.

TEXTILES OF NORTHERN THAILAND

Embroidering a striped Lahu bag

Textile production in Northern Thailand dates from the early Lanna period, and the region is known for its silk and cotton. Chiang Mai and San Kamphaeng are centers for silk clothing – also made in the Northeast *(see pp256–7)* – including the traditional *pha sin* (woman's sarong). Outlets also sell furnishings and cottonware produced in Pasang *(see p219)* such as the *pha koma* (man's sarong). Chiang Khong factory-shops produce Thai Lue cotton fabrics in stunning colors *(see p239)*, while hill tribes make and sell brightly patterned fabrics. Most textiles can be bought as lengths or as ready-made items.

A traditional cotton design

A 19th-century *pha sin*

Birds of Northern Thailand

ORTHERN THAILAND lies on the Eastern Asia Flyway, a major flight path for migrating birds. Thailand boasts some ten percent of the world's bird species, 380 of which have been recorded in the hills around Chiang Mai. Most of these are migratory birds that have flown south in winter to the warmer climes of Thailand's forested hills. In recent years, steps have been introduced to protect bird habitats under threat from deforestation. But many sites in the north, especially Doi Suthep *(see pp212–13)* and Doi Inthanon *(see pp220–21)* national parks, still provide a habitat for numerous bird species.

SELECTED MIGRATION ROUTES

━━━ ARCTIC WARBLERS

━━━ SIBERIAN RUBYTHROATS

━━━ HERONS

Black-crowned night-herons *are nocturnal birds. They have a black crest, nape, and back, whitish underparts, and gray wings. Resident in various countries, they migrate to low altitudes in Northern Thailand.*

Changeable hawk-eagle

The red-breasted parakeet, of deciduous woodlands, is threatened by the illegal trade in birds.

Red-wattled lapwings, *named for the red patch of skin in front of the eye, reside near streams and in open forest. When alarmed they emit a loud, shrill call.*

Teak tree

Silver pheasants *live at various altitudes, typically over 700 m (2,300 ft). Their red feet and long tail distinguish them from other types of pheasants. They are also bred in captivity to be sold for food – because of their depleted numbers, pheasants are protected.*

Pheasant-tailed jacanas *have long legs, toes, and claws that enable them to walk on leaves in lowland rivers, foraging for food.*

Purple herons are wetland birds that can be seen near forest streams. They have a slender, rufous (red-brown) neck.

0 – 500 M (0 – 1,640 FT) ABOVE SEA LEVEL

Coral-billed ground-cuckoos are difficult to observe because they are rare, shy birds.

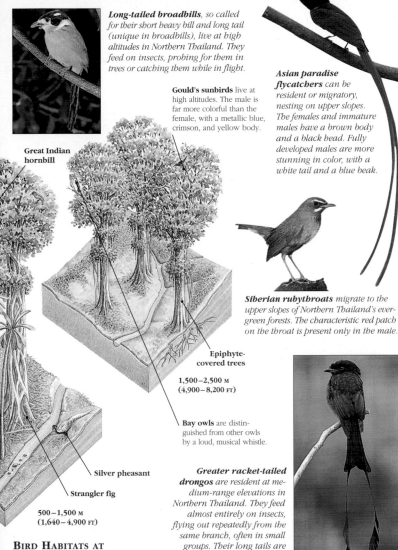

Long-tailed broadbills, *so called for their short heavy bill and long tail (unique in broadbills), live at high altitudes in Northern Thailand. They feed on insects, probing for them in trees or catching them while in flight.*

Gould's sunbirds live at high altitudes. The male is far more colorful than the female, with a metallic blue, crimson, and yellow body.

Asian paradise flycatchers *can be resident or migratory, nesting on upper slopes. The females and immature males have a brown body and a black head. Fully developed males are more stunning in color, with a white tail and a blue beak.*

Great Indian hornbill

Siberian rubythroats *migrate to the upper slopes of Northern Thailand's evergreen forests. The characteristic red patch on the throat is present only in the male.*

Epiphyte-covered trees

1,500–2,500 M (4,900–8,200 FT)

Bay owls are distinguished from other owls by a loud, musical whistle.

Silver pheasant

Greater racket-tailed drongos *are resident at medium-range elevations in Northern Thailand. They feed almost entirely on insects, flying out repeatedly from the same branch, often in small groups. Their long tails are tipped with a vane or "racket" that ripples as the bird flies.*

Strangler fig

500–1,500 M (1,640–4,900 FT)

Bird Habitats at Different Altitudes

Deciduous dipterocarp trees clothe the foothills of Northern Thailand. Here, teak forests provide a habitat for kalij pheasants, wagtails, and parakeets, and migratory wetland birds such as herons. Higher up the slopes, bazas, hornbills, hill mynas, and shikes are drawn to mixed evergreen and deciduous forests. Oaks and epiphytic plants, such as ferns, thrive on the hilltops, where arctic warblers, owls, and other small birds live.

Tips for Bird-Watching

• The best time to see birds is during the "winter" months, from January to April, when resident birds are mating and most migratory species arrive. Avoid the wet season (June–October), when heavy rain and leeches can be a problem.
• National park headquarters provide leaflets detailing bird-watching trails. Guided trips can often be arranged.
• Take binoculars, plenty of water, insect repellent, and a compass. Try to wear dark green or inconspicuous clothing.
• Many birds are shy, so be patient. Walk quietly to avoid rustling leaves, and do not walk straight toward the bird.

NORTHWEST HEARTLAND

NORTHWEST THAILAND *is the heartland of Lanna Thai. The ancient city of Chiang Mai, famed for its many fine temples and handicrafts, is the focal point for visitors. This and smaller towns are set in verdant valleys among thickly forested mountains. The Northwest is also home to a number of ethnic minorities, and the rich mix of diverse cultures and scenery is most enticing.*

Chiang Mai, superbly sited in the Ping River Valley, was once the capital of the Lanna Kingdom. In the 12th–18th centuries this kingdom, strongly influenced by Burma, ruled over what is now northern Thailand, and local Thais remain proud of their Lanna heritage. Indeed, the silverwork, woodcarving, pottery, and other crafts of the North are regarded by many as the most exquisite in Thailand. Nowhere in the country are crafts more readily available than in Chiang Mai and its environs.

Chiang Mai is also a useful base from which to explore the mountains and villages. Trekking to hill-tribe villages is a popular, though controversial, activity. Although most trekkers are genuinely interested in hill-tribe culture, there is a danger that villages will become dependent on tourism and that traditional ways of life will be lost forever.

In the west, close to the Burmese border, the remote towns of Mae Hong Son and Mae Sariang are in some ways more Burmese than Thai. The *wats*, for instance, have multiroofed *chedis* reminiscent of Burmese temples.

North of Chiang Mai, the streets of Chiang Dao are lined with two-story teak buildings, a reminder that the surrounding countryside was once rich in teak forests. To the south of Chiang Mai, Lanna influence can again be seen in temples and museum artifacts within the cities of Lampang and Lamphun. The latter also has surviving traces of the older Kingdom of Haripunchai.

Thailand's highest mountain, Doi Inthanon, lies west of Chiang Mai, within a national park with good facilities. Here can be seen dramatic waterfalls and a wide range of wildlife, including hundreds of migratory birds.

Boy lighting a candle at Wat Phra That Lampang Luang, one of several major *wats* in the Northwest

◁ Woman cleaning umbrellas in the handicraft village of Bo Sang, near Chiang Mai

Exploring the Northwest Heartland

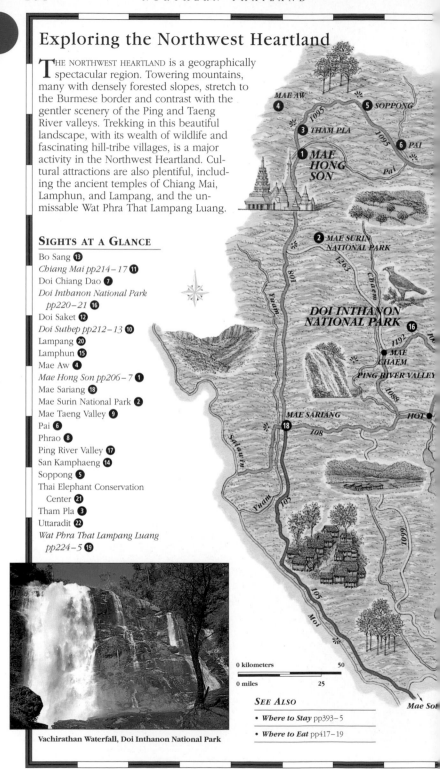

THE NORTHWEST HEARTLAND is a geographically spectacular region. Towering mountains, many with densely forested slopes, stretch to the Burmese border and contrast with the gentler scenery of the Ping and Taeng River valleys. Trekking in this beautiful landscape, with its wealth of wildlife and fascinating hill-tribe villages, is a major activity in the Northwest Heartland. Cultural attractions are also plentiful, including the ancient temples of Chiang Mai, Lamphun, and Lampang, and the unmissable Wat Phra That Lampang Luang.

SIGHTS AT A GLANCE

MAE AW ④
⑤ SOPPONG
③ THAM PLA
⑥ PAI
① MAE HONG SON
② MAE SURIN NATIONAL PARK
DOI INTHANON NATIONAL PARK ⑯
MAE CHAEM
PING RIVER VALLEY
MAE SARIANG ⑱
HOT
Mae Sot

Vachirathan Waterfall, Doi Inthanon National Park

0 kilometers — 50
0 miles — 25

SEE ALSO

- **Where to Stay** pp393–5
- **Where to Eat** pp417–19

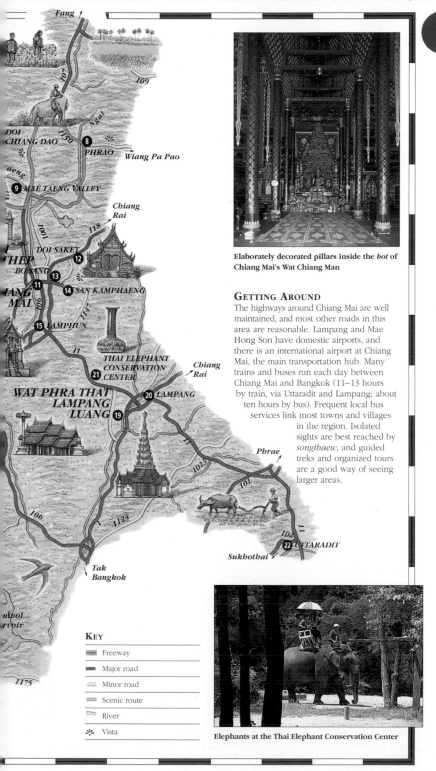

Elaborately decorated pillars inside the *bot* of Chiang Mai's Wat Chiang Man

GETTING AROUND

The highways around Chiang Mai are well maintained, and most other roads in this area are reasonable. Lampang and Mae Hong Son have domestic airports, and there is an international airport at Chiang Mai, the main transportation hub. Many trains and buses run each day between Chiang Mai and Bangkok (11–13 hours by train, via Uttaradit and Lampang; about ten hours by bus). Frequent local bus services link most towns and villages in the region. Isolated sights are best reached by *songthaew*, and guided treks and organized tours are a good way of seeing larger areas.

KEY

▬	Freeway
▬	Major road
▬	Minor road
▬	Scenic route
▭	River
☼	Vista

Elephants at the Thai Elephant Conservation Center

Street-by-Street: Mae Hong Son ❶
แม่ฮ่องสอน

BEAUTIFULLY LOCATED in a valley ringed by forested mountains, Mae Hong Son sprang up in 1831 from a small camp where elephants were tethered. The town remained largely isolated until it was linked by a paved highway to Chiang Mai in 1965. The province has traditionally been dominated by nearby Burma, as shown by its architecture. Shan and Karen people, who make up most of the population, continue to move across the border to live in Mae Hong Son and its environs. Today, the tranquil town is growing as a resort and trekking center. In the cool season, you may need to wear a sweater or jacket here.

To Airport

★ Wat Hua Wiang
This teak temple has a Burmese-style, multi-roofed design. The bot – in an advanced state of decay – houses an important brass image of Buddha, Phrachao Para La 'Khaeng, that was transported here from Burma.

The Night Bazaar sells crafts and Thai Lue fabrics.

Daily Market
This lively, pungent market, which almost spills onto the airport runway, sells a range of fresh produce, Burmese textiles, and trekking supplies. Local hill tribes are often seen here.

THE PADAUNG WOMEN

Many tours from Mae Hong Son visit the "long-neck women" of the area. These women, of the Padaung, or Kayan, tribe, are distinguished by their long necks, lengthened from childhood by brass rings. Among the explanations for this old practice are that it protects the women from tiger attacks and that it is a way of enhancing their looks. This practice had begun to die out until recently when the Padaung realized tourists would pay to photograph the women.

"Long-neck women" of the Padaung tribe

Traditional Shan teak houses can be seen along this street.

UDOM CHAONITHET

PRADIT CHONG KHAM

SINGHANAT BAMRUNG

Chong Kham Lake
This lake, which was originally a bathing pool for elephants, can be especially stunning in the early-morning mists that enshroud the town.

VISITORS' CHECKLIST

Mae Hong Son province. ↟ 48,000. ✖ 1 km (1,100 yds) NW of Chong Kham Lake. ⊞ Khumlum Phraphat Rd. ⓘ TAT, Chiang Mai (0-5324-8604). @ tatchmai@tat.or.th ⊞ Singhanat Bamrung Rd (0-5361-1952). ⊞ daily. ⊗ Poi Sang Long Festival (late Mar/early Apr); Chong Para Festival (Oct).

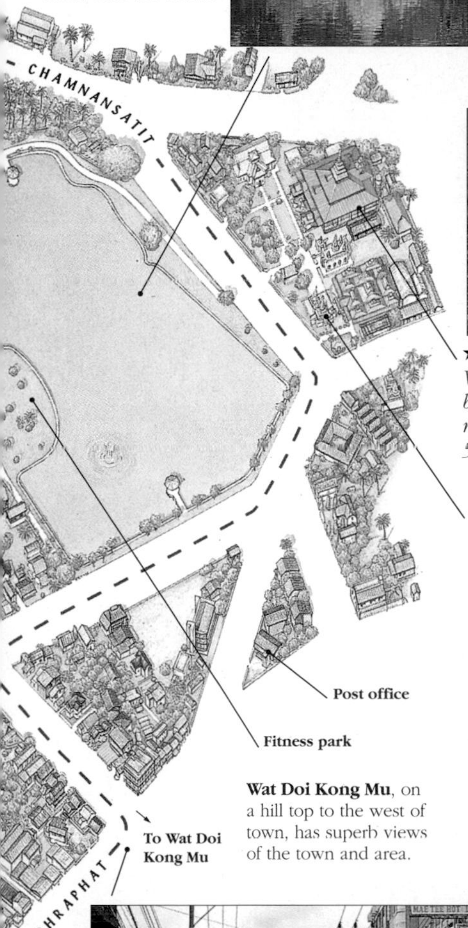

CHAMNANSATIT

★ **Wat Chong Kham**
Wat Chong Kham (c.1827), which was built by the Shan, features a multi-roofed chedi. The wat houses a revered 5-m (16-ft) seated Buddha image.

Post office

Fitness park

★ **Wat Chong Klang**
Built in the late 19th century, this temple has distinctive white and gold chedis. Painted glass panels depicting the jataka tales (see p26) can be seen on request.

Wat Doi Kong Mu, on a hill top to the west of town, has superb views of the town and area.

To Wat Doi Kong Mu

LUM PHRAPHAT

Khumlum Phraphat Road
Craft shops, restaurants, and tour companies line Mae Hong Son's main street. Hill-tribe textiles and antiques are among the items for sale.

| 0 meters | 25 |
| 0 yards | 25 |

KEY

– – – Suggested route

STAR SIGHTS

★ **Wat Hua Wiang**

★ **Wat Chong Kham**

★ **Wat Chong Klang**

The spectacular Mae Surin waterfall in Mae Surin National Park

Mae Surin National Park ❷

อุทยานแห่งชาติน้ำตกแม่สุริน

Mae Hong Son province. Park HQ 2.5 km (2 miles) off Hwy 108, 8 km (5 miles) N of Mae Hong Son [i] *TAT, Mea Hong Son (0-5361-1299); Forestry Dept (0-2562-0760 or www.dnp.go.th for bungalow bookings).* 🚌 *from Khun Yuam then songthaew.* ⭕ *daily.* 📷

THIS SMALL PARK is the highlight of the area south of Mae Hong Son. Much of its lowland forest provides a habitat for the Malaysian sun bear, Asiatic black bear, and barking deer. Bird species include drongos and hornbills.

Mae Surin waterfall, which at 100 m (330 ft) is one of the highest in Thailand, is reached from the Khun Yuam district. on a dirt road. Also accessible from this road is Thung Bua Thong ("wild sunflower meadow"), which blooms in November and December.

Raft trips along the Pai River, which flows through the park, can be arranged at guesthouses in Mae Hong Son and Pai.

Tham Pla ❸

ถ้ำปลา

Mae Hong Son province. Off Hwy 1095, 17 km (11 miles) N of Mae Hong Son. [i] *TAT, Chiang Mai (0-5324-8604).* 🚌 *Mae Hong Son, then songthaew, or join tour.* 📷

LOCATED NORTH OF Mae Hong Son, this scenic spot can be visited on a day trip from the town. Tham Pla ("fish cave") is actually a pool and stream at the base of a limestone outcrop, so named because of the huge carp that live in it. Visitors make merit by buying papaya to feed to the fish. The peaceful surrounding gardens are perhaps the site's most attractive feature.

Mae Aw ❹

แม่ออ

Mae Hong Son province. 🚶 *7,000.* 🚌 *Mae Hong Son, then songthaew, or join tour.* [i] *TAT, Chiang Mai (0-5324-8604).* 📅 *daily.* .

SITUATED in the mountains near the Burmese border, Mae Aw is a remote settlement built by members of the Kuomintang, or KMT *(see p232).* Apart from superb views, the village offers an intriguing insight into life in an isolated border village. But fighting still sometimes breaks out between rival factions over control of the local opium trade, following the overthrow of Khun Sa *(see p223)* in 1996.

The best way to get to Mae Aw is with a tour from Mae Hong Son or by jeep. Before you come, check with the local tourist information office that there is no fighting in the area.

Soppong ❺

สบป่อง

Mae Hong Son province. 🚶 *15,000.* 🚌 *from Mae Hong Son.* [i] *TAT, Chiang Mai (0-5324-8604).* 📅 *daily.*

THE VILLAGE OF Soppong (sometimes called Pang Mapha on local maps) is perched some 700 m (2,200 ft) up in the mountains. With its fine views, beautiful surround-

Highway 1095 as it passes through Soppong

Muslim children in Pai, part of the town's mixed community

Pai 6
ปาย

Mae Hong Son province. 27,000. from Mae Hong Son. TAT, Chiang Mai (0-5324-8604). daily.

PAI HAS A FAST-GROWING reputation as one of Northern Thailand's top beauty spots and is popular with trekkers and lovers of mountain scenery. Originally an old Shan settlement, the town and surrounding area have, in recent decades, become populated by Lisu and Lahu hill tribes, Muslims from Burma, and Yunnanese from China.

The yellow and white tiles and multilayered roofs of **Wat Klang**, between the bus station and the Pai River, are typical of Shan temples. The hilltop **Wat Phra That Mae Yen**, just east of Pai, was also built by the Shan. The carved wooden doors of the main *wihan* depict scenes from nature and human life. The temple has sweeping views of the valley.

Guided treks of the area *(see p211)* can be arranged at many guesthouses in town.

ing teak forests, and air of tranquility, Soppong is becoming an increasingly popular resort. Many trekkers pass through here on the way to visit local hill-tribe villages populated by Lisu and Shan (a minority originally from Burma). The village itself has a thriving market where local tribespeople congregate daily.

ENVIRONS: Tham Lot, north of Soppong, is one of the largest cave systems in Southeast Asia. The three adjoining caverns form a vast subterranean canyon, which is cut through by a large stream. The distinctive stalactites and stalagmites are especially impressive. The discovery of artifacts and huge, roughly carved teak coffins indicates that the caves were inhabited thousands of years ago. Visitors may cross the stream by raft or by elephant. Guided visits can be arranged at local guesthouses.

Tham Lot
8 km (5 miles) N of Soppong, Mae Hong Son province. daily. (for guide and lantern).

THAILAND'S ENDANGERED WILDLIFE

With its diversity of landscapes, Thailand is an ideal habitat for a vast range of flora and fauna. In the 20th century, however, poaching and deforestation have led to the extinction of many species, including the kouprey (a type of wild cattle) and Schomburgk's deer. Some animals are caught for food; some, including gibbons, are sold as pets, while others, like snakes, are killed through fear. Of Thailand's 282 mammal species, about 40 are endangered, and while laws exist to protect these animals, they are not always enforced. Almost all of Thailand's large mammals are in danger of extinction, and many others, including the white-handed gibbon, are, at best, rare. This alarming state of affairs is not confined to mammals: ten percent of the country's 405 reptiles and amphibians are also endangered.

Rock python – its favored forest habitat is rapidly disappearing

A rare white-handed gibbon

TIGERS IN THAILAND
The increasing demand for dried tiger parts in traditional Chinese medicines has led to the worldwide demise of this great creature. Of the few thousand tigers that remain in Asia, about 500 are estimated to be living in Thailand, particularly in the Khao Yai National Park *(see pp174–5)*. In 1995 the Royal Forest Department established a conservation project to try to prevent the tiger from dying out altogether in Thailand.

Pavilions and carp-filled pool in front of Tham Chiang Dao

Doi Chiang Dao **7**

ดอยเชียงดาว

12 km (7.5 miles) W of Chiang Dao, Chiang Mai province. ■ *TAT, Chiang Mai (0-5324-8604).* ■ *from Chiang Mai to Chiang Dao, then songthaew.*

A T 2,195 M (7,200 FT), Doi Chiang Dao is the third-largest mountain in Thailand. Home to several Lisu and Karen villages, it features a mixture of tropical and pine forests. Today, this peak and the surrounding area, characterized by rugged limestone scenery and dense teak forest, are more of an attraction than the nearby town, Chiang Dao.

Running for some 14 km (8.5 miles) under the mountain is a network of caves, **Tham Chiang Dao**, best reached from Chiang Dao town. Most of the caves house statues of the Buddha that, over the years, have been left by Shan pilgrims from Burma. The highlight of the bat-inhabited caves, however, is their huge stalactites and stalagmites. Lanterns and guides can be hired in order to make the most of these impressive features. The tours take visitors along an illuminated walkway through the caves.

Near the caves is a temple, **Wat Tham Chiang Dao**, with a Buddhist meditation center and a small room displaying gongs and other instruments. Beyond a huge tamarind tree, by a pond, is an old Burmese-style *chedi*. Nearby, a small market offers a wide selection of locally gathered forest roots, herbs, and spices.

East of Doi Chiang Dao, and dominated by the peak, is **Chiang Dao town**, with its traditional teak buildings along the main street. It was founded in the 18th century as a place

Façade of Wat Tham Chiang Dao, near Doi Chiang Dao

of exile for *phi pop*, ("spirit people"), who were suspected of being possessed by evil spirits. In fact, the symptoms of their true illnesses, such as malaria, had been mistaken as signs of madness.

The **Elephant Training Center Taeng Dao**, southeast of Chiang Dao, is located in a wooded area beside a stream. The daily displays feature elephants bathing, and lifting and dragging logs. Elephant rides may also be taken.

Tham Tup Tao, 48 km (30 miles) north of Chiang Dao, are two large caverns. Tham Pha Kao ("light cave") houses two large Buddha images and a stalagmite carved in the shape of a group of elephants. Inside Tham Pha Chak ("dark cave"), which can be explored only by lantern, is a bat colony.

🐾 **Tham Chiang Dao**
Off Hwy 107, 5 km (3 miles) NW of Chiang Dao. ◻ *daily.* 🏯 🎫
🏠 **Elephant Training Center Taeng Dao**
E of Hwy 107, 15 km (9.5 miles) SE of Chiang Dao, Chiang Mai province.
📞 *0-5329-8553.* ◻ *daily (displays 9–10am and 10–11am).* 🏯
🐾 **Tham Tup Tao**
W of Hwy 107, Chiang Mai province.
◻ *daily.* 🏯 🎫

Phrao **8**

พร้าว

Chiang Mai province. 🚶 *46,000.*
🚌 *from Chiang Mai.* ■ *TAT, Chiang Mai (0-5324-8604).* 🏯 *daily.*

A SMALL MARKET TOWN, Phrao is a meeting place for Thai traders and hill-tribe people. Until quite recently, Phrao was relatively isolated from other towns. Today, Highway 1150 connects it with Wiang Pa Pao (*see p242*), making it more accessible. Phrao is still off the main tourist track. The town's main sight is its covered market, which sells traditional textiles and locally grown fruit and vegetables.

ENVIRONS: Heading east towards Wiang Pa Pao, Highway 1150 passes through spectacular forest scenery. Here, several Lisu and Hmong hill-tribe villages can be seen.

ORCHIDS IN THAILAND

Seen on logos throughout Thailand, the orchid is the country's most famous flower. There are over 1,300 varieties of wild orchid in Thailand, most of which are dependent on forests. But while their natural habitat is threatened by deforestation, millions are being cultivated for export to overseas markets.

A pink orchid, one of the most popular colors for the overseas markets

Export began in the 1950s, and burgeoned in the 1980s when the first orchid farms were established. In 1991 the value of exports peaked at about $80 million. Since then, as consumer trends have changed in important markets such as Japan, this figure has started to decline.

A leisurely rafting trip along the Taeng River

Mae Taeng Valley ❾

แม่แตง

Chiang Mai province. 🚌 🚆 *Chiang Mai, then songthaew.* 🛈 *TAT, Chiang Mai (0-5324-8604).*

T HE AREA AROUND Mae Taeng, especially the vicinity of the Taeng River to the northwest of the town, is very popular with trekkers. In recent years, the land has been terraced and irrigated to improve agricultural production. The variety of crops grown has created an attractive contrast of landscapes. However, most trekkers come here not only for the peaceful surroundings but also to witness everyday scenes in the region's many Lisu, Karen, and Hmong villages. Other activities, including river rafting and elephant rides, can be combined with treks in the area. The **Mae Taman Rafting and Elephant Camp** is located amid peaceful scenery on a dirt road to the west of Highway 107 and arranges rafting trips on the Mae Taeng River. Elephant rides and bullock cart rides can also be taken. A nearby guesthouse, set on the banks of the river, offers accommodation.

🏠 **Mae Taman Rafting and Elephant Camp**
7 km (4.5 miles) W of Hwy 107. 🔲 *daily.* 📷

Hmong women, wearing their distinctive woven textiles

TREKKING AROUND CHIANG DAO

Northern Thailand is renowned for its trekking *(see p446)*. Treks in the area around Chiang Dao and Mae Taeng often combine visits to hill-tribe villages with an elephant ride or raft trip through the stunning scenery. Most three-day treks from Chiang Mai, which can be arranged by guesthouses or trekking companies in the city, incorporate this area. Among the region's interesting towns are Mae Taeng, Phrao, and Chiang Dao, all of which have long been at the interface between the Thai-dominated lowlands and the uplands, where the hill tribes live. It is vital to trek with a guide who is familiar with the area and hill-tribe etiquette. Typical routes, lasting two to three days, are marked below.

Tourists enjoying an elephant ride, Chiang Dao

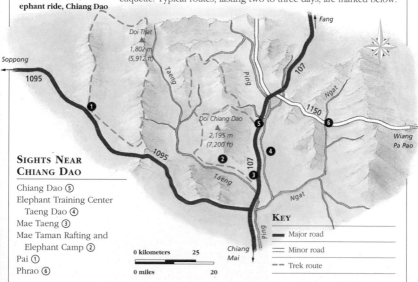

Fang

Doi That
1,802 m
(5,912 ft)

Soppong

1095

Doi Chiang Dao
2,195 m
(7,200 ft)

Wiang
Pa Pao

SIGHTS NEAR CHIANG DAO

Chiang Dao ⑤
Elephant Training Center
  Taeng Dao ④
Mae Taeng ③
Mae Taman Rafting and
  Elephant Camp ②
Pai ①
Phrao ⑥

KEY

━━ Major road

═══ Minor road

╌╌ Trek route

0 kilometers   25

0 miles   20

Chiang
Mai

Doi Suthep ⑩

ดอยสุเทพ

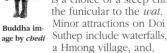

DOI SUTHEP is a much-visited, thickly forested mountain in the twin-peaked Doi Suthep-Doi Pui National Park. Near its 1,601-m (5,250-ft) summit is Wat Phra That Doi Suthep, one of the most revered Buddhist shrines in Northern Thailand. The mountain is also popular with birdwatchers and trekkers. From Chiang Mai, a paved road snakes up the hillside to a village with restaurants and souvenir shops. From here there is a choice of a steep climb or the funicular to the *wat*. Minor attractions on Doi Suthep include waterfalls, a Hmong village, and, farther along the road, the English-style gardens of Phuping Palace.

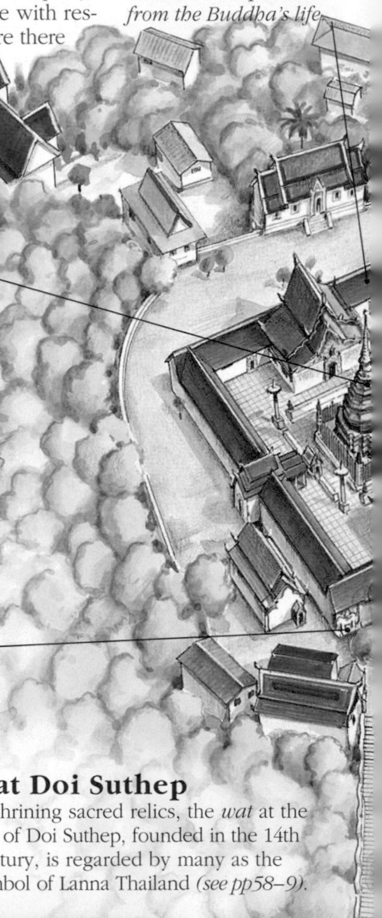

Buddha image by *chedi*

Murals in Cloister
The murals depict scenes from the Buddha's life.

★ **Central Chedi**
This striking gold-plated Lanna structure is a 16th-century extension of the original. The four multi-tiered gold umbrellas around it, onto which pilgrims apply gold leaf (see p26), are adorned with intricate filigree.

White Elephant Monument
According to legend, in the 1390s King Ku Na's elephant selected the site of the chedi by marching up the mountain, trumpeting and turning three times.

Wat Doi Suthep

Enshrining sacred relics, the *wat* at the top of Doi Suthep, founded in the 14th century, is regarded by many as the symbol of Lanna Thailand *(see pp58–9).*

Naga Staircase
Flanked by nagas, this sweeping staircase has 304 steps. The less energetic can take the funicular up to the temple.

STAR FEATURES

★ **Central Chedi**

★ **Panoramic Views**

Buddha Images in the Main Wihan

The gold Buddha images in the 16th-century wihan *are the most important within the temple complex. The huge image in the back is surrounded by several smaller ones.*

VISITORS' CHECKLIST

16 km (10 miles) NW of Chiang Mai, Chiang Mai province. 🛈 *TAT, Chiang Mai (0-5324-8604); Forestry Dept (0-2562-0760 or www. dnp.go.th for bungalows).* 🚌 *Chiang Mai then songthaew.* **Wat Doi Suthep** ⏱ *5:30am–7:30pm daily.* **Palace Gardens** ⏱ *8:30am–4pm Fri–Sun (but phone to check).* **Phuping Palace** ⛔ *to public.*

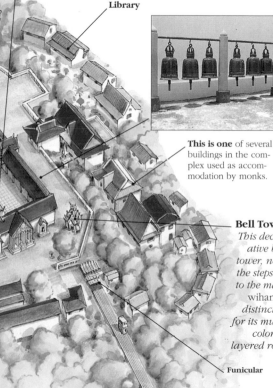

Library

Temple Bells

The original use of these small bells was to call the monks and the people to worship. Today, there is a constant tinkling from visitors ringing them for good luck.

This is one of several buildings in the complex used as accommodation by monks.

Bell Tower

This decorative bell tower, near the steps up to the main wihan, *is distinctive for its multicolored, layered roof.*

Funicular

WILDLIFE AROUND WAT DOI SUTHEP

Black-collared starling, a resident of the park

With its rich and varied wildlife, Doi Suthep-Doi Pui National Park is a great attraction for nature lovers. Despite the deforestation of the western side of the park due to agriculture and the building of tourist accommodations, the park is rich in plants, butterflies, and birds such as the green cochoa. Though people have killed or driven out many indigenous mammals, 60 species still live here, including the Burmese ferret badger.

★ Panoramic Views

From the edge of the temple complex there are breathtaking views of the forests of Doi Suthep-Doi Pui National Park and of Chiang Mai city, situated to the southeast.

Street-by-Street: Chiang Mai ⓲

เชียงใหม่

Typical Chiang Mai lantern

THAILAND'S SECOND most important city, Chiang Mai (literally, "new city"), was chosen in 1292 by King Mengrai to replace Chiang Rai *(see pp240–41)* as the capital of his Lanna Kingdom *(see pp58–9)*. Under Mengrai, Chiang Mai became a major base for Theravada Buddhism. It was during this period and the subsequent reign of King Tilok that many fine *wats* were built within the walled city, which is still the most atmospheric area. Today, visitors are increasingly drawn to Chiang Mai not only for its beautiful temples, but also for its excellent shopping and trekking facilities and upscale hotels and restaurants.

To Suan Dok Gate

Mengrai Kilns *(see p433)* sells a wide range of ceramics.

To Mengrai Kilns

SAMLAN

SOI 7

Old Chiang Mai
The first bridge across the Ping River was built in 1950. Others were later added to cope with the city's growth.

Wat Muen Ngon Kong
This wat *has exquisite latticework and a Lanna* chedi *topped by a Burmese finial.*

Wat Phra Chao Mengrai has a decorated ceremonial gate.

KEY

— — — Suggested route

STAR SIGHTS

★ Wat Phra Sing

★ Wat Chedi Luang

Wat Phan Waen
A typical Northern Thai temple, Wat Pan Waen is set within peaceful compounds, which provide relief from the city heat. The doors of the wihan *are decorated with religious images.*

★ Wat Phra Sing
This wat was built in 1345 to house King Kham Fu's ashes. The Wihan Lai Kham is a superb Lanna structure with carved and gilded pediments. Murals inside depict everyday life in 19th-century Chiang Mai.

VISITORS' CHECKLIST

Chiang Mai province. 🚶 84,000.
✈ 3 km (2 miles) SW of Chiang Mai. 🚃 Charoen Muang Rd.
🚌 Chiang Mai Arcade. 🛈 TAT, 105/1 Chiang Mai–Lamphun Rd (0-5324-8604). 🚉 main office: same address as TAT (0-5324-8974). 🚭 daily. 🎏 Flower Festival (Feb), Intakin Festival (May), Bo Sang Festival (Jan), Yi Peng Festival (Nov), Songkran (mid-Apr).

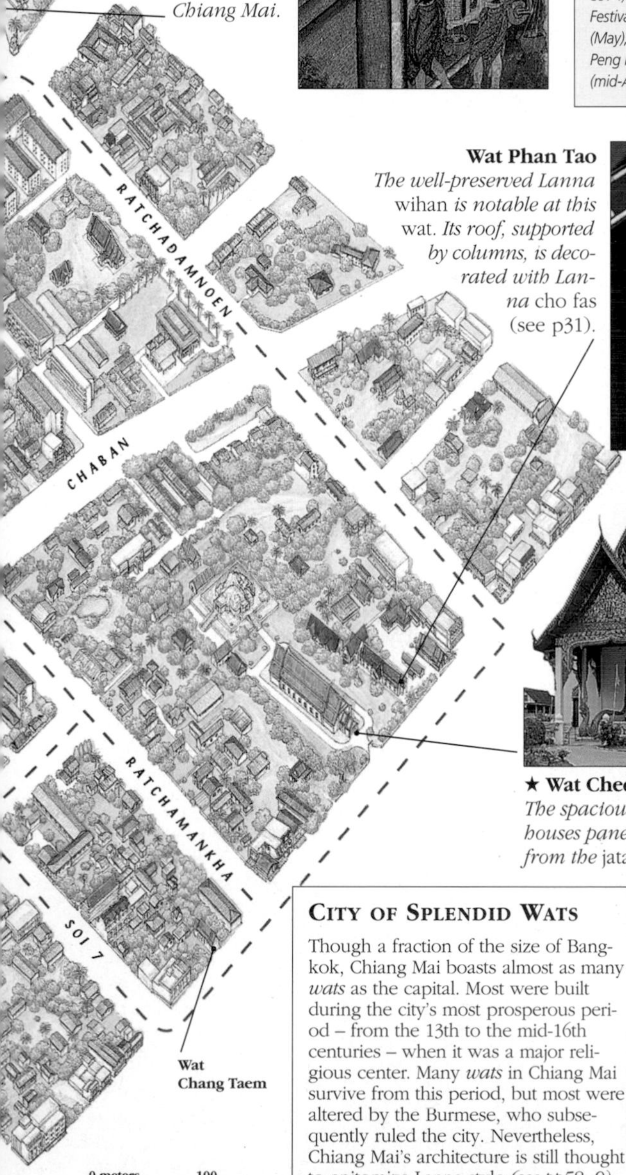

Wat Phan Tao
The well-preserved Lanna wihan is notable at this wat. Its roof, supported by columns, is decorated with Lanna cho fas *(see p31).*

★ Wat Chedi Luang
The spacious, triple-roofed wihan houses panels depicting scenes from the jataka *tales (see p26).*

RATCHADAMNOEN

CHABAN

RATCHAMANKHA

SOI 7

Wat Chang Taem

0 meters   100
0 yards   100

CITY OF SPLENDID WATS

Though a fraction of the size of Bangkok, Chiang Mai boasts almost as many *wats* as the capital. Most were built during the city's most prosperous period – from the 13th to the mid-16th centuries – when it was a major religious center. Many *wats* in Chiang Mai survive from this period, but most were altered by the Burmese, who subsequently ruled the city. Nevertheless, Chiang Mai's architecture is still thought to epitomize Lanna style *(see pp58–9)*, with features such as elaborate woodcarvings on temple pillars and doors.

The 19th-century Wihan Lai Kham, Wat Phra Sing

Exploring Chiang Mai

OFTEN CALLED the "rose of the North," Chiang Mai deserves its reputation. Its most important *wats*, notably Wat Chedi Luang and Wat Phra Sing, are situated within the old walled area of the city. The moat bounding the historic center is still intact, but the walls were largely destroyed during World War II. There is also much to see outside the old city, including Wat U Mong – one of the area's oldest forest *wats* – and the excellent National Museum. Northeast of the river is the old colonial sector, with its characteristic

Burmese carving

mansions. Chiang Mai thrives on its crafts trade *(see pp198–9)*, as shown by the wide range sold at Warorot Market and the Night Bazaar, and along Tha Phae Road.

One of the murals inside Wat Phra Sing's Wihan Lai Kham

🗿 Wat Phra Sing

วัดพระสิงห์

Samlan Rd, near Suan Dok Gate.
◯ *daily.*
Construction of this temple, the largest in Chiang Mai, began in 1345, though the *bot* dates from 1600. The Wihan Lai Kham ("gilded hall"), decorated with murals of everyday life, houses the revered golden Phra Buddha Sing. Like its namesakes in Bangkok *(see p84)* and Nakhon Si Thammarat *(see p369)*, the image is said to have originated in Sri Lanka.

🗿 Wat Chedi Luang

วัดเจดีย์หลวง

Phra Pok Klao Rd. ◯ *daily.*
Within the compound of this temple is the spot where King Mengrai was killed by lightning in 1317. The revered Emerald Buddha image was briefly housed in the *wat* in the 15th century – a previous attempt to bring it to Chiang Mai failed *(see p79)*. The *chedi*, once 90 m (295 ft) high, was damaged by an earthquake in 1465.

🗿 Wat Chiang Man

วัดเชียงมั่น

Off Ratcha Phakhinai Rd. ◯ *daily.*
King Mengrai dedicated this residence as a wat, the city's oldest, while his new capital was being built. It features Lanna teak pillars and a *chedi* surrounded by stone elephant heads. The *wihan* houses the Phra Kaeo Kao, thought to have been carved in Northern India in the 6th century BC.

⛩ Tha Phae Gate

ประตูท่าแพ

Tha Phae Gate marks the beginning of Tha Phae Road, the commercial hub of Chiang Mai. Located here are bookstores, department stores, and handicraft shops. Farther east, the road becomes Highway 1006, along which are shops and factories selling silk, celadon, lacquerware, and other crafts.

⛩ Suan Dok Gate

ประตูสวนดอก

This is the city's western gate, marking the start of Suthep Road, along which three important temples are situated.

🏬 Night Bazaar

ไนท์บาซาร์

Chang Khlan Rd. ◯ *6–11pm daily.*
With its wide range of goods at competitive prices, this easily rivals Bangkok's Chatuchak Market *(see p131)*. Inside are endless stalls selling hill-tribe crafts, leather goods, and clothing. The top floor specializes in antiques. Beware of fakes *(see p431)*, especially at the stalls outside the market. This is also a good place to try Chiang Mai's Burmese-influenced cuisine. Shops on Wualai Road, south of Chiang Mai Gate, sell the best silverware and textiles.

🏬 Warorot Market

ตลาดวโรรส

N of Tha Phae Rd. ◯ *daily.*
During the day, this covered market sells local food, clothing and hill-tribe crafts, often at lower prices than the Night Bazaar. Fruits, spices, and tasty dishes are all available. By night, it is the site of a colorful flower market.

Shoppers browsing around Chiang Mai's lively Warorot Market

ENVIRONS: There are many sights outside the city center that are worth a visit. Most can be reached by bicycle, motorbike, *songthaew*, or *tuk-tuk*. For longer excursions, most hotels and guesthouses offer trekking tours to hill-tribe villages *(see pp196–7)*. There are also many organized tour operators located on Tha Phae Road.

To the north of the city is the **Chiang Mai National Museum**. Its varied collection ranges from Haripunchai terra-cottas to Lanna heads of the Buddha, the largest of which is some 3 m (10 ft) tall.

Sited on the grounds of Chiang Mai University is the **Tribal Research Institute**. Its small museum and library detail the history of the area's ethnic minorities. Treks to hill-tribe villages can also be arranged here.

On Kaew Narawat Road, to the northeast of the city, is **McCormick Hospital**. This working hospital is typical of Chiang Mai's 19th- and 20th-

century architecture, much of which was built by missionaries and officials of the British teak logging companies who came here from Burma.

Just west of Suan Dok Gate, on Suthep Road, is **Wat Suan Dok**. The temple was built in 1383 to house relics of the Buddha, while the open-sided *wihan* was restored in the 1930s. The small *chedis* contain ashes of members of Chiang Mai's former royal family. Near the entrance is a school of Thai massage.

Farther along Suthep Road, in a picturesque forest, is the 14th-century **Wat U Mong**. Some of the original underground tunnels leading to the monks' cells can still be explored. Also of note is a disturbing image of a fasting Buddha. This temple and nearby **Wat Ram Poeng** offer meditation courses. The latter's library keeps versions of the Theravada Buddhist canon in English, Chinese, and other languages.

Buddha image, National Museum

Façade of the 14th-century Wat Suan Dok

Wat Chet Yot, distinctive for its seven-spired *chedi*, is set in spacious grounds. Its stuccoed design is based on the Mahabodhi Temple of Buddh Gaya in India, where the Buddha achieved Enlightenment.

🏛 Chiang Mai National Museum
Off Superhighway. ◯ *Wed–Sun.*
⬤ *public hols.* 🎟
🏛 Tribal Research Institute
Chiang Mai University, off Huai Kaew Rd. ◯ *Mon–Fri.* ⬤ *public hols.*

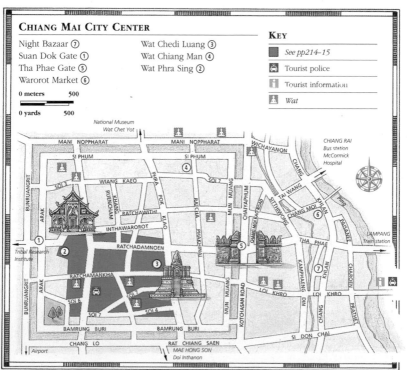

CHIANG MAI CITY CENTER

Night Bazaar ⑦
Suan Dok Gate ①
Tha Phae Gate ⑤
Warorot Market ⑥

Wat Chedi Luang ③
Wat Chiang Man ④
Wat Phra Sing ②

KEY

▮ *See pp214–15*

🚓 *Tourist police*

ℹ *Tourist information*

🛕 *Wat*

0 meters 500
0 yards 500

Doi Saket ⓬
ดอยสะเก็ด

Off Hwy 1019, 16 km (10 miles) NE of Chiang Mai, Chiang Mai province. **i** *TAT, Chiang Mai (0-5324-8604).* **ⓧ** *Chiang Mai, then songthaew.* **◯** *daily.*

FORMING A TRIANGLE with Bo Sang and San Kamphaeng, the mountain of Doi Saket is an ideal sight to combine with these two towns on a day trip from Chiang Mai.

The main reason for visiting Doi Saket is its hilltop temple, Wat Doi Saket, which offers stunning views of the Chiang Mai valley. The *wat* is reached by a steep staircase of 300 steps, flanked on either side by a *naga*. The temple complex includes a modern *wihan*, painted in red and gold, and a white *chedi*. There is a huge, seated Buddha on the hill top and seven smaller Buddhas, one for each day of the week.

Red and gold modern *wihan* of the hill top Wat Doi Saket

Women constructing ornamental umbrellas in the village of Bo Sang

Bo Sang ⓭
บ่อสร้าง

9 km (6 miles) E of Chiang Mai, Chiang Mai province. **👥** *2,600.* **ⓧ** *from Chiang Mai.* **i** *TAT, Chiang Mai (0-5324-8604).* **◯** *daily.* **🎪** *Umbrella Fair (Jan).*

BO SANG IS KNOWN throughout Thailand as the "umbrella village" on account of the decorative umbrellas produced here. The village is made up almost entirely of shops and factories involved in this craft.

Each umbrella has a wooden handle, bamboo ribs, and a covering of oiled rice paper, silk, or cotton. Craftsmen will usually add names or a personalized design in bold colors if requested. The annual fair includes competitions, exhibitions, and a beauty contest.

Other handicrafts, including silverware, celadon (a grayish-green porcelain), and lacquerware, are also sold here.

Aside from its umbrella making, Bo Sang is also the heart of a farming community. In the wet season (June–October), the rice fields are a deep green color. From November to January, the fields dry out and turn golden. Farmers then thresh the rice by hand.

Many houses in and around Bo Sang are traditional, wooden Northern Thai structures *(see p32)* with spacious rooms. They are typically built on stilts and set in small gardens.

San Kamphaeng ⓮
สันกำแพง

13 km (9 miles) E of Chiang Mai, Chiang Mai province. **👥** *44,000.* **ⓧ** *from Chiang Mai.* **i** *TAT, Chiang Mai (0-5324-8604).* **◯** *daily.*

THIS VILLAGE, with its old, wooden buildings and narrow streets, is renowned for its silk and handicraft products.

There are many factories

NAGAS: MYTHICAL SERPENTS

Naga figures, seen throughout Thailand, are protective serpents. Acting as guardians against bad spirits, they often flank the walls of temples or the staircases up to them, and may also be carved on roofs, doors, gables, and windows. The significance of *nagas* is deep-rooted throughout Buddhist Asia, though their meaning may vary slightly according to the country, with overlaps between Buddhism and Hinduism. In Buddhism, their origins can be traced back to an episode in the *jataka* tales *(see p27)* in which a *garuda*, or mythical bird, attacks and subdues a *naga* that is trying to harm the Buddha. The *naga* subsequently becomes the Buddha's guardian. Its protective powers are shown when Mucilinda, a king of the *nagas*, grows several heads to shelter the Buddha from a thunderstorm. *Nagas* are also believed to control rainfall and are worshiped as givers of water during Songkran *(see p226)*.

Two-headed *naga* of Wat Chedi Luang, Chiang Saen *(see p238)*

Geyser bursting through the ground at the San Kamphaeng Hot Springs

here selling good-quality silk, teak furniture, silverware, lacquerware, jade, or celadon. Prices can be high, though bargaining *(see p455)* often reduces the cost significantly. An interesting feature of most of the silk factories are their exhibits of the silk-making process. The whole procedure is shown *(see pp256–7)*, from silk moths, through the unraveling of the cocoons, to the weaving of dyed silk thread on traditional wooden looms.

ENVIRONS: To the east of San Kamphaeng, just past the village of Mu Song, are the caves of **Tam Muang On**, with impressive stalactites and stalagmites. Farther east are the **San Kamphaeng Hot Springs**, offering therapeutic baths in hot mineral water. Here, geysers spurt to incredible heights.

⛩ Tam Muang On
14 km (8.5 miles) E of San Kamphaeng.
◯ *daily.*
⛩ San Kamphaeng Hot Springs
20 km (12.5 miles) E of San Kamphaeng. ◯ *daily.* ▨

Lamphun ⑮
ลำพูน

Lamphun province. ▨ *97,000.* ▨
▨ ⓘ *TAT, Chiang Mai (0-5324-8604).*
▨ *daily.* ▨ *Lamyai Festival (Aug).*

THIS ANCIENT TOWN was the capital of the Haripunchai Kingdom from AD 750–1281. Today, Lamphun is made up of large wooden houses beside the Kuang River and is characterized by its peaceful atmosphere, ancient temples, and surrounding countryside of rice fields.

Lamphun's most important temple is **Wat Phra That Haripunchai**. The present compound was probably founded in AD 1044 by King Athitayarai of Haripunchai, though the 46-m (150-ft) high central *chedi*, topped by a nine-tier umbrella of pure gold, is thought to date from 897. In the 1930s, the temple was renovated by Khrubaa Siwichai, one of the most revered monks

Buddha head, Lamphun National Museum

in Northern Thailand. One unusual structure is the rare, pyramid-shaped *chedi* in the northwest of the compound. The large *bot* houses a reclining Buddha image, while a 15th-century Lanna Buddha is kept in the main *wihan*. Adjoining it is a 19th-century library, with a staircase flanked by *nagas*. To the right of the library is an open pavilion displaying a huge gong cast in 1860, alleged to be the largest in the world. Outside the main compound is a smaller *bot*, inside of which is a so-called "happy Buddha," a fat, smiling Chinese-style image.

The nearby **Lamphun National Museum** is small but excellent. It has carvings and artifacts from many periods, especially the Dvaravati, Haripunchai, and Lanna kingdoms. Modern artifacts include an ornate black and gold howdah *(see pp198–9)* and *naga* decorations. The collection of Buddha images covers many schools of sculpture.

Wat Chama Thewi (or Wat Kukut), just west of Lamphun on Highway 1015, is noted for its two *chedis*, thought to be among the oldest in Thailand. Both built in 1218, they are the last surviving examples of Dvaravati architecture. The larger, tiered structure is adorned with Buddha images, and the smaller one is decorated with Hindu gods.

⌂ Lamphun National Museum
Inthayongyot Rd, opposite Wat Phra That Haripunchai. ◯ *Wed–Sun.* ▨

ENVIRONS: Pasang, a small town 30 km (19 miles) south of Lamphun, produces excellent cottonwear of unique designs, especially sarongs and shirts. They are sold through many outlets in the town. Lamphun province, in particular the town of Nong Chang Kheun, to the north, is renowned for its *lamyai*, or longan *(see p129)* fruit. It is celebrated in a festival that features competitions and a Miss Lamyai beauty contest.

Doi Inthanon National Park ⑯

อุทยานแห่งชาติดอยอินทนนท์

The rare *hypericum garrettii*

DOI INTHANON, at 2,565 m (8,400 ft), is the highest mountain in Thailand. It is located in the 272-sq km (105-sq mile) Doi Inthanon National Park, and, only 58 km (36 miles) from Chiang Mai, is a popular destination for one-day excursions. The park has many types of habitat and a wide range of mammals, such as leopard cats, pangolins, and flying squirrels. The area is also popular for bird-watching, being home to nearly 400 bird species, many from North Asia (including mountain hawk eagles and Eurasian woodcocks). Karen and Hmong peoples *(see pp196–7)* also live here. In contrast to the rest of Thailand, the climate on Doi Inthanon can be chilly, so visitors to the park are advised to take warm clothing.

Twin Chedis
This shrine is inside one of th twin chedis of Phra That Nap amataneedon, built for King Bhumibol's 60th birthday.

Spectacular View
Walkers on Doi Inthanon are treated to impressive views. On a clear day it is possible to see for many miles over the forested landscape.

Doi Inthanon
2,565 m (8,400 ft)

Siriph
water

Mae Pan
waterfall

MAE CHAEM

Sphagnum Moss
Doi Inthanon's cool climate allows plants such as mosses, ferns, and lichens to thrive. At the mountain's summit, sphagnum mosses form a kind of bog, the only habitat of this kind in Thailand.

Montane evergreen forests are found on the upper levels of Doi Inthanon.

Timber Beetle
For protection, this beetle's markings ape the warning coloration of wasps. Its larvae are hatched in the trunks or branches of trees.

0 kilometers   2

0 miles   2

Orchids

Wild orchids are in abundance on Doi Inthanon. On the higher slopes of the mountain, 2,500 m (8,200 ft) above sea level, pink and white orchids (see p210) can be seen draped over the branches of evergreen trees.

VISITORS' CHECKLIST

Chiang Mai province. Park HQ off Hwy 1009 (which is off Hwy 108), S of Chiang Mai. *TAT, Chiang Mai (0-5324-8604); Forestry Dept, Bangkok (0-2562-0760 or www.dnp.go.th for bungalow bookings).* from Chom Thong to Mae Klang falls, then songthaew to Doi Inthanon summit.. 6am–6pm daily.

White-Crested Laughing Thrush

This bird takes its name from its distinctive white crest. Its common habitat is the forest crowning the upper slopes of Doi Inthanon.

Deciduous and submontane forests are found in low-lying areas of the national park.

Vachiratarn waterfall

Borichinda cave

Mae Klang waterfall

CHIANG MAI

Chom Thong

HOT

Hmong Tribespeople

The Hmong (see p196) have been here since the 1890s. Their slash-and-burn agriculture has led to deforestation, but government programs to reduce this are now underway.

Mae Ya Waterfall

This is estimated to be the highest waterfall in the whole of Thailand. Falling over 250 m (820 ft), Mae Ya waterfall is also one of the most beautiful sights at Doi Inthanon.

KEY

═══	Road
– –	Trail
–·–	Park border
ℹ	Park headquarters
🛆	Camping and bungalows
☆	Vista

Rural landscape around Hot, a town in the Ping River Valley

Ping River Valley ⑰
หุบเขาแม่น้ำปิง

Chiang Mai province. ℹ *TAT, Chiang Mai (0-5324-8604).* 🚌 *Chiang Mai, then songthaew.*

Nearly 600 km (370 miles) long, the Ping River is one of the major waterways in Northern Thailand. It rises on the Burmese border and flows on to the Bhumibol Reservoir before merging with the Wang, Yom, and Nan rivers. This becomes the Chao Phraya River at Nakhon Sawan, in the Central Plains. The valley is a rural area where traditional life can still be observed.

Chom Thong, just south of Chiang Mai, at the junction of Highway 108 and the road to Doi Inthanon National Park *(see pp220–21)*, is a small but busy town. It boasts one major sight, **Wat Phra That Si Chom Thong**. The *wat* was built to enshrine a relic of the Buddha and is still an important pilgrimage site for Buddhists. Many will try to make the journey at least once a year. This *wat* is also widely considered to be one of the most beautiful in Northern Thailand. The gilded *chedi*, built in 1451, is Burmese in design, as is the mid-16th-century *bot*, which features intricate woodcarvings

depicting flowers, birds, and *nagas (see p218)*. A meditation center and a room displaying thrones, religious antiques, and weapons are also located within the temple complex.

The deep Chaem River Valley, west of Chom Thong, is known locally for its many varieties of butterfly and moth. Several villages, spread along the twisting road within the valley, are known collectively as the town of **Mae Chaem**. The town, once famous for weaving, is now modernizing rapidly. Its main temple, **Wat Pa Daet**, is worth visiting for its well-preserved Lanna buildings and extensive murals.

At the southern end of the valley is the small town of **Hot**. Originally located 15 km (10 miles) farther downstream, the town was relocated to its present site in 1964, when the land was flooded to form the Bhumibol Reservoir. Today, this reservoir is a major source of Thailand's electricity. Ruins of the original town can still be seen beside the reservoir, though they are limited to only a few *chedis*. Excavation of the site has turned up amulets, stucco carvings and gold jewelry. These artifacts are now on display in Chiang Mai's National Museum *(see p217)*. Modern-day Hot, meanwhile, is an important market town and a useful staging post for journeys westward to the town of Mae Sariang.

Wooden carving on the *bot* of Wat Phra That Si Chom Thong

Mae Sariang ⑱
แม่สะเรียง

Mae Hong Son province. 🚶 *48,000.* 🚌 ℹ *TAT, Chiang Mai (0-5324-8604).* 🚤 *daily.*

Mae Sariang is a small, pleasant town on the Yuam River. The area has long historical links with nearby Burma, a fact that is reflected in Mae Sariang's architecture and by its large community of Burmese Muslims. People of the Karen hill tribe – the area's main ethnic group – can be seen in the central market.

Two temples near the bus station have Burmese features: multilayered roofs and vivid orange and yellow exterior ornamentation. **Wat Chong Sung** (also called Wat Uthayarom) was built in 1896, while **Wat Si Bunruang** dates from 1939.

Environs: The area around Mae Sariang is mountainous and forested, with many winding roads. Organized trips by boat or *songthaew* (which can be arranged in town) make the 45-km (30-mile) journey from Mae Sariang to **Mae Sam Laep**, a Karen settlement on the Burmese border next to the Salawin River. This river was once infamous for drug running and gem smuggling. Today, Mae Sam Laep is a staging post for the (mostly illegal) teak log trade. Political troubles in Burma have made this area a zone for refugees, though some Burmese minorities, such as the Lawa, have lived here longer than Thais.

***Chedi* of the 19th-century Wat Chong Sung in Mae Sariang**

The History of Opium in Thailand

Opium was first grown in Northern Thailand in the late 19th century, when hill tribes *(see pp196–7)* arrived from Southern China, where the drug was a major commodity. Grown on poor soil at high altitudes and easily transported, it was in fact their most profitable cash crop. Opium production was outlawed in Thailand in 1959, but flourished nonetheless during the Vietnam War. It was during this lucrative period that power struggles erupted

Opium poppies

for control of the Golden Triangle's *(see pp236–7)* poppy fields. The KMT *(see p232)*, allowed by the Thai government to control the illicit drugs trade, and the Shan United Army, based in Burma, were the largest of the many contenders, who also included the Thai, Burmese, and Lao armies. Opium production has been cut by more than 80 percent since the 1960s, and most hill tribes now grow other crops. However, Thailand is still used as a channel for opium produced in nearby countries.

Smoking opium *in custom-built dens became popular in parts of Asia – especially China – in the 19th century.*

Britain and China fought the Opium Wars of 1839–42 and 1856–60 over British rights to import opium from India. After the wars the drug was legalized in China and freely traded.

Short sickles, used to score poppy heads, are just some of a number of poppy-cultivating implements exhibited in the House of Opium.

The thin hillside soil easily supports poppies, which favor the low-nutrient, high-alkaline conditions at altitudes of over 1,000 m (3,300 ft).

OPIUM PRODUCTION

This mural in the House of Opium Museum, Sop Ruak *(see p238)*, is one of a series showing traditional poppy harvesting for opium production, a process normally carried out in December and January. The museum also houses artifacts depicting the war between the KMT and the Shan United Army.

Since the 1980s, new cash crops, including cabbage, tea, and coffee, have begun to replace poppies grown for opium production. Today, fields of these new crops are a common sight in Northern Thailand.

King Bhumibol, concerned about opiate addiction and the illegal drug trade in his country, has been particularly active in encouraging replacement crops.

Wat Phra That Lampang Luang 🔟
วัดพระธาตุลำปางหลวง

Buddha in Wihan Phra Phut
A huge Buddha image sits inside the 13th-century wihan, *the oldest building on the site.*

China cow by the main *chedi*, where devotees make merit

ONE OF THE MOST famous temples in Northern Thailand, Wat Phra That Lampang Luang is also one of the most attractive. The main buildings were constructed in the late 15th century on the site of an 8th-century fortress. This had been built on a mound to protect it from attack and was further fortified by three parallel earthen ramparts separated by moats. The ramparts are still visible in the village around the present *wat*. In 1736 a local hero, Tip Chang, successfully defended the temple from the Burmese. The buildings are distinctive for their graceful architecture and richly colored interiors, while the revered Phra Kaeo Don Tao image, allegedly carved from the same jadeite block as the Emerald Buddha *(see p79)*, is kept in the museum behind the main complex.

Wihan Phra Phut
With its beautifully carved façade and two-tiered roof, this wihan, *from 1802, is a masterpiece of Lanna architecture.*

Bodhi tree

Five Buddhas in Wihan Luang
The huge, open-sided main wihan, *which dates from 1496, has an elegant, three-tiered roof. Inside are five seated Buddha images.*

Main entrance

Main Staircase
Flanked by nagas, *this stairway leads up to a 15th-century ceremonial gatehouse.*

Ho Phra Phuttabat
*This small, elevated
mondop houses a
sculpture of the
Buddha's Footprint,
which is worshipped
by pilgrims during
important festivals.
Women may not
enter the building.*

Bot

Wihan Phra Chao Sila

★ Main Chedi
*The subtle green and blue
hues of the 15th-century
chedi are due to centuries of
rainfall, which have oxidized
the copper. Inside is a hair,
said to be from the Buddha.*

★ Murals in Wihan Nam Tam
*These faded murals, which depict
16th-century life and scenes from
the jataka tales (see p26), adorn the
walls of what may be Thailand's
oldest surviving wooden structure.*

Wihan Ton Kaew

Pillar Detail
*This black lac-
quered pillar,
inlaid with
gold, is typical
of the intricate
decoration of
the whole tem-
ple complex.*

**Ku in Wihan
Luang**
*The Buddha
image, Phra
Chao Lang
Thong, which
dates from
1563, sits in
this gilded
brick ku (Lao-
style prang).*

Horse-drawn carriages, the main form of transport in Lampang

Lampang ⑳
ลำปาง

Lampang province. 🚗 *94,000.*
✈ 🚉 🚌 ℹ *TAT, Chiang Mai*
(0-5324-8604). 🏛 *daily.* 🎭 *Luang*
Wiang Lakon (Feb).

THE SECOND LARGEST TOWN in Northern Thailand, Lampang is still growing rapidly as a trading center. It offers much of the historic interest of Chiang Mai, but without the overt commercialization. Lampang is also a good base for excursions and travel within Northern Thailand.

The town was originally inhabited in the 7th century. The following century, when it was still called Kelang Nakorn, it became part of the Haripunchai Empire, which was centered on Lamphun *(see p219).* In the 19th century, British traders came here from Burma and turned the town into a teak production center, bringing Burmese workers with them. The result was the many teak houses and Burmese-style temples seen throughout the town today. Teak furniture is just one of the traditional crafts still produced in Lampang; others are cottonware and ceramics.

Modern Lampang is distinctive for its brightly colored horse-drawn carriages, another surviving tradition. This mode of transportation was introduced to Lampang in the 19th century, and it is the only town in Thailand that uses it.

One of the most important temples in Northern Thailand is **Wat Phra That Lampang Luang** *(see pp224–5),* to the southwest of the town, which is famous for its impressive 19th-century murals.

Lampang town focuses on the south side of the Wang River, although the main sights are found to the north of it. Of its temples, the most interesting is **Wat Phra Kaeo Don Tao.** The *wat* is thought to have been built about the same time the town was founded, but only the 50-m (165-ft) *chedi* survives from the original buildings. The distinctive *mondop* is notable for its nine-tier teak roof with intricate carvings and a bronze Buddha in the Mandalay style.

Between 1436 and 1468 the temple housed the revered Emerald Buddha, or Phra Kaeo *(see p77),* which was later moved to Bangkok's Wat Phra Kaeo. During the same period, a similar jasper Buddha image, now in Wat Phra That Lampang Luang, was kept here. Within the compound is the **Lanna Museum,** displaying religious Lanna artifacts.

Ban Sao Nak ("many pillars house"), southeast of Wat Phra Kaeo Don Tao, is a Lanna structure built in 1896. It takes its name from the 116 square teak pillars supporting the building. Now a museum, it is furnished with Burmese and Thai antiques. The sumptuous decoration includes lacquerware, ceramics, and silverware. **Wat Pongsanuk Tai,** to the west of Ban Sao Nak, is a distinctive late 18th-century

Interior of Ban Sao Nak, Lampang, decorated with antique crafts

---

SONGKRAN FESTIVITIES IN THE NORTH

Celebrated nationwide, but most exuberantly in and around Chiang Mai, Songkran *(see p42)* is one of Thailand's major festivals. Held over three days from April 12th–14th (though celebrations carry on until the 15th in towns such as Chiang Mai), Songkran marks the start of the Buddhist New Year. This public holiday has, over the centuries, evolved from a purely religious event, in which Buddha images are bathed with water to purify them, into a much greater celebration of water in the hot season. Nowadays, buckets of water are thrown over everyone in the streets (unsuspecting tourists make the best targets). Some of Songkran's original customs, such as younger Thais paying respect to their elders and monks by sprinkling their hands with perfumed water, are also maintained.

River procession in Lampang, part of the Songkran festivities

Performance at the Thai Elephant Conservation Center near Lampang

Lanna temple with a copper *chedi*. An enclosure in the *mondop* contains a Bodhi tree that is surrounded by four Buddha images.

The 19th-century Burmese-style **Wat Si Chum**, located in the south of the city, is constructed mostly from beautifully carved teak. The exquisite lacquerwork inside the main chamber shows life in Lampang during the 19th century.

Lanna Museum
Phra Kaeo Rd. ☎ 0-5321-1364.
○ daily.

Ban Sao Nak
Ratwana Rd. ○ daily.

Thai Elephant Conservation Center ㉑
ศูนย์ฝึกลูกช้าง

Off Hwy 11, 38 km (24 miles) NW of Lampang, Lampang province.
i TAT, Chiang Mai (0-5324-8604).
☎ 0-5422-7051. 🚌 🚌 Lampang, then songthaew. ○ daily; shows 9:30–11am (2pm Sat–Sun).

ONE OF THE BEST elephant training camps in Northern Thailand, this one is less tourist-oriented than many others. About 12 animals, three to five years old, arrive here each year to be trained, and there are about 100 in total. Although their ability peaks between the ages of 40 and 50, the elephants may remain at the camp until the official retirement age of 60.

During the five-year training period the elephants learn a variety of tasks in the nearby forest, including stacking, carrying, and pushing logs.

Nowadays, such chores are part of the performances put on for tourists. Visitors can feed the elephants fruit. There is also a small museum focusing on the culture and the history of elephants in Thailand *(see p243)*.

ENVIRONS: On the opposite side of the highway is the **Thung Kwian Forest Market**. It sells a wide range of wild plants and medicinal and culinary herbs, as well as lizards, beetles, and snakes. Recent government campaigns have attempted to end the sale of endangered species *(see p209)* at the market, though some, such as pangolins (scaly anteaters), are still sold here.

Poster for Thai Elephant Conservation Center

Thung Kwian Forest Market
Off Hwy 11, 35 km (22 miles) NW of Lampang. ○ daily.

Uttaradit ㉒
อุตรดิตถ์

Uttaradit province. 🏠 102,000. 🚉
🚌 **i** TAT, Chiang Rai (0-5371-7433).
🚢 daily. 🎪 Langsat Fair (Oct).

THIS PROVINCIAL CAPITAL, relatively free of modern development and tourist paraphernalia, features on few visitors' itineraries. Nevertheless, the town's location makes it a convenient staging post between the North Central Plains and Northern Thailand.

Uttaradit rose to prominence during the Sukhothai era, and just prior to the collapse of the kingdom at the end of the 13th century the town marked its northern border. Uttaradit's most famous citizen was King Taksin, who was born here in the mid-18th century. He reunited Thailand after the Burmese sacked Ayutthaya in 1767. The town is made up of old teak buildings and narrow streets. The main temple of interest is **Wat Tha Thanon**, behind the train station. Inside is the Luang Pho Phet, a revered bronze Lanna Buddha.

To the west of Uttaradit is **Wat Phra Boromathat**, which is also known as Wat That Thung Yang. Its *wihan* is an example of the Lao Luang Prabang architectural style.

Uttaradit province is famous for the quality of its agricultural produce, particularly the *langsat* fruit.

Busy main street of Uttaradit, the birthplace of King Taksin

FAR NORTH

THE FAR NORTH *of Thailand is known as the Golden Triangle –
the meeting point of Thailand, Burma, and Laos and an area
historically associated with opium production. Nowadays,
this picturesque region with numerous hill-tribe villages attracts large
numbers of trekkers. Less well known delights in the Far North include,
southeast of the Golden Triangle, quiet towns such as Phrae and Nan.*

The fertile flood plains of the Mekong, which touch the tip of the Far North before running east into Laos, contrast with the breathtaking beauty of the mountains in the west and east of the area. Here can be found remote villages inhabited by hill tribes such as the Mien and Akha, who still preserve their traditional way of life. There are also settlements populated by ex-Chinese Nationalist soldiers and their descendants, who migrated here after Mao Tse-tung's Communist army won the Chinese civil war in 1949.

Chiang Rai is the main town in the Far North. Though not picturesque, it has a few sights and is used as a trekking base. Of greater interest are the towns strung out by the Mekong along the Burmese and Lao borders, including the ancient city of Chiang Saen and Chiang Khong, a Thai Lue settlement.

Most visitors to northern Thailand travel from Chiang Mai to Chiang Rai, and then north to the Golden Triangle; thus some sights to the east are relatively unknown. The old, walled settlement of Phrae, for instance, with some of Thailand's largest teak buildings, is visited by few tourists, despite being easily accessible from the Central Plains and Chiang Mai. The town of Nan is more remote, set in a valley far from the main highway to the Golden Triangle. The diversion is worthwhile, if only to see the murals at Wat Phumin. Northeast of here, Doi Phu Kha National Park offers superb birdwatching. To the south of Nan, and far from the beaten track, is extraordinarily diverse scenery ranging from the earth pillars of Sao Din and Phrae Muang Phi to the vast Sirikit Reservoir.

Thai Lue farmer plowing the fields in the time-honored way

◁ Young Lisu women sporting their elaborate and colorful traditional costumes

Exploring the Far North

THE NORTHERNMOST region of Thailand is, for many people, synonymous with the Golden Triangle. This semimythical region around the meeting point of three national borders still conjures up images of untamed wilderness, remote hill-tribe villages, and fugitive opium barons. There remains more than a grain of truth in this reputation, but the Far North is also developing rapidly as a tourist destination, centered around the one-time capital of the Lanna Kingdom, Chiang Rai. The major attraction for visitors is the spectacular and varied geography of the region, best explored by foot or motorbike. Touring through the mighty forested mountains along the Burmese and Lao borders, and beside the winding Mekong, as it skirts the tip of the region, is a richly rewarding experience.

SIGHTS AT A GLANCE

KEY

▬	Major road
▭	Minor road
▬	Scenic route
〰	River
✲	Vista

TACHILEK
MAE SAI 5
DOI 4
6
MAE SALONG 3
1089
GOLDEN TRIANGLE TOUR
THA TON 2
CHIANG RAI
10
FANG 1
Chiang Mai
118
MAE SARUAI 11
100
Phrao
WIANG PA PAO 12
118
Chiang Mai
PHAYAO
120
1035
Lampang
Sukhothai

0 kilometers   25
0 miles   15

A gathering of Lisu tribeswomen in traditional costume

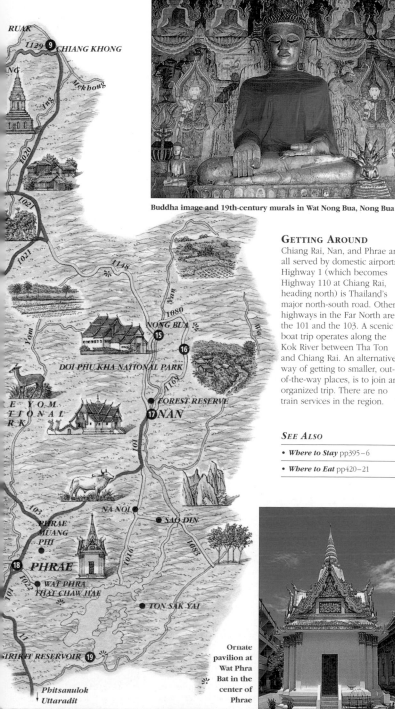

Buddha image and 19th-century murals in Wat Nong Bua, Nong Bua

GETTING AROUND

Chiang Rai, Nan, and Phrae are all served by domestic airports. Highway 1 (which becomes Highway 110 at Chiang Rai, heading north) is Thailand's major north-south road. Other highways in the Far North are the 101 and the 103. A scenic boat trip operates along the Kok River between Tha Ton and Chiang Rai. An alternative way of getting to smaller, out-of-the-way places, is to join an organized trip. There are no train services in the region.

SEE ALSO

- **Where to Stay** pp395–6
- **Where to Eat** pp420–21

Ornate pavilion at Wat Phra Bat in the center of Phrae

Karen tribespeople trading their wares at Fang's daily market

Fang ❶

ฝาง

Chiang Mai province. 👥 *111,000.*
🚌 *from Chiang Mai.* 🛈 *TAT, Chiang
Mai (0-5324-8604).* ▲ *daily.*

T HIS TOWN was founded as
a trading center in 1268
by King Mengrai, who took
advantage of the site's location at the head of a valley.
At the beginning of the 19th
century the town was des-
troyed by Burmese raiders,
and it lay deserted until 1880.
Today Fang is effectively a
border town between the
areas inhabited by Thais and
hill tribes *(see pp196–7).* The
local Mien, Karen, and Lahu
tribes sell their goods at
Fang's market, and this has
made it an important
trading center.

   Fang is characterized by
teak houses. The influence
of nearby Burma is evi-
dent in many struc-
tures, such as **Wat
Jong Paen**, located
in the north of
town. The most
impressive tem-
ple in Fang, it
features a Bur-
mese-style, multi-
roofed *wihan.*

ENVIRONS: Drug trading in the
Fang area has been significant
in the past, and fighting between rival drug factions in
Burma still occasionally spills
across the border. It is wise to
check the situation with the
local tourist office before
venturing on a guided trek.
Sights in the region include,

some 10 km (6 miles) west of
Fang, sulfur springs, whose
natural energy is used to
power a nearby geothermal
plant. To the southwest of
Fang, Highway 1249 leads to
the peak of **Doi Ang Khang**,
via several Lisu, Lahu, and
Hmong hill-tribe villages.

Tha Ton ❷

ท่าตอน

Chiang Mai province. 👥 *21,000.*
🚌 *from Chiang Mai to Fang, then*
songthaew. 🛈 *TAT, Chiang Mai
(0-5324-8604).*

L OCATED ON A BEND in the Kok
River, picturesque Tha Ton
is essentially a staging post for
riverboats that make regular
trips from here to Chiang
Rai. Excursions can be arranged at guesthouses in
town, and may often be
combined with visits
to nearby tribal vil-
lages or hot springs.
Tha Ton's chief tour-
ist attraction is **Wat
Tha Ton**, which is
notable for a huge
white Buddha
with a striking
golden topknot.
The temple domi-
nates the town from its hillside location to the west,
offering panoramic views of
the surrounding countryside.

**Imposing white Buddha
overlooking Tha Ton**

ENVIRONS: The road leading
from Tha Ton to Doi Mae Salong, 43 km (26 miles) to the
northeast, takes in impressive
mountain scenery and villages
along the Burmese border.

Mae Salong (Santikhiree) ❸

ดอยแม่สะลอง (ดอยสันติคีรี)

Chiang Rai province. 👥 *15,000.* 🚌
Chiang Rai, then songthaew. 🛈 *TAT,
Chiang Rai (0-5371-7433).* ▲ *daily.*

O NE OF THE most important
settlements in the recent
history of Northern Thailand,
the hillside town of Mae Salong
is also one of the most scenic.
Mae Salong was founded in
1962 by the Kuomintang
(KMT), or Chinese Nationalist
Army, following their defeat
in China by Mao Zedong in
1949. It became a center for
exiled Chinese soldiers, who
used it as a base for incur-
sions into China. The Thai
military agreed to let the
KMT stay if they helped to
suppress Communism, which
they believed would become
rife among the hill tribes at the
time of the Vietnam War. In
return for their help, the KMT
were allowed to control and
tax the local opium trade. As
a result, the area around Mae
Salong was relatively lawless
and dangerous until the 1980s.
   When Khun Sa, the opium
warlord *(see p223),* retreated
to Burma in the early 1980s,
the Thai government began to
have some success in pacify-
ing the area. This was helped
when, soon after the end of
this turbulent period, Mae
Salong was officially renamed
Santikhiree ("hill of peace"), in
an attempt to rid the town of
its former image. The new term
is used for both the town and
the 1,200-m (3,950-ft) peak

**Chinese medicinal herbs and spices
for sale at Mae Salong market**

Modern temple on the hill top of Doi Mae Salong

that rises above it, Doi Mae Salong. A temple was recently built at the summit, giving spectacular views of the surrounding rolling hills, which are dotted with hill-tribe villages. Akha and Mien villagers can be seen at the market in Mae Salong, but the town's main population is made up of old KMT soldiers and their descendants. The sight of low, Chinese-style houses made of bamboo and the sound of Yunnanese (a Chinese dialect) give the overall impression that Mae Salong is more of a Chinese than Thai town.

A road built to Mae Salong in the early 1980s made the settlement less isolated. Opium production is now suppressed, having been replaced by new cash crops such as cabbage, tea, and Chinese herbs and medicines. This produce is sold in the town's market.

Doi Tung **4**

ดอยตุง

Chiang Rai province. *TAT, Chiang Rai (0-5371-7433).* *from Mae Chan or Mae Sai to turn-off for Doi Tung, then songthaew to summit.*

THE MOUNTAIN of Doi Tung is an impressive limestone outcrop dominating the Mekong flood plain near Mae Sai. The narrow road snakes through beautiful monsoon forest, winding its way up to the 1,800-m (5,900-ft) peak. On a clear day the views of Burma and lowland Thailand from the summit are especially stunning.

The name of the mountain means "flag peak," so called because in AD 911 King Achutarat of Chiang Saen ordered a giant flag to be flown from the summit to mark the site where two *chedis* were to be built, allegedly to house a piece of the Buddha's collarbone. Still a major pilgrimage site, the *chedis* are at the heart of **Wat Phra That Doi Tung**, which was renovated in the early 1900s. Also here is a large, rotund Chinese-style Buddha image. Pilgrims throw coins into its navel to make merit.

The area around Doi Tung has historically been the site of opium production, the poppy fields guarded by hill tribespeople and the KMT. In recent years the area has become the focus for a rural development project aimed at increasing central government control over the area. In 1988 **Doi Tung Royal Villa** was built on the mountain as part of a plan to increase tourism in the area and to discourage nearby hill tribes from producing opium. Originally a summer residence for the late mother of King Bhumibol, the villa has an attractive flower garden and a restaurant. While the plan has largely succeeded, local villagers have become dependent on handouts from the development project and from tourists.

Doi Tung is now connected to the other main settlements of the area by good roads. These make fascinating driving into regions that were once the preserve of drug barons. Mae Salong and Mae Sai may be reached by these routes, via Lahu and Akha hill-tribe villages. Although a strong Thai army presence has reduced drug trading in the area substantially, visitors are advised not to leave main roads.

Doi Tung Royal Villa
Hwy 1149. *daily.* **Palace Gardens** *6am–6pm.*

The hillside of Doi Tung, cultivated with new crops aimed at replacing opium as the main source of income

Mae Sai ❺
แม่สาย

Chiang Rai province. 🏠 58,000.
🚉 🛈 TAT, Chiang Rai (0-5371-7433).
@ tatchrai@tat.or.th ✉ daily.

THE NORTHERNMOST town in
Thailand, Mae Sai is separated from Burma only by a
bridge. Every day, the town
bustles with traders from the
neighboring country who
come here to trade their wares.
Among the handicrafts for sale
are lacquerware, gems, and
jade items, mostly made in
Burma. Though the town itself is nondescript, there are
good views over the Sai River
to Burma. **Wat Phra That Doi
Wao** also has a good vista.

ENVIRONS: For a small fee in
US dollars, visitors may usually
cross the bridge to the Burmese town of **Tachilek**. Check
the current political situation
with the Burmese Embassy (see
p451) or with a tour operator,
as this determines whether visitors can travel farther into Burma. Tachilek looks much like
Mae Sai and thrives on its market selling a variety of goods.
South of Mae Sai is **Tham
Luang**, a large cave complex
with crystals that change color
in the light. Farther south are
more caves, **Tham Pum** and
Tham Pla, with lakes inside.

🗻 **Tham Luang**
Off Hwy 110, 6 km (3.5 miles) S of Mae
Sai. ☐ daily. 🎫 🛗
🗻 **Tham Pum and Tham Pla**
Off Hwy 110, 13 km (8 miles) S of
Mae Sai. ☐ daily. 🎫 🛗

**Brick warehouses near the Burmese
border, just outside Mae Sai**

Golden Triangle Driving Tour ❻

THE GOLDEN TRIANGLE is a 195,000 sq-km
(75,000 sq-mile) area spanning parts of
Thailand, Laos, and Burma, the three countries of the "triangle." The area is historically connected to the opium and heroin
trades (thus "golden"), but it has much more
to interest visitors. This tour takes in its best
features: superb views of the "apex" of the
Golden Triangle, where the three countries
meet; hill-tribe villages nestling amid stunning mountain scenery; and the historical
towns of Chiang Saen and Chiang Khong.
Illicit opium trading is thought to continue in
the region, however, and visitors should take extra care
near the Burmese border, which can be dangerous.

**Lanna
carving,
Chiang Saen**

Doi Mae Salong ②
This mountain, the site of the mainly
Chinese settlement of Mae Salong (see
pp232–3), is set amid beautiful
rolling scenery.

Saam Yekh Akha ③
As in every Akha vil-
lage, small sculptures
of people, represent-
ing human life, deco-
rate the village gates.
These are meant to
warn spirits that only
humans may enter.

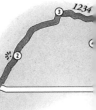

Pha Dua ④
This Mien village
sells textiles and handi-
crafts. Visitors may also see
elaborate rituals and ceremonies based on the local hill
tribe's religion, a mixture of
animism and Chinese Taoism.

Tha Ton ①
Located near the Burmese
border, Tha Thon (see p232)
is a staging post between the
lowlands and the mountains.
A huge white Buddha image,
visible from miles around,
faces eastward over the town
and surrounding countryside.

TIPS FOR DRIVERS

Tour length: 200 km (125 miles).
Stopping-off points: Mae Sai,
Chiang Saen, and Chiang Khong
all have restaurants, guesthouses,
and gas stations. Smaller roads
may be difficult for travel, especially in the wet season, so it is best
to use the numbered roads above.

0 kilometers   15

0 miles   10

Mae Sai ⑥
Wat Phra That Doi Wao, on a hilltop outside Mae Sai, is the town's best temple. The *bot* features carvings of the Buddha.

Doi Tung ⑤
This impressive mountain is the site of the Doi Tung Royal Villa *(see p233)*, which has a colorful, English-style flower garden.

Sop Ruak ⑦
This village *(see p238)*, with its restaurants and shops, thrives on its location at the meeting point of Thailand, Burma, and Laos.

BURMA (MYANMAR)

Tachilek

1290

Mekhong

LAOS

1129

THAILAND

1016

ae Chan

089

110

Kok

ng Rai

KEY

▬▬	Major road
═══	Minor road
▬ ·	International Border
☀	Vista

Chiang Khong ⑩
Though most people pass nonstop through Chiang Khong *(see p239)* en route to Laos, the town's Wat Luang is well worth seeing.

Wat Phra That Pha Ngao ⑨
This 10th-century temple *(see p239)* is superbly sited on a hilltop south of Chiang Saen, and offers exhilarating views of the surrounding countryside. It is distinctive for its bas relief work on the *wihan* and its *chedi* of shiny white marble.

Chiang Saen ⑧
Visitors should not miss this town *(see pp238–9)* of ruined temples and teak trees, once the capital of a small kingdom. Today it boasts an excellent branch of the National Museum and a daily market specializing in Thai Lue fabrics and souvenirs.

Farmers using traditional methods to cultivate rice in paddies near Chiang Saen

The Golden Triangle Apex (Sop Ruak) 7

สามเหลี่ยมทองคำ (สปรวก)

68 km (42 miles) NE of Chiang Rai, Chiang Rai province. *from Chiang Saen.* *from Chiang Saen.* *TAT, Chiang Rai (0-5371-7433).*

THE APEX OF THE Golden Triangle is the point at which the borders of Thailand, Burma, and Laos meet. The junction, at a bend in the Mekong River, is near the village of **Sop Ruak**. Historically, the "Golden Triangle" referred to a much wider region – the area of Northern Thailand, Burma, and Laos in which opium was produced *(see p223)*. Nowadays, though, the term refers to a much smaller area and is associated with Sop Ruak village.

Sop Ruak, eager to take advantage of its location, is growing rapidly as a tourist spot, as evidenced by its many shops, restaurants, and hotels. A museum, the **House of Opium**, displays artifacts relating to opium production. It details a battle between the KMT army *(see p232)* and the now-deposed opium lord, Khun Sa *(see p223)*, over control of the local opium trade. The battle, which established the notoriety of the Golden Triangle, took place in 1967.

But the area's main attraction is undoubtedly the Mekong. Boat trips give views of Laos and of the Golden Triangle Paradise Resort in Burma. The resort, with a casino, was built in Burma as gambling is illegal in Thailand.

Lanna carving, National Museum

🏛 House of Opium
212 House of Opium, SE of Sop Ruak village center. ⬜ *daily.* 📷

Mural in the House of Opium showing tools used to harvest poppies

Chiang Saen 8

เชียงแสน

Chiang Rai province. 🏯 47,000. 🚌 🚤 🛈 *TAT, Chiang Rai (0-5371-7433).* 🛍 *daily.*

ONE OF THE oldest towns in Thailand, Chiang Saen is set beautifully on the bank of the Mekong River. The town was founded in 1328 by Saenphu, the grandson of King Mengrai, as a powerful fortification with many temples. There is evidence, however, from some of Chiang Saen's monuments, that suggests the town may be much older. In 1558 Chiang Saen was captured by the Burmese. It was liberated by King Rama I in 1804, who burned it to the ground to prevent its recapture. The present town was established in the early 1880s. Today, Chiang Saen is a quiet and peaceful settlement boasting an impressive number of monuments that survived the razing. The Fine Arts Department in Bangkok lists 66 ruins inside the walled town and 75 beyond.

The largest temple in Chiang Saen is **Wat Phra That Chedi Luang**. Its 58-m (190-ft) octagonal *chedi*, built between the 12th and the 14th centuries, is a classic Chiang Saen (more commonly known as Lanna) structure. Beside the temple is a small market selling textiles and souvenirs made by the Thai

Lue, an ethnic minority from China who came to the area in the 18th century. Also nearby is the **Chiang Saen National Museum**, with a collection of stone carvings from the Lanna period, Buddha images, and artifacts relating to hill-tribe culture *(see pp196–7)*.

The town's most attractive temple is **Wat Pa Sak**, ("teak forest temple"), located outside the old walls to the west. The monument consists of seven separate ruined structures set among teak trees, which give the *wat* its name. The *chedi*, built in 1295, is the oldest in town. It is carved with flowers and mythological beasts.

On a hill to the northwest of Chiang Saen is **Wat Phra That Chom Kitti**, which may date from 10th century. The temple has little of architectural interest, it gives fine views of the town and the Mekong.

Just south of Chiang Saen is the hilltop **Wat Phra That Pha Ngao**. This temple, with a white pagoda, offers stunning views of the river and the Golden Triangle region.

🏛 **Chiang Saen National Museum**
Phahon Yothin Rd. ⬜ *Wed–Sun.*
🔴 *public hols.* 📷
🏛 **Wat Pa Sak**
Near Chiang Saen Gate. ⬜ *daily.* 📷

Typical Thai Lue fabrics for sale in Chiang Khong

Chiang Khong ❾
เชียงของ

Chiang Rai province. 🗾 *52,000.*
🚌 🚉 ℹ️ *TAT, Chiang Rai (0-5371-7433).* 🚌 *daily.*

SITUATED ON THE bank of the Mekong River, Chiang Khong town is all that remains of the much larger territory of Chiang Khong, most of which was lost to the French in 1893 when they claimed it as part of French Indochina (the rest of this land now forms part of Laos). A growing border town, Chiang Khong is largely dominated by events in Laos. The town was one of the key points of arrival for refugees after the Communist victory in Laos in 1975 *(see p285)*.

There is a large Thai Lue community here too, and shops sell their distinctive, multicolored textiles. Chiang Khong's main temple is the 13th-century **Wat Luang**, in the town center. On a hillside just northwest of town is a cemetery where some 200 Chinese KMT soldiers, killed in battles against Communists in the area since the 1960s, are buried.

ENVIRONS: Visitors can take a ferry to **Huay Xai**, just inside the Lao border. To do so, you must obtain a visa for Laos from a travel agency in Chiang Khong or from the Lao Embassy in Bangkok *(see p451)*. An important trading center, Huay Xai boasts the 19th-century **Wat Chan Khao Manirat**.

THAILAND'S TEAK INDUSTRY

The use of teak *(Tectona grandis)* in Thailand dates back many centuries. Its favorable properties, including strength and resistance to pests and disease, made it a natural choice for use in buildings and furniture, while its fine grain traditionally lent itself to intricate

Transporting teak logs on the Chao Phraya River

carving. However, reckless overlogging has led to disastrous deforestation, and, as a result, most commercial teak logging and export was banned in 1989. Pockets of teak may still be seen in its natural habitat – low-lying deciduous forests of up to 600 m (1,950 ft) in elevation, with rich, moist soil (such forest is characteristic of Northern Thailand) – or in large new plantations. The trees are easily recognizable by their huge size – they can grow up to 100 m (330 ft) when mature – and by their large, floppy leaves, which fall off during the dry period of November to May. Thailand's historic use of teak is evident in rural parts of the country, as in the old wooden houses of provincial towns, including Phrae *(see pp248–9)* and Ngao *(see p242)*, both located in the North.

Lowland teak forest in Northern Thailand

Chiang Rai ⑩

เชียงราย

THIS ANCIENT TOWN was founded in 1262 by King Mengrai. He decided that the site, in a basin between mountains, would be ideal for the new capital of the Lanna Kingdom *(see pp56–7)*. However, the capital was transferred to Chiang Mai only 34 years later, and Chiang Rai declined in importance. Today it is known as the "gateway to the Golden Triangle." While the modern town may lack the charm and architectural interest of Chiang Mai, it has a number of sights worthy of attention.

Detail of carved peacock, Wat Phra Sing

Exploring Chiang Rai

With its varied ethnic groups and beautiful surrounding scenery, Chiang Rai, the capital of Thailand's northernmost province, feels far removed from Bangkok or even Chiang Mai. Evidence of the town's historic importance can be seen in monuments such as Wat Phra Kaeo, even though modern development is becoming increasingly prominent.

The construction of new hotels for tourists, who use Chiang Rai as a trekking base, and of second homes for the wealthy people of Bangkok, has made the town one of the fastest growing in Thailand. Economic activity in the area is expected to grow even further as trade increases with China, just 200 km (120 miles) to the north. New development focuses mainly on the area between the old market off Suk Sathit Road and Phahon Yothin Road, with the newest hotels on the outskirts of town and by the airport. Resorts have been built on many of the islands in the Kok River.

🏯 Wat Phra Kaeo

วัดพระแก้ว

Trirat Rd. ◯ *daily.*
This is the city's most revered temple. According to legend, lightning struck and cracked the *chedi* in 1354, revealing a plaster cast statue encasing the Emerald Buddha (actually made of jadeite). Today Thailand's most holy Buddha image is housed in Bangkok *(see p79)*. A replica, presented in 1991, is now kept here. The *wat* dates from the 13th century and is also notable for its fine *bot*, decorated with elaborate woodcarving, and the Phra Chao Lang Thong, one of the largest surviving bronze statues from the early Lanna period *(see pp58–9)*.

🏯 Wat Chet Yot

วัดเจ็ดยอด

Chet Yot Rd. ◯ *daily.*
This small temple, named for its unusual, seven-spired *chedi*, is similar in appearance to its namesake in Chiang Mai *(see pp216–17)*. The front veranda of the main *wihan* has a mural depicting astrological scenes.

🏯 Wat Phra Sing

วัดพระสิงห์

Singhakhlai Rd. ◯ *daily.*
Built in the late 14th century, Wat Phra Sing is a typical Northern wooden structure, with low, curved roofs. The main *wihan* houses a replica of the Phra Sing Buddha in Chiang Mai's Wat Phra Sing *(see pp214–17)*. Also of interest are the carved medallions below the windows of the *bot*, which depict birds and animals. Around the Bodhi tree are images of the Buddha.

Staircase leading up to a seated Buddha image at Wat Mungmuang

🏯 Wat Mungmuang

วัดมุงเมือง

Uttarakit Rd. ◯ *daily.*
A rotund Buddha image with one hand raised in the *vitarkha mudra* position *(see p163)* dominates this *wat*. The murals in the main *wihan*, depicting local mountain scenery and scenes of flooding and pollution, reflect the concern of Thais at the rapid growth of their cities, an issue of particular relevance in Chiang Rai.

🏯 Wat Phra That Doi Thong

วัดพระธาตุดอยทอง

At-am Nuai Rd, Doi Chom Thong Hill. ◯ *daily.*
This temple, built in the 1940s, is located on a hill top outside the town. It is on this spot that King Mengrai is said to have decided upon the location of his new capital. In the *wihan* is Chiang Rai's original *lak muang*, or "city pillar," traditionally erected in Thailand to mark the founding of a new city.

Wihan of Wat Phra Sing, housing a replica of Chiang Mai's Phra Sing Buddha

Overbrook Hospital, an example of Chiang Rai's colonial architecture

Overbrook Hospital
โรงพยาบาลโอเวอร์บรุ๊ค
Singhakhlai Rd. **0-5371-1336.**
This working hospital is typical of the colonial architecture created by Westerners in the 19th and 20th centuries, when the city was a base for missionaries and traders. Such buildings are slowly being swamped in Chiang Rai as modern development proceeds apace. This trend is likely to continue as ever more trekkers and package tourists, demanding ever more comprehensive facilities, are attracted to the wild beauty of the mountainous Golden Triangle region *(see pp236–8)*.

Hill Tribe Museum
พิพิธภัณฑ์ชาวเขา
620–625 Thanalai Rd. **0-5371-9167.** 9am–8pm Mon–Sat.
This small museum and crafts center was established in 1990 by the non-profit Population and Community Development Association (PDA), also known for raising awareness of Thailand's AIDS problem *(see p112)*. In addition to informing tourists of the plight of hill tribes *(see pp196–7)*, volunteers at the center work with the tribespeople themselves, educating them on how to cope with threats to their traditional lifestyle from a rapidly modernizing society. The center displays and sells hill-tribe crafts *(see pp198–9)*. These can also be bought at the market and in shops around the center of town.

ENVIRONS: Chiang Rai is growing as a base for visiting the rest of the Far North. Vehicle rental, guided treks, and organized excursions can be arranged

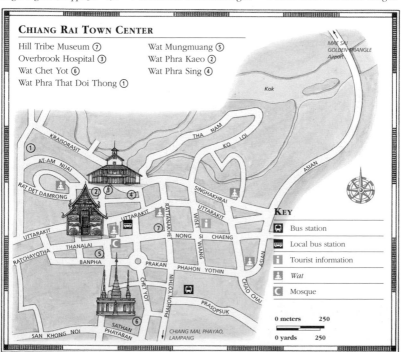

Tourists riding an elephant at Ruamit

through tour companies and many of the guesthouses in town. Also available are boat trips on the Kok River, including excursions to the village of **Tha Ton** *(see p232)*.
Ruamit, some 20 km (12 miles) west of Chiang Rai, can be reached by an hour-long boat ride. This village was originally inhabited solely by the Karen tribe, although many different hill tribes now live here. Elephants can then be taken to travel overland to other Akha and Mien villages.

CHIANG RAI TOWN CENTER

Hill Tribe Museum ⑦
Overbrook Hospital ③
Wat Chet Yot ⑥
Wat Phra That Doi Thong ①
Wat Mungmuang ⑤
Wat Phra Kaeo ②
Wat Phra Sing ④

MAE SAI
GOLDEN TRIANGLE
Airport

Kok

KEY

Bus station

Local bus station

Tourist information

Wat

Mosque

0 meters   250
0 yards   250

Mae Saruai ⑪
แม่สรวย

Chiang Rai province. 🚶 *84,000.* 🚌 *Chiang Rai, then* songthaew. 🛈 *TAT, Chiang Rai (0-5371-7433).* 🛒 *daily.*

Situated on a plain between mountains and jagged limestone outcrops, this small market town is a popular meeting place for hill tribes, particularly Akha *(see pp196–7).* Mae Saruai is modernizing rapidly, and new agriculture, including flower production, is replacing traditional crops such as rice.

ENVIRONS: Cars can be rented in Chiang Rai to visit the Akha hill-tribe villages. The remote ones are accessible on motorcycles or by trekking. Ban Saen Chareon, 10 km (6 miles) west of Mae Saruai, was the subject of a major study of the Akha.

Wiang Pa Pao ⑫
เวียงป่าเป้า

Chiang Rai province. 🚶 *61,000.* 🚌 🚐 *Chiang Mai, then* songthaew; *or* 🚐 *Chiang Rai, then* songthaew. 🛈 *TAT, Chiang Rai (0-5371-7433).* 🛒 *daily.*

An important market town, Wiang Pa Pao is picturesquely located in a long, thin, green valley surrounded by mountains. The town is composed mainly of two-story teak buildings, characteristic of Northern Thailand, and has quiet back streets shaded by teak trees. Many hill-tribe villagers who live in the area, especially Lisu and Akha, come

Chedi **and** *wihan* **of Wat Si Sutha-wat, Wiang Pa Pao's main temple**

The main street in Mae Saruai, with its two-story buildings

to trade at its market. Wiang Pa Pao's main tourist attraction is **Wat Si Suthawat**, to the east of the main road through town. This spacious old temple, with distinctive, curled *nagas* flanking the sweeping staircase that leads up to the main *wihan*, is surrounded by teak trees.

Phayao ⑬
พะเยา

Phayao province. 🚶 *21,000.* 🚌 🛈 *TAT, Chiang Rai (0-5371-7433).* 🛒 *daily.*

This quiet provincial capital, spectacularly sited beside a large lake, was possibly first settled in the Bronze Age. Later abandoned, it was resettled in the 12th century, when it became an independent city state. Today, Phayao is divided into two parts. The older district is confined to the promontory jutting into the lake. With its narrow streets and teak houses, it is more pleasant than the newer part.

Wat Si Komkam, situated just north of town by the lake, dates from the 12th century. Its modern *wihan* houses a 16th-century, 16-m (52-ft) Buddha image, which is thought to be the largest in the whole of Northern Thailand. The *wihan* is surrounded by 38 heads of the Buddha in the Phayao style – distinguished by their rounded heads and pointed noses – dating from the 14th century.

Ngao ⑭
งาว

Lampang province. 🚶 *53,000.* 🚌 *from Lampang or Chiang Rai.* 🛈 *TAT, Chiang Mai (0-5324-8604).* 🛒 *daily.*

Like many towns in Northern Thailand, Ngao's historical association with the teak trade is evident in its buildings. The suspension bridge over the Yom River offers wonderful views of the town, with its teak houses on stilts backing onto the fertile river valley.

Ngao's principal temple is **Wat Dok Ban**, on the east side of town. It is distinctive for its wall surrounded by about 100 kneeling angel figures of different colors.

ENVIRONS: Mae Yom National Park, northeast of Ngao, is centered on the Yom River, one of Northern Thailand's main waterways. More than 50 species of birds have been observed in the park, as well as many mammals, including the serow (a type of antelope), pangolin (scaly anteater), wild pigs, and barking deer.

Angel at Wat Dok Ban, Ngao

Within the park is the **Dong Sak Ngan Forest**, notable for its tall teak trees. The forest can be reached only on foot.

🏞 **Mae Yom National Park**
18 km (11 miles) NE of Ngao.
🛈 *Forestry Dept (0-2579-0529).*
◯ *daily.* 📷

Elephants in Thailand

A S WELL AS playing a very important practical role in Thai history, elephants have traditionally been of great spiritual significance. They were first mentioned centuries ago in Hindu and Buddhist texts and since then have enjoyed a higher status in Thailand than any other animal. However, although wild elephants have been protected by law since 1921, deforest-

White elephant on a former Siamese flag

ation and, to a lesser extent, poaching have reduced their numbers to just a few thousand. The introduction of machines for logging, followed by a ban on most commercial logging in 1989, has led to a sharp fall in the number of captive elephants, too. While tourists may still come across these being ridden by *mahouts*, a surer way to see them is at shows at elephant camps.

Elephants were used in war, as depicted in this old manuscript

WORKING ELEPHANTS
Although most logging is officially banned in Thailand, elephants are still used for transporting logs in some areas. They are often looked after by one handler for all their life, and cause less damage than modern machinery.

Able to run *up to 20 km (12 miles) an hour, elephants were frequently used by hunters.*

This 19th-century training manual *shows how to tame wild elephants.*

SACRED ELEPHANTS
The spiritual significance of elephants derives from Ganesh, the Hindu god of knowledge and the remover and creator of obstacles, who is a young boy with an elephant's head. The significance of white elephants *(see p102)*, the most revered of all, has its roots in Buddhism. Only the king may own them.

Mural of elephants *in one of the Buddhist heavens, Wat Suthat, Bangkok (see pp86–7).*

Royal white elephants, *said to represent the monarch's power, are the most sacred elephants.*

Nong Bua 🕔
หนองบัว

Nan province. 🏛 *5,100.* 🚌 *Nan, then songthaew.* ℹ️ *TAT, Chiang Rai (0-5371-7433).* 🏛 *daily.*

THIS PICTURESQUE TOWN, situated on a flat, fertile plain beside the Nan River, is characterized by traditional teak houses on stilts and neat vegetable gardens. It is one of a number of towns in Nan province inhabited by the Thai Lue, an ethnic minority related to the Tai people of Southern China, who began to settle in the region in 1836.

Wat Nong Bua, which was built in 1862, has features typical of a Thai Lue temple, including a two-tiered roof and a carved wooden portico. Its murals are thought to be the work of the same artists who painted those at Wat Phumin *(see pp246–7)*. Though the murals at Wat Nong Bua are more faded than Wat Phumin's, their depictions of 19th-century life are just as fascinating. As at Wat Phumin, scenes from the *jataka* tales *(see pp26–7)* are also featured here.

To the west of town is a textile factory, where traditional Thai Lue fabrics are made using hand-operated looms. The distinctive, multicolored fabrics are for sale in the adjacent store.

Nong Bua is the site of a two-day festival held every three years in December (1999, 2002, and so on), during which the villagers pay homage to their ancestors.

A 19th-century mural depicting a hunting party, Wat Nong Bua

Doi Phu Kha National Park 🕠
อุทยานแห่งชาติดอยภูคา

Visitors' Center off Hwy 1080, 85 km (42 miles) NE of Nan. ℹ️ *TAT, Chiang Rai (0-5371-7433); Forestry Dept (0-2562-0760 or www.dnp.go.th).* 🚌 *Nan, then songthaew.*

RANGED AROUND the 2,000-m (6,550-ft) peak of Doi Phu Kha, this is one of the most recently created national parks in Thailand. For years, the area was widely considered to be a hotbed of Communist infiltration. Some of the hilltribe villagers here were suspected of sympathizing with the Communists and were kept isolated from visitors. Tourism in the park is therefore still in its infancy. Doi Phu Kha has two main attractions, the most

Short-tailed magpie, Doi Phu Kha National Park

obvious being its beautiful scenery, such as caves and waterfalls. The visitors' center provides information on forest walks and opportunities for bird-watching.

The other points of interest in the park are the tribal villages, particularly Mien and Hmong *(see pp196–7)*, and lowland ethnic minorities such as the Htin and Thai Lue.

There are few good roads or tourist facilities in the park. The more adventurous will be rewarded by an area relatively free of development.

Nan 🕢
น่าน

Nan province. 🏛 *60,000.* ✈️ 🚌 ℹ️ *TAT, Chiang Rai (0-5371-7433).* 🏛 *daily.* 🎏 *Nan Provincial Fair (Oct/ Nov), Nan Boat Racing (late Oct or early Dec). Golden Orange Festival (Dec/Jan).*

NAN DEVELOPED as an isolated kingdom in the 13th and 14th centuries. It fell under the influence of the Sukothai and Lanna kingdoms *(see pp 54–7)*, then surrendered to Burmese control in 1558. In 1788 the town became a vassal state of Bangkok, though it kept its autonomy and independent rulers until it officially became part of Thailand in 1931. Today, Nan is a prosperous town on the Nan River.

Wat Phumin *(see pp246–7)*, in the south of town, is without doubt the most important sight in Nan. Just north of it (on highway 101) is the **Nan National Museum**, which is housed in an impressive

Thai Lue farmers working in the rice fields around Nong Bua

former royal palace dating from 1903. The ground floor is dedicated to the ethnic groups of Nan province, including the Hmong and Mien hill tribes. The second floor has a comprehensive selection of artifacts relating to the history of the region, including and weapons. Notable items include a "black" elephant tusk weighing 18 kg (40 lb), supported by a sculpted *khut* (mythological eagle). Thought to date from the 17th century, the tusk is actually dark brown.

The collection of Buddhas includes some rare Lanna and Lao images. Also exhibited are sky rockets made by local farmers for the Bun Bang Fai (Rocket Festival) *(see pp42–3)* held each May in Northeast and parts of Northern Thailand. Unusually for Thai mu-

Façade of the *bot* of the 14th-century Wat Suan Tan in Nan

seums, many of the exhibits are labeled in English. Nearby is **Wat Chang Kham Wora Wihan**, with a magnificent 14th-century *chedi* resting on sculpted elephant heads. The *bot* and the *wihan* are guarded by *singhas* (mythological lions). Among Nan's other temples is **Wat Suan Tan**, in the northwest of town, with a 40-m (130-ft) *chedi*, crowned by a white *prang* – a rounded, Khmer-style tower that is very rarely seen in Northern Thailand. Housed in the *wihan* is a bronze Buddha image, Phra Chao Thong Thip. The image was made to the order of the king of Chiang Mai in 1449 after he conquered Nan. According to legend, the monarch gave the city's craftsmen just one week to make it.

Just southeast of Nan is the revered **Wat Phra That Chae Haeng**. Dating from 1355, the temple is set in a square compound on a hill top overlooking the Nan valley. Its gilded Lanna *chedi* is just over 55 m (180 ft) high. This, and the huge *nagas* (serpents) flanking the staircase, can be seen from several miles around. The multilayered roof of the *wihan* is Lao in style.

"Black" elephant tusk in Nan National Museum

ENVIRONS: Despite its many attractions, the far-flung and mountainous province of Nan was, until fairly recently, one of the most remote and inaccessible areas in Thailand. In the past few years, better roads have greatly improved connections to the province, and it is now among the country's fastest growing tourist destinations.

To the north of Nan is **Tham Pha Tup Forest Reserve**, a limestone cave complex set in a forested area. There are some 17 caves here, which are impressive for their stalactites and stalagmites. About half of them can be reached by marked trails.

Another natural feature of the region is **Sao Din**, literally "earth pillars," which are located off Highway 1026, about 30 km (19 miles) to the south of Nan. These sculpted clay columns, created by erosion, stick out of depressions in the ground. The pillars have the same eerie appearance as those at Phrae Muang Phi in Phrae province *(see p249)* and have been used as a backdrop for many Thai films.

🏛 **Tham Pha Tup Forest Reserve**
Off Hwy 1080, 12 km (7 miles) N of Nan. 🛈 *Forestry Dept (0-2562- 0760 or www.dnp.go.th).* ◯ *daily.* 🈂

🏛 **Nan National Museum**
Hwy 101. ◯ *Wed–Sun.* 🈂

TRADITIONAL BOAT RACES IN NAN

Each year, at the end of October, boat races take place on the river at Nan. The races are the highlight of the two-week Nan Provincial Fair, which attracts visitors from all over Thailand. The tradition of the boat races is thought to have begun toward the end of the 19th century and marks the start of the Krathin season *(see p46)*, when the city's menfolk present new robes to the local monks. The boats, some 30 m (98 ft) in length, can hold up to 50 rowers. Each one is carved from a single log and decorated to look like a dragon-serpent or *naga (see p218)*. The sides are brightly painted with traditional motifs.

Boats competing during annual races on the Nan River

Wat Phumin
วัดภูมินทร์

O NE OF THE MOST BEAUTIFUL TEMPLES in northern Thailand, Wat Phumin was founded in 1596 by the ruler of Nan. The *wat* was renovated in the mid-19th century and again in 1991 and is notable for its cross-shaped design, elaborate coffered ceiling, and carved doors and pillars. The highlight, however, is undoubtedly its murals. These were originally thought to have been painted by Thai Lue *(see p244)* artists during the 19th-century renovation. But the apparent depiction of French troops, unknown in the area before the French annexation of part of Nan province in 1893, suggests a date in the mid-1890s. Three main themes can be picked out from the murals: the life of the Buddha, the *jataka (see p26)* tale of his incarnation as Khatta Kumara, and scenes depicting everyday life in Nan.

Rich Official
This lavishly dressed man, smoking a pipe, may depict the ruler of Nan who commissioned the murals.

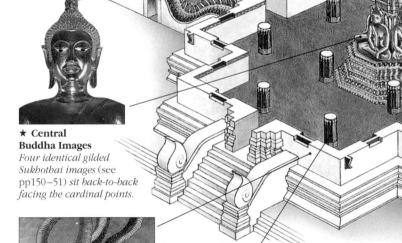

★ **Central Buddha Images**
Four identical gilded Sukhothai images (see pp150–51) sit back-to-back facing the cardinal points.

Decorative Pillars
These red, black, and gold pillars are all carved with the same floral pattern. The bases of some pillars feature elephant motifs while others depict devas *(Hindu gods).*

Descending Serpents
This mural shows poisonous snakes sent by angry gods to punish an unruly king in the story of Khatta Kumara.

STAR FEATURES

★ **Central Buddha Images**

★ **Story of the Buddha Mural**

Courting Couple
This mural gives an insight into clothing worn in 19th-century Nan. The tattooed man with a Thai Lue hair-style may be one of the artists.

VISITORS' CHECKLIST

Phumin village, south bank of Nan River, Phakong Rd, center of Nan town. ○ 8:30am – 4:30pm daily.

★ Story of the Buddha Mural
The mural on the northern wall above the main door is particularly outstanding. Located at the very top of the image is the Buddha, and on a lower plane are his disciples. In the bottom half, Khatta Kumara and his friends are depicted on their way to a city with a palace, which Khatta later rebuilds after its destruction by snakes and birds.

***Nagas* (serpents)** flank the steps at the front and back of the building.

Main entrance

The Arrival of Europeans in Nan
This scene shows characters wearing European clothes. The figures in berets may be French, and the mural could be a direct reference to the takeover of part of Nan province by the French in 1893.

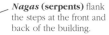

Boy, Mother, and Elephant's Footprint
In this scene, Khatta Kumara is with his mother. She bore him after drinking the god Indra's urine from an elephant's footprint. Indra had descended to earth in the form of an elephant.

Street-by-Street: Phrae ⑬

แพร่

Wᴛʜ ɪᴛs ᴅɪsᴛɪɴᴄᴛɪᴠᴇ ᴄʜᴀʀᴍ and identity, Phrae is appealing yet surprisingly seldom visited. The town was built beside the Yom River in the 12th century and remained an independent city state until it came under Ayutthayan control. In the 18th century, the town was taken by the Burmese and later became a base for Burmese and Lao teak loggers. Burmese influence is obvious in Phrae's temples, which also have Lanna features. The town prospers on agricultural produce from the surrounding fertile valley, as shown by the growing commercial district outside the walled town. Remains of the old city walls and moat can be seen in the northeast of town.

Buddhist shrine inside the museum at Wat Luang

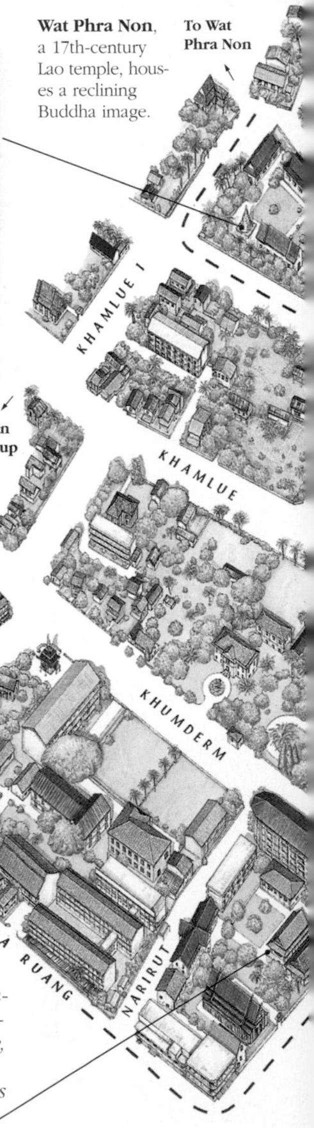

Wat Phra Non, a 17th-century Lao temple, houses a reclining Buddha image.

To Wat Phra Non

★ **Wat Luang**
Phrae's oldest temple (12th century) is entered through a section of old city wall. The octagonal Lanna chedi is notable for its elephant caryatids. Swords, jewelry, and photographs are displayed in the museum.

To Ban Prathup Chai

Wat Phra Ruang
Several architectural styles are blended at this temple. The cruciform bot is more characteristic of temples in nearby Nan. The Lao wihan has delicately carved doors, shown here. The chedi is Lanna.

Wat Phra Bat
The Lao bot of Wat Phra Bat dates from the 18th century, while the wihan, housing a revered Buddha image, is modern. Part of a Buddhist university, the temple is often bustling with monks.

Wat Si Chum

The plain interiors of the bot *and* wihan *contrast with the ornate Buddha images inside. Unfortunately, the* chedi *is in a state of ruin.*

★ Teak Houses
These teak houses are typical of Phrae. Their roofs are decorated with kalae, *a feature of Northern Thai houses (see p32).*

Public Park
This park is ideal for relaxing after visiting Phrae's sights. Unusually for Thai towns, it is located in the center.

ROBMUANG

CHAROEN MUANG

To Wat Chom Sawan and old city walls

0 meters   100

0 yards   100

KEY

– – – Suggested route

STAR SIGHTS

★ Wat Luang

★ Teak Houses

ENVIRONS: Wat Chom Sawan, in the northeast of Phrae, is an early 20th-century Shan temple with a distinctive, copper-crowned Burmese *chedi*.

To the west of Phrae is **Ban Prathup Chai**, one of Thailand's largest teak houses. The structure, with its lavish, ornate pillars and furniture, was assembled in the mid-1980s. Even though teak logging was not then banned (see p239), spare teak logs from nine other houses were used to build it.

To the southeast is **Wat Phra That Chaw Hae**, thought to date from the 12th–13th centuries. Staircases flanked by *nagas* and stone lions lead through a teak forest up to the hilltop *wat*. The temple is named after the satinlike cloth *(chaw hae)* that worshipers wrap around the 33-m (110-ft) gilded *chedi*. Inside is the revered Phra Chao Than Chai, believed to grant wishes.

Phea Muang Phi is a popular excursion from Phrae. This surreal landscape *(muang phi* means "ghost city") consists of pillars of soil and rock that rise from the ground like mushrooms. Like Sao Din in Nan province (see p245), they are the result of the erosion of clay beneath a hard crust.

Ban Prathup Chai
1 km (1,100 yards) W of Phrae. daily.

Wat Phra That Chaw Hae
8 km (5 miles) SE of Phrae, Phrae province. Phrae, then songthaew. daily.

Phea Muang Phi
Off Hwy 101, 18 km (11 miles) NE of Phrae, Phrae province. Phrae, then songthaew.

Sirikit Reservoir ⑲
เขื่อนสิริกิติ์

45 km (28 miles) SE of Phrae, Uttaradit province. Nan or Uttaradit, then songthaew.

NAMED AFTER Queen Sirikit and set amid splendid scenery, this reservoir and dam were created in the mid-1970s on the Nan River, a tributary of the Chao Phraya. Built to control flooding, the dam also provides electricity and water to farmers in the area.

NORTHEAST
THAILAND

Introducing Northeast Thailand

THE KHORAT PLATEAU, which takes up most of the Northeast, is mostly barren scrubland; its main focus is the city of Khorat. To the north and east of this region and separating it from neighboring Laos is the Mekong River Valley. Along the Thai side of the river lie small towns and villages, some with small docks and beaches. Known locally as Isan, the Northeast has an extremely rich history. One of the first areas in the world where rice was cultivated, silk woven, and bronze produced, it fell under Khmer rule in the 9th–13th centuries. Isan's proximity to Laos and Cambodia and its largely infertile land mean that it is seen by many Thais as a poor relation. Most of its people are ethnically Lao and are known for their friendly openness.

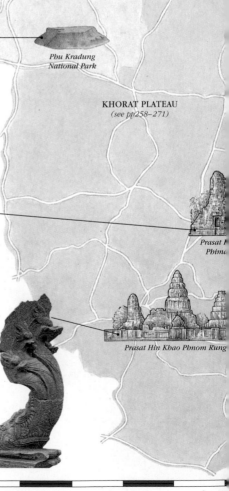

Nong Khai

Phu Kradung National Park

KHORAT PLATEAU
(see pp258–271)

Prasat Hin Phimai

Prasat Hin Khao Phnom Rung

Phu Kradung National Park
(see pp276–7), *with a steep-sided plateau at its center, is home to fabulous animal and plant life.*

Prasat Hin Phimai (see pp266–7), *dating from the 11th–12th centuries, is one of the most extensively restored Khmer temple complexes in Thailand.*

Prasat Hin Khao Phnom Rung (see pp270–71), *covering a huge area, is one of Thailand's finest examples of Khmer architecture.*

◁ **The ruins of Prasat Hin Muang Tam reflected in one of its four surrounding lotus-filled ponds**

Nong Khai (see pp282–3) is a rapidly developing commercial town that has retained a peaceful riverside atmosphere.

MEKONG RIVER VALLEY
(see pp272–293)

Wat Phra That Phanom

Wat Phra That Phanom
(see p287) was, according to legend, built shortly after the death of the Buddha. It is the Northeast's most sacred shrine.

Prasat Khao Phra Wihan

Prasat Khao Phra Wihan
(see p292) enjoys a stunning location on a mountain spur on the border between Thailand and Cambodia.

| 0 kilometers | 50 |
| 0 miles | 25 |

The Lost Khmer Temples

Lintel at Phnom Rung

W HEN EUROPEANS first saw mysterious ruins in the forests far east of Ayut-thaya, they thought they had found an ancient Chinese, or even Greek, civili-zation. It was not until the 19th century that the history of the Khmers, who ruled an area covering much of modern Cambodia and Northeast Thailand from the 9th–14th centuries, began to be un-covered. The Khmers are now acknowledged to have been among the world's greatest architects. Many sites can be visited in Thailand today; in Cambodia, war has slowed the restoration of Angkor, the old capital.

THE KHMER EMPIRE

• *Major Khmer sites*

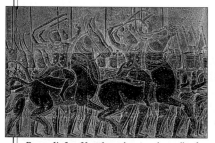

Bas-reliefs of battles *adorning the walls of many Khmer sites not only display the creative and technical abilities of the Khmer craftsmen, but have also helped scholars to write Khmer history. The Khmers' main adversaries were the Thais: in 1444 Ayutthaya finally took Angkor, and the Khmer Empire was vanquished.*

At the center of Angkor Thom stands the Bayon, with its distinctive, colossal heads.

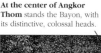

Restoration *of the most important of Thai-land's 300-odd Khmer monuments was begun in 1925. The Thai Fine Arts Department has overseen work at temple complexes such as Phimai (see pp266–7) in the late 20th century.*

ROMANCE OF THE GREAT TEMPLES

Khmer temple complexes were built to symbol-ize kingship and the universe and are awesome in their scale and beauty. The Thais borrowed elements of Khmer temple design *(see p30)*, and a scale model, made in 1922, of Angkor Wat, the largest complex, stands at Bangkok's Wat Phra Kaeo *(see pp76–9)*. European views of romantic ruins abound, as exemplified by engravings such as this made in 1866–8. A re-construction of Angkor Wat was also the center-piece of the 1931 Colonial Exposition in Paris.

A shivalinga was the main object of worship at the center of many Khmer temples. It is a phallus representing the creative force of the Hindu god Shiva.

THE REDISCOVERY OF ANGKOR

In about 1550 a Cambodian king is said to have come upon the ruins of Angkor while hunting for elephants. He cleared part of the site where his ancestors had once held court. Before long, news filtered to Europe from Portuguese and Spanish missionaries of a vast hidden city. But few ventured into the jungle, and the artistic feats of the Khmers were to remain largely unknown for another 300 years. Interest in the ruins increased when France colonized Indochina. Henri Mouhot (1826–61) earned the dubious posthumous status of "discoverer" of Angkor on publication of his engravings and drawings of the site that he made in 1860. From his work France decided to finance proper exploration. Louis Delaporte, George Coedès, Jean Boisselier, and Henri Parmentier were among others who spent much of their lives piecing together Khmer history.

The French scholar Parmentier in 1923

Scenes from the Ramayana, an ancient Indian epic, are found at many Khmer temples, and probably directly inspired the Thai version, the Ramakien (see pp36–7).

The 19th-century artists were particularly inspired by imagery of the jungle encroaching upon the ruins.

The scale of the humans shown in the engraving is fairly accurate. The larger statues in the foreground are imaginary.

Marc Riboud, a photographer for the renowned Magnum agency, visited Angkor in the 1960s and 1980s. He took some of the most evocative and widely published pictures of Angkor before and after the war in Cambodia.

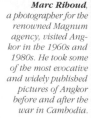

The gently smiling faces of the Buddha at the Bayon of Angkor Thom have found their way onto posters, book covers, and, here, the score of a 1921 foxtrot.

Silk Production

Leaves from the mulberry bush

Finds at the prehistoric site of Ban Chiang *(see pp50–51)* indicate that silk production in Northeast Thailand may predate even that of China, where sericulture probably originated in about 2700 BC. In Thailand, silk production was beginning to die out until an American, Jim Thompson *(see pp116–17)*, revived it in the 1940s. Today, all manner of silk products are available, with silk shirts and sarongs popular with visitors. The silk industry is centered mostly in the Northeast, due to the suitability of soil in these areas for growing mulberry bushes, the main diet of the silkworm. Silk production in these areas is still based on traditional methods and comprises the stages outlined here.

2 *In three to four weeks the eggs grow into silkworms. These are placed on large, woven bamboo trays and, protected from mice, ants, flies, and bright light, feed on mulberry leaves. In the larval stage, while they are still growing, each silkworm sheds its skin four times and increases its weight 10,000-fold.*

Silkworm moth
(Bombyx mori)

1 *Female silkworm moths spend their short life of about four days mating and laying eggs.*

SILKWORMS

REELING	DYEING

7 *The raw silk is soaked in soapy water to remove the sericin, a gumlike coating, leaving it softer and lighter.*

5 *The individual silk threads are lifted out of the pot using a special forked bamboo pole. They are twisted together to form a single, larger thread, which is then reeled onto a spool.*

6 *Silk skeins are inspected and graded. The outer layer of cocoon gives the coarsest yarn and is used for furnishings. The best silk, from the middle and inner layers, is used for weaving.*

8 *The yarn is then dyed. The strength of the dye depends on the number of times the yarn is dipped in the solution. Tie-dyed yarn (ikat) is achieved by wrapping segments of yarn with dye-resistant strings, according to the design required. The thread is then dried and the strings removed, revealing the pattern.*

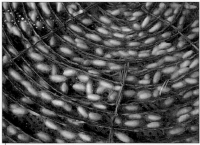

3 *At the end of the 30-day growth cycle, the fully developed silkworms are ready to spin a cocoon. They are moved to a large, circular, bamboo tray with a frame that leaves them just enough space to attach their cocoons. Silkworms build their cocoons from a single white or yellow fiber secreted from the mouth at a rate of 12 cm (4.5 in) per minute.*

Cocoons, which are spun in about 36 hours

4 *Cocoons have to be reeled within ten days or the moths will begin to hatch and damage the silk. The cocoons are placed in a pot of water just below boiling point. This kills them and releases the silk threads.*

COCOONS

PLYING	WEAVING

9 *Up to six threads can be plyed together to form a single thread, the weft.*

10 *The silk is woven on upright looms with foot treadles. The coarse weft is woven into fine, even warps, which even in traditional workshops are often prefabricated and imported from Japan, Korea, and Europe – the production of the warp is a time-consuming business by any method. The combination of fine and coarse threads gives the fabric its unique luster.*

TOOLS FOR SILK WEAVING

During the silk-weaving process, the fibers must be kept clean and free from obstructions that could tangle and damage them. Each implement has a unique and vital function: delicate brushes with ornamental wooden handles help to keep the silk free from particles of dust. Carved wooden pulleys, which are attached to traditional looms, insure that the fibers run smoothly while they are being woven.

Traditional pulley

Decorative silk brushes

11 *The distinctive, brightly colored silk is then made into umbrellas, scarves, ties, shirts, and sarongs, and sold around Thailand (see p439).*

KHORAT PLATEAU

THOUGH ONE OF THE MOST *infertile areas of Thailand, and home to the nation's poorest people, the Khorat Plateau is rich in culture and historic sites from the days when the Khmer Empire held sway over the region. The people are welcoming, the cuisine fiery hot, often served with glutinous rice and raw vegetables, and the silk and cotton handicrafts are exquisite.*

The vast, sandstone Khorat Plateau dominates the Northeast, a region that the Thais call Isan. The plateau, which is about 200 m (660 ft) above sea level, takes up almost a third of Thailand's land mass and is home to about a third of the population. The uneven rainfall of the region causes both floods and droughts and permits the cultivation of only one rice crop per year. As a result there is much rural poverty.

Although few tourists visit the region, there is much of historical interest to be discovered. To the north, at Ban Chiang, lies a site that has revolutionized archaeologists' views of prehistoric Southeast Asia. The Northeast is now thought to be one of the first areas in the world where rice growing, bronze making, and silk weaving were pioneered. Silk production has flourished again since the mid-20th century, and visitors are drawn to modern-day weaving villages where a wide range of silk and cotton goods are sold.

In the 9th century AD, the Khorat Plateau came under Cambodian control, which was to endure until the end of the 13th century. It was during this period that the region's splendid Khmer temples were built. The magnificent stone temples at Phnom Rung and Phimai, which once stood on a road linking the plateau with the Khmer capital of Angkor, have been evocatively restored in recent years.

Bung Phlan Chai, a scenic lake in the center of Roi Et town

◁ Balustraded stone windows at Prasat Hin Muang Tam

Exploring the Khorat Plateau

THE KHORAT PLATEAU occupies most of Northeast Thailand. It is a broad stretch of barren, arid hills some 300 m (985 ft) above sea level, separated from the Central Plains to the west by the Phetchabun mountain range. Much of the region is characterized by red earth and scrub forest. Khorat city, regarded as the gateway to the Northeast, is the center of the region's transportation network. Other towns and sights of interest in the region can be reached by road from here, though distances are considerable. North of Khorat lie the towns of Khon Kaen and Roi Et; farther north still, the prehistoric site of Ban Chiang. East of Khorat the main attractions are the Khmer temples of Phimai and Phnom Rung. Nearby are Ta Klang and Surin, which are linked historically with the elephant trade.

SIGHTS AT A GLANCE

Ban Chiang **2**
Ban Ta Klang **13**
Dan Kwian **8**
Khon Kaen **3**
Khorat **7**
Prasat Hin Khao Phnom Rung (see pp270–1) **11**
Prasat Hin Muang Tam **10**
Prasat Hin Phimai (see pp266–7) **6**
Prasat Ta Muen and Prasat Ta Muen Tot **9**
Roi Et **4**
Surin **12**
Udon Thani **1**
Yasothon **5**

The exquisitely restored Prasat Hin Phimai

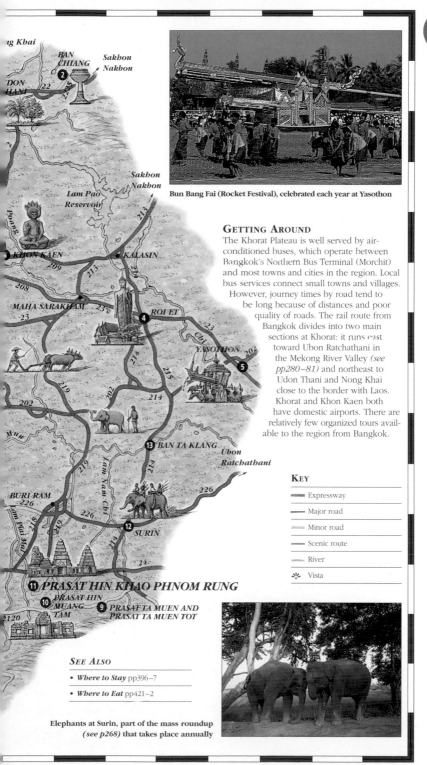

Bun Bang Fai (Rocket Festival), celebrated each year at Yasothon

GETTING AROUND

The Khorat Plateau is well served by air-conditioned buses, which operate between Bangkok's Northern Bus Terminal (Morchit) and most towns and cities in the region. Local bus services connect small towns and villages. However, journey times by road tend to be long because of distances and poor quality of roads. The rail route from Bangkok divides into two main sections at Khorat: it runs east toward Ubon Ratchathani in the Mekong River Valley *(see pp280–81)* and northeast to Udon Thani and Nong Khai close to the border with Laos. Khorat and Khon Kaen both have domestic airports. There are relatively few organized tours available to the region from Bangkok.

KEY

▬▬	Expressway
▬▬	Major road
▬▬	Minor road
▬▬	Scenic route
▬▬	River
✹	Vista

SEE ALSO

- **Where to Stay** pp396–7
- **Where to Eat** pp421–2

Elephants at Surin, part of the mass roundup
(see p268) **that takes place annually**

Nong Prachak Park, one of the more peaceful parts of Udon Thani

Udon Thani ❶

อุดรธานี

Udon Thani province. 🏙 *170,000.*
✈ 🚌 🚆 ℹ *TAT, Mukmontri Rd,
Udon Thani (0-4232-5406).* 🚢 *daily.*

DURING the Vietnam War
Udon Thani changed from
a sleepy provincial capital
into a booming support
center for a nearby
American airbase.
Since the withdrawal
of the GIs in 1976,
Udon has retained a
little of that past vi-
brancy, together with
some rather nonde-
script streets, lined
with Western-style
coffee shops, night-
clubs, and massage parlors. It
has continued to grow as an
industrial and commercial
center within the region. The
most attractive part of town is
Nong Prachak Park, where
there are some open-air restaurants. The town makes a
good base for travelers wanting to visit nearby Ban Chiang.

**Ban Chiang pot,
c.2000 BC**

Ban Chiang ❷

บ้านเชียง

Udon Thani province. 🏙 *4,680.*
🚌 *from Udon Thani.* ℹ *TAT, Udon
Thani (0-4232-5406).* 🚢 *daily.*

THE PRINCIPAL attraction for
visitors to Ban Chiang is
its archaeological site *(see
pp50–1)*. It was discovered
by accident in 1966 by an
American sociologist who
tripped over some remains.

The finds provided archaeological evidence that northeast
Thailand may have been one
of the world's earliest centers
of bronze production. Spear-
heads from the site are thought
to date from around 3600 BC,
while ceramics, dating from
between 3000 BC and AD 500,
testify to a high degree of technical and artistic skill.

Today, a collection
of these artifacts is
on display, together
with ornaments such
as bangles and rings,
at the **Ban Chiang
National Museum**.

A short walk from
the museum, 2 km
(1 mile) through
dusty streets lined with
quaint wooden shop-
houses, two covered excavation sites lie in the grounds of
Wat Pho Si Nai. Here the main
exhibits are graves containing
skeletal remains and ceramics
used for symbolic purposes in
burial. Bodies were wrapped

in perishable material and laid
on their backs. Pots were then
arranged along the edge of
the grave and over the bodies
themselves. Other grave goods
found at the burial site include
pig skulls and mandibles, jewelry, tools, weapons, and river
pebbles.

Research associated with
the discoveries at Wat Pho Si
Nai indicates that the inhabitants of Ban Chiang were a
strong, long-legged people
with wide foreheads and
prominent cheekbones with
an average life expectancy of
31 years. The main causes of
death were diseases such as
malaria. As with other early
peoples of Southeast Asia, the
exact ethnic origins of the
population of Ban Chiang
remain a mystery.

**🏠 Ban Chiang
National Museum**
On edge of Ban Chiang village.
🕐 *9am–4pm Wed–Sun.* 🎫

Khon Kaen ❸

ขอนแก่น

Khon Kaen province. 🏙 *240,000.* ✈
🚌 🚆 ℹ *TAT, 15/5 Prachasamoson
Rd, Khon Kaen (0-4324-4498).* 🚢 *daily.*
🎉 *Silk Festival (10 days Nov/Dec).*
ⓦ *www.khonkaen.com*

ONCE THE QUIET capital of
one of the poorest prov-
inces in the northeast of Thailand, this place has changed
into a bustling town. Located
at the heart of the region, it
has consequently been a focus
of regional development
projects – the town now

Khon Kaen National Museum, home to Ban Chiang and Dvaravati relics

boasts the largest university in the northeast, in addition to its own television studios. There are a number of modern hotels and shopping complexes, all of which nestle rather incongruously among the town's more traditional streets and market places.

Places of interest to tourists include **Khaen Nakhon Lake**, an artifical lake beside which are some restaurants. **Khon Kaen National Museum** has a collection of Ban Chiang artifacts and a number of Dvaravati *(see pp52–3)* stelae carved with excerpts from the life of the Buddha, as well as examples of local folk art.

 **Khon Kaen National Museum**

At intersection of Kasikhon Thungsang Rd and Lungsun Rachakhan Rd. ◯ *Wed–Sun.* ◉ *public hols.* 🚫

Roi Et ❹

ร้อยเอ็ด

Roi Et province. 🏠 *119,000.*
🚌 🚹 *TAT, Khon Kaen (0-4324-4498).* 🏪 *daily.*

Founded in 1782, Roi Et literally means "one hundred and one," a name that is thought to be an exaggeration of 11, the number of vassal states over which the town once ruled. Today it is a steadily growing provincial capital. The modern skyline is dominated by an immense brown and ocher image of the Lord Buddha, the Phraphuttha-rattana-mongkol-maha-mani, which is situated within the grounds of **Wat Buraphaphiram**. Measuring 68 m (225 ft) from its base to the tip of its flame finial, this giant standing Buddha is reputed to be one

The Phraphuttha-rattana-mongkol-maha-mani image at Roi Et

of the tallest in the world. The climb up the statue offers an impressive view of the town and surrounding area. Silk and cotton are both good buys in Roi Et and can be found along Phadung Phanit Road.

THE KHAEN

Originating in Laos, and played widely in Northeast Thailand, the *khaen* is a large, free-reed panpipe and is constructed primarily of bamboo. Although the length and pitch of the *khaen* are not standardized, the number of pipes and the tuning are. Each *khaen* is pitched according either to the personal preference of the player, or to the range of the singer it accompanies, and has a range of two octaves – this gives a total of 15 pitches. Whereas most arts in Thailand are formally taught, *khaen* players tend to learn their skills by listening to relatives and neighbors in the village. There is no written music for the *khaen*, its repertoire having been passed down through oral transmission. It was traditionally played by young men on their way to woo their sweethearts or by blind beggars in the hope of receiving a few coins for their performances. Women never play the *khaen*.

***Craftsmen** assemble the* khaen *from bamboo reeds dried in the sun. Wax from the* khisut, *an insect, is used to glue the reeds together and attach them to the carved windchest.*

The *khaen* consists varying lengths of bamboo, each producing a different pitch.

Holes in the reeds are fingered to create different levels of pitch.

Notes are made by blowing into this carved windchest.

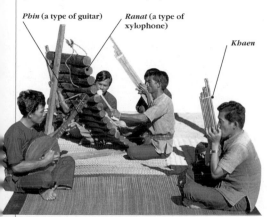

Phin (a type of guitar)   *Ranat* (a type of xylophone)   *Khaen*

Orchestra with *khaen*, *phin*, and *ranat* players

Bun Bang Fai or "Rocket" Festival held each year at Yasothon

and, perhaps surprisingly, it is Buddhist monks who possess the expertise of building and firing the rockets. The rockets are paraded on floats through the streets, surrounded by revelers, then shot into the clouds to "fertilize" them. The festival's sexual overtones come out in bawdy humor and flirtation, not encouraged at other times. The owners of those rockets that fail to go off are ritually coated in mud.

Yasothon **5**

ยโสธร

Yasothon province. 🚶 *108,000.* 🚌 ℹ️ *TAT, Ubon Ratchathani (0-4524-3770).* 🎪 *daily.* 🎆 *Bun Bang Fai (Rocket) Festival (May).*

L IKE MANY provincial towns across Thailand, Yasothon has only a few tourist sights. There are one or two temples that are worth visiting, in particular **Wat Thung Sawang** and **Wat Mahathat Yasothon**. Situated in the center of the town, the latter is home to the Phra That Phra Anon *chedi*, thought to have been built in the 7th century to house the relics of Phra Anon, the closest disciple of the Buddha.

Yasothon is best known, however, as the principal venue for the Bun Bang Fai or "Rocket" Festival *(see pp43–4)*. As a result of harsh weather in Northeast Thailand, this festival, the principal function of which is to appease a Hindu rain god, is one of great symbolic importance. Local people invest enormous sums of money in the construction of huge bamboo rockets. The gunpowder that goes into the rockets is pounded by young girls in the temple grounds,

Prasat Hin Phimai **6**

ปราสาทหินพิมาย

See pp266–7.

Khorat **7**

โคราช

Khorat province. 🚶 *207,000.* ✈️ 🚌 🚆 ℹ️ *TAT, 2102–4 Mittraphap Rd, Khorat (0-4421-3666).* 🎪 *daily.* 🎆 *Thao Suranari Festival (late Mar/early Apr), Phimai Boat Racing (Oct/Nov).*

I N FORMER TIMES, Khorat, or Nakhon Ratchasima, was two separate towns, Khorakhapura and Sema; they were joined during the reign of

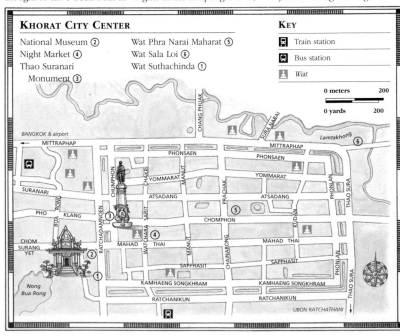

KHORAT CITY CENTER

National Museum ②
Night Market ④
Thao Suranari Monument ③
Wat Phra Narai Maharat ⑤
Wat Sala Loi ⑥
Wat Suthachinda ①

KEY

🚆 Train station
🚌 Bus station
🚶 Wat

0 meters 200
0 yards 200

Ornate pediment and façade of the *bot* at Wat Phra Narai Maharat

King Narai (1656–88). Today Khorat is a rapidly expanding business center. Its recent development stems from playing host to a nearby US airbase during the Vietnam War. At first sight Khorat appears to the visitor as a sprawl of confusing roads and heavy traffic. The city center has little of interest save for the **Night Market** that sells good-value street foods and local handicrafts.

At the city's western gate, Pratu Chumphon, is the **Thao Suranari Monument**, built in memory of Khunying Mo, a woman who successfully defended Khorat against an attack by an invading Lao army in 1826. While her husband, the deputy governor of Khorat, was away on business in Bangkok, Prince Anuwong of Vientiane (*see pp284–5*) seized the city. Khunying Mo and her fellow captives allegedly served the Lao army with liquor and were then able to kill them in their drunken stupor with whatever weapons were at hand. The Lao invasion was therefore held at bay until help arrived. Khunying Mo was given the title of Thao Suranari or "brave lady" from which the monument, built in 1934, derives its name. It shows Khunying Mo standing, hand on hip, on a tall pedestal. The

Thao Suranari Monument

base of the statue is adorned with garlands and ornamental offerings made by local people in their respect for her; a week-long festival, including folk performances of dancing, theater, and song is also held in her honor each year.

Located in the grounds of **Wat Suthachinda** is Khorat's **Maha Weerawong National Museum**. The artifacts on display here range from skeletal remains of human corpses, Dvaravati and Ayutthaya Buddha images, ceramics, and wood carvings, and were donated to Prince Maha Weerawong, from whom the museum derives its name.

Though quite a modern city, Khorat has a number of other Buddhist temples. In the *wihan* of **Wat Phra Narai Maharat** is a sandstone image of the Hindu god Vishnu, originally found at Khmer ruins near to the city.

One of the most strikingly innovative, modern Buddhist temples in northeast Thailand is **Wat Sala Loi**, or the "temple of the floating pavilion," on the banks of the Lam Takhong River. Designed in the form of a Chinese junk, the main *wihan* of this *wat* has won architectural awards. It was constructed entirely from local materials, including distinctive earthenware tiles made only at the nearby village of Dan Kwian. The original site on which

Wat Sala Loi now stands dates back to the time of Khunying Mo, and her ashes are still buried here, a fitting resting place for the heroine without whom present-day Khorat would possibly not exist.

Just outside Khorat, **Wat Khao Chan Ngam**, is the site of prehistoric finds, while at **Wat Thep Phitak Punnaram**, a large white Buddha overlooks the road.

Maha Weerawong National Museum
Ratchadamnoen Rd. ◯ *Wed–Sun.*
● *public hols.* ◩

Dan Kwian ❽
ด่านเกวียน

Khorat province. ⬛ *2,300.*
ℹ *TAT, Khorat (0-4421-3666).*

SOUTHEAST OF KHORAT is Dan Kwian, first inhabited in the mid-18th century by the Mon people traveling east from the Burmese border. Since then it has become famous for its rust-colored pottery, derived from the high iron content of the local clay.

Today Dan Kwian is essentially a collection of ceramics factories, many of which can export large items for tourists. Shops selling the local pottery line the highway at the entrance point to the village. Items for sale include jewelry, elaborately decorated vases, often in the form of upstanding fish, chicken-shaped plant pots, leaf-shaped wind chimes, and traditional water jars.

LUCKY KHORAT CATS

Silver-colored Khorat cats are named after the Khorat Plateau. They are one of the most prized breeds in Thailand. A pair of Khorat cats is sometimes given as a wedding present in the Northeast, as they are believed to bring good fortune to their owners. They are mentioned in a book of cat poems written during the Ayutthaya period. Khorat cats were first introduced to the West in 1896, but did not gain the same popularity as their cream-colored relatives, who are still known as the original Siamese cats.

Thai stamp bearing a picture of a Khorat cat

Prasat Hin Phimai ⑥
ปราสาทหินพิมาย

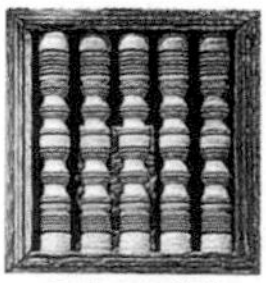

Balustraded window

IN THE SMALL TOWN of Phimai, on the banks of the Mun River, lies one of Thailand's most extensively restored Khmer temple complexes. There is no definitive date for the construction of this temple, but the central sanctuary is likely to have been completed during the reign of Suryavarman I (1001–49). Prasat Hin Phimai lies on what was once a direct route to the Khmer capital at Angkor, and, unusually, is oriented in a southeasterly direction to face that city. Originally a Brahmanic shrine dedicated to Shiva, Prasat Hin Phimai was rededicated as a Mahayana Buddhist temple at the end of the 12th century. Its famous lintels and pediments depict scenes from the Ramayana (see p36), and, unique among Khmer temples, Buddhist themes. Restoration of the site was carried out by the Fine Arts Department in 1964–9.

Front View of Central Sanctuary
The white sandstone edifice is topped with a rounded prang, the style of which may have influenced the builders of Angkor Wat (see pp254–5).

Naga Bridge
This symbolic bridge leads to the main entrance of the temple complex. The line of nagas that flank either side of the bridge are mythical guardian spirits.

CENTRAL SANCTUARY
The word *prasat*, which is used to refer to the central sanctuary, also describes the temple complex as a whole.

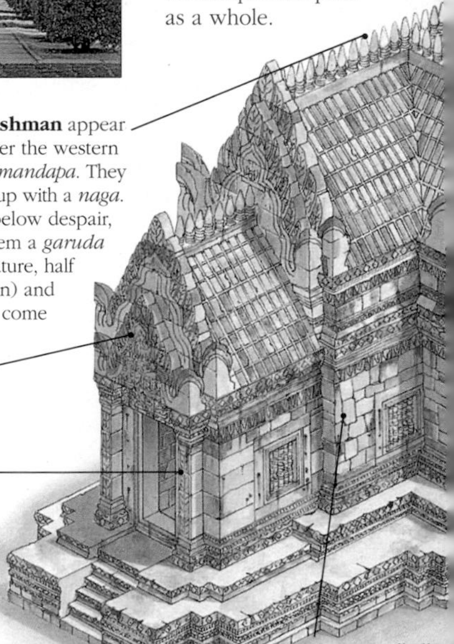

Rama and Lakshman appear on the lintel over the western entrance to the *mandapa*. They have been tied up with a *naga*. The monkeys below despair, while above them a *garuda* (a mythical creature, half bird, half human) and more monkeys come to the rescue.

Southern Pediment
The southern pediment of the mandapa *shows a dancing Shiva, a classic Khmer theme. His mount, Nandin the bull, is to the right.*

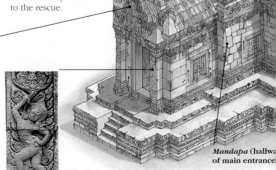

Mandapa (hallway of main entrance)

Pilaster with Vajarasattva
On the southern face of the mandapa, *this pilaster shows a Vajarasattva (guardian spirit), holding a thunderbolt and a bell, protecting the door.*

STAR FEATURES

★ Northern Porch

★ Northern Pediment

★ Buddha under Naga

Rama and his monkeys, building the causeway to Lanka – a scene from the Ramayana *(see p36)* – can be seen on the western pediment of the *prang*.

Prang (tower)

★ **Northern Porch**
The centerpiece of the northern porch is this lintel depicting a three-headed, six-armed Vajarasattva. Below him crouch a group of dancing girls.

VISITORS' CHECKLIST

Centre of Phimai town, Khorat province. ℹ TAT, Khorat (0-4421 -3666). @ tatsima@tat.or.th ✕ 🚌 🚏 Khorat, then songthaew. ⏱ 6am–6pm daily. 📷 📹 Phimai Temple Festival (Nov).

★ **Northern Pediment**
This scene from the Ramayana includes Vishnu holding a conch, a lotus, a discus, and a staff.

★ **Buddha under Naga**
Seated atop a coiled naga and protected by an umbrella formed by the beast's head, this reproduction of a 13th-century Buddha is in the Bayon (see p254) style.

The God of Justice, on the pediment of the eastern porch, judges a feud between Rama and Tosakan *(see p37)*, good and evil.

Trilokayavijaya, the most important Mahayana Bodhisattva (Enlightened being), can be seen on the interior lintel of the eastern porch.

Novice Monks
Though Prasat Hin Phimai does not function as a working wat, it is sometimes the setting for Buddhist gatherings and celebrations.

PLAN OF COMPLEX

1 Central sanctuary
2 Inner compound
3 Outer compound
4 Royal pavilions
5 *Gopuras* (entrance pavilions)
6 *Naga* (serpent) bridge

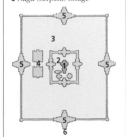

Prasat Ta Muen and Prasat Ta Muen Tot ⑨

ปราสาทตาเมือนและตาเมือนโต๊ด

Off Hwy 214, Surin province.
ℹ *TAT, Khorat (0-4421-3666).* 🚉
🚌 *Surin, then preferably by organized tour.* ⭕ *daily.* 📷

IN THE DISTRICT of Ta Muen, in Surin province, the remains of two Khmer *prasats* stand 100 m (330 ft) apart. One, Prasat Ta Muen, is a laterite chapel marking what would once have been a resting place on the long, arduous road between Angkor *(see pp254–5)* and Prasat Hin Phimai *(see pp266–7)*. The other, Prasat Ta Muen Tot, is more decayed and was originally a hospital to care for travelers along this route. Both were built by King Jayavarman VII (1181–1220).

Although both *prasats* are today largely in ruins, with their brickwork gripped and overrun by the roots of towering fig trees, they are potent reminders of the powerful Khmer Empire that once held sway over the Khorat Plateau. Because of their location along the rather dangerous Cambodian border, Ta Muen and Ta Muen Tot are best seen as part of a tour organized by one of the guesthouses in Surin, and may require a military escort. They are not easily accessible to lone tourists and cannot be visited at times of disputes and skirmishes between the various rival factions in the area.

Border police who act as armed escorts for visitors, Prasat Ta Muen

Prasat Hin Muang Tam ⑩

ปราสาทหินเมืองต่ำ

Off Hwy 214, Buri Ram province.
ℹ *TAT, Khorat (0-4421-3666).*
🚌 *from Surin to Prakhon Chai, then songthaew.* ⭕ *daily.* 📷

MUANG TAM, or "the lower city," stands at the foot of Khao Phnom Rung, an extinct volcano on top of which lies the Khmer site of Prasat Hin Khao Phnom Rung *(see pp270–1)*. Muang Tam postdates the earliest stages of construction of the more elaborate and well-preserved temple above and was built in brick, sandstone, and laterite between the 10th and 12th centuries as a residence for the local governor. Today little remains, and at first sight Muang Tam appears to be nothing more than an exotic heap of decaying brickwork.

The remains of four brick sanctuaries surround what would once have been a central temple containing religious icons. The reliefs on the Muang Tam lintels indicate that these icons are most likely to have been Hindu. The lintel over the northern sanctuary shows Shiva and his consort Parvati riding on Nandin the bull, another lintel depicts the four-headed Hindu god of creation, Brahma.

All the sanctuaries in the complex face east and are encircled by galleries (now collapsed). On each side there are

---

THE SURIN ELEPHANT ROUNDUP

In the third weekend of November, Surin is transformed by the annual Elephant Roundup. The first roundup was held here in 1960, though nowadays the elephants are used less as working animals than as performers. Some 150 to 200 elephants from local farms are led into Surin by their riders. Shows include demonstrations of how elephants are captured and raised. There are war parades celebrating King Naresuan of Ayutthaya (1590–1605), who fought the Burmese on elephant back. Soldiers, dressed in Ayutthayan costume, march toward an imagined enemy with spears and shields poised. There are also demonstrations of the elephants' strength and intelligence, as well as a chance for spectators to take rides.

Elephants and riders in traditional costume, Surin

also four *gopuras* or entrance pavilions. Beyond these lie four L-shaped ponds, decorated at each corner with majestic, multiheaded *nagas*. The ponds themselves are filled with colorful lotus blossoms.

An immense reservoir or *baray*, 1,200 m (3,950 ft) wide and 500 m (1,650 ft) long, is situated to the north of Muang Tam, pointing to the fact that this site probably once supported a sizeable population.

Prasat Hin Khao Phnom Rung ⓫
ปราสาทหินเขาพนมรุ้ง

See pp270–1.

Boiling silkworm cocoons to release the silk threads, Surin

Surin ⓬
สุรินทร์

Surin province. 🏘 214,000. 🚉 🚌
ℹ TAT, Khorat (0-4421-3666). 🏛
daily. 🐘 Elephant Roundup (Nov).

S URIN IS FAMOUS for its silk, its elephants, and its first ruler, Phraya Surin Phakdi Si Narong Wang, from whom it derives its name. A modern statue in the town depicts the leader dressed to go into battle. A member of the Suay tribe, Phraya Surin became ruler of Surin in 1760 when, according to legend, he was instrumental in recapturing an escaped royal white elephant *(see p102)*.

The process of silk production *(see pp256–7)* can be seen in the surrounding villages.

There are over 700 patterns used by silk weavers in Surin province. Rhomboid designs are especially popular.

During the 1970s, when the Khmer Rouge seized control of, and terrorized, neighboring Cambodia, thousands of Cambodian refugees crossed the Banthat mountains into Surin province and took up residence there, alongside already established Lao refugees, Thais, and Suay tribespeople. Although most immigrants have been repatriated, some remain.

Surin's main attraction is undoubtedly the annual Elephant Roundup, at the **Surin Sports Park**. At other times of the year, artifacts associated with elephant capture and training can be seen at the **Surin Museum**, including buffalo-hide ropes used by Suay tribesmen to catch wild elephants. There are also exhibits of the protective clothing and amulets, inscribed with magical incantations, worn during elephant hunts. The capture and training of elephants in Surin is traditionally a male preserve. In fact, women are strictly forbidden to touch the paraphernalia of the hunt, in case they destroy the magic needed to catch the elephants.

Statue of Phraya Surin

🏠 **Surin Museum**
Chitramboong Rd. ⭘ Wed–Sun.

Road sign advertising Ban Ta Klang, the Elephant Village

Ban Ta Klang ⓭
บ้านตากลาง

Surin province. 🏘 15,000. ℹ TAT, Khorat (0-4421-3666). 🏛 daily. 🐘 Elephant Roundup (Nov).

T HE SUAY TRIBESPEOPLE make up the population of Ban Ta Klang, which is also known as the Elephant Village, a name that reflects the Suay people's skill in capturing and training wild elephants. The Suay are thought to have migrated to Thailand from Central Asia in the early 9th century and to have been the first people to make use of elephants for building, in particular for the construction of Khmer temples. Nowadays, Ban Ta Klang is the primary training ground for the Surin Elephant Roundup. Every October, approximately one month before the roundup in Surin itself, Suay tribesmen begin to practise their skills. In the days leading up to the roundup, the training becomes intense. To participate in the roundup, the riders must walk their elephants the 50 km (32 miles) or so south to the outskirts of Surin.

An elephant feeding while the trainer takes a break, Surin

Prasat Hin Khao Phnom Rung ⑪

ปราสาทหินเขาพนมรุ้ง

Carved stone elephants

Crowning the extinct volcano of Khao Phnom Rung is the splendid Khmer temple complex Prasat Hin Khao Phnom Rung. A Hindu temple, it was built here to symbolize Shiva's abode on Mount Krailasa; hence the processional way leading to the central sanctuary, its stairways, and *naga* bridges extending in total for 200 m (655 ft). The temple's construction began early in the 10th century, and, like other Khmer sites, it lies on a route to Angkor Wat in Cambodia *(see pp254–5)*. Its buildings are aligned so that at Songkran *(see p44)*, the rising sun can be seen through all 15 doors of the western *gopura*.

Western Porch Pediment
This carving shows monkeys rescuing Sita in a chariot that is itself a model of the temple.

★ **Central Sanctuary**
The corncob-shaped prang of the central sanctuary is the cosmological summit of the processional way.

Brick Sanctuary
Located just southeast of the central sanctuary, this 13th-century Bayon-style, laterite structure was a late addition to the compound. It was built as a library.

★ **Naga Bridge**
This naga bridge, which is located inside the main temple compound, links the east-facing entrance gopura to the central sanctuary. The body of the naga forms the bridge's balustrade.

STAR FEATURES

★ **Central Sanctuary**

★ **Naga Bridge**

★ **Ornamental Ponds**

★ **Processional Way**

Pediment over Porch of Mandapa
The carving on this pediment represents Shiva Nataraja, the dancing Shiva, his ten arms splayed out in a dance of death and destruction.

VISITORS' CHECKLIST

50 km (31 miles) S of Buriram, off Hwy 24, Buriram province.
ℹ TAT, Khorat (0-4421-3666).
🚌 from Khorat or Surin to Ban Ta Ko, then songthaew.
🕐 9am–5pm daily. 📷 🚻 🎫
Phnom Rung Festival (Apr).

Nandin the Bull
This image of Nandin the bull, the mythical mount of the Hindu deity Shiva, is located in the first, eastern chamber of the central sanctuary.

Main temple compound

Gopura

★ **Ornamental Ponds**
Located at the front of the entrance to the main temple compound are four ponds. They supposedly represent the four sacred rivers of the Indian subcontinent. In the background, a naga *bridge leads into the complex.*

Main entrance   *Naga* bridge

The stairway forms part of the processional way to the principal temple compound.

★ **Processional Way**
This processional walkway was built to symbolize the spiritual journey from earth to Hindu heaven.

MEKONG RIVER VALLEY

SOME 2,000 KM (1,250 MILES) *from its source in the Tibetan Himalayas, having passed through China, Burma, the tip of northern Thailand, then Laos, the Mekong River reaches Chiang Khan in Northeast Thailand. From here the river forms the border with Laos until it flows into Cambodia. Although relatively few tourists visit this border country, it has many natural and cultural attractions.*

The agricultural basin of the Mekong River Valley stands in contrast to the dusty, parched Khorat Plateau to the south and west and the rugged mountains on the Lao side of the river. The Mekong River Valley's relatively fertile land means fruit and vegetables can be produced on a marketable scale. Furthermore, due to its distance from Bangkok, the area has escaped widespread development and remains one of the most beautiful, unspoilt regions in the country.

Lively Nong Khai is the most important border town in the region and the access point to the Lao capital, Vientiane. The stretch of river to the west of here is dotted with numerous picturesque towns and villages with traditional teak houses. At Phu Phrabat Historical Park (near Ban Phu), a variety of mesmerizing sandstone rock formations can be seen. Nearby are the extraordinary huge Buddhist and Hindu statues of Wat Khaek.

As the river winds its way east and then south, past Nakhon Phanom, it passes one of the most important Buddhist pilgrimage sites in Thailand, Wat Phra That Phanom. The temple supposedly dates from the death of the Lord Buddha in 543 BC.

Farther downriver is Pha Taem, a cliff face painted with huge prehistoric figures and unusual geometrical patterns. Not far away, at Khong Chiam, the Mun River flows into the Mekong, creating the phenomenon of the "two-colored river." From here the Mekong flows into Laos and then Cambodia. The Cambodian border with Thailand has been the scene of skirmishes between rival factions and, as a result, it is not always possible to reach one of the most magnificent of all Khmer monuments, Prasat Khao Phra Wihan.

View from Nakhon Phanom, looking over the Mekong River and into Laos

◁ **Distinctive rock formations – a feature of the Northeast – near Phu Kradung**

Exploring the Mekong River Valley

THE MIGHTY MEKONG RIVER forms a 750-km (465-mile) border between Northeast Thailand and Laos. The valley along which it flows is a relatively fertile area in an otherwise arid region of Thailand. It is possible to follow the length of the Mekong from Chiang Khan to Pha Taem by road. Some of the most attractive areas are west of Nong Khai, where visitors pass through sleepy towns and villages of pretty wooden houses. South of the northern stretch of the Mekong lie the Phu Rua, Phu Kradung, and Phu Hin Rong Kla national parks. Farther south is Ubon Rachathani, by far the largest city in the region.

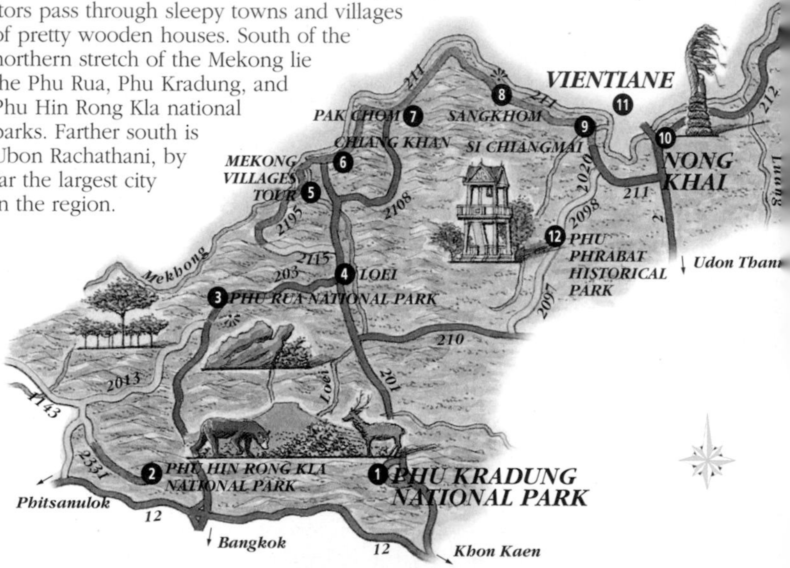

VIENTIANE

PAK CHOM 7   SANGKHOM   8

CHIANG KHAN   SI CHIANGMAI   9

MEKONG VILLAGES TOUR 5   6   NONG KHAI

10

12 PHU PHRABAT HISTORICAL PARK   ↓ Udon Thani

Mekong

4 LOEI

3 PHU RUA NATIONAL PARK

11

PHU HIN RONG KLA NATIONAL PARK   2

Phitsanulok

1 PHU KRADUNG NATIONAL PARK

↓ Bangkok   12   Khon Kaen

The colorful Phi Ta Khon Festival, held in Loei

SIGHTS AT A GLANCE

GETTING AROUND

Nong Khai, Loei, Nakhon Phanom, and Ubon Ratchathani are the best bases from which to tour the area. Two train lines run through the region: a direct line, which divides at Khorat, connects Bangkok to Ubon Ratchathani and to Udon Thani. Travelers can pick up a connection from Udon Thani to Nong Khai. The best way to get around is by bus, rented car, or *songthaew*. Long-tail boats run on some sections of the Mekong River.

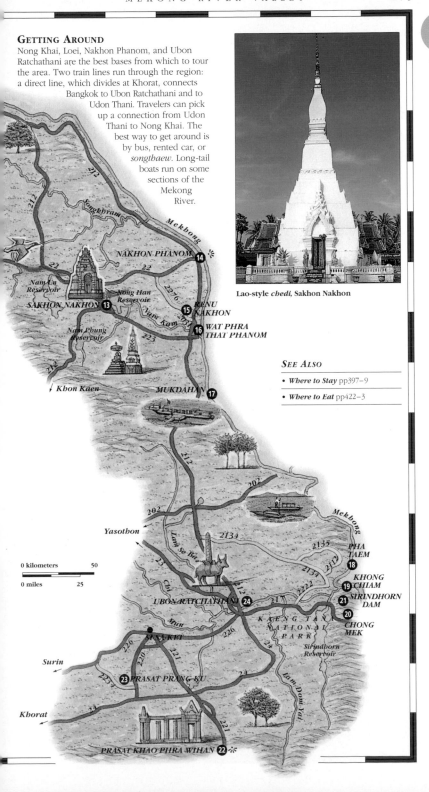

Lao-style *chedi*, Sakhon Nakhon

SEE ALSO

• *Where to Stay* pp397–9
• *Where to Eat* pp422–3

Phu Kradung National Park ❶

อุทยานแห่งชาติภูกระดึง

Thai flower

THERE ARE TWO LEGENDS connected to Phu Kradung, or "bell mountain": the first is that the sound of a bell, said to be that of the god Indra, once rang out from its peak; the second is that the mountain rings like a bell when struck with a staff. This steep-sided, flat-topped mountain is now a national park covering 348 sq km (135 sq miles), its 60-km (37-mile) plateau 1,350 m (4,450 ft) above sea level. This plateau has a climate cool enough for plants that cannot survive in other parts of Thailand; many animals also live in its thin pine forests and grasslands.

Asiatic Black Bear
This bear lives in forests all over Southeast Asia; it feeds on ants, insect larvae, nuts, and fruit.

Waterfalls
Waterfalls are dotted all over Phu Kradung. They are most impressive in October (the end of the rainy season).

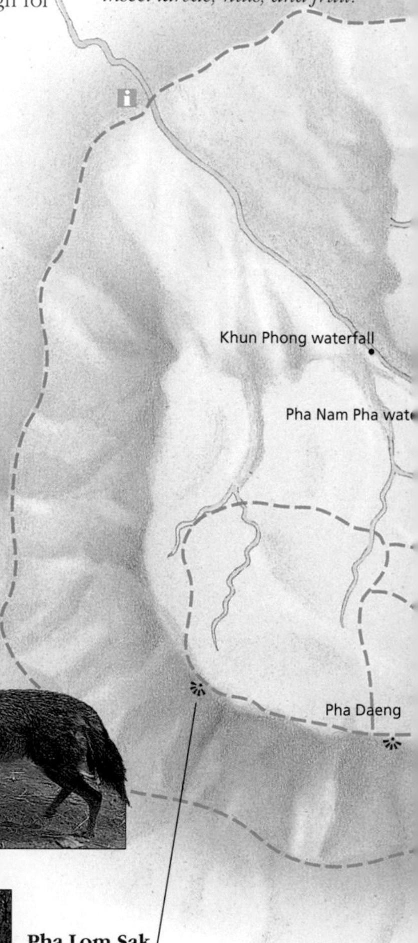

Asian Jackal
Thailand has two wild dogs. The handsome Asian jackal, which lives on Phu Kradung, has a bushy tail. The other common species is the red dog.

Khun Phong waterfall

Pha Nam Pha wat

Pha Daeng

Pha Lom Sak
This unusually shaped sandstone ledge is situated on the southern edge of the plateau. It provides beautiful vistas over the rolling hills and valleys. In summer, lines of people gather to photograph this popular and scenic attraction.

Pha Nok An
"Swallow cliff," situated at the eastern edge of the plateau, offers breathtaking sunrise views. Its name refers to the many families of swallows who build their nests under the cliff's overhang.

VISITORS' CHECKLIST

Loei province. Park HQ about 8 km (5 miles) off Hwy 2019, on Hwy 2019. *TAT, Udon Thani (0-4232-5406); Forestry Dept (0-4287-1333 inc bungalow bookings).* *Bus to Pha Nok Kao then* songthaew. *Access to plateau on foot only.* *mid-Jul–early Sep (rainy season).*

Pitcher Plants
Common in Phu Kradung, carnivorous pitcher plants gather nutrients lacking in the local acidic soil by "eating" insects.

Phen Pop Mai waterfall
Tharn Yai waterfall
Tharn Sawan waterfall
Sa Anodat pond
LOEI

Phone Phop waterfall is named after the first World Champion Thai boxer, Phone Kingphet, who stumbled upon it when he was training. Phone chose the plateau as a training ground because its cool climate prepared him for fights abroad.

Park entrance

0 kilometers 10

0 miles 10

KEY

- Road
- Trail
- National park office
- Camping and bungalows
- Vista

THE BALLAD OF PHU KRADUNG

Phu Kradung was the inspiration for a long poem in 1969 by the award-winning Thai poet and artist Angkhan Kalyanaphong, who eulogized its unspoiled, natural beauties. *Lam Nam Phu Kradung* ("the ballad of Phu Kradung") reflects Angkhan's interest in nature and Buddhism. This excerpt translates poorly into English:

"Each time the sun went down
I would sit at the Makduk cliff
And watch the beams of colored light
Pierce the clouds and set alight the sky."

Sa Anodat pond, one of many inspiring sights

Rapids in Phu Hin Rong Kla National Park

Phu Hin Rong Kla National Park ❷

อุทยานแห่งชาติภูหินร่องกล้า

Phitsanulok province. Park HQ off Hwy 2331, 31 km (19 miles) SE of Nakhon Thai. **i** *TAT, Phitsanulok (0-5525-2743); Forestry Dept (0-2562-0760 or www.dnp.go.th for bungalow bookings).* 🚌 *from Loei or Phitsanulok to Nakhon Thai, then songthaew.* 🏞

COVERING AN AREA of 307 sq km (120 sq miles), Phu Hin Rong Kla National Park has a wide variety of flora and fauna and an unusual open-air museum with exhibits of the Communist camp based

here in the 1960s and '70s. The spread of Communism in Southeast Asia from the 1950s alarmed the Thai goverment, and hostilities between the Communist Party of Thailand (CPT) and the military commenced in 1964. Soon after, the open forests of the Phu Hin Rong Kla mountain range became a CPT stronghold. An average elevation of 1,000 m (3,300 ft), proximity to Laos – run by the Communist Pathet Lao from 1975 (*see p285*) – and the access this facilitated to headquarters, at Kunming in China, all made it an ideal site. The CPT was active after 1976, when thousands of students fled here after a coup in Bangkok. By 1979, disillusioned with Communism, many began to take advantage of an amnesty from the Thai government. Dwindling support and government attacks on Phu Hin Rong Kla in the early 1980s led the site to fall to the authorities in 1982.

Two years later it opened as a national park. Its highest peak, Phu Man Khao, rises to a height of 1,620 m (5,300 ft).

Phu Rua National Park ❸

อุทยานแห่งชาติภูเรือ

Loei province. Park HQ off Hwy 203, 60 km (30 miles) W of Loei. **i** *TAT, Udon Thani (0-4232-5406); Forestry Dept (0-2562-0760 or www.dnp. go.th for bungalow bookings).* 🚌 *from Loei to Phu Rua village, then songthaew.* 🏞

PHU RUA or "boat mountain" gets its name from its peak, which is shaped like a junk. It stands some 1,365 m (4,500 ft) above sea level and offers spectacular views of the town of Loei to the south and toward Laos. A modern Buddha image sits looking out over the plains in contemplation of their beauty.

It is possible to drive to the summit of Phu Rua, passing several bizarre rock formations on the way. The most remarkable is Hin Ta or "tortoise rock," with two huge sandstone boulders stacked one on top of the other, surmounted by a third, giving the structure the appearance of a giant mushroom.

For the traveler with time to explore the 121 sq km (47 sq miles) of this national park, a number of marked trails lead

Unusual rock formation at Phu Rua National Park

through a beautiful landscape of meadows, rock gardens, and pine and evergreen forests. Views across the surrounding lowlands can be seen from Phu Kut and the cliffs of Pha Lon Noi, Pha Dong Tham San, Pha Yat, and Pha Sap Thong. There are also several waterfalls located around the park, namely Huai Phai, Huai Ta Wat, and Lan Hin Taek.

Animals at Phu Rua National Park include barking deer, wild pigs, a wide variety of birds, including pheasant, and the rare *tao puru*, or Siamese big-headed turtle. Phu Rua is also famed for being one of the coolest areas of Thailand, with a record low temperature of -4° C (25° F) having been recorded here in 1981.

Relics of the war between the military and the CPT, Phu Hin Rong Kla

Rolling hills near Loei, typical of this part of the Northeast

Loei ❹

เลย

Loei province. 🏠 86,000. ✈ 🚉 ℹ
TAT, Udon Thani (0-4232-5406). 🛒 daily.
🎉 Cotton Blossom Festival (Feb), Phi Ta
Khon Festival, Rocket Festival (both May).

IN THAI, the word *loei* means "beyond" or "to the farthest extreme," a fitting name for a town and province that lie in the northernmost part of Northeast Thailand, straddling the edge of the Khorat Plateau. Though the province is administrated as part of Isan (the Northeast), its climate and landscape are more similar to those of Northern Thailand. In winter it is cold and foggy, in summer searingly hot. In the past, bureaucrats who had fallen out of favor with the Siamese government, based in Bangkok, were posted to the remote town of Loei as punishment for their inefficiency. One fortunate aspect of Loei's isolation is that it firmly retains its traditional flavor.

Lying along the west bank of the Loei River, Loei has a few sights of interest to visitors. There is a lively market by the bridge across the river, and next to the bridge is the **Lak Muang** or "city pillar." The town also has an old Chinese shrine, **Chao Pho Kut Pong**, a popular place of worship for the local people. The surrounding valley is rich in minerals and also produces some of the finest cotton in Thailand. Examples of this can be bought in Loei, in shops along Charoenraj Road and Ruamchai Road.

Loei also has a reasonable amount of cheap accommodations, making it a good base from which to visit Phu Rua and Phu Kradung *(see pp276–7)* national parks.

PHI TA KHON FESTIVAL

Although a less lively version of this festival is held in the provincial capital of Loei in July, its real home is in the town of Dan Sai, 80 km (50 miles) to the west. Here Phi Ta Khon takes place in June at the beginning of the rainy season *(see pp43–5)*. Its purpose is to make Buddhist merit and call for rain. The festival's origins are in the Buddhist tale of Prince Vessandorn, the Lord Buddha's final incarnation before he attained *nirvana*. Apparently, when Vessandorn returned to his city, the welcoming procession was so enchanting that the spirits emerged to celebrate. Today, the young men of Dan Sai dress up as spirits *(phi ta khon)*, draped in robes of patchwork rags and sporting painted masks made out of coconut tree trunks with huge, gaping mouths, beaklike noses, and wickerbasket crowns. During the three-day festival, they make playful jibes at onlookers as they parade a sacred Buddha image around the town. Monks also recite the story of Vessandorn to the crowd. On the third day, the "spirits" bring the festival to a close by circumambulating the main building of the local *wat* three times, before finally casting their colorful masks into a nearby river.

Phi Ta Khon
costume

Young men, dressed as spirits, preparing to parade a sacred Buddha around Loei town

Phi Ta Khon "spirits" making fun of onlookers

Ornate, Lao-style façade of Wat Tha Kok, Chiang Khan

Chiang Khan ❻

เชียงคาน

Loei province. 🏯 *52,000.* 🚌 *from Loei or Nong Khai.* 🛈 *TAT, Udon Thani (0-4232-5406).*

CHIANG KHAN CONSISTS of two two-kilometer-long parallel streets running along the south bank of the Mekong River and lined with run-down teakwood shop-houses, restaurants, and temples. Those temples most worth a visit are Wat Santi, Wat Pa Klang, built over 100 years ago by Lao immigrants, Wat Si Khun Muang, Wat Tha Kok, and Wat Mahathat. The last is the oldest temple in Chiang Khan, its *bot* having been built in 1654. Like Wat Tha Kok, it shows French colonial influence in its colonnades and shutters.

Wat Tha Khok has a beautiful, painted ceiling. Its exterior walls are stained red, like the river, from dust. This possibly stems from deforestation in nearby Laos, which exposes the local red topsoil.

ENVIRONS: Located 2 km (1 mile) farther east from Wat Tha Kok along the Mekong River is Wat Tha Khaek. Neglected for years, this temple is now undergoing major reconstruction in a mixture of traditional and modern styles. A further 2 km (1 mile) down river are the scenic Kaeng Kut Khu rapids.

Pak Chom ❼

ปากชม

Loei province. 🏯 *29,000.* 🚌 *from Loei or Nong Khai.* 🛈 *TAT, Udon Thani (0-4232-5406).* 📅 *daily.*

PAK CHOM IS LITTLE MORE than a picturesque settlement of ramshackle wooden buildings clustered by the bank of the Mekong River, 40 km (25 miles) northeast of Chiang Khan. It's a good place to stop for refreshments and to enjoy the scenery. In the 1970s and 1980s the town had a somewhat higher profile thanks to Ban Winai, a Lao-Hmong *(see p196)* refugee camp of some 15,000 inhabitants. It was established when these tribespeople fled Laos in the wake of the Pathet Lao *(see p285),* who overthrew the Lao monarchy and took control of the country in 1975. In 1992 the camp was disbanded and the Hmong moved to Chiang Kham in the Chiang Rai province of Northern Thailand.

Mekong Villages Tour ❺

AS WELL AS VILLAGES, this tour takes in temples, lush forest, and great river views. No river in the world is quite like the 4,025-km (2,500-mile) Mekong, with its distinctive red waters. Its source is in the Himalayas, and it separates Laos and Thailand for 750 km (470 miles) before flowing through Cambodia and Vietnam out into the South China Sea. Rich in agriculture, its floodplain has been a source of wealth in an otherwise infertile region.

Ban Muang ④
Fishermen casting their nets are a common sight at this point in the Mekong River.

Pha Baen ②
This small village is one of many with picturesque wooden buildings and river views.

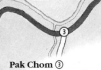

Pak Chom ③
The journey along the stretch of river between Chiang Khan and Pak Chom can be made by road or by long-tail boat.

Chiang Khan ①
Many of the temples and shop-houses in Chiang Khan show Lao influences.

TIPS FOR TRAVELERS

Length: *120 km (75 miles).*
Stopping-off points: *Chiang Khan has a couple of restaurants, and four or five good guesthouses serving food. Pak Chom, Sangkhom, and Si Chiangmai all have good guesthouses offering food. Some guesthouses rent out bicycles. Food vendors can be found in most villages and towns.*
Public transport: *Local buses run between the main towns along the route. It is also possible to travel from Chiang Khan to Pak Chom by long-tail boat.*

KEY

━━ Tour route
╌╌ Other roads
〰 Rivers

Sangkhom ⑧
สังคม

Nong Khai province. 🚶 *19,000.*
🚌 *from Loei or Nong Khai.* ℹ *TAT,*
Udon Thani (0-4232-5406).

THE MAIN ATTRACTIONS of this town are its peace and quiet and its location in a particularly lush part of the Mekong River Valley. Ranged along the bank of the river are some quaint wooden buildings. Sangkhom also makes a good base for excursions into the surrounding countryside.

ENVIRONS: The **Than Thip falls** are a major highlight of this area. Just outside Sangkhom, 3 km (2 miles) off the main highway, they are hidden in the middle of jungle and banana groves. The two main, and most accessible, levels of this waterfall have pools at their bases, making them ideal for a refreshing swim. More intrepid travelers can explore a further three levels higher up the falls.

Topiary in the gardens of the Fisheries Department, near Si Chiangmai

Si Chiangmai ⑨
ศรีเชียงใหม่

Nong Khai province. 🚶 *23,000.*
🚌 *from Loei or Nong Khai.* ℹ *TAT,*
Udon Thani (0-4232-5406). 🕙 *daily.*

THIS TOWN overlooks the Lao capital of Vientiane *(see pp284–5)* on the other side of the Mekong River and has a large population of Lao and Vietnamese refugees. Its main claim to fame is as the world's largest producer of spring roll wrappers. When the weather is good, they can be seen along the roadsides, spread out on bamboo racks to dry in the sun.

ENVIRONS: Located 5 km (3 miles) outside Si Chiangmai are the gardens of the **Fisheries Department**, featuring unusual elephant-shaped topiary.

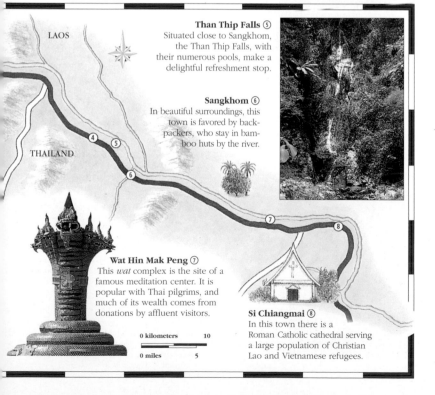

Than Thip Falls ⑤
Situated close to Sangkhom, the Than Thip Falls, with their numerous pools, make a delightful refreshment stop.

Sangkhom ⑥
In beautiful surroundings, this town is favored by backpackers, who stay in bamboo huts by the river.

LAOS

THAILAND

Wat Hin Mak Peng ⑦
This *wat* complex is the site of a famous meditation center. It is popular with Thai pilgrims, and much of its wealth comes from donations by affluent visitors.

Si Chiangmai ⑧
In this town there is a Roman Catholic cathedral serving a large population of Christian Lao and Vietnamese refugees.

0 kilometers   10

0 miles   5

Nong Khai ⑩
หนองคาย

Village Weaver shop sign

ONCE A SLEEPY BORDER TOWN, Nong Khai has recently been transformed into one of the busiest commercial centers in the Northeast, partly because of the opening of the Friendship Bridge. The first bridge to span the Mekong River between Thailand and Laos, its construction in 1994 was a factor in an increase in trade between the two countries. Nevertheless, the town center retains much of its original charm, and Nong Khai's main attraction for travelers is still its peaceful riverside character.

Relative peace and quiet on Nong Khai's Meechai Street

Exploring Nong Khai
Nong Khai's streets and *sois* are lined with traditional wooden shop-houses. Its most vibrant neighborhood is around the Sadet riverboat pier, with its market and adjacent restaurants overlooking the Mekong River. A recent influx of prosperity in the town is made obvious by the burgeoning number of restaurants as well as modern shopping centers and banking facilities.

Intricate carving on the rear of the Lao-style Wat Si Muang

🏬 Indochina Market
ตลาดอินโดจีน
Off Rimkhong Rd, Tha Sadet. ◯ *daily.*
This market remains the focus of lively, local trade carried out between Thailand and Laos. Reciprocal visa arrangements allow merchants from either country to visit Vientiane *(see pp284–5)* or Nong Khai for up to three days. Merchandise that can be bought at the market includes clothing, pots and pans, foodstuffs, pestles and mortars, fishing nets, and tables woven from bamboo.

Prap Ho Monument
อนุสาวรีย์ปราบฮ่อ
Janjopthit Rd.
The Prap Ho Monument, a symbol of municipal pride, was built to honor those who held off Ho Chinese invasions in 1855 and 1877. Built in 1886, and bearing Thai, Lao, Chinese, and English inscriptions, it is the site of annual celebrations on March 5.

🏛 Prajak Road
ถนนประจักษ์
Along Prajak Road, visitors can pay a call at the Village Weaver shop, where traditional silk weaving is carried out. The factory/shop specializes in *mut mee,* the name given to a method of tie-dying used in the Northeast. It was established as part of a program to encourage local girls to stay and work in Nong Khai, rather than moving to larger urban centers such as Bangkok. There is also a market on Prajak Road, to the rear of the bus station.

🛕 Wat Si Muang
วัดศรีเมือง
Off Meechai Rd. ◯ *daily.*
The temple buildings and *chedi* of Wat Si Muang are Lao in style. The *wat* has an ornate shrine at the main entrance, cluttered with Buddhist merit offerings. Wat Si Muang is one of many such temples that line the main Meechai Road leading west toward Wat Pho Chai.

🛕 Wat Pho Chai
วัดโพธิ์ชัย
Pho Chai Rd. ◯ *daily.*
The newly restored and somewhat gaudy Wat Pho Chai lies in the southwest of the city, adjacent to a street market of the same name. Its main chapel sports imposing *naga* balustrades and a pair of roaring lions at the top of the entrance stairs, protecting the highly revered Luang Pho Phra Sai Buddha image

Guardian lion, Wat Pho Chai

housed inside. This solid gold Buddha with a ruby-studded, flame finial was originally molded in the ancient Lao kingdom of Lan Xang. It later resided in Vientiane *(see pp274–5).* In 1778 it was taken by Prince Chakri, later Rama I (1782–1809), following the first Thai invasion of Laos. As he attempted to ferry it across the Mekong, it fell into the river and, according to legend, miraculously resurfaced. After it had been rescued it was placed in Wat Pho Chai. Murals in the temple give a pictorial account of this story.

Luang Pho Phra Sai Buddha image, housed in Wat Pho Chai

🅱 Other Wats

Apart from its major sights, Nong Khai has a number of minor *wats* worth a visit. All of them have Lao-influenced architecture and include **Wat Haisoke**, **Wat Lamduan** and **Wat Si Sumang**, which all offer views of the Mekong River, and **Wat Si Khun Muang**.

ENVIRONS: Though always a major crossing point for tourists and traders bound for the Lao capital of Vientiane, Nong Khai gained significance as a commercial border post with the opening of the **Friendship Bridge** in 1994. Built with Thai, Lao, and Australian cooperation, it

links Ban Chommani on the western outskirts of Nong Khai to Tha Na Laeng on the opposite bank, some 20 km (12 miles) from Vientiane. By the foot of the bridge, on the Thai side, is a stretch of sand known as Chommani beach, a popular spot for picnicking Thais during the dry season, when the waters of the Mekong River are low.

Closer to the town center is the Lao *chedi* of **Phra That Nong Khai**, which collapsed into the Mekong River in 1847. Over the years it has slowly drifted farther and farther into the middle of the river to the point where it can now be seen only when the water is low.

By far the most unusual site of interest at Nong Khai lies some 5 km (3 miles) to the east of the town. **Wat Khaek**, also known as Sala Kaew Ku, was founded in 1978 by the charismatic Luang Pu Bunleua Surirat. This Thai-Brahmin shaman allegedly trained under a Hindu guru in Vietnam, moved on to Laos, and was then forced to Thailand by the hostile attentions of the Pathet Lao *(see p285)*. Wat Khaek is essentially an

Seven-headed *naga*, Wat Khaek

VISITORS' CHECKLIST

Nong Khai province. 🅷 83,000. 🚆 3 km (2 miles) W on Kaeo Worawut Rd. 🚌 Praserm Rd. 🅸 TAT, Udon Thani (0-4232-5406). 🛥 daily. 🎉 Nong Khai Festival (Mar), Bun Bang Fai (Rocket) Festival (May); Naga Fireballs (Oct).

open-air theme park of enormous, concrete Hindu and Buddhist sculptures.

Among the giant gods, saints, and demons that are depicted here are Rahu, the god of eclipses and, tallest of all, a 25-m (82-ft) high seven-headed *naga* with a tiny Buddha seated on its coils. The atmosphere of a walk through this eccentric collection of images is intensified by incense and piped music. The shrine building is an exhibition hall on two floors that contains, among other things, numerous photographs of the Luang Pu or "Venerable Grandfather." He is said to have such charisma that anyone drinking holy water offered by him will immediately donate all their belongings to the temple.

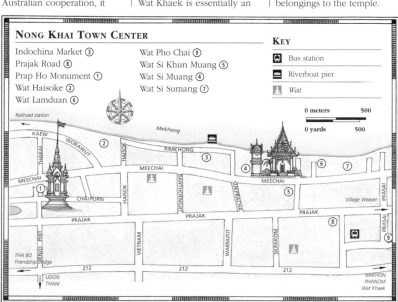

NONG KHAI TOWN CENTER

Indochina Market ③
Prajak Road ⑧
Prap Ho Monument ①
Wat Haisoke ②
Wat Lamduan ⑥

Wat Pho Chai ⑨
Wat Si Khun Muang ⑤
Wat Si Muang ④
Wat Si Sumang ⑦

KEY

🚌 Bus station
🚤 Riverboat pier
🅰 *Wat*

0 meters 500
0 yards 500

Vientiane ⑪

เวียงจันทน์

Temple door

IN ITS 1,000-YEAR HISTORY, Vientiane has come under Khmer, Vietnamese, Thai, and French colonial influence. It was capital of the Lan Xang Kingdom in the 16th century and later a vassal of Ayutthaya. The Thais sacked Vientiane in 1828. In 1893 the French annexed Laos and made Vientiane its capital. Laos gained independence in 1953; in 1975 it became a Socialist Republic. A day trip from Nong Khai (see pp282–3), today Vientiane shows a side of Southeast Asia that is fast disappearing.

Exploring Vientiane

Vientiane has been isolated from change for generations. However, trade with Thailand, encouraged by the Friendship Bridge (see p283), means that the city is likely to start changing as fast as some Thai towns across the Mekong River.

Vientiane was one of three important French Indochinese cities; the others were Ho Chi Minh City (or Saigon) and Phnom Penh. French colonial influence can still be felt in the city with its broad, tree-lined boulevards and shuttered villas that sit somewhat incongruously next to traditional Lao- and Thai-influenced structures. Some drab apartment blocks, built with Russian aid, have also sprung up.

Shop-house in Vientiane

🛕 Haw Pha Kaew

Setthathirat Rd. ◯ Tue–Sun.
● public hols. 📷
This temple was once home to the Phra Kaeo or Emerald Buddha (see p79), which was

taken by the Thais in 1778 and placed in Wat Phra Kaeo in Bangkok. (Phra Kaeo is the preferred transliteration in Thai; Pha Kaew in Lao.) A replica, a symbol of renewed friendship, was given to Laos by Thailand in 1994. The sack of 1828 left the temple in ruins. Restored in the 20th century, it is now a museum. The beautifully carved main door is all that remains of the original wat.

🛕 Wat Sisaket

Lane Xang Rd. ◯ Tue–Sun.
● public hols. 📷
This wat, built in 1818, was one of the few buildings to survive the sack of 1828. It is now the oldest wat in Vientiane and one of the most interesting to visit. Its most memorable feature is the 2,052 tiny Buddha images made of terra-cotta, bronze, and wood that fill niches in the walls of the cloister. Over 300 Buddha images also rest on a long shelf below the niches.

🏛 Lao Revolutionary Museum

Samsenthai Rd. ◯ daily. ● public hols. 📷
Artifacts and photographs here detail the period of French colonialism, independence in the 1940s and '50s, and the rise of the Pathet Lao.

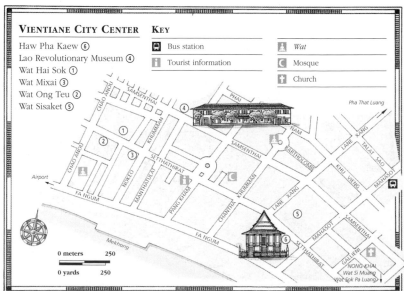

VIENTIANE CITY CENTER

KEY

Haw Pha Kaew ⑥
Lao Revolutionary Museum ④
Wat Hai Sok ①
Wat Mixai ③
Wat Ong Teu ②
Wat Sisaket ⑤

🚌 Bus station
ℹ️ Tourist information

🛕 Wat
🕌 Mosque
✝️ Church

Pha That Luang

Airport

Mekhong

0 meters   250
0 yards   250

NONG KHAI
Wat Si Muang
Wat Sok Pa Luang

Wat Mixai

Setthathirat Rd. ⬤ *daily.*

Its gates flanked by two *nyaks* or guardian giants, parts of this *wat* complex were built in 19th-century Rattanakosin style.

Wat Ong Theu

Setthathirat Rd. ⬤ *daily.*

One of the most important *wat* complexes in all Laos, Wat Ong Theu was originally founded in the early 16th century. Destroyed in 1828, it was rebuilt in the 19th and 20th centuries. The *wat* houses a large, 16th-century bronze Buddha image, with two standing Buddhas either side of it. The *wat* also houses a school for monks.

Wat Hai Sok

Setthathirat Rd. ⬤ *daily.*

Like other *wats* in Vientiane, Wat Hai Sok recently underwent restoration. Its most distinctive feature is an impressive five-tiered roof.

ENVIRONS: The **Pha That Luang**, which perches, somewhat out of the way, halfway up a hill on the northeastern outskirts of the city, is the most important national and Buddhist monument in Laos. According to legend a *chedi* was built here in the 3rd century BC to house a breastbone of the Lord Buddha. More tangible evidence

suggests this was the site of a Khmer *prasat*. The present structure was built in 1566, when Vientiane became the capital of the Lan Xang Kingdom. It was damaged in the 18th and 19th centuries and restored, albeit badly, by the French in 1900. A better restoration of the site was undertaken in the 1930s.

Wat Si Muang, to the southeast of the city center, is the most popular place of worship in Vientiane. According to legend, the site was chosen by Lao sages in 1563.

Wat Sok Pa Luang is known for its instruction in *vipassana*, a type of Buddhist meditation.

Ho Nang Ussa, a rock formation in Phu Phrabat Historical Park

Phu Phrabat Historical Park ⑫

อุทยานประวัติศาสตร์ภูพระบาท

Off Hwy 2021, 10 km (6 miles) W of Ban Pheu, Udon Thani province. ⓘ TAT, Udon Thani (0-4232-5406). 🚌 from Nong Khai or Udon Thani to Ban Phu, then songthaew. ⬤ *daily.* 📷

THE DISTINCTIVE sandstone formations that are the central attraction of this historical park cannot fail to leave their imprint on the imagination. The local population has shrouded the site in many fantastic myths and legends. According to one of these, Princess Ussa was sent to Phu Phrabat by her father to study. However, she fell in love with Prince Barot. Outraged, her father challenged the prince to a temple-building duel, but lost. A huge sandstone slab in the park, known as Kok Ma Thao Barot, is supposedly Prince Barot's stable. The mushroom-shaped Ho Nang Ussa apparently represents Princess Ussa's residence, where she pined away many long years in exile.

The 6,000-year-old human history of this site is testified to by cave paintings found on the underside of two natural rock shelters, known locally as Tham Wua and Tham Khon or "ox cave" and "people cave."

At the entrance to the historical park stands a crude replica of Wat Phra That Phanom (see p287); the **Wat Phraphutthabat Bua Bok** houses the Bua Bok Buddha Footprint and is an important pilgrimage site for local Thais.

THE PATHET LAO

The Lao Patriotic Front was formed after World War II and, with ties to Ho Chi Minh's Communist Party in Vietnam, opposed French rule. In 1953 Laos was declared a constitutional monarchy, backed by France and the US. The LPF's armed wing, the Pathet Lao, mounted an armed struggle against the government in the 1960s. During the Vietnam War the US repeatedly bombed Laos in order to stamp out Pathet Lao support for the North Vietnamese. With the withdrawal of American forces from the region in 1975, the Pathet Lao staged a bloodless coup and declared Laos the Lao People's Democratic Republic.

ກອງແລະເສນະຂະນາຍຂະເນຂະປະຂາທະເປະຂະອ່ນ
ພາຍໃຕ້ການນຳພາຂອງພັກແນ່ນຂະນາງໄປສູ່ຄວາມວັດທະນາເຕາອນ

Poster supporting the Lao People's Democratic Party

Wat Phra That Choeng Chum, the main *wat* in the old, once Khmer, town of Sakhon Nakhon

Sakhon Nakhon ⑬

สกลนคร

Sakhon Nakhon province.
🏃 *120,000.* ✈ 🚌 🚏 *TAT, Nakhon Phanom (0-4251-3490).* 🚢 *daily.*
🎎 *Wax Castle Ceremony (Oct).*

THERE ARE TWO SIGHTS of interest in the friendly town of Sakhon Nakhon. **Wat Phra That Choeng Chum** is a beautiful temple complex with a large *bot* and *wihan*, a 10th-century Khmer *prang*, and a whitewashed, 24-m (80-ft) Lao-style *chedi* built during the Ayutthaya period.

The old *prang* is reached through a door in the *wihan*. Etched into the *prang's* base is an ancient Khmer inscription, and around it are Lao and Khmer images of the Buddha. Also in the compound is an interesting display of *luk nimit,* which are Brahmin foundation markers that somewhat resemble giant cannon balls.

The five-layered, 11th-century Khmer *prang* of **Wat Phra That Narai Cheng Weng** was built as a Hindu monument. The name Cheng Weng is taken from the princess responsible for its construction; Narai is a Thai and Khmer name for Vishnu. The most important lintel – over the only entrance, to the east – shows Shiva dancing to the destruction of the universe, as he tramples the head of a lion. On the northern portico is a splendid depiction of Vishnu, with a lotus and baton in two of his four hands.

Nakhon Phanom ⑭

นครพนม

Nakhon Phanom province.
🏃 *114,000.* ✈ 🚌 🚏 *TAT, 1841 Soontornvijit Rd, Nakhon Phanom (0-4251-3490).* 🚢 *daily.* 🚤 *Illuminated Boats Procession (Oct).* @ *tat.ne@npu.msu.ac.th*

NAKHON PHANOM – "city of hills" – is a good town in which to spend a few relaxing days by the Mekong. In the dry season a beach by the river, **Hat Sai Tai Muang**, becomes exposed, and it is possible to walk out almost as far as Laos. However, this town cannot be used as a place to procure a visa for, or as an entry point into, Laos.

To celebrate the end of the rains, during the night of the full moon in the 11th lunar month, there is a resplendent procession of illuminated boats on the river here. Measuring some 10 m (33 ft) in length, the boats are traditionally crafted from bamboo or banana trees. They are filled with lighted candles, incense, kerosene lamps, and offerings of fragrant flowers and candies.

Renu Nakhon ⑮

เรณูนคร

Nakhon Phanom province.
🏃 *39,000.* 🚌 *from Nakhon Phanom.* 🚏 *TAT, Nakhon Phanom (0-4251-3490).* 🚢 *Wed.*

RENU NAKHON is a village known primarily for its weaving and fine embroidery. At the popular Wednesday market, colorful cottons and silks are sold by the *phun*, a measure 75 cm (2 ft) long. Ready-made garments and furnishings from all over the Northeast and Laos are also sold. There is a more permanent gathering of textile stalls around **Phra That Renu**. This was built in 1918 and modeled loosely on the nearby *chedi* at That Phanom.

Shop selling a range of locally made textiles, Renu Nakhon

Wat Phra That Phanom ⑯

วัดพระธาตุพนม

THIS WAT, in the remote town of That Phanom, is the most revered shrine in Northeast Thailand, famous for its central, Lao-style brick and plaster *chedi*. The *chedi* was constructed some 1,500 years ago, although according to legend it was built eight years after the death of the Buddha in 535 BC, when local dignitaries erected it as a burial place for his breastbone. The monument has been restored many times, most recently after devastating rains in 1975. Each year at the full moon of the third lunar month, during a farming holiday, a week-long temple festival attracts thousands of pilgrims from Thailand and Laos.

VISITORS' CHECKLIST

Center of That Phanom, Nakhon Phanom province. 🛈 *TAT, Nakhon Phanom (0-4251-3490).* 🚌 *from Nakhon Phanom, Sakhon Nakhon, or Mukdahan.* ◻ *6am–7pm daily.* 🔲 🎫 *Phra That Phanom Festival (Feb/Mar).*

Pilgrims at Wat Phra That Phanom
Thousands come to pay homage at festival time and throughout the year. Many devotees are from Laos – the monument is the second most sacred site to them, the first being That Luang in Vientiane.

CENTRAL CHEDI

The famous 57-m (185-ft) high *chedi* at the center of the temple is in the shape of a stylized, elongated lotus bud. The present structure, rebuilt in 1977, is modeled on That Luang in Vientiane, Laos.

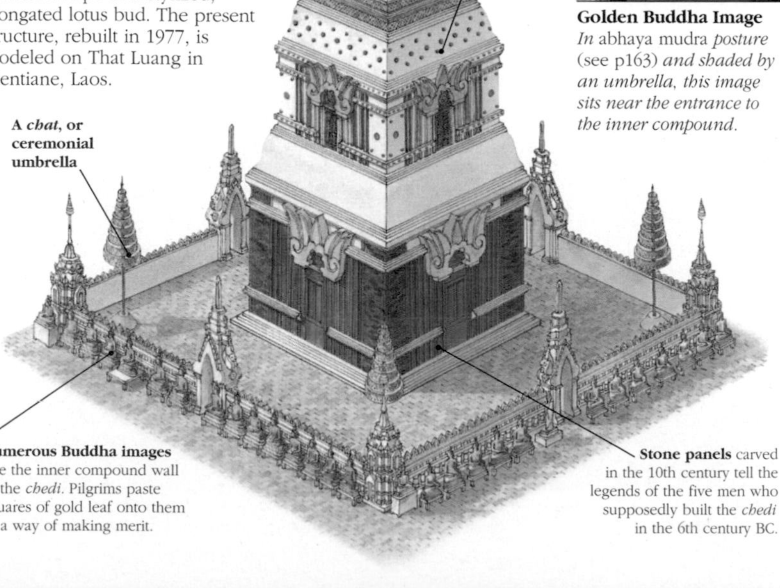

Stone Lion
One of two on either side of the outer compound's central path, this fierce mythical beast is a temple guardian who wards off evil forces.

Gold decoration in the shape of a multi-leaved lotus flower represents the path to Enlightenment.

The *chedi* is studded with gemstones and gold rings.

Golden Buddha Image
In abhaya mudra *posture (see p163) and shaded by an umbrella, this image sits near the entrance to the inner compound.*

A *chat*, or ceremonial umbrella

Numerous Buddha images
line the inner compound wall of the *chedi*. Pilgrims paste squares of gold leaf onto them as a way of making merit.

Stone panels carved in the 10th century tell the legends of the five men who supposedly built the *chedi* in the 6th century BC.

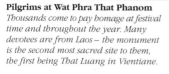

The market along the river at Mukdahan, where Lao and Vietnamese merchandise is sold

Mukdahan ⑰

มุกดาหาร

Mukdahan province. ⬛ 83,000.
⬛ 🏢 TAT, Nakhon Phanom
(0-4251-3490). ⬛ daily. ⬛ Ruam
Pao Thai Ma Kham Wan Chai
Khong Fair (Jan).

MUKDAHAN IS THE CAPITAL of one of Thailand's newest provinces, created in 1980 from areas that were formerly part of Nakhon Phanom and Ubon Ratchathani provinces.

By far the most interesting street is Samran Chai Khong Road, which runs along the Mekong River front. It faces the second largest city in Laos, Suwannakhet, on the

Seated Buddha at Wat Yot Kaew Siwichai, Mukdahan

opposite bank. As a result of its proximity to this city, Mukdahan has grown up as a busy trading center, and both Lao and Thai boats can be seen at the pier, loading and unloading their goods. Tourists with a visa *(see p451)* can cross into Laos at this point.

A market also runs most of the length of the riverside, between **Wat Si Mongkol Tai** and **Wat Yot Kaew Siwichai**. Goods for sale may be disappointing because there are few examples of traditional Lao and Vietnamese merchandise. Expect an excess of plastic ephemera, though the market is worth a visit for the local sweetmeats and its colorful atmosphere.

Wat Si Mongkhol Thai was built in 1956 by Vietnamese immigrants in the town and is distinguished by statues of mythical creatures at the entrance to its main chapel.

The gaudier Wat Yot Kaew Siwichai houses an enormous, seated, golden Buddha image. The figure sits in an open-fronted *wihan* with paneled glass on two of its sides. Near Wat Yot Kaew Siwichai, on Song Nang Sathit Road, is the Chinese **Chao Fa Mung Muang shrine**, home to Mukdahan's guardian spirit. Also here is the **Lak Muang**, or City Pillar, which is usually draped in colorful plastic garlands.

ENVIRONS: Excellent views of the entire provincial capital can be captured from the 500-m (1,650-ft) peak of **Phu Manorom**. There is a pavilion at the top of the hill sheltering a replica of the Buddha's Footprint.

🏯 Phu Manorom

Off Hwy 2034, 5 km (3 miles) S of
Mukdahan. ⬛ daily. ⬛

Pha Taem ⑱

ผาแต้ม

18 km (11 miles) N of Khong Chiam,
Ubon Ratchathani province. 🏢 TAT,
Ubon Ratchathani (0-4524-3770).
@ tatubon@tat.or.th ⬛ from Ubon
Ratchathani to Khong Chiam, then
tuk-tuk. ⬛ daily. ⬛

THE ROUTE, 18 km (11 miles) from Khong Chiam up to Pha Taem or "painted cliff," is a circuitous one, really accessible only by rental car or *tuk-tuk*. Along the way, a few kilometers before you arrive at the cliff top, an unusual, sandstone rock formation can be seen at the side of the road. Known as Sao Chaliang, it is reminiscent of the Ho Nang Ussa at Phu Phrabat Historical Park *(see p285)*.

At the end of the journey, an unmarked trail leads from the parking lot to the cliff face. This is decorated with huge figures and geometrical designs. Painted in an indelible red pigment derived from soil, tree gum, and fat, the paintings are thought to date back some 4,000 years. Covering 170 m (560 ft) along the cliff face, they include depictions of fish traps, wild animals, giant cockroachlike fish, angular human beings, and a 30-m (98-ft) stretch of handprints. The artists who created these decorations are thought to be related to the early inhabitants of Ban Chiang (see p262) and were rice cultivators rather than cave dwellers.

Prehistoric cliff-painting, Pha Taem

Pha Taem is particularly beautiful at sunset, when it has tremendous views across the Mekong and of the wild Lao jungle beyond.

Khong Chiam ⑲
โขงเจียม

Ubon Ratchathani province.
🏠 30,000. 🚌 🛈 TAT, Ubon Ratchathani (0-4524-3770). 🛍 daily.

KHONG CHIAM IS NEAR the confluence of the muddy red Mekong and the indigo-blue Mun rivers, which creates the phenomenon of the *maenam song si* or "two-colored river." The differing colors of the rivers derive from the amounts of sand and clay suspended in their waters.

Scenic views are offered from the bank at **Wat Khong Chiam**, and boat trips out to the confluence point itself allow a full appreciation of the blend of colored waters, clearest in April. It is also possible to cross from Khong Chiam to the Lao town on the opposite side of the river, but this cannot be used by travelers as an official crossing point into Laos.

Visitors to Khong Chiam can also watch traditional conical fish traps being made out of wicker.

Chong Mek ⑳
ช่องเม็ก

Ubon Ratchathani province.
🏠 4,900. 🚌 from Ubon Ratchathani. 🛈 TAT, Ubon Ratchathani (0-4524-3770). 🛍 daily.

ON THE BORDER between Thailand and Laos, Chong Mek is one of the few places at which tourists can cross into Laos. Other Lao entry points include Nong Khai, (see pp282–3) and Chiang Khong (see p239). Visitors need a valid visa (see p451), which can be obtained in advance from Bangkok. For those who do not have a visa, it is possible, even without a passport, to walk some 200 m (660 ft) over the border to browse around the open-air market and duty-free shops that are set up there.

Chong Mek has all the feel of a remote frontier post, and its Lao market, although small, is interesting and friendly. Young women vendors and children sell fruit, French bread

Making wicker fish traps, Khong Chiam

sticks, textiles, and round wicker tables called *tok*, around which the Lao, Northern, and Northeastern Thais traditionally squat to eat.

In the market there may also be groups of old women selling rare plants and flowers. However, many of the plants are, sadly, taken from a fast-disappearing Lao jungle. Visitors to the market are advised not to buy these.

Boat on the Sirindhorn Dam

Sirindhorn Dam ㉑
เขื่อนสิรินธร

Ubon Ratchathani province. 🛈 TAT, Ubon Ratchathani (0-4524-3770). For information about tourist accommodation call 0-2436-3179. 🚌 from Ubon Ratchathani to Chong Mek, then songthaew.

NAMED AFTER the second daughter of King Bhumibol, the Sirindhorn Dam was built in 1971. The reservoir it created is 43 km (27 miles) from north to south; the turbines produce 24,000 kilowatts of electricity.

There is a park at the dam HQ, and a restaurant and bungalows. It is possible to walk out over the dam and to take a boat on the reservoir.

Dams in Thailand have been funded by the World Bank since the 1950s to meet Thailand's ever-increasing need for electricity. They are given support mainly by politicians and the business community. Recently, residents and environmental groups have begun to campaign against the construction of new dams.

Huge, intricately carved candles paraded through the streets of Ubon Ratchathani during the Candle Festival ▷

Prasat Khao Phra Wihan 🄬

ปราสาทเขาพระวิหาร

Off Hwy 221, S of Ubon and Sisaket, just inside Cambodia. 🛈 *TAT, Ubon Ratchathani (0-4524-3770).* 🚌 *from Ubon or Sisaket to Kantharalak, then songthaew.* ◯ *daily.* 📷

THE EXTRAORDINARY SITE of this early Khmer temple, laid out along a spur of the Dongrek Mountains, makes it one of the most distinctive Khmer structures outside of Angkor *(see pp254–5).* Possibly older than Angkor, sadly, it was long the victim of disputes between Thailand and Cambodia. After much disagreement between the two countries, in 1962 a decision was taken by the World Court: while the easiest access to the temple is through Thailand, the temple stands firmly in Cambodia.

During the mid-1970s, the years of the Khmer Rouge regime in Cambodia, the temple became a strictly no-go area. After the Vietnamese invaded Cambodia in 1978, conflicts between rival factions continued in the area until the late 1980s. The site was finally cleared of land mines and opened to the public in the early 1990s, but as civil unrest

Three ruined *prangs*, all on a single base, at Prasat Prang Ku

continues in Cambodia, this magnificent temple is forced to close down periodically.

When Khao Phra Wihan is open, tourists can walk through army checkpoints to ascend a series of grand staircases, pass through stone *gopuras*, and then walk along an 850-m (2,800-ft) *naga*-lined causeway to arrive at the central sanctuary, or *prasat*. Dedicated to the Hindu god Shiva, it is now largely in ruins. The *prang* in particular is in need of restoration. Views from the sheer cliffs here, over the Cambodian plateau, are exhilarating. If the temple is closed, elegant Khmer reliefs carved in the cliff can be viewed from the Thai side of the border.

Stone relief on the Cambodian sight of Prasat Khao Phra Wihan

Prasat Prang Ku 🄪

ปราสาทปรางค์กู่

Off Hwy 2234, 70 km (43 miles) SW of Si Sa Ket, Si Sa Ket province. 🛈 *TAT, Ubon Ratchathani (0-4524-3770).* 🚌 *from Ubon or Sisaket to Kantharalak, then songthaew* ◯ *daily.* 📷

LOCATED IN THE DISTRICT of Prang Ku in Si Sa Ket province, this 11th-century Khmer monument comprises three brick *prangs* on a single platform. The most remarkable feature is a well-preserved lintel, divided horizontally into two sections by the tails of two long *nagas*. In the

center stands Vishnu on his mount, a *garuda*. On either side of the *garuda* are two lions with garlands of flowers in their open mouths. The top half of the lintel is decorated with dancing deities. In front of Prasat Prang Ku is a 1-km (1,100-yd) long Khmer *baray* (reservoir), a welcome feeding ground for birds.

Ubon Ratchathani 🄭

อุบลราชธานี

Ubon Ratchathani province. 🚶 118,000. ✈ 🚌 🚐 🚉 🛈 *TAT, 264/1 Khuan Thani Rd, Ubon Ratchathani (0-4524-3770).* @ *tatubon@tat.or.th* 🏠 *daily.* 🎉 *Ubon Candle Festival (late Jul).*

FROM THE 10TH CENTURY, Ubon Ratchathani province, often simply known as Ubon, was part of the Khmer Empire. It later fell under the control of the Ayutthaya Kingdom *(see pp56–7).* The provincial capital, the city of Ubon Ratchathani was founded by Lao immigrants on the northern bank of the Mun River at the end of the 18th century, and Lao influence can still be seen in the architectural features of some of the city's religious buildings. Following the rapid growth of Ubon during the Vietnam War, when it played host to a nearby American air base, the city is, today, one of the largest in Thailand.

At first sight, Ubon appears to be a great concrete sprawl, but the **Ubon National Museum** is one of the best in the Northeast, and some fascinating

A beautifully preserved stone *gopura*, Prasat Khao Phra Wihan

temples are dotted around the city. The museum is housed in the former country residence of King Vajiravudh (1910–25) and contains displays of Khmer, Hindu, and Lao Buddhist iconography, as well as traditional tools, utensils, and handicrafts. One of the rarest and most impressive exhibits is a giant bronze drum, dating back as far as the 4th century AD, that was used originally for ceremonial purposes.

The most interesting of Ubon's temples is **Wat Thung Si Muang** on account of its teakwood library. Founded by King Rama III (1824–51) the *wat* houses 150-year-old murals showing some of the *jatakas* (*see p26*). The complex also includes a *mondop* with a Buddha Footprint.

In 1853 King Mongkut (1851–68) gave his support to the construction of **Wat Supattanaram Worawihan** as the first temple in the Northeast dedicated to the Thammayut sect – a strict branch of Theravada Buddhism – of which the king was also a member. It consists of a highly eclectic blend of architectural styles, having been built by Vietnamese craftsmen who were under instruction to incorporate an unusual mixture of Khmer, Thai, and European architectural influences.

The more modern **Wat Phra That Nong Bua** was built in 1957 to commemorate the 2,500th anniversary of the death of the Lord Buddha. Its two four-sided, whitewashed towers are decorated with standing Buddha images in niches and reliefs of tales of the Buddha in his previous lives. Ubon also has a small number of other interesting temples: **Wat Cheng**, with its elegant Lao-style wooden carvings; **Wat Si Ubon Rattanaram**, built in 1855 and housing a topaz Buddha image, originating from

Figure atop Wat Supattanaram

Carved Buddha images in niches at Wat Phra That Nong Bua

Chiang Saen; and the main temple, **Wat Maha Wanaram**, in which local people worship.

Ubon becomes a place of pilgrimage at the beginning of Buddhist Lent, when, during the Ubon Candle Festival (*see p45*), large, sculpted candles are carried through the streets.

⌂ Ubon National Museum
Khuan Thani Rd. **☎** 0-4525-5071.
○ *Wed–Sun.* ● *public hols.* ⌘

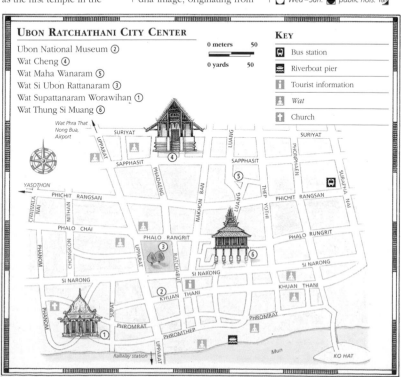

UBON RATCHATHANI CITY CENTER

Ubon National Museum ②
Wat Cheng ④
Wat Maha Wanaram ⑤
Wat Si Ubon Rattanaram ③
Wat Supattanaram Worawihan ①
Wat Thung Si Muang ⑥

0 meters 50
0 yards 50

KEY

🚌 Bus station
🛳 Riverboat pier
ℹ Tourist information
卍 Wat
✝ Church

THE GULF OF THAILAND

Introducing the Gulf of Thailand

THAIS AND FOREIGNERS flock to the Gulf's resorts to unwind, relax on the many superb beaches, and eat delicious seafood. Bangkok weekenders have long favored Cha-am and Hua Hin, while built-up Pattaya draws lovers of sports and hectic nightlife. The towns of Chaiya and Phetchaburi contain architectural and artistic treasures and have the lively ethnic and cultural mix typical of the Western Seaboard and farther south. Inland, breathtaking flora and fauna abound in beautiful, crowd-free national parks. Several islands burgeoned in popularity in the 1990s: sunworshipers frequent Ko Samui's long, sandy beaches on the Western Seaboard, while other visitors favor Ko Samet and the sand, simplicity, and solitude of Ko Chang, both on the east coast. The Gulf's sunniest days are from December to August.

Phetchaburi

WESTERN SEABOARD
(see pp314–331)

Phetchaburi (see pp318–20) *is an important cultural center with more than 30* wats, *including the splendid Wat Mahathat, founded in the 14th century. Despite a history dating back to the 11th century and an attractive old quarter, the town receives few visitors.*

Angthong National Marine Park
(see pp330–31), *easily accessible from Ko Samui, is a stunning group of tiny islands teeming with wildlife.*

Angthong National Marine Park

Ko Samui
(see pp326–8) *is the premier beach destination of the Western Gulf. This large island caters to tourists on all budgets.*

Ko Samui

◁ **Vacationers enjoying the sun, sand, and sea on a section of Jomtien beach, Pattaya**

EASTERN
SEABOARD
(see pp302–313)

Ko Samet

Ko Chang

Ko Samet (see pp308–9) *is the east coast's top destination for budget travelers seeking low-cost accommodations, beautiful white sand beaches, and clear waters.*

Pattaya (see p307) *attracts an unlikely mix of families eager to take advantage of the beaches and excellent sports facilities, and hedonists equally eager to enjoy the renowned nightlife of the discos, go-go, and beer bars.*

Ko Chang (see pp312–13) *is part of an archipelago of 52 islands that has only attracted limited development. It is an ideal retreat for those seeking seclusion and the pleasures of beach life.*

0 kilometers   50

0 miles   25

Beach Life and Leisure in the Gulf

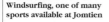

Windsurfing, one of many sports available at Jomtien

THAI BEACH CULTURE dates from the 1920s with the opening of both the railroad from Bangkok to Hua Hin and the first golf club, the Royal Hua Hin, designed by Scottish railroad engineer AO Robins. Hua Hin and its modern neighbor, Cha-am, continue to attract Thai weekenders from Bangkok, whose leisure pursuits center more around seafood dining than swimming and sunbathing. Foreigners, meanwhile, are attracted to the Gulf's clear waters and fine sands, and exceptionally good water sports. The development of resort hotels and golf courses in the Gulf continues to boom, to the alarm of many environmentalists. However, it is still possible to find seclusion and simplicity, such as on Ko Chang.

Bangpra Golf Course, Pattaya, is one of many courses within the forested hills of Chon Buri province (see p445).

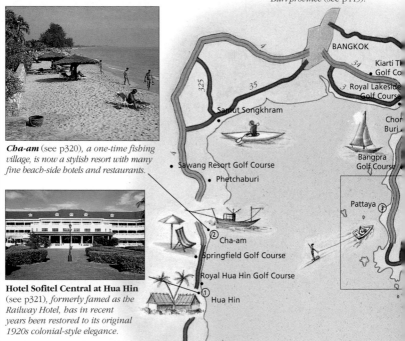

Cha-am (see p320), a one-time fishing village, is now a stylish resort with many fine beach-side hotels and restaurants.

Hotel Sofitel Central at Hua Hin (see p321), formerly famed as the Railway Hotel, has in recent years been restored to its original 1920s colonial-style elegance.

BEST BEACHES OF THE NORTHERN GULF

Hua Hin Beach ①
Thailand's first beach resort. Good for the charm of the town and its seafood restaurants.

Cha-am Beach ②
Popular with Thai weekenders but quiet during the week. Outstanding seafood restaurants.

Jomtien Beach, Pattaya ③
A 14-km (9-mile) long beach. Suitable for families and has excellent water sports facilities.

Glass Sand Beach (Hat Sai Kaeo), Ko Samet ④
Longest and liveliest beach on the island with

sand so clean it squeaks when walked on. Beautifully clear water, and good for water sports.

White Sand Beach (Hat Sai Khao), Ko Chang ⑤
The best and busiest beach on an unspoiled island. Fishing, snorkeling, and boat trips.

PATTAYA

Thailand's biggest, brashest resort attracts single males and family package tourists in equal numbers. The former are drawn by the neon-lit go-go bars and a reputation acquired when Pattaya was used for R&R by US servicemen during the Vietnam War. Families, meanwhile, are attracted by the restaurants, golf courses, and beaches, particularly Jomtien beach (south of Pattaya beach), which has the best water sports facilities in the country.

Si Racha
Ko Sichang
Laem Chabang
Golf Course
Pattaya
Phoenix
Golf Course
Eastern Star
Golf Course
Sattahip   Rayong

0 kilometers   20
0 miles   10

Water sports – a major attraction of Pattaya

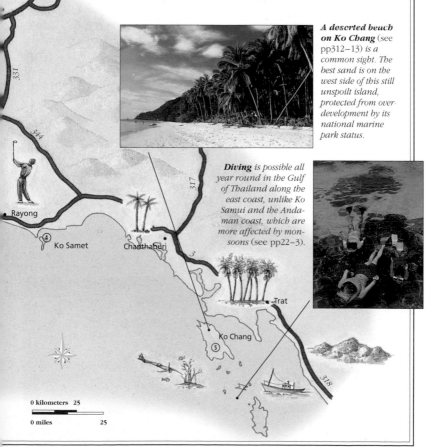

A deserted beach on Ko Chang (see pp312–13) *is a common sight. The best sand is on the west side of this still unspoilt island, protected from over-development by its national marine park status.*

Diving is possible all year round in the Gulf of Thailand along the east coast, unlike Ko Samui and the Anda-man coast, which are more affected by mon-soons (see pp22–3).

331
344
317
Rayong
Ko Samet
Chanthaburi
3
Trat
Ko Chang
318

0 kilometers   25
0 miles   25

Thai Gemstones

SINCE THE 15TH CENTURY, Chanthaburi ("city of the moon") has been known to Western travelers for its abundance of gemstones. As a trading city its history dates back to the Khmer Empire in the 9th century *(see pp52–3)*. Along with Bangkok, Chanthaburi is world-renowned as a gem center, and for its skilled gem cutters. The gemstones – mainly rubies and sapphires, with associated deposits of zircon, spinel, and garnet – are found in alluvial deposits either on the surface or up to 6 m (20 ft) underground. Although rubies and sapphires are now overmined around Chanthaburi, farmers have previously found gemstones while plowing. Over 70 percent of the world's rubies have come from Thailand.

Star ruby ring

GEM-MINING AREAS

■ *Ruby and sapphire mines*

This machine is pumping gravel and water that may contain gemstones such as rubies.

Examining gemstones *in the host rock helps formulate the correct cutting plan. This ensures that the best yield and shapes are obtained.*

Simple grinding wheels *are often used in small businesses, which are commonly run from the owner's home. More sophisticated operations use modern equipment such as diamond saws.*

MINING FOR GEMSTONES

In Chanthaburi, gem stores can arrange visits to mines. Due to over-mining locally, many of the stones cut in Chanthaburi come from mines in Cambodia or Vietnam.

FACETING GEMSTONES

Thai workers have a worldwide reputation for their skill and dexterity in faceting (precisely cutting) gemstones, often using simple equipment and judging angles by eye. A modern faceting machine may use a diamond blade or laser to improve speed and accuracy. After cutting, the stones are sorted and graded by size and quality, with quality being determined by sparkle, color, brilliance, and the presence or absence of imperfections.

Modern faceting equipment used to cut gemstones

Most gem buyers *prefer to buy gems "in the rough," using their expertise to judge the potential of the uncut material. Later the buyers arrange the cutting of the stones, often in their own workshops. Untrained buyers should beware of potential scams (see p456).*

Bargaining *in gem-mining towns such as Bo Rai (see p311) is common practice. Since opinions differ as to the potential of rough material and the quality of cut stones, bargaining is hard but good natured.*

Designing and making jewelry *from gems demands a delicate touch and a keen eye, qualities renowned in Thai craftsmen and women. Most jewelry is made to highlight the beauty of the gems.*

Whole families can often be seen searching for gemstones. Children may begin helping at a very young age.

Pans are often used to scoop up gravel that may contain gemstones. The gemstones sink to the bottom of the pan.

Of all the Thai gemstones, deep blue sapphires and blood-red rubies are highly prized, as are unusually colored (such as yellow) sapphires. Sometimes the color is enhanced permanently by heating the stones to almost 2,000° C (3,650° F).

Star sapphire

Star ruby

Green sapphire

Zircon

Ruby

Peridot

Yellow sapphire

EASTERN SEABOARD

The EASTERN SEABOARD of the Gulf of Thailand, stretching from Bangkok to the Cambodian border, is a region of contrasts. Remarkably picturesque and unspoiled islands lie within easy reach of brash, over developed resorts; oil refineries and industrial complexes are scattered along much of the coast, but not far inland are little-visited and spectacular national parks.

The Eastern Seaboard was a frontier between the Khmer and Sukhothai empires in the early 15th century. As Khmer power waned, large numbers of ethnic Tais settled here and discovered gem-rich deposits in the lush countryside. Chanthaburi became a centre for gem trading and in the 18th and 19th centuries had to expel first Burmese then French occupying forces. Numerous Vietnamese refugees have since settled in the town.

Though still a forested region with orchards, gem-mining, and fishing communities, the Eastern Seaboard has seen dramatic changes in the late 20th century as the oil and tourist industries have grown dramatically. However, some seaside towns have retained their charm, and in Si Racha excellent seafood can be sampled in open-air restaurants overlooking the bay. In contrast to this are the neon lights of Pattaya, an infamous destination for US marines on R&R during the Vietnam War. Despite a seedy image, it is an excellent center for water sports.

South and east of Rayong there are beautiful mountainous islands and dense rainforest sheltering a wealth of fauna and flora. Trails, waterfalls, and eerie limestone caves characterize Khao Chamao, Khao Kitchakut, and Khao Sabap national parks.

The relaxed island of Ko Samet is a popular vacation destination, with its squeaky-sand beaches. Farther south, Ko Chang has many idyllic deserted beaches and coves. It can be accessed from the market town of Trat, which is also the starting point for day trips to the gem market at Bo Rai.

Temple boys in a shrine cave within the Khao Chamao-Khao Wong National Park

◁ Enjoying the good life on the blissfully quiet Ko Chang

Exploring the Eastern Seaboard

BLESSED WITH miles of idyllic beaches and soaring temperatures, the Eastern Seaboard is a sun-lover's paradise. Whether you want to unwind and sample the local seafood or try out water sports, there is much to choose from. Beach resorts range from the chaotic Pattaya, with its lively nightlife, to lesser-known – and relatively undeveloped – islands such as Ko Chang, which is part of a stunning national marine park. The three other national parks in this region, characterized by tropical forests, mountains, and waterfalls, are home to a wealth of wildlife. The main town in the area is Chanthaburi, center of the thriving gem mining industry.

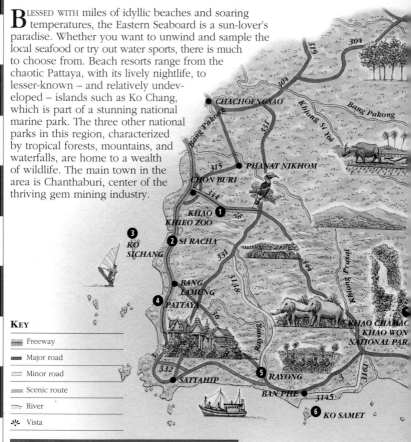

KEY

▨	Freeway
▬	Major road
▭	Minor road
▭	Scenic route
▭	River
☆	Vista

Relaxing on Ko Samet's beautiful white beaches

SIGHTS AT A GLANCE

GETTING AROUND

The Eastern Seaboard's transport system is comprehensive on the mainland and connects to the main islands. A twice daily train service runs from Hua Lamphong Station in Bangkok to Si Racha and Pattaya. Chon Buri and Sattahip are served by domestic airports. Buses are the easiest way to get around the Eastern Seaboard: there is a regular service from Bangkok's Eastern Bus Terminal to the main towns. To visit places not on bus routes, charter a *songthaew* from a local bus station. Transportation in the mainland towns is provided by *songthaews*, rickshas, and *tuk-tuks*.

Several ferries leave Ban Phe each day for Ko Samet. On the island, *songthaews* service the main beaches, and fishing boats can be hired to surrounding islands. Ko Chang and Ko Mak are reached by ferry from Laem Ngop. Infrastructure on these islands is poor, though motorcycles and *songthaews* can be hired to get around the rough roads.

The opulent interior of the main hall of Wat Khao Sukim

SEE ALSO

- *Where to Stay* pp399–401

- *Where to Eat* pp423–5

| 0 kilometers | 25 |
| 0 miles | 15 |

ARANYAPRATHET

HAO KITCHAKUT

9

8 WAT KHAO SUKIM

10 CHANTHABURI

KHAO SABAP 11   12 BO RAI
NATIONAL
PARK

14 TRAT

13 KO CHANG

KHLONG YAI 15

BAN HAT
LAK

Bungalows on palm fringed Ko Chang

Khao Khieo Zoo ❶
สวนสัตว์เขาเขียว

Off Route 3144, 10 km (6 miles) SE of
Chon Buri, Chon Buri province.
📞 0-3829-8195. 🚌 🚲 *Chon Buri,
then samlor.* ⏰ *8am–6pm daily;
Night Safari 6–9pm daily.* 🅿

THIS OPEN ZOO has over 50
species of birds and ani-
mals, including deer, zebras,
and tigers. The animals
inhabit spacious, semifree
enclosures, and the birds are
kept in a large aviary. The zoo
is in a peaceful, hilly setting
amid woodland scenery and is
best reached by car.
For bird enthusiasts, 20 km
(12 miles) south of Khao Khieo
is the beautiful wild marshland of **Bang Phra Reservoir**,
where, among other species,
the brown-spotted wimbrel
can be seen in winter.

Si Racha ❷
ศรีราชา

Chon Buri province. 👥 *27,000.*
🚌 🚲 ⛴ ℹ️ *TAT, Pattaya (0-3842-
7667).* 🛥 *daily.*

FAMED FOR ITS SEAFOOD and its
spicy Si Racha sauce *(nam
phrik si racha)* – Thailand's
answer to Tabasco – this small
seaside town is the launching
point for trips to Ko Sichang.
Running off busy Jermjompol
Road, Si Racha's main waterfront street, are several tenta-
cle-like piers. At the end of the
piers are breezy, open-air restaurants ideal for sampling the
local delicacies: oysters *(hoi
nang rom)* or mussels *(hoi
thot)* dipped in Si Racha sauce.

Wat Atsadangnimit, Rama V's meditation chamber on Ko Sichang

On a rocky promontory, which
is also an occasional ferry pier,
is **Ko Loi**, a Thai-Chinese Buddhist temple. Of interest are
a Buddha Footprint, an image
of Kuan Yin (the Chinese goddess of mercy), and a pond
full of turtles. Buddhists feed
the turtles as an act of merit-
making *(see p125)*.
The streets of Si Racha (and
Ko Sichang) resonate to the
sound of spluttering motorcycle rickshas. They are
unique to the area – their side-
cars are positioned at the rear.

Ko Sichang ❸
เกาะสีชัง

Chon Buri province. 👥 *4,600.*
⛴ *from Si Racha.* ℹ️ *TAT, Pattaya
(0-3842-7667).*

A FORMER HAUNT of King
Chulalongkorn (Rama V),
this small island, with a rugged coastline, once functioned
as the customs checkpoint for
Bangkok-bound ships. Now it
is a relatively quiet place with
some architectural ruins and
a handful of guesthouses catering to visitors who want to
avoid the bustle and commer-
cialism of the resorts.
There is only one ramshackle
fishing village, **Tha Bon**, on
the eastern side of the island.
Just north of it is the **Chinese
Temple**, with colorfully
decorated shrine caves.
On the west coast of the
island are the quiet beaches
of **Hat Sai Khao** and **Hat
Tham**. On the southern side,
sprawling over a hillside, are
the overgrown ruins of **Rama
V's Summer Palace**. The
palace was built in the 1890s
but abandoned after a fleeting

Motorcycle rickshas provide the transport on Si Racha and Ko Sichang

occupation by the French in 1893. In 1901 it was moved and reconstructed as Vimanmek Palace at Dusit Park in Bangkok *(see pp98–101)*.

Restoration work on the remains of the palace complex is being carried out – two elegant, pistachio-green villas, just behind the beach at **Hat Tha Wang**, are now finished.

For the most part, though, only foundations remain – a riddle of staircases, rock pools, and tattered mosaic floors and fragrant frangipani trees. The only structure to remain intact is the circular **Wat Atsadangnimit**, at the top of the hill and crowned by a crumbling *chedi*. This was once a meditation chamber used by King Chulalongkorn.

The deserted rocky hilltop offers pleasant walks and fine views. It is home to nesting seabirds and the yellow squirrel, which is endemic here.

Pattaya ➍

พัทยา

Chon Buri province. 👤 *94,000.* 🚉
🚌 ⛴ 🛈 *TAT, 382/1 Mu 10 Chaihat Rd, Pattaya (0-3842-7667).* 🚤 *daily.* 🎉 *Pattaya Festival (Apr).*

PATTAYA'S faded beauty is now difficult to discern. The once-idyllic beaches attracted visitors as early as the 1950s and later became a destination for American troops on R&R during the Vietnam War. Now dubbed "Patpong by the Sea" *(see p112)*, the

A jet ski sitting ready for use on one of Pattaya's beaches

town has become one of Thailand's infamous red light districts, with a menagerie of neon lights, go-go bars, and glitzy transvestite shows.

Despite its seedy image, families come in the thousands to Pattaya on two-week package tours. They come for the good, cheap accommodations, extensive beaches (though the sea is often polluted), excellent restaurants, and the best sports facilities in Thailand.

Pattaya consists of three bays. At its center is the 3-km (2-mile) long **Pattaya beach**. Central Pattaya Road is packed with condominiums, fast-food restaurants, and souvenir shops. South Pattaya Road or "the strip," as the locals call it, is

Parrot fish, a common sight for divers in Pattaya's waters

where the sex industry plies its trade. North Pattaya Road, on the other hand, is more sedate, with open-air drinking spots called bar beers.

Many tourists prefer the more family-oriented 14-km-long (9-mile) **Jomtien beach**, around the southern headland of Pattaya. This is also the best place for water sports, as the sea here is cleaner. Scores of companies offer water-skiing and jet-skiing, windsurfing, sailing, parasailing, game-fishing, and scuba diving. Landbased activities include golf (there are numerous golf courses), target shooting, horseback riding, and tennis.

Quieter **Naklua bay**, to the north of Pattaya beach, has a fishing village that, despite tourism, has kept its charm.

Picnicking Thais relaxing at Suan Son, a beach park near Rayong

Rayong ➎

ระยอง

Rayong province. 👤 *95,000.* 🚌 ⛴
🛈 *TAT, 153/4 Sukhumvit Rd, Rayong (0-3865-5420).* 🚤 *daily.* 🎉 *Fruit Fair (May).*

RAYONG is a busy and prosperous fishing town best known locally for its statue of Thailand's most famous poet, Sunthorn Phu *(see p309)*.

The main attractions lie outside the town. For good beaches, head 25 km (16 miles) southeast to **Ban Phe**. A 20-km (12-mile) coast road winds along from here to Laem Mae Phim.

From Ban Phe there are boats to Ko Samet *(see pp308–9)*. Ferries also run to nearby **Ko Saket**, **Ko Man Nok** and **Ko Man Klang** – the latter two islands are part of the Laem Ya-Mu Ko Samet National Park. The park authorities have managed to limit excessive development here, although jet-skiing is gradually eroding the coral reef.

Five km (3 miles) past Ban Phe is the beach park of **Suan Son** ("pine park"). This has crystal-white sand beaches and is a popular picnic area for Thais. It offers seafood snacks and homegrown water sports such as wave riding on inner tubes.

Rayong province is known for its succulent fruit, particularly the pineapple and durian *(see p309)*, and its *nam pla* (fish sauce) and *nam phrik kapi* (shrimp paste).

Ko Samet ➏
เกาะเสม็ด

Rayong province. 🏠 *1,464.* 🚢 *from Ban Phe (Rayong) to Ao Wong Duan and Ao Phrao.* 🛈 *TAT, Rayong (0-3865-5420).* 🎫 *daily.*

K O SAMET, blessed as it is with clear blue waters and crystalline sand, is popular with foreigners and Thai weekenders. Because it is only 6 km (4 miles) long and 3 km (2 miles) wide, most of the island is accessible on foot. The interior's dense jungle, home to the usual geckos and hornbills, is riddled with trails.

Although the island now has some tourist accommodation, when it attained national park status in 1981 all but the most rustic development was halted. In 1990 the park authorities closed Ko Samet to overnight visitors but met angry opposition from local residents and businessmen. The island was reopened after four days.

The small fishing town of **Na Dan**, which links Ko Samet to Ban Phe on the mainland, was an ancient checkpoint for Chinese junks. Legend has it that its calm, sheltered waters were once the hunting ground of pirates. Several beaches on Ko Samet offer one-way boat trips back to Ban Phe.

The kite-shaped island's finest beaches are on the east coast. With its clear shallow waters, **Hat Sai Kaeo** ("glass sand beach") is the longest and liveliest beach. Water sports on the beach include windsurfing.

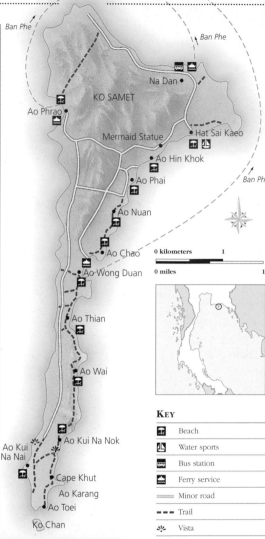

KEY

🏖	Beach
🏄	Water sports
🚌	Bus station
⛴	Ferry service
▦▦▦	Minor road
▬ ▬ ▬	Trail
☀	Vista

Sunset walk along the coast of picturesque Ko Samet

Boat trips around Ko Samet and snorkeling day trips to nearby islands leave from here.

Heading southward along the east coast are the equally popular **Ao Hin Khok**, **Ao Phai** and **Ao Nuan**. Near the first is a wind-battered statue of the prince and the mermaid in *Phra Aphaimani*, a poem by Sunthorn Phu, Thailand's most famous poet.

Farther south, the bays are less crowded, with the exception of the wide beach at **Ao Wong Duan** ("moon bay"), which can get quite busy. At the narrow isthmus of **Ao Kui**, solitude and beauty are guaranteed. It is merely a short stroll between sunrise and sunset vistas of Ao Kui Na Nok and Ao Kui Na Nai. The island's best coral is found just off the southern tip.

The only area to have undergone development on the largely inaccessible west coast is **Ao Phrao** ("paradise bay"). Due to its isolation, the beach here doesn't receive as many overnight visitors as those on the east coast.

There have been reports of malaria on Ko Samet in the past, so precautions are necessary. A health clinic, located near Na Dan, can deal with any urgent problems.

Wat Khao Sukim's cable car, which transports visitors up to the temple

Upscale bungalows on peaceful Ao Phrao, Ko Samet

Khao Chamao–Khao Wong National Park ❼

อุทยานแห่งชาติเขาชะเมา–เขาวง

Rayong province. Park HQ 17 km (11 miles) N of Hwy 3 at Klaeng. ℹ *TAT, Rayong (0-3865-5420).* @ *tatrayong @tat.or.th Forestry Dept, Bangkok (0-2562-0760 or 0-3889-4378 inc bungalow bookings).* 🚌 *Rayong or Chanthaburi, then songthaew.* ♿

THE TWO MOUNTAINS in this national park, Khao Wong and Khao Chamao, loom above the farming lowlands of the Eastern Seaboard.

Tigers, elephants, and Asiatic black bears find refuge in the park's tropical, broadleaved, evergreen forests, away from farmers and hunters. Also resident is the *tor soro* carp. Folklore claims that the name of Chamao mountain, which

means "to get drunk," derives from the curious giddy feeling induced by eating the carp.

Park highlights include the pools of the **Khao Chamao waterfall** and the 80 or so **Khao Wong caves**. Tham Pet ("diamond cave") and Tham Lakhon ("theater cave"), situated 4 km (2 miles) southeast of the park headquarters, are the most spectacular of these limestone caverns. When the waters are low it is possible to proceed to **Hok Sai waterfall** and camp on the summit.

There are few developed trails in the park. The best route climbs alongside the cascading Khao Chamao waterfall and ends near the top of the falls at Chong Kaep.

From the park's northwest station former elephant trails lead through the fertile and wildlife-rich forest of the stunning Khlong Phlu valley.

Wat Khao Sukim ❽

วัดเขาสุกิม

Khao Bay Si, Tha-Mai district, 20 km (13 miles) N of Chanthaburi, off route 3322. ℹ *TAT, Rayong (0-3865-5420).* 🚌 *Chanthaburi, then songthaew.*

THIS HUGE, pale orange *wat* is perched on the side of Sukim mountain The temple, the home of Luang Pho Somchai, one of Thailand's most popular meditation masters, is reached via a cable car or the *naga*-lined staircase. Inside are a number of tables inlaid with mother-of-pearl, while exhibits housed in a museum include an ostentatious display of jewelry and a collection of Bencharong, Khmer, and Ban Chiang pottery. They show the surprising wealth that a revered monk can accumulate from donations by merit-makers.

THE POETRY OF SUNTHORN PHU

Sunthorn Phu (1786–1855) is Thailand's most respected poet. His long, lyrical travel verses, often with a moral lesson, made him the favorite poet of kings Rama II and Rama III. The epic *Phra Aphaimani*, Sunthorn Phu's first poem, was inspired by the surroundings of Ko Samet (then called Ko Kaew Pisadan), where he settled. The poem tells the story of a prince, Phra Aphaimani, exiled to an underwater kingdom ruled by a giant-ess, who is in love with him. Helped by a mermaid, the prince escapes by fleeing to Ko Samet. The giantess follows, but is defeated when the prince plays his magic flute, sending her to sleep. The prince is subsequently betrothed to a beautiful princess.

Statue on Ko Samet depicting characters in *Phra Aphaimani*

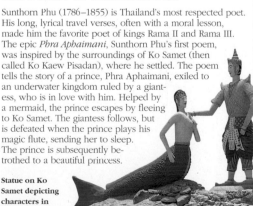

Khao Kitchakut National Park ⑨
อุทยานแห่งชาติเขาคิชฌกูฏ

Chanthaburi province. Park HQ off Hwy 3249, 24 km (15 miles) NE of Chanthaburi. **ℹ** *Park HQ (0-3945-2074).* **🚌** *Chanthaburi, then songthaew.* 🚻

COVERING AN AREA of just 59 sq km (23 sq miles), this is one of Thailand's smallest national parks. It encompasses Khao Kitchakut, a granite mountain just over 1,000 m (3,300 ft) high. The park's best known site, the 13-tier **Krathin waterfall**, is located near park headquarters. From here a relatively easy trail can be taken to the top.

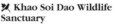
Logo of the Thai national parks

More ambitious hikers and large numbers of pilgrims make the arduous four-hour climb to the summit of the impressive Phrabat mountain. They come to see two sights: an image of the Buddha's Footprint, which is etched here in granite, and a strange collection of natural rock formations shaped like an elephant, a large turtle, a pagoda, and a monk's bowl.

Khao Kitchakut is near the much larger, but less visited, **Khao Soi Dao Wildlife Sanctuary** (745 sq km, 290 sq miles). Both protected areas enclose some of the last surviving tracts of a once-great lowland forest. They are vital to the economy of the region as their slopes collect water for orchards. They also provide protection for many endangered species, including sun bears, spot-bellied eagle owls, silver pheasants, spiny-breasted giant frogs, binturongs (bear cats), and elephants. The upland forests of Khao Soi Dao provide a habitat for the tree-dwelling pileated gibbon.

🐾 Khao Soi Dao Wildlife Sanctuary
Off Hwy 317, 25 km (16 miles) NW of Chanthaburi. **ℹ** *TAT, Rayong (0-3865-5420).* **🚌** *Chanthaburi, then songthaew.* 🚻

A refreshing shower at the base of Krathin waterfall, Khao Kitchakut

Shrine inside the Church of the Immaculate Conception, Chanthaburi

Chanthaburi ⑩
จันทบุรี

Chanthaburi province. **🏠** *48,000.* **🚌 ℹ** *TAT, Rayong (0-3865-5420).* **🛒** *daily.* **🎉** *Fruit Festival (May/Jun).*

SURROUNDED BY verdant chili and rubber plantations, this prosperous and friendly town is arguably Thailand's most charming settlement. Known as a center for gem trading *(see pp300–1)* since the 15th century, Chanthaburi has attracted a wide ethnic mix. Vietnamese refugees form the largest group. They came in three waves: in the 19th century, fleeing the anti-Catholic persecutions of Cochin China; in the early 20th century, escaping French colonial rule; and after the 1975 victory in South Vietnam by North Vietnamese Communists. The Vietnamese quarter, running parallel to the river on Rim Nam Road, is lined with latticework wooden shop-houses.

The monarch most revered in the town today is King Taksin. In the 18th century he expelled the Burmese from the town, their last Thai stronghold, thus reuniting Thailand. Two monuments celebrate Taksin and his famous victory: **San Somdej Prachao Taksin** on Tha Luang Road is a huge statue in the shape of Taksin's hat. **Taksin Park** sports a dynamic bronze statue of the king in battle as seen on the 20-*baht* note.

On the bank of the Chanthaburi River is the **Church of the Immaculate Conception**, a French-style Catholic cathedral built on the site of

MAYTIME FRUIT FESTIVALS

Held in three neighboring provinces – Rayong, Chanthaburi and Trat – this annual fruit festival, lasting for a few days in either May or June (whenever the harvest is ripe), is a colorful, celebratory affair. These provinces are known for their flavorsome rambutan, durian, and mangosteen, which all come into season during May. Stalls selling the produce of local orchards are set up on the main streets of each town. Parades of floral-and-fruit floats are held along with gaudy beauty pageants, which are a ubiquitous element of every provincial Thai festival. Contests for the ripest durian or most beautifully shaped fruit, among other titles, are a highlight of the year for local farmers and a great spectacle for tourists. Visitors can also see cultural shows and excellent displays of local handicrafts. In Chanthaburi there are many stalls selling one of the specialties of the province: intricately woven straw mats.

Fruit festival float, Chanthaburi

an 18th-century missionary chapel. It is the largest cathedral in the country and a legacy of French occupation. The French held Chanthaburi hostage from 1893 to 1904 as a guarantee that Thailand would relinquish her hold on Lao and Cambodian land. To keep the country intact, King Chulalongkorn reluctantly agreed to surrender the territories.

The **Gem Quarter** (*talat phloi*), at the intersection of Si Chan and Thetsaban 4 roads, attracts gem traders from all over the world. On weekends a rainbow array of gemstones from Burma, Cambodia, and the rich mines of Chanthaburi province are traded at street stalls. However, most of the best quality stones are dispatched directly to Bangkok.

Statue of King Taksin, Chanthaburi

also a haven for wildlife, with over 156 species of birds and 32 of mammals, including the Asiatic black bear, tiger, leopard, barking deer, and macaque. The park's other attractions are its spectacular waterfalls – the most impressive being **Phliu waterfall**. Facing this are two *chedis*: the Alongkon *chedi* and a 3-m (10-ft) high pyramid-shaped *chedi*, built by King Chulalongkorn in honor of one of his queens, Sunantha, who drowned at Bang Pa-in (*see p171*) in 1876. The region was much loved by Chulalongkorn.

A harder hike is required to reach the 20-m (66-ft) roaring Trok Nong falls and the forest-encircled Klang waterfall. The entrance road to the park is lined with souvenir shops.

Khao Sabap National Park ⓫

อุทยานแห่งชาติน้ำตกพลิ้ว

Chanthaburi province. Park HQ off Hwy 3, 14 km (9 miles) SE of Chanthaburi. ⓘ TAT, Rayong (0-3865-5420); Forestry Dept (0-2562-0760 or www.dnp.go.th for bungalow bookings). 🚌 Chanthaburi, then songthaew. 🅿

IMMENSELY POPULAR with Thais, this 135-sq km (52-sq mile) park contains some of Thailand's richest rainforest. It is

Bo Rai ⓬

บ่อไร่

Trat province. 🚶 25,000. 🚌 ⓘ TAT, 100 Mu 1 Trat–Laem Ngop Rd, Laem Ngop, Trat province (0-3959-7255). 🚌 daily.

THIS SMALL TOWN used to be the thriving center of the Eastern Seaboard's gem trade. The surrounding mines, once renowned for the quality of their rubies (*tab tim*), have almost dried up, so today the Bo Rai gem trade is small. Only one morning market of any significance, the **Khlong Yaw market**, remains. The market has a reverse system of buying and selling – buyers sit at makeshift tables and vendors stroll around displaying their wares.

Sadly, gem mining has destroyed large areas of Trat province, exposing the topsoil and leaving acres of despoiled land in rusty-orange mud.

Customer carefully inspecting a vendor's gems in Bo Rai market

Bungalows amid coconut trees along Khlong Phrao, Ko Chang

Ko Chang ⓭

เกาะช้าง

Trat province. 🏠 *5,800.* 🚢 *from Laem Ngop.* 🛈 *TAT, 100 Mu 1 Trat– Laem Ngop Rd, Laem Ngop, Trat province* 📞 *0-3959-7255.*

Mountainous ko chang is the largest of the 50 or so islands that form the Ko Chang National Marine Park, which covers an area of 650 sq km (250 sq miles), two-thirds of which is ocean. Despite their crystal-clear waters and postcard-perfect beaches, the islands' tourist industry is, surprisingly, still in its infancy. One drawback is that several of the islands in the group consist solely of expensive, privately owned resorts.

Since Thai-Chinese agricultural families first settled on Ko Chang in the mid-19th century, most of the island's wildlife has been destroyed, although some small mammals, including the barking deer, stump-

tailed macaque, and small Indian civet, remain. Also resident are some 75 bird species, and reptiles and amphibians such as monitor lizards, pythons, king cobras, and the endemic Ko Chang frog.

Inland exploration is difficult because of the rugged terrain. The coast road, which was begun in the early 1990s, is the first construction to improve accessibility on the island. Ko

Map

Laem Ngop

Ban Khlong Son

Hat Sai Khao

Laem Ngop

Dan Mai

Khlong Phlu waterfall

Ban Khlong Phrao

Hat Khlong Phrao

KO CHANG

Ban Sa Lak Phet

Ao Bang Bao

Ao Sa Lak Phet

Ko Mai Si Yai

Ko Laoya

Ko Ngam

Ko Khlum

Ko Wai

Ko Pai Dong

Ko Kut, Ko Rang, Ko Mak, Ko Kradat

0 kilometers   5

0 miles   5

KEY

🏖	Beach
🤿	Water sports
🛈	Tourist information
🚢	Ferry service
▬	Minor road
🔆	Vista

Chang's best beaches are on the west coast, especially along Ao Sai Khao, where the shell-sprinkled, bungalow-lined **Hat Sai Khao** ("white sand beach"), the island's longest and busiest beach, is located. An information center on the beach arranges boat trips, fishing, and snorkeling. Most guesthouses also offer fishing, snorkeling, and motorcycle rental. **Hat Khlong Phrao**, south of here, is more attractive and quieter. Nearby is a fishing village, Ban Khlong Phrao. Because tourism is growing only gradually on the island, fishing is still the main industry.

The beaches in the south are still relatively isolated. Of these, the beach at the sheltered bay of **Ao Bang Bao**, in the southwest corner, is particularly beautiful. East of here is a long beach encircling a bay, Ao Sa Lak Phet, where there are a few fishing villages and bungalows. The wrecks of two Thai Navy ships can be visited off the coast here.

Of the island's many waterfalls, two are worth the hike. On the east coast, near the park headquarters, is the three-tiered **Than Mayom waterfall,**

View of Hat Khlong Phrao, one of the best beaches on Ko Chang

which has good views of the island. The other is **Khlong Phlu waterfall**, along Khlong Phrao on the west coast. The uppermost level, accessible by a gentle 3-km (2-mile) hike, has a freshwater pool.

For snorkelers, divers, and day-trippers there are stunning smaller islands off the coast of Ko Chang, with a good variety of hard and soft corals and a proliferation of giant clams.

Ko Kut, the second largest island within the group, falls outside the park boundaries. It has excellent beaches and breathtaking waterfalls.

The rocky, coral-lined coast of **Ko Wai**, south of Ko Chang, is popular for fishing. Around **Ko Rang**, farther south, is a cluster of rocky coral islets.

Ko Mak, a predominantly flat island, is covered mainly in coconut plantations. It has a secluded beach on the northwest bay, a fishing village, and good coral reefs.

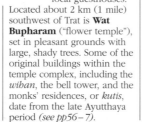

Barrel sponge, seen off Ko Chang

Northeast of Ko Mak is the coconut-fringed **Ko Kradat**, a tiny island with some of the prettiest beaches in the island cluster. Although the entire island is a privately owned resort with expensive hotels, bungalows can also be hired.

Sandflies and mosquitoes are a problem on the islands, so precautions are necessary.

Trat ⑭

ตราด

Trat province. 🚶 72,000. 🚌 🚆 🛈 TAT, 100 Mu 1 Trat–Laem Ngop Rd, Laem Ngop, Trat province (0-3959-7255). 🏛 daily. 🎏 Rakham Fruit Fair (May–Jun).

THIS PROVINCIAL CAPITAL is a small but busy commercial town. Currently, most tourists pass through Trat only en route to Ko Chang. However, the town's popularity is likely to increase in line with that of the archipelago. Trat has several attractions, including its markets, most of which are centered around Tait Mai and Sukhumvit roads. The covered market on Sukhumvit Road has a good selection of food and drink stalls. Also of interest are the gem-mining villages around Trat, such as Bo Rai, where rubies are mined (see pp300–1). Trips can be arranged at local guesthouses. Located about 2 km (1 mile) southwest of Trat is **Wat Bupharam** ("flower temple"), set in pleasant grounds with large, shady trees. Some of the original buildings within the temple complex, including the *wihan*, the bell tower, and the monks' residences, or *kutis*, date from the late Ayutthaya period (see pp56–7).

Durian vendor at one of Trat's bustling markets

Khlong Yai ⑮

คลองใหญ่

Trat province. 🚶 15,000. 🛈 TAT, 100 Mu 1 Trat–Laem Ngop Rd, Laem Ngop, Trat province (0-3959-7255). 🏛 daily.

SITUATED near the Cambodian border, this picturesque seaside town sports a handful of bustling Thai-Cambodian markets and stalls selling delicious noodles with seafood.

The road from Khlong Yai to the border checkpoint of **Hat Lek** passes through spectacular scenery: Cambodia's Cardamom Mountains are on one side, fish farms and sea on the other. Hat Lek is Thailand's narrowest point and marks the end of Sukhumvit Road, which starts in Bangkok (see p132). Currently, visitors may not cross into Cambodia.

Fishing trawlers, harbored on Ko Chang, which provide the main source of income on the island

WESTERN SEABOARD

THE ROLLING LANDSCAPE *of the Western Seaboard extends some 600 km (370 miles) from Bangkok to Surat Thani. Its major attraction is, without doubt, the islands that make up the beautiful Ko Samui archipelago, such as Ko Pha Ngan, Ko Tao, and the Ang Thong National Marine Park. Yet visitors should not ignore the many charms of the mainland – lively towns, fine beaches, and national parks.*

Miles of remote sandy beaches dominate long stretches of the Western Seaboard, which unites the Buddhist heartland of the nation with the maritime, Muslim-influenced South. Temples reflecting pre-Thai influences, simple fishing villages, verdant fruit orchards, and sand-rimmed resorts characterize this region.

The Tenasserim Mountains, rising to 1,329 m (4,350 ft), form a spine down the peninsula. They absorb much of the rain that falls during the southwest monsoon, keeping the coastal strip relatively dry. However, this coastal region is still a fertile growing area, famed for its pineapples, corn, sugar cane, "lady-finger" bananas, asparagus, and mangosteens.

Beaches easily reached from the capital cater primarily to weekenders from Bangkok. Particularly popular are the casuarina-lined waterfronts of Cha-am and Hua Hin. The latter was Thailand's first beach resort. The many golf courses within easy reach of these two tourist centers make this area arguably the country's premier golf destination. Farther south, the stunning islands of the Ko Samui archipelago offer excellent diving and sunbathing, and a well-developed tourist infrastructure.

Trekkers and bird-watchers will be drawn to Khao Sam Roi Yot and Kaeng Krachan national parks, where migratory birds rest and feed in the salt marshes from August to April.

Among the most interesting of the towns along the Western Seaboard is Phetchaburi, with its crumbling architectural remnants of the Khmer, Mon, Ayutthaya, and Rattanakosin epochs. Farther to the south, Chaiya still contains archeological remains that reveal its important role in the Srivijaya Empire *(see pp336–7).*

Fishing boats in the bay of the peaceful town of Prachuap Khiri Khan

◁ Devotees making offerings inside Phetchaburi's Wat Mahathat

Exploring the Western Seaboard

THIS LONG, NARROW COASTAL STRIP, backed by mountains along the Burmese border, stretches from the cultural center of Phetchaburi to the commercial town of Surat Thani. In the north is one of Thailand's oldest beach resorts, Hua Hin, while farther north still is the modern resort of Cha-am. The area also offers natural beauty inland in the huge, hilly Kaeng Krachan National Park and the limestone outcrops of the coastal Khao Sam Roi Yot National Park. The more recently developed islands of the stunning Ko Samui archipelago are the major attractions farther south. Ko Samui itself is the main resort island, while Ko Tao and Ko Pha Ngan are popular with backpackers. For spectacular, unspoiled island scenery, it is hard to beat the beautiful Angthong National Marine Park.

SIGHTS AT A GLANCE

Towering stacks of TV aerials on the houses along the Phet River in the center of Phetchaburi

Lapping up the sun on Ko Samui's Chaweng beach

GETTING THERE

Most of the attractions of the Western Seaboard are easily accessible from the main highways 4 and 41. The major towns are linked to each other and Bangkok by several air-conditioned bus services and trains daily (Bangkok to Hua Hin is 3–4 hours by bus or train; Bangkok to Surat Thani is 11 hours by bus, 11–13 hours by train). Ko Samui, Surat Thani, Prachuap Khiri Khan, and Hua Hin have domestic airports. *Songthaews* and bicycle rickshas can be hired for trips to local sights. Cha-am, Hua Hin, and Ko Samui have car rental facilities. Surat Thani and Don Sak are the main gateways to the Ko Samui archipelago. Ko Tao is also accessible via Chumphon. The train/bus/ferry journey from Bangkok to Ko Samui takes 16 hours.

SEE ALSO

• *Where to Stay* pp401–3
• *Where to Eat* pp425–7

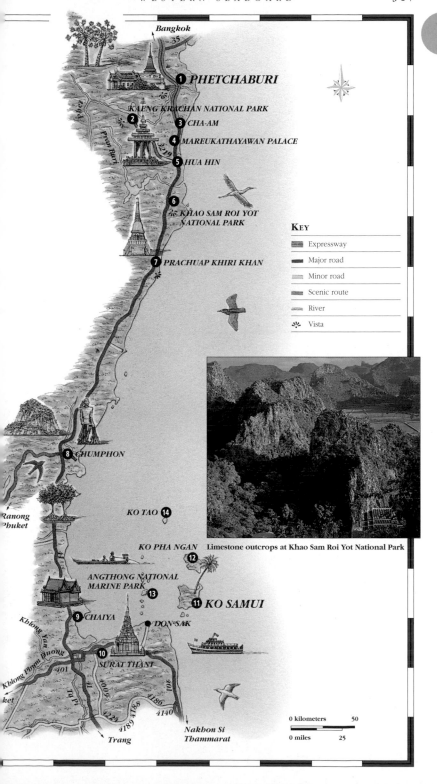

Limestone outcrops at Khao Sam Roi Yot National Park

1 *PHETCHABURI*

KAENG KRACHAN NATIONAL PARK

2

3 *CHA-AM*

4 *MAREUKATHAYAWAN PALACE*

5 *HUA HIN*

6

KHAO SAM ROI YOT NATIONAL PARK

7 *PRACHUAP KHIRI KHAN*

8 *CHUMPHON*

Ranong
Phuket

KO TAO **14**

KO PHA NGAN

12

ANGTHONG NATIONAL MARINE PARK

13

11 *KO SAMUI*

9 *CHAIYA*

DON SAK

Khlong Yan

Khlong Phum Duong
ket

10 *SURAT THANI*

Trang

Nakhon Si Thammarat

Bangkok
35

Phet Buri

Pran Buri

4219

401
411
4009
4188
4189
4224
4140
4186
401

KEY

▬▬	Expressway
▬▬	Major road
▬▬	Minor road
▬▬	Scenic route
▬▬	River
※	Vista

0 kilometers 50

0 miles 25

Street-by-Street: Phetchaburi ❶

เพชรบุรี

Detail, Phra
Nakhon Khiri

SETTLED SINCE AT LEAST the 11th century, Phetchaburi (often spelled Phetburi) is one of Thailand's oldest towns. It has long been an important trading and cultural center, and Mon, Khmer, and Ayutthayan influences can be seen in its 30 temples. During the 19th century it became a favorite royal retreat, and King Mongkut built a summer house here on a hill, Khao Wang, west of the center. This is now part of the Phra Nakhon Khiri Historical Park (see p320). Other major sights are the 17th-century Wat Yai Suwannaram, the five Khmer prangs of Wat Kamphaeng Laeng, and an old quarter that has retained much of its original charm. Despite such attractions, accommodation is scant. Most visitors come on day trips from Bangkok, 123 km (76 miles) away.

Phra Song Road
Several wats are located on this busy road.

To Phra Nakhon
Khiri Historical
Park

NOK

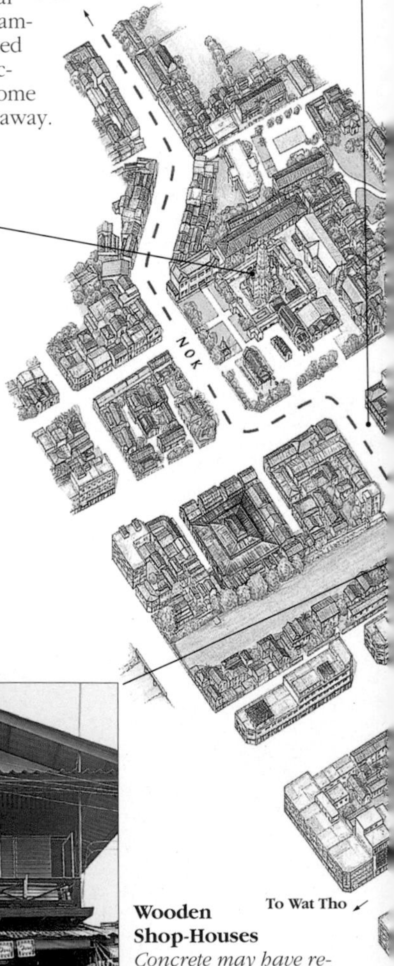

Wat Mahathat
The five white Khmer-style prangs of this much-restored 14th-century temple dominate the town's central skyline. The figures of angels and gods decorate the roofs of the main wihan and bot.

STAR SIGHTS

★ **Phra Nakhon Khiri Historical Park**

★ **Wat Kamphaeng Laeng**

★ **Wat Yai Suwannaram**

To Wat Tho

Wooden Shop-Houses
Concrete may have replaced wood in many Thai towns, but attractive wooden buildings, many lining the river bank, are still a feature of Phetchaburi.

★ Phra Nakhon Khiri Historical Park

As an avid astronomer, King Mongkut had this observatory conveniently built next to his hilltop summer palace; this is now a museum (see p320). The magnificently landscaped and forested surrounding park offers extensive views of Phetchaburi.

To Wat Chisa-in

CHAROEN KASEM

CHISA-IN

PHET

PHANIT JEROEN

PONGSURIYA ROAD

PHRA SONG

MATAYAWONG

Market

To Wat Kamphaeng Laeng

★ Wat Yai Suwannaram

Built during the Ayutthaya period (see pp56–7), the temple is notable for the lovely original murals of Hindu gods in the bot. A scripture library stands on stilts in the middle of a large pond on the grounds.

To Wat Yai Suwannaram

| 0 meters | 75 |
| 0 yards | 75 |

KEY

 — — — Suggested route

★ Wat Kamphaeng Laeng

This is one of the few surviving Khmer shrines in Thailand outside the Northeast. The five laterite prangs of the temple, in varying states of disrepair, are typically Khmer in design and may date from the 12th century. Originally a Hindu temple, it was later adapted for Buddhist use.

Phra Nakhon Khiri, Rama IV's ambitious 19th-century palace complex

Exploring Phetchaburi's Outer Sights

Phetchaburi is divided by the Phet River, which weaves its way past this provincial capital's 30 historic temples. Many, especially the Ayutthayan *wats*, are excellently preserved, their pinnacles dominating the skyline. In the distance, to the west, three large hills loom imperiously over the city.

Phra Nakhon Khiri, locally referred to as Khao Wang, translates as the "celestial city of the mountain." This palace complex, perched on top of 92-m (302-ft) Maha Samana hill, was commissioned by King Mongkut (Rama IV) as a summer house in the 1850s. Extravagant use of European, Chinese, and Japanese architectural styles make this a bold study in Thai and foreign architecture. Set among natural woods, rocks, and caverns, it also offers fine vistas of Phetchaburi town and panoramic views of the province.

The complex extends over three peaks. The Royal Palace and the Ho Chatchawan Wiangchai, an observatory tower (Rama IV was an accomplished amateur astronomer), are both perched on the west rise; the Phra That Chomphet, a white *chedi* erected by Rama V, stands on the central rise; and Wat Maha Samanaram, containing some fine murals, takes up the east rise. In 1988 the complex was made a Historical Park. A cable car takes visitors up the steep ascent to the palace buildings.

A short distance north of town is **Tham Khao Luang**, a cave containing stalactites,

chedis, and Buddha images. To the right of the cave's mouth lies **Wat Bun Thawi**, notable for its intricately carved wooden door panels.

🏠 **Phra Nakhon Khiri**
Khao Wang, Phetchaburi. 📞 0-3242-5600. ⬜ daily. 🎫
🛕 **Tham Khao Luang**
Hwy 3173, 3 km (2 miles) N of Phetchaburi. ⬜ daily. 🎫 donation.

Kaeng Krachan National Park ❷
อุทยานแห่งชาติแก่งกระจาน

Phetchaburi province. Park HQ off Hwy 3175, 60 km (37 miles) S of Phetchaburi. 🛈 TAT (0-3247-1005); Forestry Dept (0-2562-0760 or www. dnp.go.th for bungalow bookings). 🚌 Phetchaburi then songthaew. 🎫

THAILAND'S LARGEST national park is home to at least 40 species of large mammal, such as tiger, leopard, elephant, gibbon, two types of Asiatic bear, and two types of leaf-monkey (langur). Established in 1981, this 2,920-sq km (1,150-sq mile)

Tiger, one of many species at Kaeng Krachan National Park

preserve covers nearly half of Phetchaburi province and contains some of the most pristine tracts of tropical evergreen forest in the country.

The park is relatively unknown to tourists but offers some excellent hiking.

Its western flank is marked out by the dramatic Tenasserim mountain range and the Thai-Burmese border. Streams and rivers are the water source for the 45-sq km (17-sq mile) **Kaeng Krachan reservoir**, which can be explored by boat. Thousands of migratory birds coming from as far afield as China and Siberia rest, feed, and breed in the salt marshes.

Horse for hire at Cha-am beach

Cha-am ❸
ชะอำ

Phetchaburi province. 🏘 20,000. 🚌 🚆 🛈 TAT, 500/51 Phetkasem Rd, Cha-am (0-3247-1005). 🚤 daily.

SINCE THE MID-1980s Cha-am has experienced a dramatic surge in popularity. It has been developed from a quiet fishing and market village into a lively playground for Bangkok weekenders. Tall condominiums and huge resort hotels have sprung up alongside the long, sandy beach. During the week, however, it can be remarkably quiet.

The resort caters primarily to Thais, who focus their attentions on eating and drinking rather than swimming. At umbrella-shaded tables strung along the beach like a high tide mark, visitors feast on delicious grilled fish, squid, shrimp, and mussels. Spicy dips and cold beer complete the culinary adventure.

Those who prefer more formal eating will find restaurants serving the same range of succulent fare at the northern end of the beach.

Mareukathayawan Palace ❹
พระราชนิเวศน์มฤคทายวัน

Off Hwy 4, 9 km (5 miles) S of Cha-am. 🚹 TAT, Cha-am (0-3247-1005). 🚌 from Cha-am. ⏰ 8:30am–4:30pm daily. 💰 donation. 🚫 in bedroom.

MAREUKATHAYAWAN PALACE ("the palace of love and hope") was the summer residence of Rama VI. Built midway between Cha-am and Hua Hin, this grand golden teak building was designed by an Italian architect and constructed in just 16 days in 1923. However, it was abandoned when Rama VI died two years later and stood neglected for decades. The palace has undergone restoration since the 1970s and is now close to its original appearance.

The building is cool and airy; its wooden halls, verandas, and royal chambers are decorated simply and painted in pastel shades. Although the palace is easily accessible, it is rarely visited by tourists.

Hua Hin ❺
หัวหิน

Prachuap Khiri Khan province. 🏠 33,000. 🚉 🚌 🚗 🚹 Municipality Tourist Office, 114 Phetkasem Rd, Hua Hin (0-3247-1005). ✉ daily.

HUA HIN WAS Thailand's first beach resort. Its rail connection to Bangkok, completed in 1911, was central to its success, making the 190-km (118-mile) journey from Bangkok a manageable seaside excursion.

A nine-hole golf course, commissioned by King Rama VI, and the splendid colonial style Railway Hotel were built in 1922 and 1923.

Hua Hin Station, vital to the resort's early success

Following the international trend for recuperative spa resorts at the time, Hua Hin became a popular retreat for minor Thai royalty, Bangkok's high society, and affluent foreigners. Prince Chulachakrabongse built a summer palace in the town which he called **Klai Klangwon** (meaning "far from worries") in 1926. It is still used by the Royal Family and is not open to the public. Although Hua Hin's fortunes declined after World War II,

its historical connections have helped it become popular again with a new generation of Bangkokians. Activities such as pony riding, seafood dining, golf, and shopping for polished seashell curios in the town's market give Hua Hin a relaxed, family feel.

For an insight into the Hua Hin of the 1920s, visit the Railway Hotel, now called the **Hotel Sofitel Central**. By the 1960s it had fallen into disrepair, but a sensitive restoration of the elegant 1920s' decor, museum tea room, and intricate topiaries won it an Outstanding Conservation Award from the Architects' Association of Thailand in 1993. Before its refurbishment the hotel and its environs were used extensively in the making of the film *The Killing Fields*, where it stood in for the Phnom Penh Hotel.

South of Hua Hin's main beach lies Khao Takiap (or "chopstick hill"), which is covered with miniature *chedis* and shrines. Nearby stands **Wat Khao Lad**, fronted by an impressive 20-m (66-ft) standing Buddha, which faces the sea.

The majestic open hall and first-floor gallery in the north wing of Mareukathayawan Palace

Khao Sam Roi Yot National Park ❻

อุทยานแห่งชาติเขาสามร้อยยอด

Prachuap Khiri Khan province. Visitors' Centre off Hwy 4, 37 km (23 miles) S of Pranburi. 🛈 TAT, Cha-am (0-3247-1005); Forestry Dept (0-2562-0760 or www.dnp.go.th for bungalow bookings). 🚌 Pranburi, then songthaew.

THIS SMALL COASTAL PARK sits in the narrowest part of the Thai peninsula, overlooking the Gulf of Thailand. Covering 98 sq km (38 sq miles), it is a region of contrasts: sea, sand, and marsh backed by mountains and caves. The park is best known for its distinctive limestone pinnacles (Khao Sam Roi Yot means "mountain of 300 peaks") that rise vertically from the marshland to a height of 650 m (2,150 ft).

The park's wetlands provide a sanctuary for water birds. Millions of migratory birds flying from Siberia to Sumatra and Australia rest, feed, and breed here between August and April. It is home to many other animals such as the rare dusky langur, the nocturnal slow loris, and the crab-eating macaque. **Tham Phraya Nakon** houses a grand pavilion, built for King Rama V in 1896, and **Tham Sai** contains fossilized falls.

Wat Chong Kra Chok, overlooking sedate Prachuap Khiri Khan

Prachuap Khiri Khan ❼

ประจวบคีรีขันธ์

Prachuap Khiri Khan province. 🚶 60,000. 🚌 🚆 🚢 🛈 TAT, Cha-am (0-3247-1005). 🛒 daily.

PRACHUAP KHIRI KHAN means "town among the mountain chain." And it is certainly true that its coastal sugar-loaf limestone outcrops at either end of a sandy bay give it a "little Rio" appearance. The local economy relies primarily on fishing; freshly caught seafood can be purchased from a number of good restaurants and stalls along the promenade. This peaceful administrative town has pleasant swimming beaches to the north and south

Beware monkeys sign, Khao Sam Roi Yot

of its main bay. The top of the delightful **Wat Chong Kra Chok** – perched on one of the surrounding hills – offers the best view of the area. About 200 macaques live on the hill, and every evening they climb to the top to feed from the lovely frangipani trees.

Chumphon ❽

ชุมพร

Chumphon province. 🚶 84,000. 🚌 🚆 🚢 🛈 TAT, Surat Thani (0-7728-8818). @ tatsurat@samart.co.th 🛒 daily. 🎉 Luang Suan Buddha Image Parade and Boat Race (5 days in Oct).

CHUMPHON IS REGARDED by some as the point of cultural transition between the heartland of the Buddhist Tai peoples, and the peninsular south of the country, where Muslim culture is strong. The town was the home of Prince Chumphon, the Father of the Royal Thai Navy, who died in 1923. Nearby, the 68-m (225-ft) long **HMS Chumphon** torpedo boat, decommissioned in 1975, has been preserved. It forms a distinctive landmark.

The reefs around the 47 tiny islands off Chumphon's 222-km-long coast (140-mile) are becoming increasingly popular with divers. Tour companies in town will arrange diving day trips to such islands as **Samet**, **Mattra**, **Ngam Yai**, and **Ngam Noi**. Chumphon is also the most convenient place from which to get a ferry to Ko Tao (see p331).

CHAIYA'S ROLE IN THE SRIVIJAYA EMPIRE

Srivijayan votive tablet

The Mahayana Buddhist Empire of Srivijaya (see pp52–3) dominated the whole Malaysian peninsula and parts of Indonesia between the 7th and 13th centuries AD. Although the majority of scholars now believe that Palembang in Sumatra was the Srivijayan capital, discoveries of temple remains and some exquisite stone and bronze statues (many now in the National Museum in Bangkok) in Chaiya provide evidence of Chaiya's importance. Its strategic geographical position, as a then coastal port, meant the town played an important role in the east-west trade between India, the peninsula, and China. In fact, Chaiya was mentioned in the writings of the Chinese monk I Chinga, who, while visiting the area in the late 7th century, testified to its religious and cultural sophistication. It is known that some of Chaiya's rulers were connected by marriage to those of central Java. Furthermore, it is possible that the name "Chaiya" originated as a contraction of "Siwichaiya" (a different transliteration of Srivijaya), which follows the local tendency to emphasize the final syllable of a word.

8th-century bronze found at Chaiya

A line of Buddha images at Phra Boromathat Chaiya, one of the few remaining temples from the Srivijaya period

Chaiya ⑨

ไชยา

Surat Thani province. 👥 34,000.
🚉 🚌 🅷 TAT, Surat Thani (0-7728-
8818). 🛗 daily. 🎭 Chak Phra
Festival (Oct–Nov).

DESPITE THE SOMEWHAT dreary look of the small railroad town of Chaiya, the settlement is actually one of the oldest and most historically significant in Southern Thailand. A number of superb examples of sculpture dating from the Srivijaya period (7th–13th centuries) have been found here.

Many of the sculptures show clear Mon and Indian influences, depicting figures such as Bengali-style Buddha images and multiarmed Hindu deities. These, and a variety of votive tablets, can be seen at the **Chaiya National Museum**. It also holds examples of Ayutthayan art. The museum is 2 km (1 mile) west of Chaiya and a ten-minute walk from the train station.

Right beside the museum is **Phra Boromathat Chaiya** (see pp336–7), an important Srivijayan temple. Within the main compound is the central chedi, which has been painstakingly restored. Square in plan, it has four porches that ascend in tiers and are topped with small towers. The 8th-century chedi is built of brick and vegetable mortar. Although the site is old, it is the memory of Phra Chaiya Wiwat, a locally venerated monk who died in 1949, that attracts the majority of worshipers today.

🏛 Chaiya National Museum

Phra Boromathat Chaiya. 📞 0-7743-
-1066. ⏱ Wed–Sun. ⬤ public hols.
🎟

ENVIRONS: The International Dhamma Hermitage (see p446), based at **Wat Suan Mok**, southwest of Chaiya, is a popular and famous retreat for Buddhists from all over the world. Its attraction is its back-to-basics religious philosophy established by the wat's founder, Buddhadhasa Bhikkhu, who died in 1993. Within the temple a regimen of

Murals relating the story of the Buddha at Wat Suan Mok

physical labor underpins a simple monastic life devoid of elaborate religious ceremony. Ten-day residential meditation retreats are held here, starting on the first day of each month.

🏛 Wat Suan Mok

7 km (4 miles) S of Chaiya off Hwy 41.
📞 0-7743-1552. ⏱ daily.

Surat Thani ⑩

สุราษฎร์ธานี

Surat Thani province. 👥 31,000.
✈ 🚉 Phun Phin, 14 km (9 miles) W
of Surat Thani, then bus. 🚌 ⛴ Ban
Don (in town); Thong, 6 km (4 miles)
E of town. 🅷 TAT, 5 Talat Mai Rd,
Surat Thani (0-7728-8818). @ tatsurat
@tat.or.th 🎭 Rambutan Fair (Aug),
Chak Phra Festival (Oct–Nov).

SURAT THANI, a business center and port dealing in rubber and coconuts, first grew to prominence in the Srivijaya period since it was strategically located at the mouth of the Tapi and Phum Duang Rivers. The riverside is still intriguing today with its numerous small boats ferrying people to the city's busy waterfront markets, which sell fresh products and flowers. But Surat Thani is best known as a transportation gateway to the beaches of Ko Samui and Ko Pha Ngan.

Lofty palm trees and clear blue waters of a near-deserted beach on Ko Samui ▷

Ko Samui ⓫

เกาะสมุย

A T 247 SQ KM (95 SQ MILES), Samui is Thailand's third largest island, after Ko Phuket and Ko Chang. Dubbed the biggest coconut plantation in the world until the first backpackers arrived in the 1970s, this island has now seen tourism

Coconuts, a key crop on Samui

become its main income earner. Samui's beaches are world famous – its long, perfect strands attract around 500,000 visitors each year. Chaweng beach, in particular, has a reputation as something of a hangout for an international party crowd. It is likely, however, that as more and more luxury accommodation is built for package tourists, the character of Ko Samui will change somewhat.

Naton

Naton is Samui's capital and main ferry port. The island was first settled in the 1850s by Chinese merchants who had come in search of trade in cotton and coconuts. Naton was founded around 1905, when the site was chosen as the island's administrative center.

Few visitors stay here, except in order to take an early morning boat to Surat Thani on the mainland. The town has a supermarket, post office, and money changing facilities.

The main transport route on the island is the 50-km (31-mile) circular road, which passes through Naton. *Songthaews* departing from Naton ferry port travel either northward (clockwise) toward Chaweng beach and the airport, or southward (counterclockwise) toward Lamai.

The 12-m (38-ft) "Big Buddha" on Ko Faan, just off the Samui coast

Maenam

This 4-km (2-mile) long beach is the most westerly stretch of sand on the north coast. It has extensive views of Ko Pha Ngan *(see p329)*. Visitors flock here for the excellent windsurfing opportunities, which are aided by the strong directional breezes that blow on-

KEY

🏖	Beach
🏄	Water sports
ℹ	Tourist information
🛕	Wat
✈	Airport
🚌	Bus station
⚓	Ferry service
▬▬	Main road
═══	Minor road
☀	Vista

Maenam, on the north coast, one of the quietest beaches on Ko Samui

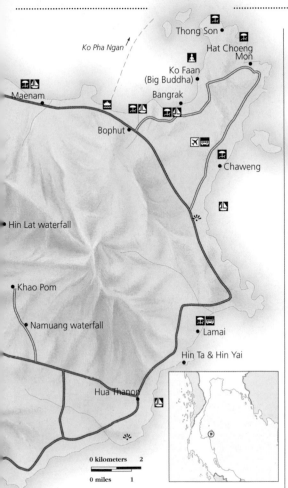

Ko Pha Ngan

Thong Son

Hat Choeng
Mon

Ko Faan
(Big Buddha)

Maenam

Bangrak

Bophut

Chaweng

Hin Lat waterfall

Khao Pom

Namuang waterfall

Lamai

Hin Ta & Hin Yai

Hua Thanon

0 kilometers   2

0 miles   1

VISITORS' CHECKLIST

Surat Thani province. 42,000.
23 km (14 miles) from Naton.
from Surat Thani, Tha Thong
and Don Sak. TAT, Naton (0-
7742-0504) or TAT, Surat Thani
(0-7728-8818); Songserm Travel,
Naton (0-7728-9894, for ferry
bookings). 3 km (2 miles) S of
Naton (0-7742-1281). daily.
W www.samui.sawadee.com

**Paragliding over Chaweng beach,
one of many activities**

shore during the northeasterly
monsoon from December to
February. However, the beach
is narrow and not as attractive
as others on the island.

Bophut

Bophut has better facilities
than Maenam. Its village, at
the eastern end of the next
bay to the east, includes bungalows, a bank, bars, restaurants, and a range of water
sports. The tranquil 2-km
(1-mile) long beach is popular
with families and backpackers.
From Bophut there is a daily
boat service to Hat Rin, a
beach on Ko Pha Ngan.

Bangrak

Adjacent to Bophut is Bangrak,
also known as "Big Buddha"
beach. The sea is not as clear
here as it is off Chaweng and

Lamai beaches *(see p328)*, but
it does offer plenty of budget
accommodations. A causeway
links the eastern end of
Bangrak beach to the tiny
island of Ko Faan, home to
the large, gold-covered Big
Buddha. The imposing statue
is popular with islanders and

Asian tourists, who come here
to make merit *(see p125)*. A
gaudy bazaar of souvenir stalls
and cafés has sprung up at
the foot of the *naga* staircase
leading to the Buddha image.

Thong Son and Choeng Mon

Farther along the coast, on
Samui's northeastern cape, is
a series of secluded rocky
coves. Hat Thong Son is a
peaceful inlet with marvelous
views across to Ko Pha Ngan.
Most of the accommodation
on the headland is concentrated at Ao Choeng Mon, an
attractive bay with a pleasant
beach and good swimming.

Palm trees shading typical beachside huts on Ko Samui

Exploring Ko Samui: the East Coast and Minor Sights

THE BEAUTIFUL BEACHES and buzzing nightlife of Chaweng and Lamai on Samui's east coast draw tourists from all over the world. Many visitors never stray from these resorts, leaving the quieter beaches on the south and west coasts, the island's *wats*, and Samui's spectacular mountainous and forested interior relatively untouched.

Muslim fishermen landing their boats on Samui's east coast

Chaweng

Chaweng is the longest, busiest, and most beautiful beach on the island, stretching 5 km (3 miles) down the east coast. Its warm waters, white sands, and back-to-nature beach bungalows have attracted budget travelers for many years. Today, though, more and more upscale developments are being built to accommodate package tourists.

At the northern end of Chaweng is a tranquil 1-m (3-ft) deep lagoon, ideal for children and novice windsurfers. The long, inviting sweep of the middle and southern end of the beach is bordered by coconut palms. Chaweng is at its most scenic along its southern section where large boulders alternate with discreet sandy coves.

For the active, the beach has a wide range of sports including windsurfing, canoeing, paragliding, scuba diving, tennis, and volleyball.

Chaweng has the most developed tourist infrastructure on Samui with travel agencies, banks, supermarkets, and car and bike rental among the facilities available. Although it does attract a few families, Chaweng is still predominantly visited by young travelers. Many come to enjoy the ever-increasing numbers of bars, restaurants, and clubs.

Lamai

Samui's second largest beach caters primarily to the European budget tourist. The main focus is at the center of the 4-km (2-mile) long beach. Behind the beach are riotous bars, nightclubs, and restaurants serving Western food.

Lamai village is at the quieter, northern end of the beach, away from the crowds. It still has many old teak houses with thatched roofs.

The village's main sight is Wat Lamai Cultural Hall, built in 1826, which has a small folk museum dedicated to arts and crafts found on Samui.

On the southern promontory of Lamai beach are the Hin Ta and Hin Yai rock formations that are famous for their similarity in shape to male and female sexual organs.

South and West Coasts

There are many quiet beaches with simple huts along the south and west coasts, such as around Thong Krut. Another is Thong Yang which – although only 1.5 km (1 mile) south of the pier where the vehicle ferries from Don Sak dock – which is perfect for those seeking peaceful seclusion.

Swimming in Namuang waterfall, in the center of Samui

The Interior

For visitors tiring of the beach, the interior of Samui offers an adventurous alternative. The mix of dense tropical forest and large coconut plantations seems impenetrable, but there are rough trails – which can be negotiated by four-wheel-drive vehicle or by motorcycle – and two roads leading to Samui's picturesque waterfalls.

Namuang, an impressive 30-m (98-ft) high waterfall, is a popular destination for picnics and swimming. It is situated 10 km (6 miles) from Naton and 5 km (3 miles) from the circular coast road. Hin Lat, 3 km (2 miles) from Naton, is smaller than Namuang and less interesting. Both falls are at their most spectacular in December or January at the end of the rainy season, when they swell with rainwater.

Chaweng, the longest and most attractive beach on Ko Samui

Ko Pha Ngan ⑫

เกาะพะงัน

Surat Thani province. 👤 8,400.
🚢 from Naton on Ko Samui to
Tong Sala. ℹ TAT, Surat Thani
(0-7728-8818). 🚢 daily.

K O PHA NGAN is 15 km (9
miles) north of Ko Samui,
and is two-thirds its size. The
island has the same tropical
combination of powdery
beaches, accessible coral reefs,
and rugged, forested interior.
Budget travelers come to enjoy a bohemian life, staying
in rattan huts beside idyllic
bays. The island is much less
developed for tourism than
Samui, due mainly to its bad
road system. Much of it is accessible only by sea or along
rutted tracks by pickup truck.

Tong Sala
This town is the entrance port
to Ko Pha Ngan, and, like
Naton on Ko Samui, acts as a
service town with a bank, post
restante, supermarket, travel
agent, and photoprocessing
store. Next to the pier, an
armada of *songthaeus* waits to
take visitors around the island.

Hat Rin
The greatest number of bungalows on the island is at Hat
Rin, located at the southeastern
tip, 10 km (6 miles) from Tong
Sala. It has become a popular
destination with backpackers,
many of whom now consider
Samui's resorts to be too
commercialized. Hat Rin has
two wide beaches flanking
the headland. Its accommodations are often fully booked
for a week either side of the
monthly full moon beach

**The white sands of Hat Rin beach
on Ko Pha Ngan**

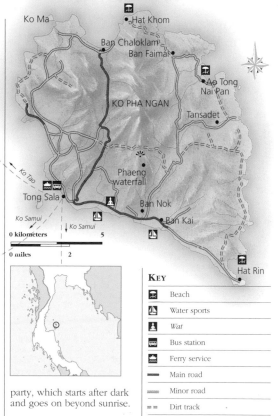

party, which starts after dark
and goes on beyond sunrise.

Chaloklam
A strong smell of dried, salted
fish emanates from Chalo-
klam's storefronts. Asian visitors often stop here to buy
fish after visiting the
revered Chao Mae
Koan Im shrine in the
center of the island.
In Chaloklam, fishing-
related activities such
as mending nets and
gutting fish coexist
with shop-houses
selling pizza and
other tourist snacks.
The beaches near the
town tend to be rath-
er dirty but improve
farther to the east, especially
as far out of town as Khom
beach.

**Dried fish at
Chaloklam village**

Tong Nai Pan
Although the majority of the
beaches are on the east side
of the island, most are accessible only from a rough track
running along the coast. The
twin bays of Tong Nai Pan Noi
and Tong Nai Pan Yai in the

northeast offer arguably the
most attractive scenery. They
can be reached by pickup
truck from Tong Sala
or, between January
and September, by
long-tail boats, which
sail from Maenam
beach on Ko Samui.
 Tansadet, 3 km (2
miles) to the south,
is the island's biggest
stream and waterfall.
It owes its name,
"royal stream," to
the ten visits King
Chulalongkorn made
between 1888 and 1909. Since
then most Thai monarchs have
left large stone inscriptions on
rocks alongside the stream –
finding the signatures requires
scrambling among the rocks.
The stream has two falls, Sam-
pan and Daeng. Both are suitable for swimming, but heavy
rainfall from September to December makes the stream bed
too dangerous to walk along.

KEY
🏖	Beach
⚓	Water sports
🚶	*Wat*
🚌	Bus station
⛴	Ferry service
▬	Main road
═	Minor road
＝＝	Dirt track
🌸	Vista

Angthong National Marine Park ⑬

อุทยานแห่งชาติทางทะเลอ่างทอง

Surat Thani province. Park HQ on Ko Wua Talab. ⛴ *from Ko Samui.* ⓘ *TAT, Surat Thani (0-7728-8818); Park HQ (0-7728-6025); Forestry Dept (0-2562-0760 inc bungalow bookings).* ◑ *Nov–Dec.*

THE 40 VIRTUALLY uninhabited islands of the Angthong National Marine Park display a rugged beauty distinct from palm-fringed Ko Samui 31 km (19 miles) away to the southeast. The Angthong ("golden basin") islands, covering an area of 102 sq km (39 sq miles), are the submerged peaks of a flooded range of limestone mountains that, farther south in Nakhon Si Thammarat province, rise to 1,835 m (6,000 ft).

Angthong's pristine beauty owes much to being the preserve of the Royal Thai Navy, and therefore off-limits until 1980 when it was declared a National Marine Park. Now naval boats have been replaced by tourist ferries. Most visitors come on day-trips from Ko Samui to relax on the mica-white sands, explore the lush forests and limestone caves, sea canoe around the islands' jagged coastlines, and snorkel among the colorful fan corals.

Another attraction is the abundant wildlife, both on land and in the sea. Leopard cats, squirrels, long-tailed macaques, sea otters, and pythons may be glimpsed, and a lack of natural predators has made the endearingly friendly dusky langur easy to spot. Among the 40 bird species found in the archipelago are the black baza, the edible-nest swiftlet, the brahminy kite, and the Eurasian woodcock.

Divers taking advantage of the excellent coral off **Ko Sam Sao** will probably see short-bodied mackerel *(pla thu),* a staple of the Thai diet. The sea around the islands is favored by the fish as a breeding ground. It is also possible to spot dolphins, although they are wary of humans because fisherman catch them for their meat.

Ko Naayphud

Ko Hindab

Ko Wuakantang

Ko Sam Sao

Ko Mae Ko

Ko Phi

🏖ⓘ🏄 National Park Headquarters

Ko Wua Talab

Ko Samui

ANGTHONG NATIONAL MARINE PARK

Ferry to Angthong National Marine Park

Ko Tao-Pun

Ko Phaluai

0 kilometers 2

0 miles 1

View from a trail on Ko Wua Talab, Angthong National Marine Park

Boat for carrying visitors from the ferry to the beach on Ko Mae Ko

The park headquarters, and the islands' only tourist accommodations and facilities, are located on the largest island, **Ko Wua Talab** ("sleeping cow island"). A steep 400-m (1300-ft) climb from here leads to a vista offering wonderful panoramas of the whole archipelago and beyond to Ko Pha Ngan, Ko Samui, and the mainland. The view is at its best at sunrise and sunset.
Another fairly tough climb leads to Tham Buabok ("waving lotus cave"), so named because of the shape of some of its stalactites and stalagmites.

On **Ko Mae Ko** there is a swimming beach as well as the stunning Thale Noi, a wide turquoise lake bordered by sheer cliffs. This is the "golden basin" that gives the islands their name.

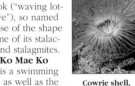

Cowrie shell, Ko Tao

Ko Tao ⑭

เกาะเต่า

Surat Thani province. 1,300.
from Chumphon or Ko Samui. TAT, Surat (0-7728-8818).

LOCATED 40 KM (25 miles) north of Ko Pha Ngan, "turtle island" is the smallest and prettiest of the islands in the Samui archipelago that offer visitors accommodations.

Ko Tao's major attraction is its superb offshore diving. Excellent visibility, a wide range of diving sites, and a rich variety of coral and marine life make for some of the most rewarding diving in the country. The main dive sites are Green Rock, Chumphon Pinnacle, and Southwest Pinnacle. Many

sites are suitable for beginners thanks to the shallow inshore bays and clear waters. In May water visibility can approach 40 m (130 ft), which is often claimed to be the maximum possible. The island has about ten dive companies that operate all year round, although the main season is from December to April.

The island itself is rugged, with dense forest inland, quiet coves along the east coast, and a fine sweep of sandy beach on the west side. Plenty of simple bungalow accommodation is available, although it can be difficult to find a room in tourist season.

Just to the northwest of Ko Tao lie three immensely scenic islands known collectively as **Ko Nang Yuan**. Linked by sandbars and surrounded by coral, these are a delightful place to linger for a few days.

Diving among the rich marine life and fine coral off Ko Tao

Birds' nests: a regional delicacy

BIRD'S-NEST SOUP

Unlike such misleadingly named delicacies as Bombay duck, the main ingredient of bird's-nest soup is, indeed, birds' nests. Not just any nest will do, however. Only the homes of birds such as the brown-rumped swift, the edible-nest swiftlet, and the sea swallow are acceptable. When these delicate, saliva-thread constructions are cooked they are transformed into smooth, noodlelike strands that are considered to have aphrodisiac properties by peoples throughout Southeast and East Asia. Such is the perceived potency of the soup that the nests change hands for huge sums of money. A government license is required to collect the nests, and many of the most important sites, such as those in caves on Ko Phi Phi Ley (see p363) are protected by armed guards. The dangerous job of nest harvesting is allowed only between February and April and in September, when agile collectors must scale the cave walls on flimsy bamboo scaffolds.

SOUTHERN
THAILAND

Introducing Southern Thailand

The narrow peninsula of Southern Thailand, stretching from Ranong, on the Burmese border, to Malaysia, is a unique region with a rich, multicultural heritage. Forested mountains run along much of the interior, and the hinterland and islands of Phangnga Bay in the Andaman Sea form Thailand's most spectacular natural landscape. Here the shallow waters are dotted with limestone stacks and craggy islands 300 m (985 feet) high. Some of the country's best sandy beaches and diving sites are also found along the southern coasts and around the Andaman islands. Though the beach resorts of Phuket and Krabi draw the most visitors to the area, the South also offers historic cultural sites, such as the towns of Songkhla and Nakhon Si Thammarat. Sadly, many parts of the region's coast were hit by the tsunami in 2004 and some 5,300 people were killed. However, the Thais responded rapidly and the rate of reconstruction has been impressive.

UPPER ANDAMAN COAST *(see pp342–363)*

Phangnga Bay

Phuket

Phangnga Bay (see pp354–7), *with its weird and wonderful towering limestone stacks, is one of Southern Thailand's most famous natural beauty spots. Due to massive erosion the bay can no longer be accessed by tourist boats, but can be viewed from a distance.*

Phuket (see pp348–53) *is Thailand's largest island and richest province. Prosperous even during the 19th century, when Chinese merchants used the island as a base for sea trade, today it is one of the most popular tourist resorts in Thailand. Phuket is now a largely upscale destination with luxury hotels, restaurants, and shops lining many of the island's stunning beaches. A wide range of water sports is available, including superb diving facilities.*

◁ **A row of golden, seated Buddha images in the interior courtyard of Wat Wang, near Phatthalung town**

Nakhon Si Thammarat (see pp368–9), *once the regional capital of the Srivijaya Empire (see pp 336–7), is today the South's cultural center. Despite some fine sights, including Southern Thailand's holiest shrine, Wat Mahathat, and one of the few remaining* nang talung *shadow puppet theaters, the city is still not visited by many tourists.*

Songkhla National Museum (see pp374–5), *contains an eclectic collection of ceramics, art, and furniture. It occupies the one-time deputy governor's residence, a splendid 19th-century Chinese-style mansion.*

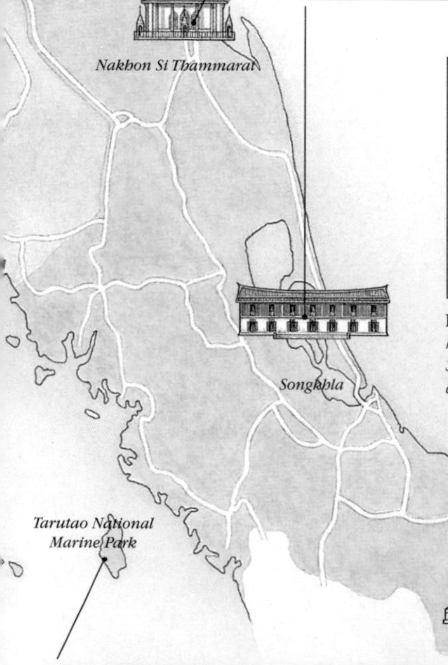

Nakhon Si Thammarat

Korlae *fishing boats* (see p378), *with painted hulls, are a colorful feature of the Muslim South. Some of the best ones can be seen at Pattani, once an independent Muslim state.*

Songkhla

0 kilometers 50

0 miles 25

Tarutao National Marine Park

Pattani

DEEP SOUTH
(see pp364–379)

Tarutao National Marine Park (see p376) *has a wide diversity of wildlife and offers some of the most stunning, unspoiled beaches and island scenery in Thailand.*

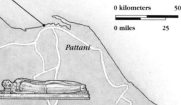

The Peninsula as a Cultural Crossroads

For over 2,000 years, the peninsula that is now divided between Malaysia, Thailand, and Burma has been a major cultural crossroads. Finds from the Isthmus of Kra (especially the historic trading centers of Nakhon Si Thammarat, Chaiya, Sathing Phra, and Takua Pa) testify to strong links with China, India, the Middle East, and even the Roman Empire before the first millennium AD. In the 7th–13th centuries the Hindu-Buddhist Srivijaya Empire held sway over much of the region. After Srivijaya's decline, Burma and Siam, both Buddhist, pushed south, while Islam, brought by Arab traders, made a lasting impact in the southernmost part of the peninsula. There was even greater cultural diversity from the 16th century, when the British, Dutch, Portuguese, and other colonial powers developed trade routes through the Straits of Malacca.

Islam, *the main religion in Malaysia, is widely practiced in Southern Thailand today – minarets compete with Buddhist shrines in many towns.*

Prehistoric paintings *can be found in Phangnga Bay (see pp354–7) and other parts of the peninsula. Humans have lived here at least since the last Ice Age, when the peninsula did not exist as such – the area from Borneo to Sumatra was then dry land.*

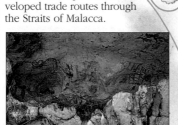

Ceremonial drums *found at the ancient cities of Chaiya and Nakhon Si Thammarat and in Sumatra, were made in Dong Son in North Vietnam c.500 BC, testifying to early trade.*

The Srivijaya Empire *ruled the peninsula as far north as Chaiya in the 7th–13th centuries. As first a Hindu and then a Mahayana Buddhist state, it produced many statues of Bodhisattvas – enlightened beings who delay nirvana in order to save mankind.*

TRADE ROUTES

The Straits of Malacca have always been a natural channel for sea routes. Chinese, Indian, and Arab vessels were trading, gathering provisions, and "wintering" at posts along the peninsula at least 2,000 years ago. European ships joined them from the 16th century. As seafaring technology developed ships became less dependent on some ports, which subsequently declined.

0 kilometers		1,000
0 miles		500

KEY

— Local routes (c. 5th century BC onward)

— Major routes during the Srivijaya period (7th–13th centuries AD)

— Major European routes (16th century onward)

This Dutch East India Company cannon is in Nakhon Si Thammarat, an ancient town in Southern Thailand (see pp368–9). The company traded all over Southeast Asia and was drawn to the peninsula by access to Chinese and Japanese goods.

SRIVIJAYAN ARCHITECTURE

The Srivijaya Empire controlled trade at ports such as Chaiya *(see pp322–3)* and Takua Pa, on the Isthmus of Kra. Numerous Srivijayan artifacts have been found in the Gulf and South of Thailand, but most *chedis*, which were built of stucco and brick, have been built over. The main example to survive is an outstanding, complete *chedi* at Wat Phra Boromathat in Chaiya. Cruciform in shape, it has four tiers, decreasing in size as they ascend. On each corner is a smaller *chedi*. Built in the 9th–10th centuries, it has been restored many times, most recently in 1930.

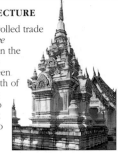

***Chedi* of the Javan-influenced Wat Phra Boromathat, Chaiya**

TO CHINA

VIETNAM

THAILAND

CAMBODIA

S O U T H C H I N A S E A

THMUS RA

MALAYSIA

BORNEO

SUMATRA

JAVA

O AFRICA, EUROPE

TO THE SPICE ISLANDS (MOLUCCAS)

This European engraving *shows a march in Pattani (see p378), one of several Muslim states in the peninsula that lost autonomy to Bangkok in the early part of the 20th century.*

The Thais and Burmese *battled over the northern peninsula after Srivijaya waned. A fight for Phuket, or Junkceylon (see pp348–53), took place in 1785.*

European trade *led to extensive mapping of Southeast Asia. This 17th-century French map shows the local trade route up the east coast of the peninsula, from Batavia (Jakarta) in Java to the city of Ayutthaya in Siam.*

Coral Reefs

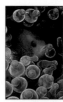

Red saddleback anemonefish

THAILAND'S BEST CORAL REEFS are found in the Andaman Sea. These reefs, which are composed of countless tiny marine animals, grow extremely slowly: 1 m (3 ft) of coral reef can take 1,000 years to form. As a coral reef is an excellent source of food and shelter, it provides the base for a unique and diverse marine ecosystem. The reef consists of reef builders (mainly hard corals, whose limestone skeletons form the basis of the reef) and reef dwellers, such as sea urchins, whose remains may also help build the reef when they die. Although the 2004 tsunami did damage many reefs, particularly those of the Surin, Similan, and Phi Phi islands, initial reports of great devastation were inaccurate.

Snorkeling *is a low-cost and easy way to explore a coral reef. Many reefs can be found in relatively shallow, clear water, which is excellent for snorkeling.*

Gobies *– small, spiny-finned fish with large heads – live mainly in tropical waters. They often share sand burrows with shrimp.*

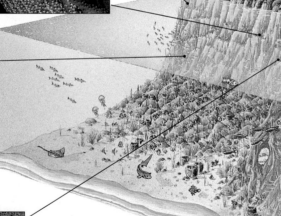

Coconut grove

West-facing wall

The clown trigger-fish *has an upright spine in its dorsal fin. The spine is raised to wedge the fish under rocks and ledges; this stops predators from pulling the fish out.*

A TYPICAL REEF

On the island's east side, the reef flat slopes away from the beach, rises to a crest, then slopes steeply to the sea bed. Mostly hard corals are found on the east side. The reef's west walls tend to be much steeper and rockier than the east side. Its boulders provide protection for soft corals and nooks in which creatures such as eels live.

Moray eels *are voracious predators, hiding in crevices and lunging out at unsuspecting prey swimming by. Food left between a moray's teeth may be picked clean by hungry cleaner shrimp.*

Leopard sharks, *also known as zebra sharks, pose no threat to people. At Shark Point, near Ko Phi Phi, divers often see these timid creatures resting or cruising along the outskirts of the coral reef.*

Many species of sea bird *gather around islands with coral reefs to feed on the abundant fish life. This is a great egret, a large wading bird that feeds by stabbing small fish with its razor-sharp bill.*

Scuba diving *is an excellent way to experience diverse reef ecosystems (see p444). In the South, Phuket has the most diving operators offering instruction, equipment rental, and trips to offshore islands such as Ko Phi Phi. When exploring a coral reef, you should not touch the delicate corals, as this causes permanent damage to the reef.*

Sandy beach

Reef flat

Reef crest

Rays *are often seen around coral reefs. Manta rays have impressive wingspans of up to 6 m (20 ft), while blue-spotted rays have a poisonous spine in their tail.*

Snapper *often follow schools of feeding goatfish, devouring any small fish that escape the latter.*

Reef slope

CORAL: THE REEF'S BUILDING BLOCK

Coral is made of the skeletons of polyps, small animals related to sea anemones and jellyfish. Polyps are unusual in that they build their skeletons outside their bodies. As the polyps divide, the coral colony slowly builds up. There may be as many as 200 different species of coral in a reef, divided into hard corals such as brain coral, and colorful soft corals, which have no stony outer skeleton.

Giant hermit crabs *are soft-bodied crustaceans. They protect their bodies by living and moving around the sea bed in the empty shells of mollusks such as whelks.*

Hard, rocklike coral

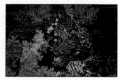

Soft, plantlike coral

Mangrove Forests

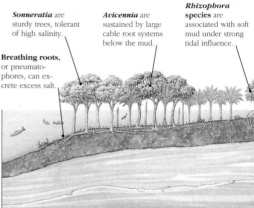

White-throated kingfisher

MANGROVE FORESTS develop only in the tropics, in brackish and saltwater areas of estuaries. In Thailand they are found in pockets of the South, particularly at Phangnga Bay *(see pp354–7)*. Mangrove species are the only trees to have adapted to the inhospitable conditions of these muddy, intertidal zones. The forests typically cover networks of channels and levees created from the buildup of silt that becomes trapped in the cage-like root systems of the trees. Though often dismissed as wasteland, in its natural state a mangrove forest is a vital ecosystem – a fertile spawning, nursing, feeding, and sheltering ground for crustaceans, fish, birds, snakes, and even mammals. "Primary" mangrove grows to over 25 m (80 ft) high. However, most mangrove in Thailand is "secondary," meaning it has been cut by humans and reaches only 5–10 m (16–33 ft).

The characteristic stiltlike roots of most mangrove trees support the tree against the constant movement of tidal waters. As well as holding the trunk of the tree above the high tide level, the roots trap nutrient-rich sediments.

The upward-growing roots (pneumatophores) of some trees have special "breathing" pores used during low tide.

Sonneratia are sturdy trees, tolerant of high salinity.

Avicennia are sustained by large cable root systems below the mud.

Rhizophora species are associated with soft mud under strong tidal influence.

Breathing roots, or pneumatophores, can excrete excess salt.

The mud skipper, so called for its skipping gait across mud flats at low tide, is the ubiquitous mangrove dweller. It can survive for short periods out of water.

CROSS SECTION OF A MANGROVE LEVEE

This cross section shows a typical gradation of trees in a Thai mangrove forest. The waters are at high tide, a time when small fish and invertebrates feed in the sheltered, nutrient-rich waters around the roots of the trees. At low tide, when the roots of the trees are exposed, crabs and wading birds scour the mud flats for trapped fish and decaying matter.

The estuarine crocodile was once king of the mangroves. Nowadays it is bred in farms and is very rarely seen in the wild.

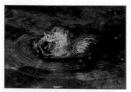

Small-clawed otters are often spotted in mangrove regions. They eat the smaller inhabitants such as mollusks and crabs.

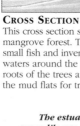

Male fiddler crabs sift the silt with their one enlarged claw, selecting tiny organic particles to eat. As with most other types of crab, their colorful claws are also used in courtship displays.

Rhizophora *trees*, *such as these at Phangnga Bay, are common in Thai mangrove forests. Their colonizing ability is largely due to the unusual shape of their seed pods. With dagger-shaped stalks, these penetrate the ooze rather than floating away with the tide.*

Yellow-ringed cat snakes*, like other mangrove snakes, are adept swimmers and tree climbers. They rest by day and hunt fish and frogs by night.*

Nipa palms thrive in soft mud away from wave action. Nipa is used by Thais to wrap tobacco and as an ingredient in candies and alcohol.

Bruguiera trees grow in compacted mud that is inundated with water only during high spring tides.

Crab-eating macaques *inhabit Thai mangrove forests; they are capable swimmers and forage for crabs at low tide. Seeds also form part of the macaques' diet.*

THE DESTRUCTION OF THAILAND'S MANGROVE FORESTS

Despite the provision of a national mangrove management program (set up in 1946), some 60 percent of Thailand's mangrove has been cleared since the 1960s – just 300,000 acres were thought to remain by 1996. Not only has this loss of habitat decimated marine life, but coastal erosion has also started to become a problem in parts of the South. Without the roots of mangrove trees to trap it, estuarine silt is deposited over a progressively larger area, and seawater seeps over more and more of the land. The rate of loss peaked in the late 1980s with the boom in tiger shrimp farming in former mangrove areas. After

Shrimp farm in a former area of mangrove forest

clearing mangrove trees to make way for shrimp farms, farmers use the tide-flushed mangrove channels to discharge nutrient-rich excreta from the prawn pools. This reduces oxygen levels in the adjacent natural breeding grounds of shrimp, fish, and crabs. Charcoal production is also to blame: tall mangrove species have been select-cut for decades in order to be incinerated and turned into charcoal. The fuel is sold cheaply in Thailand or shipped to Singapore for distribution within Asia. Road and harbor construction are other factors responsible for the loss of mangrove forests in Thailand.

UPPER ANDAMAN COAST

THE ABIDING IMAGE *of Thailand's Andaman Coast is of long sandy beaches backed by swaying palms and a verdant hinterland of rainforest. Centered on Ko Phuket, the upper half of this coast has many attractions. This region suffered the most from the 2004 tsunami, in particular Ranong, the Surin, Similan, and Phi Phi islands, but rebuilding and environmental restoration work has been swift.*

The Andaman Coast around Phuket has long been a magnet for Thais and foreigners. Merchants were drawn by its strategic position on the spice routes between East and West *(see pp336–7)*; prospectors came for the rich tin deposits. This is a lush, fertile region. Much of the interior is cloaked in rainforest, and rubber, coffee, cashew, banana, and durian plantations are common.

The outstanding natural beauty of the Andaman Coast is known the world over. The biggest draw in the region is Phuket, now a resort island, which has superb beaches, excellent diving facilities, and the most developed tourist infrastructure in Southern Thailand. Over the last 20 years, many traditional sea gypsy and Muslim fishing villages on Phuket and around Krabi have been transformed into vacation resorts. Long-tail boats take visitors to sights like the extraordinary limestone stacks of Phangnga Bay. In remote mangrove channels – accessible only by canoe – otters, monkeys, and sea eagles still live undisturbed.

There is outstanding scenery and diving around Ko Phi Phi, though it is now firmly on the tourist trail. Visitors wanting sand and sun without the crowds head for relatively undeveloped islands such as Ko Lanta. Unspoiled beach resorts can be found along the stretch of coast from Ranong to Phuket, and the virgin rainforest of Khao Sok National Park is located inland. West of here, the Ko Surin and Ko Similan archipelagos offer some of the world's best dive sites.

The southwest monsoon, which lasts from about June to October, makes some of the outer islands inaccessible.

A typical beach scene in this part of Thailand: sun, sand, and water sports

◁ Not just a vacation island – the productive rice paddies of Phuket

Exploring the Upper Andaman Coast

THIS PART OF THAILAND'S Andaman Sea coast contains some of the most inviting beach scenery in Southeast Asia. Using the international resort of Phuket as a base, visitors have 12 long sandy beaches on their doorstep and a full range of shopping, dining, entertainment, land and water sport services. The towering limestone stacks of Phangnga Bay can readily be explored in a day. An alternative base is quieter Krabi, which combines fine beaches with spectacular cliff landscapes. The idyllic island scenery of Ko Phi Phi is accessible from Krabi and Phuket. The monsoon forests of the Tenasserim mountain range provide a backdrop to the little frequented beaches of Khao Lak. Avid divers and snorkelers can visit the remote Similan and Surin archipelagos acclaimed for their superlative corals and aquatic life.

Yachting off the coast of the un-spoiled Similan archipelago

```
0 kilometers    25
0 miles    15
```

A deserted beach on Ko Phi Phi – still possible to find despite its ever-increasing popularity

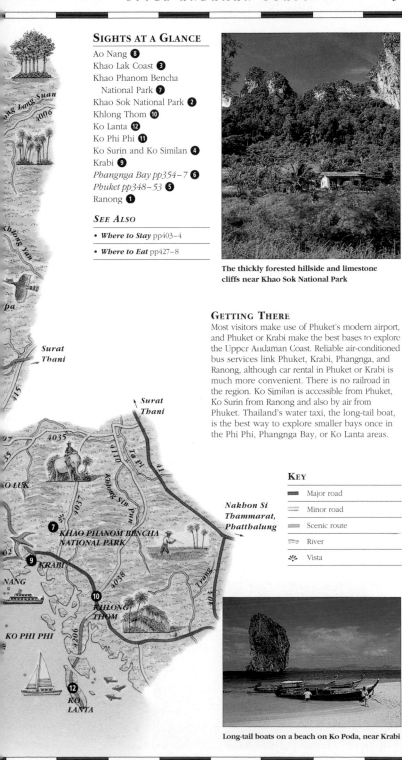

The thickly forested hillside and limestone
cliffs near Khao Sok National Park

GETTING THERE

Most visitors make use of Phuket's modern airport,
and Phuket or Krabi make the best bases to explore
the Upper Andaman Coast. Reliable air-conditioned
bus services link Phuket, Krabi, Phangnga, and
Ranong, although car rental in Phuket or Krabi is
much more convenient. There is no railroad in
the region. Ko Similan is accessible from Phuket,
Ko Surin from Ranong and also by air from
Phuket. Thailand's water taxi, the long-tail boat,
is the best way to explore smaller bays once in
the Phi Phi, Phangnga Bay, or Ko Lanta areas.

KEY

▬▬	Major road
▭▭	Minor road
▬▬	Scenic route
▭▭	River
☆	Vista

Long-tail boats on a beach on Ko Poda, near Krabi

Collecting water from one of Ranong's geothermal springs

Ranong ❶

ระนอง

Ranong province. 🏃 *69,000.* 🚗 ⛴ 🚌 *daily.* ℹ️ *TAT, Surat Thani (0-7728-8818).*

RANONG WAS originally settled in the late 18th century by Hokkien Chinese who were hired to work as laborers in the region's tin mines. The area grew rich, and Ranong is now a major border town. From here Thai nationals may travel to **Victoria Point** in Burma on a half- or full-day boat trip. Referred to as Kaw Thaung by the Burmese, the town is well known for bargain duty-free goods and handicrafts. Officially, foreigners may not go to Victoria Point without a visa, but this is not always enforced.

In Ranong, the natural hot springs are the main attraction. They rise beside the Khlong Hat Sompen River at **Wat Tapotaram**, 1 km (1,100 yds) east of the town center, and

are channeled into three concrete tubs called Mother, Father, and Child. At an average temperature of 65° C (150° F), the water is too hot for bathing. A short walk down the river, the Jansom Thara Spa Resort Hotel has tapped and cooled the water to a more bearable 42° C (110° F). Those not staying at the hotel can take a spa bath for a nominal fee.

Khao Sok National Park ❷

อุทยานแห่งชาติเขาสก

Surat Thani province. Park HQ off Hwy 401, 40 km (25 miles) E of Takua Pa. ℹ️ *TAT, Surat Thani (0-7728-8818) or Forestry Dept (0-2562-0760 or www. dnp.go.th for bungalow bookings).* 🚌 *from Surat Thani or Takua Pa.* 📷

TOGETHER WITH nearby preserves, Khao Sok National Park forms the largest and most dramatic tract of virgin forest in South Thailand. The 738-sq km (285-sq mile) park rises to a height of 960 m (3,150 ft) and includes 100 spectacular islands, formed when the Rachabrapha Dam was built in 1982.

Elephants, tigers, bears, boars, and monkeys live in the park, along with at least 188 species of birds, including hornbills and the argus pheasant. Sightings of the larger mammals are usually at night and animal tracks, are regularly seen along the park's many marked trails.

Sadly, poaching of tigers and elephants persists despite the efforts of national park officers. The area is popular with tourists eager to trek, canoe, watch birds, and spot animals. The park also contains interesting flora, such as the rare giant Rafflesia flower. Many of the hiking trails are suitable for all levels, with more demanding hikes for the experienced. Khao Sok receives the brunt of both summer and winter monsoons, causing a long wet season from May to November. The best time to visit the park is between January and April, when the skies are clear.

Khao Lak Coast ❸

เขาหลัก

Phangnga province. ℹ️ *TAT, Phuket (0-7621-1036).* 🚌 *from Takua Pa or Phuket.*

THE COASTLINE south of Takua Pa consists of long stretches of rocky and sandy beaches. Commercial development along this once quiet coast is on the increase and a variety of accommodation can now be found here. Khao Lak, halfway between Takua Pa and Thai Muang, has a fine beach and is a good base from which to explore the area. The nearby **Khao Lak (Lam Ru) National Park** is famous for its spectacular scenery.

Barking deer at Khao Lak

Steep ridges of monsoon forest extend to the winding coast. Barking deer and small bears are among the wildlife still living in the forest but, sadly, the park is plagued by encroachment and poaching.

Because of its proximity to the Similian Islands (4 hrs by boat) many visitors come here to book their dive trips. Between November and April, Tap Lamu fishing port and Hat Khao Lak operate as ferry points for Ko Similan.

🥾 **Khao Lak (Lam Ru) National Park** Park HQ 25 km (16 miles) S of Takua Pa. ℹ️ *Forestry Dept (0-2562-0760).* 📷

Khao Sok, a wilderness of virgin forest, limestone cliffs, and waterfalls

Similan's boulders, under which are massive underwater grottoes

Ko Surin and Ko Similan ❹

เกาะสุรินทร์และสิมิลัน

Phangnga province. ■ *TAT, Phuket (0-7621-1036) or Forestry Dept (0-2562-0760 inc bungalow bookings for Similan).* **Surin** ⬛ *from Khuraburi Pier, 2 km (1 mile) off Hwy 4.* 🍴 **Similan** ⬛ *from Tap Lamu, off Hwy 4, 39 km (24 miles) S of Takua Pa; or by diving trips from Khao Lak Coast or Ko Phuket.* ☐ *Best time for diving is Dec–early May.* ● *mid-May–mid-Nov.* 🏊

K O SURIN and Ko Similan, 60 km (37 miles) off the west coast and 100 km (62 miles) apart, are the most remote islands in Thailand. Because of the southwesterly monsoon, from May to October they are virtually inaccessible. In season, however, the two archipelagos offer some of the best diving sites in the world and some of the most spectacular wildlife and scenery in Thailand.

The five **Surin** islands are virtually uninhabited, home only to a few sea gypsies and national park officials. There is a park dormitory on Ko Surin Nua, but most people camp on the islands.

The two largest islands, Ko Surin Nua and Ko Surin Tai, are heavily forested with tall hardwood trees. Sea eagles, monitor lizards, and crab-eating macaques are common sights. The surrounding sea offers an outstanding array of soft corals and frequent sightings of

shovel-nose rays, bow-mouthed guitar fish, and whale sharks. However, overfishing has led to the depletion of the marine life of Ko Surin, and many divers maintain that the best sightings of sealife are around the Similans instead.

Of the nine **Similan** islands 4, 7, 8, and 9 were damaged by the 2004 tsunami but are still open to tourists and divers. The name Similan is thought to derive from the Malaysian word *sembilan*, meaning nine, and the islands are numbered Ko 1 through to Ko 9. Ko 4 (Ko Miang) has the park HQ, a restaurant, bungalows, and campsite (with a supply of two-person tents). Also important is Ko 9, where the ranger sub-

station can be found. The interiors of these islands consist of crystal-white sand and lush rainforest, while the headlands are made up of distinctive, giant granite boulders the size of houses. Beneath these rocks are underwater grottoes and swim-through tunnels, which appeal to divers and snorkelers.

The sea bed is decorated with staghorn, star, and branching corals, and a range of fish, including manta rays, and giant sea turtles. Other, more threatening, fish include giant groupers, and poisonous stonefish, and lionfish. Sharks around the islands include black and white tips, leopard sharks, hammerheads, bull sharks, and whale sharks.

Diver exploring the colorful coral around Ko Similan

THE WORLD'S LARGEST FLOWER

Khao Sok is one of the few places in the world where the giant *Rafflesia kerri* grows. This foul-smelling tropical plant has no roots or leaves and is wholly parasitic. For most of the year it lies dormant in the form of microscopic threads inside the roots of a host tree. Once a year, however, a small flower breaks the surface of the host's bark. Over a period of months the bud swells to the size of a watermelon

and eventually opens to become the world's largest flower, with a diameter up to 80 cm (31 inches). The flower's fetid smell attracts insects that assist in the pollination process. After a few days the orange-red flower shrivels to a vile, unsightly, putrescent mass. Occasionally a Rafflesia in flower may be found at the end of a marked path at Khao Sok.

Rafflesia flower in full bloom, Khao Sok National Park

Phuket ❺

ภูเก็ต

PHUKET IS THAILAND'S largest island and one of the most popular vacation destinations in Southeast Asia, attracting up to one million visitors each year. At 48 km (30 miles) long and covering 543 sq km (210 sq miles), it is a province in itself – and the wealthiest in the country. Originally this prosperity was based on tin production, but tourism is now the major earner. The northern tip of the island is separated from the mainland by only a narrow channel of sea, over which runs the 700-m (765-yd) long Sarasin Bridge.

Patong beach on Phuket

Game fishing
Tuna, barracuda, and other fish are hunted from boats.

Half-Buried Buddha
Wat Phra Tong is built around an unusual, gold-leafed Buddha image, half buried in the ground. Legend says that whoever tries to remove it will die.

★ West Coast Beaches
The clearest waters, best sand, and most luxurious hotels are on the west coast. Patong is the most densely developed resort; Karon and Kata are quieter.

KEY

🏖	Beach
🏄	Water sports
ℹ	Tourist information
🛕	*Wat*
✈	Airport
🚌	Bus station
⛴	Ferry service
▬	Main road
▭	Minor road
☀	Vista

STAR SIGHTS

★ **West Coast Beaches**

★ **Thai Village**

★ **Marine Research Center**

Sarasin Bridge •

Hat Sai Kaeo •

Hat Mai Khao •

Hat Nai Yang •

Hat Nai Thon •

Wat Phra To

Thalang

Ao Bang
Tao

Hat Pansea •

Hat Surin •

Hat Kamala

Phuket
FantaSea •

Kathu
waterfall •

Hat Patong •

• Hat Karon Noi

Wat Chalong

Hat Karon •

Hat Kata Yai •

Hat Kata Noi •

Hat Nai Harn •

Hat
Rav

Cape Promthep   Ko Bon

Cape Promthep is the southernmost point on Ko Phuket. The views from this rugged headland are some of the most stunning on the island, particularly at sunset.

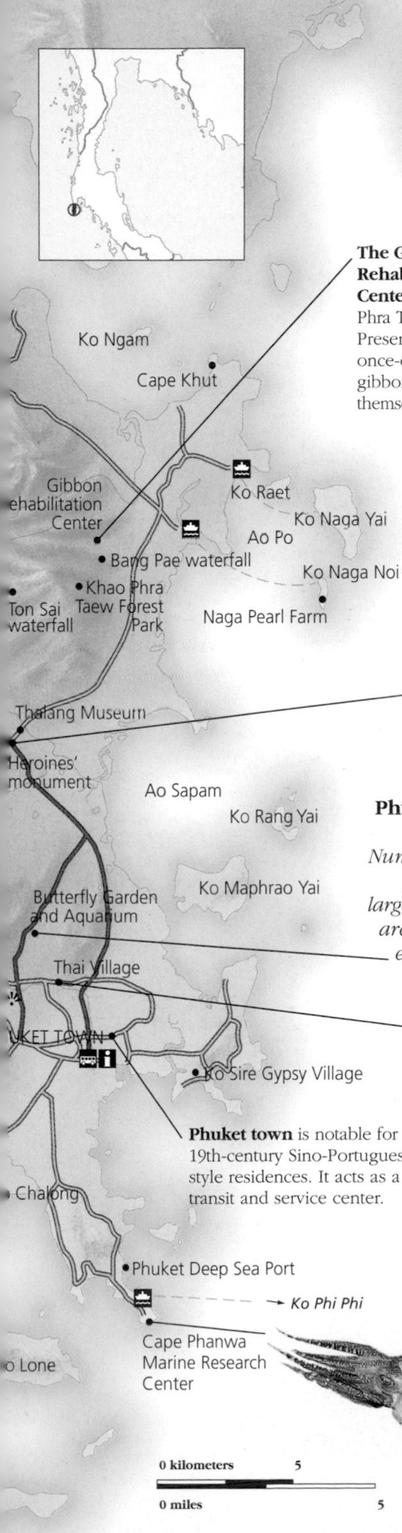

VISITORS' CHECKLIST

Phuket province. 🏘 102,000.
✈ 29 km (18 miles) N of Phuket
town. 🚌 Phangnga Rd, Phuket
town. ⛴ from Ko Phi Phi to
Phuket Deep Sea Port. 🛈 TAT,
73–75 Phuket Rd (0-7621-1036).
@ tatphuket@tat.or.th
📠 Phuket Rd (0-7621-2046).
🎪 Vegetarian Festival (late Sep/
early Oct, for nine days),
King's Cup Regatta (Dec).
🌐 www.phuket.com

The Gibbon Rehabilitation Center in the Khao Phra Taew Forest Preserve encourages once-domesticated gibbons to fend for themselves in the wild.

Ko Ngam

Cape Khut

Gibbon
Rehabilitation
Center

Ko Raet

Ao Po

Ko Naga Yai

Bang Pae waterfall

Ko Naga Noi

Khao Phra
Taew Forest
Park

Ton Sai
waterfall

Naga Pearl Farm

Heroines' Monument
Two brave sisters rallied the women of Phuket to success- fully defend the island against Burmese invaders during the Battle of Thalang in 1785.

Thalang Museum

Heroines'
monument

Ao Sapam

Ko Rang Yai

Ko Maphrao Yai

Butterfly Garden
and Aquarium

Thai Village

Phuket Butterfly Garden and Aquarium
Numerous species of butter- flies are cultivated in a large, covered garden. There are also 50 fish tanks with examples of local sealife.

UKET TOWN

Ko Sire Gypsy Village

Phuket town is notable for its 19th-century Sino-Portuguese- style residences. It acts as a transit and service center.

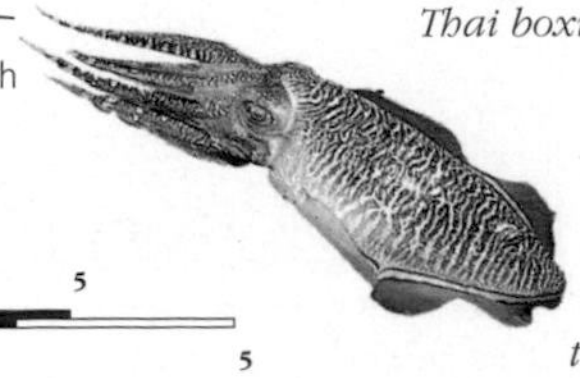

Chalong

Phuket Deep Sea Port

Ko Phi Phi

Cape Phanwa
Marine Research
Center

o Lone

0 kilometers   5

0 miles   5

★ Thai Village
Orchids are sold at this village, and there is a show on Thai culture with elephants, Thai boxing, and classical dancing.

★ Marine Research Center
A well-designed aquarium at the center includes salt- and freshwater fish, lobsters, turtles, and mollusks.

Phuket Town

PHUKET TOWN grew to prominence around the beginning of the 19th century, when the island's tin resources attracted thousands of Chinese migrants. Many merchants made fortunes from tin, built splendid residences, and sent their children to British Penang to be educated. Hokkien-speaking tin-mining families soon intermarried with the indigenous Thai population. Today, the bustling downtown area retains some of its earlier charm, though, unlike most of the island, it is geared toward residents rather than tourists. The Chinese heritage is preserved in the Sino-Portuguese shop-houses, temples, the local cuisine, and the Vegetarian Festival.

Dragon detail at a temple

One of the grand old Sino-Portuguese mansions in Phuket town

🏠 Chinese Mansions
Thalang, Yaowarat, Dibuk, Krabi, and Phangnga roads.
The heart of Phuket town is the old Sino-Portuguese quarter with its spacious, if now rather run-down, colonial-style residences set in large grounds. Most date from the reigns of Rama IV and Rama V (1851–1910). Among the best examples are those used today as offices by the Standard Chartered Bank and Thai Airways on Ranong Road. Unfortunately, no one has yet seen fit to convert any of the old mansions into a museum, and none can be visited. Many of the commercial Chinese shop-houses are also dilapidated.

🏠 Thavorn Hotel Lobby Exhibition
ห้องแสดงของเก่าโรงแรมถาวร
74 Rasada Rd. ☎ 0-7621-1334.
🕐 daily.
The owner of this hotel in the center of town has assembled a collection of Phuket artifacts

and pictures that he now displays in the lobby and adjacent function rooms. Among the exhibits are models of tin mines, pictures of the town

center in the 19th century, Chinese treasure chests, and weavers' tables, all of which are imaginatively displayed.

🍜 Fresh Produce Market
ตลาดสด
Ranong Rd. 🕐 daily.
The 24-hour wet market is a treat that assaults the senses. The market and adjacent lanes are full of colorful characters hawking condiments, dried herbs and spices, pungent pickled *kapi* fish, squirming eels, and succulent durians.

🍂 Rang Hill
เขารัง
On the top of this hill overlooking the town stands a statue of Khaw Sim Bee Na-Ranong (1857–1913), governor of Phuket for 12 years from 1901. He enjoyed considerable autonomy from Bangkok but is credited with bringing the island firmly under central rule, and also with importing the first rubber tree into Thailand.

🏛 Bang Niew Temple
ศาลเจ้าบางเหนียว
Phuket Rd. 🕐 daily.
This temple is where *naga* devotees climb knife ladders during the Vegetarian Festival. The inner compound is devoted to a number of Chinese mythological gods, the most prominent being Siew, Hok, and Lok, who represent longevity, power, and happiness.

PHUKET TOWN'S VEGETARIAN FESTIVAL

At the start of the ninth Chinese lunar month, Phuket town hosts a nine-day Vegetarian Festival accompanied by gruesome rites. The tradition began over 150 years ago when a troupe of Chinese entertainers in Phuket recovered from the plague by adhering to austere rituals practised in China. Today, believers use the festival to purge the body and soul of impure thoughts and deeds. Devotees dress in white, follow a vegetarian diet, and refrain from alcohol and sex. The high-

Nagas **parading through the town**

light is the parade of *nagas* (spirit mediums) with their flesh pierced by metal rods. Other *nagas* climb ladders of knives, plunge their hands into hot oil, or walk on burning coals. The worse the suffering, the greater reward for the *naga* and his temple.

Wat Mongkol Nimit, a typical example of Rattanakosin architecture

🏯 Wat Mongkol Nimit
วัดมงคลนิมิต
Yaowarat Rd. ⭕ *daily.*
This large, Rattanakosin-style
temple has finely carved doors.
Its compound acts as a community center where monks
play *takraw* with the laity.

🏯 Chui Tui Temple
ศาลเจ้าจุ้ยตุ่ย
Ranong Rd. ⭕ *daily.*
A steady flow of people visit
this Chinese temple to shake
numbered sticks from a canis-
ter dedicated to vegetarian god
Kiu Wong In. Each number
corresponds to a preprinted
fate that, according to belief,
the person will inherit.

ENVIRONS: Three km (2 miles)
to the north of Phuket town is
the **Phuket Butterfly
Garden and Aquarium**. The
garden's warm and humid
atmosphere provides ideal
conditions for hundreds of
tropical butterflies as well as
scorpions, stag beetles, other
assorted insects, and a playful
otter. Among the highlights of
the aquarium are the strange
dog-face pufferfish and the
black-tip sharks.

The **Thai Village**, located
4 km (2.5 miles) north of
Phuket town, puts on cultural
performances and animal
shows from the different
regions of Thailand.

There are demonstrations of
muay thai boxing *(see pp40–
41)*, traditional dancing, cock
fighting, sword fighting, and a
reenactment of a Thai wedding. The fisherman's, tin
miner's, and rubber-tapping
dances were invented here.
There is also an elephant
show. The village is a good
place to buy *yan lipao (see
p101)* reed grass bags and
ornaments, made by a
weaving method unique to
Southern Thailand. You can
watch the artisans at work.
There is also an **Orchid
Garden**, with orchids for
sale – 40,000 are grown
here each year.

🌺 **Phuket Butterfly
Garden and Aquarium**
Yaowarat Rd. 📞 *0-7621-5616.*
⭕ *9am–5pm daily.* 🎫
🌺 **Thai Village and
Orchid Garden**
Thepkasattri Rd. 📞 *0-7621-4860.*
⭕ *daily.* 🎫

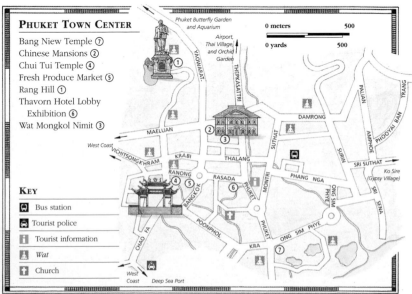

PHUKET TOWN CENTER

Bang New Temple ⑦
Chinese Mansions ②
Chui Tui Temple ④
Fresh Produce Market ⑤
Rang Hill ①
Thavorn Hotel Lobby
  Exhibition ⑥
Wat Mongkol Nimit ③

KEY

🚌	Bus station
🚓	Tourist police
ℹ️	Tourist information
🏯	*Wat*
✝️	Church

Exploring Phuket

PHUKET WAS CALLED Junkceylon by early European traders, but its modern name may derive from the Malay word *bukit*, meaning hill. On arrival, many visitors head straight for a beach resort and do not leave it for the duration of their vacation – the best of the island's beaches are strung out along the west coast. However, there are several historical and cultural sights to complement the beachside attractions, and the lush, hilly interior is also worth exploring.

Hibiscus flower, typical of Phuket

High-rise hotel overlooking the popular, tree-lined beach at Patong

Hat Patong

Phuket's most developed beach is the 3-km (2-mile) long Hat Patong. Once a quiet banana plantation, it is now almost a city by the sea. The area has a lively nightlife, with a vibrant mix of hotels, restaurants, discos, and bars. During the day there are many water activities, such as parasailing, waterskiing, diving, and deep-sea fishing.

Although Patong continues to expand, the beaches along the southern headland of Patong bay are far quieter. It is possible to ride to the cape on elephant back.

Hat Karon and Hat Kata

South of Patong, and almost as popular, are the beaches of Karon and Kata. Karon has one long stretch of sand lined with accommodations, and a second beach at tiny Karon Noi. Kata's beaches, along the bays of Kata Yai and Kata Noi, are smaller and prettier, sheltered by rocky promontories. There are a number of good restaurants on the headland between Karon and Kata.

Other Western Beaches

North of Patong, fringed by palm-covered headlands, lie the smaller beaches of Kamala, Surin, and Pansea. Hat Kamala is relatively undeveloped, with some Muslim fishermen's houses and a few restaurants. Just to the south, however, is **Phuket FantaSea**, a huge Las Vegas-style cultural theme complex that hosts a spectacular live night-time stage show with music, dance, special effects and elephants.

Farther north from Hat Kamala, Hat Bang Tao offers a quiet, enchanting retreat, popular with families. Fronted by a few exclusive hotels, the beach is good for water sports.

Round the next few headlands are three beaches: Hat Nai Thon, a gorgeous, undeveloped stretch; Hat Nai Yang, which is visited by Thais on weekends; and Hat Mai Khao, a deserted 12-km (7.5-mile) stretch of sand.

🏠 Phuket FantaSea
99 Kamala Beach. **[** 0-7627-1222.
🕐 5:30–11:30pm Wed–Mon. 🈂️ 🍴

Cape Promthep, one of the best vistas on Phuket – a good place for spectacular sunsets

SEA GYPSIES OF THE ANDAMAN SEA

Sea gypsies, known as *chao ley* in Thai, may originate from the Andaman or Nicobar islands, across the Andaman Sea from Thailand. Phuket's sea gypsy population settled the area around 200 years ago, following routes from the Mergui archipelago, west of the Burmese mainland. Today, they can be found in Phuket at Rawai, Ko Sire, near Sapam village, and in northern Phuket's villages of Laem La and Nua. Ethnically, they comprise three groups: Moklen, Moken, and Urak Lawoi. Sea gypsies live throughout the Andaman Sea at Ko Surin, Ko Phra Tong in Phangnga, and farther south at the islands of Phi Phi, Lanta, Talibong, Tarutao, and Langkawi. They speak their own language and have animistic beliefs. Once a year they hold a spiritual cleansing ceremony, placing human mementoes on a small boat before pushing it out to sea to get rid of bad spirits.

Cleaning fish, an everyday part of life for Andaman sea gypsies

Southeastern Capes and Bays

Ao Nai Harn, a bay near the southern tip of Phuket, is the home of the exclusive Phuket Yacht Club. The beach (open to all) is one of the most beautiful on the island. Cape Promthep, 2 km (1 mile) away on the southern tip of Phuket, offers wonderful views, especially at sunset.

Ghost crab at Marine Center

North of Promthep, on the east side of the island, are Hat Rawai, and farther along, Ao Chalong. The sands around this bay are not as white as those on the west coast, but there are many excellent seafood shacks here. Ao Chalong acts as an anchorage for international yachts exploiting its sheltered location, and is also a departure point for boat excursions to the charming islands of Lone, Hai, and Bon, where there is good snorkeling.

Farther up the coast at Cape Phanwa is the interesting and much-visited Phuket Aquarium, which forms part of the **Marine Research Center**.

Marine Research Center
Tip of Cape Phanwa. 0-7639-1126. 8:30am–4pm daily.

Northeast Coast

Ko Naga Noi, an island off Phuket's northeast coast, has a tranquil, sandy beach that makes a fine halt for swimming and relaxing. The island is home to the **Naga Pearl Farm**, whose owners give demonstrations of the process of culturing South Sea pearls.

At Phuket's northeasternmost point, on the Cape Khut headland, there are sweeping views of the monoliths of Phangnga Bay *(see pp354–7)*. The placid waters of the narrow channel between Phuket and Phangnga province are exploited by Muslim fishermen who farm sea bass here.

Naga Pearl Farm
Ko Naga Noi. 0-7626-0216. daily.

Thalang

This town in central Phuket was the site of a famous battle in 1785 against the Burmese, which is commemorated by the Heroines' Monument 8 km (5 miles) to the south. A short walk east of the monument is the Thalang Museum, which outlines the rich heritage of Phuket. Among the exhibits are

5th-century religious icons, Chinese porcelain, life-size figures recreated from the Burmese battle, and information on the sea gypsies.

In Thalang itself there is a good market and, nearby, Wat Phra Tong. In the center of the *wat* lies a gold-covered Buddha image, half buried in the ground. Legend has it that disaster will come to anyone who tries to move the image.

Thalang National Museum
Off Hwy 402, opposite Heroines' Monument. 0-7631-1025, 0-7631-1426. daily. public hols.

Khao Phra Taew Forest Park

Four km (2.5 miles) east of Thalang is the spectacular Khao Phra Taew Forest Park. The preserve is important as it preserves the last of Phuket's primary rainforest.

Within the park are two fine waterfalls. Ton Sai waterfall is the prettiest and is at its best from June to December. On the eastern fringe of the preserve is the Bang Pae waterfall.

Near the latter is the **Gibbon Rehabilitation Center**. This volunteer-run program aims to reintroduce domesticated gibbons into the forest by encouraging them to fend for themselves. Visitors' donations buy food for the gibbons.

Khao Phra Taew Forest Park
Thalang district. daily.
Gibbon Rehabilitation Center
Near Bang Pae Falls. daily.

A barrel of limes for sale at Thalang market in central Phuket

Phangnga Bay ❻
อ่าวพังงา

NO ONE AREA EPITOMIZES the splendor of the South's landscape as succinctly as 400-sq km (155-sq mile) Phangnga Bay. Its scenic grandeur derives from towering limestone stacks rising sheer from calm, shallow waters up to 350 m (1,150 ft) high. Inside many of the 40-odd stacks are narrow tunnels and sea caves. Inland, too, this coastal area boasts majestic, scrub-clad pinnacles.

Sea eagle, Phangnga Bay

Phangnga is, in fact, the most spectacular remnant of the once mighty Tenasserim Mountains, which still form a spine through Thailand to China.

Protected Mangroves
The heavily silted northern end of Phangnga Bay, where several rivers meet the sea, is Thailand's largest and best preserved area of mangrove (see pp340–41).

Undercut Cliffs
The action of waves erodes the base of the stacks at a rate of about 1 m (3 ft) every 5,000 years.

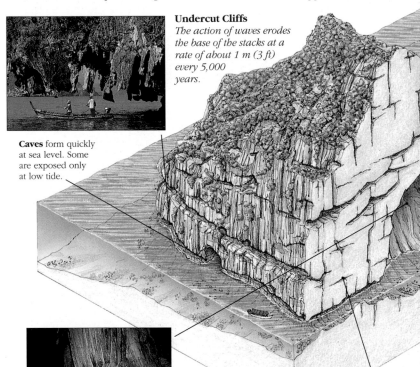

Caves form quickly at sea level. Some are exposed only at low tide.

Fissures allow water to penetrate and erode the limestone.

Calcite Deposits in Caves
Within most caves are stalagmites, stalactites, and other structures formed from dripping calcite.

CROSS SECTION OF TYPICAL STACKS IN PHANGNGA BAY
The limestone landscape at Phangnga Bay is known by geologists as drowned karstland. Karst is characterized by its internal drainage system, whereby water finds its way into the interior of the limestone through fissures, then erodes the rock from within. A riddle of tunnels is typical; chasms and vast sea chambers *(hongs)* are also common at Phangnga.

Aerial view of Stacks in Phangnga Bay
The stacks at Phangnga make striking coastal scenery.

Forest scrub clings to cracks in the limestone.

The weakened roof of the cave will eventually collapse.

Isolated Stacks
There are a number of sheer, thin stacks in the bay. These columns of rock are splinters of limestone that have been heavily eroded by the sea.

HOW PHANGNGA BAY WAS FORMED

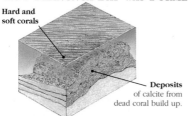

Hard and soft corals

Deposits of calcite from dead coral build up.

130 million years ago *the area was under water and part of a vast coral reef. Calcite deposits from dead coral built up in thick layers.*

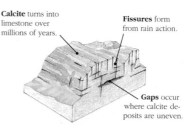

Calcite turns into limestone over millions of years.

Fissures form from rain action.

Gaps occur where calcite deposits are uneven.

75 million years ago *plate movements pushed these deposits, which had turned to limestone, out of the ocean. The rigid rock ruptured.*

Meltwater from ice caps begins to flood Phangnga.

The gap erodes into a cave.

20,000 years ago, *at the end of the last Ice Age, the sea level rose, flooding Phangnga. Wave and tide action accelerated the process of erosion.*

Wave action sculpts the stacks.

The cave is much larger.

8,000 years ago *the sea reached its highest level, about 4 m (13 ft) above its present height, sculpting a shelf, visible on most of the stacks.*

Exploring Phangnga Bay

UNTIL RECENTLY BOAT TOURS of the bay took in the best-known sights, such as the fishing village built over water in the shadow of Ko Panyi, and "James Bond Island," as well as a number of fascinating caves. Some of the eerie caverns contain prehistoric paintings and Buddhist shrines.

Seashell, Phangnga

Due to massive erosion however, tourist boats are currently banned from large areas of Phangnga Bay though viewing is still possible from a distance. The karst scenery continues inland to the east, where cliffs soar above hidden valleys with cascading rivers.

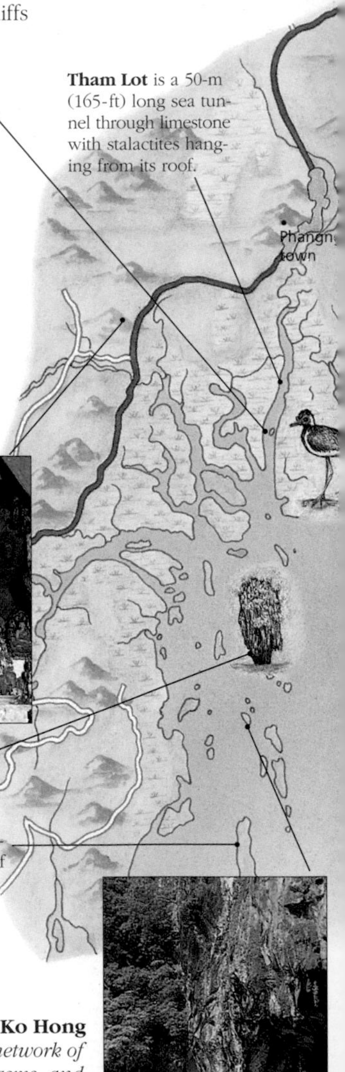

Tham Lot is a 50-m (165-ft) long sea tunnel through limestone with stalactites hanging from its roof.

Phangnga town

★ Panyi Fishing Village
About 120 Muslim families live in this village, which is built on stilts above the water. Islanders sell fish sauce, dried shrimp, and shrimp paste.

Suwan Kuha Cave (Wat Tham)
A reclining Buddha, tiny shrines, and chedis are found among stalactites and stalagmites in this cave temple.

Ko Phanak contains a number of sea *hongs* with vegetation-clad walls and marooned snakes and monkeys.

★ James Bond Island
This island (Ko Khao Phing Kan) and nearby Ko Tapu ("nail island") both appeared memorably in the 1974 James Bond classic, The Man With the Golden Gun.

Ko Hong
A vast network of lagoons, chasms, and tunnels runs underneath this island. As a conservation measure access to the area is forbidden at present.

Areas of Mangrove
It is possible to explore many mangrove channels in a small boat at high tide, though skillful piloting is required.

Rubber Plantations
Rubber is a major industry around Phangnga. Latex, tapped from rubber trees, is left to harden in shallow trays.

Tham Hua Gralok ("skull cave") contains prehistoric paintings, in black and red pigment, of humans and strange animals.

Ao Luk •

Tanboke Koranee National Park
In Ao Luk district, this national park is known for its series of miniature waterfalls amid beautiful limestone scenery.

0 kilometers   10

0 miles   5

JAMES BOND AND THE ISLAND HIDEOUT

In the film *The Man With the Golden Gun* (1974), James Bond (Roger Moore) comes to the Orient in search of the villain Scaramanga (Christopher Lee). Bond is eventually taken to Scaramanga's hideout, an island just off China. In fact, the island seen is Ko Khao Phing Kan in Phangnga Bay; the sheer rock nearby, containing the secret weapon, is Ko Tapu.

Scaramanga and Bond

STAR SIGHTS

★ **Panyi Fishing Village**

★ **James Bond Island**

The extraordinary Ko Tapu ("nail island") in Phangnga Bay ▷

Khao Phanom Bencha National Park ❼

อุทยานแห่งชาติเขาพนมเบญจา

Krabi province. Park HQ off Hwy 4, 20 km (12.5 miles) N of Krabi. 🛈 *TAT, Phuket (0-7621-2213); Forestry Dept (0-2562-0760).* 🚍 *Krabi, then local bus.* 🅿

THIS 500-SQ KM (193-sq mile) national park of mostly tropical monsoon forest is named for the five-shouldered peak of Khao Phanom Bencha, which rises to a height of 1,350 m (4,400 ft).

Despite illegal logging and poaching, the park's rainforest still holds at least 156 species of bird, including the white-crowned hornbill and the striped wren-babbler. Among the 32 mammal species catalogued are the Asiatic black bear, Malaysian sun bear, clouded leopard, wild boar, binturong, and serow.

Clouded leopard in Khao Phanom Bencha

The thundering **Huay To waterfall** and **Huay Sadeh waterfall** are located less than 3 km (2 miles) from the park headquarters. Park attendants can arrange treks to the summit. The climb is difficult but rewarding – from the top there are spectacular views of the surrounding forest.

Ao Nang ❽

อ่าวนาง

18 km (11 miles) W of Krabi town, Krabi province. 🛈 *TAT, Phuket (0-7621-2213).* 🚍 *Krabi, then songthaew.*

FROM NOVEMBER TO APRIL this scenic bay becomes a popular vacation base for tourists who are seeking a less hectic atmosphere than Phuket.

Until the early 1980s, fishing and coconut, and rubber plantations were the mainstay for the Muslim villagers at Ao Nang. Today the 2-km (1-mile) sandy beach sports a growing number of hotels, seafood restaurants, scuba diving outlets, and canoe tour companies. Visitors can rent a sea canoe to paddle in the turquoise waters in the shadow of the 100-m (330-ft) rocky eastern end of the bay. Nearby is uncrowded Pai Plong beach.

In season, Ao Nang is a pleasant base for day trips by longtail boat to the striking **Railae-Phra Nang headland**, located 3 km (2 miles) to the southeast. Its sheer limestone cliffs, pure white sand, and emerald sea attract many visitors.

Hat Phra Nang, west of the Phra Nang headland, is the most attractive beach in the area. Rising above it is a high

Strolling along a beach on Ko Poda, a small island near Ao Nang

limestone cliff into which **Tham Phra Nang Nok** ("outer princess cave") is carved. Inside is a shrine to the lost spirit of a princess, Phra Nang, whose ship allegedly sank near the beach in the 4th century BC. Today, local fishermen place offerings of incense, fruit, and water at the shrine to bring them a plentiful catch. Inside the cliff is **Sa Phra Nang**, a lagoon reached by a steep path.

Flanking Phra Nang are the white sand beaches of East and West Railae, the latter being much finer. There are boats from West Railae and Phra Nang beaches to **Ko Poda**, southwest of Phra Nang, where striped tiger fish can be fed by hand from the shallow shore, and **Ko Hua Khwan**, or Chicken Island, located farther south. Both islands offer excellent diving and snorkeling.

On **Ko Hong**, 25 km (16 miles) northwest of Ao Nang, the prized nests of the edible-nest swiftlet *(see p331)* are collected from the island's intricate network of caves.

The headquarters of the **Phi Phi-Hat Nopparat Thara National Marine Park**, to the west of Ao Nang, overlook stunning beaches. The park covers an area of 390 sq km (150 sq miles), which includes Ko Phi Phi *(see pp362–3)*, Ko Mai Phai, and Ko Yung (also known as Ko Mosquito).

🏊 **Phi Phi-Hat Nopparat Thara National Marine Park**
Park HQ 3 km (2 miles) W of Ao Nang. 🛈 *TAT, Krabi office (0-7561-2740).* 🚍 *Krabi, then songthaew.*

Idyllic bay within the Phi Phi-Hat Nopparat Thara National Marine Park

Krabi ❾
กระบี่

Krabi province. 👥 68,000. 🔲 ⛴
🛬 ℹ️ TAT, Phuket Rd, Phuket
(0-7621-7138). 🛳 daily.
🌐 www.krabi.sawadee.com

THIS SMALL FISHING TOWN, the capital of beautiful Krabi province, has an important role as the ferry embarkation point for islands such as Ko Lanta to the south, Ko Phi Phi to the southwest, and the beaches around Ao Nang to the west. Set on the banks of the Krabi Estuary, the town takes its name from a sword, or *krabi*, allegedly discovered nearby. It is surrounded by towering limestone outcrops, similar to those in Phangnga Bay *(see pp354–7)*, which have become the symbol of Krabi province. Among the most notable are **Kanap Nam twin limestone peaks**, which stand like sentinels at each side of the river. To the east, the town is flanked by mangrove-lined shorelines. These outcrops and mangroves can be toured by renting a long-tail boat from the Chao Fa pier in the center of town.

ENVIRONS: Located 8 km (5 miles) north of town is **Wat Tham Sua** ("tiger cave temple"), named after a rock formation that resembles a tiger paw. It is one of the most renowned forest *wats* in Southern Thailand, with the main hall, where meditation is practiced, built inside a cave.

Swimmers enjoying a hot spring spa in the forest near Khlong Thom

A circular path in the nearby forest hollow offers a pleasant walk among towering, buttressed trees and *kutis*, simple huts inhabited by monks and nuns. A 300-m-high staircase (985-ft) leads to a large Buddha image and Buddha Footprint on top of the cliff. From here there are panoramic views of the province.

Buddha image on the cliff top by Wat Tham Sua, Krabi province

Khlong Thom ❿
คลองท่อม

Krabi province. 👥 60,000. 🔲 ℹ️
TAT, Phuket (0-7621-2213). 🛳 daily.

SOME 40 KM (25 MILES) south of Krabi town, Khlong Thom is known locally for the small museum within **Wat Khlong Thom**. The temple's abbot has assembled an array of archaeological icons and weapons from the area. One of the most interesting exhibits is a collection of distinctive beads called *lukhat*.

A maritime port, Kuan Lukbat, was once located on the site of Khlong Thom. From the 5th century AD onward, the port was used by foreign merchants and emissaries crossing the peninsula to Nakhon Si Thammarat and Surat Thani *(see pp336–7)*. Few traders wanted to sail through the treacherous, pirate-infested Straits of Malacca, so they traveled overland instead.

ENVIRONS: A bumpy 12-km (7.5-mile) ride inland from Khlong Thom leads to a natural hot spring in the forest, which is ideal for swimming.

About 8 km (5 miles) farther on is the rewarding **Tung Tieo forest trail** in Khao No Chuchi lowland forest. The well-marked paths lead through this protected area, skirting emerald pools along the way. The surrounding woodland is the only known area in the world where the colorful ground-dwelling Gurney's pitta survives. Previously, this bird was thought to be extinct.

CLIMBING KRABI'S STACKS

Krabi and Ko Phi Phi are the only places in Thailand where organized rock-climbing takes place. The honeycombed limestone stacks around the Phra Nang headland, near Krabi, and Ko Phi Phi offer challenging climbers from around the world. Only the south of France is said to offer such arduous climbs. They vary in difficulty from an easy "4" according to the French system, to a very difficult "8b." Climbers can cool off with a swim between climbs.

Climber on Thaiwand Wall, Tham Phra Nang near Ao Nang

Ko Phi Phi ⑪

เกาะพีพี

Krabi province. 🏠 *7,700.* 🚢 *from Phuket or Krabi.* ℹ️ *TAT, Phuket (0-7621-2213).* ⓦ *www.phi-phi.com* 🎎 *Chinese New Year (Feb), Songkran (Apr), Loykratong (Nov).*

S PECTACULAR Ko Phi Phi, pronounced "PP," 40 km (25 miles) south of Krabi town, is in fact two separate islands: Phi Phi Don and Phi Phi Ley. Both islands belong to the **Phi Phi-Hat Nopparat Thara National Park**, which also takes in part of the mainland near Ao Nang *(see p360).*

The islands are famed for their spectacular landscapes. Rock climbers are attracted by the breathtaking cliffs *(see p361),* with tall sheer walls of limestone rising to 314 m (1,030 ft) on Phi Phi Don, and 374 m (1,230 ft) on Phi Phi Ley. Nature lovers will find a haven in the islands' coral beds, teeming with sea life.

Phi Phi Don

The two sections of Phi Phi Don, the larger of the two islands, are linked by a 1-km (1,100-yd) isthmus of sand. Here stands the island's original Muslim fishing village, Ban Ton Sai. This area was badly damaged by the 2004 tsunami but extensive reconstruction work is ongoing. Since development began on Phi Phi Don following the arrival of the first visitors in the 1970s, the island has given itself up

KEY

🏖️	Beach
🏄	Water sports
⚓	Ferry service
- - -	Trail
🌟	Vista

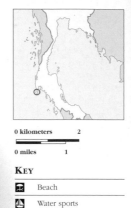

to tourism. However, there is still plenty of natural beauty to enjoy here. A pleasant one-hour coastal walk from Ban Ton Sai leads to Hat Yao ("long beach"), with tantalizing white sands, vibrant offshore marine life, and unhindered views of the soaring flanks of Phi Phi Ley, 4 km (2.5 miles) away.

It is also worth climbing the steep trails on Phi Phi Don's two massifs, which afford wonderful vistas of the island. The eastern route is well marked and the least strenuous.

Superb coral beds at Hin Pae off Hat Yao, and at Ko Phai ("bamboo island"), to the northeast of Phi Phi Don, provide some of the best diving and snorkeling in Thailand.

To the north is Ban Laem Tong. This village's sea gypsy population still survives on fish caught in the isolated coves of nearby Laem Tong.

A typical view of Ko Phi Phi's stunning scenery, now enjoyed by large numbers of vacationers

One of Ko Phi Phi's enticing, dazzling, white-sand beaches

Phi Phi Ley

In contrast to Phi Phi Don, Phi Phi Ley remains uninhabited and unspoiled, though the island was hit by the 2004 tsunami. Boats from Phi Phi Don bring visitors on day trips to see the paintings in Viking Cave. Another feature of the cave are the nests of the edible-nest swiftlet *(see p331)*, which are used in bird's nest soup. Agile collectors climb rickety bamboo scaffolding to reach the nests, which are so valuable that the caves are protected by armed guards and staying overnight on the island is prohibited. There is excellent snorkeling at the coral reefs of Ao Maya.

ENVIRONS: Many of the islands in the area shelter endangered bird species such as the white-bellied sea eagle and the *mukimaki* flycatcher.

Ko Lanta ⑫

เกาะลันตา

Krabi province. 🏠 *26,000.* 🚢 *from Krabi or Bo Muang.* 🛈 *TAT, Phuket (0-7621-2213).*

CLOSE TO THE MAINLAND in the southeast corner of Krabi province, Ko Lanta is a group of 52 islands, 15 of which belong to the Ko Lanta National Marine Park. The park is home to many animals, including lemurs, langurs, civets,

---

CAVE PAINTINGS OF THE ANDAMAN ISLANDS

There are many prehistoric paintings in Phangnga *(see pp354–9)* and Krabi *(see p361)* provinces, especially in caves on the Andaman Islands. Most are stylized red and black outlines depicting human forms, hands, fish, and, in some cases, broken line patterns that are thought to have had symbolic value. Some of the unidentifiable images are of monstrous beings – half-human, half sea-creatures – that still mystify archaeologists. Such paintings may have been drawn as part of magical-religious rituals to bring good fortune for hunting, fishing, food gathering, and tribal battles. Many paintings can be reliably dated to Neolithic times, but the drawings of junklike boats at Phangnga Bay and in the misleadingly named Viking Cave on Phi Phi Ley may be only a few hundred years old.

Paintings of boats in a cave at Phangnga Bay

---

mouse deer, and over 100 types of bird. Most of the wildlife is on the smaller, remoter islands.

The ramshackle wooden port of Ban Sala Dan is the gateway to **Ko Lanta Yai**, a predominantly Muslim fishing island. Some 25 km (15 miles) long, this is the main island in the archipelago. It is covered with undulating forested hills sweeping down to numerous west-facing sandy bays, and, although it cannot match Ko Phi Phi for scenery, it is a good alternative for those seeking solitude.

A rare white-bellied sea eagle

Monkey and lizard footprints are still more common on its beaches than human prints.

The Laem Kaw Kwang headland in the northwest of the island has views across to Ko Phi Phi. At the southern tip, a 3-km (2-mile) coastal trail leads to a solar-powered lighthouse on a steep promontory beside the park headquarters.

Sea gypsies inhabit the nearby village, Ban Sangka-u. They are renowned for their colorful rituals, such as the *loi rua* ceremony. As part of the festivities, a 2-m (6-ft) replica boat is sent out to sea to banish the ill fate built up throughout the past year.

Bungalow accommodations on the unspoiled island of Ko Lanta

DEEP SOUTH

T HE DEEP SOUTH OF THAILAND *has more in common with Malaysia than with the distant Thai heartland to the north. Many visitors come here to experience the region's distinct culture, dialect, and food, and to learn about the local history and religion. The scenery, with spectacular mountains in the interior of the peninsula and unspoiled beaches and islands on the west coast, is equally alluring.*

In many ways Thailand's Deep South doesn't feel like Thailand at all. The influence of Indian, Chinese, and Malaysian culture can be seen in the region's architecture and ethnic makeup. Skin tones are noticeably darker than the rest of the country. The population speaks an unusually intonated dialect of Thai, and Yawi, a language related to Malay and Indonesian. Also, the food is spicier, characterized by often bitter curries laced with turmeric.

South of Songkhla, especially near the coasts, most people are Muslim, and the minarets of mosques replace the gilded peaks of Buddhist temples. Indeed, Pattani, an important Malay kingdom in the 17th century, is still a center of Islamic scholarship. Even so, Wat Phra Mahathat in Nakhon Si Thammarat, the South's cultural capi-

tal, is one of the most revered Buddhist temples in Thailand. Also, numerous Hindu shrines and customs, not least the Hindu-inspired *manohra* dance, are evidence of Nakhon's role as a major religious center on the ocean trade routes between India and China.

Modern Songkhla has become the educational capital of the South. Nearby Hat Yai has grown from an agricultural service and railroad town into an important shopping and entertainment center. However, tourism is still low-key around the west coast's superb beaches and on the stunning islands of the Tarutao National Marine Park. The wild interior is even less developed. A few tigers, elephants, and Negrito tribes still roam the South's forested mountains, which, until the mid-1970s, sheltered bands of Communist guerrillas.

Two Muslim girls – the Islamic religion is strong in the Deep South

◁ **Detail from the staircase to Wat Pha Kho, Sathing Phra**

Exploring the Deep South

THE EASTERN LOWLANDS of the Deep South are among the most fertile in the country. Year-round heat and high humidity are ideal conditions for fast-growing coffee beans, pineapples, cashews, rambutans, and oil and rubber palms. The South's commercial capital, Hat Yai, is in this region, but Nakhon Si Thammarat and Songkhla are the cultural centers. In the west, the Trang coast and Tarutao archipelago both have fine sand beaches, spectacular corals, and few visitors by virtue of undeveloped tourist facilities. The east coast offers fewer natural attractions, but charming towns such as Songkhla are well worth visiting. The three provinces south of Hat Yai – Yala, Pattani, and Narathiwat – are strongly influenced by Muslim Malaysia. The differences in language, cuisine, and religion are obvious even to casual visitors. Densely forested mountains near the Malaysian border shelter tigers, elephants, and other wildlife.

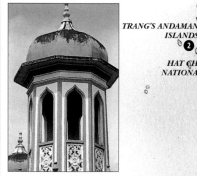

Minaret of Friday Mosque, Nakhon Si Thammarat

SIGHTS AT A GLANCE

Typically deserted beach in the Tarutao archipelago

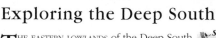

Getting Around

Hat Yai is the main transportation hub of the Deep South. The 930-km (580-mile) trip to Hat Yai from Bangkok takes about 14 hours by bus and 17 by train. Most of the other big towns have bus and rail connections. Highways 4 and 41 are the major north-south roads. Most roads are paved, and local buses run to many sights. There are six small regional airports. Many Singaporeans and Malaysians visit the area on tours; most other visitors are independent travelers. A rental car is the easiest way to get around. The east coast islands can be reached from Pak Meng, Pak Bara, and Kantang.

Fishing village in Narathiwat province

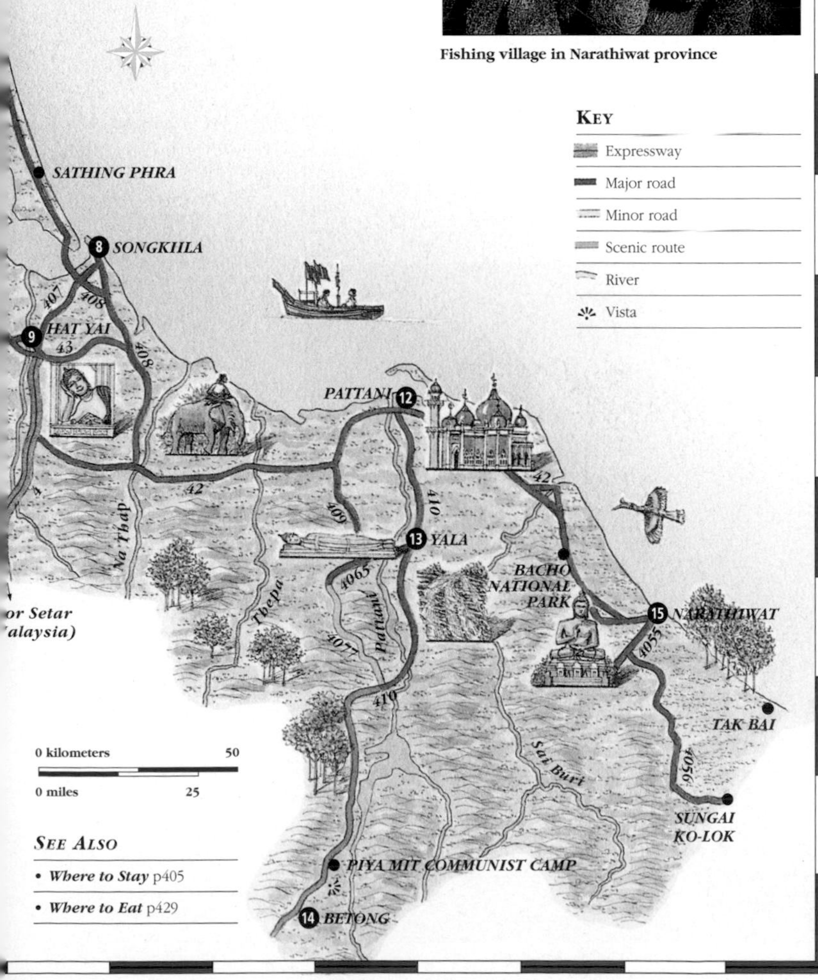
SATHING PHRA
8 SONGKHLA
407
408
9 HAT YAI
43
408
PATTANI 12
42
409
410
42
13 YALA
Na Thap
Thepa
4065
4077
Pattani
BACHO NATIONAL PARK
15 NARATHIWAT
4055
410
TAK BAI
Sai Buri
4056
SUNGAI KO-LOK
PIYA MIT COMMUNIST CAMP
14 BETONG
or Setar
alaysia)
KEY
Expressway
Major road
Minor road
Scenic route
River
Vista
0 kilometers 50
0 miles 25

See Also

- ***Where to Stay*** p405
- ***Where to Eat*** p429

Nakhon Si Thammarat ❶

นครศรีธรรมราช

ALTHOUGH NAKHON SI THAMMARAT is featured on few tourist itineraries, the most historic town in the South is a lively center with several attractions. Under the name of Ligor, it is thought to have been the capital of Tambralinga, a peninsular kingdom prior to the 7th century. From the 7th–13th centuries it was an important city of the Srivijaya Empire *(see pp336–7)*, when it became a religious center with the Sanskrit name Nagara Sri Dhammaraja, meaning "city of the sacred dharma king." Many Indian traders settled in Nakhon – as the town is popularly known – and Hindu shrines are a feature here, together with *nang talung* shadow puppet plays *(see p373)* and intricately etched nielloware *(see p433)*.

Silver figure

The relaxing way to take in Nakhon's sights

🔲 Wat Phra Mahathat

วัดพระมหาธาตุ
Rachadamnoen Rd, 2 km (1 mile) S of train station. ◯ *daily.*

Wat Phra Mahathat is one of Thailand's most sacred temples. Although its age is disputed, the *wat* is thought to be at least 1,500 years old. The present *chedi* dates from the 13th century and was supposedly built to house relics of the Buddha that were brought

here from Sri Lanka. It is 77 m (255 ft) high and topped with gold variously estimated to weigh between 600 and 1,000 kg (1,350 to 2,200 lbs).

The Wihan Luang chapel has an intricately painted 18th-century ceiling, although the Wihan Phra Ma hall is perhaps more impressive. It features an elaborate, emerald-inlay door from the Sukhothai period, carved with the figures of

Phrom and Vishnu. A small museum displays an evocative but unlabeled selection of archaeological finds, jewelry, and religious sculptures including Dvaravati pieces from the 6th to 13th centuries.

🔲 Nakhon Si Thammarat National Museum

พิพิธภัณฑสถานแห่งชาตินครศรีธรรมราช
Rachadamnoen Rd, 2.5 km (1.5 miles) S of train station. 🔲 *0-7534-1075.* ◯ *Wed–Sun.* ⬤ *public hols.* 🔲

The centerpiece of this branch of the National Museum is the 9th-century statue of Vishnu in the Pala style of South India. It was found in the base of a tree in Kapong district near Takua Pha in Phangnga, then a major transit point for Indians colonizing the south.

Two rare bronze drums made by the Dong Son people of northern Vietnam are another highlight. The Thai gallery displays religious art from Dvaravati and Srivijayan periods to the Rattanakosin era. Look out for Buddha images in the distinctive local Sing style, characterized by stumpy features and animated faces.

🔲 Shadow Puppet Theater (Suchart House)

บ้านหนังตะลุงสุชาติ
10/18 Si Thammasok Soi 3. 🔲 *0-7534-6394.* ◯ *daily.*

The *nang talung* workshop of Suchart Subsin keeps alive a uniquely Southeast Asian form of entertainment in danger of dying out. Visitors can watch the puppets being cut from leather and buy the finished product. Sometimes impromptu shows are staged.

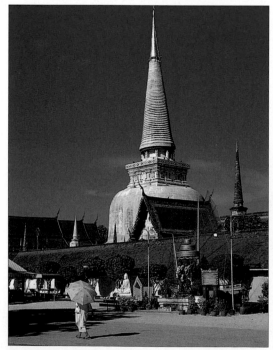

The gold-topped *chedi* of Nakhon's splendid Wat Phra Mahathat

🖼 Ho Phra I-suan (Shiva)
หอพระอิศวร

Rachadamnoen Rd. ⭕ daily.

In the hall of this shrine is a 1-m (3-ft) *shivalinga*, a phallic image of the Hindu god Shiva, that may date back to the 6th century AD. The worship of Shiva was a potent force in the early peninsular city-states of the first millennium AD.

🖼 Ho Phra Buddha Sihing
หอพระพุทธสิหิงค์

Rachadamnoen Rd. ⭕ Wed–Sun.

The Phra Buddha Sing is one of Thailand's most revered images. The replica kept in this shrine is of an original cast in Sri Lanka in AD 157 and brought to Nakhon at the end of the 13th century. Local

Ho Phra Buddha Sing, home of the sacred Phra Buddha Sing image

artisans put their characteristic stamp on the Buddha by giving it a half smile, a rounder face, and a full chest. It is similar to Buddha images in Wat Phra Sing in Chiang Mai.

🖼 Ho Phra Narai
หอพระนารายณ์

Rachadamnoen Rd. ⭕ daily.

Five *lingas* (phallic sculptures) discovered on the site of this shrine may date from before AD 1000. They are now in the Wat Mahathat Museum.

🏠 Tha Chang Road
ถนนท่าช้าง

The tradition of gold and silver shops along this road dates from 1804, when migrants from Saiburi district moved to Nakhon. Only skilled gold- and silversmiths were allowed to settle here, to the west of Sanam Na Muang parade ground.

Typical nielloware pot

🏠 Ancient City Wall & North Gate
กำแพงเมืองเก่า

Just E of Rachadamnoen Rd.

The ancient city wall originally contained an area 400 m by 2,230 m (440 yds by 2,450 yds). The red brick North Gate is a reconstruction of the original.

🖼 Wat Sao Thong Tong
วัดเสาธงทอง

Rachadamnoen Rd ⭕ daily.

Adjoining the compound of Wang Tawan Tok temple, this *wat's* main attraction is the Southern Thai wooden house, started in 1888 and finished in 1901. It is actually three houses joined together and features delicately carved wooden door panels, gables, and window surrounds. The Architects' Association of Thailand gave a conservation award to the building in 1993.

🏠 Bovorn Bazaar
บวรบาซาร์

Rachadamnoen Rd. ⭕ daily.

The city center bazaar is a peaceful courtyard and popular meeting place with cafés, bars, and two good restaurants.

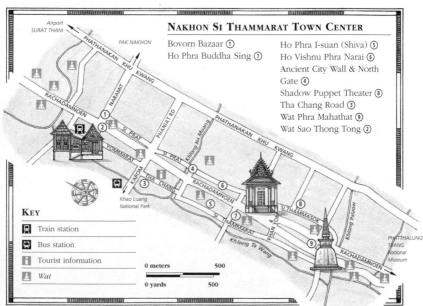

NAKHON SI THAMMARAT TOWN CENTER

Airport
SURAT THANI
PAK NAKHON
PHATHANAKAN KHU KWANG
RACHADAMNOEN
NARAMIT
SI PRAT
YOMMARAT
PHANIAT RD
Khlong Na Muang
SI PRAT
PHATHANAKAN KHU KWANG
KARUM
THA CHANG
Khao Luang National Park
RACHADAMNOEN
SI THAMMARAT
PHAN YORM
SI THAMMASOK
Khlong Palaow
Khlong Ta Wang
RACHADAMNOEN
PHATTHALUNG TRANG National Museum

KEY

🚉	Train station
🚌	Bus station
ℹ	Tourist information
🖼	Wat

0 meters 500
0 yards 500

Lush lowland scenery at Hat Chao Mai National Park

Trang's Andaman Islands ❷
หมู่เกาะอันดามันจังหวัดตรัง

Trang province. 🚤 *long-tail from Kantang to Ko Muk, Ko Kradan and Ko Libong, and from Pak Meng to Ko Hai and Ko Muk.* **ℹ** *TAT, Nakhon Si Thammarat (0-7534-6515); Forestry Dept (0-2562-0760).*

Tourist development has barely touched the 50 or so small islands off the coast of Trang province. Their stunning sands, pristine corals, and rich bird and marine life remain the preserve of a handful of solitude seekers.

Forested **Ko Hai**, or **Ko Ngai**, is the island most easily reached from Pak Meng on the mainland and offers the widest choice of accommodation. There are wonderful beaches, particularly on the east coast, and magnificent coral offshore.

Ko Muk, 8 km (5 miles) southeast of Ko Hai, is best known for Tham Morakhot ("emerald cave") on its west coast. A long limestone tunnel leads from the sea to an inland beach surrounded by vegetation-clad cliffs. It can be entered only by boat at low tide.

Arguably the most beautiful and remotest of Trang's Andaman islands, **Ko Kradan** offers white sand beaches and good snorkeling.

Farther south and close to the mainland, **Ko Libong** is the largest of the islands. It is famed for its spectacular birdlife, which is at its best during March and April.

Hat Chao Mai National Park ❸
อุทยานแห่งชาติหาดเจ้าไหม

Trang province. **ℹ** *TAT, Nakhon Si Thammarat (0-7534-6515); Forestry Dept (0-2562-0760 inc bungalow bookings).* 🚌 *from Trang to Kantang, then songthaew.*

Around 50 km (31 miles) west of Trang town, the varied coastal landscape of Hat Chao Mai National Park includes mangrove creeks, coastal karsts, and hidden beaches, accessed through caves around Yao and Yongling beaches. The casuarina trees lining Pak Meng beach in the north of the park is popular. This is also the main departure point for boat tours around Trang's islands, nine of which are also under park control. Dugongs can sometimes be spotted between the mainland and the islands.

Tuk-tuk **in Trang town**

Trang ❹
ตรัง

Trang province. 👥 *83,000.* ✈ 🚉 🚌 **ℹ** *TAT, Nakhon Si Thammarat (0-7534-6515).* ⛴ *daily.* 🎋 *Vegetarian Festival (Oct).*

Trang has been a trading center since at least the 1st century AD. It grew to prosperity between the 7th and 13th centuries during the Srivijaya period and remains an important commercial town today. Rubber, palm oil, and fishing are the mainstays of its economy. Tourism has not yet made much impact, although this may change if Trang's Andaman islands start to be more intensively developed.

The town has a strong Chinese character (and good Chinese restaurants) as a result of an influx of immigrant labor in the latter half of the 19th century. Trang's Vegetarian Festival, mirroring its better-known counterpart on Phuket *(see p350)*, is renowned for the intensity of its ascetic rites, which include body piercing.

The **Rubber Museum** displays tools used in making the pressed rubber sheets that can be seen hanging to dry outside plantation houses all over Southern Thailand. It also explains the right and wrong ways to tap rubber.

A monument to Khaw Sim Bee Na-Ranong, the first governor of Trang from 1890 to 1901, stands in the Fitness Park at the eastern end of Phatthalung Road. The statue

Tranquil landing pier on the estuary of the Trang River

attracts many merit-makers, especially on April 10, the day dedicated to the former governor. The Clarion MP Hotel is notable for being partially built in the shape of an ocean liner.

🏛 Rubber Museum

Trang Non-Formal Education Center, Phatthalung Rd. 📞 0-7521-8440. 🕐 Mon–Fri.

ENVIRONS: Trang province was dependent on tin mining until the first rubber tree seedlings were brought into Thailand around 1901. The first rubber tree can still be seen in Kantang, 22 km (14 miles) southwest of Trang, near a small museum dedicated to Khaw Sim Bee Na-Ranong. Boats run from Kantang to many of the nearby islands.

Dense rainforest on the steep slopes of the Banthat Mountains

Slender rubber trees in one of Trang province's many plantations

the Sakai tribe still maintain their hunter-gatherer existence. These ethnically unique Negrito people speak a language related to Mon-Khmer. Traditionally they live in groups of 10 to 30 in simple lean-to leaf and grass shelters near running water, and hunt with poison blow darts. Forest clearance and exposure to lowland culture has led to some Sakai becoming agricultural laborers.

The mountains are also home to many amphibian and reptile species, including dwarf geckos and wrinkled frogs. Rare birds include hornbills, spiderhunters, hawk cuckoos, and the narcissus flycatcher. A worthwhile excursion is to the **Khao Chong Nature and Wildlife Study Center**, 20 km (12 miles) east of Trang off

Highway 4. It contains an impressive open zoo and two waterfalls. Just to the south, a bird sanctuary at **Khlong Lamchan** has a reservoir that attracts many species of duck.

The minor road heading south along the western flanks of the Banthat Mountains gives access to a series of spectacular waterfalls, caves, and shady picnic places. Highlights include the huge **Ton Tay falls**, the spray rainbow that often forms by mid-afternoon over the **Sairung falls**, and the stalactites and stalagmites of **Tham Chang Hai** ("lost elephant cave") near Muansari village in Nayong district.

Much farther south, and easily accessible from Satun, is the spectacular Thale Ban National Park (see p376).

Banthat Mountains ❺

เขาบรรทัด

Trang province. 🏛 TAT, Nakhon Si Thammarat (0-7534-6515); Forestry Dept (0-2562-0760).

THE VERDANT Banthat Mountains, which run down the peninsula as far as the Malaysian border, mark the eastern boundary of Trang province.

The forested higher elevations of the mountains, which rise to 1,350 m (4,430 ft) at Khao Ron, are one of the few places in South Thailand where

DUGONGS

The once common dugong, or sea cow, was brought to the brink of extinction in Thai waters by hunting and by accidental drowning in commercial fishing nets. Today numbers are slowly increasing. The area around the Trang islands of the Andaman Sea is one of the few places they can be spotted. These herbivores feed on the seagrass beds around Ko Libong and the Trang Estuary. They grow up to 3 m (10 ft) long and can weigh 400 kg (880 lbs). In local folklore, the tears of a dugong act as a love potion.

The dugong – a rare, gentle giant now protected by law

Phatthalung ⑥
พัทลุง

Phatthalung province. 🏯 *81,000.*
🚌 🚕 🚤 🛈 *TAT, Nakhon Si
Thammarat (0-7534-6515).* 🏪 *daily.*
🎏 *Phon Lak Phra Competition
(3 days in Oct or Nov).*

ONE OF THE FEW rice-grow-
ing areas in Southern
Thailand, Phatthalung province has earned a steady income from the crop throughout its history. It is better
known, though, as the place
where *nang talung* (shadow
puppetry) was first performed
in Thailand – the name *nang
talung* may even derive from
Phatthalung. This theater, related to Indonesian shadow
puppetry, is performed mainly in Phatthalung and Nakhon
Si Thammarat provinces.

Phatthalung town was established in the 19th century
during the reign of Rama III
(see pp60–1). Today's modern
town is set out in a grid and is
surrounded by limestone hills
to the north and the fertile
Thale Luang lake to the east.

Phatthalung lies between
two attractive peaks: **Khao
Ok Talu** ("punctured chest
mountain"), to the northeast,
and **Khao Hua Taek** ("broken
head mountain") to the northwest. According to local
legend, these two mountains,
"the mistress" and "the wife,"
fought over Khao Muang (the
male mountain), located to
the north. It is said that they
still nurse their battle scars
from this confrontation. In
fact, Khao Ok Talu has a
naturally occurring tunnel in
its peak (the punctured chest),

Khao Ok Talu ("punctured chest mountain") overlooking Phatthalung

while Khao Hua Taek has a
dent in its peak (the broken
head). In the latter are the
Buddhist grottoes of **Wat
Tham Kuha Sawan**. Inside
the lower cave are statues of
monks and the Buddha, while
the upper cave has views of
Khao Ok Talu and most of
Phatthalung and the
surrounding area.

ENVIRONS: Lush rice fields surround Phatthalung. At **Lam
Pam**, a small fishing village

6 km (4 miles) east of Phatthalung, slow-flowing canals
empty into the large Thale
Luang inland sea. The breezy
but peaceful area at Sansuk
beach has a few restaurants
serving good seafood. Boats
can be hired to the nearby
islands, Ko Si and Ko Ha.

Two km (1 mile) before
Lam Pam is **Wat Wang**, Phatthalung's oldest temple,
thought to have been founded
at the same time as the town.
Next to the *chedi* is a *bot*
with faded murals depicting
Buddhist and Ramakien *(see
pp36–7)* themes.

The restored **Governor's
Palace** occupies a peaceful
site nearby. Built in 1889, the
palace comprises two individual buildings. The outer teak
structure, nearer the road,
functioned as living quarters
for the governor's family. The
main building, beside the river,
is built around a courtyard
with a large tree.

🏯 **Governor's Palace**
Hwy 4047, 4 km (2 miles) E of
Phatthalung. 🕐 *8:30–4pm daily.*

The elevated structures of the Governor's Palace in Lam Pam

Thale Noi Waterfowl Park ❼
ทะเลน้อย

32 km (20 miles) NE of Phatthalung, Phatthalung province. ℹ️ *TAT, Nakhon Si Thammarat (0-7534-6515); Forestry Dept, Bangkok (0-2562-0760 or www.dnp.go.th 🖱️ from Phatthalung, then hire a long-tail.* 🕗 *8:30–4pm daily.* 📷

Long-tail boat at Thale Noi Waterfowl Park

THE LARGEST wetland bird sanctuary in Thailand, this park serves as a resting and feeding ground for thousands of exotic migratory birds flying to Sumatra and Australia to escape winter in Siberia and China. The best way to explore the watery preserve, covering 30 sq km (12 sq miles), is by long-tail boat, which can be hired from Phatthalung for a two-hour round trip.

Thale Noi has the appearance of a swamp, but it is predominantly a freshwater lake, with a depth of up to 1.5 m (5 ft). Only in periods of high southerly winds does the lake become brackish, when saltier water

White-throated kingfisher

from Thale Luang and Songkhla Lake to the south is pushed northward.

Dawn is the best time for bird-watching, especially between the months of January and April. Many of the 150 or so species of birds who visit the park arrive during this time, swelling its population to as much as 100,000. In May the population begins to shrink, and from October to December there are only small numbers of native species left. A view-

ing platform in the lake is the ideal place for bird-watching. Among the birds here are the purple swamp hen, bronze-winged jaçana, whistling teal, white-throated kingfisher, the long-legged *nok i-kong*, and the white ibis and gray heron.

One of the major forms of vegetation in the park is *don kok*, a reed which the *nok i-kong* use to build "platforms".

Around 100 families live along the shores of Thale Noi, mostly in raised wooden houses. They make a living from fishing and by weaving bulrush reeds into mats.

SHADOW PUPPETS – NANG TALUNG

Nang talung is the popular Thai version of shadow puppetry, an art form that originated as early as 400 BC in Asia. *Nang talung* performances, which begin late at night and last several hours, are still an essential part of village life in the Deep South. It is the task of a single person, the *nai nag* (puppet master), to create the whole show. Sitting behind an illuminated screen, he maneuvers up to six puppets per scene. The puppets, about 50 cm (20 in) high, are made from leather, or *nang*, which is carved, colored, and rendered movable by joints. The changing tone of the puppeteer's voice differentiates between the charac-

Shadow puppet of a Ramakien character

A puppeteer, sitting behind a screen, using his skills to perform *nang talung*

ters, while a band of musicians adds tension to the plot. While the more formal *nang yai* is based on the Ramakien *(see pp36–7)*, *nang talung* takes its inspiration from everyday life, with themes such as family problems. Each story is created by the *nai nag* and includes easily recognizable characters, such as comic figures with exaggerated features. Once a year the apprentices commemorate the puppet master in a *wai kru* ("paying respect to the teacher") ceremony.

The audience's view of *nang talung*

Songkhla **8**

สงขลา

Songkhla province. 🏠 *86,000.*
✈ 🚌 *at Hat Yai, 36 km (22 miles)*
SW of Songkhla. 🚌 🚤 🚆 🏢 *TAT,*
Hat Yai (0-7424-3747). @ *tatsgkhl*
@tat.or.th 🚌 *daily.*
🎎 *Chinese Lunar Festival (Sep/Oct).*

ONCE KNOWN as Singora
("lion city"),
Songkhla grew to
prominence during
the Srivijaya period
(see pp336–7). It
once had a reputa-
tion as a pirate base
but gradually at-
tracted Arab, Indian,
Khmer, and Chinese
traders. The cuisine
and language of
Songkhla reflect its
multicultural heritage, and a
subtle Portuguese influence is
evident in the architecture of
the houses along Nakhon
Nok and Nakhon Nai roads.

Today the city, built on the
headland between the Gulf of
Thailand and Thale Sap – the
country's largest lake – is a
fishing port and an administrative and educational center.
Songkhla's main beach, **Hat
Samila**, which is presided over
by a bronze **mermaid statue,**
has several good seafood restaurants. Farther south, at

Wat Chai Mongkhon,
Songkhla

Khao Seng, is a Muslim fishing village where colorful
korlae fishing boats *(see p378)*
can be seen. A local myth
says that if you can move the
Nai Bang's Head boulder on
the headland beside the
village, you will inherit the
gold buried underneath.

The beautiful, evocative
building housing the **Songkhla
National Museum** is
an attraction in itself.
It was built in 1878
in the Southern Thai-
Chinese style as the
residence of deputy
Songkhla governor
Phraya Suntharanur-
aksa. A hidden grass
courtyard flanks two
spiraling staircases
leading to the wood-
en paneled second
story where most exhibits are
kept. Highlights include Bencharong pottery, earthenware
jars recovered from the sea
around Songkhla, 7th- to 9th-
century Dvaravati plinths and
Buddha images, and Ban
Chiang pottery said to date
from 3000 BC.

The **Patsree Museum** in
Wat Matchimawat (sometimes
called Wat Klang), south of the
National Museum, is no less
important. Its 35-cm (14-in)
stone image of Ganesh, the elephant god, is thought to date

from the late 6th century, making it the earliest such image
found in the peninsula. Chinese painted enamelware from
the Qwing Ching dynasty,
15th-century U Thong wares,
and 18th-century European
plates all indicate the importance of Songkhla's former
maritime trade links.

The city's other main temple, **Wat Chai Mongkhon**,
has a Buddha relic from Sri
Lanka buried beneath it.

Songkhla is an attractive
city to walk around, taking in
the topiary garden at **Khao
Noi** and the view of Thale
Sap from the peak of **Khao
Tung Kuan**. Restaurants and
live music bars can be found
around Chaiya Road.

**Elaborately decorated door at the
Songkhla National Museum**

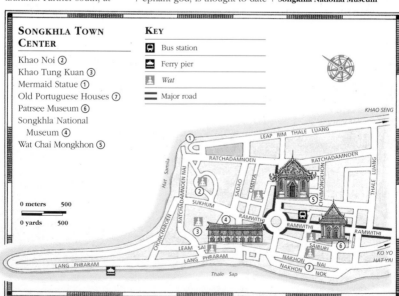

**SONGKHLA TOWN
CENTER**

Khao Noi ②
Khao Tung Kuan ③
Mermaid Statue ①
Old Portuguese Houses ⑦
Patsree Museum ⑥
Songkhla National
    Museum ④
Wat Chai Mongkhon ⑤

KEY

🚌 Bus station
🚤 Ferry pier
🏛 *Wat*
━━ Major road

0 meters   500
0 yards   500

⚄ Songkhla National Museum
Wichianchom Rd. ☐ *Wed–Sun.*
● *public hols.* 📷

⚄ Patrsee Museum
Wat Matchimawat, Saiburi Rd.
☐ *Wed–Sun.* ● *public hols.* 📷

ENVIRONS: The Prem Tinsula-
nond bridge connects Songkhla
with the narrow coastal strip to
the north. The longest bridge
in Thailand, it traverses Thale
Sap via the island of **Ko Yo** on
the western side of the lake.
The link has boosted the island's active cotton-weaving
industry and fish farms.

Ko Yo is home to the excellent **Folklore Museum**, on a
hilltop overlooking the lake.
The museum, which aims to
preserve the rich folk traditions
of the South, houses displays
on history, ethnology, and religion. Exhibits include fabrics,
pottery, and metalware, and
traditional arts from the South.
Examples of these Southern
crafts are rattan and brassware
from Ranong, Muslim *kris*
knives from Pattani, *krajude*
grass mats from Chumphon,
and dove cages from Songkhla.

Wat Pha Kho, in **Sathing
Phra** district, to the north of
Songkhla, is believed to be
the oldest temple in Songkhla
province. Archaeological finds
around the *wat* suggest Sathing
Phra was once an important
port selling ceramics, produced
at nearby Pa-o, to Khmer,
Cham, and Chinese traders.

⚄ Folklore Museum
Institute of Southern Thai Studies, Ko
Yo, 14 km (8 miles) SW of Songkhla.
☐ *daily.* 📷

Three young devotees venerating a Buddhist shrine in Hat Yai

Hat Yai ⑨
หาดใหญ่

Songkhla province. 🏠 *70,000.* ✈
12 km (7 miles) W of Hat Yai. 🚉 🚌
ℹ *TAT, 1/1 Soi 2, Niphat U-thit Rd, Hat
Yai (0-7424-3747).* 🚌 *next to TAT
(0-7424-6733).* 🛒 *daily.* 📷
Chinese Lunar Festival (Sep/Oct).

ALTHOUGH IT IS the
commercial and
transport capital of
Southern Thailand,
Hat Yai wins no
prizes for beauty.
It has grown afflu-
ent due to its
strategic railroad
junction, its cut-
price products,
and a constant
flow of Malaysian tourists
who converge on the city on
weekends to enjoy its dining,
shopping, and nightlife.
Malay, English, Yawi, Hokkien,
Mandarin, and the clipped
syllables of Southern Thai dialect can be heard around the

**Seller displaying
produce at Hat Yai market**

cosmopolitan downtown area.
Be aware that some parlors
here advertising "ancient
massage" will probably offer
more than a quick rubdown.

As Hat Yai's cultural attractions are few, most visitors
spend daylight hours shopping in Thailand's third largest
city. Electrical goods at the
Kim Yong market, durians
and apples from street
vendors, and
Bangkok-
made leather
goods and fash-
ions in the dep-
artment stores are
a few of Hat Yai's
popular buys.
Bullfighting takes
place in the city
on the first Saturday of every
month at different locations.
Bulls are pitted against each
other, and the winner is the
animal that forces its opponent
to retreat. The furious betting
is often as much of a spectacle as the fight itself.

Wat Hat Yai Nai, 2 km (1
mile) west of the city center,
has the third largest reclining
Buddha image in the world,
measuring 35 m (115 ft) long
and 15 m (49 ft) high. You can
walk inside the image, entering
via a small shrine room. Herbal
saunas and massages are offered in the temple grounds.

ENVIRONS: Ton Nga Chang
("elephant tusk") waterfall, 24
km (15 miles) west of Hat Yai,
takes its name from the two
streams of water that tumble
over the seven tiers of falls.
They are best seen in the cool
season, starting in November.

Extensive fish farms beside Ko Yo on Thale Sap lake, near Songkhla

Taking the ferry from Pak Bara to Tarutao National Marine Park

Thale Ban National Park ⑩

อุทยานแห่งชาติทะเลบัน

Satun province. Off Hwy 4184, 37 km (23 miles) from Satun. 🛈 *TAT, Hat Yai (0-7423-1055); Forestry Dept (0-2562-0760 inc bungalow bookings).* 🚌 *Satun, then songthaew.*

Thale ban is a lush expanse of dense tropical rainforest scattered with waterfalls that extends over the Banthat Mountains *(see p371)* close to the Malaysian border. It covers only 102 sq km (40 sq miles) but contains a staggering variety of wildlife including sun bears, tigers, and rare birds such as bat hawks. The park has some marked trails, the Yaroy waterfall, 5 km (3 miles) north of the park headquarters, and several swimming pools.

Satun is the nearest town and gateway to the park. It is within easy reach of Pak Bara, from which ferries depart for Tarutao, and the west coast.

Tarutao National Marine Park ⑪

อุทยานแห่งชาติตะรุเตา

Satun province. 22 km (14 miles) from Pak Bara. 🛈 *TAT, Hat Yai (0-7423-1055) or Park HQ (0-7472-9002).* 🚢 *from Pak Bara; regular crossings mid-Nov to mid-Apr only.*

The 51 islands of the Tarutao National Marine Park are the most southwesterly in Thailand, located only 8 km (5 miles) from the Malaysian island of Langkawi. Tarutao is renowned for its superb diving sites, considered to be among the best in the world.

Offshore sightings of sperm and minke whales, dugongs, and dolphins are common. There is also a rich concentration of fish life with 92 species of coral fish and around 25 percent of all the world's fish species in the surrounding seas.

For centuries the islands had a more sinister reputation as a lair for pirates. It wasn't until the 1960s that the British Royal Navy finally curtailed the pirate raids. The archipelago, extending over 1,490 sq km (580 sq miles), became Thailand's first national marine park in 1974.

The park includes spectacular, unspoiled scenery, a wide variety of wildlife, and good coral. However, these attractions are accessible to visitors only from mid-November to mid-May as monsoon storms make the ferry trip from Pak Bara too risky at other times.

Hawksbill turtle, a resident of Tarutao

The largest island in the group, 26-km (16-mile) long **Ko Tarutao**, offers the greatest scenic variety. Tropical rainforest covers most of its surface, which reaches a height of 708 m (2,300 ft). Most accommodations and the best facilities for visitors are found near the wonderful, pristine beaches of the west coast.

Ferries from Pak Bara dock at Ao Phante Malaka, which is where the park headquarters, bungalows, two restaurants, and the island's only store are located. Worthwhile excursions from here include the half-hour climb to To-bo cliff with its fine views, particularly at sunset, and the 2-km (1-mile) boat trip to stalagmite-filled Crocodile cave. No crocodiles have been seen for many years, but the island does support a wide variety of fauna including deer, wild pigs, macaques, otters, and soft-shelled turtles.

Ko Adang and **Ko Lipey** are the only other islands in the park to offer (rudimentary) accommodations and food for visitors.

Rugged Ko Adang, 62 km (39 miles) west of the mainland, rises to 703 m (2,300 ft). It is thickly forested and has many year-round waterfalls, such as the Rattana falls on the southwest coast. Here, you can take a freshwater rock pool swim while overlooking the sea.

The smaller island of Ko Lipey, 2 km (1 mile) south of Ko Adang, has pleasant footpaths through coconut plantations and the immaculate sands of Pattaya beach. It is also home to a community of sea gypsies, displaced from Ko Rawi and Ko Adang when the park was created. Relations between the gypsies and the park authorities are strained.

Ko Kra, off Lipey's east coast, has excellent corals, as does Ko Yang, midway between Rawi and Adang islands.

Tiny Ko Khai ("egg island"), west of Tarutao, has a dramatic rock arch and is surrounded by fine sands. These are a major breeding ground for sea turtles, hence the island's name.

Colorful corals, part of a reef in the Tarutao National Marine Park

Seafood of the South

O NE OF THE GREATEST culinary treats Thailand provides is the abundant fresh seafood of the South. Throughout the year, a wide range of fish, crabs, lobsters, mussels, shrimp, mollusks, and squid are available along both the Gulf of Thailand and Andaman Sea coasts. Although flash-frozen and container-freighted seafood is avail-

Ho mok, a seafood mousse with fresh mint

able all over the country today, it is hard to beat the flavor of a freshly caught fish, simply cooked and served up whole on a plate by the shore. Nor does it have to be expensive: for every five-star restaurant offering lobster bisque there are half a dozen street cafés serving an enormous range of seafood cooked in an amazing variety of styles.

Hoi nang rom sot, *a simple Thai hors d'oeuvre of fresh oysters, is served out of the shell with slices of zesty lime.*

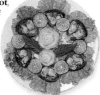

Green mussels from the Gulf of Thailand

Whelks from the Andaman Sea

Andaman Sea cockles

Fresh crab from Phuket

Saltwater tiger shrimp

Charamet fish, *prized for its succulent, soft flesh, is cooked here in sweet plum sauce* (neung buay), *accompanied by ginger, lemon grass, and chili peppers.*

BARBECUED SEAFOOD

Barbecued seafood, known as *thale phao*, is popular with both Thais and foreign visitors. Diners make their selection of freshly caught fish and shellfish displayed on banks of crushed ice. Pricing is usually by weight.

Thot man kung (deep fried shrimp cakes) *are served with a sweet sauce dip. This is a favorite dish with those who don't like very spicy food.*

Meuk op sos noei (squid baked in butter sauce) *is decorated with exquisitely carved vegetable "flowers" and "leaves." Garnishes of this type accompany many Thai dishes and are generally not eaten.*

Phanaeng kung makheuathet *is a creamy, fragrant dish of tomatoes stuffed with a shrimp and coconut milk curry. It is a specialty of Hat Yai and Phuket.*

Kung mangkon phat phrik phao (barbecued lobster with chili sauce) *is particularly popular around Phuket, where lobsters abound.*

Pattani ⑫
ปัตตานี

Pattani province. 👥 74,000. ☎
🚉 🛈 *TAT, Narathiwat (0-7351-6144).* 🚌 *daily.* 🎭 *Lim Ko Niaw Festival (Mar).*

FOUNDED IN THE EARLY 15th century, Pattani was once a semiautonomous Malay-speaking sultanate. Today, it is the heart of Muslim South Thailand (75 percent of the province's population are followers of Islam). There is also a sizable Chinese presence, and the cultural mix between these two communities is the most interesting feature of modern Pattani.

Apart from the **Matsayit Klang** mosque there are few notable sights, but the town is lively, particularly around the harbor with its brightly colored boats.

ENVIRONS: The mosque of **Kru Se**, 7 km (4 miles) east of town, is unremarkable in design but has an interesting story behind it. In the 1570s, Lim To Khieng, a Chinese merchant, married a local woman

Muslim women in Pattani

and converted to Islam. To show his devotion to his new faith he started the construction of a mosque. His sister, Lim Ko Niaw, sailed from China to protest about his conversion, and he swore he would return to China as soon as the mosque was finished. However, he made sure that it never was, and his sister, on her deathbed, cursed the building and anyone who attempted to complete it. Her shrine and the still unfinished mosque attract huge numbers of devotees.

Wat Khuha Phimuk, with its adjacent cave containing a reclining Buddha

Yala ⑬
ยะลา

Yala province. 👥 93,000. 🚉 🚌
🛈 *TAT, Narathiwat (0-7351-6144).* 🎭 *ASEAN Barred Ground Dove Festival (1st weekend Mar); Yala City Pillar Celebrations (May 25–30).*

YALA, OFTEN HERALDED as the cleanest town in Thailand, is laid out in an orderly fashion with a grid pattern of streets and tree-lined boulevards. It's a prosperous and rather staid place, at its most lively during the annual cooing competition of the ASEAN Barred Ground Dove Festival, which attracts entrants from all over Southeast Asia. Yala's mosque is the largest in Thailand.

ENVIRONS: For many people, the main reason to visit Yala is to see **Wat Khuha Phimuk**, called Wat Na Tham locally, located 8 km (5 miles) outside the town. It is one of the most sacred and important archaeological sites in South Thailand. A cave next to the temple contains a 25-m-long (82-ft) reclining Buddha. The statue, which allegedly once had the head of the Hindu god Vishnu, dates from the 8th century, the beginning of the Srivijaya period.

Among the priceless icons from that era found here are votive *stupas* from Northeast India and 9th-century bronze standing Buddha images in the style of South India.

The small museum hall, at the foot of the *naga* staircase leading up to the temple cave, displays a range of Srivijayan artifacts found in the area.

KORLAE FISHING BOATS

Along mainly the east coast of the peninsula, from Ko Samui southward, colorful, painted fishing boats called *korlae* have been built and decorated by Muslim fishermen for hundreds of years. The finest examples of this now declining industry originate in the boatyards of Saiburi district, Pattani. Originally sailboats, they are now run with engines by fishermen. Among the characters commonly depicted in the superbly detailed hull designs are the *singha* lion, the *gagasura* horned bird, *payanak* sea serpent, and the *garuda* bird from Asian mythologies. Artists, however, don't feel anything is amiss if they add a Swiss Alpine background.

Battling mythical beasts, intricately painted on a *korlae* boat

Betong

เบตง

Yala province. 29,000.
Sungai Kolok, Narathiwat
(0-7361-2126). daily.

BETONG IS THE southernmost town in Thailand. It sits high in the hills, 5 km (3 miles) from the Malaysian border and 140 km (87 miles) from Yala.

The surrounding countryside is of more interest than the town itself, which has few sights other than the 40-m-high (130-ft) *stupa* in **Wat Phuttha Tiwat**. This was built in the late 1980s in a modified Srivijayan style.

ENVIRONS: The winding road from Yala to Betong climbs through remote mountain forests where bands of the Sakai tribe still hunt.

From the 1940s until the 1980s this dense forest was home to an active unit of the Communist Party of Malaya, taking refuge in Thailand. A paved road leads to their former underground guerrilla camp, **Piya Mit**, which has now been converted into a museum. Around 180 Communists lived here undetected in 1 km (1,100 yds) of tunnels, 10 m (33 ft) below the surface.

The end came peacefully in 1989 when "an honorable settlement" was reached with the Malaysian and Thai governments. Most of the former revolutionaries settled in the area, and some now guide visitors through the network of dank tunnels and explain the camp's facilities. The cleverly constructed kitchen area has a flue that would disperse smoke on the other side of the hill, thus concealing the camp's location. It was so successful that the stronghold remained undetected until the end. Other items on display include old shoes, uniforms, knives, and torches used by the fugitive comrades. Simple accommodations are available in modern bungalows.

Piya Mit
Betong province. Off Hwy 410, 19 km (12 miles) N of Betong. daily.

Narathiwat

นราธิวาส

Narathiwat province. 68,000.
TAT region 3, 102/3
Muz, Kaluwonuea, Muang, Narathiwat
(0-7351-6144). tatnara
@cscoms.com. Chao Mae Toe
Moe Festival (late Apr or early May),
Narathiwat Fair (3rd week Sep).

THE TOWN of Narathiwat is visited by few tourists, but it makes a useful base for exploring the surrounding region. It has a few decent hotels and restaurants and an atmosphere befitting one of Thailand's smallest provincial capitals. The Muslim fishing village is a good place to see the traditional painted *korlae* boats. There are a number of good beaches near the town – the best is Ao Manao, 6 km (4 miles) to the south.

Immense golden-tiled Buddha on Khao Kong, Narathiwat

ENVIRONS: Taksin Palace, south of town, is the summer residence of the King and Queen It is open to the public when the royal family is not in residence. The gardens have views of the adjacent beach and contain an aviary with peacocks and cockatoos.

On the road to Rangae is the hill **Khao Kong**, perched upon which is the tallest seated Buddha image in Thailand. The 24-m (79-ft) statue is covered in golden tiles.

Close to the Malaysian border, 34 km (21 miles) south of Narathiwat, is the village of **Tak Bai**. Its main attraction is Wat Chonthara Sing He: an outpost of Thai Buddhism in an almost exclusively Malay-speaking, Muslim area. The *wat* was erected in 1873 by King Chulalongkorn to stake his claim to a region that the British wanted to incorporate into Malaya (Malaysia).

The architecture of the temple mixes Southern Thai with Chinese influences, the latter being particularly evident in the tiered roof. One of the buildings in the large grounds contains a reclining Buddha decorated with Chinese ceramics from the Song dynasty. Another is adorned with fine murals depicting many aspects of local life painted during the reign of King Mongkut.

Taksin Palace
Off Hwy 4084, 8 km (5 miles) S of Narathiwat. daily. usually Aug & Sep.

A lively scene of daily life from a mural at Wat Chonthara Sing He

TRAVELERS' NEEDS

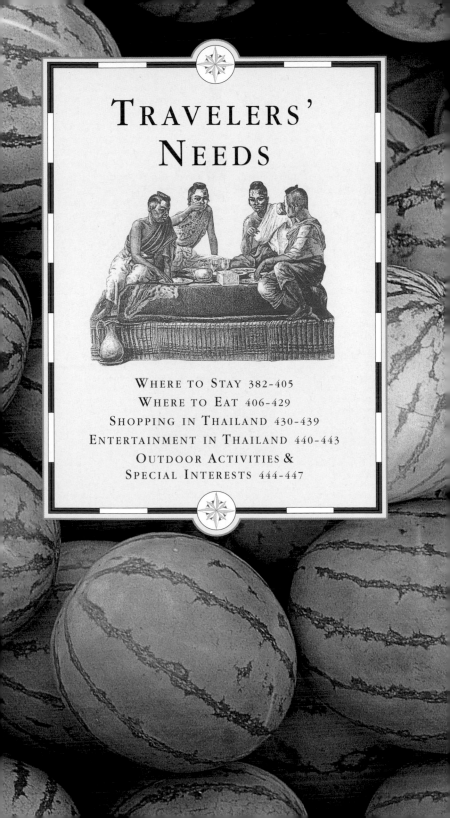

WHERE TO STAY

ACCOMMODATIONS IN THAILAND come in all price ranges, although the distribution of hotels is very uneven: massive development in the beach resorts contrasts with basic guesthouses (or no facilities at all) in many rural areas. All major cities have at least one international-class hotel, while Bangkok boasts of some of the best hotels anywhere in the world. These are equipped with swimming pools, gyms, restaurants, business services, and other luxury facilities. Middle-range accommodation is available in most towns

Bellboy at the Oriental Hotel

and, although much lacks character, it is uniformly clean, efficient, and friendly. Western-style bathrooms are the rule rather than the exception, air-conditioning is widespread (though some middle-range hotels may offer fan rooms as well), and services such as laundry and safe deposit are standard. Guesthouses provide remarkably cheap accommodations for budget travelers. Other alternatives include, for the hardy, camping or staying in bungalows in the national parks, and, for the ascetic, bedding down in a monastery.

HOTEL GRADING AND FACILITIES

HOTELS ARE not officially graded, although some are registered with the **Thai Hotels Association**. Price is therefore the only indication of what to expect *(see p384)*. Accommodations range from basic to luxury. At the low end of the market cleanliness is not always a priority.

Often the best value is to be found in the once-luxury establishments that have been downgraded since the arrival of international luxury chains. These hotels offer the facilities available in first-class hotels at a fraction of the cost.

LUXURY HOTELS

THAILAND'S LUXURY HOTELS are probably the equal of any in the world – and their number and standards are rising year after year. Expect to be treated like a visiting dignitary in the air-conditioned oases of Bangkok and the other major cities. Rooms are sure to have every conceivable luxury, from a king-size bed and massive television to a well-stocked minibar and perhaps even a marble Jacuzzi. In such world-famous hotels as the Oriental and the Shangri-La in Bangkok, the magnificent views of the Chao Phraya River are an added privilege.

These first-class hotels offer their guests a huge range of facilities, including business centers, banqueting halls, con-

Hilton Hua Hin Resort & Spa, noted for fine sea views *(see p402)*

ference rooms, shopping malls, coffee shops, fitness centers, and swimming pools, as well as numerous food outlets.

All luxury hotels in Thailand provide an extensive range of cuisines, some having as many as ten restaurants; Thai is, of course, standard, and Chinese – often with a regional variant such as Cantonese or Szechuan – is common. Italian and French restaurants are very popular, usually complete with imported European chef. Less popular, but increasingly available, are German, English, Japanese, and Mexican cuisines. Compared with similar establishments in the West, these hotels offer an excellent value for the money.

RESORT HOTELS

LIKE THE URBAN luxury hotels, the resort hotels of Thailand are unsurpassed in style, comfort, and elegance by the majority of their counterparts elsewhere in the world. They also usually offer stunning views. Such resorts as the Regent in Chiang Mai, Maiton Island in Phuket, and the Dusit Resort in Cha-am are luxury designer-built oases of tranquility and opulence. You should expect – and will usually get

The Conrad Room at the Oriental Hotel, Bangkok *(see p390)*

◁ **Fresh watermelons on display at the Damnoen Saduak Floating Market, near Bangkok**

Felix River Kwai Resort, Khwae Yai River, Kanchanaburi *(see p391)*

– the very best of everything. Charming service is provided by traditionally dressed waiting staff, and you should not be surprised if waitresses approach your table on their knees. (Height etiquette dictates that you, as an honored guest, should be physically higher than servants.) The food available is varied and generally of an excellent standard.

Most resorts offer their guests a wide range of entertainments and distractions, such as swimming – for which there might be several pools – outdoor Jacuzzis, saunas, tennis courts, water sports facilities, and even riding or polo. In Chiang Mai, resorts may be able to organize elephant trekking.

GUESTHOUSES

GUESTHOUSES are a relatively new phenomenon in Thailand, dating from the backpacker explosion of the 1970s. Still frequented primarily by Western travelers, they offer a superb value for the money and often a lot of charm.

In Bangkok, Khao San Road is the primary haunt of budget travelers. Offering low-cost accommodation in an otherwise expensive capital city seems to have taken priority over comfort, and, with few exceptions, Bangkok guesthouses are at best unremarkable.

Outside the capital, however, and especially in Chiang Mai, guesthouses are usually clean, friendly, and astoundingly cheap. Most have rooms with air-conditioning or fans, as well as bathrooms. Some establishments offer swimming pools, restaurants, and good service for around 400 *baht* a

night, just a fraction of the cost of a top resort hotel. Cheap guesthouses may cost as little as 100 *baht*, but for this expect basic facilities, with communal Asian toilets and showers, although the quality of service should still be good.

THAI AND CHINESE HOTELS

THAI AND CHINESE hotels can be found just about everywhere in Thailand, though relatively few foreign visitors choose to stay in them. They generally offer basic facilities, often without Western-style toilets (they are clean, but you must squat rather than sit), and are cheap, functional, and unexceptional.

Thai hotels are architecturally unexciting, generally being multistory concrete blocks containing numerous identical rooms. As ever in Thailand, however, they are usually clean and the service is

friendly. Most will offer you a choice between air-conditioned rooms *(hong air)* and fancooled rooms *(hong patlom)*.

Chinese hotels, by contrast, are readily identifiable by a number of distinctly "Middle Kingdom" features – and not just the serious-looking concierge who usually guards the keys. Wall partitions generally stop a foot short of the ground, and several feet below the ceiling, making privacy distinctly elusive. Mirrors are strategically placed to repel evil spirits, and Chinese decorative features, such as dragons and red-and-gold Chinese characters (for good luck), are much in evidence.

Only a few Thai and Chinese hotels are equipped with restaurants. However, in some remote areas, particularly little-visited areas of the Central Plains and Northeast Thailand, these hotels may well provide the only option for travelers.

STAYING IN MONASTERIES

MONASTERIES are traditionally places of refuge and contemplation. Whether you are a Buddhist, or want to learn more about Buddhism, it is often possible to stay overnight in a *wat* for a small donation.

Facilities are basic, and early rising is the norm. Mixed-sex accommodation is not available. Clean, tidy dress and an appropriate demeanor are also important. For temple etiquette see page 455.

Nong Sam Guest House, Chiang Khan, Northeast Thailand *(see p397)*

RENTALS

RENTAL accommodations are widely available throughout Thailand at very reasonable rates. However, rental is an option rarely taken up by short-term visitors. This is for a number of reasons: dining out is inexpensive in Thailand; landlords rarely speak other languages; and advertisements of apartments for rent are generally aimed solely at Thais. However, it may make sense for visitors staying in one place for more than a few weeks to rent a room or a small apartment. Thai friends will normally be happy to act as intermediaries in arranging a short-term lease.

STAYING IN NATIONAL PARKS

THE MAJORITY of national parks allow camping (for a minimal fee), although the facilities provided are invariably extremely basic when compared to those available in Europe and North America. Camping has never taken off in Thailand, as Thais do not understand why anyone would choose to sleep under canvas when there is a cheap hotel

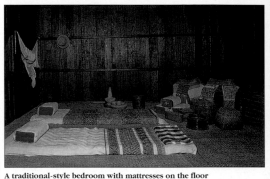

A traditional-style bedroom with mattresses on the floor

nearby. Additionally, campers have to face the perils of the outdoors. Mosquito nets and coils and copious amounts of insect repellent are essential.

In many national parks visitors can also stay in clean, if usually charmless, concrete bungalows. As there are only limited numbers of these, it is advisable to book ahead by phoning the **Forestry Department** in Bangkok.

PRICES

THAILAND'S EXTRAORDINARY range of accommodations includes something to suit every visitor's budget. At the top end of the market, which includes such hotels as Bangkok's Oriental and Chiang Mai's Regent, the sky is the limit. Celebrities and heads of state may take suites at 40,000 *baht* a night, although for more everyday luxury expect to pay between 10,000 and 15,000 *baht* a night.

Tourist accommodations cost from 1,000 to 5,000 *baht* a night in Bangkok, Chiang Mai, Pattaya, Phuket, or Ko Samui. A comfortable air-conditioned room in a standard provincial hotel goes for between 700 and 1,500 *baht*, depending on the season. Prices everywhere are at their highest in the cool season. In the hot season (March to May) and the rainy season (May to October) rates often fall, except in the capital, which is open for business all year round. A clean but spartan room in a Thai or Chinese hotel in Bangkok will cost around 500 *baht*, falling to 150 to 250 *baht* in the regions.

Local factors should also be taken into consideration. For example, in Surin the hotel prices soar during the Elephant Roundup in November, when rooms in this otherwise moderately priced city are booked up months in advance.

The best deals available are probably the guesthouses of Chiang Mai and other tourism-oriented towns. It is possible to stay in traditional Thai houses, with teak walls and stilts, for between 100 and 500 *baht* a night. This is difficult to beat, and visitors often stay for weeks longer than planned. Beach bungalow accommodations are similarly priced, but less comfortable, and more prone to invasion by insects.

An idyllic setting: tent and bungalows at Ao Phrao on Ko Samet

BOOKING

ADVANCE BOOKING is advisable for luxury hotels and mid-range establishments, especially during national and local festivals. Thai and Chinese hotels and guesthouses are unlikely to take bookings. In popular tourist areas, and at luxury hotels, staff speak English. Elsewhere, making a booking may be difficult unless you speak some Thai. TAT offices are able to make bookings on behalf of tourists.

TAXES

THE TAX SITUATION in Thailand is rather confusing and apparently anomalous. All hotels should charge seven percent VAT (value added tax), and some luxury hotels will also add a 10 percent service charge on top of their basic rates. Some of the top hotels – such as the Oriental, Shangri-La, and others in this category – include tax in the room rates quoted. Less expensive hotels, catering to tourists, may simply add on tax when the final bill is presented. Thus, it is important to ask whether it is included in the price when booking or before checking in.

At small hotels outside the main resorts, tax is rarely (if ever) charged, and service is paid for (if at all) by tipping.

BARGAINING

IT IS ALWAYS a good idea to ask about "special rates" or the possibility of a reduction in price. The worst that can happen is a polite refusal, and

very often, especially outside Bangkok and out of season, such an inquiry can lead to substantial savings. It is not considered impolite to ask, but it is bad manners to press the point. Many hotels give discounts if bookings are low, and if special rates are available, most Thai proprietors will certainly let you know.

TIPPING

OUTSIDE THE CAPITAL and the major destinations of Ko Samui, Phuket, Pattaya, and Chiang Mai, tipping is unusual. Porters will expect a tip, and staff are rewarded for good service. Use your discretion: if you have received particularly good service, then leave a tip if you wish. Thanks, and a smile, are also much appreciated.

There are no hard and fast rules, and the standard British 10 percent – let alone the American 15 percent – would be far too much on a large bill. Between 10 and 50 *baht* is adequate in almost every circumstance. Expensive hotels will automatically include a service charge on the bill.

FACILITIES FOR CHILDREN

THAIS LOVE CHILDREN and are incredibly tolerant of them, especially if they are blond-haired and blue-eyed. Such kids seem as exotic and doll-like to Thais as their own offspring do to the average Westerner. However, very few mid-range hotels have facilities for children or nursing mothers, and supervised play areas are rare.

By contrast, the majority of seaside resorts and luxury hotels offer some kind of babysitting services, and children can often stay in their parents' room for free. Paddling pools may be provided, but you must look after your own children.

Khon Kaen Hotel, Northeast Thailand *(see p397)*

DISABLED TRAVELERS

EVEN LUXURY HOTELS have few facilities for disabled visitors. Wheelchair ramps are beginning to make an appearance in newly commissioned luxury hotels, and nearly every luxury or tourist-class establishment has an elevator. However, that is the limit of facilities in most hotels.

Thailand has a fast developing economy and a booming tourist trade, but it is likely to be many years before a serious awareness of the needs of the disabled develops. Hotels should be carefully chosen, with the help of the Thai Hotels Association, and bookings made well in advance.

Bungalows and coconut palms on Ko Chang

Thailand's Best Luxury Hotels

Thailand boasts a remarkable number of superb, international-class hotels. These tend to be clustered in major cities like Bangkok and Chiang Mai, and around the big resorts such as Pattaya and on Phuket. However, as tourism keeps on increasing in Thailand, fine new hotels are appearing in smaller towns and resorts, and few countries in Southeast Asia can boast a similar range and quantity of first-rate accommodation. Many hotels also represent excellent value for the money when compared with similar standard hotels in Europe and the US. Some Thai hotels, such as the renowned Oriental in Bangkok and Amanpuri Resort on Phuket have been acclaimed the best in the world. Listed here are the top luxury hotels in each region.

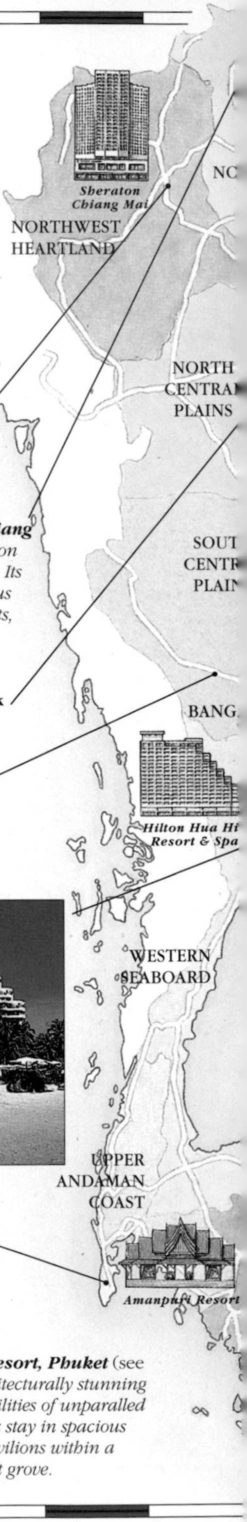

Sheraton Chiang Mai *(see p394),* attracts the rich and famous, providing luxury at high prices.

Dusit Island Resort, Chiang Rai (see p395), *is located on an island in the Kok River. Its attractions include spacious grounds, pool, tennis courts, and excellent restaurants.*

Pailyn Hotel, Phitsanulok *(see p392),* offers stylishly furnished rooms with river views, a sauna, and two good restaurants.

Felix River Kwai Resort, Kanchanaburi *(see p391),* is artfully set in landscaped grounds next to the Khwae River. Extensive amenities include two swimming pools, 24-hour room service, and rooms for nonsmokers and the disabled.

Hilton Hua Hin Resort & Spa (see p402), *stands on the beachfront of this popular, long-established resort. In addition to international-standard facilities, all rooms have balconies with sea views.*

Amanpuri Resort, Phuket (see p404), *is architecturally stunning and offers facilities of unparalleled luxury. Guests stay in spacious individual pavilions within a shady coconut grove.*

NC

Sheraton Chiang Mai

NORTHWEST HEARTLAND

NORTH CENTRAL PLAINS

SOUT CENTR PLAIN

BANG

Hilton Hua Hi Resort & Spa

WESTERN SEABOARD

UPPER ANDAMAN COAST

Amanpuri Resort

Sima Thani Hotel, Khorat
(see p397), situated out of the center of town, is spacious and attractively decorated. Amenities are first rate and include swimming pool, fitness center, sauna, two restaurants, and two bars. The five-story atrium lounge is particularly striking.

Pathumrat Hotel, Ubon Ratchathani (see p399), *is a modern seven-story hotel near the town center. Rooms are comfortably furnished and come equipped with air-conditioning, minibar, and TV. Facilities include a coffee shop and a swimming pool.*

MEKONG
RIVER
VALLEY

KHORAT
PLATEAU

Pathumrat Hotel

Grand
Hyatt
Erawan

EASTERN
SEABOARD

Oriental Hotel, Bangkok
(see p390), *has long been recognized as one of the world's great hotels. Its standards of luxury and superlative service make a stay here a memorable experience.*

Grand Hyatt Erawan, Bangkok (see p390), *is one of the finest luxury hotels in the capital.*

Royal Cliff Beach Resort, Pattaya (see p400), *located near Jomtien beach, is the best family resort in the area. It offers high quality accommodations, excellent service, and a wide range of sports and leisure facilities. Most rooms have sea views.*

DEEP
SOUTH

Royal Crown Hotel, Songkhla *(see p405),* is a popular hotel, notable for its central location, friendly service and restaurant.

0 kilometers   200

0 miles   100

Choosing a Hotel

THE HOTELS in this guide have been selected across a wide price range for their locations and value. Many have excellent facilities, and some are splendidly designed. The chart lists the hotels by region, starting with Bangkok; color-coded thumb tabs show the regions covered on each page. For restaurant listings see pages 412–29.

		Credit Cards	Swimming Pool	Western Bathrooms	Coffee Shop	Garden/Terrace

BANGKOK

OLD CITY: *BK Guest House.* **Map** 2 D3.   (B)
11/1 Soi Surao, Chakrabongse Rd. [0-2281-3048. FAX 0-2222-4416.
Clean, very low-priced rooms with shared bathrooms. Well placed for the Chao Phraya River and the Old City. *Rooms: 25.*
— Western Bathrooms: ■

OLD CITY: *Peachy Guest House.* **Map** 1 C4.   (B)
10 Phra Athit Rd. [0-2281-6471.
A pleasant garden makes this place stand out among the many inexpensive guesthouses in and around Banglamphu. *Rooms: 47.* 🗐 15.
— Western Bathrooms: ■, Garden/Terrace: ■

OLD CITY: *Khao San Palace.* **Map** 2 D4.   (B)(B)
139 Khao San Rd. [0-2282-0578.
In recent years Khao San Road has replaced Soi Ngam Duphli to the south of Lumphini Park as the backpackers' haunt in Bangkok. This place is among the best – though rates are high for the area. *Rooms: 62.* 🗐 62.

OLD CITY: *Nith Jaroen Hotal.* **Map** 2 D4.   (B)(B)
183 Khao San Rd. [0-2281-9872.
A quiet, clean guest house set back from the busy Khao San Rd. All rooms have ceiling fans and en-suite bathrooms. *Rooms: 28.* 🗐 0.
— Western Bathrooms: ■

OLD CITY: *Phra Athit Mansion.* **Map** 1 C4.   (B)(B)(B)   MC V
22 Phra Athit Rd. [0-2280-0744. FAX 0-2280-0742.
Basic, clean, airy accommodations very close to the Phra Athit ferry pier. Suitable for young travelers watching their funds. *Rooms: 35.* 🗐 0.
— Western Bathrooms: ■

OLD CITY: *Royal.* **Map** 2 D4.   (B)(B)(B)   MC V
2 Ratchadamnoen Klang Ave. [0-2222-9111. FAX 0-2224-2083.
One of Bangkok's oldest hotels. Majestic accommodations, despite its recent history: in 1992 there was much bloodshed in the foyer during a pro-democracy demonstration. 🍴 24 TV *Rooms: 300.* 🗐 300.
— Swimming Pool: ●, Western Bathrooms: ■, Coffee Shop: ●

CHINATOWN: *River View Guest House.* **Map** 6 F3.   (B)(B)   AE V
768 Soi Phanu Rang Si, Songwat Rd. [0-2234-5429. FAX 0-2237-5428.
A real bargain, right by the river. The view from the 8th-floor restaurant is wonderful, even if the food is only mediocre. A clean and friendly establishment, though the service is a little slow. 🍴 TV *Rooms: 45.* 🗐 12.
— Western Bathrooms: ■

CHINATOWN: *White Orchid.* **Map** 6 E2.   (B)(B)(B)   AE DC MC V
409–421 Yaowarat Rd. [0-2226-0026. FAX 0-2221-8101.
Plain but respectably turned-out establishment, well located for the many gold and herbalist shops in the main shopping area of Chinatown, Sampeng Lane. 🍴 TV *Rooms: 330.* 🗐 330.
— Western Bathrooms: ■, Coffee Shop: ●

CHINATOWN: *Grand China Princess Hotel.* **Map** 6 F2.   (B)(B)(B)(B)   AE DC MC V
215 Yaowarat Rd. [0-2224-9977. FAX 0-2224-7999.
Mid-range, plain hotel situated right in the heart of Bangkok's busy Chinatown. Good access to diverse restaurants in the area serving Thai, Japanese, and Chinese cuisine. 🍴 TV 📶 *Rooms: 155.* 🗐 155.
— Western Bathrooms: ■, Coffee Shop: ●

DUSIT: *Bangkok International Youth Hostel.* **Map** 2 F2.   (B)
25/2 Phitsanulok Rd. [0-2281-0361. FAX 0-2281-6834.
Clean, with reasonable rates and a downstairs restaurant serving good food. Usual youth hostel rules apply. Situated close to Vimanmek Palace in the relatively peaceful Dusit quarter. 🍴 TV *Rooms: 20 (64 beds).* 🗐 15.
— Western Bathrooms: ■, Coffee Shop: ●, Garden/Terrace: ■

DUSIT: *D & D Inn.* **Map** 2 D4.   (B)(B)
68–70 Khao San Rd. [0-2629-0526. FAX 0-2629-0529. [W] www.khaosanby.com
The D & D Inn offers a very high standard of service in clean, pleasant surroundings. Facilities include hot showers, internet access, a beauty salon and Thai massage. 🍴 24 TV *Rooms: 99.* 🗐 99.
— Swimming Pool: ●, Garden/Terrace: ■

Price categories for a standard double room per night, including tax for luxury hotels.

ⓑ under B350
ⓑⓑ B350–800
ⓑⓑⓑ B800–1,600
ⓑⓑⓑⓑ B1,600–3,200
ⓑⓑⓑⓑⓑ over B3,200

CREDIT CARDS
AE American Express; DC Diners Club; MC MasterCard; V VISA; JCB Japanese Credit Bureau.

WESTERN BATHROOMS
Indicates sit-down, flush toilets; showers and/or baths. Others have squat toilets and trough-and-dipper baths.

COFFEE SHOP
Hotel with coffee shop.

GARDEN/TERRACE
Hotel with garden, courtyard, or terrace.

	Credit Cards	Swimming Pool	Western Bathrooms	Coffee Shop	Garden/Terrace
DUSIT: *Trang.* **Map** 2 D2. ⓑⓑⓑ 99/1 Wisut Kasat Rd. ☎ 0-2282-2141. FAX 0-2280-3610. A mid-range hotel near the river north of the Old City. Particularly well placed for the key sights of Dusit. ⫫ ⫫ TV *Rooms:* 181. ▤ 181.	AE MC V	●	●	●	
DUSIT: *Royal Princess.* **Map** 3 A4. ⓑⓑⓑⓑ 269 Lan Luang Rd. ☎ 0-2281-3088. FAX 0-2280-1314. W www.royalprincess.com A luxurious establishment conveniently located for the sights of Dusit and the Old City. Excellent Chinese restaurant, as well as Italian and meticulously prepared Japanese fare. ⫫ ⫫ 24 TV ⛱ *Rooms:* 167. ▤ 167.	AE DC MC V JCB	●	●	●	●
DOWNTOWN: *Niagara.* **Map** 7 B5. ⓑⓑ 26 Soi Suksa Witthaya. ☎ 0-2233-5783. FAX 0-2233-6563. The best low-cost accommodations in the Silom area. Just far enough from Patpong to escape the late-night bar and traffic noise. ⫫ *Rooms:* 90. ▤ 48. ⫫ 24 TV			●	●	
DOWNTOWN: *White Lodge.* **Map** 7 C1. ⓑⓑ 36/8 Soi Kasem San 1. ☎ 0-2216-8867. FAX 0-2216-8228. Clean, friendly, and a good bargain. Located in the center of Siam Square business district. Jim Thompson's House can be found nearby. ⫫ *Rooms:* 26. ▤ 26.			●	●	
DOWNTOWN: *Bangkok Palace.* **Map** 4 F5. W www.bangkokpalace.com ⓑⓑⓑ City Square, 1091/336 New Petchaburi Rd. ☎ 0-2253-0510. FAX 0-2253-0556. Huge complex with special facilities for business travelers, 11 function rooms and a ballroom. ⫫ ⫫ 24 TV ⛱ *Rooms:* 644. ▤ 644.	AE DC MC V JCB	●	●	●	
DOWNTOWN: *Indra Regent.* **Map** 4 E5. ⓑⓑⓑⓑ 120/126 Ratchaprarop Rd. ☎ 0-2208-0022. FAX 0-2208-0388. W www.indrahotel.com Located in the busy Pratunam area, this 1970s hotel has business facilities and luxurious rooms. Most long-distance, air-conditioned, luxury buses to Bangkok stop in this area. ⫫ ⫫ 24 TV ⛱ *Rooms:* 439. ▤ 439.	AE DC MC V JCB	●	●	●	●
DOWNTOWN: *Mandarin Bangkok.* **Map** 7 B3. ⓑⓑⓑⓑ 662 Rama IV Rd. ☎ 0-2238-0231. FAX 0-2237-1620. W www.mandarin-bkk.com This reasonably priced downtown hotel has spacious guest rooms. The breakfast buffet is extensive. ⫫ ⫫ 24 TV ⛱ *Rooms:* 400. ▤ 400.	AE DC MC V JCB	●	●	●	
DOWNTOWN: *Amari Watergate.* **Map** 4 E5. ⓑⓑⓑⓑⓑ 847 Petchaburi Rd. ☎ 0-2653-9000. FAX 0-2653-9045. W www.amari.com Attractive luxury accommodations in the core of the Pratunam business district. This establishment has several in-house restaurants – the Italian regularly attracts high praise. ⫫ ⫫ 24 TV ⛱ *Rooms:* 569. ▤ 569.	AE DC MC V JCB	●	●	●	●
DOWNTOWN: *Asia.* **Map** 3 C5. ⓑⓑⓑⓑⓑ 296 Phaya Thai Rd. ☎ 0-2215-0808. FAX 0-2217-0109. W www.asiahotel.co.th Established in 1964, the Asia has five good restaurants serving Chinese, Vietnamese, and Thai food. Convenient for the Siam Center, Siam Square, and the World Trade Center. ⫫ ⫫ 24 TV ⛱ *Rooms:* 650. ▤ 650.	AE DC MC V JCB	●	●	●	
DOWNTOWN: *Conrad Hotel.* **Map** 8 D3. ⓑⓑⓑⓑⓑ All Seasons Place, 87 Wireless Road. ☎ 0-2690-9999. FAX 0-2190-9000. This hotel is located in the heart of the central business district and within walking distance of the skytrain and Lumphini park. Newly built, modern establishment offering all the luxuries of a five-star hotel. ⫫ ⫫ 24 TV ⛱ *Rooms:* 392. ▤ 392.	AE DC MC V JCB	●	●	●	●
DOWNTOWN: *Dusit Thani.* **Map** 8 D4. ⓑⓑⓑⓑⓑ 946 Rama IV Rd. ☎ 0-2236-9999. FAX 0-2236-6400. W www.dusit.com One of the best views of Bangkok can be seen from the top-floor restaurant. This 23-story hotel has pyramid-style architecture, a relaxing, tree-lined pool area, and eight restaurants. ⫫ ⫫ 24 TV ⛱ *Rooms:* 517. ▤ 517.	AE DC MC V JCB	●	●	●	●

For key to symbols see back flap

Price categories for a standard double room per night, including tax for luxury hotels.

Ⓑ under B350
ⒷⒷ B350–800
ⒷⒷⒷ B800–1,600
ⒷⒷⒷⒷ B1,600–3,200
ⒷⒷⒷⒷⒷ over B3,200

CREDIT CARDS
AE American Express; DC Diners Club; MC MasterCard; V VISA; JCB Japanese Credit Bureau.

WESTERN BATHROOMS
Indicates sit-down, flush toilets; showers and/or baths. Others have squat toilets and trough-and-dipper baths.

COFFEE SHOP
Hotel with coffee shop.

GARDEN/TERRACE
Hotel with garden, courtyard, or terrace.

	CREDIT CARDS	SWIMMING POOL	WESTERN BATHROOMS	COFFEE SHOP	GARDEN/TERRACE

DOWNTOWN: *Four Season Hotel Bangkok.* **Map** 8 D2. ⒷⒷⒷⒷⒷ
155 Ratchadamri Rd. 0-2250-1000. FAX 0-2253-9195.
A world-class, centrally located, luxury hotel offering every facility including yoga and ballroom dancing. 🍴 🍽 24 TV 🛁 *Rooms: 340.* 📋 *340.*
— AE DC MC V JCB — ● ■ ● ■

DOWNTOWN: *Grand Hyatt Erawan.* **Map** 8 D1. ⒷⒷⒷⒷⒷ
494 Ratchadamri Rd. 0-2254-1234. FAX 0-2254-6308. W www.bangkok.hyatt.com
Spacious rooms and luxurious decoration are features of this stylish hotel, which has a four-story atrium and an extensive art collection.
🍴 🍽 24 TV 🛁 *Rooms: 428.* 📋 *428.*
— AE DC MC V JCB — ● ● ● ● ●

DOWNTOWN: *Holiday Inn Silom Bangkok.* **Map** 7 A5. ⒷⒷⒷⒷⒷ
981 Silom Rd. 0-2238-4300. FAX 0-2238-5289. W www.bangkok-silom.holiday-inn.com
Immaculate, marble-clad establishment offering every comfort. Positioned towards the western end of Silom Road near Bangkok's financial, shopping, and sightseeing areas. 🍴 🍽 24 TV 🛁 *Rooms: 726.* 📋 *726.*
— AE DC MC V JCB — ● ● ●

DOWNTOWN: *Montien.* **Map** 7 C3. ⒷⒷⒷⒷⒷ
54 Surawong Rd. 0-2234-8060. FAX 0-2236-5218. W www.montien.com
Rooms are a little plain for this price range, but the location for business and pleasure is perfect: close to Silom business district and just a stone's throw from the nightlife in Patpong. 🍴 🍽 24 TV 🛁 *Rooms: 475.* 📋 *475.*
— AE DC MC V JCB — ● ■ ●

DOWNTOWN: *Nai Lert Park Bangkok.* **Map** 8 E1. ⒷⒷⒷⒷⒷ
2 Witthayu (Wireless) Rd. 0-2253-0123. FAX 0-2253-6509.
Absolutely everything you would expect in a Raffles International hotel; luxury, comfort, taste – there is even a Thai Brahmin fertility shrine in the hotel grounds. 🍴 🍽 24 TV 🛁 *Rooms: 338.* 📋 *338.*
— AE DC MC V JCB — ● ● ● ■

DOWNTOWN: *Oriental.* **Map** 6 F4. ⒷⒷⒷⒷⒷ
48 Oriental Ave. 0-2659-9000. FAX 0-2659-0000. W www.mandarin-oriental.com
Excelling in comfort, elegant decor, and service, this legendary establishment, founded in 1876 *(see p110),* still ranks as one of world's top hotels. Notable, too, are its gardens and river view. 🍴 🍽 24 TV 🛁 *Rooms: 393.* 📋 *393.*
— AE DC MC V JCB — ● ■ ● ■

DOWNTOWN: *Royal Orchid Sheraton.* **Map** 6 F3. ⒷⒷⒷⒷⒷ
2 Captain Bush Lane, Si Praya Rd. 0-2266-0123. FAX 0-2236-8320.
This stylish, spacious, business hotel shares a helicopter service to the airport with the Oriental. There are startlingly good views of the Chao Phraya River from its 28 floors . 🍴 🍽 24 TV 🛁 *Rooms: 740.* 📋 *740.*
— AE DC MC V JCB — ● ● ● ■

THON BURI: *Royal City* W www.royalrivergroup.com ⒷⒷⒷⒷ
800 Borom Ratchonni Rd. 0-2435-8888. FAX 0-2434-3636. This Thon Buri hotel near the Chao Phraya River offers first class accommodations, rather off the beaten track. A garden café and stylish French restaurant add to its appeal. 🍴 🍽 24 TV 🛁 *Rooms: 401.* 📋 *401.*
— AE DC MC V JCB — ● ● ● ■

THON BURI: *Royal River.* **Map** 1 A2. W www.royalrivergroup.com ⒷⒷⒷⒷ
219 Charan Sanit Wong Rd. 0-2422-9222. FAX 0-2433-5880.
Generally considered to be the best, well-facilitated, luxury hotel on the west bank of the Chao Phraya River. 🍴 🍽 24 TV 🛁 *Rooms: 436.* 📋 *436.*
— AE DC MC V JCB — ● ■ ● ■

THON BURI: *Bangkok Marriott Resort & Spa.* **Map** 6 E4. ⒷⒷⒷⒷⒷ
257/1–3 Charoen Nakhon Rd. 0-2476-0022. FAX 0-2476-1120.
Set on the west bank of the Chao Phraya River, this spacious luxury hotel has five restaurants (one international), 11 acres of landscaped gardens, and a hot spa that can take up to ten people. 🍴 🍽 24 TV 🛁 *Rooms: 413.* 📋 *413.*
— AE DC MC V JCB — ● ■ ● ●

FARTHER AFIELD: *Namsin Hotel* Ⓑ
2/16 Kraiphet Rd, Ratchaburi. 0-3233-7551. FAX 0-3233-7633.
This simple Ratchaburi hotel doesn't offer upmarket accomodation, but does provide great value for money. Spacious, comfortable rooms come with either ceiling fans or air conditioning. TV *Rooms: 78.* 📋 *10.*

FARTHER AFIELD: *Ambassador* W www.amtel.co.th ⒷⒷⒷ
171 Soi 11, Sukhumvit Rd. 📞 0-2254-0444. FAX 0-2253-4123.
A good value hotel, with every service, located in the busy heart of
Sukhumvit. This one, though, has a selection of ethnic restaurants on the
ground-floor terrace. 🍴 📶 24 📺 🔒 *Rooms: 750.* 🗐 *750.*
AE DC MC V JCB

FARTHER AFIELD: *Fortune Hotel Bangkok* ⒷⒷⒷⒷ
Fortune Town Building, 1 Ratchadaphisek Rd. 📞 0-2641-1500. FAX 0-2641-1530.
A large and comfortable establishment with a good business center. Has
three Asian-based restaurants, a coffee shop, and a bar. Well located for the
Thailand Cultural Center. 🍴 📶 24 📺 🔒 *Rooms: 406.* 🗐 *406.*
AE DC MC V JCB

FARTHER AFIELD: *Park Hotel* ⒷⒷⒷ
6 Sukhumvit, Soi 7. 📞 0-2255-4300. FAX 0-2255-4309.
Very comfortable indeed – with pool, gym and sauna facilities – yet
reasonably priced for western Sukhumvit. Close proximity to the expressway allows easy access to the airport. 🍴 📶 24 📺 🔒 *Rooms: 139.* 🗐 *139.*
AE DC MC V JCB

FARTHER AFIELD: *Amari Airport* W www.amari.com ⒷⒷⒷⒷⒷ
333 Chert Wudthakas Rd, Don Muang. 📞 0-2566-1020. FAX 0-2566-1941.
A plush hotel connected by walkway to the International and Domestic
terminals of Bangkok Airport and Don Muang train station. Ideal for
passengers in transit, but overpriced. 🍴 📶 24 📺 🔒 *Rooms: 432.* 🗐 *432.*
AE DC MC V JCB

FARTHER AFIELD: *Landmark Plaza.* Map 8 F2. ⒷⒷⒷⒷⒷ
138 Sukhumvit Rd. 📞 0-2254-0404. FAX 0-2253-4259. W landmarkbangkok.com
Near to the National Convention Center and ideal for downtown
Sukhumvit, this extensive complex has a four-floor shopping plaza and
ten quality restaurants. 🍴 📶 24 📺 🔒 *Rooms: 415.* 🗐 *415.*
AE DC MC V JCB

FARTHER AFIELD: *Sukhothai Bangkok.* Map 8 D4. ⒷⒷⒷⒷⒷ
13/3 Sathorn Tai Rd. 📞 0-2344-8888. FAX 0-2344-8889. W www.sukothai.com
A series of courtyards, pagodas, and small ponds peacefully set in six
acres of landscaped gardens make this hotel very attractive. Near the top
of the price range for Bangkok. 🍴 📶 24 📺 🔒 *Rooms: 224.* 🗐 *224.*
AE DC MC V JCB

SOUTH CENTRAL PLAINS

AYUTTHAYA: *New BJ Guest House* Ⓑ
19/29–33 Naresuan Rd. 📞 0-3521-4046.
Centrally located and clean – the best place for budget travelers visiting
Ayutthaya. Bicycle rentals and good food are available. 🍴 *Rooms: 10.* 🗐 *0.*

AYUTTHAYA: *U Thong Inn* ⒷⒷⒷ
210 Rodjana Rd. 📞 0-3524-2236. FAX 0-3524-2235. W www.uthonginn.com
The best-appointed hotel in Ayutthaya, within easy striking distance of all
the most important historical sights. 🍴 📶 24 📺 🔒 *Rooms: 209.* 🗐 *209.*
AE DC MC V

BANG PA-IN: *Phra Intaracha* ⒷⒷ
136 Mu 7, Tambon Chiangraknoi. 📞 0-3536-1081.
Few people stay in Bang Pa-in – it's too convenient a day trip from Bangkok.
But if you do stop here, then this hotel is better than most. *Rooms: 53.* 🗐 *18.*

KANCHANABURI: *Jolly Frog Back-Packers* Ⓑ
28 Soi China Maenam Kwai Rd. 📞 0-3451-4579.
Original name, original concept: a unique bamboo "motel" situated right
on the river bank, with a very popular restaurant. 🍴 *Rooms: 55.* 🗐 *0.*

KANCHANABURI: *Felix River Kwai Resort* ⒷⒷⒷ
9/1 Mu 3, Thamakham. 📞 0-3451-5061. FAX 0-3451-5095.
Luxurious hotel with landscaped gardens, next to the Khwae River.
Facilities include tennis courts, two good-sized swimming pools, and a
private safe in every room. 🍴 📶 24 📺 🔒 *Rooms: 255.* 🗐 *255.*
AE DC MC V

LOP BURI: *Lopburi Inn* ⒷⒷ
28/9 Narai Maharat Rd. 📞 0-3641-2300. FAX 0-3641-2457.
One of the best hotels in the Central Plains, with pleasant, air-conditioned
rooms. However, it is more than 3 km (2 miles) from Lop Buri's historic
sites. 🍴 24 📺 🔒 *Rooms: 126.* 🗐 *126.*
AE MC V

LOP BURI: *Lopburi Inn Resort* ⒷⒷⒷ
114 Phaholyothin Rd. 📞 0-3661-4790. FAX 0-3661-4195.
Opposite Lop Buri Plaza, this is one of the biggest hotels in Lop Buri,
offering good value for money. 🍴 📶 📺 🔒 *Rooms: 90.* 🗐 *90.*
MC V

For key to symbols see back flap

Price categories for a standard double room per night, including tax for luxury hotels.

- (B) under B350
- (B)(B) B350–800
- (B)(B)(B) B800–1,600
- (B)(B)(B)(B) B1,600–3,200
- (B)(B)(B)(B)(B) over B3,200

CREDIT CARDS
AE American Express; DC Diners Club; MC MasterCard; V VISA; JCB Japanese Credit Bureau.

WESTERN BATHROOMS
Indicates sit-down, flush toilets; showers and/or baths. Others have squat toilets and trough-and-dipper baths.

COFFEE SHOP
Hotel with coffee shop.

GARDEN/TERRACE
Hotel with garden, courtyard, or terrace.

Listing	Price	Credit Cards	Swimming Pool	Western Bathrooms	Coffee Shop	Garden/Terrace
NAKHON PATHOM: *Nakhon Inn* 55 Ratwithi Rd. 0-3425-1152. FAX 0-3425-4998. A pleasant, clean place offering all the usual facilities. Without much character, but stylish compared with other options. TV **Rooms:** 70. 70.	(B)(B)			■	●	■
SANGKHLA BURI: *P Guesthouse* 81 Mu 1 Tambon Noog Loo, Sangkhla Buri. 0-3459-5061. FAX 0-3459-5139. This comfortable lakeside guesthouse is beautifully situated for views over the lake to the Mon village. There are also bungalows to rent with views over the lake. **Rooms:** 24. 2.	(B)					

NORTH CENTRAL PLAINS

Listing	Price	Credit Cards	Swimming Pool	Western Bathrooms	Coffee Shop	Garden/Terrace
KAMPHAENG PHET: *Phet Hotel* 90 Wichit Rd. 0-5571-2810. Near the market in the south of Khampaeng Phet, this clean hotel with a small pool offers a good value for the money. 24 TV **Rooms:** 235. 235.	(B)(B)	MC V	●	■	●	■
KAMPHAENG PHET: *Cha Kang Rao* 123/1 Thesa Rd. 0-5571-1315. FAX 0-5571-1326. In the newer part of Khampaeng Phet, yet within easy distance of the old historic city. There are also tennis courts. 24 TV **Rooms:** 90. 90.	(B)(B)(B)	MC V		■	●	
MAE SOT: *Central Mae Sot Hill Hotel* 100 Asia Highway. 0-5553-2601. FAX 0-5553-2600. Features include tennis courts, disco, cocktail lounge, ballroom, supper club, and an excellent restaurant. Children are particularly well catered to, with a water spa and children's pool. 24 TV **Rooms:** 120. 120.	(B)(B)(B)	AE DC MC V	●	■	●	■
PHITSANULOK: *Phitsanulok Youth Hostel* 38 Sanam Bin Rd. 0-5524-2060. This friendly youth hostel occupies an old, jasmine-covered wooden house with a large teak veranda. **Rooms:** 21. 0.	(B)			■		■
PHITSANULOK: *Pailyn* 38 Baromatrailokanart Rd. 0-5525-2412. FAX 0-5525-8185. The best hotel in Phitsanulok, offering luxurious, tastefully furnished rooms, river views, and two restaurants. 24 TV **Rooms:** 240. 240.	(B)(B)(B)	AE MC V		■	●	
SAWANKHALOK: *Muang Inn* 21 Kasem Rat Rd. 0-5564-1753. FAX 0-5564-1662. The only place worth staying in Sawankhalok. Pleasant atmosphere, with good Central Thai cooking available in the restaurant. **Rooms:** 39. 20.	(B)(B)			■		
SUKHOTHAI: *Sawasdiphong* 56/2–5 Singhawat Rd. 0-5561-1567. FAX 0-5561-2268. Clean, comfortable, and unremarkable accommodations in New Sukhothai, though the restaurant is highly rated. **Rooms:** 23. 15.	(B)			■		
SUKHOTHAI: *Thai Village House* 214 Charotvithwong Rd. 0-5561-1049. FAX 0-5561-2583. Attractive teak bungalows owned by the Sukhothai Cultural Center. The only place to stay in Old Sukhothai itself – book ahead. **Rooms:** 80. 80.	(B)(B)	MC V		■		■
SUKHOTHAI: *Ananda Museum Gallery Hotel* 10 Mu 4 Bantum. 0-5562-1885. FAX 0-5562-2428. www.ananda-hotel.com A comfortable mixture of Thai and contemporary-style furnishings adorn this hotel which opened in 2004. 24 TV **Rooms:** 32. 32.	(B)(B)(B)(B)	AE MC V		■		■
TAK: *Wiang Tak* 25/3 Mahathai Bamrung Rd. 0-5551-1950. FAX 0-5551-2169. Tak has only a small number of plain hotels, which line the town's main street. This is the largest and best establishment. **Rooms:** 100. 100.	(B)(B)	AE MC V JCB		■	●	

UMPHANG: *Umphang Country Huts* (B)(B)
141 Mu, 1 Tambon Umphang. [0-5556-1079.
These basic huts on the outskirts of Umphang are the most comfortable
"jungle" accommodations in the province. [] *Rooms: 18.* 目 *0.*

NORTHWEST HEARTLAND

CHIANG DAO: *Chiang Dao Hills* (B)(B)(B)
28 Mu 6, Ping Kong, Chiang Dao. [0-5323-2434. FAX 0-5325-1372.
An isolated and tranquil bungalow resort set in rolling hill country. The
hotel restaurant is highly recommended. [] *Rooms: 36.* 目 *0.*

CHIANG MAI: *Daret's Guest House* (B)
4/5 Chaiyaphum Rd. [0-5323-5440.
Long-established and popular backpacker hangout in the central Tha
Phae Gate area. Good information on activities is provided, and Daret's
restaurant is well known for cheap, non-spicy, tasty fare. [] *Rooms: 28.* 目 *0.*

CHIANG MAI: *Hollanda Montri House* (B)
365 Charoenrat Rd. [0-5324-2450. [W] www.hollandamontri.com
Budget accommodation with private bathrooms, a good standard of
service and wonderful views of the Mae Ping river. [] *Rooms: 16.* 目 *7.*

CHIANG MAI: *Al Farooq* (B)(B)
341 Charoen Prathet Rd. [0-5382-1107. FAX 0-5382-1106.
A mid-range hotel located in Chiang Mai's Muslim neighborhood in the
south of the city. Notable mainly for its restaurant, where vegetarian fare
and excellent halal dishes are prepared. [] 24 TV *Rooms: 85.* 目 *85.*

CHIANG MAI: *Anodard* (B)(B) — MC V
57–59 Ratchamankha Rd. [0-5327-0755. FAX 0-5327-0759.
An old-fashioned hotel in the heart of the walled city. Clean and
unpretentious. [] 24 TV *Rooms: 120.* 目 *42.*

CHIANG MAI: *Baan Jong Come* (B)(B)
47 Tha Phae Rd, Soi 4. [0-5327-4823.
Central but quiet location in one of Chiang Mai's many back lanes. Has a
pleasant garden atmosphere and friendly staff who are well informed on
trekking and other activities in the area. [] *Rooms: 24.* 目 *5.*

CHIANG MAI: *Chatree Guest House* (B)(B) — MC V
11/10 Suriyawong Rd. [0-5327-9221. FAX 0-5327-9085.
This place offers an approachable, relaxed atmosphere rather removed
from its location in the Night Bazaar area. [] 24 TV *Rooms: 120.* 目 *120.*

CHIANG MAI: *Lai Thai Guest House* (B)(B) — AE MC V
111/4–5 Khotchasan Rd. [0-5327-1725. FAX 0-5327-2724.
A guesthouse with good facilities next to the moat surrounding Chiang Mai's
walled city. This is an ideal place to stay during the Songkran Festival in
April, when you can see revelers hurling water. [] 24 TV *Rooms: 120.* 目 *40.*

CHIANG MAI: *Tapae Place* (B)(B) — AE DC MC V JCB
2 Tha Phae Rd, Soi 3. [0-5327-0159. FAX 0-5327-1982.
This hotel has a lot of charm and character and is situated on one of
Chiang Mai's quiet and attractive back lanes. Within easy striking distance
of Tha Phae Gate and the Night Bazaar. [] 24 TV *Rooms: 90.* 目 *90.*

CHIANG MAI: *Top North Guest House* (B)(B) — MC V
15 Mun Muang Rd, Soi 2. [0-5327-8900. FAX 0-5327-8485.
This modern building, with Northern Thai style motifs, is in the old
walled city close to the small bar strip on Mun Muang Road. Provides
motorbike rental as well as trekking services. [] 24 *Rooms: 90.* 目 *50.*

CHIANG MAI: *Diamond Riverside* (B)(B)(B) — AE DC V JCB
33/10 Charoen Prathet Rd. [0-5327-0080. FAX 0-5327-1482.
A luxury hotel by the Ping River right in the city center, within easy walking
distance of the Night Bazaar. A fine, 150-year-old teak house functions as
a restaurant on the grounds. [] [] 24 TV [] *Rooms: 423.* 目 *423.*

CHIANG MAI: *River View Lodge* (B)(B)(B) — MC V
25 Charoen Prathet Rd, Soi 4. [0-5327-1110. FAX 0-5327-9019.
Looks like a large Swiss chalet from the outside, while all the rooms have
touches of traditional Lanna style. The lodge has fine views of the river,
and you can swim in its riverside pool. [] *Rooms: 36.* 目 *36.*

For key to symbols see back flap

Price categories for a standard double room per night, including tax for luxury hotels.

- (B) under B350
- (B)(B) B350–800
- (B)(B)(B) B800–1,600
- (B)(B)(B)(B) B1,600–3,200
- (B)(B)(B)(B)(B) over B3,200

CREDIT CARDS
AE American Express; DC Diners Club; MC MasterCard; V VISA; JCB Japanese Credit Bureau.

WESTERN BATHROOMS
Indicates sit-down, flush toilets; showers and/or baths. Others have squat toilets and trough-and-dipper baths.

COFFEE SHOP
Hotel with coffee shop.

GARDEN/TERRACE
Hotel with garden, courtyard, or terrace.

CHIANG MAI: *Chiang Mai Orchid*   (B)(B)(B)   AE DC MC V JCB
23 Huai Kaeo Rd. 0-5322-2091. FAX 0-5322-1625.
Popular with high society, this long-established, grand hotel has a reputation for fine wine and extensive cellars. Facilities include a health club. Located in the northwest part of town. *Rooms: 364. 364.*

CHIANG MAI: *Lotus*   (B)(B)(B)(B)   AE DC MC V JCB
99/4 Huai Kaeo Rd, Mu 2. 0-5322-4333. FAX 0-5322-4493.
Linked to one of the biggest shopping complexes in Chiang Mai, this hotel attracts visitors who like shopping and nightlife. The adjacent Kad Theater is the largest in Southeast Asia. *Rooms: 690. 690.*

CHIANG MAI: *Novotel Chiang Mai*   (B)(B)(B)   AE DC MC V JCB
183 Chang Puek Rd. 0-5322-5500. FAX 0-5322-5505.
A modern, airy hotel in northern Chiang Mai. The adjacent theme park, run by the hotel, features Mexican food and has fountains, pools, and a wave-making machine. *Rooms: 159. 159.*

CHIANG MAI: *Four Seasons Resort Chiang Mai*   (B)(B)(B)(B)(B)   AE DC MC V JCB
Mae Rim–Samoeng Old Rd. 0-532-98181. FAX 0-5329-8189.
In the Mae Sai valley with 20 acres of landscaped gardens featuring lakes, lily ponds, and terraced rice fields, the Regent has the most spectacular setting of the Chiang Mai luxury hotels. *Rooms: 64. 64.*

CHIANG MAI: *Imperial Chiang Mai Resort*   (B)(B)(B)(B)(B)   AE DC MC V JCB
284 Mu 3, Tambon Don Kaew, Mae Rim. 0-5329-8330. FAX 0-5329-7897.
Fabulous sports facilities with everything available from horseback riding to swimming in the Olympic-size pool. Even if you aren't athletic, its beautiful location is a great draw. *Rooms: 48. 48.*

CHIANG MAI: *Sheraton Chiang Mai*   (B)(B)(B)(B)(B)   AE DC MC V JCB
318/1 Chiang Mai–Lamphun Rd. 0-5327-5300. FAX 0-5327-5299.
The Westin has some of the most expensive rooms in Chiang Mai, which gives it an exclusivity that attracts the rich and famous. Notable guests have included Elizabeth Taylor. *Rooms: 570. 570.*

LAMPHUN: *Suan Kaew Bungalow*   (B)
209 Lamphun–Lampang Highway, Mu 4. No telephone.
Good value, basic hotel just outside a town with little accommodations. A far nicer place to stay than the run-down Si Lamphun Hotel. *Rooms: 8. 0.*

LAMPANG: *Asia Lampang*   (B)(B)   MC V
229 Boonyawat Rd. 0-5422-7844. FAX 0-5422-4436.
An old hotel that has been refurbished to compete with other local establishments like the Wiengthong. Now with an air of plushness, this hotel is still a good bargain. *Rooms: 73. 73.*

LAMPANG: *Lampang Wiengthong*   (B)(B)(B)   AE DC MC V JCB
138/109 Paholyothin Rd. 0-5422-5801. FAX 0-5422-5803.
A luxurious hotel in downtown Lampang, in stark contrast to the town's average, dirty hotels. Very comfortable, with all modern conveniences, including business facilities. *Rooms: 235. 235.*

MAE HONG SON: *Piya Guest House*   (B)
1/1 Khunlum Phrapat Rd. 0-5361-1260. FAX 0-5361-1308.
Perfectly located on the shores of Chong Kham Lake, this is the best place for budget travelers wanting to check out Mae Hong Son's famous early morning mists. For this reason it is often full. *Rooms: 20. 20.*

MAE HONG SON: *Golden Pai & Suite Resort*   (B)(B)(B)   MC V
285 Mu 1 Pangmu. 0-5361-2265. FAX 0-5361-2265.
A Lanna-style resort, close to the Pai river, set in beautiful mountain scenery for an authentic back-to-nature experience. *Rooms: 63. 63.*

MAE HONG SON: *Imperial Tara*　　　　ⒷⒷⒷⒷ
149 Mu 8, Tambon Pang Mu. 📞 0-5368-4444. ℻ 0-5368-4440.
In the heart of trekking country, a short distance out of town, is this
resort hotel with grand Northern architecture. It is set in landscaped,
tropical gardens. 🍴 📺 📺 🔧 *Rooms: 104.* 📋 *104.*

| | AE DC MC V JCB | ● | ■ | ● | ■ |

MAE HONG SON: *Rooks Holiday Resort & Hotel*　　　　ⒷⒷⒷⒷ
114/5–7 Khunlum Phrapat Rd. 📞 0-5361-2324. ℻ 0-5361-1524.
Nestling at the foot of Doi Kong Mu, there is a choice of detached
bungalows or modern rooms. 🍴 24 📺 🔧 *Rooms: 114.* 📋 *114.*

| | AE DC MC V | ● | ■ | ● | ■ |

PAI: *Rim Pai Cottages*　　　　ⒷⒷ
17, Mu 3, Viang Tai Rd. 📞 0-5369-9133. ℻ 0-5369-9234.
The best place to stay in the small town of Pai, by the river. Thai houses
are available. The price includes breakfast. 🍴 *Rooms: 37.* 📋 *7.*

| | | | ■ | | ■ |

FAR NORTH

CHIANG KHONG: *Ruanthai Sophapan*　　　　Ⓑ
83 Mu 8 Sai Klang Rd. 📞 0-5379-1023. ℻ 0-5379-1446.
A handful of clean and attractive rooms in a teak house. Its terrace, right
on the bank of the Mekong, allows good views of Laos. 🍴 *Rooms: 40.* 📋 *40.*

| | | | ■ | | |

CHIANG RAI: *Boonbundan Guest House*　　　　Ⓑ
1005/13 Chet Yot Rd. 📞 0-5371-7040. ℻ 0-5371-2914.
In a quiet, shaded area not far from the town center, and with an
attractive outdoor restaurant. Fans cool down the bungalows; air-
conditioning is in the newer, main building. 🍴 *Rooms: 53.* 📋 *16.*

| | | | ■ | | |

CHIANG RAI: *Golden Triangle Inn*　　　　ⒷⒷ
590/2 Paholyothin Rd. 📞 0-5371-1339. ℻ 0-5371-3936.
A mid-range hotel with a Japanese garden and rooms in traditional Thai
decor. The price includes American breakfast. 🍴 *Rooms: 31.* 📋 *31.*

| | MC V | | ■ | ● | ■ |

CHIANG RAI: *Dusit Island Resort*　　　　ⒷⒷⒷⒷ
1129 Kraisora Sit Rd. 📞 0-5371-5777. ℻ 0-5371-5801. 🌐 www.dusit.com
Set on an island in the middle of the Kok River, and so a great place from
which to view the river activity, this attractive hotel has a relaxed atmosphere
and a lovely outdoor restaurant. 🍴 📺 24 📺 🔧 *Rooms: 271.* 📋 *271.*

| | AE DC MC V JCB | ● | ■ | ● | ■ |

CHIANG RAI: *Little Duck*　　　　ⒷⒷⒷⒷ
199 Paholyothin Rd. 📞 0-5371-5620. ℻ 0-5371-5639. @ chitpong@chmai.loxinfo.co.th
Despite its name, this is not a little place at all, rather, a massive hotel complex wedded to a shopping mall with many facilities, including a pool hall
and convention rooms. 🍴 24 📺 🔧 *Rooms: 330.* 📋 *330.*

| | AE DC MC V JCB | ● | ■ | ● | ■ |

CHIANG RAI: *Rimkok Resort Hotel*　　　　ⒷⒷⒷⒷ
6 Mu 4, Thaton Rd. 📞 0-5371-6445. ℻ 0-5371-5859.
On the banks of the Mae Kok river and only 5 km from downtown and the
airport. Excellent service, meticulous rooms, and comprehensive facilties. Its
Thai restaurant is one of the best in town. 🍴 🔧 24 📺 *Rooms: 256.* 📋 *256.*

| | AE MC V D | ● | ■ | ● | ■ |

CHIANG RAI: *Wiang Inn*　　　　ⒷⒷⒷⒷ
893 Paholyothin Rd. 📞 0-5371-1533. ℻ 0-5371-1877.
A fairly typical, large, provincial hotel with every sort of facility including
disco and masseurs. 🍴 24 📺 🔧 *Rooms: 260.* 📋 *260.*

| | AE DC MC V JCB | ● | ■ | ● | |

CHIANG SAEN: *Gin's Guest House*　　　　Ⓑ
71 Chiang Saen–Sop Ruak Rd Mu 8. 📞 0-5365-0847. ℻ 0-5365-1023.
Set in a lychee orchard, this guesthouse offers secluded, pretty bungalows
and bicycles for visiting the Golden Triangle. 🍴 *Rooms: 13.* 📋 *0.*

| | | | ■ | | ■ |

DOI MAE SALONG (SANTIKHIREE): *Mae Salong Resort*　　　　ⒷⒷ
Chiang Rai–Mae Chan Rd. 📞 0-5376-5014. ℻ 0-5376-5135.
The best hotel with the finest views, over the mountains on the Thai-
Burmese border, in a beautiful, remote town. The restaurant has a
considerable reputation for Yunnanese food. 🍴 24 📺 *Rooms: 92.* 📋 *0.*

| | MC V | | ■ | | ■ |

GOLDEN TRIANGLE: *The Imperial Golden Triangle Resort*　　　　ⒷⒷⒷⒷ
222 Golden Triangle, Sop Ruak. 📞 0-5378-4001. ℻ 0-5378-4006.
All rooms at this comfortable hotel overlook the river and offer a
lovely view of the Golden Triangle – the confluence of the Ruak and
Mekong rivers. The excellent restaurant serves both Thai and
Western cuisine. 🍴 24 📺 🔧 *Rooms: 73.* 📋 *73.*

| | AE DC MC V | ● | ■ | ● | ■ |

For key to symbols see back flap

Price categories for a standard double room per night, including tax for luxury hotels.

- (B) under B350
- (B)(B) B350–800
- (B)(B)(B) B800–1,600
- (B)(B)(B)(B) B1,600–3,200
- (B)(B)(B)(B)(B) over B3,200

CREDIT CARDS
AE American Express; DC Diners Club; MC MasterCard; V VISA; JCB Japanese Credit Bureau.

WESTERN BATHROOMS
Indicates sit-down, flush toilets; showers and/or baths. Others have squat toilets and trough-and-dipper baths.

COFFEE SHOP
Hotel with coffee shop.

GARDEN/TERRACE
Hotel with garden, courtyard, or terrace.

	CREDIT CARDS	SWIMMING POOL	WESTERN BATHROOMS	COFFEE SHOP	GARDEN/TERRACE
GOLDEN TRIANGLE: *Anantara Resort & Spa Golden Triangle* (B)(B)(B)(B) 229 Mu 1, Golden Triangle, Sop Ruak. ☎ 0-5378-4086. FAX 0-5378-4090. Probably one of Northern Thailand's most luxurious hotels, designed in traditional style. A lively resort specializing in mountain biking, elephant rides, boat trips, and assorted tours. 🍴 🛎 24 TV 🏊 *Rooms: 110.* ▤ 110.	AE DC MC V JCB	●	■	●	■
MAE SAI: *Mae Sai Plaza* (B) 386/2 Sailomchoi Rd. ☎ 0-5373-2230. Having the appearance of a medieval fortress, this extraordinary collection of rooms and huts is built into the side of a cliff. Views of the river toward Burma are captivating. 🍴 *Rooms: 60.* ▤ 0.			■		
MAE SAI: *Mae Sai Guest House* (B)(B) 688 Paholyothin Rd. ☎ 0-5373-2021. Attractive, relaxing bungalow accommodations by the fascinating Sai River. So close to Burma that you can watch the women washing clothes on the opposite bank each morning. 🍴 TV *Rooms: 25.* ▤ 0.			■		■
NAN: *Sukkasem* (B) 119–121 Ananta Worarittidet Rd. ☎ 0-5471-0141. FAX 0-5477-1581. A basic, ferro-concrete hotel in history-steeped Nan, with little to recommend it but low price and relatively clean rooms. 🍴 *Rooms: 42.* ▤ 4.			■		
NAN: *Dheveraj* (B)(B)(B) 446 Sumon Dheveraj Rd. ☎ 0-5471-0094. FAX 0-5471-1365. The best hotel in Nan, albeit somewhat in need of modernization. Built around a courtyard featuring a fountain. Large, clean rooms and friendly staff. 🍴 24 TV *Rooms: 154.* ▤ 115.	MC V		■	●	
PHRAE: *Mae Yom Palace* (B)(B) 181/6 Yantrakit Koson Rd. ☎ 0-5452-1029. FAX 0-5452-2904. Definitely the best hotel in town, offering tours to hill-tribe villages. Well run, amiable, and with spotless rooms. 🍴 24 TV 🏊 *Rooms: 104.* ▤ 104.	AE MC V	●	■	●	■
PHRAE: *Nakhon Phrae Tower* (B)(B) 3 Muang Hit Rd. ☎ 0-5452-1321. FAX 0-5452-3503. This highrise hotel has comfortable rooms with all modern facilities. Tours can be organized to visit hill-tribe villages and nearby craft centers. 🍴 24 TV 🏊 *Rooms: 139.* ▤ 139.	AE DC MC V JCB		■	●	■
THA TON: *Mae Kok River Lodge* (B)(B)(B) 3 Chiang Mai–Fang Rd. ☎ 0-5345-9328. FAX 0-5345-9329. A small hotel in a beautiful, remote location, by the Burmese border. Specializes in "Track of the Tiger" trekking. 🍴 *Rooms: 22.* ▤ 0.	AE MC V		■		
KHORAT PLATEAU					
BURIRUM: *Wong Tong* (B)(B)(B) 512/1 Chira Rd. ☎ 0-4461-2540. FAX 0-4462-0859. Right in the city center, this three-story hotel provides a high standard of service. Rooms are decorated in Northern style. 🍴 TV *Rooms: 71.* ▤ 71.	MC V		■	●	
CHAIYAPHUM: *Lertnimitra* (B) 447/1 Nivesrat Rd. ☎ 0-4481-1522. FAX 0-4482-2335. Chaiyaphum is the most convenient base for visiting the nearby silk villages. This hotel offers some air-conditioned bungalows as well as fan and air-conditioned rooms in the main building. 🍴 TV *Rooms: 79.* ▤ 59.	MC V JCB		■	●	
KHON KAEN: *Suksawat* (B) 4/3 Klang Muang Rd. ☎ 0-4323-6472. An old wooden building located on the quiet back streets of this busy Northeastern city. No special facilities, but with more personality and character than many of the larger establishments. *Rooms: 38.* ▤ 0.			■		■

KHON KAEN: *Khon Kaen* (B)(B)
43/2 Pimpasute Rd. [C] 0-4323-7177. FAX 0-4324-2458.
Large, modern hotel with nightclub and karaoke. The restaurant serves good Thai, Western, and Japanese fare. [] [24] [TV] **Rooms:** 134. 134.
AE DC MC V

KHORAT: *Doctor's House* (B)
79 Sup Siri Rd, Soi 4. [C] 0-4425-5846.
Fine, very reasonably priced rooms, and a relaxing garden seating area. Helpful staff are always glad to give you information on local area. Guests keep coming back because of the family atmosphere. [] **Rooms:** 4. 0.

KHORAT: *Siri* (B)
688 Pho Klang Rd. [C] 0-4424-2831.
Quiet and friendly accommodations, popular with budget travelers. On the ground floor is the Veterans of Foreign Wars Café – Khorat was a US air base during the Vietnam War. Serves US-style fast food. [] **Rooms:** 40. 10.

KHORAT: *Royal Princess* (B)(B)(B)
1137 Sura Nari Rd. [C] 0-4425-6629. FAX 0-4425-6601.
Luxurious hotel decorated tastefully in Northeastern Thai style. The Empress Chinese restaurant is excellent; it has a reputation for serving good local food, too. [] [24] [TV] [] **Rooms:** 188. 188.
AE DC MC V JCB

KHORAT: *Sima Thani* (B)(B)(B)
Mittraphap Rd. [C] 0-4421-3100. FAX 0-4421-3121.
The top hotel in Khorat, but quite far from the center of town. All modern facilities, very spacious, and with a pleasant garden atrium dotted with Khmer-style sculptures. [] [] [24] [TV] [] **Rooms:** 265. 265.
AE DC MC V JCB

PHIMAI: *Old Phimai Guest House* (B)
214 Mu 1 Chomsudasadet Rd. [C] 0-4447-1918.
Under friendly management, and with a tranquil atmosphere, this enchanting wooden guesthouse has attractive bedrooms and a pleasant roof garden. Very close to the temple at Phimai. [] **Rooms:** 8. 2.

ROI ET: *Saket Nakorn Hotel* (B)(B)
60–80 Haisok Rd. [C] & FAX 0-4351-1741.
A typical Thai provincial hotel: clean, but plain. Ask for rooms away from the road, which can be noisy at night. [] [24] [TV] **Rooms:** 151. 151.
MC V JCB

SURIN: *Petchkasem* (B)(B)(B)
104 Chitbumrung Rd. [C] 0-4451-1274. FAX 0-4451-4041.
Medium-sized luxurious hotel with large, air-conditioned rooms, good business facilities, and attentive staff. [] [24] [TV] [] **Rooms:** 162. 162.
MC V

SURIN: *Tong Tarin* (B)(B)(B)
60 Sirirat Rd. [C] 0-4451-4281. FAX 0-4451-1580.
Surin's top hotel, located slightly out of town. It has a cool, airy feel with a marble atrium and all the usual trappings and facilities of a luxury hotel. [] [24] [TV] **Rooms:** 240. 240.
MC V

UDON THANI: *Charoen* (B)(B)(B)
549 Phosri Rd. [C] 0-4224-8155. FAX 0-4224-1093.
The Charoen is a large, well-appointed business hotel with air-conditioned rooms and glitzy bar and disco. [] [24] [TV] [] **Rooms:** 250. 250.
AE DC MC V

UDON THANI: *Charoensri Grand Royal* (B)(B)(B)
277/1 Prajak Rd. [C] 0-4234-3555. FAX 0-4234-3550.
Luxury tower hotel providing the best accommodations for miles around. Lacks character, but its clean, spacious bedrooms with good views from the upper floors more than make up. [] [] [24] [TV] [] **Rooms:** 255. 255.
MC V JCB

MEKONG RIVER VALLEY

CHIANG KHAN: *Nong Sam Guest House* (B)
407 Mui, Rim Kong Rd. [C] 0-4282-1457.
Very friendly establishment run by an Englishman and his Thai wife, consisting of large, comfortable, screened rooms in brick and wood bungalows. Try the delicious, home-cooked Thai food. [] **Rooms:** 5. 0.

LOEI: *Phuluang* (B)(B)
55 Charoen Rat Rd. [C] 0-4281-1532. FAX 0-4281-2558.
A typical upcountry Thai hotel – clean, spartan rooms complemented by adequate facilities and a small nightclub. [] [TV] **Rooms:** 78. 78.

Price categories for a standard double room per night, including tax for luxury hotels. **B** under B350 **BB** B350–800 **BBB** B800–1,600 **BBBB** B1,600–3,200 **BBBBB** over B3,200	**CREDIT CARDS** AE American Express; DC Diners Club; MC MasterCard; V VISA; JCB Japanese Credit Bureau. **WESTERN BATHROOMS** Indicates sit-down, flush toilets; showers and/or baths. Others have squat toilets and trough-and-dipper baths. **COFFEE SHOP** Hotel with coffee shop. **GARDEN/TERRACE** Hotel with garden, courtyard, or terrace.	CREDIT CARDS	SWIMMING POOL	WESTERN BATHROOMS	COFFEE SHOP	GARDEN/TERRACE

	CREDIT CARDS	SWIMMING POOL	WESTERN BATHROOMS	COFFEE SHOP	GARDEN/TERRACE
MUKDAHAN: *Hua Nam* **B** 36 Samut Sakdarak Rd. 0-4261-1197. No facilities whatsoever, but clean and reasonably priced, with large rooms. Close to the pier for Suwannakhet in Laos. **Rooms:** 30. 10.					
MUKDAHAN: *Mukdahan* **B** 8/8 Samut Sakdarat Rd. 0-4261-1619. This is a no-frills hotel, just out of town near the river, but it is clean and friendly, and Northeastern food is available. **Rooms:** 43. 43.			■	●	■
MUKDAHAN: *Mukdahan Grand* **BBB** 78 Songnang Sathit Rd. 0-4261-2025. FAX 0-4261-2021. With good views across the Mekong to Suwannakhet in Laos and high standards unmatched in Mukdahan. 24 TV Rooms: 203. 203.	AE MC V		■	●	■
NAKHON PHANOM: *River Inn* **B** 19 Apiban Bancha Rd. 0-4251-1305. A rather shabby and run-down hotel in one of Thailand's oldest towns, but well located beside the Mekong River. **Rooms:** 16. 8.			■	●	■
NAKHON PHANOM: *Maenam Khong Grand View* **BBB** 527 Sunthorn Wichit Rd. 0-4251-3564. Nakhon Phanom's most luxurious accommodations, with every modern convenience. Spectacular views across the Mekong River to Laos make staying here a memorable experience. 24 TV Rooms: 116. 116.	DC MC V		■	●	■
NONG KHAI: *Mut Mee Guest House* **B** 1111/4 Kaew Worawut Rd. 0-4246-0717. FAX 0-4241-2182. @ mutmee@mutmee.com In a beautiful mango orchard overlooking the Mekong, this welcoming establishment, run by an Englishman and his Thai wife, consists of rooms or bamboo huts. Bicycles can be rented. **Rooms:** 28. 0.					■
NONG KHAI: *Nong Khai Grand* **BBB** 589 Nong Khai–Ponephisai Rd. 0-4242-0033. FAX 0-4241-2026. A mid-range hotel to the south of the main city on the route to Wat Khaek. Facilities include a disco. 24 TV Rooms: 130. 130.	AE DC MC V JCB	●	■	●	
NONG KHAI: *Royal Mekhong Nong Khai* **BBB** 222 Had Jommani Rd. 0-4242-0024. FAX 0-4242-1280. A luxurious, riverside establishment near the Friendship Bridge, which opened in 1993 in anticipation of the increased number of visitors crossing to and from Laos. 24 TV Rooms: 208. 208.	AE DC MC V JCB	●	■	●	
THAT PHANOM: *Chai Wan Hotel* **B** 38 Phanom Phanarak Rd. 0-4254-1391. A traditional Thai hotel built around an inner courtyard. All the rooms are fan-cooled and private Thai-style bathrooms are available. **Rooms:** 20. 0.					■
PHU KRADUNG: *Phu Kradung National Park Bungalows* **BB** Phu Kradung National Park. 0-2562-0760. Attractive, well-appointed bungalows arranged in the lee of a hill in the middle of the national park. Book well in advance. **Houses:** 16. 0.			■		■
UBON RATCHATHANI: *Tokyo* **B** 360 Upparat Rd. 0-4524-1739. FAX 0-4526-3140. The Tokyo is a friendly, reasonably priced hotel with clean rooms. Popular, despite lacking distinguishing features. **Rooms:** 70. 10.			■		
UBON RATCHATHANI: *Regent Palace* **BB** 265–271 Chayankun Rd. 0-4524-5046 or 0-452-45047. FAX 0-4524-5597. Facilities include a billiards club and a cocktail lounge. The hotel is clean, comfortable and quiet, but not particularly inspiring. 24 TV Rooms: 120. 120.	MC V		■	●	

UBON RATCHATHANI: *Pathumrat* ⒷⒷⒷ — AE MC V
337 Chayangkun Rd. 【 0-4524-1501. 𝐅𝐀𝐗 0-4524-2311.
A luxury hotel, close to the town center. Favored by tour companies, facilities include a disco and nightclub. 🍴 24 TV *Rooms: 169.* 🗐 *169.*

EASTERN SEABOARD

BANG SAEN: *Bang Saen Resort* ⒷⒷⒷ — V
325 Longhaet Rd, Chonburi. 【 0-3838-1772. 𝐅𝐀𝐗 0-3838-1772.
One of several resort hotels north of Si Racha, but the only one which is actually on the beach. Facilities include a swimming pool and cool airy restaurant. 🍴 TV 🛏 *Rooms: 74.* 🗐 *74.*

CHANTHABURI: *Chanthaburi Riverside* ⒷⒷ — V
63 Mu 9, Chantanimit Rd. 【 0-3931-1726. 𝐅𝐀𝐗 0-3931-1726.
A very plush resort hotel near the river, with courteous, efficient staff and good attention to detail. With regard to facilities, it has just about everything, including its own botanical garden. 🍴 24 TV *Rooms: 72.* 🗐 *72.*

CHANTHABURI: *KP Grand* ⒷⒷⒷ — AE DC MC V JCB
35/200–201 Trirat Rd. 【 0-3932-3201. 𝐅𝐀𝐗 0-3932-3215.
Luxurious and spacious hotel offering perhaps the best accommodations in town. Try the sticky rice and durian at the restaurant when this fruit is in season (Mar–May). 🍴 🍸 24 TV 🛏 *Rooms: 202.* 🗐 *202.*

KO CHANG: *White Sand Beach Resort* ⒷⒷ
Hat Sai Khao. 【 0-1863-7737, 0-1865-0375. 𝐅𝐀𝐗 0-9244-8954.
Paradise – sturdy bungalows for 2–8 people roofed with nipa palm; hammocks strung between palm trees, and white coral sands. 🍴 *Rooms: 99.* 🗐 *0.*

KO CHANG: *Ko Chang Resort & Spa* ⒷⒷⒷⒷ — AE DC MC V
Klong Prao Beach. 【 0-3955-1082 𝐅𝐀𝐗 0-3955-7080.
Lovely bungalows set amid leaning palms overlooking the South China Sea – a Robinson Crusoe-style getaway. 🍴 TV 🛏 *Rooms: 145.* 🗐 *145.*

KO SAMET: *Naga* Ⓑ
Ao Hin Kok. 【 0-3861-4035.
Simple bungalows set on a low hill overlooking Hin Kok bay. The attached restaurant sells delicious homemade bread and cakes. 🍴 *Rooms: 29.* 🗐 *0.*

KO SAMET: *Ao Kiu Coral Beach Bungalows* ⒷⒷ
Ao Kui Na Nok. 【 & 𝐅𝐀𝐗 0-3865-2491.
Set right on the quietest beach on the island, the bungalows at Ao Kiu Na Nok are friendly, clean, and well built, with hot water. Less expensive huts and bungalows are also available. 🍴 *Rooms: 27.* 🗐 *0.*

KO SAMET: *Wongduan Resort* ⒷⒷ — MC V
Ao Wong Duan. 【 0-3865-1777. 𝐅𝐀𝐗 0-3865-1819.
Comfortable bungalow resort next to the calm, azure waters of Wong Duan bay. Unfortunately, the peace is often broken by jet-skiers. It is out of the price range of most backpackers. 🍴 *Rooms: 54.* 🗐 *30.*

KO SAMET: *Saikaew Villa* ⒷⒷⒷⒷ — MC V JCB
Hat Sai Kaew. 【 0-3864-4144. 𝐅𝐀𝐗 0-3864-4012.
Located at the heart of Saikaew Beach and offering a variety of bungalows. All accommodation is fully equipped with 24-hour electricity and water supply. Beautiful surroundings. 🍴 *Rooms: 100.* 🗐 *49.*

KO SAMET: *Moo Ban Talay* ⒷⒷⒷⒷ — AE DC MC V JCB
Ao Noi Na. 【 0-1838-8682. 𝐅𝐀𝐗 0-3864-4251. ⓦ www.moobantalay.com
Each bungalow here is built on stilts and to a unique design. Occupying a long stretch of private beach, the resort provides water sports courses and free resort transfers four times a day. 🍴 TV *Rooms: 11.* 🗐 *11.*

PATTAYA: *Diamond Beach* ⒷⒷ — AE DC MC V JCB
South Pattaya. 【 0-3842-9885. 𝐅𝐀𝐗 0-3842-4888.
If you want to stay in the vibrant heart of South Pattaya's "strip," then this is the place for you. A beauty salon, videotheque, and massage parlor are among the facilities. 🍴 🍸 24 TV 🛏 *Rooms: 138.* 🗐 *138.*

PATTAYA: *Diana Inn* ⒷⒷ — AE MC V
Central Pattaya. 【 0-3842-9675. 𝐅𝐀𝐗 0-3842-4566.
Friendly, clean, and very good value. The restaurant has a wide range of reasonably priced Thai and Western fare. 🍴 24 TV *Rooms: 111.* 🗐 *111.*

Price categories for a standard double room per night, including tax for luxury hotels.
- Ⓑ under B350
- ⒷⒷ B350–800
- ⒷⒷⒷ B800–1,600
- ⒷⒷⒷⒷ B1,600–3,200
- ⒷⒷⒷⒷⒷ over B3,200

CREDIT CARDS
AE American Express; DC Diners Club; MC MasterCard; V VISA; JCB Japanese Credit Bureau.

WESTERN BATHROOMS
Indicates sit-down, flush toilets; showers and/or baths. Others have squat toilets and trough-and-dipper baths.

COFFEE SHOP
Hotel with coffee shop.

GARDEN/TERRACE
Hotel with garden, courtyard, or terrace.

	CREDIT CARDS	SWIMMING POOL	WESTERN BATHROOMS	COFFEE SHOP	GARDEN/TERRACE
PATTAYA: _Little Duck Pattaya Resort_ ⒷⒷ 336/22 Pattaya Klang Rd. 📞 0-3842-8065. FAX 0-3842-6043. This hi-tech, medium-sized hotel is located in the center of Pattaya's entertainment area. Hosts a popular disco. 🍴 24 📺 **Rooms: 146.** 🛏 146.	AE DC MC V	●	■	●	
PATTAYA: _Mermaid's Beach Resort_ ⒷⒷ 75/102 Mu 12, Nong Pru Jomtien Beach Rd. 📞 0-3823-2210. FAX 0-3823-1906. One of the best run and most attractive hotels on family-oriented Jomtien beach, with a good reputation for fresh seafood. 🍴 📺 **Rooms: 112.** 🛏 112.	AE DC MC V	●	■	●	■
PATTAYA: _Peace Resort_ ⒷⒷ 179/40 Mu 5, Pattaya–Naklua Rd. 📞 0-3842-6605. FAX 0-3842-6607. As the name suggests, this is a refuge from the noisy, southern part of town. The landscaped gardens are lovely. 🍴 24 📺 🛏 **Rooms: 80.** 🛏 80.	MC V	●	■	●	■
PATTAYA: _Palm Garden_ ⒷⒷ 240/1 Mu 9, Pattaya 2nd Rd. 📞 0-3842-9386. FAX 0-3842-9188. Located in the quiet, northern part of town, this hotel is clean, reasonably priced, and has attractive gardens. 🍴 24 📺 **Rooms: 115.** 🛏 115.	AE MC V	●	■	●	■
PATTAYA: _Grand Jomtien Palace_ ⒷⒷⒷ 356 Jomtien Beach Rd. 📞 0-3823-1405. FAX 0-3823-1402. Situated far down Jomtien Road to the south of Pattaya's bustling night life, with fine views across Jomtien bay. 🍴 24 📺 🛏 **Rooms: 252.** 🛏 252.	AE MC V	●	■	●	■
PATTAYA: _Woodland Resort_ ⒷⒷⒷ 164/1 Mu 5, Pattaya–Naklua Rd. 📞 0-3842-1707. FAX 0-3842-5663. Attractive colonial-lodge style resort set in well-maintained gardens far from the traffic fumes of central Pattaya. 🍴 24 📺 🛏 **Rooms: 135.** 🛏 135.	AE DC MC V	●	■	●	■
PATTAYA: _Amari Orchid Resort_ ⒷⒷⒷⒷ 204 Mu 5, Pattaya Beach Rd. 📞 0-3842-8161. FAX 0-3842-8165. 🌐 www.amari.com/orchid Situated in extensive grounds at the quiet, north end of Pattaya's crescent-shaped bay, hidden from noisy discos and beer bars. The resort has Asian and Western restaurants. 🍴 24 📺 🛏 **Rooms: 236.** 🛏 236.	AE DC MC V	●	■	●	■
PATTAYA: _A-One Royal Cruise_ ⒷⒷⒷⒷ 499 Beach Rd North. 📞 0-3825-9500. FAX 0-3842-4242. Designed to resemble a cruise liner, with spectacular views of Pattaya bay. Facilities include a disco, barber shop, beauty shop, and shopping arcade. 🍴 🍷 24 📺 🛏 **Rooms: 200.** 🛏 200.	AE DC MC V JCB	●	■	●	
PATTAYA: _Asia Pattaya_ ⒷⒷⒷⒷ Pratumnak Rd. 📞 0-3825-0401. FAX 0-2215-2642. On a low cliff overlooking Ao Noi or "little bay" is this very private, very exclusive, hotel with good views. Facilities include tennis courts, a golf course, and water sports equipment. 🍴 🍷 24 📺 🛏 **Rooms: 320.** 🛏 320.	V	●	■	●	■
PATTAYA: _Central Wong Amat_ ⒷⒷⒷⒷ 277–8 Mu 5, Pattaya–Naklua Rd. 📞 0-3842-6999. FAX 0-3842-8599. Well-appointed establishment with everything on the premises from videotheque to tennis courts. 🍴 24 📺 🛏 **Rooms: 178.** 🛏 178.	AE DC MC V JCB	●	■	●	■
PATTAYA: _Royal Cliff Beach Resort_ ⒷⒷⒷⒷⒷ 353 Mu 12, Pratumnak Rd. 📞 0-3825-0421. FAX 0-3825-0511. 🌐 www.royalcliff.com Quite simply an institution. Every conceivable facility, including four swimming pools and eight restaurants, and set on top of a cliff overlooking Jomtien bay. 🍴 🍷 24 📺 🛏 **Rooms: 1,072.** 🛏 1,072.	AE DC MC V JCB	●	■	●	■
RAYONG: _Rayong_ Ⓑ 65/1–3 Sukhumvit Rd. 📞 0-3861-1073. A reasonably priced Thai hotel with a friendly staff and clean rooms. Restaurant and food stalls nearby. **Rooms: 51.** 🛏 14.			■		■

RAYONG: *Purimas Beach Hotel & Spa*   ⓑⓑ
4/5 Mu 3, Pae Klang Kam Rd. 【 0-3863-0382. FAX 0-3863-0380. W www.purimas.com
With its own private beach, overlooking the Gulf of Siam, Purimas offers
quiet efficiency with five-star facilities and impeccable service. 🍴 📠 TV
🔒 *Rooms: 79.* 🗒 *79.*

| | AE MC V JCB | ● | ■ | ● | ■ |

RAYONG: *Hin Suay Nam Sai*   ⓑⓑⓑⓑ
250 Mu 2, Klang. 【 0-3863-8264. FAX 0-3863-8034. W www.hinsuaynamsai.com
Luxury resort set in landscaped grounds with a private beach. A haven
for racket sports enthusiasts. 🍴 📠 24 TV 🔒 *Rooms: 174.* 🗒 *174.*

| | AE DC MC V JCB | ● | ■ | ● | ■ |

RAYONG: *Novotel Coralia Rimpae*   ⓑⓑⓑⓑ
4/5 Mu 3, Pae Klang Kam Rd. 【 0-3864-8008. FAX 0-3864-8002.
A spectacularly well-appointed resort hotel, which is not at all unusual
along this part of Thailand's Gulf coast, but in this case there are no less
than four swimming pools. 🍴 📠 24 TV 🔒 *Rooms: 189.* 🗒 *189.*

| | AE MC V JCB | ● | ■ | ● | ■ |

TRAT: *Laem Ngop Inn*   ⓑ
19/14 Tambon Laem Ngop. 【 0-3959-7044. FAX 0-3959-7144.
For most people Laem Ngop will be no more than a brief halt on the
way to or from Ko Chang. This basic hotel is actually the best in Trat
province, and it has lovely views of Ko Chang. TV *Rooms: 31.* 🗒 *26.*

| | | | ■ | | |

TRAT: *Muang Trat*   ⓑⓑ
40 Wichitjanya Rd. 【 0-3951-1091.
An unremarkable hotel located in downtown Trat, but it is clean and
comfortable and has a courteous staff. 🍴 TV *Rooms: 144.* 🗒 *65.*

| | MC V | | ■ | | |

WESTERN SEABOARD

CHA-AM: *Santisuk Bungalows and Beach Resort*   ⓑⓑⓑ
263/3 Ruamchit Rd. 【 0-3247-1212.
Tastefully decorated, popular and reasonably priced establishment
offering both rooms and bungalow accommodations. 🍴 *Rooms: 62.* 🗒 *3.*

| | MC V | | ■ | ● | ■ |

CHA-AM: *Beach Garden*   ⓑⓑⓑⓑ
949/21 Cha-am Beach. 【 0-3247-1334. FAX 0-3247-1291.
South of central Cha-am on a clean, wide beach, this hotel offers water
sports, four swimming pools, tennis, fishing, and miniature golf. It is
favored by European tour groups. 📠 24 TV 🔒 *Rooms: 230.* 🗒 *230.*

| | AE DC MC V JCB | ● | ■ | ● | ■ |

CHA-AM: *Cha-am Methavalai*   ⓑⓑⓑ
220 Ruamchit Rd. 【 0-3243-3250. FAX 0-3243-1590. W www.methavalai.com
Well suited to families, with several multiroomed bungalows. Clean,
quiet, and attractive. 🍴 24 TV 🔒 *Rooms: 215.* 🗒 *215.*

| | AE DC MC V | ● | ■ | ● | ■ |

CHA-AM: *Regent Cha-am*   ⓑⓑⓑⓑ
849/21 Phetkasem Rd. 【 0-3245-1240. FAX 0-3247-1492. W www.regent-chaam.com
Luxurious hotel and cottage accommodations on an enormous site –
about 300 acres altogether – almost a village in its own right. Facilities
include squash and tennis courts. 🍴 📠 24 TV 🔒 *Rooms: 700.* 🗒 *700.*

| | AE DC MC V JCB | ● | ■ | ● | ■ |

CHA-AM: *Dusit Resort and Polo Club* @ polo@dusit.com   ⓑⓑⓑⓑ
1349 Phetkasem Rd. 【 0-3252-0009. FAX 0-3252-0296. W www.dusit.com
A stylish resort with an English country and polo club theme. Rooms are big
and luxurious with oversized marble bathrooms. Facilities include horse-
back-riding, polo, and water sports. 🍴 📠 24 TV 🔒 *Rooms: 298.* 🗒 *298.*

| | AE DC MC V JCB | ● | ■ | ● | ■ |

CHUMPHON: *Chumphon Cabana Resort & Diving Center*   ⓑⓑⓑ
69 Mu 8, Hat Thung Wua Laen. 【 0-7756-0246. FAX 0-7756-0247. @ info@cabana.co.th
This hotel offers well-furnished rooms, suites, and bungalows close to the
beach. The resort is also the local dive center. 🍴 *Rooms: 133.* 🗒 *133.*

| | AE DC MC V JCB | ● | ■ | ■ | ■ |

HUA HIN: *Ban Boosarin*   ⓑⓑ
8/8 Poonsuk Rd. 【 0-3251-2076. FAX 0-7751-2089.
Hua Hin was Thailand's first beach resort when it became popular back
in the 1920s. This is good, cheaper accommodations in a town of expensive, luxurious resorts, and it's close to the beach. TV *Rooms: 10.* 🗒 *10.*

| | | | ■ | | ■ |

HUA HIN: *Anantara Resort & Spa*   ⓑⓑⓑⓑ
45/1 Phetkasem Rd. 【 0-3252-0250. FAX 0-3252-0259.
Traditional Thai housing set amid large, lush, tropical gardens. Rooms are
Thai-style with teak and rattan furniture. Sports available include golf,
sailing, surfing, and ocean kayaking. 🍴 TV 🔒 *Rooms: 187.* 🗒 *187.*

| | AE DC MC V JCB | ● | ■ | ● | ■ |

For key to symbols see back flap

<table>
<tr><td colspan="2">

Price categories for a standard double tax room per night, including tax for luxury hotels.

B under B350
BB B350–800
BBB B800–1,600
BBBB B1,600–3,200
BBBBB over B3,200

</td>
<td colspan="5">

CREDIT CARDS
AE American Express; DC Diners Club; MC MasterCard; V VISA; JCB Japanese Credit Bureau.

WESTERN BATHROOMS
Indicates sit-down, flush toilets; showers and/or baths. Others have squat toilets and trough-and-dipper baths.

COFFEE SHOP
Hotel with coffee shop.

GARDEN/TERRACE
Hotel with garden, courtyard, or terrace.

</td>
</tr>
</table>

	CREDIT CARDS	SWIMMING POOL	WESTERN BATHROOMS	COFFEE SHOP	GARDEN/TERRACE
HUA HIN: *Chom View Hotel & Resort* BBBB 93 Soi Talay 12. 0-3251-1383. FAX 0-3251-1662. A five-minute drive south of Hua Hin, Chom View is an extremely quiet and relaxing place to stay. Located right on the beach, with luxury serviced apartments as well as less expensive rooms. ❚❙ 24 TV **Rooms: 43.** 43.	AE DC MC V JCB	●	■		■
HUA HIN: *Hilton Hua Hin Resort & Spa* BBBB 33 Naresdamri Rd. 0-3251-1006. This luxurious, high-rise hotel stands right on Hua Hin's beach and offers every facility. A big bonus is that all rooms have balconies that provide excellent ocean views. ❚❙ ❙❙ TV ❙ **Rooms: 225.** 225.	AE DC MC V JCB	●	■	●	■
HUA HIN: *Hua Hin Marriott Resort & Spa* BBBB 107/1 Phetkasem Rd. 0-3251-1881. FAX 0-3251-2422. A large and luxurious resort for those in search of good sports facilities, which include golf, tennis, and water sports. Also boasts a shopping arcade and a children's playground. ❚❙ ❙❙ 24 TV ❙ **Rooms: 218.** 218.	AE DC MC V JCB	●	■	●	
HUA HIN: *Sofitel Central Hua Hin Resort* BBBBB 1 Damnoen Kasem Rd. 0-3251-2021. FAX 0-3251-1014. A luxurious and architecturally impressive colonial-style hotel (*see pp298 and 321*). It has parklike grounds that include a topiary garden, wide lawns, and an orchid and butterfly farm. ❚❙ ❙❙ 24 TV ❙ **Rooms: 207.** 207.	AE DC MC V JCB	●	■	●	■
KO PHA NGAN: *Island View Cabana* B 106 Mu 7, Mae Hat Beach. 0-7737-7019. Clean, friendly, basic accommodations on the island's northwestern coast. Its restaurant serves fresh seafood. Ko Mae, a small island just offshore, makes a beautiful backdrop to this beach paradise. ❚❙ **Rooms: 33.** 0.					■
KO PHA NGAN: *Nice Beach Bungalow* BB Thong Nai Pan Yai Beach. 0-7722-94745. @ nicebeach@kohphangan.com Pleasant and quiet accommodation on a beautiful white sand beach, which is one of the best for swimming and snorkeling. ❚❙ **Rooms: 33.** 33.		●	■	●	
KO SAMUI: *Coral Cove Chalet* BBB 210 Mu 4 Coral Cove Beach, Tong Takian Beach. 0-7742-2260. FAX 0-7742-2496. At the top end of Lamai beach accommodations, very comfortable and with great views. The bright chalets, grouped around a pool, are set in a cove framed by thousands of coconut palms. ❚❙ **Rooms: 72.** 72.	AE MC V	●	■	●	■
KO SAMUI: *Golden Sand Resort* BBB 124/2 Lamai Beach. 0-7745-8111. FAX 0-7742-4430. W www.goldensand-resort.com This lively beach resort includes a billiards club, tennis court, and videotheque. There's no swimming pool, but access to the appealing, shimmering ocean is easy. ❚❙ TV **Rooms: 66.** 66.	MC V		■		■
KO SAMUI: *Chaweng Blue Lagoon* BBBB 99 Mu 2, Chaweng Beach. 0-7742-2037. FAX 0-7742-2401. Beautiful Thai buildings flanking Chaweng beach are complemented by a large swimming pool, children's pool, and playground. Extensive water sports facilities include ocean kayaking. ❚❙ ❙❙ TV ❙ **Rooms: 60.** 60.	AE DC MC V JCB	●	■	●	■
KO SAMUI: *Coral Bay Resort* BBBBB 9 Mu 2, Tambon Bophut. 0-7742-2223. FAX 0-7742-2392. W www.coralbay.net Located at the northern end of Chaweng beach, this all-bungalow resort offers every comfort and a wide range of water sports. The bungalows are furnished with coconut wood furniture. ❚❙ **Rooms: 42.** 42.	MC V	●	■	●	■
KO SAMUI: *Central Samui Beach Resort* W www.samuibeach.com BBBBB 38/2 Mu 3, Bophut, Chaweng Beach. 0-7723-0500. FAX 0-7742-2385. Immaculate gardens and marvelous beach views from the most beautiful, central stretch of Chaweng beach. ❚❙ ❙❙ 24 TV ❙ **Rooms: 208.** 208.	AE DC MC V JCB	●	■	●	■

KO SAMUI: *Chaweng Regent Hotel* W www.samuibeach.com ⓑⓑⓑⓑ
155/4, Mu 3 Chaweng Beach. 🅒 0-7742-2008. FAX 0-7742-2222.
Yet another beautifully appointed luxury resort with fine views over Chaweng beach. The restaurant specializes in delicious crayfish, lobster, crab, and giant sizzling shrimp. 🍴 🍴 24 TV 🏊 *Rooms: 145.* 🛏 *145.*
Cards: AE DC MC V JCB

KO SAMUI: *Poppies Samui Seaside Cottages* ⓑⓑⓑⓑⓑ
21/8 Mu 3, Chaweng. 🅒 0-7742-2419. FAX 0-7742-2420.
A village of tastefully furnished, luxurious cottages, each secluded from its neighbors by lush tropical gardens. 🍴 TV *Rooms: 24.* 🛏 *24.*
Cards: AE DC MC V

KO TAO: *Nang Yuan Dive Resort* ⓑⓑⓑ
Ko Nang Yuan, nr Ko Tao, Surat Thani. 🅒 0-7742-7046.
This bungalow and cottage resort is located on an island in a small, three-island archipelago, encircled by a turquoise ring of coral. Excellent diving around the island. 🍴 *Rooms: 55.* 🛏 *41.*
Cards: MC V

PHETCHABURI: *Khao Wang Hotel* ⓑⓑ
123 Ratwithi Rd. 🅒 0-3242-5167. FAX 0-3241-0750.
This basic hotel, in one of the country's oldest towns, is well positioned for the attractions of the extravagant architecture of Khao Wang Palace and the surrounding temples on Phra Nakhon Khiri hill. TV *Rooms: 49.* 🛏 *10.*

PRACHUAP KHIRI KHAN: *Hadthong* ⓑⓑ
7 Susuk Rd. 🅒 0-3260-1050. FAX 0-3260-1057.
Comfortable modern hotel offering the best lodgings in town. Views both over the bay and of nearby "mirror mountain." 🍴 TV *Rooms: 142.* 🛏 *142.*
Cards: AE MC V

SURAT THANI: *Wang Tai* ⓑⓑⓑ
1 Talat Mai Rd. 🅒 0-7728-3020. FAX 0-7728-1007.
The coffee shop of this modern hotel tower, just out of town, has wide ranging views of the Tapi estuary. The hotel also has a restaurant, a bar, a discotheque, and a golf course. 🍴 24 TV *Rooms: 230.* 🛏 *230.*
Cards: AE DC MC V JCB

UPPER ANDAMAN COAST

KO PHI PHI: *Phi Phi Banyan Villa* ⓑⓑⓑⓑ
129 Mu 7, Ao Nang, Ko Phi Phi Don. 🅒 0-7561-1233. FAX 0-1892-6242.
A comfortable villa adjacent to the public beach. Every room has views overlooking Ton Sai Bay. 🍴 TV 🏊 24 *Rooms: 79.* 🛏 *0.*

KO PHI PHI: *Phi Phi Island Cabana* ⓑⓑⓑⓑ
Ton Sai Beach, Ko Phi Phi Don. 🅒 & FAX 0-7561-2132.
Phi Phi comprises two islands: Phi Phi Don is the busier, Ton Sai bay its main accommodations center. These well-appointed bungalows are in a jungle setting with superb ocean views. 🍴 TV 🍴 *Rooms: 222.* 🛏 *140.*
Cards: AE MC V

KO PHI PHI: *Holiday Inn Resort* ⓑⓑⓑⓑⓑ
Laem Tong, Ko Phi Phi Don. 🅒 0-7621-4654.
The most exclusive resort on the island. The design of its luxury cottages and larger, family-style suites has won a design award. Facilities include tennis courts, a freshwater pool, and a Jacuzzi. 🍴 🍴 TV *Rooms: 80.* 🛏 *80.*
Cards: AE DC MC V

KO LANTA: *Khaw Kwang Beach Bungalows* ⓑ
16 Mu 1, Tamboon Saladan, Ko Lanta Yai. 🅒 0-7562-1373.
Situated to the west of Ban Sala Dan, these are well-separated thatched bungalows, all with private bath. *Rooms: 45.* 🛏 *0.*

KO LANTA: *The Narima Bungalow Resort* W www.narima-lanta.com ⓑⓑⓑⓑ
98 Mu 5, Klong Nin. 🅒 0-7560-7700. FAX 0-7560-7709.
This resort is set in pleasant, peaceful surroundings and is very close to the beach. Accommodation consists of small bungalows sleeping two to three people. Good food. Book well in advance. 🍴 *Rooms: 32.* 🛏 *32.*
Cards: MC V JCB

KRABI: *Best Western Ban Ao Nang Resort* ⓑⓑⓑⓑ
31/3 Mu 2, Ao Nang.Beach 🅒 0-7563-7074. FAX 0-7563-7070.
A moment's walk from an idyllic beach, this three-story modern hotel is friendly, clean, and comfortable. 🍴 TV *Rooms: 109.* 🛏 *104.*
Cards: AE MC V

KRABI: *Krabi Resort* ⓑⓑⓑⓑ
232 Mu 2 Ao Nang Beach. 🅒 0-7563-7030. FAX 0-7563-7051. W www.krabiresort.net
The most luxurious accommodations available at Ao Nang. Stay in the modern hotel buildings or try the beach-facing, thatched-roof bungalows. The gardens are well tended and colorful. 🍴 TV *Rooms: 103.* 🛏 *103.*
Cards: AE DC MC V JCB

For key to symbols see back flap

Price categories for a standard double room per night, including tax for luxury hotels.

B under B350
BB B350–800
BBB B800–1,600
BBBB B1,600–3,200
BBBBB over B3,200

CREDIT CARDS
AE American Express; DC Diners Club; MC MasterCard; V VISA; JCB Japanese Credit Bureau.

WESTERN BATHROOMS
Indicates sit-down, flush toilets; showers and/or baths. Others have squat toilets and trough-and-dipper baths.

COFFEE SHOP
Hotel with coffee shop.

GARDEN/TERRACE
Hotel with garden, courtyard, or terrace.

	CREDIT CARDS	SWIMMING POOL	WESTERN BATHROOMS	COFFEE SHOP	GARDEN/TERRACE

KRABI: *Phra Nang Inn* BBBB
119 Mu 2, Ao Nang Beach. [0-7563-7130. FAX 0-7563-7134.
This hotel has a rustic feel and is constructed out of pine and palms. It has good views over Ao Nang beach. Facilities include a restaurant and a small pool. ♦ TV **Rooms:** 83. ≣ 30.
Credit Cards: AE MC V — Swimming Pool ● · Western Bathrooms ■ · Coffee Shop ● · Garden/Terrace ■

KRABI: *Sheraton Krabi Beach Resort* BBBB
1 Tungfah Rd. [0-7562-8000. FAX 0-7562-8028.
This expensive establishment offers every facility including a beauty salon. The hotel is close to Krabi town, but some distance away from the main beach attractions. ♦ ♦ 24 TV ♦ **Rooms:** 221. ≣ 221.
Credit Cards: AE MC V — Swimming Pool ● · Western Bathrooms ■ · Garden/Terrace ■

PHANGNGA: *Phangnga Bay Resort* BBB
20 Thadan Rd, Panyi. [0-7641-2067. FAX 0-7641-2070.
A mid-range, modern resort on the edge of Phangnga Bay. Views are disappointing, but facilities include a swimming pool and a recommended restaurant. ♦ TV **Rooms:** 88. ≣ 88.
Credit Cards: AE MC V — Swimming Pool ● · Western Bathrooms ■ · Garden/Terrace ■

PHUKET: *Felix Karon Phuket* W www.phuket.com/felix BBBB
4/8 Patak Rd, Karon Beach. [0-7639-6666. FAX 0-7639-6853. @ felix@phuket.com
This hotel has good facilities for families with children and is well located for popular Karon Beach. ♦ TV ♦ **Rooms:** 81. ≣ 81.
Credit Cards: AE DC MC V — Swimming Pool ● · Western Bathrooms ■ · Coffee Shop ● · Garden/Terrace ■

PHUKET: *Thara Patong Beach Resort* BBBB
81 Thaweewongse Rd. [0-7634-0135. FAX 0-7634-0446. @ tharapatong@phuket.com
An attractive seaside resort with just about everything from an outdoor Jacuzzi to tennis courts and a sauna room. There is a pool for children, and an excellent seafood restaurant. ♦ ♦ 24 TV ♦ **Rooms:** 128. ≣ 128.
Credit Cards: AE DC MC V — Swimming Pool ● · Western Bathrooms ■ · Coffee Shop ● · Garden/Terrace ■

PHUKET: *Pearl Village* W www.phuket.com/pearlvillage BBBB
Nai Yang Beach and National Park. [0-7632-7006. FAX 0-7632-7338.
This resort lies on the fringes of a national park, north of Phuket town. Facilities include two pools, one with a waterfall. Famous guests have included Prince Philip and Michael Jackson. ♦ ♦ 24 TV ♦ **Rooms:** 226. ≣ 226.
Credit Cards: AE DC MC V JCB — Swimming Pool ● · Western Bathrooms ■ · Coffee Shop ● · Garden/Terrace ■

PHUKET: *Amanpuri* W www.amanresorts.com BBBBB
Pansea Beach 118 Mu 3, Sri Santhorn Rd. [0-7632-4333. FAX 0-7632-4100.
Amanpuri is a Sanskrit word meaning place of peace and is aptly applied to this elegant pavilion complex. In the evening there is a cultural performance including dancing and sword fights. ♦ ♦ 24 **Rooms:** 40. ≣ 40.
Credit Cards: AE DC MC V JCB — Swimming Pool ● · Western Bathrooms ■ · Garden/Terrace ■

PHUKET: *Banyan Tree Resort* @ banyantree@lagunaphuket.com BBBB
33 SMoo 4, Sri Sunthorn Rd, Pathong. [0-7632-4373. FAX 0-7632-4356.
Luxurious resort with magnificent villas and a beautifully groomed beach. The restaurants are also outstanding. ♦ 24 TV ♦ **Rooms:** 108. ≣ 108.
Credit Cards: AE DC MC V JCB — Swimming Pool ● · Western Bathrooms ■ · Garden/Terrace ■

PHUKET: *Diamond Cliff Resort & Spa* W diamond@diamondcliff.com BBBBB
284 Pra Baramee Rd, Kalim, Pathong. [0-7634-0501. FAX 0-7634-0507.
This resort nestles on the hillside above the clear waters of Patong bay, yet is only a short walk from Patong's vibrant nightlife. Has a fine choice of Asian and European restaurants. ♦ ♦ 24 TV ♦ **Rooms:** 333. ≣ 333.
Credit Cards: AE DC MC V JCB — Swimming Pool ● · Western Bathrooms ■ · Coffee Shop ● · Garden/Terrace ■

PHUKET: *Laguna Beach Club* BBBBB
323 Sri Sunthorn Rd, Cherngtalay. [0-7632-4320. FAX 0-7632-4174.
Another resort with just about everything in the way of amenities. Of special interest to parents, there is a supervised "Kids Club" where children can be safely left to play. ♦ ♦ 24 TV ♦ **Rooms:** 252. ≣ 252.
Credit Cards: AE DC MC V JCB — Swimming Pool ● · Western Bathrooms ■ · Coffee Shop ● · Garden/Terrace ■

PHUKET: *The Maiton Resort* W www.phuket.com/maiton BBBBB
100 Moo 7 Sakdidej Rd, Maiton Island. [0-7621-4954. FAX 0-7621-4959.
Maiton is an isolated, offshore island about 2 km (1 mile) long and just 400 m (1,300 ft) wide. There is no town or village – the resort offers peace and quiet in extraordinary comfort. ♦ ♦ TV ♦ **Rooms:** 75. ≣ 75.
Credit Cards: AE DC MC V JCB — Swimming Pool ● · Western Bathrooms ■ · Garden/Terrace ■

DEEP SOUTH

HAT YAI: *Garden Home* ⒷⒷ MC V
51/2 Hoi Muk Rd. 🅒 0-7423-4444. FAX 0-7423-4444.
Attractive modern hotel built around a waterfall and garden. Well located for the tasty food stalls at the junction of Kimpradit and Phadung Phakdi roads and a good value for the money. 🍴 24 📺 *Rooms: 103.* 🛏 *103.*

HAT YAI: *Diamond Plaza* ⒷⒷⒷ AE MC V
62 Niphat Uthit 3 Rd. 🅒 0-7423-0130. FAX 0-7423-9824.
This hotel is friendly and reasonably priced. It is located near the center of Hat Yai's nightlife. 🍴 24 📺 *Rooms: 272.* 🛏 *272.*

HAT YAI: *J B Hotel* 🆆 www.jb-hotel.com ＠ jb@.jb-hotel.com ⒷⒷⒷⒷ AE DC MC V JCB
99 Chuti Anusorn Rd. 🅒 0-7423-4300. FAX 0-7423-4328.
The classiest hotel in Hat Yai, but some distance from the city center on the north side of town. 🍴 🍸 24 📺 *Rooms: 432.* 🛏 *432.*

KO TARUTAO: *National Park Bungalows* ⒷⒷ
Tarutao and Adang National Marine Park. 🅒 0-7472-9022.
Rather short on facilities, but in incredibly beautiful natural surroundings. The national park authority has an effective monopoly. 🍴 *Rooms: 16.* 🛏 *0.*

NAKHON SI THAMMARAT: *Taksin* ⒷⒷ
1584/23 Sriprad Rd. 🅒 0-7534-2790. FAX 0-7534-2794.
Most of Nakhon Si Thammarat's hotels are undistinguished, and this is no exception. However, rooms are clean, the staff friendly, and the tariff a remarkably good value. Large rooms. 🍴 📺 *Rooms: 120.* 🛏 *120.*

NAKHON SI THAMMARAT: *Thai* ⒷⒷ MC V
1373 Rachadamnoen Rd. 🅒 0-7535-6505. FAX 0-7534-4858.
Conveniently located two blocks from the railroad station, this clean but unremarkable hotel boasts a videotheque, a discotheque, and a shopping mall. 🍴 📺 *Rooms: 215.* 🛏 *120.*

NARATHIWAT: *Tanyong* ⒷⒷ MC V
16/1 Sopha Phisai Rd. 🅒 0-7351-1477. FAX 0-7351-1834.
Chinese-style hotel with good Malay cuisine. Try the mangoes and sticky rice specialty during the hot season. 🍴 📺 *Rooms: 84.* 🛏 *84.*

PATTANI: *My Garden* ⒷⒷ MC V
8/28 Charoen Pradit Rd. 🅒 0-7333-1055. FAX 0-733-36217.
Located about 1 km (1,100 yds) out of town. The best accommodations in Pattani, with a very popular disco. Try the Diana Restaurant directly opposite, which specializes in seafood. 🍴 📺 *Rooms: 136.* 🛏 *109.*

PHATTHALUNG: *Lam Pam Resort* ⒷⒷ V
88 Mu 6, Tambon Lam Pam. 🅒 0-7461-1486. FAX 0-7461-2013.
This resort has clean, simple chalets, a good restaurant, and is situated 15 minutes' drive out of town on the banks of the Thale Sap lake. Many think it is the best option available in Phatthalung. 📺 *Rooms: 76.* 🛏 *76.*

SONGKHLA: *Lake Inn* ⒷⒷ AE DC MC V
301–3 Nakhon Nok Rd. 🅒 0-7432-1441. FAX 0-7443-7275.
A mid-range establishment located on the western side of Songkhla, overlooking the main fishing wharf for the Thale Sap lake. As might be expected, the Lake Inn serves good seafood. 🍴 📺 *Rooms: 79.* 🛏 *79.*

SONGKHLA: *Royal Crown Songkhla* ⒷⒷⒷ AE MC V
38 Sai Ngam Rd. 🅒 0-7431-1918. FAX 0-7432-1027.
A clean, pleasant, and centrally located establishment, popular with Songkhla's expatriate oil workers and their families. 🍴 24 📺 *Rooms: 52.* 🛏 *52.*

TRANG: *Clarion MP Resort Hotel* ⒷⒷⒷ MC V
184 Trang–Phatthalung Rd. 🅒 0-7521-4230. FAX 0-7521-1177.
Shaped like a luxury liner, this opulent establishment offers every sort of facility including a lovely garden restaurant, extensive swimming pools, karaoke, and lobby bar. 🍴 🍸 24 📺 🏊 *Rooms: 190.* 🛏 *190.*

TRANG: *Thumrin Thana Hotel* ⒷⒷⒷ AE MC V
69/8 Trang Thana Rd. 🅒 0-7521-1211. FAX 0-7522-3288. 🆆 www.thumrin.co.th
An upscale, high-rise hotel located in central Trang near the railroad station. It is starting to look a little shabby nevertheless, it still ranks as one of the better hotels in Trang. 🍴 📺 *Rooms: 289.* 🛏 *289.*

For key to symbols see back flap

WHERE TO EAT

THAILAND IS FORTUNATE in being a land of plenty. As much of the land is fertile and the population has always been small relative to the size of the country, famine is all but unknown. In the 13th century King Ramkamhaeng of Sukhothai, the first Thai kingdom, recorded: "This land is thriving . . . in the water are fish, in the fields there is rice." He might also have mentioned the wide range of tropical fruits, vegetables, and spices – to which have been added, since his day, a wealth of imports from

The usual eating implements

tropical America, thriving in their new Old World setting. The range of dishes, as well as the variety and freshness of the ingredients, make for one of the world's great cuisines. Thais love to eat: six or seven times a day is not uncommon. Wherever there are people there are restaurants and food stands. As well as flavor and freshness, Thais also appreciate the harmonious presentation of food. The dishes of even a modest meal will often be garnished with flowers and rosettes carved out of colorful vegetables and fruit.

The Grand Ballroom of the Holiday Inn on Silom Road, Bangkok

RESTAURANTS

THERE IS A GREAT RANGE of eating establishments, from "hole in the wall" cafés, to the leafy *suan ahan* "garden restaurants," to air-conditioned oases of luxury. Unlike the ubiquitous roadside stands, all these are fairly restricted in their opening times. Most urban restaurants, especially those serving Western food, open at about 11am and close between 10pm and midnight. This is not really a problem, since opening times – together with details of credit cards accepted – are usually posted on the door. But it can mean that finding an early Western-style breakfast is difficult away from the tourist scene, in which case a Thai omelete may have to serve as a substitute.

Virtually every major city and resort in Thailand has at least one free tourist magazine.

They can be picked up in hotel reception lobbies, at banks and money changers, as well as in many restaurants. These list restaurants by cuisine and specialty, often giving details of how to get there, along with telephone numbers for booking tables. Away from the major tourist destinations, you can be sure that the main hotels in every

Restaurant in the Sadet Market at Nong Khai, by the Mekong River

town will have air-conditioned restaurants offering a mixture of Thai and Chinese cuisine.

Thais have taken to Western cuisine, and especially to the Western fast food culture, with enthusiasm. McDonald's and Kentucky Fried Chicken are increasingly visible, but the most popular imports appear to be pizza and pasta, which can be found in just about any provincial capital. However, quality does vary from place to place.

COFFEE SHOPS

IN TOURIST RESORTS and international hotels, coffee shops are just that – places to sit and drink cappuccino or espresso, eat snacks, refresh oneself, or kill time. In this they differ little from their counterparts in New York or London. It is not so in the smaller provincial towns or Thai hotels, however. Here, "coffee bars" are more like nightclubs, with live music, darkened windows, and a plethora of "hostesses" whose job it is to entertain the customer and encourage the spending of money. It is generally easy to tell the difference between the two types of establishment, even from the outside.

ROADSIDE AND MARKET FOOD STANDS

SOME OF THE BEST and most reasonably priced food in Thailand can be found at any of the numerous roadside food stalls. Generally speaking, such establishments are clean and

Street vendor's cart selling fruit and drinks, Phuket

unpretentious. These stands are often mobile, allowing the proprietors to push them home and clean them every night. The ingredients are openly displayed behind glass panels. Fast cooking processes, such as flash-frying, grilling over charcoal, or boiling are often used. This means that the fare, invariably fresh, should also be well cooked and safe to eat.

A sure way of measuring a stall's popularity, as anywhere in the world, is by its patrons. If there are plenty of locals sitting at the simple tables most stalls provide, then the chances are the food is good. Don't be surprised to find a businessman with a Mercedes parked nearby sitting at the same stall as a *tuk-tuk* driver. Thais from all sectors of society know how to appreciate good, cheap food.

Menus are rarely in English, so it is a good idea to memorize the names of your favorite dishes from the food glossary *(see pp410–11)*. Alternatively, you can point and ask to taste – few Thais expect foreign visitors to speak their language, and they are always willing to help and advise.

KHANTOKE DINING

A TRADITIONAL STYLE of dining in Northern Thailand, *khantoke* dinners are often arranged for guests by hotels in Chiang Mai and other Northern cities. Diners sit on raised platforms around a circular table. The meal includes a variety of Northern dishes such as *nam phrik num* (a very spicy dip), *kap mu* (pork skin) and *kaeng kai* (a chicken and vegetable curry), all of which are served with *khao niaw* (sticky rice) and washed down with local beer. A *khantoke* dinner is often accompanied by displays of traditional Thai dancing.

PRICES

B UYING MEALS is one of the cheapest aspects of a visit to Thailand. The cost of alcohol, however, can often be more than the meal itself. It is common practice for prices to be displayed. Menus invariably list them next to each dish. The prices for shellfish are often given by weight. In larger establishments and international-class hotels a service charge and tax will usually be levied. These extra costs will be clearly detailed on the check.

Even at very small establishments prices are nearly always fixed and marked (in Arabic numerals) on a board. Bargaining for foodstuffs is rare – surprising in a country where shoppers delight in haggling.

Neon sign for a restaurant

TIPPING

T IPPING WAS once unknown, but its popularity is increasing as Thais grow accustomed to tips from tourists. Do not apply a percentage: ten percent of 50 *baht* may well be appropriate, but ten percent of an expensive meal would be far too much.

EATING HABITS IN THAILAND

T HE THAI PHILOSOPHY of nutrition is simple – if you are hungry, eat. Nothing should stand in the way. Most Thais, moreover, eat little but often, sometimes snacking six or seven times a day. The concept of three meals simply does not apply in Thailand. Even though people do indeed eat breakfast, lunch, and dinner, they may also stop for a bowl of noodles, a fried snack, or a sweet at any time of day.

Eating is a simple pleasure and does not involve complex rituals of etiquette, although visitors should note a few rules. Thais eat with a fork held in the left hand and a spoon held in the right hand. The fork is used solely to push food onto the spoon; eating straight from a fork is considered crude. Since food – especially meat – is cut into pieces before it is cooked, knives are not needed.

Thai noodle dishes are often strongly influenced by Chinese culinary traditions, and they are eaten using chopsticks and a spoon. Another exception to the general rule is sticky rice *(khao niaw)*, which is eaten – delicately – with the fingers.

Food in Thailand is generally served communally in a series of large bowls. Only small rice bowls are reserved for individual use. Rice is traditionally served first, and then a spoon is used to ladle two or three spoonfuls from the communal bowls on top of the rice. You should feel free to come back later for more as necessary. Overloading your plate is regarded as uncouth – there is no hurry, and there is always plenty more in the kitchen.

Street vendor cooking satay for passersby in a Bangkok park

What to Eat in Thailand

THAI FOOD IS FAMOUS for its spicy qualities. Chili peppers were imported to Thailand from the New World, in the 16th century by European traders *(see p153)*. The Thais took to them (especially the small, fiery ones) with great enthusiasm. In spite of this, mild dishes are also widely available in Thailand. Rice is, of course, the staple food, while rice noodles come second, appearing in dry, fried dishes and in soups. The cuisine is nutritious and flavorful: meats are lightly fried, the vegetables boiled.

Three chili varieties

Rice porridge (jok) *is a standard breakfast. Often an egg is added, which cooks as it is stirred in. The best condiment for this dish is chilies in rice vinegar.*

Condiment of chilies in fish sauce *(nam pla phrik)*

Condiments of fish sauce and chili flakes

Noodle soup (kuaytiaw nam) *is the only Thai dish to be eaten with chopsticks. It includes vegetables and usually meat balls.*

Fried rice dishes (khao phat), *made with egg, slivers of meat, and vegetables, are a delicious and filling all-in-one meal that can be enjoyed any time of day.*

Phat thai *is a mixture of flat rice noodles fried with bean curd, vegetables, egg, peanuts, and dried shrimp. It is claimed to be Thailand's national dish.*

Wheat noodles served with slices of red pork (bami haeng mu daeng) *is a typical dish that can be bought from street vendors throughout the country.*

Tom yam, *typically made with shrimp and tomatoes, is the most famous of all Thai soups. It is spiced with coriander, lemongrass, and chilies and is often cooked and served in a tureen.*

Mu sap bai kraphao *(fried pork flavored with holy basil) is a delicious meat dish that may form part of a communal meal.*

Phanaeng curry (kaeng phanaeng) *is a "dry" chicken curry. Ingredients include shrimp, coriander seeds, red chilies, and a small amount of basil.*

Green curry (kaeng khiaw wan), *like many Central Thai curries, is cooked in coconut milk, which gives it an almost sweet flavor. Green chilies add spice and heat.*

Steamed rice (khao suay), *the mainstay of communal meals in Thailand, is always served first. It is the best thing for cooling the mouth when eating very hot food.*

Sticky rice (khao niaw) *cooked and served in a covered basket is common in the North and Northeast. This glutinous rice is eaten with the fingers; sometimes the rice is rolled into a ball and used to carry food to the mouth.*

Raw Thai
eggplant

Carved raw
carrot

Crispy
pork
rinds

**Nam phrik
ong**, a pork
and chili dip

Carved
yellow
eggplant

Nam phrik *is a family of popular dishes where an elaborately prepared chili paste is eaten as a dip with raw vegetables and deep-fried meat. Regional specialties include* nam phrik ong *from Northern Thailand, with pork rinds. On special occasions and at fancy restaurants, the vegetables are carved, often in the shape of flowers.*

Fried water lilies (phat pak bung) *are just one of many simple, mild dishes that may be served as part of a main meal. They take only a minute to cook.*

Papaya salad (som tam) *is very popular throughout Thailand. The papaya is sliced thin and mixed with chilies. Chicken is a good accompaniment.*

Seafood salad (yam thalay) *is often served as an appetizer in the South. Like many other Thai salads, the warm, cooked seafood is placed on a bed of lettuce.*

Mango with sticky rice (khao niaw mamuang), *which is sweetened with coconut cream, is the country's best known dessert. Only the sweetest mangoes are used.*

DRINKS

Thailand has a wealth of fruits *(see p129)*, many of which can be juiced. Coconut juice, drunk with a straw straight from the coconut, is also popular. Tea and coffee are usually served chilled. Beer is the preferred alcoholic accompaniment to meals – it complements spicy food better than wine. Plain water *(nam plao)* is served with main meals.

Pumpkin custard (sangkhaya) *is a dessert of coconut milk, eggs, and sugar. It may be served either with sticky rice or baked in a hollowed out pumpkin.*

**Roselle
juice**

**Iced
tea**

**Singha
beer**

**Chang
beer**

A Glossary of Typical Thai Dishes

THAI CUISINE IS FAMOUSLY creative and varied *(see pp34–5)*. Even street vendors delight in their culinary skills, and it is not uncommon to see food being encased in a banana leaf as delicately as if it were being gift wrapped. Such artful presentations and the sheer range of dishes can be bewildering to newcomers: it may not even be obvious what

Khanom khrok – **coconut puddings**

is savory or sweet. This glossary covers typical dishes; phonetic guidance for food words is on page 503.

CHOOSING DISHES

RESTAURANT MENUS in tourist areas may include descriptions in English, and sometimes other languages. The Thai names of dishes often derive simply from the main elements – for instance, the dish *khao mu daeng* translates literally as "rice, pork, red." Thus, the basic components of any dish can often be worked out with only a little knowledge of Thai. If there is

no menu, the dishes of the day will be on display. If you don't recognize the dish, pointing and saying *"nee arai na?"* ("what's this?") should elicit a list of ingredients.

Vegetarians should find it easy to order food without meat *(mai ao nua)*, but ought to be aware that fish sauce is used in many dishes. Dairy products feature only rarely in Thai cuisine, so vegans should not fare worse than vegetarians.

A street vendor cooking over charcoal on a road-side stall

Thais are accustomed to foreigners asking if a dish is spicy *(phed mai?)*, or requesting a non-spicy meal *(mai ao phet na)*. To enliven any dish, diners can use the ubiquitous condiments of chilies in vinegar, chili flakes, sugar (for savory dishes), and fish sauce usually found on tables.

SNACKS

Thais love to snack. Almost every street corner has a selection of food stalls selling raw and freshly cooked snacks.

Bami mu daeng
บะหมี่หมูแดง
Egg noodles with red pork.
Khai ping
ไข่ปิ้ง
Charcoal-roasted eggs.
Kai yang
ไก่ย่าง
Charcoal-grilled chicken.
Khanom beuang
ขนมเบื้อง
Filled, sweet, crisp pancakes.

Chicken satay

Khanom khrok
ขนมครก
Coconut puddings.
Khao tom mud
ข้าวต้มมัด
Sticky rice served in banana leaves.
Kluay ping
กล้วยปิ้ง
Charcoal-grilled bananas.
Look chin ping
ลูกชิ้นปิ้ง
Meatballs with a chili sauce.
Po pia
ปอเปี๊ยะ
Deep-fried spring rolls.
Sai krok
ไส้กรอก
Thai beef or pork sausages.

Satay
สะเต๊ะ
Slivers of beef, pork, or chicken grilled on a stick, served with peanut sauce and cucumber.
Tua thod
ถั่วทอด
Roasted cashews or peanuts.

NOODLES

Rice noodles come as *sen yai* (broad), *sen lek* (medium), and *sen mi* (thin). *Bami* are egg noodles. *Woon sen* are thin, transparent soy noodles.
Bami nam
บะหมี่น้ำ
Egg noodles in a broth with vegetables and meat or fish.
Kuaytiaw haeng
ก๋วยเตี๋ยวแห้ง
Rice noodles served "dry" with vegetables and meat or fish.
Kuaytiaw nam
ก๋วยเตี๋ยวน้ำ
Rice noodles in a broth with vegetables and meat or fish.
Look chin pla
ลูกชิ้นปลา
Fishballs with noodles.
Phad thai
ผัดไทย
Rice noodles fried with beancurd, egg, dried shrimp, peanuts, bean sprouts, and chili.

Street sellers and their customers in a Bangkok market

RICE DISHES

Rice is the staple food. A familiar Thai greeting, equivalent to "how are you?" is *kin khao mai?*, literally "have you eaten rice?"

Khao man kai
ข้าวมันไก่
Chinese-style chicken with rice cooked in chicken stock.

Khao mok kai
ข้าวหมกไก่
Thai-style chicken biriyani.

Khao mu daeng
ข้าวหมูแดง
Chinese-style red pork served on a bed of fragrant rice.

Khao na ped
ข้าวหน้าเป็ด
Roast duck served on a bed of fragrant rice.

Khao phad mu/kung
ข้าวผัดหมูหรือกุ้ง
Fried rice with pork or shrimp.

SOUPS

Soups are diverse and inventive. Some, such as *jok*, are eaten for breakfast. The word *"sup"* is widely recognized.

Jok
โจ๊ก
Ground rice soup with minced pork and ginger.

Khao tom
ข้าวต้ม
Rice soup with a selection of meat and vegetable side dishes.

Tom jeud tao hu
ต้มจืดเต้าหู้
Mild broth with beancurd and minced pork.

Tom kha kai
ต้มข่าไก่
Chicken soup with galingale, coconut milk, and lemon grass.

Tom yam kung
ต้มยำกุ้ง
Shrimp, mushrooms, lemon grass, galingale, and coriander.

CURRIES

Curries are served either *rat khao* (on a plate of rice) or in a bowl as an accompaniment to a central bowl of rice.

Kaeng kari kai
แกงกะหรี่ไก่
Indian-style chicken and potato.

Kaeng khiaw wan
แกงเขียวหวาน
Slightly sweet green curry.

Fragrant green leaves make a perfect wrapping for sticky rice

Kaeng matsaman
แกงมัสมั่น
A mild curry from the Muslim South with beef, peanuts, potatoes, and coconut milk.

Kaeng phanaeng
แกงแพนง
Southern-style "dry" curry with coconut and basil.

Kaeng phed
แกงเผ็ด
A hot curry with red chilies, lemon grass, and coriander.

Kaeng som
แกงส้ม
Hot and sour curry, often with fish.

SEAFOOD

An amazing variety of seafood is available at reasonable prices, particularly in the South.

Hoi malaeng pu op
หอยแมลงภู่อบ
Steamed green mussels.

Hoi thod
หอยทอด
Oysters fried in batter with egg on a bed of beansprouts.

Hu chalam
หูฉลาม
Shark's fin soup.

Southern seafood, including crab

Kung mangkon phao
กุ้งมังกรเผา
Grilled lobster.

Pla meuk yang
ปลาหมึกย่าง
Roasted sliced squid.

Pla nung khing
ปลานึ่งขิง
Steamed fish with ginger, chili, and mushrooms.

Pla thod
ปลาทอด
Deep fried fish.

Pu neung
ปูนึ่ง
Steamed crab.

REGIONAL DISHES

Kaeng hang le
แกงฮังเล
Pork, peanut, and ginger curry from Chiang Mai.

Khao soi
ข้าวซอย
Chicken or beef curry served with wheat noodles, fresh lime, and pickled cabbage. A Northern specialty.

Larb ped
ลาบเป็ด
Northern spicy minced duck.

Som tam
ส้มตำ
Green papaya salad with peanuts, from the Northeast.

Yam thalay
ยำทะเล
Southern spicy seafood salad.

DESSERTS

Known as *khong wan* or "sweet things," these are mostly coconut or fruit based.

Foy thong
ฝอยทอง
Sweet, shredded egg yolk.

Khao niaw mamuang
ข้าวเหนียวมะม่วง
Fresh mango served with sticky rice and coconut milk.

Kluay buat chi
กล้วยบวดชี
Bananas in coconut milk.

Mo kaeng
หม้อแกง
Thai-style egg custard.

DRINKS

Bia
เบียร์
Beer. Usually served in bottles.

Cha ron
ชาร้อน
Tea with condensed milk.

Kafae
กาแฟ
Coffee, often instant.

Nam cha
น้ำชา
Chinese-style tea without milk.

Nam kuad
น้ำขวด
Bottled water.

Coconut seller on the Floating Market

Choosing a Restaurant

THE RESTAURANTS in this guide have been selected for their good value, exceptional food, and interesting location. This chart highlights some of the factors that may influence your choice. Use the color-coded thumb tabs, which indicate the regions covered on each page, to guide you to the relevant sections of the chart.

	CREDIT CARDS	THAI SPECIALTIES	ASIAN (NON-THAI) DISHES	WESTERN DISHES	OUTDOOR TABLES
BANGKOK					
OLD CITY: *Vegetarian Restaurant.* **Map** 2 D4. 85/2 Soi Wat Bawon, off Tanao Rd. 🍴 *No telephone.* A wide range of good-value vegetarian food, such as Indian-style potato curries, *khanom chin* (noodles), and coconut-milk desserts.	Ⓑ		●	▣	
OLD CITY: *Maharajah.* **Map** 2 D4. Khao San Rd. 🍴 *No telephone.* Tasty Indian food at reasonable prices is served at this restaurant, which caters chiefly to budget travelers on hectic Khao San Road. 🍽	ⒷⒷ			▣	
OLD CITY: *Sorn Daeng.* **Map** 2 E4. 77 Ratchadamnoen Klang Ave. 🍴 *0-2224-3088.* Enjoy tasty Thai food and seafood at this eatery near the Democracy Monument. The dishes, which are a bargain, include Southern Thai specialties such as *kaeng matsaman* (beef curry). 🍽	ⒷⒷ	AE MC V JCB	●		●
CHINATOWN: *Nai Sow.* **Map** 6 F1. 3/1 Maitri Chit Rd. 🍴 *0-2222-1539.* This Chinese-Thai restaurant is famous for what many believe to be the best *tom yum kung* (shrimp in a hot and sour soup) in Bangkok.	Ⓑ	MC V	●	▣	
CHINATOWN: *Royal India.* **Map** 6 D1. 392/1 Chak Phet Rd. 🍴 *0-2221-6565.* Good, solid, North Indian cooking at reasonable prices that should not be missed. Both vegetarian and nonvegetarian dishes are featured on the menu. Try the Indian breads, which are especially tasty. 🍽	Ⓑ			▣	
CHINATOWN: *Samrat.* **Map** 6 D1. Chak Phet Rd. 🍴 *No telephone.* Set in a tiny alley to the side of the ATM Department Store, this friendly Sikh-run establishment dishes up wonderful dhals and curries. These can all be washed down with *chai* (hot, sweet, Indian tea).	Ⓑ			▣	
DUSIT: *Empress.* **Map** 3 A4. Royal Princess Hotel, 269 Lan Luang Rd. 🍴 *0-2281-3088.* A well-known Chinese restaurant, in the Royal Princess Hotel, with a considerable reputation for its Southern Chinese cuisine. Cantonese specialties such as dim sum are recommended. 🍽 🍷	ⒷⒷⒷ	AE DC MC V JCB		▣	
DUSIT: *Piccolo.* **Map** 3 A5. Royal Princess Hotel, 269 Lan Luang Rd. 🍴 *0-2281-3088.* A fine restaurant, specializing in North Italian food. Some delicious dishes feature veal – this is unusual, as it's a rarity in Bangkok. The various pasta dishes are also recommended. 🍽 🍷	ⒷⒷⒷⒷ	AE DC MC V JCB			●
DOWNTOWN: *Thai Room* 30/37 Patpong, Soi 2. 🍴 *0-2233-7920.* Set in the heart of Patpong, most regulars patronize this old favorite for its tasty Mexican specialties, such as tacos, nachos, and fajitas. There are also over 100 Thai dishes and delicious club sandwiches. 🍽	ⒷⒷ	AE MC V	●	▣	●
DOWNTOWN: *Arirang.* **Map** 8 C4. 106–108 Silom Rd, Soi 4. 🍴 *0-2234-1096.* The Korean barbecued beef here is so tender it virtually melts in the mouth. Try the *kimchi* (pickled garlic) dishes. Friendly staff. 🍽	ⒷⒷⒷ	AE		▣	
DOWNTOWN: *Bobby's Arms.* **Map** 7 C3. 1st Floor, Car park bldg, Patpong, Soi 2. 🍴 *0-2233-6828.* This enduringly popular English pub is tucked away behind the second floor of Patpong parking lot. It serves the whole gamut of pub food, from steak and kidney pie to bangers and mash. 🍽 🍷	ⒷⒷⒷ	AE DC MC V			●

Price categories for an evening meal for one, including service, but not alcohol:

B under B100
BB B100–200
BBB B200–500
BBBB B500–1,000
BBBBB over B1,000

THAI SPECIALTIES
The restaurant has Thai dishes.

ASIAN (NON-THAI) DISHES
Cuisine from other parts of Asia, such as China, Korea, Japan, or India, is served.

WESTERN DISHES
French, Italian, or other Western fare is on the menu.

OUTDOOR TABLES
Facilities for eating outdoors *(suan ahan)*, on a terrace, or in a garden or courtyard.

	CREDIT CARDS	THAI SPECIALTIES	ASIAN (NON-THAI) DISHES	WESTERN DISHES	OUTDOOR TABLES
DOWNTOWN: *Bussaracum*. **Map** 7 C4. BBB Sethiwan Bldg, Silom Rd. 0-2266-6312. This renowned restaurant concentrates on Royal Thai cuisine *(see p34)*. Specialty dishes, such as *foy thong*, or "golden threads," (an egg-yolk concoction), are enhanced by the elegant surroundings. ▤ ▟	AE DC MC V JCB	●			
DOWNTOWN: *El Gordo's Cantina*. **Map** 7 C4. BBB 130/8 Soi 8, Silom Rd. 0-2237-1415. Popular Mexican and Tex-Mex food. If you crave burritos, nachos, tortillas, and other Mexican dishes, this is the place to come. The management is deservedly proud of its margaritas. ▤ ▟	AE DC MC V JCB			●	
DOWNTOWN: *Gaddi's Grill*. **Map** 7 B3. BBB Mandarin Bangkok Hotel, 662 Rama IV Rd. 0-2238-0230. This prestigious grillroom offers a wide range of imported food. Choose from American steaks, New Zealand lamb, Scottish smoked salmon, and local seafoods. Desserts include French cheesecake. ▤ ▟	AE DC MC V JCB			●	
DOWNTOWN: *Himali Cha Cha* BBB 1229/11 Charoen Krung (New) Rd. 0-2235-1569. Mouthwatering Mogul-style cooking in one of Bangkok's oldest Indian restaurants. The fresh breads are delicious, the dhals superb. ▤ ▟	AE MC V		▪		
DOWNTOWN: *Royal Kitchen*. **Map** 8 E4. BBB Sukhumvit 55. 0-2391-9634. Silver chopsticks and a series of beautifully-decorated small dining rooms add to the pleasure of eating some of the very finest southern Chinese food in Bankok. Lunchtime dim sum is excellent too. ▤	AE DC MC V		▪		
DOWNTOWN: *Sichuan Garden*. **Map** 8 E1. BBB World Trade Center, Ratchadamri Rd. 0-2255-9840. Sichuan cuisine is spicier, sharper, and more pungent than other Chinese styles of cooking and is very popular in Bangkok. Here it is served in stylish, agreeable surroundings. ▤ ▟	AE DC MC V JCB		▪		
DOWNTOWN: *Trattoria da Roberto*. **Map** 7 C4. BBB 37/9 Patpong, Soi 2. 0-2233-6851. Savor fine Italian food in an authentically Italian ambience, right in the heart of Bangkok's premier night entertainment area. The veal *parmigiano* is memorable, the seafood spaghetti sublime. ▤ ▟	AE DC MC V			●	
DOWNTOWN: *Mayflower*. **Map** 8 D4. BBBB Dusit Thani Hotel, 946 Rama IV Rd. 0-2200-9000 ext 2799. An award-winning Chinese restaurant – one of the best in Bangkok – specializing in Cantonese cuisine. The sumptuous, intricately designed interior features authentic Chinese antiques. ▤ ▟	AE DC MC V JCB		▪		
DOWNTOWN: *Noble House*. **Map** 8 E1. BBBB Nai Lert Park Bangkok, 2 Witthayu (Wireless) Rd. 0-2253-0123. Superior Cantonese cuisine in surroundings designed to resemble an old Chinese trading house. The lunchtime dim sum, served by waitresses dressed in Chinese traditional dress, is exceptional. ▤ ▟	AE DC MC V JCB		▪		
DOWNTOWN: *Le Banyan*. BBBBB 59 Sukhumvit Soi 8. 0-2253-5556. Classic French cuisine, including Duck *Foie Gras*, is served here in a traditional Thai house. Open for dinner only. ▤ ▟ ▜	AE DC MC V			●	
DOWNTOWN: *Le Normandie*. **Map** 6 F4. BBBBB Oriental Hotel, 48 Oriental Ave 0-2659-9000. Michelin three-star chef Georges Blanc is permanent consulatant in the kitchens of this unforgettable French restaurant. Enjoy the stunning views over the Chao Phraya river. ▤ ▟ ▜	AE DC MC V JCB			●	

For key to symbols see back flap

Price categories for an evening meal for one, including service, but not alcohol: Ⓑ under B100 ⓑⓑ B100–200 ⓑⓑⓑ B200–500 ⓑⓑⓑⓑ B500–1,000 ⓑⓑⓑⓑⓑ over B1,000	**THAI SPECIALTIES** The restaurant has Thai dishes. **ASIAN (NON-THAI) DISHES** Cuisine from other parts of Asia, such as China, Korea, Japan, or India, is served. **WESTERN DISHES** French, Italian, or other Western fare is on the menu. **OUTDOOR TABLES** Facilities for eating outdoors *(suan ahan)*, on a terrace, or in a garden or courtyard.			

	CREDIT CARDS	**THAI SPECIALTIES**	**ASIAN (NON-THAI) DISHES**	**WESTERN DISHES**	**OUTDOOR TABLES**
DOWNTOWN: *Spice Market*. **Map** 8 D2. ⓑⓑⓑⓑ Four Seasons Hotel, 155 Ratchadamri Rd. ☎ 0-2251-6127. One of the city's best Thai restaurants, offering a wide range of dishes in a setting decorated to resemble an old Thai spice shop. Enjoy delicious curries and old-fashioned Thai sweets. 🍽 🍷	AE DC MC V JCB	●			▪
THON BURI: *Rim Nam*. **Map** 6 D2. ⓑⓑ 111 Somdet Phra Pin Klao Rd. ☎ 0-2424-1112. Enjoy Thai- and Chinese-style seafood at reasonable prices on the bank of the Chao Phraya, next to Phra Pin Klao Bridge. 🍽 🍷	V	●	▪		▪
THON BURI: *Sala Rim Nam*. **Map** 6 F4. ⓑⓑⓑⓑ Opposite Oriental Hotel, 597 Charoen Nakorn Rd. ☎ 0-2437-3080. Good food in a romantic riverside setting. Across the river from the Oriental pier (with regular ferry links to the hotel), the restaurant is renowned for its excellent seafood and classical Thai dancing. 🍽 🍷	AE DC M V JCB	●			▪
FARTHER AFIELD: *Cabbages and Condoms* Ⓑ 10 Sukhumvit, Soi 12. ☎ 0-2229-4610. A distinctive restaurant serving organically grown Thai food. The unusual name derives from the work of Mechai Viravaidya, a promoter of family planning. Profits go towards his work. 🍽 🍷	AE DC MC V JCB	●			
FARTHER AFIELD: *Mangsawirat* Ⓑ Just off Ratwithi Rd, Nakhon Pathom, Nakhon Pathom province. ☎ *No telephone.* A popular vegetarian restaurant offering a wide range of tasty dishes. Well worth trying is the *kaeng kari* (Indian-style potato curry).		●			
FARTHER AFIELD: *Nakhon Inn* ⓑⓑ 55 Ratwithi Rd, Nakhon Pathom, Nakhon Pathom province. ☎ 0-3425-1152. This restaurant and coffee shop prepares standard Central Thai fare like *tom yam kung* (spicy soup with shrimp) and some basic Western cuisine. If you want steak and fries, this is the place. 🍽 🍷	AE	●		●	
FARTHER AFIELD: *Bei Otto* ⓑⓑⓑ 1 Sukhumvit, Soi 20. ☎ 0-2260-0869. A popular German establishment with its own *bierhaus*, delicatessen, and bakery. The house specialties include a mixed sausage platter, leg of pork with sauerkraut, wiener schnitzel, and *rösti*. 🍽 🍷	AE DC MC V			●	
FARTHER AFIELD: *Bourbon Street* 🅦 www.bourbonstbkk.com ⓑⓑⓑ Washington Square, Sukhumvit, Soi 22. ☎ 0-2259-0328. Located quite unexpectedly in downtown Bangkok is this Cajun-Creole restaurant. Gumbo, jambalaya, red beans and rice, blackened redfish, and Cajun boiled fish are among the dishes. 🍽 🍷	AE MC V			●	
FARTHER AFIELD: *Cedar* ⓑⓑⓑ 4/1 Sukhumvit, Soi 49/9. ☎ 0-2391-4482. Middle Eastern and Greek dishes are a feature of this restaurant decorated to resemble a (rather sophisticated) Arab tent. Try the wonderful tzatziki, moussaka, hummus, falafel, and kebabs. 🍽 🍷	AE DC V		▪	●	
FARTHER AFIELD: *Le Dalat* ⓑⓑⓑ 47/1 Sukhumvit, Soi 23. ☎ 0-2258-4192. One of three branches of the most celebrated Vietnamese restaurant in Bangkok. Enjoy *cha glo* (spring rolls) or *naem meuang* (spicy grilled meatballs wrapped in lettuce leaves) in elegant surroundings. 🍽 🍷	AE DC MC V		▪		
FARTHER AFIELD: *Huntsman Pub*. **Map** 8 F2. ⓑⓑⓑ Landmark Plaza Hotel, 138 Sukhumvit Rd. ☎ 0-2254-0404. An upscale, British-style pub serving typical dishes such as a mixed grill and steak and kidney pie, as well as general Thai food. There is a well-stocked bar and live entertainment every night. 🍽 🍷	AE DC MC V JCB	●		●	

FARTHER AFIELD: *Kisso* ⒷⒷⒷ — AE DC MC V JCB — ▪
Westin Grand Sukhumvit, 259 Sukhumvit Rd. ⓒ 0-2651-1000.
This exclusive Japanese restaurant excels in sushi, tempura, sashimi, *teppanyaki*, and other classic dishes. Choose from the fixed-price lunch menu, the à la carte dinner, and the Japanese buffet on weekends. 🍴 🍷

FARTHER AFIELD: *Lemongrass* ⒷⒷⒷ — AE DC MC V — ● ▪
5/1 Soi 24, Sukhumvit Rd. ⓒ 0-2258-8637.
This popular establishment cooks up moderately spiced Central Thai food in an elegant old wooden house. The specialty is *kai yang phak phanaeng* (sweet and spicy Southern-style grilled chicken). 🍴 🍷 🍵

FARTHER AFIELD: *Man Ho*. **Map** 8 F2. ⒷⒷⒷ — AE DC MC V — ●
JW Marriott Hotel, 4 Sukhumvit, Soi 2. ⓒ 0-2656-7700.
Excellent Chinese food from this restaurant inside the JW Marriot hotel. The emphasis is on fresh seafood and vegetables. 🍴 🍷

FARTHER AFIELD: *Nang Yuan Restaurant* ⒷⒷⒷ — AE DC MC V — ▪
Fortune Town Bldg, 1 Ratchadaphisek Rd. ⓒ 0-2641-1500.
Chinese specialties, including steamed bird's nest with red dates and ginseng. The dim sum lunch buffets are recommended. 🍴 🍷

FARTHER AFIELD: *Pan Pan 33* ⒷⒷⒷ — AE DC MC V — ●
Soi 33, Sukhumvit Rd. ⓒ 0-2258-5071.
Everything is delicious, from the salami and wood-fired calzone, salads, and pasta dishes to the rich, dark coffee. 🍴 🍷

FARTHER AFIELD: *Seafood Town* ⒷⒷⒷ — AE DC MC V — ● ▪ ●
7 Soi 24, Sukhumvit Rd. ⓒ 0-2661-0037.
This is definitely the place to go if you like your seafood served up fast and tasty. Lunchtime is when the place is at its most buzzing, so maybe evening is the time to pay a visit. 🍴

FARTHER AFIELD: *Señor Pico* ⒷⒷⒷ — AE DC MC V JCB — ●
Rembrandt Hotel, Sukhumvit, Soi 18. ⓒ 0-2261-7100.
Some of the best Mexican and Tex-Mex cuisine in town, including fajitas, nachos, and combination platters, as well as good steaks. These are served in a bright and cheery atmosphere. 🍴 🍷

FARTHER AFIELD: *Stable* ⒷⒷⒷ — AE DC MC V — ● ● ▪
Soi 8, Sukhumvit Rd. ⓒ 0-2253-3410.
This is the best place to go in Bangkok if you find yourself assailed by a craving for Danish food. If you are, make straight for the Big Smorgaas buffet. 🍴

FARTHER AFIELD: *Celadon*. **Map** 8 D4. ⒷⒷⒷⒷ — AE DC MC V JCB — ● ▪
Sukhothai Bangkok Hotel, 13/3 Sathorn Tai Rd. ⓒ 0-2287-0222.
This superb Thai restaurant features delicious specialties such as *gai hor phai toey* (chicken grilled in screw pine leaves) and *tom kha kai* (chicken soup flavored with coconut and galangal). 🍴 🍷 🍵

FARTHER AFIELD: *Trader Vic's* ⒷⒷⒷⒷ — AE DC MC V JCB — ▪ ●
Marriott Royal Garden Riverside, Charoen Nakhon Rd. ⓒ 0-2476-0021.
Polynesian cuisine – dishes such as suckling pig, and smoked or fried breadfruit – in addition to some international food. Veal cutlets are a specialty: try them pan fried. 🍴 🍷 🍵

SOUTH CENTRAL PLAINS

AYUTTHAYA: *Chainam* ⒷⒷ — ● ▪ ● ▪
36/2 Uthong Rd. ⓒ 0-3525-2013.
Good Thai and Western dishes for reasonable prices are characteristic of this restaurant. It is a good place to go for Western breakfasts.

AYUTTHAYA: *Phae Krung Kao* ⒷⒷ — AE MC V — ● ▪
4 Mu 2, Uthong Rd. ⓒ 0-3524-1555.
This attractive, floating restaurant specializes in seafood, but the menu also has a wide range of chicken and pork dishes. The cuisine is mainly Thai, but some Chinese delicacies are also available. 🍴 🍷

KANCHANABURI: *Mae Nam* ⒷⒷ — ●
End of Lak Muang Rd. ⓒ 0-3451-2811.
A large floating restaurant with fish and seafood specialties. A band plays Thai pop or light Western music in the evenings.

For key to symbols see back flap

Price categories for an evening meal for one, including service, but not alcohol:

(B) under B100
(B)(B) B100–200
(B)(B)(B) B200–500
(B)(B)(B)(B) B500–1,000
(B)(B)(B)(B)(B) over B1,000

THAI SPECIALTIES
The restaurant has Thai dishes.

ASIAN (NON-THAI) DISHES
Cuisine from other parts of Asia, such as China, Korea, Japan, or India, is served.

WESTERN DISHES
French, Italian, or other Western fare is on the menu.

OUTDOOR TABLES
Facilities for eating outdoors (suan ahan), on a terrace, or in a garden or courtyard.

		Credit Cards	Thai Specialties	Asian (Non-Thai) Dishes	Western Dishes	Outdoor Tables
KANCHANABURI: *New Isaan* 292/1–2 Saengchuto Rd. No telephone. A simple, clean establishment serving typical Northeastern delicacies. Try the *kai yang* (grilled chicken) or the *som tam* (papaya salad).	(B)(B)		●			
KANCHANABURI: *Punnee Café and Bar* Saengchuto Rd. 0-3451-3503. This café has a mix of Western-style Thai and Thai-style European dishes on its menu. It also advertises "the coldest beer in town."	(B)(B)		●		●	■
LOP BURI: *Sala Mangsawirat (Vegetarian Pavillion)* 26/47 Soonkangkha Manora. No telephone. For vegetarians and meat-eaters alike, this is an inexpensive place to sample the delights of Thai vegetarian cuisine. As with most vegetarian restaurants in Thailand, opening hours are limited. after 2pm.	(B)		●			
LOP BURI: *Asia Lopburi Hotel* 1/7–8 Surasak Rd. 0-3641-8893. Quality Chinese and Thai food at reasonable prices and in comfortable surroundings. This is an ideal place to try *priaw wan* (sweet and sour) dishes or *kai phat pet mamuang* (chicken fried with cashew nuts).	(B)(B)		●	■		
SUPHAN BURI: *Wang Kung* Nang Pim Rd. No telephone. A pleasant restaurant with inexpensive Chinese and Thai-Chinese food. It is easily identified by the Chinese lanterns hanging outside.	(B)(B)	MC V	●	■		

NORTH CENTRAL PLAINS

		Credit Cards	Thai Specialties	Asian (Non-Thai) Dishes	Western Dishes	Outdoor Tables
KAMPHAENG PHET: *Malai* 77 Thesa Rd. 0-5571-1630. A small eatery serving tasty Northeastern Thai food. There is no English sign, so look out for the rice baskets hanging outside. Try the *nam phrik* pepper-based dips.	(B)		●			■
KAMPHAENG PHET: *Phayao* 217–219 Thesa Rd. 0-5571-2174. This popular bakery offers bread and a variety of sweet pastries, washed down with tea or coffee. It is a good place to enjoy breakfast in Kamphaeng Phet.	(B)				●	
KAMPHAENG PHET: *Ruan Phae Rim Ping* 120 Soi 1, Thesa 2 Rd. 0-5571-2767. Located on the bank of the Ping River, this pleasant garden restaurant rustles up *miang sawoei* – a spicy Thai hors d'oeuvre with fresh ginger, peanuts, and piquant sauces – among other specialties.	(B)(B)	MC V	●	■		■
MAE SOT: *Pim Hut* 415/11–12 Intharakiri, Tang Kim Chiang Rd. 0-5553-2818. One of a number of clean, reasonably priced restaurants along this road, Pim Hut has a selection of Western, Thai, and Chinese dishes. The moderately priced Western breakfasts are recommended.	(B)		●		●	
MAE SOT: *Kangtung* 2/1 Sri Phanich Rd. 0-5553-2030. Excellent Cantonese cuisine in the best Chinese restaurant in town. Dim sum is a delicious option at lunchtime on most days.	(B)(B)			■		
PHITSANULOK: *Laap Phet Nong Khai* 275 Singha Decha Chokechai. No telephone. The specialty of the house here is a delicious *lap phet* (duck salad). Many other Central and Northeast dishes, including *khao niaw mamuang* (mango with sticky rice), are also available.	(B)		●			

PHITSANULOK: *Rim Nam Food Market* (B)
Phuttha Bucha Rd. *No telephone.*
This large group of food stalls is a good place for *phak bung loy fa*
(flash-fried morning glory) – tossed spectacularly through the air from
chef to server – for which Phitsanulok is renowned.

PHITSANULOK: *Fah Thai* (B)(B)
Reua Pier, Wang Chan Rd. *0-5524-2743.*
This boat-restaurant cruises the Nan River each evening. Its extensive
Thai menu includes *kluay tak* (sweet banana), a local specialty.

PHITSANULOK: *Ketnikaa* (B)(B) MC V
66 Phuttha Bucha Rd. *0-5524-1333.*
Seafood specialties such as local freshwater shrimp, are offered at this
rather plush establishment. There is a live band every night.

SUKHOTHAI: *Night Market* (B)
Off Nikhon Kasem Rd. *No telephone.*
A great variety of tasty Thai favorites are available here. Try the *phat
thai* (spicy rice noodles fried with dried prawn and beansprouts), the
mussel omelettes, and the *kai ping* (charcoal-roasted eggs).

SUKHOTHAI: *Coca Sukhothai* (B)(B) MC V
Sawasdiphong Hotel, 56/2–5 Singhawat Rd. *0-5561-1567.*
A Thai-style *suki* place: that is, where diners cook their own food at
the table. Meals are a delicious concoction of fresh fish, chicken, pork,
beef, and assorted seafood with fresh vegetables in a tasty broth.

SUKHOTHAI: *Dream Café and Antique House* (B)(B) MC V
86/1 Singhawat Rd. *0-5561-2081.*
An extensive selection of Thai and Western food in this atmospheric
restaurant decorated with 19th-century Thai antiques. Choose from a
range of Thai herbal liquors, which are said to boost stamina.

TAK: *Jintana* (B)(B)
2/46 Paholyothin Rd. *0-5551-1638.*
A large restaurant with a pleasant garden terrace. The house
specialties include fish dishes and spareribs cooked with garlic.

NORTHWEST HEARTLAND

CHIANG MAI: *Galare Food Centre* (B)
89/2 Chang Khlan Rd. *0-5327-2067.*
This good selection of food stalls close to the Night Bazaar includes a
wide range of Northern and Central Thai dishes, Indian food, and seafood. On most nights traditional Thai dancers perform next to diners.

CHIANG MAI: *New Lamduan Faham Khao Soi* (B)
North of Rama IX Bridge, Charoen Rat Rd. *No telephone.*
This restaurant, which serves delicious food in unpretentious surroundings, enjoys the distinction of royal patronage. HM King Bhumibol is
said to favor the *khao soi* (chicken and noodles in a spicy broth).

CHIANG MAI: *Raan Khao Soi Islam* (B)
Charoen Prathet Rd, Soi 1. *0-5327-1484.*
A halal establishment with the best *khao soi* (broth served with
noodles) in Thailand. Other dishes include samosas, and *khao mok
kai* (chicken biryani). It is clean and the staff are friendly. *after 3pm.*

CHIANG MAI: *Sri Pen* (B)
103 Inthawarorot Rd. *0-5321-5328.*
Top quality Northern Thai food. Local specialties are cooked to the
highest standards and come with a selection of fresh green vegetables
and sticky rice. An incredibly good value for the money. *after 3pm.*

CHIANG MAI: *Brasserie Restaurant* (B)(B) MC V
37 Charoen Rat Rd. *0-5324-1665.*
Pla meuk krathiam phrik tai (fried, stuffed squid with garlic and pep-
per) is just one of the good dishes at this riverside restaurant.

CHIANG MAI: *Chiang Mai Ban Yuan* (B)(B)
8 Phra Pok Klao Rd, Soi 11. *0-5381-1258.*
Delicious Vietnamese specialties include *nam nyang* (barbecued
pork), cooked to a secret family recipe.

For key to symbols see back flap

Price categories for an evening meal for one, including service, but not alcohol:

ⓑ under B100
ⓑⓑ B100–200
ⓑⓑⓑ B200–500
ⓑⓑⓑⓑ B500–1,000
ⓑⓑⓑⓑⓑ over B1,000

THAI SPECIALTIES
The restaurant has Thai dishes.

ASIAN (NON-THAI) DISHES
Cuisine from other parts of Asia, such as China, Korea, Japan, or India, is served.

WESTERN DISHES
French, Italian, or other Western fare is on the menu.

OUTDOOR TABLES
Facilities for eating outdoors *(suan ahan)*, on a terrace, or in a garden or courtyard.

	Price	CREDIT CARDS	THAI SPECIALTIES	ASIAN (NON-THAI) DISHES	WESTERN DISHES	OUTDOOR TABLES
CHIANG MAI: *Gallery* 25–29 Charoen Rat Rd. 0-5324-8601. Excellent food such as *nam phrik ong* (spicy tomato and minced pork curry) in a delightful garden by the river. Booking is essential.	ⓑⓑ	MC V	●		●	■
CHIANG MAI: *JJ Bakery* 2–6 Ratchadamnoen Rd. 0-5341-8090. This is an enduringly popular place with both travelers and locals. The menu features good Thai food, though most people come here for the salads, sandwiches, and other snacks.	ⓑⓑ	AE MC V	●		●	■
CHIANG MAI: *Rosemary Irish Pub* 24/1 Rachawithi Rd. 0-5321-4554. Irish and English home cooking, with favorites such as sandwiches and ice cream dished up in a welcoming Irish-pub atmosphere. The fresh breads include baguettes and delicious soda bread.	ⓑⓑ		●		●	■
CHIANG MAI: *Smiling Monkey* 40/1 Bamrung Buri Rd. 0-5327-7538. A lovely garden restaurant under English management. Try one of the tasty dishes such as *kaeng khiaw wan* (green curry), or have a drink at the bar in the charming, old teak house.	ⓑⓑ	MC V JCB	●			
CHIANG MAI: *Whole Earth* 88 Si Don Chai Rd. 0-5328-2463. A long-established vegetarian and South Asian restaurant set in attractive grounds, not far from the Night Bazaar. It is one of the few restaurants in Chiang Mai offering Indian cuisine.	ⓑⓑ		●	■		
CHIANG MAI: *Antique House* 71 Charoen Prathet Rd. 0-5327-6810. Enjoy a delicious Northern or Central Thai meal in a late 19th-century restored wooden house, or dine in its small garden, which is decorated with antique Lanna furniture and handicrafts.	ⓑⓑⓑ	MC V	●	■		■
CHIANG MAI: *Babylon* 100/63 Huai Kaew Rd. 0-5321-2180. The atmosphere is that of a small, charming, Italian village café. Spaghetti with blue cheese is just one of the superb dishes.	ⓑⓑⓑ	MC V			●	
CHIANG MAI: *Kaeng Ron Ban Suan* 149/3 Soi Chom Doi. 0-5321-3762. Beautifully located at the foot of Doi Suthep, this restaurant specializes in Northern Thai food. Try the *sai wua* (Northern-style sausage) or the *pak kut* (a Thai vegetable harvested only in the wild).	ⓑⓑⓑ	AE DC MC V	●			■
CHIANG MAI: *Khun Pad's Kitchen* 49/1–8 Arrak Rd, Suandok Gate. 0-5381-4558. This charming restaurant, in Paddy Fields Hotel, serves fine Thai cuisine in relaxed surroundings. Its delightful ambience attracts locals and tourists, too. Ask for a table on the garden terrace.	ⓑⓑⓑ	MC V	●			
CHIANG MAI: *Old Chiang Mai Cultural Center* 185/3 Wualai Rd. 0-5320-2993. This is a good place to enjoy a traditional Northern Thai *khantoke* dinner, with classical Thai dance and music. The restaurant is set in a series of old Lanna-style houses. ● *after 9pm.*	ⓑⓑⓑ	MC V	●			■
CHIANG MAI: *Le Coq d'Or* 68/1 Koh Klang Rd. 0-5328-2024. Chiang Mai's best French restaurant is part of an elegant house that once belonged to the first British consul in Chiang Mai. The wine list is unusually comprehensive for Thailand.	ⓑⓑⓑⓑ	AE DC MC V			●	

CHIANG MAI: *Piccola Roma Palace* ⒷⒷⒷⒷⒷ
144 Charoen Prathet Rd. 【 *0-5327-1256.*
A first-class restaurant whose fresh seafood is flown in daily. The
Italian owner, Angelo, has a wine list unsurpassed in Northern Thailand. Luxurious surroundings are matched by authentic food. 🍴 🍷

	AE MC V			●	

LAMPANG: *Mackenna Pub* Ⓑ
Tipchang Rd, next to Riverside Bar and Restaurant. 【 *No telephone.*
Popular for *kap klaem* (snacks), which can accompany iced beer or
Thai whisky. Dine on the excellent *mu sap bai kaprao* (minced pork
with holy basil) while enjoying views of the Yom River. 🍴

	MC V	●			■

LAMPANG: *Baan Rim Nam* ⒷⒷ
328 Tipchang Rd, next to Mackenna Pub. 【 *0-5422-1861.*
A very popular place situated, as its name suggests, by the river. The
cuisine is excellent, including Thai dishes such as *phat kari pu* (crab
meat in yellow curry sauce). There is live folk music every night.

	MC V	●		●	■

LAMPANG: *Khrua Tai Rim Nam* ⒷⒷ
Pamai Rd, Amphur Wiang Neua. 【 *No telephone.*
Located on the bank of the Wang River in a large teak house, this is
the best restaurant in the old Wiang Neua part of the city. Try the *tot
man kung* – shrimp cakes with a sweet tamarind sauce. 🍴 🍷

		●			■

LAMPANG: *Suki Bhami Coca* ⒷⒷ
138/72–74 Paholyothin Rd. 【 *0-5431-6440.*
Thai-style *suki* cuisine, where diners cook their own food at the table
on hotplates. Enduringly popular with the locals. 🍴

	MC V	●	■		

LAMPHUN: *Ba-Mii Kwangtung* Ⓑ
On the corner of Rot Kaew and Inthayongyot roads. 【 *No telephone.*
An excellent selection of fresh noodles makes this just about the best
place to eat in Lamphun. There is no English sign, but as the cooking
is done by the entrance, it is easy to find. ● *by nightfall most evenings.*

		●			

MAE HONG SON: *Good Luck Restaurant* Ⓑ
Khunlum Phraphat Rd. 【 *No telephone.*
This little place juggles a remarkably international range of dishes – Thai,
Greek, Turkish, Jewish, Arab, and vegetarian – all to a high standard.

		●	■	●	

MAE HONG SON: *Bai Fern* ⒷⒷ
87 Khunlum Phraphat Rd. 【 *0-5361-1374.*
An attractive restaurant in a large wooden house, offering a variety of
good, inexpensive Central Thai and Chinese food, as well as simple
Western dishes. A pleasant atmosphere adds to the experience.

		●		●	■

MAE HONG SON: *Khai Muk* ⒷⒷ
71 Khunlum Prapas Rd. 【 *0-5361-2092.*
Chinese and Thai dishes in simple yet attractive surroundings make
this place a favorite with locals and visitors alike. The *kai phat met
mamuang* (chicken fried with cashew nuts) is recommended.

		●	■		■

MAE HONG SON: *Golden Teak* ⒷⒷⒷ
Imperial Tara Hotel. 【 *0-5361-1021.*
This resort hotel, 3 km (2 miles) outside town, serves delicious Thai
food. Outside tables overlook the lush terraced valley. 🍴 🍷

	AE DC MC V	●			■

MAE SARIANG: *Inthira Restaurant* Ⓑ
Wiang Mai Rd. 【 *0-5368-1529.*
The Inthira is deservedly popular for serving the best Thai and
Chinese food in remote Mae Sariang. The restaurant is well known for
its lunchtime *kop krob* (batter-fried frogs).

		●	■	⌡	

PAI: *Own Home Restaurant* Ⓑ
Ratchadamrong Rd. 【 *No telephone.*
Good-quality mixed cuisine in this out-of-the-way spot. Try the falafel
with hummus, tzatziki, and other Middle Eastern fare. The menu also
includes Indian samosas, Mexican burritos, and vegetarian Thai food.

		●	■	●	■

PAI: *Tai Yai Restaurant* Ⓑ
Ratchadamnoen Rd. 【 *No telephone.*
Enjoy the best Western breakfast in Pai, featuring home-baked whole
wheat bread, muesli, and locally grown coffee. The majority of Pai's
restaurants are closed by 10pm – this stays open later than most.

		●		●	

For key to symbols see back flap

<table>
<tr><td colspan="2">

Price categories for an evening meal for one, including service, but not alcohol:

B under B100
BB B100–200
BBB B200–500
BBBB B500–1,000
BBBBB over B1,000

</td><td colspan="2">

THAI SPECIALTIES
The restaurant has Thai dishes.

ASIAN (NON-THAI) DISHES
Cuisine from other parts of Asia, such as China, Korea, Japan, or India, is served.

WESTERN DISHES
French, Italian, or other Western fare is on the menu.

OUTDOOR TABLES
Facilities for eating outdoors (suan ahan), on a terrace, or in a garden or courtyard.

</td></tr>
</table>

		CREDIT CARDS	THAI SPECIALTIES	ASIAN (NON-THAI) DISHES	WESTERN DISHES	OUTDOOR TABLES
FAR NORTH						
CHIANG KHONG: *Lawt Tin Lu* — B			●	■		
Sai Klang Rd, Soi 2. No telephone. Simple but delicious Chinese and Thai food is served at this branch of a renowned Shan-Chinese restaurant in Kengtung, eastern Burma.						
CHIANG RAI: *Mae Oui Kiaw* — B			●			
106/9 Ngam Muang Rd. No telephone. An exceptional place for Northern Thai cuisine, with all the common dishes, including *nam phrik ong* (a spicy curry of tomato and minced pork) and *kaeng hang le* (pork and ginger curry). ● after 6pm.						
CHIANG RAI: *Raan Ahaan Islam* — B			●			■
142 Itsaraphap Rd. No telephone. One of the top halal establishments in town. The house specialties include *khao mok kai* (chicken biryani) and *khao soi* (a wheat noodle and coconut milk curry with beef or chicken). ● after 3pm.						
CHIANG RAI: *Golden Triangle International Café* — BB		MC V	●		●	
590 Paholyothin Rd. 0-5371-1339. Central Thai food made to Western tastes – not too hot unless requested. Many Western dishes, too, including breakfasts. ▤						
CHIANG RAI: *Yunnan* — BB				■		
2211/9 Khwae Wai Rd. 0-5371-3263. Specializing in regional Chinese food including Sichuan, with dishes such as Yunnanese ham and Kunming-style fried milk. ⚟						
CHIANG RAI: *Chinatown* — BBB		AE DC MC V JCB		■		
Dusit Island Resort, 1129 Kraisorasit Rd. 0-5371-5777. An extremely extensive Chinese menu. Dim sum is a lunchtime specialty, while Peking duck is an excellent dish served in the evenings in a classy ambience. ▤ ⚟						
CHIANG RAI: *Giovanni's Pizza* — BBB					●	
595 Paholyothin Rd. No telephone. Chiang Rai's best Italian restaurant. The menu features a wide range of antipasto, pizza, pasta, and meat dishes. A favorite with the town's ex-patriate community. ▤ ⚟						
CHIANG SAEN: *Bierstübe* — BBB					●	
897/6 Paholyothin Rd. 0-5371-4195. If you're pining for rich, hearty German fare, then this is the place to come. All the usual German favorites – such as wiener schnitzel (veal in breadcrumbs) – come with draught beer or schnapps. ▤ ⚟						
DOI MAE SALONG (SANTIKHIREE): *Mae Salong Villa* — BBB		AE MC V	●	■	●	■
5 Mu 1, Doi Mae Salong. 0-5376-5115. A popular restaurant with good views across the hills. Often at night, a barbecue is held around a warming log fire. The menu consists of Chinese – in particular, Yunnanese – specialties. ⚟						
FANG: *Parichat Road* — B			●			
Rawp Wiang Rd. No telephone. This small, clean Thai restaurant specializes in noodles. Try the excellent *khao soi* – a bowl of wheat noodles served in a chicken or beef curry broth, eaten with lime and chili peppers.						
GOLDEN TRIANGLE: *Border View* — BBB		AE DC MC V	●	■	●	
Delta Golden Triangle Hotel, 222 Golden Triangle, Sop Ruak. 0-5378-4001. Elegant dining on a terrace overlooking the Mekong. Excellent Thai and Chinese food, as well as good, genuine Western cuisine. ▤ ⚟						

GOLDEN TRIANGLE: *Sala Maenam* ⒷⒷⒷ
Anantara Resort & Spa. 🔲 *0-5378-4086.*
Despite its name, this upscale establishment does not offer Lao food, but Thai, Chinese, and Western cuisine. The dishes are good, and the setting, at the heart of the Golden Triangle, is even better. 🔲 🍷

AE DC MC V JCB

MAE SAI: *Jo Jo's Café* Ⓑ
233/1 Mu 1 Paholyothin Rd. 🔲 *0-5373-1662.*
A varied menu of delicious Thai and Western food is on offer here at reasonable prices. Try the *khao soi* (rice noodles in curry sauce) or *khao mok kai* (Muslim chicken biryani). 🔲

MAE SAI: *Rabieng Kaew* ⒷⒷ
356/1 Mu 1, Paholyothin Rd. 🔲 *0-5373-1173.*
Excellent Central and Northern Thai food, as well as some unexpected Asian specialties. Try the fresh, tender Korean barbecued beef. Northern Thai music is played in the evenings. 🔲

NAN: *No Name* Ⓑ
38/1 Suriyapong Rd. 🔲 *No telephone.*
Noodle dishes at very reasonable prices. Try the *kuaytiaw reua* – literally "boat noodles" – a delicious, spicy broth.

PHRAE: *Night Market* Ⓑ
Pratuchai intersection. 🔲 *No telephone.*
Not an individual restaurant, but a collection of food stalls with street-side tables and chairs. An excellent place to enjoy incredibly cheap and tasty Central Thai and Thai-Chinese food.

PHRAE: *Ban Fai* ⒷⒷⒷ
57/6 Mu 1, Yantrakit Koson Rd. 🔲 *0-5452-3114.*
On the menu at this large restaurant is good Central Thai food, and perhaps the best seafood in town. 🔲 🍷

MC V

KHORAT PLATEAU

BURIRAM: *Phnom Rung Park* Ⓑ
Phnom Rung Hill. 🔲 *No telephone.*
These stalls and small restaurants offer a delicious array of dishes including *som tam* (papaya salad), grilled chicken, and sticky rice. This is the only refreshment stop at Prasat Hin Khao Phnom Rung.

CHAIYAPHUM: *Phaibun* Ⓑ
Ratchathan Rd. 🔲 *No telephone.*
Good Central Thai and Chinese cuisine is offered at this large, comfortable, clean, and dependable restaurant. Try the *mu prio wan* (sweet and sour pork) or the *kaeng khiaw wan* (green curry). 🔲 🍷

KHON KAEN: *Nong Lek* ⒷⒷ
67/19–20 Mitraphab Rd. 🔲 *0-4326-1759.*
Good Thai and Chinese food in a restaurant patronized by locals. The specialties are *khao na pet* (duck served with rice) and seafood.

KHON KAEN: *Pa Uan J.C. Esan* ⒷⒷ
Laub Baeng Rd. 🔲 *0-4332-0182.*
The Northeast Thai dishes served here are popular with the locals but are very hot, so be careful! Specialties include grilled fish, northeastern-style beef soup with chilli and *somtam* (papaya salad).

KHORAT: *VFW (Veterans of Foreign Wars) Café* Ⓑ
167–168 Phok Klang Rd. 🔲 *0-4424-2831.*
This café, founded by ex-US servicemen, specializes in American-style fast food and simple Thai dishes. It is a good place for breakfast. 🔲

KHORAT: *Great Wall* ⒷⒷ
Chomphon Rd. 🔲 *No telephone.*
Khorat has an extensive Sino-Thai population, and this Chinese estab-lishment is one of the community's favorite eating places. Enjoy the excellent Cantonese cuisine in comfortable, relaxing surroundings. 🔲

MC V JCB

PHIMAI: *Bai Toey* Ⓑ
Chomsuda Sadet Rd. 🔲 *0-4447-1725.*
Simple Thai and Western fare in a garden setting. Try the vegetarian dishes and the sweets made from sticky rice and coconut milk.

Price categories for an evening meal for one, including service, but not alcohol:	THAI SPECIALTIES — The restaurant has Thai dishes.
Ⓑ under B100	ASIAN (NON-THAI) DISHES — Cuisine from other parts of Asia, such as China, Korea, Japan, or India, is served.
ⒷⒷ B100–200	WESTERN DISHES — French, Italian, or other Western fare is on the menu.
ⒷⒷⒷ B200–500	OUTDOOR TABLES — Facilities for eating outdoors (suan ahan), on a terrace, or in a garden or courtyard.
ⒷⒷⒷⒷ B500–1,000	
ⒷⒷⒷⒷⒷ over B1,000	

	Price	Credit Cards	Thai Specialties	Asian (Non-Thai) Dishes	Western Dishes	Outdoor Tables
ROI ET: *Neua Yang Kaolee* Rim Beung Plan Chai Rd. 🔲 No telephone. This excellent garden restaurant is located on the northeastern side of Beung Phlan Chai Lake, in the center of town. It is named after the house specialty, Korean barbecued beef, which is cooked at the table.	ⒷⒷ	MC V		■		■
SURIN: *Paetee* 2/4–5 Tessabali Rd. 🔲 0-4451-1682. One of the biggest Chinese restaurants in town, with a wide-ranging menu that has become popular with both visitors and locals. ▤	ⒷⒷⒷ			■		
UDON THANI: *Rung Thong* Hor Nalika Clock Tower. 🔲 0-4222-3154. A simple establishment that excels at delicious, reasonably priced Central and Northeastern food, including Thai curries. Try the *tom kha kai* (chicken soup with coconut milk and lemon grass).	Ⓑ		●			
UDON THANI: *Madame Kiu* Adunyadet Rd. 🔲 No telephone. A late-night place that stays open until 4am providing good Central Thai and Chinese food, as well as some basic Western fare. *Kung phat phrik phao* (shrimp fried with chilies) is one of the specialties. ▤	ⒷⒷ		●	■	●	
UDON THANI: *Mayfair* Charoen Hotel, 549 Phosri Rd. 🔲 0-4224-8155. This award-winning restaurant has the best reputation for good food in Udon Thani. There is an extensive menu that features Thai and Chinese cuisine in addition to good Western breakfasts. ▤ 🍷	ⒷⒷⒷ	AE DC MC V JCB	●	■	●	
MEKONG RIVER VALLEY						
CHIANG KHAN: *Suksomboon Hotel* 243/3 Chai Khong Rd. 🔲 0-4282-1064. Situated on the Mekong River. If you have the stomach for it, sample the *gung ten* – live shrimp taken straight from the river, immersed in a bowl of lemon and chili sauce, and eaten while still alive.	Ⓑ		●	■	●	
LOEI: *Savita* 317/2 Loeidansai Rd. 🔲 0-4281-2499. Savita is a restaurant/coffee shop, serving Central Thai food and Thai-style Western fast food including burgers and sandwiches. ▤	ⒷⒷ	MC V	●		●	
MUKDAHAN: *Night Market* Songnang Sathit Rd. 🔲 No telephone. This extensive group of food stalls near the bus station sells Thai, Lao, and Vietnamese specialties at excellent prices.	Ⓑ		●	■		
MUKDAHAN: *Riverside* Samran Chai Khong Rd. 🔲 No telephone. A shady riverside terrace that has pleasant views of Suwannakhet in Laos across the water. The menu features Thai and Chinese cuisine and cold beer. One of the best dishes is *lap phet* (spicy duck salad).	ⒷⒷ		●	■		■
NAKHON PHANOM: *Nawt Laap Phet* 494 Aphiban Bancha Rd. 🔲 0-4251-1994. Northeastern specialties, as well as common dishes such as spicy grilled chicken and papaya salad. Especially recommended is the *yang seua rong hai* – literally "grilled crying tiger" – beef with chilies.	Ⓑ		●			
NAKHON PHANOM: *Mekhong Golden Giant Catfish* 417 Sunthon Wichit Rd. 🔲 0-4251-1218. *Pla buk* – giant Mekong catfish – is the specialty here. Try it stir-fried with holy basil (*phat kraphao*) or baked in a clay pot (*op mo din*). 🍷	ⒷⒷ	AE MC V	■		●	■

NONG KHAI: *Udom Rot* Ⓑ
423 Rim Khong Rd. (0-4241-2561.
Good views of the Mekong and the river traffic to Laos. Enjoy the excellent *phat tai*, which is thin rice noodles fried with bean sprouts, egg, pork, and dried shrimp, served with a slice of fresh lime.

NONG KHAI: *Indochine* ⒷⒷ
189/1 Meechai Rd. (No telephone.
This is an excellent place to sample Vietnamese cooking. Among the typical dishes are spring rolls accompanied by fresh green vegetables, barbecued sausages, and various egg-based concoctions.

THAT PHANOM: *That Phanom Pochana* Ⓑ
31 Phanom Phanarak Rd. (0-4254-1189.
Situated near the triumphal arch in the center of town, this restaurant specializes in reasonably priced Thai and Chinese fish dishes.

UBON RATCHATHANI: *Jiaw Kii* Ⓑ
Khuan Thani Rd. (No telephone.
An excellent place for breakfast, whether you like Thai *khao tom* (rice soup) or Western-style ham and eggs with warm buns. 🍴

UBON RATCHATHANI: *Indochine* ⒷⒷ V
Wat Chang, 168–170 Sapphasit Rd. (0-4524-5584.
People travel from all over the country to enjoy the great Vietnamese cooking – the omelettes in particular are praised – and the pleasant, relaxed atmosphere of this old teak house.

EASTERN SEABOARD

CHANTHABURI: *Chanthon Phochana* Ⓑ
126/4 Benchamarachutit Rd. (0-3932-1240.
Tasty Thai and Chinese fare is served at this spotlessly clean restaurant. Chanthaburi is known for its noodle dishes, and this is the place to taste dishes such as *sen mi phat pu* (crab fried with noodles).

CHANTHABURI: *Mangsawirat* Ⓑ
Tha Chalab Rd, Soi 3. (No telephone.
A tiny vegetarian establishment next to Taksin Park. As well as delicious, reasonably priced food, there are many fresh fruit juices, including guava, *roselle* (similar to blackcurrant), coconut, and tamarind.

KO CHANG: *Sunset (Tawanplob)* ⒷⒷⒷ MC V
39 Mu 4, Ko Chang. (no telephone.
An upscale place for this relatively undeveloped island, with seafood specialties and a wide range of dishes. 🍴

PATTAYA: *Poteen Still* Ⓑ
219/68 Soi Yamato. (0-3842-0644.
Uniquely, this place serves a mixture of Irish pub fare, such as fish and chips, together with various Thai dishes. 🍴

PATTAYA: *Ali Baba* ⒷⒷ AE V MC
1/13–14 Central Pattaya Rd. (0-3842-9262.
This restaurant has two menus: good North Indian cuisine inside, and South Indian vegetarian food outside. Choose from a variety of curries, dhals, Indian breads, and cooling raitas. 🍴 🍴

PATTAYA: *Bahay Filipino* ⒷⒷ MC V
485/3 Pattaya 2nd Rd. (0-3842-6191.
This establishment features Filipino specialties, accompanied by live music. Try the suckling pig, *gambas al ajillio* (raw shrimp in garlic and olive oil), or *gambas rebosado* (shrimp baked in butter). 🍴 🍴

PATTAYA: *Nang Loi* ⒷⒷ AE MC V
214/10 South Pattaya Beach Road. (0-3842-8478.
On Pattaya's well-known 'strip', this is a great place for seafood. Choose your own fish and your preferred cooking method. The huge steaks are delicious too. A patio overlooks the sea for outdoor dining.

PATTAYA: *Russkii* ⒷⒷ
205/8–9 Pattaya 2nd Rd. (0-3842-9662, 0-1268-6569.
This is the best Russian place in the resort. Try the borscht (beet soup), *pelmeni* (small dumplings), or chicken Kiev. 🍴

For key to symbols see back flap

Price categories for an evening meal for one, including service, but not alcohol:

Ⓑ under B100
ⒷⒷ B100–200
ⒷⒷⒷ B200–500
ⒷⒷⒷⒷ B500–1,000
ⒷⒷⒷⒷⒷ over B1,000

THAI SPECIALTIES
The restaurant has Thai dishes.

ASIAN (NON-THAI) DISHES
Cuisine from other parts of Asia, such as China, Korea, Japan, or India, is served.

WESTERN DISHES
French, Italian, or other Western fare is on the menu.

OUTDOOR TABLES
Facilities for eating outdoors *(suan ahan),* on a terrace, or in a garden or courtyard.

	Price	Credit Cards	Thai Specialties	Asian (Non-Thai) Dishes	Western Dishes	Outdoor Tables
PATTAYA: *Vientiane* 485/18 Pattaya 2nd Rd. 0-3841-1298. Pattaya's foremost Indochinese restaurant has a varied menu that features Lao, Vietnamese, Thai, and Chinese dishes, as well as seafood. 🍽	ⒷⒷ	AE V	●	■	●	■
PATTAYA: *Bruno's Restaurant & Wine Bar* Central Shopping Arcade, Pattaya 2nd Rd. 0-3836-1073. An unpretentious yet elegant restaurant, featuring an international menu with several house specialties on offer. The wine bar has a walk-in cave that serves as a wine cellar, supplying 150 different wines. 🍽 🍷	ⒷⒷⒷ				●	■
PATTAYA: *Delaney's* Pattaya 2 Rd. 0-3871-0641. A traditional Irish pub setting with live music most evenings. The place is popular at lunchtime, when you can order Delany's famous "Irish Curry." This is a lively venue at any time and usually fills up quickly with a trendy, mixed crowd. 🍽	ⒷⒷⒷ	AE DC MC V			●	
PATTAYA: *Green Bottle* Diana Inn, 216/6–9 Pattaya 2nd Rd. 0-3842-9675. Great food in this friendly English-style pub. The specialties include lobster thermidor, roast duck in a red wine sauce and fillet steak stuffed with goose liver paté and wrapped in bacon. 🍽 🍷	ⒷⒷⒷ	AE DC MC V	●		●	
PATTAYA: *La Gritta* Amari Orchid Resort, 240 Mu 5, Pattaya Beach Rd. 0-3842-8161. Allegedly Pattaya's top Italian restaurant, specializing in seafood. Typical fare includes pizza and pasta dishes, as well as monthly promotions featuring local produce cooked Italian style. 🍽 🍷 🍴	ⒷⒷⒷ	AE MC V			●	
PATTAYA: *Lobster Pot* 228 Beach Rd, South Pattaya. 0-3842-6083. A fine seafood restaurant. The extensive menu is matched by a pleasant atmosphere. Renowned for its fresh seafood – this is the best place for lobster thermidor in Pattaya. 🍷	ⒷⒷⒷ	AE MC V	●		●	
PATTAYA: *Mai Kai Supper Club* Hotel Tropicana, Pattaya Beach Rd. 0-3842-8645. Polynesian specialties and standard Western fare in air-conditioned comfort overlooking Pattaya bay. At Mai Kai Supper Club there is live music from a Haitian band every evening. 🍽 🍷	ⒷⒷⒷ	AE DC MC V		■	●	
PATTAYA: *Pan Pan San Domenico* 313-313/1 Tappaya Rd. 0-3825-1874. An outstanding Italian restaurant. Everything about this place, from the food to the decor, is first class. The rather limited menu is rescued by a wide range of fresh desserts and pastries. 🍽 🍷	ⒷⒷⒷ	AE MC V JCB			●	
PATTAYA: *Pattaya Park Tower* 345 Jomtien Beach Rd. 0-3825-1201. The food is good and the views are superb at this revolving seafood restaurant located on the 52nd floor of Pattaya's tallest building. The buffet includes Japanese, Thai, Chinese, and European food. 🍽	ⒷⒷⒷ	AE MC V	●	■	●	
PATTAYA: *PIC Kitchen* Soi 5, Pattaya Beach Rd. 0-3842-8387. Top quality traditional Thai food at a restaurant composed of a series of beautiful teak houses complete with floor cushions. Classical Thai dancing is a feature every week. 🍽 🍷	ⒷⒷⒷ	AE MC V	●		●	■

PATTAYA: *Red Baron*   ⓑⓑⓑ
Amari Orchid Resort, 240 Mu 5, Pattaya Beach Rd. 【 *0-3842-8161.*
German and Swiss specialties are the order of the day at this stylish
restaurant. The location is peaceful and near to the beach. 🍽 🍷
AE DC MC V

PATTAYA: *Ruen Thai*   ⓑⓑⓑ
485/3 Pattaya 2nd Rd. 【 *0-3842-5911.*
Thai food of great quality is served in a cluster of open-air wooden
pavilions, accompanied by jazz music and classical Thai dancing every
night. The children's facilities include a playground. 🍽 🍷
AE MC V

PATTAYA: *Sugar Hut*   ⓑⓑⓑ
391/18 Tappaya Rd. 【 *0-3825-1686.*
Sumptuous teak houses in a setting that is hard to fault. The menu
focuses on Central Thai cuisine, with delicious and well-presented
dishes. It is excellent value for the money. 🍽 🍷
AE DC MC V

SI RACHA: *Chua Li*   ⓑⓑⓑ
46/22 Sukhumvit Rd. 【 *0-3831-1244.*
An excellent seafood place, concentrating on Thai and Chinese dishes.
Si Racha gives its name to the local specialty: a delicious, spicy sauce
called *nam phrik si racha.* Try it with grilled lobster or crayfish. 🍽
MC V

TRAT: *Sang Fah*   ⓑⓑ
157–159 Sukhumvit Rd. 【 *0-3951-1222.*
An extensive menu featuring many seafood dishes; the *tom yam pla
chon* (spicy fish stew) is recommended. 🍽

WESTERN SEABOARD

CHA-AM: *Family Shop*   ⓑⓑ
Ruamchit Rd. 【 *No telephone*
This basic restaurant offers delicious, fresh seafood barbecues right on
the seashore. Enjoy the huge, succulent giant shrimp.

CHA-AM: *Sorndaeng*   ⓑⓑ
Cha-am Methavali Hotel, 220 Ruamchit Rd. 【 *0-3243-3250.*
Cha-am is well known for its seafood, and this restaurant serves some
of the best, cooked to both Western and Thai recipes. 🍽 🍷

HUA HIN: *Maria Ice Cream*   ⓑ
54/2 Decha Nuchit Rd. 【 *No telephone.*
Wonderful homemade ice cream, ideal for cooling down in the heat.
Choose from a whole spectrum of flavors, including papaya, durian,
watermelon, and coconut. Simple Thai snacks are also on the menu.

HUA HIN: *Museum*   ⓑⓑ
Hotel Sofitel Central, 1 Damnoen Kasem Rd. 【 *0-3251-2036.*
In keeping with its surroundings in the Sofitel (formerly Railway)
Hotel *(see p321),* the Museum is decorated in 1920s style. Traditional
high tea, with delicious pastries, can be taken here. 🍽 🍷
AE DC MC V

HUA HIN: *Charlie's Seafood*   ⓑⓑⓑ
Naresdamri Rd. 【 *No telephone.*
A wide range of freshly caught seafood at reasonable prices. House
specialties worth sampling include *pla samli* (cotton fish), *pla kapong*
(perch), and *hoi malaeng pu* (mussels).

HUA HIN: *Goya*   ⓑⓑⓑ
Hilton Hua Hin Resort & Spa, 33 Naresdamri Rd. 【 *0-3251-2888.*
One of Thailand's very few Spanish restaurants. The menu features
Iberian favorites such as paella, gazpacho, and various tapas. The
seafood specialties are particularly good. 🍽 🍷 🍷
AE DC MC V

HUA HIN: *Railway*   ⓑⓑⓑ
Hotel Sofitel Central, 1 Damnoen Kasem Rd. 【 *0-3251-2036.*
This restaurant in the former Railway Hotel specializes in French and
Asian cuisine, and there is a daily buffet with either Italian or Thai
food. Eat against the backdrop of a 1920s railroad station. 🍽 🍷
AE DC MC V

HUA HIN: *Saeng Thai*   ⓑⓑⓑ
By the pier on Naresdamri Rd. 【 *0-3251-2144.*
Right on the waterfront with outdoor tables, this is one of the oldest
seafood restaurants in town. Popular with residents and visitors alike.
MC V

Price categories for an evening meal for one, including service, but not alcohol: B under B100 BB B100–200 BBB B200–500 BBBB B500–1,000 BBBBB over B1,000	**THAI SPECIALTIES** The restaurant has Thai dishes. **ASIAN (NON-THAI) DISHES** Cuisine from other parts of Asia, such as China, Korea, Japan, or India, is served. **WESTERN DISHES** French, Italian, or other Western fare is on the menu. **OUTDOOR TABLES** Facilities for eating outdoors *(suan ahan)*, on a terrace, or in a garden or courtyard.			

		CREDIT CARDS	THAI SPECIALTIES	ASIAN (NON-THAI) DISHES	WESTERN DISHES	OUTDOOR TABLES
HUA HIN: *Suan Luang* BBBB Anantara Resort & Spa, 43/1 Phetkasem Rd. 📞 *0-3252-0250.* Excellent Thai food is served here in a traditional antique Thai setting. Live classical Thai music accompanies the meal. 🍽 🍴			●			
HUA HIN: *Palm Pavilion* BBBBB Hotel Sofitel Central, 1 Damnoen Kasem Rd. 📞 *0-3251-2036.* Another elegant, 1920s restaurant within this delightful hotel. Food includes a creative seafood menu and fine cuts of imported beef and lamb. It is very popular, so reservations are recommended. 🍽 🍴 🍷		AE DC MC V	●		●	■
KO PHA NGAN: *Island View Cabana* B Mae Hat Beach. 📞 *0-7737-7019.* Travelers in search of reasonably priced, international fare should go to this quiet, outdoor restaurant. When it is available, the steak *pla chalam* (chargrilled fresh shark steak) is memorable.				●	●	■
KO SAMUI: *Brasserie* BB Beach Comber Hotel, 3/5 Mu 2, Chaweng Beach. 📞 *0-7742-2041.* The usual excellent seafood for which Ko Samui is famous, but with a difference: at this restaurant the chefs specialize in Italian cooking. 🍴		MC V	●		●	■
KO SAMUI: *Happy Elephant* BB 79/1 Mu 1, Tambon Bophut. 📞 *0-7724-5347.* Both Thai and Western dishes, at reasonable prices. The seafood specialties are good, particularly the *kung pan oy* (shrimp cakes grilled on fresh sugar cane sticks, then dipped in sweet tamarind sauce). 🍴			●		●	
KO SAMUI: *Captain's Choice* BBB 83 Boathouse Hotel, Choeng Mon Beach. 📞 *0-7742-5041.* One of Ko Samui's top restaurants, with a wide range of fresh seafoods. All the usual maritime favorites, including shrimp, squid, crab, lobster, and crayfish, plus less common seafoods such as shark. 🍽 🍴		AE DC MC V JCB	●	■	●	■
KO SAMUI: *Coral Cove Chalet Restaurant* BBB Lamai Beach. 📞 *0-7742-2260.* A beautiful location, matched by tasty and fresh food. The specialties include *tom kha kai* (chicken cooked in coconut milk) and *kung phao* (grilled shrimp). Good Western breakfasts are also available. 🍴		AE MC V	●		●	■
KO SAMUI: *Island Restaurant* BBB North Chaweng Beach. 📞 No telephone. Reputed to give the largest helpings on Ko Samui, this restaurant specializes in seafood and Italian dishes. Imported meat, including Australian beefsteaks and New Zealand lamb, is another feature. 🍴		AE MC V	●		●	■
KO SAMUI: *Kinaree* BBB 14/3 Mu 2, Tambon Bophut. 📞 *0-7742-2015.* This chic, fern-filled restaurant offers seafood dishes including lobster thermidor, stuffed crab, and many other delicious specialties. 🍽 🍴		AE DC MC V	●		●	
KO SAMUI: *Laguna Terrace* BBB Blue Lagoon Chaweng, 99 Mu 2, Chaweng Beach. 📞 *0-7742-2037.* A combination of seafood, Thai, and European cuisine. The lunchtime buffet, on Tuesdays, Thursdays and Saturdays, is huge and reasonably priced. There is Thai dancing in the evenings. 🍴		AE MC V	●	■	●	■
KO SAMUI: *Chez Andy* BBBB 164/2 Chaweng Beach Rd. 📞 *0-7742-2593.* A Swiss restaurant serving Swiss, German, Thai and International cuisine. The head chef is Swiss, and insists that he serves the very best steak in town! 🍴		V			●	■

Ko Tao: *Ko Tao Cottage*   ⒷⒷ
19/1 Chalok Ban Khao Beach. 📞 *0-7745-6133.*
One of the best restaurants on this tiny island, pleasantly isolated from the main center of activity at Ban Hat Sairee. Not surprisingly, the menu features seafood, as well as Thai and Western dishes.

Phetchaburi: *Ban Khanom Thai*   Ⓑ
130 Petchkasem Rd. 📞 *0-3242-8011.*
Phetchaburi is famed for its Thai sweets, and the name of this establishment means "house of Thai desserts." Sample the *khanom mo kaeng*, a firm custard of mung beans, eggs, coconut, and sugar.

Prachuap Khiri Khan: *Phloen Samut*   ⒷⒷⒷ
44 Beach Rd. 📞 *0-3260-1866.*
A good place to try the local specialty, *pla samli taet diaw*, which is flash-fried, sun-dried cotton fish, served with mango salad. 🔯

Surat Thani: *Suan Isaan*   ⒷⒷ
Off Donnok Rd, 1 Damnoen Kasem Rd. 📞 *No telephone.*
A traditional Thai house with delicious Northeastern food, such as *kai yang* (grilled chicken), *som tam* (papaya salad), and other delicacies.

UPPER ANDAMAN COAST

Ko Lanta: *La Crêperie*   ⒷⒷ
Ko Lanta Yai. 📞 *No telephone.*
Seafood is the mainstay of Ko Lanta cooking, and at this restaurant it is given a French touch. The seafood pancakes are outstanding.

Ko Phi Phi: *The Rock Restaurant*   ⒷⒷ
Ton Sai Village, Ko Phi Phi Don. 📞 *0-7561-2402.*
Enjoy traditional Thai dishes in this unique restaurant with tables on raised terraces among the trees. The red curry with prawns is particularly good, or try the Rock Babeque, which you cook at your own table.

Ko Phi Phi: *Patcharee Seafood*   ⒷⒷⒷⒷ
Ton Sai Village, Ko Phi Phi Don. 📞 *No telephone.*
Excellent fresh seafood at relatively steep prices. Indulge in the barbecued shark steak, just one of several great dishes available.

Krabi: *Panan Makanan Islam*   Ⓑ
At the corner of Ruen Rudi and Maharat roads. 📞 *No telephone.*
Malay cuisine is popular in Krabi. Try the biryanis and satay, or the more unusual *kaeng matsaman*, beef curry with a peanut sauce.

Krabi: *Kotung*   ⒷⒷ
36 Kongkha Rd. 📞 *0-7561-1522.*
A seafood restaurant serving Central and Southern Thai dishes. Clean, friendly, and cheap, this place can be relied upon. The *tom yam kung* (a spicy broth with shrimp and mushrooms) is recommended. ● *Sun.*

Phangnga: *Duang*   Ⓑ
122 Phetkasem Rd. 📞 *0-7641-2216.*
Chinese and Southern Thai cuisine are featured on this restaurant's menu. The seafood is particularly fresh, with tasty dishes such as *tom yam thalay* (spicy seafood stew) and *kung phao* (grilled shrimp).

Phuket: *Somjit Noodles*   Ⓑ
214/6 Phuket Rd. 📞 *No telephone.*
A small, clean, unassuming place that makes really excellent Thai and Hokkien noodles. Try the island's best known dish – *khanom chin nam ya phuket* (Chinese noodles in a curried fish sauce).

Phuket: *Baan Rim Pa*   ⒷⒷ
100/7 Kalim Beach Rd, Patong. 📞 *0-7634-0789.*
Set on the cliff at the northern end of Patong beach, dining on the terrace here gives some lovely views of the island. The food is classical Thai, with suggested menus to make ordering simple.

Phuket: *Pop & Jazz*   ⒷⒷ
43 Phuket Villa 1, Soi 1 Yaowarat Rd. 📞 *No telephone.*
Unusually for Phuket, this establishment features Central Plains and Northern Thai specialties. Enjoy *khao soi* (a spicy, curried broth with chicken or beef) and *nam phrik ong* (a spicy pork curry). ▤

For key to symbols see back flap

Price categories for an evening meal for one, including service, but not alcohol:

(B) under B100
(B)(B) B100–200
(B)(B)(B) B200–500
(B)(B)(B)(B) B500–1,000
(B)(B)(B)(B)(B) over B1,000

THAI SPECIALTIES
The restaurant has Thai dishes.

ASIAN (NON-THAI) DISHES
Cuisine from other parts of Asia, such as China, Korea, Japan, or India, is served.

WESTERN DISHES
French, Italian, or other Western fare is on the menu.

OUTDOOR TABLES
Facilities for eating outdoors *(suan ahan),* on a terrace, or in a garden or courtyard.

	Price	Credit Cards	Thai Specialties	Asian (Non-Thai) Dishes	Western Dishes	Outdoor Tables
PHUKET: *Bluefin Tavern* 111/17 Taina Rd, Kata Beach. **C** 0-7633-0856. This New England-style pub serves up a range of tasty dishes. Typical favourites include corned beef, pastrami, roast beef sandwiches, Cuban black bean soup, Texas chili, and fish chowder.	BBB				●	■
PHUKET: *Giorgio's* Beach Rd, Patong. **C** No telephone. Mainly Italian food in a lush tropical garden setting. Choose from pizza, pasta, and specialties such as seafood soup. The Swiss pastries are good, and the list of Italian wines is extensive.	BBB	AE MC V			●	■
PHUKET: *Kan Eang Seafood* Chalong Bay. **C** 0-7638-1661. Diners can select their own seafood from the display at this restaurant. The Thai cuisine is delectable, with specialties such as *ho mok* (curried seafood mousse).	BBB	AE DC MC V	●			■
PHUKET: *Kiko* Diamond Cliff Resort, 284 Kalim Beach, Patong. **C** 0-7634-0501. A beachside restaurant that creates fine Japanese food with ingredients imported fresh from Japan. The house specialties are traditional dishes such as *teppanyaki*, sushi, and sashimi.	BBB	AE DC MC V JCB		■		
PHUKET: *Pae Thip* Pearl Village Hotel, Nai Yang Beach and National Park. **C** 0-7632-7006. Set in the middle of a lake and surrounded by landscaped gardens, this restaurant specializes in Japanese cuisine and Korean barbecues. Beautifully prepared Thai food is also available.	BBB	AE DC MC V JCB	●	■		■
PHUKET: *Lighthouse* Cape Panwa Hotel, Ao Makham. **C** 0-7639-1123. The Lighthouse has an extensive and sophisticated seafood menu. Oysters, lobster thermidor, and stuffed crab are all featured.	BBBB	AE DC MC V			●	
PHUKET: *Saffron* Banyan Tree Hotel, 393 Mu 2, Cherngtalay. **C** 0-7632-4374. An assortment of Middle Eastern and South Asian dishes. The *fukulmas peggadu badun* (stir-fried chicken livers with onions) and the Singapore chili crab are both recommended.	BBBB	AE DC MC V		■		
PHUKET: *Thainaan* 16 Wichitsongkhram Rd. **C** 0-7622-6164. Thai, Chinese, Japanese and Western cuisine, including freshly prepared seafood and exotic delicacies, all served in beautiful surroundings.	BBBB	AE MC V	●	■	●	■
PHUKET: *La Trattoria* Dusit Laguna Resort, 390 Sri Sunthorn Rd, Cherngtalay. **C** 0-7632-4324. Traditional Italian food of excellent quality is served in this open-air setting. The dishes are not cheap by Phuket standards, but this is the place to go if you want first-rate Italian food.	BBBB	AE DC MC V JCB			●	■
PHUKET: *Regatta Bar and Grill* Le Royal Meridien Phuket Yacht Club, Nai Harn Beach. **C** 0-7638-1156. Top-of-the-line *nouvelle cuisine* is prepared by the Regatta's resident European chef. Enjoy stunning views of Nai Harn bay as you dine. The ambience is wonderful, with live music every night.	BBBBB	AE DC MC V JCB			●	
RANONG: *Khun Nunt* 35/3 Luang Rd. **C** 0-7782-1910. Despite its simply furnished dining room, this is one of the best places on the west coast to try the deep-fried soft-shell crabs for which Ranong is famous. Don't miss the grilled venison in season.	BB		●			

RANONG: *Palm Court* ⓑⓑⓑ AE MC V
Jansom Hot Spa Hotel, 2/10 Phetkasem Rd. **[** 0-7781-1510.
The best restaurant in Ranong has a wide selection of Thai and
Chinese dishes. The house specialty is grilled suckling pig. **Ⓨ**

DEEP SOUTH

HAT YAI: *Ruby* ⓑ
Niyomrat Rd. **[** No telephone.
An extensive range of North Indian dhals, curries, biryanis, and tan-
doori dishes in this Muslim establishment, where all the food is halal.

HAT YAI: *Sumatera* ⓑⓑ
Cheevanusorn Rd. **[** No telephone.
This restaurant specializes in Malay cuisine with a distinct Indonesian
flavor. Try the *mee goreng* (noodles with eggs and shrimp), the *nasi
goreng* (rice with eggs and shrimp), or the *rojak* (peanut sauce salad).

HAT YAI: *Hua Lee* ⓑⓑⓑ AE DC MC V
Niphat Uthit 3 Rd. **[** No telephone.
Enjoy Chinese dishes such as *rang nok* (bird's-nest soup) and *hu
chalam* (shark's-fin soup). This place is popular with Hat Yai's Chinese
community, and stays open late into the night.

NAKHON SI THAMMARAT: *Hao Coffee* ⓑ
Bovorn Bazaar, Ratchadamnoen Rd. **[** No telephone.
A very pleasant coffee shop, attractively decorated with Thai antiques.
Tasty Thai snacks, good Western breakfasts, and international coffees.

NAKHON SI THAMMARAT: *Tamnak Thai* ⓑⓑⓑ
378 Omkhai Rd. **[** No telephone.
A delightful series of pavilions, ornamented in the Northern Thai
style, set in a lake with fountains and connected by walkways.
The cuisine (mainly Thai) and the atmosphere are good, with
live bands. ▤

NARATHIWAT: *Rim Nam* ⓑⓑ
Jaturong Ratsami Rd. **[** No telephone.
Well worth the 2-km (1-mile) trip out of town, this is Narathiwat's best
restaurant. Good Southern Thai and Malay seafood and curries, such
as *kaeng matsaman* (a curry of beef and peanut sauce).

PATTANI: *Chong Ah* ⓑⓑ
190 Prida Rd. **[** No telephone.
An extensive selection of Southern Thai, Central Thai, and Chinese
dishes. This place is popular with the locals, which is a recommen-
dation, but means you may have to wait for a table.

PHATTHALUNG: *Khrua Cook* ⓑ
Prachabamrung Rd. **[** No telephone.
Excellent seafood – try the *pla samli taet diaw* (fried cotton fish served
with fresh mango salad) or the deep-fried shrimp served with a dip.

SONGKHLA: *Khunying* ⓑ
Srisuda Rd. **[** No telephone.
Enjoy curries and noodle dishes here, including *khanom chin nam ya*
(noodles with fish curry) and *kaeng khiaw wan* (green curry).

SONGKHLA: *Bua Kaew Seafood* ⓑⓑ MC V
20 Ratchadamnoen Rd. **[** 0-7732-2939.
This restaurant conjures up first-class seafood at reasonable rates. Try
the *phat pla meuk* (spicy fried squid) or the *phat kari pu* (yellow
curried crab). Chinese dishes are also available. ▤

SONGKHLA: *Ou-en* ⓑⓑ
Srisuda Rd. **[** No telephone.
Mandarin-style cuisine and various Southern Thai dishes at this very
popular Chinese restaurant. The house specialty is Peking duck.

TRANG: *Khao Tom Phui* ⓑ
111 Talat Rd. **[** 0-7521-0127.
This establishment serves Thai and Chinese food, such as tasty
pumpui kha na fai daeng (stir-fried greens in a bean sauce) and *pla
kaphong nam daeng* (sea bass in a sweet, piquant sauce).

For key to symbols see back flap

Shopping in Thailand

THAILAND IS WELL KNOWN as a country that offers good shopping. The high quality, wide variety, and low prices of many Thai goods are a major attraction for tourists. Arts and crafts are probably the most tempting buys. These range from inexpensive wicker rice steamers to valuable antiques, and include many typically Thai items such as triangular cushions, colorful hill-tribe artifacts, and finely crafted silver jewelry. Many are available from specialty crafts centers. Thai silk has an

Market stall selling herbs

international reputation and comes in a huge variety of designs, both traditional and modern. Tailors, particularly in Bangkok, can make clothes in silk or any other fabric to high standards for low prices. The country is also known for its rich supply of gems, and the capital is a major gem trading center. With the appearance of huge, luxurious shopping malls in Bangkok alongside vibrant, chaotic markets and street stands, Thailand offers shoppers a mix of the contemporary and the traditional.

Asia Books – one of the best book chains in Thailand

Opening Hours

MOST SMALL STORES open from about 8am to 8pm or 9pm, while department stores, shopping malls, and tourist shops typically open from 10am until 9pm or 10pm in busy areas. Business days are normally Monday to Saturday, but most shops in Bangkok, tourist areas, and resorts also open on Sundays and public holidays. During the Chinese and Thai new years (in February and April) many shops shut for several days. Market hours are usually dawn to mid-afternoon for fresh produce, or late afternoon to midnight or even later for tourist markets.

How to Pay

THE THAI BAHT, linked to the US dollar, has been a stable currency since the mid-1980s. *Baht* will always be accepted throughout the country (and in Laos). Credit cards can be used in many stores in Bangkok and resorts, and

increasingly so in provincial towns. VISA and American Express are probably the most widely accepted, followed by MasterCard. Upscale places usually take all major cards. Be warned, though, that many shops will add on a surcharge of up to five percent if you pay by credit card.

Rights and Refunds

WHEN BUYING expensive items, ask for a written receipt (*bai set*) with the shop's address and tax number. For goods on which you want to reclaim the seven percent sales tax, shops should fill out a form for you to present to customs at the airport. However, the hassle and handling fees involved mean that this is rarely worth the trouble.

If you are arranging to have goods shipped home make sure you confirm all the costs involved with the supplier in advance, including insurance, tax, and shipping charges.

Refunds are almost unheard of, but exchange of faulty or poorly fitting non-sale goods from reputable stores should be possible, if sometimes complicated. In small shops you may succeed through charm.

Bargaining

THE TREND IN CITIES, especially Bangkok, is toward chain stores with fixed prices and endless discount sales. However, the Thai love of bargaining means you can still often negotiate at small shops, specialty retailers, and, of course, market stands. There are a few tips for successful bargaining. Be aware of the going rate for items so as not to offer embarrassingly low sums. Talking in Thai numbers may restrain the vendor's initial bid. You can try faking disinterest if the seller's bids remain high. This is a better policy than enthusiastically bargaining, then deciding not to buy when the vendor agrees on your price.

Jewelry stall on Khao San Road, Bangkok

Fashion Island: one of Bangkok's new hi-tech shopping malls

DEPARTMENT STORES AND MALLS

INTERNATIONAL-STYLE department stores are a mainstay
of Bangkok shopping. How-
ever, Thai market habits die
hard, and many stores fill
their aisles with bargain stands.

The two main Thai chains
are **Robinson's**, which has
branches in Bang Rak district
on Silom and Sukhumvit roads
among others; and the more
upscale **Central** at the Silom
Complex, farther down Silom
Road, Chidlom and Lad Phrao.

The scale of the change in
Thai shopping habits is remarkable. Residents of Bangkok
already have countless downtown malls, such as **Peninsula
Plaza**, to choose from, as well
as luxury shopping complexes
like **Emporium**, **Central
World Plaza** and **Siam
Paragon**. But the trend is for
vast new malls out of the
center of the city – such as
Fashion Island on Ramindra
Road. These are the focus for
growing suburbs and
resemble self-contained, air-
conditioned towns, selling not
only fashion and domestic
items, but even houses and
cars. They incorporate huge
food courts, water parks, movie
theaters, concert halls, skating
rinks, bowling alleys and
entertainment theme parks.

Two of the world's five
biggest shopping malls are in
outer Bangkok. **Seacon
Square** on Srinakharin Road,
southeast of the city, contains
a fun fair and stretches for
more than 1 km (1,100 yds).

The rest of Thailand has yet
to experience such excesses,
but a few modern malls are
now appearing in the larger
towns and resorts. Examples
include **Kad Suan Kaew** in
Chiang Mai and the **Mike
Shopping Mall** in Pattaya.

ENGLISH-LANGUAGE BOOKSTORES

THAILAND HAS THREE English-
language book and maga-
zine chains: **Asia Books**,
Kinokuniya, and **Bookazine**.
All have several branches in
Bangkok; there are two DK
outlets in Chiang Mai, and a
Bookazine in Pattaya. DK's
Seacon Square branch is South-
east Asia's largest bookstore.

MARKETS AND STREET VENDORS

THERE IS A MARKET at the heart
of every Thai town. Even
the smallest will offer a good
range of fresh produce, and
the larger markets often sell
everything from arts and crafts
to fruit and vegetables and
household items. The most notable are Chatuchak Market
(see p131), north of Bangkok,
the massive Chiang Mai Night
Bazaar *(see p216)*, and the
smaller night market in Chiang
Rai. For markets in central
Bangkok, see pages 436–7.

Impromptu roadside stands
are also found all over the
country. Some sell devotional
items such as jasmine rings
(see p27), and others are good
for souvenirs (though many
of the goods are of dubious
legality). Chiang Mai, Pattaya,
and Patong in Phuket have
many such stands. In Bangkok
they are found on Silom and
Sukhumvit roads, and in Bang-
lampu and Patpong districts.

FACTORIES AND CRAFT CENTERS

TOURS OF FACTORY outlets and
craft centers are popular,
particularly in the North and
Northeast. No bargaining is
required as prices are fixed,
but be aware that guides take
commissions.

FAKE GOODS

Thailand's trade in fakes is so notorious that many people
seek out the most kitsch items as souvenirs. Most prized are
goods with a deliberately fake quality, using famous logos on
products they'd never normally grace, such as Louis Vuitton
fanny packs or Chanel T-shirts. Conversely, identical copies
with spoof labels like Live's
Jeans are even becoming
collectors' items. Original
manufacturers are under-
standably outraged by the
piracy. Although it could be
argued that aping an original
is a way for a developing
country to gain skill on which
to build new industries, it is
still illegal. In fact, a growing
copyright clampdown has
shrunk the trade in fakes and
even led to some forgers becoming official import agents.
Be warned that customs officers may confiscate fakes.

Street stall in Pattaya selling fake versions of expensive watches

THAI SILK

THE ANCIENT ART of Thai silk-weaving *(see pp256–7)* was revived by American Jim Thompson *(see pp114–15)* after World War II and is now a booming export business. Silk can be plain, patterned, or in the subtle *mut mee* style made from pre-tie-dyed *(ikat)* thread. Aside from Thai designs, this heavy, bright, and slightly rough cloth is now imaginatively used for ties, dresses, shirts, skirts, and other Western fashion items, plus cushions, hangings, and sundry ornaments. Many shops will tailor clothes to your measurements, even to your own designs.

Most silk comes from the Northeast and the North, but some is woven in and around Bangkok. For range and quality, Surawong Road in Bangkok is reliable, particularly **Jim Thompson's** and **Khanitha**, as well as **Shinawatra** on Sukhumvit Road. Chiang Mai's San Kamphaeng Road is renowned for its silk, the most famous producer being **T. Shinawatra Thai Silk**.

The Thai Silk Fair is held annually in Khon Kaen in late November or early December, when the town is packed with vendors and their bolts of cloth. If you miss the fair, **Prathamakant** sells a superb selection of silk all year round.

A dazzling selection of swatches of colorful Thai silk

CLOTHES

THAI TAILORS can make suits and dresses to order for low prices. Resist the rip-off 24-hour package deals including a "free gift." You get better service by seriously assessing

Made-to-measure suits are a specialty of many Thai tailors

the designs, fabric, and cut, and insisting on one or two intermediate fittings. In Bangkok, countless Chinese and Indian tailors advertise in tourist magazines and outside their shops along Sukhumvit, Charoen Krung, and Khao San Roads. Designs are usually copied, often with considerable skill, from magazines or catalogues of famous brands such as Armani and Hugo Boss. The quality of workmanship can vary considerably. Ask around for recommendations.

Other popular items of Thai clothing include baggy fishermen's pants; batik sarongs (especially in the South, such as at Ko Yo, Songkhla); vests and trousers made from hill-tribe fabrics; Thai silk and other Northeastern fabrics.

ARTS AND CRAFTS

MOST THAI HANDICRAFTS are produced in the North and Northeast, and Chiang Mai is undoubtedly where visitors will find the widest choice of goods. The vibrant, diverse Night Bazaar sells everything from lacquerware to teak furniture, and you will need several hours if you want to peruse the often overpriced shops on San Kamphaeng Road (Highway 1006).

Prathamakant in Khon Kaen stocks a fine selection of Northeastern items such as the colorful triangular pillows.

Ayutthaya is a good source of crafts and antiques, particularly around Wat Phra Si Sanphet and on Si Sanphet Road,

where you can find unique stone carvings at **Kim Jeng**. Nearby **Bang Sai Folk Arts and Crafts Center** is the focus of Queen Sirikit's SUPPORT Foundation, which enables villagers to make a living from preserving their traditions *(see p101)*. The fine pieces they produce are also sold at the dozen **Chitrlada** shops around Thailand. High-quality ethnic crafts at fixed prices are available from boutiques in most top hotels, **Silom Village**, **River City**, and the less expensive **Narayanaphand** department store in Bangkok. In the South, **Thai Village and Orchid Farm** in Phuket town is a good bet.

HILL-TRIBE ARTIFACTS

THE COSTUMES and artifacts of the hill tribes make fascinating anthropological souvenirs. Items might include Akha coin headdresses, Lahu geometric blankets and cushion covers, Hmong red-ruffled black jackets, brightly colored Lisu tunics, wooden cattle bells, almond-shaped bamboo boxes, wooden boxes with carvings, and woven rattan.

Some of the best outlets in Chiang Mai are the **Hill Tribe Products Foundation**, **Thai Tribal Crafts**, and the **Old Chiang Mai Cultural Center**. The **Chiang Rai Handicraft Center** also has a large range. In Bangkok, the best selection is found at Chatuchak Market *(see p131)*. Buying from the shop at **Cabbages and Condoms** will ensure that your money goes to the tribes.

Lisu tribeswoman, selling tribal goods at a Chiang Rai bazaar

Roadside basket seller in Northern Thailand

WOOD, BAMBOO, AND RATTAN

BAMBOO, RATTAN, and wooden items are very cheap and can be shipped home. Carved wooden friezes, screens, headboards, doors, and lintels are readily available. Chiang Mai is the best source – **Boss Decor** is excellent for wooden furniture; **Pen Phong** is good for rattan/bamboo. Woodcarving is a specialty of Mae Tha and Ban Luk near Lampang, as well as the Bo Hang district of Chiang Mai. Hang Dong and Saraphi, south of Chiang Mai, are known for their intricate basketware.

Be aware that if you buy wooden items, you may be contributing to Thailand's already disastrous deforestation.

Attractive celadon and blue and white ceramics in Bangkok

CERAMICS

DELICATE BENCHARONG pottery was historically made in China and sent to Thailand to be decorated with intricate floral patterns using five colors. Today the entire process occurs in Thailand. You can buy complete dinner services in Bencharong, and myriad designs, including the more typical spherical pots. In Bangkok,

Chatuchak Market is cheaper and offers a wider choice than the downtown shops. The heavy celadon pottery style is distinguished by its etched designs under a thick, translucent green, blue, or brown glaze with a cracked patina. It's best bought direct from the potteries in Chiang Mai, where the top producer is **Mengrai Kilns**, but is also available in Bangkok from **Thai Celadon House** and many craft shops including those on Silom and Charoen Krung roads.

Lampang is notable for its fine blue and white ceramics, produced by companies such as **Indra Ceramics**.

LACQUERWARE

LACQUERWARE is a Northern Thai specialty. It usually has floral, flame, or portrait designs in black and gold on bamboo and wood. More common is the Burmese style of red ocher on bamboo and rattan with pictorial scenes or floral designs. Traditional items include boxes for food and jewelry. Lacquerware is plentiful in the craft shops of Chiang Mai and Bangkok.

NIELLOWARE AND PEWTERWARE

NIELLOWARE, the intricate process of silver (or, more rarely, gold) inlay in a black metal amalgam in floral and flame patterns, makes for beautiful items like cufflinks, pill boxes, and jewelry. Some of the finest is from Nakhon Si Thammarat.

Southern Thailand has significant tin deposits, so pewterware has become a major craft. Typical items include tankards, plates, vases, and boxes. Department stores in Bangkok and stores in Phuket town stock good selections.

KALAGA TAPESTRIES

THE WEAVING of *kalaga* tapestries involves metallic and multicolored threads, beads, patches, and sequins sewn onto a padded black background. It is a 200-year-old Burmese art but has only recently been revived, so antique examples are rare and very expensive. The ubiquitous modern embroideries are often gaudy and sloppily made, but the more carefully constructed (and more expensive) simple traditional designs can make attractive cushions, hangings, bags, and even caps. Towns near to the Burmese border such as Mae Sot and Mae Sai are usually the best sources.

MUSICAL INSTRUMENTS, MASKS AND PUPPETS

MUSICAL INSTRUMENTS including *khaens* (Northeastern "pan pipes"), *piphat* ensemble gongs, and drums make impressive souvenirs. They are available at Chiang Mai's Night Bazaar and at Silom Village, Narayanaphand, Chatuchak, and Nakorn Kasem markets in Bangkok. These places are also good sources of *khon* masks and theatrical items such as intricate *hoon krabok* puppets and *nang taloong* and *nang yai* shadow puppets.

In the South, Nakhon Si Thammarat is the place for shadow puppets. They can be bought from the **Shadow Puppet Theater**, and, if you phone in advance, the master puppet-maker will show you how the puppets are made.

Narayanaphand department store in Bangkok

ANTIQUES

THE DELICACY and charm of Thai antiques are so appealing to shoppers that the few antiques remaining in the country are very expensive, fakes, or illegally obtained. Thailand is, in fact, one of the principal outlets for antiques from all over Southeast Asia. Some shops resemble museums, jumbled with tapestries, statues, cabinets, bells, puppets, ceramics, baskets, lacquerware, and temple artifacts. They're enchanting even if you're not buying.

Bargains are rare, although prices are lower than in Hong Kong or Singapore. Chiang Mai's Tha Phae and Loi Khro Roads are a bit cheaper than the main sources in Bangkok: Charoen Krung Road, River City, Chatuchak Market, and in Chinatown at Wang Burapha and Nakorn Kasem Market. There are antique auctions at River City on the first Saturday of each month. The excellent copies available are a cheaper, more culturally responsible alternative.

Recommended shops include **Amaravadee Antiques** and **Borisoothi Antiques** in Chiang Mai, and Bangkok's **The Fine Arts** and **NeOld**.

Export permits are required for antiques and all Buddha images from the Fine Arts Department via the **National Museum** and take at least a week to obtain *(see p451)*. Not surprisingly, given that so much of their cultural heritage has left the country, Thai customs officers are vigilant in enforcing this regulation.

Antiques in one of Bangkok's more exclusive shops

Shoppers admiring gold jewelry in Bangkok's Chinatown

JEWELRY

THAI JEWELRY tends to be large and expressive, often with superb detailing. The country has a long history of silverwork, particularly in the North and Northeast and among the hill tribes. The Wualai Road shops in Chiang Mai offer a good selection.

Necklaces, bracelets, earrings, and Lao-style belts are typical in employing silver thread and filigree detail, often incorporating silver beads and large, plate-like pendants. Contemporary and international styles are increasingly preferred in cities and resorts. More affordable modern costume jewelry sells well in Siam Square and Chatuchak Market in Bangkok, where you can buy inexpensive ethnic wares and jewelry imaginatively created from such diverse materials as nuts, seeds, shells, and beans.

Intricate bejeweled silver pendant

Some of Thailand's best jewelry is found in Bangkok's **Peninsula Plaza** shopping mall as well as hotels such as the Dusit Thani. Some shops will work to your own specifications, notably **Uthai's Gems** in Bangkok and **Shiraz** in Chiang Mai. Richard Brown designs personalized Vedic astrological jewelry at **Astral Gemstone Talismans**.

Gold is a popular, age-old form of portable wealth, and the most common type is the very yellow, Chinese-style gold. There are Chinese-owned gold shops in most sizable towns.

Be warned that amulets are not classed as jewelry and the trade in these sacred items is widely disapproved of, not least by the Buddhist authorities who believe it exploits and encourages superstition. You need a licence to export them.

GEMS

BANGKOK IS POSSIBLY the world's biggest gem trading center. The local stones are rubies, red and blue spinels, orange and white zircons, and yellow and blue sapphires *(see pp300–301)*. Markets operate around Chanthaburi, Kanchanaburi, Mae Sai, and in Mae Sot on the Burmese border, where gems are cheaper than in Bangkok. However, you'll need an expert eye to pick out the bargains and should be wary of illegally smuggled gems. Phuket is Thailand's only good source of high quality pearls (try **Pearl Center** in Phuket town).

Gem scams are notorious in Bangkok and Chiang Mai, so run a mile if someone friendly says it's a public holiday so there's a government suspension of tax. Countless people have fallen for this ruse before being coaxed into parting with large sums of money by clever salesmanship and even, sometimes, drugged drinks.

It is possible to learn gemology and have stones authenticated and graded (but not valued) at the **Asian Institute of Gemological Sciences** in Bangkok.

DIRECTORY

DEPARTMENT STORES AND MALLS

Central Department Store
Silom Complex, 191 Silom Rd, Bangkok. **Map** 7 A4.
[0-2231-3333.

Central World Plaza
Ratchadamri Rd, Bangkok.
Map 8 D1.
[0-2255-9400.

Emporium
Sukhumvit Rd, Prompong, Bangkok. **Map** 8 F1,
[0-2664-8000.

Fashion Island
5/5 Ramindra Rd, Bangkok.
[0-2947-5000.

Kad Suan Kaew
99/4 Mu 2, Huai Kaew Rd, Chiang Mai.
[0-5322-4444.

Mike Shopping Mall
262 Mu 10, Pattaya Beach Rd, Pattaya.
[0-3841-2000.

Peninsula Plaza
153 Ratchadamri Rd, Bangkok. **Map** 8 D1.
[0-2253-9762.

Robinson's
2 Silom Rd, Bang Rak, Bangkok. **Map** 8 D3.
[0-2266-3340.

Seacon Square
904 Srinakharin Rd, Bangkok.
[0-2721-8888.

Siam Paragon
Rama I Rd, Bangkok.
Map 7 C1.
[0-2658-3000.

ENGLISH-LANGUAGE BOOKSTORES

Asia Books
221 Sukhumvit Rd, Bangkok.
[0-2651-0428.

Bookazine
Floor 1, CP Tower, 313 Silom Rd, Bangkok.
Map 7 C4.
[0-2231-0016.

Kinokuniya
Floor 6, Isetan, Ratchadamri Rd, Bangkok.

Map 8 D1.
[0-2255-9834.

THAI SILK

Jim Thompson's
9 Surawong Rd, Bangkok.
Map 7 C3.
[0-2632-8100.

Khanitha
113–5 Surawong Rd, Bangkok. **Map** 7 C3.
[0-2235-0464.

Prathamakant
79/2–3 Ruenrom Rd, Khon Kaen.
[0-4322-4080.

Shinawatra
94 Sukhumvit Rd, Soi 23, Bangkok.
[0-2258-0295.

T. Shinawatra Thai Silk
145/1–2 Chiang Mai-San Kamphaeng Rd, Chiang Mai. [0-5333-1187.

ARTS AND CRAFTS

Bang Sai Folk Arts and Crafts Center
Tambon, Bang Sai, Ayutthaya province.
[0-3536-6092.

Chitrlada Shop
Chitrlada Palace, Bangkok. **Map** 3 B2.
[0-2282-8435.

Kim Jeng
12 Mu 2, Kamang, Ayutthaya.

Narayanaphand Department Store
127 Ratchadamri Rd, Bangkok. **Map** 8 D1.
[0-2252-4670.

River City
23 Trok Rongnamkaeng, Yotha Rd, Bangkok. **Map** 6 F3. [0-2237-0077.

Silom Village
286 Silom Rd, Bangkok.
Map 7 A4.
[0-2233-9447.

Thai Village and Orchid Farm
52/11 Thepkasattri Rd, Muang Phuket.
[0-7621-4860.

HILL-TRIBE ARTIFACTS

Cabbages and Condoms
10 Sukhumvit, Soi 12, Bangkok. **Map** 8 F1.
[0-2229-4611.

Chiang Rai Handicrafts Center
732 Mu 5 Rimkok, Phahon Yothin Rd, Chiang Rai.
[0-5371-3355.

Hill Tribe Products Foundation
21/17 Suthep Rd, Chiang Mai.
[0-5327-7743.

Old Chiang Mai Cultural Center
185 Wualai Rd, Chiang Mai.
[0-5327-5097.

Thai Tribal Crafts
208 Bamrung Rad Rd, Chiang Mai.
[0-5324-1043.

WOOD, BAMBOO, AND RATTAN

Boss Decor
12/7 Loi Khro Rd, Chiang Mai.
[0-5320-7011.

Pen Phong
189/25 Nongkaew Rd, Hangdong, Chiang Mai.
[0-5343-3745.

CERAMICS

Indra Ceramics
382 Lampang–Denchai Rd, Lampang.
[0-5422-1189.

Mengrai Kilns
79/2 Araks Rd, Chiang Mai.
[0-5327-2063.

Thai Celadon House
8/3–8/5 Ratchadapisek Rd, Sukhumvit, Bangkok.
[0-2229-4383.

PUPPETS

Shadow Puppet Theater
110/18 Si Thammasok Soi 3, Nakhon Si Thammarat.
[0-7534-6394.

ANTIQUES

Amaravadee Antiques
141 Chiang Mai–Hot Rd, Chiang Mai.
[0-5344-1628.

Borisoothi Antiques
15/2 Chiangmai-San Kamphaeng Rd, Chiang Mai.
[0-5333-8460.

National Museum
Fine Arts Department, 1 Na Phra That Rd, Bangkok.
Map 1 C4.
[0-2224 -1370.

NeOld
149/2–3 Surawong Rd, Bangkok. **Map** 7 B4.
[0-2235-8352.

The Fine Arts
3/F Room 354 River City, Bangkok.
Map 6 F3.
[0-2237-0077 ext.354.

JEWELRY

Astral Gemstone Talismans
Sri Hrisikesh Plaza, C3 Building, Joe Louis Theater, Lumpini Night Bazaar, Bangkok.
[0-2252-1230.

Shiraz
170 Thapae Rd, Chiang Mai.
[0-5325-2382.

Thai Lapidary
1009–11 Silom Rd, Bangkok. **Map** 7 C4.
[0-2236-2134.

Uthai's Gems
28/7 Soi Ruam Rudi, Phloen Chit Rd, Bangkok.
Map 8 F2.
[0-2253-8582.

GEMS

Asian Institute of Gemological Sciences
33rd Floor, Jewellery Trade Center, 919/1 Silom Rd, Bangkok. **Map** 7 A4.
[0-2267-4315.

Pearl Center
83 Ranong Rd, Soi Phutorn, Phuket town.
[0-7621-1707.

Bangkok's Markets

MARKETS ARE A FUNDAMENTAL part of Bangkok life. Both specialty and general markets provide great browsing, whether you are interested in flowers or fabrics, sarongs or stamps. Do not try to take in too many markets in one outing – focus on one area and explore that in depth. Nancy Chandler's *Market Map and Much More*, readily available in Bangkok, can be a great help in planning a market sortie.

Market vendor selling Thai flowers

Thewet Flower Market *(see p100)*, located in a sedate backwater of the city, offers a riotously colorful spectacle of flowers and plants from all over Thailand.

Banglamphu Market *is a typical neighborhood market with general stalls displaying food, shoes, clothes, and assorted bric-a-brac.*

Khao San Road Market *may take up only one tiny road, but it has become a legend among backpackers as a source of almost anything imaginable. In addition to rucksacks, hiking boots, and other travelers' equipment, it is good for second-hand books, jewelry, clothes, bags, and pirated cassette tapes.*

Bo Be Market, on the corner of Krung Kasem and Lan Luang roads, is one of the city's main cloth markets and a good source of Chinese silk.

Pak Khlong Market (see p94) *is the most lively and atmospheric wholesale fresh produce market in the capital. Open 24 hours a day, it is best viewed – and cheapest – between 10pm and 5am, when exotic blooms line the pavements along with fruit and vegetables.*

KEY TO MARKET LOCATIONS IN BANGKOK

Banglamphu Market ②
Bangrak Market ⑬
Bo Be Market ④
Kao Market ⑩
Khao San Road Market ③
Nakorn Kasem
  (Thieves' Market) ⑤
Pak Khlong Market ⑧
Patpong/Silom Market ⑫
Phahurat Market ⑦
Pratunam Market ⑪
Sampeng Lane Market ⑨
Stamp Market ⑥
Thewet Flower Market ①

Phahurat Market (see p94) *is the commercial hub of Bangkok's Indian community. Fabric sellers and tailors predominate, and the air is filled with the aroma of Indian food and spices.*

Nakorn Kasem (see p94), otherwise known as the Thieves' Market, in Chinatown was once a focus for stolen goods. Today, it is a good place to pick up pots and pans, antiques, ceramics, and furniture. Hard bargaining and a sharp eye for spotting fakes is recommended.

| 0 meters | 500 |
| 0 yards | 500 |

The Stamp Market is held every Sunday outside the General Post Office on Charoen Krung Road. Thailand has long been issuing fine stamp designs, collected by philatelists around the world.

Pratunam Market *(see pp114–15)* occupies a maze of covered stalls. It is particularly good for cheap Indian fabrics and sewing accessories, and it also has general domestic items.

Kao Market, *(see pp92–3)* between Yaowarat Road and Sampeng Lane, has been supplying the Chinese community with traditional ceremonial and decorative items – from lanterns to paper models for cremations – for more than 200 years.

Sampeng Lane Market (Soi Wanit) in a former red light district has bargain-priced quality fabrics, toys, household goods, Chinese decorative items, and stationery.

Patpong/Silom Market *(see pp111–12)* is a neon-lit jumble of stalls displaying cheap souvenirs and fake goods. Stalls on Silom Road have fashionable clothes.

Bangrak Market (see p111) *is a small but thriving local bazaar. Many of the top hotels buy their fruit, vegetables, meat, and sea-food from here. The market also has fabric and clothes stands.*

What to Buy in Thailand

Toy tuk-tuk

THAI MARKET STALLS, craft centers, and specialty shops offer a wide and tempting range of souvenirs and gifts. Handicrafts are particularly good buys, and there are few regions of the country without their own specialty. In the south you can find delicately worked niello-ware, pewter, and shadow puppets; colorful hill-tribe artifacts, lacquerware, and silver jewelry are made in the North; the Northeast is famed for its silk and cushions. The widest selection is available in major cities such as Bangkok and Chiang Mai.

TRADITIONAL MASKS AND PUPPETS

Thailand has a rich tradition of masked dance and puppetry, and although performances are becoming increasingly rare, masks and puppets make evocative souvenirs. Most depict characters from the Ramakien *(see pp36–7)* and include huge leather *nang yai* figures, smaller *nang taloong* shadow puppets, *boon krabok* marionettes, and the smaller *boon lek (see pp38–9)*. Puppets can be bought in the South as well as at markets such as Chatuchak in Bangkok.

Nang taloong **puppet**

Figure of a Thai musician

Khon **mask of a demon**

Rattan and wickerwork come in many guises, from simple rice steamers to attractive and durable sets of rattan furniture. Trays, boxes, and bags are popular and can be found for sale in many Thai markets, particularly in Bangkok and Chiang Mai. Reputable shops can arrange for large items to be shipped overseas.

Nielloware is an ancient craft that has been practiced in the South of Thailand for several centuries. Nakhon Si Thammarat province is the center of Thai nielloware production today. The process involves the decorative etching of silver and gold items that are then rubbed with a black metal alloy. Jewelry and small boxes are the most affordable items.

Wood-carving is a highly skilled profession, and visitors can buy everything from tiny carved bowls and pill boxes to huge screens, cabinets, and beds. However, be aware that some hardwood items may be made from illegally felled trees.

Lacquerware items include jewelry boxes, bangles, bowls, and trays. The process of coating split bamboo or wood with lacquer and then adding delicate hand-paintings is a specialty of the north. The two most common styles of decoration are gold on black lacquer and the Burmese style of yellow and green on red. Chiang Mai is the best source.

Hill-tribe artifacts are sold in towns and villages all over Northern Thailand, although Chiang Mai undoubtedly has the widest range of handicrafts. Among the most attractive items are patchwork bags, brightly colored blankets, delicately wrought silver jewelry, and hand-embroidered jackets and hats. If you go on a trek it is likely that you will visit at least one hill-tribe village, enabling you to buy the local handicrafts direct from the producers and, sometimes, see them being made.

Ceramics have been produced in Thailand for hundreds of years. Although many styles show a pronounced Chinese influence, there are also several types of ceramics that are given a distinctive Thai stamp. One is the colorfully enameled Bencharong pottery that is most commonly found as small pots and vases. Celadon is another example. It is recognizable by its characteristic crazed surface on a typically light green glaze.

Blue and white dinner service

Bencharong pot

Celadon vase

Silverware is another traditional Northern Thai craft. Beaten silver bowls, vases, and boxes, often with expertly worked relief patterns, are popular buys, particularly in Chiang Mai. Delicate silver jewelry in traditional and modern designs is also widely available throughout the North and in Bangkok.

Orchid jewelry

Yellow and blue sapphire ring

A selection of sapphires

Silver bird

Silver bowl

Hanuman on silver box lid

Jewelry and gems are particularly tempting purchases in Thailand. Not only is the country one of the world's major sources of rubies and sapphires, but it is also well known for skillfully crafted jewelry. Jewelers who display their work in the shops within the top hotels usually offer good quality at fair prices, but it is unwise to buy gems with the intention of reselling at a profit unless you are an expert.

THAI FABRICS

Silk is without doubt the best known Thai fabric and probably the number-one buy for visitors *(see p432)*. It comes in an enormous range of styles, weights, and designs, both ancient and modern, including tie-dyed *mud mee*. Thai cotton goods are also excellent – *pha sin* skirts and triangular *mawn sam liam* cushions often feature complex patterns. The hill tribes are known for their bold, geometric fabric designs. In the South, batik sarongs and baggy fishermen's trousers are widely available.

Colorful silk hanging

Mawn sam liam **cushion**

Patterned silk tie

Scarf of raw Thai silk

Traditional cotton fishermen's trousers

Cotton *pha sin* skirt

ENTERTAINMENT IN THAILAND

MODERN THAILAND MAY have adopted many foreign pursuits, from Hollywood movies to karaoke, but traditional entertainments still flourish. Although the graceful movements of classical *khon* dance-dramas survive mainly as tourist shows, the grassroots following of such typically Thai obsessions as *muay thai* boxing remains as strong

Thai dancers at the Rose Garden, Bangkok

as ever. High-spirited *sanuk* (fun) is an all-embracing activity, even on the most serious of occasions such as religious festivals. Indulging in the local passions is essential to understanding life in Thailand, whether it be a song-filled night out at a bar or folk music club, a colorful temple fair, a classical concert, a *takraw* game, or watching the latest Thai movie.

The Thailand Cultural Center, the country's premier concert venue

INFORMATION SOURCES

DETAILS OF THE major events and festivals throughout Thailand are provided in a booklet available from TAT offices. For more detailed entertainment listings, *Metro* is not only the best source for what's going on in the capital, but also provides useful information on events in the rest of the country. It is also worthwhile consulting the English-language newspapers, the *Bangkok Post* and the *Nation*, and the many free tourist magazines. Good hotels should also be able to provide information.

Bangkok's listings magazine

BOOKING TICKETS

MAJOR HOTELS and travel agencies can book tickets for cultural shows and sports events. Alternatively, you can buy tickets direct from venues or, for major events, from Thai Ticketmaster counters at Central Department Store *(see p435)*. To book by phone call 0-2262-3456, or visit www.thaiticketmaster.com.

TRADITIONAL THEATER AND DANCE

WATCHING THE STYLIZED royal all-male masked dance *khon* is like seeing the murals of Wat Phra Kaeo come to life. Sadly, popular interest in the mostly Ramakien-based dance-dramas is waning, and performances of *khon*, and of the equally elaborate but less formal *lakhon*, are becoming increasingly rare. In even greater danger of extinction are the *hoon lek* marionette shows *(see pp38–9)*.

The most atmospheric place to watch traditional dance is at Sanam Luang on the evening of royal ceremonies such as the king's birthday or a funeral. At such times dozens of stages provide entertainment long into the night. Complete performances can last days, so abridged scenes are chosen for shows at the **National Theater** (indoors on the last Saturday and Sunday of the month; outdoors every Saturday and Sunday from December to May) and the hi-tech **Royal Chalermkrung Theater** in Bangkok and at the **Old Chiang Mai Cultural Center**.

Countless tourist dinner shows in the major cities and resorts offer bills of dances from all over the country. Chiang Mai's famous *khantoke* dinners *(see p34)*, including dancing, can be experienced at the

Khantoke Palace, **Khum Kaew Khantoke Palace**, and **Lanna Khantoke**. Reliable venues in Bangkok include the **Rose Garden** and **Silom Village**, while the Oriental's **Sala Rim Nam** restaurant presents authentic *khon*. *Lakhon* can also be witnessed at Bangkok's Lak Muang near Sanam Luang, and the Erawan Shrine. Traditional Thai puppetry can be seen at the **Joe Louis Theater**.

The most widespread dance-drama is *likay*, a regular feature of temple fairs, festivals, and TV. Its bawdy, slapstick, and satirical elements have allowed it to retain a popular contemporary following. The ancient equivalent from the South of Thailand is *manora*.

Still widespread in Malaysia and Indonesia, *nang talung* shadow puppet shows survive only in the Deep South at Phatthalung and Nakhon Si Thammarat *(see p373)*. Performances of *nang talung* at local festivals can run all night, but an hour or two is usually enough for most tourists. Even rarer are performances of *nang yai*, in which enormous, flat leather puppets are manipulated by a team of puppeteers.

A traditional *khon* performance

CONCERTS, EXHIBITIONS, AND MODERN THEATER

THAILAND'S MAJOR concert and exhibition halls are located in Bangkok. The state-of-the-art **Thailand Cultural Center** has the country's best performance facilities and attracts international names. **Saeng Arun Arts Center** holds interesting occasional events, but mostly in Thai. The German **Goethe-Institut** and the **Alliance Française** host first rate exhibitions, concerts, and art movies. Top stars frequently perform in the ballrooms of hotels such as the **Dusit Thani** (*see pp389–90*).

Bangkok Playhouse frequently stages plays in English and also houses **Art Corner** gallery, though **Tadu** is the best place to see contemporary Thai art. The **Patravadi Theater** puts on superb, highly visual musicals based on classical stories, which are easily understandable to non-Thais.

Hand-painted movie poster – a common sight in Thai cities

theaters in Bangkok (such as **The Lido** and **Siam Cinema**), Chiang Mai, Pattaya, Phuket, and Hat Yai show movies with their original soundtracks.

DISCOS, BARS, COMEDY, MUSIC, AND FOLK CLUBS

CHALLENGED BY international rock and sugary Thai pop, folk music has retained its popularity. It can be heard on the radio and TV, in bars, at festivals, and impromptu gatherings, particularly outside the capital, although concerts are rarely publicized in English. It is also played in the unsalubrious cafés staging *talok* (comedy), which don't welcome tourists.

The main styles include the exuberant, rhythmic *rum wong*, which is often accompanied by a jocular dance; *look thung* ("country music"), combining big band music, costumed dance troupes, and singing; and the schmaltzy, ballad-based *look krung*. Favored by bus and taxi drivers, the faster Northeastern *mo'lam* sound is distinguished by *khaen* pipes and rap-like vocals. The Khmer-style *kantrum* music of the southern region of the Northeast can be heard in Surin's **Petchkasem Hotel** on weekends. The plain-

tive, radical *phleng phua chiwit* ("songs for life") emerged during the student protests of the 1970s and has dedicated spots such as **Raintree**.

Emerging rock bands often play at **O'Reilly's Irish Pub**, while hotels host classier venues: **Riva's** (Sheraton Grande), **Spasso** (Grand Hyatt Erawan), **Angelini** (Shangri-La), and the Oriental's **Lord Jim's** and jazzy **Bamboo Bar**.

Friends sharing food and whisky while listening to live music is the nightlife formula throughout Thailand, although karaoke, discos, and themed bars are gaining ground. In Bangkok, fashionable districts come and go at great speed. Sarasin is an enduring strip, where arty types frequent **Blue's Bar**. The original trendy hangout, Silom Soi 4, is still packed with young "glitterati," while the gay scene is centered on Silom Soi 2 and the multipurpose center, **Utopia**. The most impressive internet café is **Cyberia**. In Chiang Mai, **The Riverside** leads a string of venues beside the Ping River.

Discos can be found in all the major resorts. The large Bangkok clubs include the ever popular **Narcissus**, flashy **Fogo Vivo**, and upscale **La Lunar**.

The flesh-trade districts such as Patpong (*see p112*), Nana Entertainment Plaza (Sukhumvit Soi 3), and Soi Cowboy (off Soi Asoke) in Bangkok, plus Pattaya and Patong in Phuket, are notorious for their bizarre gynecological "entertainments." Rip-offs are common, although the King's Group's bars are among the most "reputable." One of Thailand's most infamous and popular attractions on stage and TV is its cross-dressing *katoeys*, or "lady-boys." Tourists flock to their sanitized transvestite shows at **Calypso Cabaret** in Bangkok, **Blue Moon Cabaret** in Chiang Mai, **Simon Cabaret** in Patong, and **Alcazar** in Pattaya, which boasts the best performers.

Cabaret-style, costumed dancers performing at a country music concert.

MOVIES

THAIS ARE AVID movie-goers. Bangkok now has huge multiplexes, but there are still 2,000 mobile units in the country that offer impromptu open-air screenings in villages.

The Thai film industry has a long, erratic history and, despite socially aware classics like *Luk Isan* (1978), tends to produce formulaic melodramas, comedies, and violent action films. Hong Kong action movies have long been popular but, since the early 1990s, Hollywood movies have dominated the Thai market. Some

"Adult" entertainment from the King's Group

TEMPLE FAIRS AND FESTIVALS

THE THAI CALENDAR is packed with national holidays and local festivals *(see pp42–7)*. These festivals may be religious or in honor of a local hero, to promote seasonal produce, or dedicated to other activities like boat racing and kite flying.

As well as often hosting other events, most *wats* stage temple fairs. But apart from scheduled major fairs such as the Golden Mount Temple Fair in Bangkok at Loy Krathong *(see p46)*, it's usually a matter of chance whether you encounter one. The sideshows are often as entertaining as the ceremonies with vendors selling food and trinkets, colorful characters like the cross-dressing *katoeys*, folk music such as *likay* and *lam wong*, beauty contests, and who-can-eat-the-hottest-*som-tam* competitions. Other activities might include cock fighting or Siamese fighting fish contests.

Staged spectaculars aimed at tourists include the sound-and-light, fireworks, and other festivities at the Sukhothai ruins during Loy Krathong in November and during the Khwae River Bridge Week at Kanchanaburi *(see p46)*.

Parade during the Loy Krathong festival in Lampang

MUAY THAI AND KRABI-KRABONG

THAI KICK BOXING, *muay thai*, is a national passion *(see pp40–41)*. Most provinces have a boxing arena, but the nation's top two venues are in the capital. **Lumphini Stadium** has bouts on Tuesdays, Fridays, and Saturdays, and boxing can be seen at

Muay thai boxing – passionately followed all over Thailand

Ratchadamnoen Boxing Stadium on Mondays, Wednesdays, Thursdays, and Sundays. If you are interested in learning, rather than simply watching, the skills involved in *muay thai*, then contact the **International Amateur Muay Thai Federation**, who should be able to recommend suitable gyms and instructors.

Another revered, long-established Thai martial art is *krabi-krabong*, named "swordstaff" after some of the hand weaponry used. The techniques are taught to ancient standards, although skill and stamina rather than injuries inflicted are now the measures of an accomplished fighter. Demonstrations are often included in tourist cultural shows, and you can learn the intricacies of *krabi-krabong* at the **Buddhai Sawan Fencing School of Thailand**.

TAKRAW

THE ACROBATIC Southeast Asian sport of *takraw* is played by young males at seemingly any clear patch of ground in Thailand. The idea is to keep a woven rattan ball in the air using any part of your body except your hands. The players' extraordinary agility, balletic leaps, and speed of reactions are a revelation to visitors reared on more ponderous sports.

There are elaborate versions emphasizing individual skill, but the classic original style has a team trying to get the ball into a basketball-like net more times in a set period than their rivals. Despite the

competitive version, *sepak takraw*, which resembles volleyball, now being incorporated into the Olympics and Asian Games, professional games are played surprisingly rarely.

The remarkably acrobatic *takraw*

SOCCER, RUGBY, AND SNOOKER

IN RECENT YEARS Thais have developed a feverish enthusiasm for soccer. In 1996 a professional soccer league was introduced. Rugby has also sparked remarkable interest, with established clubs competing in a league and the Hong Kong Sevens. Games are mostly held in Bangkok at the **Pathumwan Stadium**, **Hua Mark Stadiums**, **Army Stadium**, and **Royal Bangkok Sports Club**.

Thailand is the most successful non-Anglophone country to adopt snooker, which has become hugely popular. Its dangerous association with underground gambling makes it hard for players to emulate champions like James Wattana, though there are some safe clubs around. Thailand hosts world ranking tournaments in March and September.

DIRECTORY

TRADITIONAL THEATER AND DANCE

Joe Louis Theater
1875 Rama IV Rd, Bangkok.
[0-2252-9683.

Khantoke Palace
288/19 Chang Khlan Rd, Chiang Mai.
[0-5327-2757.

Khum Kaew Khantoke Palace
252 Phra Pok Klao Rd, Chiang Mai.
[0-5321-0663.

Lanna Khantoke
33/10 Charoen Prathet Rd, Chiang Mai.
[0-5327-0080.

National Theater
1 Na Phra That Rd, Bangkok. **Map** 1 C4
[0-2224-1342.

Old Chiang Mai Cultural Center
185/3 Wualai Rd, Chiang Mai.
[0-5327-5097.

Rose Garden
Off Hwy 4, 32 km (20 miles) W of Bangkok.
[0-2295-3261.

Royal Chalermkrung Theater
66 Charoen Krung Rd, Bangkok. **Map** 6 D1.
[0-2222-0434.

Sala Rim Nam
Oriental Hotel, 48 Oriental Ave, Bangkok.
Map 6 F4.
[0-2236-0400.

Silom Village
286 Silom Rd, Bangkok.
Map 7 A4.
[0-2635-6810.

CONCERTS, EXHIBITIONS, AND MODERN THEATER

Alliance Française
29 Sathorn Tai Rd, Yannawa, Bangkok.
Map 8 D4.
[0-2670-4200.

Bangkok Playhouse/Art Corner
2884/2 New Phetchaburi Rd, Bangkok.
[0-2319-7641.

Goethe-Institut
18/1 Soi Atthakan Prasit, Sathorn Tai Rd, Bangkok.
[W] www.goethe. de/bangkok **Map** 8 E4.
[0-2287-0942.

Patravadi Theater
69/1 Soi Wat Rakhang, Arun Amarin Rd, Thon Buri, Bangkok. **Map** 1 B5.
[0-2412-7287.

Saeng Arun Arts Center
5th floor, Plan Bldg, 4 Soi Suksa Witthaya, Bangkok.
Map 7 B5.
[0-2237-0080 (extension 801–7).

Tadu
Barcelona Motor Building, Tiem Ruammitr, Bangkok.
[W] www.tadu.net
[0-2645-2461.

Thailand Cultural Center
Ratchadaphisek Rd, Bangkok.
[0-2245-7742.

MOVIES

The Lido
256 Rama I Rd, Siam Square, Bangkok.
Map 7 C1.
[0-2252-6498.

Siam Cinema
Siam Square, Rama I Rd, Bangkok. **Map** 7 C1.
[0-2251-1735.

DISCOS, BARS, COMEDY, MUSIC, AND FOLK CLUBS

Alcazar
Pattaya Second Rd, Pattaya.
[0-3841-0225.

Angelini
Shangri-La Hotel, 89 Soi Wat Suan Phu, Bangkok.
Map 6 F5.
[0-2236-7777.

Blue Moon Cabaret
5/3 Mun Muang Rd, Chiang Mai.
[0-5327-8818.

Blue's Bar
231/16 Soi Sarasin, Ratchadamri Rd, Bangkok.
Map 8 E3.
[0-2252-7335.

Calypso Cabaret
Asia Hotel, 296 Phayathai Rd, Bangkok.
[0-2216-8937.

Fogo Vivo Brazilian Bar & Restaurant
President Tower Arcade, Intercontinental Hotel, Bangkok.
[0-2253-0444.

La Lunar
Sukhumvit Soi 26, Bangkok **[** 0-2261-2207.

Lord Jim's/ Bamboo Bar
Oriental Hotel, 48 Oriental Ave, Bangkok. **Map** 6 F4.
[0-2236-0400.

Ministry of Sound
2 Sukhumvit Soi 12, Bangkok.
[0-2229-5850.

Narcissus
112 Sukhumvit Soi 23, Bangkok.
[0-2258-2549.

O'Reilly's Irish Pub
62 Silom Rd, Bangkok.
Map 8 C4.
[0-2632-7515.

Petchkasem Hotel
104 Chitbumrung Rd, Surin.
[0-4451-1274.

Raintree
116/64 Soi Rang Nam, off Phaya Thai Rd, Bangkok.
[0-2245-7230.

Riva's
Sheraton Grande Hotel, 250 Sukhumvit Rd, Bangkok.
[0-2653-0333.

The Riverside
9–11 Charoenraj Rd, Chiang Mai.
[0-5324-3239.

Simon Cabaret
100/6–8 Mu 4, Karon Rd, Patong, Phuket.
[0-7634-2011.

Spasso
Grand Hyatt Erawan Hotel, 494 Ratchadamri Rd, Bangkok.
Map 8 D1.
[0-2254-1234.

Sphinx
100 Silom Soi 4, Bangkok.
[0-2234-7249.

MUAY THAI AND KRABI-KRABONG

Buddhai Sawan Fencing School
5/1 Phet Kasem Rd, Thon Buri, Bangkok.
Map 5 A4.
[0-2421-1906.

International Amateur Muay Thai Federation
Pathumwan Stadium, 54 Rama I Rd, Bangkok.
Map 7 B1.
[0-2214-0120 ext 1475.

Lumphini Stadium
Rama IV Rd, Bangkok.
Map 8 E4.
[0-2252-8765.

Ratchadamnoen Boxing Stadium
1 Ratchadamnoen Nok Rd, Bangkok. **Map** 2 F4.
[0-2281-4205.

SOCCER, RUGBY, AND SNOOKER

Army Stadium
Wiphawadirangsit Rd, Bangkok.
[0-2278-5095.

Hua Mark Indoor and Outdoor Stadiums
2088 Ramkhamhaeng Rd, Bangkok.
[0-2318-0946.

Pathumwan Stadium
154 Rama I Rd, Bangkok.
Map 7 B1.
[0-2214-0120.

Royal Bangkok Sports Club
1 Henri Dunant Rd, Pathumwan, Bangkok.
Map 8 D2.
[0-2652-5000.

OUTDOOR ACTIVITIES & SPECIAL INTERESTS

I N THAILAND an impressive range of special interest activities is available. The south's spectacular coastline is ideal for aquatic fun, from sailing, water skiing, and windsurfing to big game fishing and diving to see some of the most spectacular coral reefs in the world. Northern Thailand's mountainous forests are famous for their waterfalls, caves, and wildlife, including rare birds, gibbons, elephants, and tigers. Trekking in this beautiful region to see hill tribes has become controversial in recent years, and care should be taken

Windsurfing off the coast

in choosing a responsible trekking company with knowledgeable guides. Thailand has an extensive network of beautiful national parks. Exciting ways to explore Thailand's natural wilderness include sea canoeing, leisurely bamboo rafting, thrilling whitewater rafting, elephant riding, and rock climbing. Some visitors take advantage of the country's growing number of excellent golf courses. Others come to learn cultural skills such as Buddhist meditation, traditional massage, and Thai cooking techniques, which include vegetable carving.

Spectacular diving around the reefs off Thailand's coasts and islands

DIVING AND SNORKELING

A BUNDANT CORAL REEFS thronging with aquatic life – serviced by countless diving operations – make Thailand one of the world's most accessible and rewarding destinations for underwater exploration. The Andaman coast and islands *(see pp338–63)* in particular have some stunning reefs, ocean drop-offs, and submerged pinnacles – plus visibility often exceeding 30 m (100 ft). A rich variety of marine life can be spotted, such as whale sharks off the Burma Banks.

Much of the best diving is to be found in the national marine parks containing the Surin, Similan, and Tarutao archipela-

gos in the Andaman Sea, Angthong in the western Gulf of Thailand, and Ko Chang in the eastern Gulf. The once magnificent Ko Phi Phi has not been protected by this preserve status, though, and has been heartbreakingly damaged by careless anchoring and snorkelers breaking the coral. Reckless fishing with dragnets, harpoons, and explosives has also killed some reefs, while siltation and pollution pose growing threats.

Because of rough weather brought on by monsoons *(see pp22–3)*, the Andaman sites are accessible from November to April; the shallower waters of the western Gulf coast are best visited between January and October. The Eastern Seaboard is accessible all year.

Trips vary in length from one to several days, and many tours include snorkeling. Access to many untouched reefs around Burma's Andaman islands is slowly becoming established via Phuket. In Bangkok, **Dive Info** runs special trips. Selected dive companies are listed in the directory *(see p447)*, and fuller listings and details of sites appear in the books *Asian Diver Scuba Guide: Thailand* (Asian Diver) and *Diving in Thailand* (Asia Books).

PADI- and NAUI-approved diving courses are widely available. The main centers offering courses are Phuket, Pattaya, Khao Lak, Ko Tao, Ko Samui, Ko Phi Phi, and Krabi.

Basic diving rules include: inspect your equipment and get the right fit; don't dive unless you are confident in your instructor and have been well trained; make sure there's a buddy system; check that your group is small enough for the divemasters to monitor; and never touch the coral.

SAILING

T HAILAND'S DRAMATIC coastline is popular with the yachting fraternity, who come to Phuket every December for the King's Cup Regatta. Chartering a yacht or joining a crew is possible from Hua

Hin and with **Ocean Marina** from Pattaya. However, the best facilities and scenery, and the widest choice of sailing companies, are found on Phuket. Some of the best are **Thai Marine Leisure**, **Sunsail**, and **Southeast Asia Live-aboards**.

Sea canoeing – the best, and often only, way to explore the coast

WATER SPORTS

RECENT YEARS HAVE witnessed a mushrooming in the popularity of water sports, although the disturbance they cause is of concern. In places such as Krabi water sports are banned. However, in most resorts windsurfing boards can be rented, and jet skis and "inflatable banana rides" are becoming commonplace even in national marine parks such as Ko Samet.

For the best range of water sports, including paragliding, waterskiing, and motorboat rental, head for Jomtien beach at Pattaya; Hua Hin and Cha-am; and Patong and Karon beaches on Phuket.

Anglers make for the excellent facilities for big game fishing at Pattaya and Phuket.

Sea canoeing is not just the most peaceful way to enjoy the strange karst islets of the Angthong archipelago, but also the only way to explore their collapsed sea caves. Ringed by forest and often containing tiny beaches, many of these spectacular *hongs* were first discovered by **Sea Canoe Thailand**, who run the most responsible tours to these fragile "lost worlds."

WHITEWATER RAFTING

SEDATE BAMBOO RAFTING is a popular tourist pastime, particularly on the rivers in the north. More exciting, though, is whitewater rafting on hardy inflatables. The upper reaches of the Pai and Moei rivers are ideal for this fast-growing sport, and Umphang's Mae Klong district near Mai Sat is particularly notable for world class rafting. **Thai Adventure Rafting** and **The Wild Planet** are two of the best trip organizers.

GOLF

GOLF IS REACHING near fanatical popularity levels in Thailand, which has hosted international competitions at its fast-growing number of courses. The many around Bangkok are mostly flat and uninteresting, but there are some staggeringly scenic backdrops at golfing resorts in Phuket, Khao Yai, Chiang Mai, and Kanchanaburi.

Exclusivity is a feature of many clubs, but golfing vacation packages are particularly popular at places such as Pattaya, Phuket, and Hua Hin. The best guides to courses are the *Thailand Golf Map* and *Thailand Golf Guide*, and TAT publishes a free directory of the country's top 75 courses. For improving your handicap, there's a David Leadbetter Academy of Golf at the excellent **Thana City Golf and Country Club**.

Enjoying the unique sensation of elephant riding through the forest

ELEPHANT RIDING

AFTER THE MECHANIZATION of logging, and then its supposed ban in 1989, working elephants found themselves unemployed. Offering rides is a positive means of ensuring the survival of this national symbol since their lowland forest habitat has been largely destroyed. However, some unscrupulous *mahouts* ply their mounts with drugs to lengthen their working day and some groups have voiced concern over the treatment of elephants in Thailand.

An hour's ride is all you need to appreciate the pachyderm's vehicular novelty, take photos, lurch through forest, and be sprayed by its trunk. Most treks include rides, which are also available from elephant camps. Most of these are clustered around Chiang Mai and include the **Elephant Training Center Taeng Dao**, **Mae Sa Elephant Camp**, and **Thai Elephant Conservation Center**. Bangkok's **Dusit Zoo** and **Safari World** also offer rides.

Natural Park Golf Club, Pattaya: superb golf and a spectacular backdrop

TREKKING

THAILAND HAS SOME ideal terrain for hiking, from the precipitous karst forests of Krabi and Khao Sok to the undulating mountains surrounding Mae Hong Son and Loei.

Aside from the country's natural beauty, it is the opportunity to visit hill tribes that has undoubtedly caused the trekking business to boom. The novelty of encountering hill tribespeople in elaborate costumes undeniably adds cultural frisson to a trek. However, over time traditional tribal values cannot but be eroded by continued exposure to tourists. Additionally, there is the problem of trekkers feeling like voyeurs, particularly at cynical freak shows such as the long-necked Padaung *(see p206)*. Try to establish a rapport with tribespeople and ask their permission before taking photos.

Villages close to Chiang Mai and Chiang Rai (and, increasingly, Pai and Mae Hong Son) are all depressingly exploited. Be wary of Burmese border areas, especially in Tak, where there is the chance of encountering fighting. Malaria is also a risk here, as it is in Kanchanaburi. In general, the health risks increase the farther you travel away from the towns.

For exclusively nature-based treks, head for Khao Yai *(see pp174–5)* and the south. Most treks also include an elephant ride and, if the rivers are high enough, poling on a bamboo raft. Treks can last a week, but most are over two to three

Trekkers resting on a trail in the popular Khao Yai National Park

nights and include a visit to at least one village. Scams are commonplace, and TAT keeps lists of companies recognized by the professional **Guide Association of Chiang Mai** or the **Jungle Tour Club of Northern Thailand**, but word of mouth is often best.

All treks should be led by at least two competent guides (who should speak the tribal languages and be aware of local customs). Check that the group doesn't exceed about eight trekkers, that the trek is registered with the police, and that transportation is not by public buses. Tips include lining backpacks with plastic bags to keep wet clothes in and damp out; always sleep in dry clothes – even if it means putting on wet clothes by day; wear a sun hat and cream, long trousers to protect against leeches, insect repellent (Jaico is the best), and worn-in

Delicately carved vegetables

hiking boots or at least supportive athletic shoes. Nights are cold in the mountains, so take warm layers – thermal tops and leggings, and silk sleeping bags. The best times to trek are November to February and early in the wet season in June and July.

Eco-tourism is an abused term, but **Siam Safari**, **The Trekking Collective**, and **Phuket Trekking Club** have a good reputation, and **Friends of Nature** organize ecological treks. **The Wild Planet** is equally well respected and, like **Bike and Travel**, runs professional mountain bike trips into the wild.

CULTURAL STUDY

COURSES IN MEDITATION and Buddhism can give a great insight into Thai culture and a skill for life. For meditation sessions in English and longer, disciplined retreats, contact the **World Fellowship of Buddhists**. Non-Thais are most welcome at the **Northern Insight Meditation Center's** month-long retreats; at the strict **Wat Pa Nanachat Beung Rai**; at the **Dhammakaya Foundation**'s retreats and Sunday sessions; and at the modern-minded **International Dhamma Hermitage** over the first ten days of each month. The latter two are most accepting of women; many *wats* are male-only.

Visitors also come to Thailand to study traditional Thai massage, a vigorous combination of yoga, reflexology, and acupressure. Popular training in English is conducted at **Wat Pho** *(see pp88–9)* and in Chiang Mai's subtler style at centers including the **Old Medicine Hospital** and **Institute of Thai Massage**.

The techniques of Thai cuisine – including fruit and vegetable carving – can be learned at the cooking schools in the **Dusit Thani** and **Oriental** hotels *(see pp389–90)* and **UFM Baking and Cooking School**, and **Community Services of Bangkok**.

Leisurely rafting down the Ping River near Chiang Mai

DIRECTORY

DIVING AND SNORKELING

Andaman Divers
Hat Patong, Phuket.
0-7634-1126.

Dive Info
Chitlom BTS Station,
Bangkok.
0-2655-4646.
www.diveinfo.net

Fantasea Divers
219 Rat U-thit Rd,
Patong, Phuket.
0-7634-0088.
info@fantasea.net

Hippo Diving Center
Phi Phi Island, Cabana,
Ko Phi Phi.
0-1894-0853.

Samui International Diving School
Angthong Rd, Naton,
Ko Samui & Ko Tao.
0-7723-1242.

Sea Dragon Dive Center
9/1 Mu 7, T. Khuk Khak,
A. Takua Pa, Phang Nga,
Khao Lak.
0-7642-0420.

Sea Hawk Divers
2/4 Soi Kuan Yang,
Prabaramee Rd,
Phuket.
0-7634-1179.

SAILING

Ocean Marina
274 Sukhumvit Rd,
Jomtien, Pattaya.
0-3823-7310.

Southeast Asia Live-aboards
225 Rat-U-thit, 200 Years
Rd, Patong Beach, Phuket.
0-7634-0406.
www.seal-asia.com

Sunsail
20/5 Mu 2, Ko Kaew,
Phuket.
0-7623-9057.
www.sunsail.com

Thai Marine Leisure
Boat Lagoon 20 – 7/8,
Ko Kaew, Phuket.
0-7623-9111.
www.thaimarine.com

WATER SPORTS

Deutsches Haus
(deep-sea fishing)
Soi 4 Beach Rd, Pattaya.
0-3842-8725.

Game Fishing
6/16 Chalong Bay, Phuket.
0-1723-1392, 0-7628-0996.

Santana Canoeing
92/18 Sawatdirak Rd,
Patong, Phuket.
0-7629-4220.
www.santanaphuket.com
adrea@santanaphuket.com

Sea Canoe Thailand
367/4 Yaowarat Rd,
Muang Phuket.
0-7621-2172.
www.seacanoe.net
info@seacanoe.net

Sun & Sand Tour
Pearl Hotel, Montri Rd,
Phuket town.
0-7621-1044.
www.pearlhotel.com

WHITEWATER RAFTING

Thai Adventure Rafting
73/7 Charoenprathet Rd,
Chiang Mai.
0-5327-7178.
www.activethailand.com
rafting@active.thailand.com

The Wild Planet
666 Sukhumvit 24, Bangkok.
0-2261-4412.
www.thewildplanet.com
info@thewildplanet.com

GOLF

Natural Park Golf Club
Off Hwy 3, km 83, near
Pattaya.
0-3839-3001.

Thana City Golf and Country Club
Bang Na Trat Rd,
off Hwy 34, km 14,
near Bangkok.
0-2336-1968.

ELEPHANT RIDING

Elephant Training Center Taeng Dao
Off Hwy 107, 56 km
(35 miles) N of Chiang Mai.
0-5329-8553.

Mae Sa Elephant Camp
535 Mu 1 Mae Rim,
20 km (12 miles) N of
Chiang Mai.
0-5329-7060.

Thai Elephant Conservation Center
Thung Kwian, 37 km
(23 miles) NW of
Lampang.
0-5324-8604 (TAT).

TREKKING

Bike and Travel
802/756 River Park Mu
12, Lam Lukka,
Pathum Thani.
0-2990-0900.

Friends of Nature
133/21 Ratchaprarop Rd,
Bangkok.
Map 4 E4–5.
0-2642-4426.

Guide Association of Chiang Mai
Sarika Tour Co, 1/1
Nimmanhamin Soi 4,
Chiang Mai.
0-5321-2942.
tatami@samart.co.th

Jungle Tour Club of Northern Thailand
Gem Travel Company,
Charoen Prathet Rd,
Chiang Mai
0-5381-8754.
www.thaifocus.com

Phuket Trekking Club
58/5 Soi Patong Resort,
Bangla Rd, Patong, Phuket.
0-7634-1453.
trekking@phuket.ksc.co.th

Siam Safari
PO Box 296, Phuket 3000.
0-7628-0116.

The Trekking Collective
25/1 Ratchawithi Rd,
Chiang Mai.
0-5341-9079.
info@trekkingcollective.com

CULTURAL STUDY

Dhammakaya Foundation
23/2 Mu 7 Khlong Sam,
Khlong Luang, Pathum
Thani.
0-2524-0257.

Community Services of Bangkok
15/1 Sukhumvit Rd,
Soi 33, Bangkok.
0-2258-5652.

Institute of Thai Massage
17/7 Morakot Rd,
Chiang Mai.
0-5321-8632.

International Dhamma Hermitage
Wat Suan Mok, Chaiya,
Surat Thani.
0-7743-1552.

Northern Insight Meditation Center
Wat Ram Poeng, Canal
Rd, Chiang Mai.
0-5327-8620.

Old Medicine Hospital
78/1 Soi Moh Shivagah
Komarapaj, Wualai Road,
Chiang Mai.
0-5327-5085.

UFM Baking and Cooking School
593/29–39 Sukhumvit Soi
33/1, Bangkok.
0-2259-0620
(extension 288).

Wat Pa Nanachat Beung Rai
Baan Bung Wai, Amphoe
Warinchamrab, Ubon
Ratchathani.

World Fellowship of Buddhists
616 Sukhumvit 24, Bangkok.
0-2661-1284-7.

SURVIVAL
GUIDE

PRACTICAL INFORMATION

THAILAND CATERS WELL to its growing number of tourists. The 12 million people who visit each year find one of the biggest and best-organized tourist industries in Asia. The headquarters of the helpful Tourism Authority of Thailand (TAT) is in Bangkok, and there are offices across the country and several overseas branches. The relevant address and telephone number is given for each town and sight throughout this guide. The tourist industry is developing rapidly, and the adventurous traveler no longer need be restricted to organized tours or major tourist destinations such as Bangkok and Phuket, as the country becomes more accessible to independent travelers. There are many reputable travel agencies all over Thailand. They offer advice, book flights and accommodations, and organize sightseeing tours. Some pre-travel planning is necessary to avoid the worst of the rainy season and holiday periods such as the Chinese New Year *(see pp44–7).*

Changing of the Royal Guard, Bangkok

WHEN TO GO

THAILAND'S WEATHER can be tempestuous, with year-round humidity, rocketing temperatures, and rains of biblical proportions. However, the optimum time to visit is during the cooler, drier months from November to February. It is no coincidence that this is the peak tourist season, when sights may get crowded. The hot season, from March to July, can be unbearable, while the rainy season, which generally lasts from June to October, is the least predictable of the three periods. Climate and rainfall charts can be found on pages 44–7.

WHAT TO TAKE

AS THE CLIMATE in Thailand is generally hot and humid, it is advisable to dress in cool, nonrestricting clothes made from natural fibers. A sweater may be needed in northern and northeastern regions during the cool season. Throughout Thailand, the rainy season brings sudden downpours; a light raincoat is handy. If visiting temples, appropriate dress is required *(see p455)*, as is easily removable footwear. A first-aid kit is also useful *(see p458)*.

ADVANCE BOOKING

BANGKOK IS a popular launching point for other Southeast Asian destinations, so it is necessary to book airline tickets well in advance. This is especially so during Thailand's peak tourist season, November to February, when flights and hotels are heavily booked. If you plan to travel during this period, it is wise to make arrangements at least three to six months prior to departure.

VISAS AND PASSPORTS

MANY NATIONALITIES, including the citizens of most European countries, Australia, and the US, can enter Thailand for up to 30 days without a pre-arranged visa. Proof of a confirmed return flight or other on-going travel arrangements must be presented upon arrival in Thailand. This 30-day period is not extendible. Nationals of several smaller European countries, such as Andorra, must obtain a visa before traveling. For those wishing to stay longer, a 60-day tourist visa can be arranged from a Thai embassy or consulate prior to arrival in Thailand. This usually takes two to three working days to process, but may take longer during busy periods.

A 90-day nonimmigrant visa must be applied for in your home country and requires a letter of verification from a Thai source giving a valid reason, such as business or study, for spending three months in Thailand. This visa is slightly more expensive than the 60-day tourist visa.

With all visas, entry into Thailand must occur within 90 days of issue. Visa extensions are at the discretion of the **Immigration Department** in Bangkok or any other immigration office in Thailand. Over-staying a visa carries a fine of 100 *baht* per day and can result in serious penalties. Reentry visas, allowing the

Tourists relaxing in the sun at Patong beach, Phuket

◁ **A row of *samlors* at the market in Lop Buri**

visitor to leave the country and return within 60 days, can be applied for at the Bangkok Immigration Department. Proof of funds sufficient to support the traveler while in Thailand may be required in some cases. Strictly speaking, travelers entering Thailand should have at least six months left on their passport. It is best to confirm all such details with a Thai embassy or consulate before traveling.

Crossing the border into neighboring countries generally depends on the current political situation *(see p456)*. A four-week tourist visa for Burma can be obtained from the Burmese Embassy in Bangkok (there will be a charge). A 15-day tourist visa for Laos can be issued by the Lao Embassy, but it is often quicker to apply for it at a travel agency in major cities such as Bangkok or Chiang Mai. A 15-day tourist visa is available free of charge upon arrival at Phnom Penh airport.

IMMUNIZATION

THERE ARE no legal immunization requirements unless you are traveling from a country known to be infected with yellow fever. It is recommended that everyone be immunized against polio, tetanus, typhoid, and hepatitis A. In addition – for those travelers going to remote or rural areas, or who are staying more than two to three weeks – BCG (tuberculosis), hepatitis B, rabies, diphtheria, and Japanese encephalitis are advised *(see pp458–9)*. For the latest advice, contact your doctor, who will also be able to advise on the current guidelines for malaria prevention, as the drug recommendations change fairly often.

Some vaccines need to be given separately or in stages. Malaria tablets, meanwhile, are started a week before leaving and continued for several weeks after returning. For these reasons it is advisable to contact your doctor at least six weeks before departure.

CUSTOMS INFORMATION

CUSTOMS REGULATIONS in Thailand are standard. During an inbound flight you will be given a customs form that must be filled in and handed over at the customs desk after claiming your baggage. Thai customs restrictions for goods carried into the country are the following: 200 cigarettes, one liter of wine or spirits. For complete details about export declarations, duty payments, and VAT refunds visit www.customs.go.th

A car or motorbike can be brought into the country for touring purposes for up to six months, but this requires prior arrangement through the Thai embassy in your home country. The carrying of drugs *(see p456)*, firearms, or pornography is strictly prohibited.

Although there are no restrictions on the maximum amount of money an individual may bring into the country, there is a minimum requirement, that varies according to the type of visa on which you are traveling. Check with your local Thai embassy for current requirements.

Antiques and Buddha images are not allowed out of Thailand without authorization. If you wish to export such items, you must first contact the **Fine Arts Department** of the National Museum in Bangkok at least five days before the date of shipment to fill in a form accompanied by two frontal photographs of the object being purchased (no more than five pieces to be shown in one photograph). Contemporary "works of art," such as paintings bought in markets, can be taken out of the country without permission. It is illegal to leave Thailand with more than 50,000 *baht* without the correct authorization.

DEPARTURE TAX

FOR INTERNATIONAL FLIGHTS out of Thailand *(see pp466–7)* there is a departure tax of 500 *baht* per person. For domestic flights the departure tax is 50 *baht*. Check with the airline whether these taxes are included in the price of your ticket.

Buddha images wrapped and ready for sale

TAT Duty Free logo

TOURIST INFORMATION

THE MANY BRANCHES of the Tourism Authority of Thailand (TAT) are very helpful, offering plenty of practical and background information on sights and festivals, as well as maps, brochures, miniguides, and posters. They also have a useful list of reputable travel agents and hotels. There is a small information booth in Don Muang airport. Many of the provincial capitals in Thailand have a TAT office (listed throughout this guide), as do some overseas countries.

Logo of TAT

ADMISSION CHARGES

ADMISSION CHARGES to sights in Thailand are usually nominal, ranging from 10–50 *baht* for government-run establishments (including most national parks), to 100 *baht* or more for private museums. Occasionally, foreigners may (legitimately) be charged a higher admission price than locals, on the assumption that they earn more than most Thais. Major tourist *wats* charge a set fee; in others there is usually a box for donations.

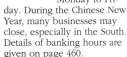

Typical entrance tickets to major historical sites

OPENING HOURS

THIS GUIDE INDICATES the days of the week when sights are open. Almost all destinations and sights in Thailand can be visited throughout the year, though accommodations on, and ferries to, some of the southern islands may be limited during the rainy season. In general, major tourist attractions open at 8am or 9am and close any time between 3:30pm and 6pm. A few also shut for lunch between noon and 1pm. Most major sights are open daily, but some national museums close for public holidays and on Mondays and Tuesdays.

Large department stores are usually open daily 10am–9pm, and smaller shops are open 8am–9pm. In small towns markets are usually held on a daily basis. Commercial offices are invariably open 8am–noon and 1pm–5pm Monday to Friday. Government offices are open 8:30am–noon and 1pm–4:30pm Monday to Friday. During the Chinese New Year, many businesses may close, especially in the South. Details of banking hours are given on page 460.

FACILITIES FOR THE DISABLED

THERE ARE few facilities for disabled travelers in Thailand. Sidewalks can be uneven and pedestrian bridges are often accessed only by steep steps. Wheelchair access is limited to the top-class hotels in major cities. The easiest way to travel is to book an organized tour *(see p471)* or to contact the **Association of Physically Handicapped People** for further information.

Phra Si Rattana Chedi, Wat Phra Kaeo, Bangkok

Colorful tourist brochures about Thailand, available from TAT

FACILITIES FOR CHILDREN

THAIS ADORE CHILDREN and will go out of their way to help you make them happy. The larger hotels have baby sitting services, and TAT offers advice on attractions that have special appeal to kids, such as zoos. Hats and sunblock are a must for children (and adults) out in the sun. There are plenty of fast-food outlets and adaptable chefs who will willingly provide a choice of suitable alternatives to spicy meals.

CENTERS OF WORSHIP FOR VISITORS

THERE ARE MANY FACILITIES for visitors to undertake Buddhist studies *(see p446)*. The **International Buddhist Meditation Center** has details of English-language courses at *wats* in and around Bangkok. Most other religious denominations are represented in Thailand – listed below are religious centers in Bangkok offering services in English. **Christ Church** holds Anglican and Episcopalian services. The **Holy Redeemer Catholic Church** holds services every Sunday. The Jewish Association of Thailand has occasional services at the **Jewish Community Center**. The **Haroon Mosque** has services for Muslims. Places of worship are listed in the telephone directories available in hotels and guesthouses in Bangkok and provincial capitals.

KEEP CLEAN

A sign at Hat Phrao, Ko Samet, asking visitors to keep the beach clean

LANGUAGE

IT IS USEFUL to learn a few Thai phrases *(see pp500–504),* and Thais will be delighted that you have made the effort. Many local people in popular tourist towns speak some English, as do most hotel receptionists. Sight and road names in these areas are transliterated, and menus are often in English as well as Thai. Prices and road numbers are in Arabic numerals. Transliterated spellings vary wildly in different maps and guides, and on signs. Note that "j" and "ch" are interchangeable, as are "d" and "t." The letters "ph" (e.g. as in Phuket) are pronounced "p," never "f." Likewise, the "h" in "th" is always silent (e.g., Thailand).

THAI TIME SYSTEM AND CALENDAR

BANGKOK TIME is seven hours ahead of Greenwich Mean Time (GMT), and 12 hours ahead of Eastern Standard Time, and 15 hours ahead of Pacific Standard Time (6, 11, and 14 during Daylight Savings). Although the standard clock and 24-hour clock are used and widely understood, Thailand also has its unique own system. Thais divide the day into four segments of six hours each. For example, 7am for us is one in the morning for them. See Phrase Book, page 504.

Two calendars are used in Thailand: the Gregorian (Western) and the Buddhist calendars. The Buddhist Era (BE) starts 543 years before the Gregorian era. To convert from the Gregorian calendar to the Buddhist calendar, add 543 years. For example, AD 1957 is the equivalent of 2500 BE.

MEASUREMENTS

THE METRIC SYSTEM is generally used in Thailand, although traditional weight and measurement systems are sometimes used in markets and outside Bangkok. As well as being a unit of currency, the *baht* is also a unit of weight that is used when pricing gold.

CONVERSION CHART

US Standard to Metric
1 inch = 2.54 centimeters
1 foot = 30 centimeters
1 mile = 1.6 kilometers
1 ounce = 28 grams
1 pound = 454 grams
1 US quart = 0.947 liter
1 US gallon = 3.6 liters

Metric to US Standard
1 centimeter = 0.4 inch
1 meter = 3 feet 3 inches
1 kilometer = 0.6 mile
1 gram = 0.04 ounce
1 kilogram = 2.2 pounds
1 liter = 1.1 US quarts

ELECTRICITY

THE ELECTRIC CURRENT for the whole of Thailand is 220 volts AC, 50 cycles. Dual-prong rounded plugs as well as flat-pin plugs can be used in sockets. Major hotels in Bangkok also have 110-volt outlets for electric razors. Adaptors can be bought in any depart-

DIRECTORY

TAT Headquarters
1600 New Phetburi Rd, Bangkok.
📞 0-2250-5500.

Association of Physically Handicapped People
73/7–8 Tivanond Rd, Talad Kwan, Nonthaburi. 📞 0-2951-0567.

CENTERS OF WORSHIP FOR VISITORS

Christ Church
11 Convent Rd, Bangkok.
📞 0-2234-3634.

Haroon Mosque
Off Charoen Krung Rd, Bangkok.
📞 0-2630-9435.

Holy Redeemer Catholic Church
123/19 Soi Ruam Rudi, 5 Witthayu (Wireless) Rd, Bangkok.
📞 0-2256-6305.

International Buddhist Meditation Center
Wat Mahathat, 3 Maharaj Rd, Bangkok.
📞 0-2623-6325.

International Church
Soi Pridi 31, Klongton, Bangkok.
📞 0-2713-2232.

Jewish Community Center
121 Soi Sainamtip 2, Soi 22 Sukhumvit Rd, Bangkok.
📞 0-2663-0244.

ment store or electrical store. These outlets also sell power-surge cables, which are vital if you are traveling with a laptop computer.

Power failures are increasingly rare but not unheard of in smaller towns, especially during the rainy season. In some rural areas it is a good idea to keep a flashlight handy.

PHOTOGRAPHY

CAMERA FILM in Thailand should be stored in relatively cool conditions as heat and humidity lead to rapid deterioration. As in any country, it is polite to ask first before photographing people, especially monks or tribespeople, whose spiritual beliefs may not welcome such intrusions.

A range of plugs and adaptors that can be used in Thailand

Etiquette

IT IS NOT BY ACCIDENT that Thailand is often referred to as "the land of smiles." The Thais are exceptionally friendly and helpful people, and getting along with them is easy – simply smile wide and laugh a lot. Being Buddhists, they are an amazingly tolerant people. Avoiding offensive behavior can generally be achieved through simple courtesy and common sense. A few taboos do exist, though, mostly with regard to the monarchy and Buddhism. Visitors should be particularly careful to behave respectfully at *wats* and in front of any Buddha image. Confrontation is also considered extremely rude, and Thais will bend over backward to avoid arguments of any sort. Losing your temper or shouting, whatever the situation, is seen as an embarrassing loss of face.

King Bhumibol taking part in a ceremony, Wat Benchamabophit

Two Thais addressing each other with a *wai*, the traditional greeting

GREETING PEOPLE

THE THAI GREETING is known as the *wai* and consists of the palms being pressed together and lifted towards the chin. The *wai* evolved from an ancient greeting used to show that neither party was carrying weapons. The *wai* is layered with intricacies of class, gender, and age: each of these dictates a certain height at which the two hands must be held. The inferior party initiates the *wai* and holds it higher and for longer than the superior, who returns it according to his or her social standing. Non-Thais are not expected to be familiar with these complexities, and the easiest method is simply to mirror whatever greeting you receive. As a general rule of thumb, however, you should not *wai* children or workers such as waiters, waitresses, and street vendors.

Thais use first names to address people, even in formal situations. The polite form of address is the gender-neutral title Khun, followed by the first name or nickname. Every Thai person has a nickname, usually a one- or two-syllable name with a simple meaning, such as Moo (pig) or Koong (shrimp).

BODY LANGUAGE

THE HEAD IS CONSIDERED a sacred part of the body by Thais. Never touch someone's head, not even that of a child. The feet are seen as the lowliest part of the body and to point your feet toward someone or rest them on a table is considered rude. When sitting on the floor, especially inside a temple, tuck your legs away behind you or to the side and try not to step over people sitting around you; allow them time to move out of your way.

ROYALTY

THE ROYAL FAMILY is the most revered institution in Thailand. Criticizing or defaming it in any way can be considered lèse-majesté. Not only could this mean a jail sentence, but Thai people will nearly always be deeply offended. Coins, bills, and stamps bear the images of kings and therefore should not be treated lightly. Similarly, you cannot photograph certain sacred sights connected to royalty, such as the *bot* of Wat Phra Kaeo, which houses the highly revered Emerald Buddha image.

THE NATIONAL ANTHEM

THE NATIONAL ANTHEM is played twice a day, at 8am and 6pm, on the radio and through tannoys in small towns and some public parks and buildings such as Lumphini

Devotees kneeling before a Buddha, their feet facing away from the image

A man offering food to a line of monks on the daily alms round

Park and Hua Lamphong Station in Bangkok. At these times it is polite to stop whatever you are doing and stand still. In theaters the national anthem is played before all performances. When it is playing the audience stands in silent respect to a portrait of the king on the screen.

MONKS

THE MONKHOOD *(sangha)* is a respected institution that comes just below royalty in the social hierarchy. Most taboos in dealing with monks concern women: it is prohibited for a monk to touch a woman or for him to receive anything directly from her. Therefore, when traveling by public transportation, women should avoid sitting near or next to a monk. If she has to offer anything to a monk she should either use a middleman or place the item nearby for him to pick up. These rules are confined to monks and do not apply to nuns.

It is not forbidden for people to talk to monks – many are eager to try out their English. However, monks never return *wais*.

ETIQUETTE AT WATS

AS IN CHURCHES and other houses of worship, a certain decorum should be observed when entering the grounds of any *wat*. Temples are calm, quiet places, so try

to avoid disturbing the peace. Dress should be clean, respectable, and unrevealing (strictly speaking, the upper arms and legs down to mid-calf should be covered). Shoes should be removed when entering any temple building. Step over, not on, the thresholds of *wat* buildings as Thais believe that one of the nine spirits that inhabit buildings lives in the threshold.

All Buddha images are sacred no matter how small, ruined, or neglected, and you must never sit with your feet pointing toward them.

Some areas of a temple may be off limits for women – there is usually a sign indicating so.

SUITABLE DRESS

BECAUSE THE THAIS are a modest people, clothing should be kept respectable whether you are in the city or in the country. Women especially should take care not to wear revealing skirts, shorts, or skimpy tops. In formal settings and restaurants you will rarely see Thai women with bare shoulders; sleeveless dresses or tops are considered too revealing for such

"No shoes" sign outside
Wat Phra Kaeo, Bangkok

situations. Topless sunbathing is frowned upon greatly – regardless of whether others are doing it – even in resorts dominated by Western tourists. Most Thais find the practice embarrassing and many of them find it offensive.

COMMUNICATING

BARGAINING is common throughout Thailand *(see p430)*. Though everyone develops a personal technique – whether it involves smiling or remaining poker-faced – it is important not to get too tough or too mean. Likewise, be patient with receptionists, waitresses, and others whom you may deal with. In general, you should avoid raising your voice or becoming obviously irritable – Thais learn in childhood always to speak softly and avoid direct conflict. Foreigners who may be used to getting results if they show impatience are likely to find Thais ignoring them rather than attempting to continue communicating with them.

Tourists bargaining with vendors on the platform of Hua Hin Station

TIPPING

TRADITIONALLY, tipping is not common practice in Thailand, though in Westernized establishments it is fast becoming so. Taxi drivers expect tips – as a rule you should round up the fare to the nearest ten *baht*. Porters, hairdressers, and barbers also often expect tips. A service charge of ten percent is common on upscale restaurant and hotel bills, even if they also charge government tax *(see p391)*.

SMOKING

MOST RESTAURANTS in Thailand provide smoking areas. The exception is Western fast food chains, where smoking is generally banned. Today, smoking is prohibited in all public areas such as theaters, department stores and on all public transit in Bangkok.

Personal Security and Health

Thailand is a fairly safe country, and simple health and safety precautions keep the vast majority of travelers out of trouble. For instance, ignore hustlers, keep away from troubled border areas, take care of valuables, and avoid staying or eating in unsanitary conditions. The infrastructure of emergency services for both health and crime is efficient throughout Bangkok and provincial capitals. As a rule of thumb, the more remote the area, the higher the health risk and less support available in the event of any mishap. The main hospitals in Bangkok, Chiang Mai, the main resorts, and other large cities have modern equipment and well trained doctors, many of whom speak some English.

Tourist policeman wearing a beret, and an ordinary officer

IN AN EMERGENCY

There are no national emergency telephone lines, and operators do not speak English. For English-speaking help, call the Tourist Assistance Center, which will contact the appropriate service for you. Lines are open from 8am to midnight, after which you will have to rely on English-speaking hotel staff. During office hours, TAT *(see p452)* may also be able to help. The Metropolitan Mobile Police cover general emergencies in Bangkok. All Bangkok's hospitals have 24-hour accident and emergency departments.

Fire engine

Ambulance

GENERAL PRECAUTIONS

Despite its size, Bangkok is relatively safe. Crime and violence do exist in the city, but the vast majority of travelers remain untouched by it. Usually discretion and sobriety are the best means of avoiding problems. Be on your guard at tourist sights, and at bus and train stations, which are rife with hustlers and pickpockets. Do not flash large amounts of cash or leave your luggage unattended. If you are leaving valuables in a hotel safe, make sure to get a receipt, and do not let credit cards out of your sight when paying for shopping.

The drugging, then robbing, of tourists on long-distance trains and buses has occurred, so politely decline food or drink from strangers. Thailand is an excellent place to buy gems *(see p434)*, but do not be tempted into buying large quantities to sell back at home unless you are familiar with the market and its pitfalls. Extra care is necessary in remote areas of the country, or in poorer parts of cities at night, or if traveling alone.

DRUGS

Thai law prohibits the sale or purchase of opium, heroin, or marijuana. Charges for possession, smuggling, or dealing can lead to a 2–15 year jail sentence or, in extreme cases, the death sentence. Border areas in the north attract drug runners. Be wary of strangers in these areas, and do not leave baggage unattended, or offer to check in a "friendly" stranger's suitcase at airports.

DANGER SPOTS

Border areas are sometimes precarious places. Changing political conditions, tribal skirmishes, and the haziness of border lines have made some areas of Thailand dangerous. Khmer Rouge insurgents are sometimes a threat along the Cambodian border, as are land mines and booby-traps.

There are frequent clashes on the Burmese border, and it is best to avoid traveling alone along remote roads in the region. In some parts of the Deep South, the militant Malay-Muslim group, PULO (Pattani United Liberation Organization) can present danger. Again, common sense should prevail and it is wise to stay away from the most remote border areas.

WOMEN TRAVELERS

Female travelers are unlikely to be harassed in Thailand. Bangkok itself is not dangerous for women; hotels are safe, and taxis are readily available.

Patrol car used by the tourist police, seen mainly in cities

If traveling alone it is a good idea to keep in touch with someone in Bangkok and let them know where you are going and for how long. Note that Thais perceive lone travelers as people to be pitied, and may offer to accompany you without any ulterior motive.

Tourist Police

THERE ARE tourist police stations in the main tourist cities. Tourist police officers all speak some English and are attached to TAT offices. Set up in 1982 to deal with tourist-related crime, they are happy to help with anything from credit card scams to ludicrous bar surcharges. They are also helpful in emergencies, and can act as an English-speaking liaison. The Bangkok branch of the tourist police is located in front of the southwest entrance to Lumphini Park. The Tourist Assistance Center is also helpful in emergencies, and is experienced in dealing with complaints such as fraudulent business charges.

Badge identifying the tourist police

Legal Assistance

SOME INSURANCE POLICIES cover legal costs, for example, after an accident. If involved in an accident when driving a rental car, it may be wiser to go to the nearest telephone and call the tourist police or the Tourist Assistance Center than remain at the scene. In Thailand there are no legal bodies specifically representing foreigners.

In an emergency, contact your embassy *(see p451)*. At night there is an answering service, giving the number of the duty officer. If you are not insured for legal proceedings, then you should contact your nearest consulate for advice.

Pharmacy sign found throughout Thailand

Logo of the Thai Red Cross Society, part of Chulalongkorn University

Medical Facilities

MEDICAL INSURANCE is advisable when traveling in Thailand. Some policies pay bills direct, while others refund you later. Hospitals in Bangkok, both public and private, are modern, clean, and efficient, although waiting times are longer at public ones. Some doctors are Western-trained and speak good English.

Outside the capital the best facilities are in the large towns: Khon Kaen in the northeast, Chiang Mai in the north, or Phuket in the south. Emergency care is available from military hospitals, which treat tourists in emergency cases. For dental or eye care, it is best to seek treatment in Bangkok. The Thai Red Cross on Rama IV Road does not offer medical treatment, but is able to deal with vaccinations and snake bites.

Pharmacies

THERE IS NO SHORTAGE of well-stocked pharmacies in Bangkok – there will be several on every main street and shopping mall, and supermarkets will have drugstore kiosks. They are all supplied with up-to-date medications and can dispense antibiotics over the counter without a prescription.

Most pharmacies are open from 8am to 9pm. In the central areas of Bangkok, around Silom and Sukhumvit Roads, a few stay open until 10pm or 11pm. Pharmacy signs are the same all over the country. In small towns pharmacies are less prolific and have fewer supplies. For instance, disposable diapers and tampons can be hard to find in remote areas.

Public Toilets

ALL HOTELS AND MANY guesthouses have Western-style flush toilets. In general, paper is erratically supplied. Some toilets have a water spray, which is used instead of toilet paper. In some restaurants and at many major sights, you will encounter the Asian squat toilet. Nearby will be a ladle and a bucket of water, which are used to wash the body and to sluice out the toilet after use. Paper is disposed of in a bin.

Coping with the Heat

Acclimatization to the sometimes oppressive humidity and heat of Thailand can often take longer than expected. In the first few days it is not advisable to exert yourself.

Make sure you drink lots of fluids, take plenty of rest in the shade, and avoid being out and about in the midday sun. Once you are acclimatized, dehydration and salt deficiency can still be a problem – always keep up a high intake of fluids, especially bottled water, or special electrolyte drinks.

A fan to beat the heat

Minor fungal infections can occur due to the heat, especially if tight clothing or shoes are worn. Perspiration trapped beneath the skin can cause the itchy rash called prickly heat. The local remedy and prophylactic for this is a talcum powder that contains a tingling cooling agent. Clothing should be loose and light – 100 percent cotton is best.

The sun, especially at midday and on the islands, is very powerful; sunscreen and a wide-brimmed hat are indispensable.

Treatment for prickly heat

First-Aid Kit

Although most first-aid items can be obtained from any pharmacy in main towns, when traveling to rural areas or quiet islands it is advisable to carry a basic first-aid kit. This should include the following: any personal medication; aspirin or pain killers for fevers and minor aches and pains; an antiseptic for minor

Tiger Balm – provides relief from aches, pains, bites, and strains

cuts and bites; a digestive preparation to soothe upset stomachs; insect repellent; bandages; scissors, tweezers, and a thermometer. Tiger Balm, available at any pharmacist, is Asia's miracle cure-all, relieving headaches, muscle pains, and insect bites.

Minor Stomach Upsets

Diarrhea, a common complaint for travelers the world over, is caused by bacteria in food and water.

Should diarrhea occur, eat plain foods for a few days and drink plenty of fluids. It is never wise to drink tap water – bottled water is readily available over most of the country. Ice should be fine in main hotels and restaurants, but avoid crushed iced drinks from street vendors. Eating in hotels and good restaurants is generally safe. It is when you venture into the street vendors' moveable feasts that the danger of "Bangkok belly" can arise. Choose food stalls that are popular with locals, and watch how the dishes are prepared. It can take time for visitors' stomachs to adjust to new foods. If your constitution is delicate, stick to unpeeled fruits and well-cooked foods, and eat dishes while they are still hot. Avoid eating spicy dishes on an empty stomach. Fried noodle or rice dishes and noodle soups are usually easy to digest.

Drugs such as Lomotil and Imodium can bring relief to diarrhea, but rehydrating solutions, available at pharmacies, are usually the best remedy. For immediate relief, a single 500 mg dose of the prescription called Ciprofloxacin is effective and safe.

Cuts and Bites

Always take precautions in rural areas: wear boots and long trousers when walking through grassland or forested areas to protect against snakebites and leeches (in the rainy season). Few snakebites

are dangerous. If you are bitten, apply an elastic bandage firmly to the bite, keep the limb immobile, and seek immediate medical help.

Jellyfish stings are painful – vinegar will soothe the wound. Coral cuts are slow to heal as coral contains a mild poison. Cuts should be treated with an antiseptic to prevent infection. Bandages keep wounds wet so should be used only sparingly.

Insect-Borne Diseases

Seven of thailand's 410 mosquito species carry malaria. Symptoms of the disease include headache, fever, and violent chills. If you experience such symptoms, seek medical advice immediately. Pollution in the main towns and resorts keeps them largely free of malarial mosquitoes. The areas of greatest risk are the Burmese and Cambodian border regions and, to a lesser degree, some rural areas north of Chiang Mai. However, malarial zones are continually changing. For up-to-date information and advice on the most suitable prophylactic drug, call a travel clinic or, in the US, the **Thai National Tourist Office**, for information on health matters (*see p457*).

Mosquitoes have become resistant to certain malaria tablets. Prevention is by far the best defense against the disease. Malarial mosquitoes are active from sundown till sunrise, during which time you should spray on plenty of repellent, wear long-sleeved clothing in light colors (dark attracts mosquitoes), and use mosquito nets and coils. Another mosquito-borne disease

Essentials for the outdoor life – mosquito coil and insect repellent

Spicy curries from food stalls – best avoided if your stomach is delicate

Tuberculosis is prevalent throughout Asia, but the visitor is not at serious risk. Vaccines are available, and unpasteurized dairy products should be avoided, particularly by children.

Bilharzia is contracted from tiny worms that infect some types of freshwater snail. They burrow into the skin and cause a general feeling of sickness followed by abdominal pain. Avoid swimming in untested rivers and lakes.

FOOD- AND WATER-BORNE DISEASES

DYSENTERY IS A severe form of food or water poisoning. Bacillary dysentery – characterized by stomach pains, vomiting, and fever – is highly contagious but rarely lasts longer than a week. Amebic dysentery has similar symptoms but takes longer to develop. It can recur and cause chronic health problems. Medical help should be sought without delay if you suspect you have either type.

Hepatitis A is passed on in conditions of poor sanitation – contaminated water or food – and can now be prevented with a vaccine. Symptoms include extreme fatigue, aching, fever, chills, and jaundice. Little can be done to treat the disease beyond rest.

Cholera is a waterborne disease, and symptoms include severe diarrhea, weakness, and cramps. A vaccination is available but is generally considered to be unreliable. Fluid replacement is the most important treatment, while the best prevention is to avoid unsanitary conditions and areas where cholera is present.

Typhoid is transmitted through contaminated water or food, so the same precautions apply. Symptoms are similar to those of flu but quickly accelerate to high fever, weight loss, and severe dehydration. Medical attention is essential as complications such as pneumonia can easily occur. Although a vaccination is available, it is not always reliable.

– dengue fever – is a risk during the daytime. However, few mosquitoes are infected with the virus, and the symptoms, though intense and unpleasant, are rarely fatal. These include fever, headache, severe joint and muscle pains, and a rash. No preventive treatment or vaccination is available.

In Northern Thailand and some rural areas there is a risk of contracting Japanese encephalitis. Spread by nightbiting mosquitoes and ticks, the symptoms are headache, fever, chills, and vomiting. Vaccination is advisable if your plans include traveling to rural areas (particularly during the rainy season), or trekking. Should any of the above symptoms occur seek immediate medical help.

As with malaria, the best way to counter the risk of dengue fever and Japanese encephalitis is to try to avoid being bitten in the first place.

PEOPLE- AND ANIMAL-BORNE DISEASES

ACQUIRED IMMUNE deficiency syndrome (AIDS) is passed through bodily fluids. Blood transfusion methods in Thailand are not always reliable – it is safest to seek treatment in the main hospitals. The same goes for inoculations – make sure needles are new or bring your own supply. Be wary of any procedure involving needles, including tattooing, ear-piercing, and dentistry.

The high turnover of clients in Thailand's infamous and pervasive sex industry means that unprotected sex carries a serious risk *(see p112)*. Not only AIDS, but other sexually transmitted diseases are commonplace. Some strains have become so virulent that they are penicillin-resistant.

Hepatitis B is also transmitted through bodily fluids. Symptoms include fever, nausea, fatigue, and jaundice, and it can lead to severe liver damage. A prophylactic vaccine is available.

Rabies is carried in the saliva of infected animals and can be passed on by a bite or lick to a wound or scratch. Any bite from a dog, cat, or monkey should be cleaned immediately and checked by a doctor. If rabies is detected, treatment involves a long series of inoculations. A prophylactic vaccine is now available.

Tetanus is a potentially lethal disease transmitted through infected cuts and animal bites. The first symptoms are difficulty in swallowing (tetanus is also known as lockjaw) and muscle stiffness in the neck area, which can lead to convulsions. As with rabies, all wounds should be speedily cleaned and examined by a doctor. Effective vaccinations are available, and a booster is necessary every ten years.

Bottled water

Banking and Local Currency

Commercial Bank credit card logo

Throughout Bangkok and the main provincial towns, banking facilities and exchange services are plentiful, well-run, and easy to access. In the major centers, tellers often speak some English. Exchange booths are usually located in the central parts of towns, and mobile exchange units are stationed near larger tourist attractions. Automatic Teller Machines (ATMs) can be found in all cities. Smaller towns are less likely to have exchange facilities, but most have banks or ATMs. Rural villages, unless they are tourist destinations, probably will not have banking or currency exchange services.

HSBC, an international bank operating in Bangkok

BANKS AND BANKING HOURS

The three main banks are the Bangkok Bank, the Thai Farmers Bank, and the Siam Commercial Bank. The Bank of Ayudhya and Bankthai also have branches throughout the country. Foreign-owned banks offering full commercial banking services include the Bank of America, Banque Indosuez, Citibank, Chase Manhattan Bank, Deutsche Bank, Hongkong and Shanghai Bank, and Standard Chartered Bank.

Banking hours are generally 8:30am–3:30pm, Monday to Friday. Some banks have branches in department stores which are open 8am–8pm. Exchange booths are often open daily, early until late. As well as providing day-to-day banking services, the major banks can also organize international money transfers. Most banks, especially in cities, will have an associated ATM.

ATM SERVICES

Most atm services provide instructions in both Thai and English. Any ATM

Automatic Teller Machines, found in Bangkok and many Thai towns

displaying the VISA or Master-Card sign will accept these cards and dispense cash in *baht* using your regular PIN.

There are surcharges for such transactions. If you are planning to stay in Thailand for several months or more, it might be a good idea to open an account at a Thai bank. This allows access to any ATM or main bank without having to worry about exchange rates or charges. Although not all banks have application forms in English, one of the tellers should be able to help. The account should not take more than a week to set up.

CHANGING MONEY

Banks almost always offer the best exchange rates, and rates differ little between banks. Hotels usually offer the worst rates, while those at exchange booths can vary considerably. US dollars are the mostly widely accepted foreign currency when buying *baht*, although sterling is also generally taken. In Bangkok, hole-in-the-wall exchange booths can be found in most major department stores and shopping malls

---

DIRECTORY

THAI BANKS

Bangkok Bank
333 Silom Rd, Bangkok.
☎ 0-2231-4333.

Bank of Ayudhya
1222 Rama 3, Bangkok.
☎ 0-2296-2000.

Siam Commercial Bank
9 Rachadaphisak Rd, Bangkok.
☎ 0-2544-1111.

Bankthai
44 North Sathorn Rd, Bangkok.
☎ 0-2633-9000.

Thai Farmers Bank
1 Thai Farmers Lane, Ratburana Rd, Bangkok.
☎ 0-2470-1122.

FOREIGN BANKS

Bank of America
CRC Tower, 33rd Floor, Wireless Rd, Bangkok.
☎ 0-2305-2800.

Citibank
82 North Sathorn Rd, Bangkok.
☎ 0-2232-2000.

Credit Agricole Indosuez
152 Wireless Rd, Bangkok.
☎ 0-2651-4590.

Deutsche Bank
208 Wireless Rd, Bangkok.
☎ 0-2250-1917.

Hongkong and Shanghai Bank
Rama IV Rd, Bangkok.
☎ 0-2614-4000.

Standard Chartered Bank
990 Rama IV Rd, Abdul Rahim Building, Bangkok.
☎ 0-2724-4000.

CARDS

American Express
☎ 0-2273-5544,
0-2273-5522.

MasterCard
☎ 001-800-11-887-0663.

VISA
☎ 001-800-441-3485.

and on major roads. Mobile exchange units can often be found near tourist attractions and around tourist market areas. These are generally open daily between 7am and 9pm. Exchange rates are published daily in the *Bangkok Post* and the *Nation*.

CREDIT AND DEBIT CARDS

CREDIT CARDS are accepted in major hotels, department stores, and upscale shops and restaurants. They can also be used at major banks (and some exchange kiosks) for cash advances. A surcharge will be applied. VISA and MasterCard are the most widely accepted cards; the use of Diners Club and American Express is more limited.

MasterCard debit cards can be used to withdraw cash at most foreign exchange booths, and at Bangkok Bank and Siam Commercial Bank. VISA debit cards can do the same at the Thai Farmers Bank. Debit cards can also be used at local ATMs, but a surcharge will be levied.

As the popularity of plastic money increases, so too does the incidence of credit-card fraud. Visitors should always carefully check what they sign.

CURRENCY

THE THAI UNIT OF currency is the *baht*, usually seen abbreviated to "B." There are 100 *satang* in a *baht*, but the *satang* represents such a small sum today that it is scarcely used. You may hear 25 *satang* referred to as a *saleung*. However, inflation is rendering this colloquial term redundant. Banknotes come in the following denominations: 10 *baht* (slowly

Bangkok Bank
The Asian International Bank

Logo for one of Thailand's long-established banks

being phased out), 20 *baht*, 50 *baht*, 100 *baht*, 500 *baht*, and 1,000 *baht*.

Changing large denomination notes in rural areas may prove difficult. The coin denominations are 25 *satang* (1 *saleng*), 50 *satang*, 1 *baht*, 5 *baht*, 10 *baht*. Possible confusion over different sized coins of the same denomination is becoming less likely as older, larger 1 and 5 *baht* coins are gradually phased out in favor of smaller versions. Old coins feature Thai numerals only, while newer coins have both Thai and Arabic numerals.

TRAVELERS' CHECKS

BANKS, MAIN HOTELS, and most exchange booths cash travelers' checks, but banks provide the best value as their surcharge is minimal. Travelers' checks are the safest method of carrying money and are exchanged at better rates than cash. Banks charge a fee per check cashed, so using large-domination checks works out cheapest.

VAT

THAILAND IMPOSES a 7 percent Value Added Tax (VAT) on goods and services, generally levied only in upscale hotels, restaurants and shops. It is not possible to claim VAT back.

20 baht

50 baht

100 baht

500 baht

1,000 baht

Coins come in the following denominations:

25 satang　*50 satang*　*1 baht*　*5 baht*　*10 baht*

Communications

A domestic phone booth

Thailand's communication network is becoming increasingly sophisticated. The telephone system is run by the Telephone Organization of Thailand (TOT) under the umbrella of the Communications Authority of Thailand (CAT). It is possible to make international calls and send faxes from all business centers and main hotels. Public phones can be found on all main roads and many minor ones. The postal system, however, can be erratic; if you are sending valuables it is advisable to use courier services. Many major international newspapers and magazines can be easily obtained. Locally published English-language newspapers and magazines can be bought in almost every hotel and bookstore, and at many curbside news stands.

A green card-phone for local and long distance domestic calls

INTERNATIONAL CALLS

All major hotels and most guesthouses offer international dialing services, but will add a surcharge of 30–40 percent. Business centers in small towns offer fax and phone services which are accompanied by high surcharges.

Bangkok's Central Post Office on Charoen Krung New Road and some major post offices around the country have a CAT center that can arrange collect and credit card calls. In Bangkok these are open from 7am to midnight, with reduced hours in the provinces.

To dial directly from a hotel room, either contact the desk, or dial 001 (for an international line) followed by the country code and telephone number. Alternatively, dial the international operator at 100. Full rates are charged from 7am to 9pm, with a 30 percent discount between midnight and 5am, and a 20 percent discount at other times.

Blue and yellow international pay phones can be found on the street, in shopping malls, and in airports. These take some credit cards, and Lenso phonecards, which are sold in the post office and by agents displaying the Lenso logo.

USING AN INTERNATIONAL PHONE

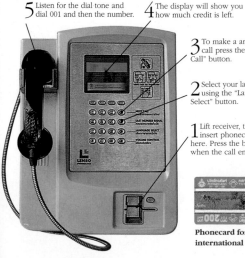

5 Listen for the dial tone and dial 001 and then the number.

4 The display will show you how much credit is left.

3 To make a another call press the "Next Call" button.

2 Select your language using the "Language Select" button.

1 Lift receiver, then insert phonecard here. Press the button when the call ends.

Phonecard for international calls

LOCAL CALLS

Local phone calls can be made from any public pay phone other than the blue and yellow Lenso phones which can be used for international calls only.

Domestic calls can be made from blue and silver coin phones or green card-phones. Coin-operated phones accept one *baht*, five *baht* and ten *baht* coins; only red phones will not accept ten *baht* coins. Hotel phones may accept only five *baht* coins. Local calls (within the same area code) cost one *baht* a minute. There are also some red coin phones, from which it is possible to make only local calls, but these are being phased out.

The long-distance domestic service covers Malaysia and Laos as well as regional Thai calls. These countries can be dialed directly using the appropriate area code.

Green and orange card-phones can be found in department stores and airports throughout the country. Cards for these can be bought at most post offices, bookstores, and hotels and come in several denominations: 25 *baht*, 50 *baht*, 100 *baht*, and 240 *baht*.

Comprehensive telephone directories are published by Shinawatra. An English edition can be found in major hotels and most restaurants in Bangkok. Such directories are to be found in most provincial capitals, but outside these there is unlikely to be an English edition available.

TELEVISION AND RADIO

THAILAND HAS FIVE television channels; programs are mostly in Thai, though in Bangkok some are broadcast with an English simulcast on FM radio. Some towns may receive only one national channel and a local station. Satellite and cable networks are fast expanding all over Asia, and most international English-language networks such as the BBC and CNN are readily available. Many hotels provide satellite and cable television as well as an in-house video channel. Check the *Bangkok Post* and the *Nation* for details.

There are over 400 radio stations nationwide. In Bangkok, there are 41 FM and 35 AM stations. The vast majority of these are in Thai, but English-language stations manned by local DJs are listed in the *Outlook* section of the *Bangkok Post*. The national public radio station, Radio Thailand, broadcasts English-language programs on 107 and 105 FM 24 hours a day, and listings for short-wave frequencies receiving the BBC, VOA, Radio Australia, Radio Canada, RFI (French), and Deutsche Welle are found in the *Focus* section of the *Nation*.

NEWSPAPERS AND MAGAZINES

THE TWO MAIN English-language newspapers, arguably the best in Asia, are the *Bangkok Post* and the *Nation*. These provide reliable local, regional, and international coverage. Their daily broad-

Two popular English-language newspapers in Thailand

sheet inserts *Outlook (Post)* and *Focus (Nation)*, include features on lifestyle, travel, and human interest as well as listings for food, films, concerts, and exhibitions in Bangkok. Both are widely sold in news kiosks and shops throughout Bangkok.

A smaller, less comprehensive newspaper, which relies heavily on the wire service, is *Business Day*. The *Asia Times,* which was launched in 1996, is a Thailand-based regional business paper. The Singapore edition of the

---

DIRECTORY

DIRECTORY ASSISTANCE

Greater Bangkok Metropolitan Area
℡ 1133.

Provincial Areas
℡ 1133.

OPERATOR

International Service or Auto Long Distance Service from Thailand to Malaysia, Myanmar, Cambodia and Laos
℡ 007 or 008.

Road-side newspaper kiosk selling a variety of publications

International Herald Tribune and the *Asian Wall Street Journal* are sold in hotels and English-language bookstores such as Asia Books and Bookazine, which also stock a good selection of international magazines such as *Esquire, Cosmopolitan,* and *Vanity Fair.* News weeklies *The Economist, Time,* and *Newsweek* are widely available, as are their Hong Kong-based Asian counterparts, *Far Eastern Economic Review* (FEER) and *AsiaWeek.*

Among the local English-language monthly publications are the useful listings guide *Metro*, the business and lifestyle magazine *Manager,* and society rag *Thailand Tatler.* Free guides available in restaurants, bars, and bookstores include *This Week Thailand, Bangkok Guide,* and the pocket-sized *Bangkok Dining and Entertainment.*

USEFUL DIALING CODES

- In 2001 the old area codes were incorporated into every telephone number. So, whether calling from within or outside the province, you need to dial a 9-digit number for Bangkok, Nonthaburi, Pathumtani and Samutprakarn (beginning with 02), or 10-digit number for other provinces.
- For international calls, dial 007, then the country code.
- Country codes are: UK 44; Ireland 353; France 33; US & Canada 1; Australia 61; New Zealand 64. It may be necessary to omit the first digit of the destination area code.

- For directory assistance dial 1133 from anywhere in the country.
- To put a call through the international operator, or to report technical problems, dial 101.
- To speak to the domestic operator, dial 101.
- To make a reverse charge (collect) call dial the international operator at 101.
- Note that the speaking clock and similar telephone services such as directory assistance are all in Thai.
- For a wake-up call, contact your hotel switchboard or front desk.

Phra Sing Post Office, in the center of Chiang Mai

MAIL

LETTERS AND POSTCARDS generally take at least one week to reach Europe and North America from Thailand. Stamps are available at all post offices and can also be bought at many hotels. The major hotels will also mail letters and packages for you.

Be wary of sending valuable items through the mail as parcels have been known to go astray. Greater reliability can usually be assured by sending letters and packages by registered mail or via International Express Mail (EMS).

Parcels must be wrapped in officially approved packaging. This will be done for you at a special counter at most post offices. Having lined up to have your parcel packed, you might find that you must then line up again for the parcel to be weighed, and once again to buy the stamps.

General delivery facilities are available at all main post offices in the country. Letters will normally be held for up to three months. To claim mail from general delivery it is necessary to show your passport and sometimes pay a

small fee. Letters should be addressed to you (with your last name written in capitals and underlined), poste restante, GPO, address, town, Thailand. Thus for Bangkok's main GPO, correspondents should send mail care of GPO, Charoen Krung Road, Bangkok.

Larger post offices are usually open from Monday to Friday between 8am and 8pm and at weekends between 8am and 1pm. Smaller post offices in cities, and those in most provincial towns, are generally open Monday to Friday between 8:30am and 4:30pm and between 9am and 12 noon on Saturdays.

FAX, TELEX, AND TELEGRAPH SERVICES

MAJOR HOTELS often provide fax and telex facilities for guests. However, you should be aware that, as with phone calls, hotels add a heavy markup for the use of such services.

It can be cheaper to take advantage of the fax, telex, and telegraph services available at the Overseas Telegraph and Telephone offices. These can be found in many towns and, usefully, are often open 24 hours a day. Additionally, some of the TAT offices and independent agencies may offer fax facilities.

Thai mailbox

COURIER SERVICES

THE MAJOR INTERNATIONAL courier companies, such as **DHL**, **FedEx** and **UPs**, operate in Thailand so it is easy to have goods air freighted home. However, for very heavy or large items, such as furniture, the cost is prohibitive, and shipping will be the only viable option. Many shops will arrange this for you and provide the necessary paperwork.

ADDRESSES

THAI ADDRESSES are complicated. What may look like a street number may in fact be a block number. For instance, 349/2–3 Sukhumvit Road, indicates block number 349 with the premises occupying numbers 2–3 of that block. Most main roads have numerous numbered *sois* (lanes) leading off them. Sometimes these are written before the road name, sometimes after. Thus, 123 Sukhumvit Soi 14, Khlong Toey, Bangkok indicates house number 123 on Soi 14 off Sukhumvit Road in Bangkok's Khlong Toey district. Some major *sois* have a name as well as a number.

An added complication is *moo* numbers. These refer to a specific, small geographical area, which is often a village. However, *moo* numbers may still be encountered in cities, reflecting the expansion of the cities as they encompassed outlying settlements within their boundaries.

Addresses outside large cities are usually the number and street name, village, village group, district, and province.

The familiar figure of King Bhumibol on all the standard issue Thai stamps

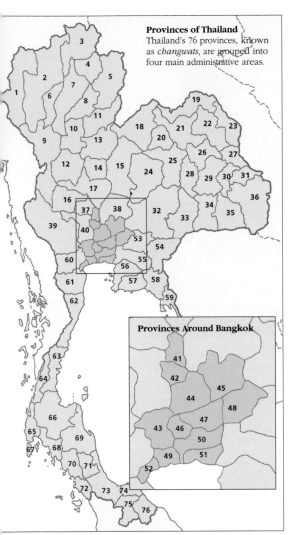

Provinces of Thailand
Thailand's 76 provinces, known as *changwats*, are grouped into four main administrative areas.

Provinces Around Bangkok

THE PROVINCES OF THAILAND

PAK NUA

1 Mae Hong Son
2 Chiang Mai
3 Chiang Rai
4 Phayao
5 Nan
6 Lamphun
7 Lampang
8 Phrae
9 Tak
10 Sukhothai
11 Uttaradit
12 Kamphaeng Phet
13 Phitsanulok
14 Phichit
15 Phetchabun
16 Uthai Thani
17 Nakhon Sawan

PAK ISAN

18 Loei
19 Nong Khai
20 Nong Bua Lum Phu
21 Udon Thani
22 Sakhon Nakhon
23 Nakhon Phanom
24 Chaiyaphum
25 Khon Kaen
26 Kalasin
27 Mukdahan
28 Maha Sarakham
29 Roi Et
30 Yasothon
31 Amnat Charoen
32 Khorat (Nakhon Ratchasima)
33 Buri Ram
34 Surin
35 Si Sa Ket
36 Ubon Ratchathani

PAK KLANG

37 Chai Nat
38 Lop Buri
39 Suphan Buri
40 Suphan Buri
41 Sing Buri
42 Ang Thong
43 Nakhon Pathom
44 Phra Nakhon Si Ayutthaya
45 Saraburi
46 Nonthaburi
47 Pathum Thani
48 Nakhon Nayok
49 Samut Sakhon
50 Krung Thep Maha Nakhon (Bangkok)
51 Samut Prakan
52 Samut Songkhram
53 Prachin Buri
54 Sa Kaeo
55 Chachoengsao
56 Chon Buri
57 Rayong
58 Chanthaburi
59 Trat
60 Ratchaburi
61 Phetchaburi
62 Prachuap Khiri Khan

PAK TAI

63 Chumphon
64 Ranong
65 Phangnga
66 Surat Thani
67 Phuket
68 Krabi
69 Nakhon Si Thammarat
70 Trang
71 Phatthalung
72 Satun
73 Songkhla
74 Pattani
75 Yala
76 Narathiwat

ADMINISTRATIVE REGIONS

THAILAND'S 500,000 sq km (193,000 sq miles) are home to 62 million people. The country is split into four main regions: Pak Nua (the North), Pak Isan (the Northeast), Pak Klang (Bangkok, the Central Plains and the Gulf of Thailand), and Pak Tai (the South).

The regions are subdivided into 76 provinces (*jangwats*), each administered by a governor. Provincial capitals are known as *amphor muangs*. Each province consists of a number of *amphors*, or dis-

tricts (722 in total), which are headed by a district officer. These are, in turn, divided into subdistricts (*king amphors*), and then into village groups (*tambons*). There are a total of 7,109 of these village groups in the country, each of which is administered by a *kamnan*. At the most basic level are the 64,450 individual villages (*moo bans*). Every village is represented by its own elected headman or *phuyaiban*.

These administrative boundaries are useful to understand when working out addresses or traveling to locations that are off the beaten track.

TRAVEL INFORMATION

FOR MOST VISITORS, flying is the most convenient way of getting to Thailand – the only other routes at present are by ferry, road, and rail via Malaysia, or by limited but rapidly improving road links via Laos. Domestic flights within Thailand are easy and cut journey times considerably, with provincial airports dotted generously around the country. Flights to surrounding countries are cheaper if booked

Thai Airways logo

within Thailand. Regular rail services run between Bangkok and Singapore, via Kuala Lumpur, Butterworth (for Penang), and some Southern Thai towns. Rail travel is efficient, clean, and comfortable, but there is a limited number of lines. Long-distance and provincial buses of varying quality run to all towns and most villages. At a local level there is a variety of taxis, *songthaews, tuk-tuks,* and rickshas.

A Boeing 747 in the traditional livery of Thai Airways

ARRIVING BY AIR

THAILAND IS SERVED BY numerous airlines from all over the world. Direct flights are available from North America, Europe, Australasia, and Asia. A flight from the US will take as long as 24 hours and may entail an overnight stay in Japan. **Thai Airways** operates direct flights from Los Angeles to Bangkok, and **British Airways**, **United**, and **Northwest** have a connecting service from New York. Flights from Asian countries may land at Phuket, Chiang Mai, or Hat Yai.

AIR FARES

THE COST OF FLYING to and from Thailand varies according to the destination, the airline and the time of year. In the northern hemisphere the low fares are available from September to April, and in the southern hemisphere from March to November. Bangkok is one of the cheapest cities in the world to fly out of due to loose government restrictions on air fares and fierce competition between the airlines and Bangkok's travel agencies.

DON MUANG AIRPORT

BANGKOK'S INTERNATIONAL airport is the entry point for the vast majority of visitors to Thailand. The airport is well equipped and is one of the most efficient in Asia. Though immigration lines can be slow the baggage claim is reliable, and the green customs channel (nothing to declare) nearly always runs smoothly.

There are two international terminals, 1 and 2, as well as a domestic terminal. The international terminals are within easy walking distance of each other, and an elevated walkway connects them to the domestic terminal. There is also a free shuttle-bus service that runs every 15 minutes along the short distance between the terminals. The arrivals hall of Terminal 1 has by far the best facilities, including currency exchange booths, automatic teller machines (ATM), a 24-hour post office with international telephone facilities, an airport clinic, a tourist information booth, and a

hotel reservation desk. At the latter you can book rooms in any of the hotels that belong to the Thai Hotels Association (*see p382*) for a small commission. The departure hall of Terminal 1 has restaurants and bars, as well as a luggage room for up to four months. There are fewer facilities at Terminal 2.

The airport is within 100 m (110 yards) of a busy metropolitan area with a market, stores, restaurants, food stalls, and even a *wat*. Nearby hotels offer daytime "ministays" of three hours as well as overnight accommodations.

A new international airport to be called Suwannabhumi is under construction and due to open in mid-2006.

GETTING TO AND FROM DON MUANG AIRPORT

TRAVEL TIME BY ROAD between the airport and central Bangkok depends on the traffic conditions. The expressway (for which a toll must be paid) can take as little as 20 minutes in optimum conditions. However, it may take over three hours if there is heavy congestion, so try to avoid rush hours. There are a variety of ways to travel the 25 km (16 miles) into

Planes on the tarmac at Bangkok airport

An ordinary city taxi, characterized by yellow registration plates

A licensed airport taxi, with yellow registration plates

An airport limousine, identified by its pale green registration plates

Bangkok from Don Muang. If you are already booked into a hotel, you should check to see if it offers a complimentary limousine or minibus service from the airport. The Thai Hotels Association desk should have this information. One or two luxury hotels operate a helicopter service to and from the airport for their guests. Thai Airways offers limousines, taxis, and a minibus service to major hotels. The taxi ranks are now controlled by the airport. This rule applies even to meter taxis. Ignore anyone offering cheap rates (they may not be all they seem), and seek out the taxi desk in the arrivals hall of each terminal, where a price will be set for your trip (typically 300 *baht*). Licensed airport limousines and airport taxis can be identified by their respective pale green or yellow licence plates. An experimental airport bus service to town began in 1996.

The train station, directly opposite the airport, is reached via a covered walkway from the arrivals hall. Trains depart from here every 15–30 minutes for Hua Lampong Station in the center of Bangkok. Normal meter taxis operate in the city.

The following bus services run between the airport and city center: AB1 to Silom Road; AB2 to Sanam Luang; AB3 to Sukhumvit 55; AB4 to Hualam Pong railway station. Women traveling alone are advised to take either an airport-licensed taxi, or the minibus service that is provided by Thai Airways.

DOMESTIC FLIGHTS

LOCAL CARRIERS **Thai Airways** and **Bangkok Airways** fly to all major provincial capitals such as Chiang Mai, Hat Yai, and Phuket. They also serve towns such as Ranong, Mae Sot, and Phrae. Other local airlines now in operation include Air Andaman, Orient Thai Airlines, PB Air and Phuket Airlines. Air tickets can be bought through travel agents and hotels, or booked directly through the airlines – in this case you will need to pick up your ticket at the airport at least one hour before flying.

On the many public holidays (*see p47*) and on weekends, when there are more people traveling, it can be difficult to get a flight, so try to book tickets well in advance or travel during the week.

Bus from Don Muang airport to the center of Bangkok

AIRPORT	INFORMATION	DISTANCE TO TOWN OR RESORT	AVERAGE TAXI FARE	AVERAGE JOURNEY TIME
Bangkok domestic:	0-2535-1111 0-2535-1253	City center 25 km (16 miles)	300 *baht*	Rail: 50 minutes Road: 1–2 hours
Chiang Mai	0-5327-0222	City center 4 km (2.5 miles)	100 *baht*	Road: 30 minutes
Phuket	0-7632-7230-7	Patong 32 km (20 miles)	550 *baht*	Road: 45 minutes
Ko Samui	0-7724-5601	Chaweng 26 km (16 miles)	150 *baht*	Road: 30 minutes

Traveling Around by Train, Bus, and Boat

THAILAND HAS AN efficient railroad system known as the SRT (State Railway of Thailand), with four major lines connecting Bangkok with the North, Northeast, East, and South. Though trains are comfortable and safe, trip times are similar, sometimes even longer, than by bus, and the number of towns on the network is limited. Phuket and Chiang Rai, for instance, do not have train stations. By contrast, well-maintained, long-distance buses connect all major cities to Bangkok, and provincial buses serve all smaller towns and many villages. The main islands are accessible via scheduled ferry services.

RAILROAD NETWORK

THE MAIN STATION in Bangkok is Hua Lampong, which serves all four major lines. The first line runs to Chiang Mai via the Central Plains. A second, which later divides in two, runs to Nong Khai and Ubon Ratchathani in Northeast Thailand. A third connects Bangkok to the Eastern Seaboard and Cambodia, and a fourth runs down the peninsula to Malaysia. However, Thon Buri Station in Bangkok Noi is the principal departure point for trains to the South. It also has lines to Kanchanaburi and Suphan Buri.

Window of a first-class train coach

TRAINS

TRAIN SERVICES are labeled Special Express (the fastest), Express, Rapid (slower than Express), and Ordinary. Travel times, even on Express trains, can be longer than by road. The trip from Bangkok to Chiang Mai, for instance, takes 11 to 13 hours.

First-class coaches (available on Express and Special Express trains) consist of individual cabins with air-conditioning. Second-class coaches have reclining seats and a choice of fans or air-conditioning. Sleepers in this class have individual seats that are converted into curtained-off beds at night. Toilets (there should be at least one Western toilet) and washing facilities are at the end of coaches.

Most tourists find that second class is comfortable enough for long distances and far more relaxing than a bus journey.

Third-class coaches have wooden benches, each seating two or three passengers: they are cheap but not recommended for long distances.

Lining up for tickets at Hua Lampong Station in Bangkok

Most trains are clean and well maintained. Uniformed vendors stroll up and down the aisles with refreshments, and buffet cars are attached to trains on long-distance routes.

TRAIN TICKETS AND FARES

A TRAIN TIMETABLE in English is available from Hua Lamphong Station in Bangkok. Trains at peak periods (weekends and holidays) can be sold out days in advance. Hua Lampong has an advance booking office with English-speaking staff. Some travel agents will also book train tickets.

Fares depend on the speed of the train and the class of the carriage. A second-class ticket between Bangkok and Chiang Mai is about 280 *baht*, with supplements of around 50–80 *baht* for Rapid and Express services. Shorter trips, such as from Bangkok to Ayutthaya, cost anything between 15–120 *baht*.

Tourists can also buy 20-day rail passes. These cost 1,000–2,000 *baht*. Information about these is available from Hua Lampong Station.

LONG-DISTANCE BUSES

LONG-DISTANCE buses run from the Eastern (Ekamai), Northern (Morchit), and Southern (Pin Kloo) bus terminals in Bangkok. Most provincial capitals can be reached direct

Fountain in front of Hua Lampong Station, Bangkok

EASTERN & ORIENTAL EXPRESS

The world-renowned Eastern & Oriental Express operates between Bangkok and Singapore. The journey takes three days and two nights, including stops at Butterworth (Penang) and Kuala Lumpur in Malaysia. The 22 carriages are bedecked with fabrics and fittings evocative of 1930s rail travel. Double and single cabins come in private and presidential classes, and there are two restaurants, a saloon car, a bar, and an observation deck. Such luxuries are, of course, reflected in the price.

Dining car on the Eastern & Oriental Express

from Bangkok. Large cities such as Chiang Mai, Phitsanulok, Khorat, and Surat Thani also act as transit hubs, with both long-distance and local connections. Buses can be faster than trains: Bangkok to Chiang Mai takes about ten hours. Vehicles are air-conditioned, with a toilet, reclining seats, and plenty of leg room. "VIP" buses have the best facilities, including free refreshments served by a stewardess. Overnight services are popular, though they can get rather chilly – blankets should be provided.

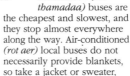

Typical train tickets

BUS TICKETS AND FARES

FARES FOR long-distance bus trips are similar in price to second-class train tickets. "VIP" buses are at the top of the price range. Book well in advance through a travel agent or at the bus station if traveling on the weekend or during a public holiday. Otherwise, just turn up at the coach station at least half an hour before departure. Tickets are always bought as one-way.

PROVINCIAL BUSES

THE GOVERNMENT bus company is called *Bor Kor Sor* (BKS). Its buses are frequent, relatively reliable, and the cheapest form of transportation in Thailand. Booking is rarely necessary. On many buses simply pay the driver or conductor. Almost every town will have a BKS terminal. The non air-conditioned (*rot thamadaa*) buses are the cheapest and slowest, and they stop almost everywhere along the way. Air-conditioned (*rot aer*) local buses do not necessarily provide blankets, so take a jacket or sweater, especially at nighttime.

Traveling on provincial buses is a good way to meet local people and reach many villages and sights. Beware, though, that refreshment and toilet stops may be infrequent, the buses may be in a poor state of repair, and the road skills of drivers will vary. Local services are nearly always slow and crowded. Back seats are reserved for monks, so be prepared to move or stand. Women should avoid sitting next to monks (*see p455*).

(*see p455*).

A blue and white air-conditioned (*rot aer*) bus

DIRECTORY

TRAIN INFORMATION

Hua Lampong Station
Krung Kasem Rd, Bangkok.
℡ *1609.*
Advance booking office
open 7am–4pm daily.

Thon Buri/Bangkok Noi Station
Arun Amarin Rd, Bangkok Noi.
℡ *0-2411-3102.*

Chiang Mai Station
Charoen Muang Rd, Chiang Mai.
℡ *0-5324-5363.*

Eastern & Oriental Express
℡ *(020) 7805 5060 (UK).*
℡ *(866) 674-3689 (US).*
℡ *0-2255-9150 (Bangkok).*
℡ *(65) 392 3500 (Singapore).*
ⓦ *www.orient-express.com*

BUS TERMINALS

Bangkok
Eastern/Ekamai Bus Terminal
Sukhumvit Rd, Bangkok.
℡ *0-2391-4164.*

Northern and Northeastern/Morchit Bus Terminal
Kampheng Phet Rd, Morchit, Bangkok.
℡ *0-2936-3670 (N).*
℡ *0-2936-0657 (NE).*

Southern/Pin Klao Bus Terminal
Nakhon Chai Si Rd, Phra Pin Klao, Bangkok. ℡ *0-2435-5605.*

Chiang Mai
Chiang Mai Arcade, Kaew Nawarat Rd, Chiang Mai.
℡ *0-5324-2664.*

BOATS TO THE ISLANDS

SCHEDULED FERRIES are always erratic, since their service is dependent on the weather conditions. Regular services are available to Ko Samui, Ko Pha Ngan, and Ko Tao from Surat Thani. Ko Phi Phi is served by ferries from Phuket and Krabi. Smaller islands have less regular services – sometimes just a makeshift ferry run by local fishermen. Travel agents will be able to give you rough timetables, but these may be dependent on filling enough seats in the boat. Many services stop in the rainy season.

Local Transportation

BANGKOK IS POSSIBLY the world's most congested city, with notorious traffic jams and pollution. You can avoid the worst congestion by using the Skytrain, an elevated rail system which opened in 1999, and the Chao Phraya Express riverboat service. Local transportation in the provinces is less frenetic, where bicycle rickshaws *(samlors)* and colorful *tuk-tuks* run alongside services such as *songthaews*, and bargaining for the fare on *samlors* is part of the Thai experience. Do not climb on before agreeing to a price, and beware being taken for a ride in more ways than one.

Bangkok tuk-tuk

A *songthaew* – uncomfortable, but cheaper and safer than a *tuk-tuk*

GETTING AROUND BANGKOK

THE SKYTRAIN makes for fast and efficient traveling in the Downtown area. There are two lines: the Sukhumvit route from Morchit Station in the north of town to Onnut Station, and the Silom route from National Stadium to Taksin Bridge, with an interchange between the two routes at the Siam Center. Other forms of city transport include riverboats, public buses, limousines and tour buses run by hotels, as well as taxis and *tuk-tuks*. A new subway, due to open in late 2004, will dramatically improve city transport.

Express riverboats with conductors serve popular piers on the Chao Phraya River, running every 10–20 minutes. Ferries also link east and west banks, and it is possible to rent a longtail boat *(see pp70–71)* at some piers to explore the *khlongs*.

In Bangkok, one-way bus lanes can make buses the fastest form of road transport. The *Tourist Map Bangkok City* and *Tour 'n' Guide Map Bangkok* show the bus routes. Blue air-conditioned buses ("AC" in the transport details for each Bangkok sight), and pink and gray microbuses (indicated by "M") are comfortable and cover the popular routes. Ordinary (non air-conditioned) buses are cheap, cover all of Bangkok, and run into the night. City buses outside Bangkok are not easy to use for non-Thai speakers but taxis, *tuk-tuks*, and *songthaews* are readily available and convenient.

TAXIS

METER TAXIS operate in Bangkok, Chiang Mai, and Hat Yai, distinguishable, by a prominent "Taxi-Meter" sign on the roof. Drivers tend to know only the names and locations of the major hotels and sights. In nonmeter taxis

TAXI-METER

Sign on the roof of a metered taxi in Bangkok

(in Bangkok these are now quite rare and not recommended), you need to bargain for the fare before getting in.

Motorcycle taxis operate in some towns. Drivers tend to congregate near markets and long *sois* and can be identified by their colorful numbered vests. Prices are negotiated.

SONGTHAEWS, SAMLORS, AND TUK-TUKS

SONGTHAEWS (literally translated as "two rows") are vans with two rows of seats in the back. They are more common than city buses outside Bangkok and run popular routes for set fares, typically between 20 and 40 *baht*. Drivers may wait until they are at least half full before starting out. Routes are sometimes written in English on the sides of the vans. *Songthaews* can be rented like taxis, but are less comfortable.

Samlors are three-wheeled vehicles that can transport one or two people up to a few kilometers. Motorized *samlors* are known as *tuk-tuks* – their two-stroke engines, introduced by the Japanese during World War II, are notoriously noisy. In heavy traffic or during the rainy season, *tuk-tuks* can be uncomfortable and unstable, but are always popular with tourists. Nonmotorized *samlors* are often in the form of bicycle rickshas. You need to negotiate a price before climbing into either type: 30–60 *baht* is reasonable for short hops.

Three-wheeled bicycle ricksha, or *samlor*, in a seaside resort

Organized Tours

H UNDREDS OF TOUR COMPANIES are based in Bangkok, Chiang Mai, and major resorts such as Phuket, and most hotels throughout the country offer tours of one sort or another. Typical excursions available range from one-day city tours covering the main sights to more comprehensive itineraries taking in several towns and locations over several days. Costs are naturally higher than taking public transit, but in some cases – for instance many sights in the Greater Bangkok region – much time and effort simply in getting to the destination may be saved. The drawback of most organized tours is, of course, that there is rarely time to linger.

as are jeeps for gaining access to remote areas. Most vehicles are well maintained and safe.

Boat tours are popular in many resorts, though the majority of operators follow the same routes. Day trips to islands, including opportunities for water sports, are common. Transfers to and from hotels are often part of the deal. Trips to remote islands, often with diving facilities on board *(see p446)*, can span several days, and accommodation may be provided on the boat itself.

BOOKING A TOUR

I T SHOULD BE POSSIBLE to book a tour of Thailand from your home country that will include all travel and accommodations. Such all-inclusive tours typically last between one and two weeks and include a few nights in Bangkok followed by excursions to Chiang Mai and other Northern locations, or to a beach resort. Other packages are more specialized, concentrating, say, on trekking in the North *(see p446)*, and may vary from a few days to several weeks in duration. Based in Bangkok, **Thai Overlander Travel & Tour** and **NS Travel & Tours** are major operators.

Most regional hotels and many guesthouses offer tours of the surrounding area, or are in close contact with local tour companies. The local TAT office will also be able to recommend reputable tour companies. Day trips to the most popular sights can usually be booked just one day in advance. Tours to more distant sights should include arrange-

ments for accommodations, and usually have at least one departure day each week. In most cases, the tour company will pick you up direct from your hotel or guesthouse.

TOUR BUSES AND BOATS

M ANY TOUR COMPANIES use luxury, or "VIP" coaches, with reclining seats, on-board refreshments, air-conditioning, and a toilet. Air-conditioned minibuses are also common,

GUIDED TOURS

B ILINGUAL GUIDES accompany many tours, especially to cultural sights such as Ayutthaya. In Northern Thailand a knowledgeable guide is essential for safety reasons when trekking through the jungle and visiting hill-tribe villages. The quality of guides varies considerably· a listing of reputable ones is published by the Professional Guide Association and available from TAT.

Elephant trekking, a popular tour option in Northern Thailand

DIRECTORY MAJOR TOUR COMPANIES **Arlymear Travel** 6th Floor, CCT Building, 109 Surawong Rd, Bangkok. 📞 *0-2236-9317.* **Diethelm Travel** Kian Gwan Building II, 140 Witthayu Rd, Bangkok. 📞 *0-2255-9150.*	**JR Chiang Mai Travel** 24 Kampaengdin Rd, Chiang Mai. 📞 *0-5327-6310.* **NS Travel & Tours** 133/19–20 Ratchaprarop Rd, Bangkok. 📞 *0-2246-5659.* **P & O Regale Travel** 191/1-2 Sathorn 12, Bangkok. 📞 *0-2635-2450.*	**Silver Queen** 291 Chaofa Rd, Phuket. 📞 *0-7622-2623.* **Songserm Travel** 51–53 Satun Rd, Phuket. 📞 *0-7622-2573.* **STA Travel** 14th Floor, Wall Street Tower Building, Suriwong Rd, Bangkok. 📞 *0-2236-0262 ext 211.*	**Thai-Indochina Tour Co** 869 Rama IV Rd, Bangkok. 📞 *0-2219-1975.* **Thai Overlander Travel & Tour** 407 Sukhumvit Rd, Bangkok. 📞 *0-2258 4779.* **World Travel Service Ltd** 1053 Charoen Krung Rd, Bangkok. 📞 *0-2233-5900.*

Renting a Car, Moped, or Bicycle

Kilometer marker

D RIVING IN THAILAND is not for the faint-hearted. Hazards come in the form of potholed roads, confusing intersections, poorly maintained vehicles, and dangerous driving. For many visitors wanting to explore away from the usual tour routes, hiring a car with a driver who is used to the roads is by far the best option. International car rental firms operate in Bangkok and provincial capitals. The standard of local rental companies varies enormously. In the resorts, mopeds and jeeps are popular with tourists.

Sign for a local car rental company: check if insurance is included

RENTING A CAR

A VALID INTERNATIONAL driver's license is a necessity for most visitors, while those from ASEAN countries (Association of Southeast Asian Nations) need only have a license from their home countries. International rental agencies offer safe cars and the most extensive insurance and backup services. **Avis** and **Budget** have desks at some airports and in major cities. Charges range from about 1,800 *baht* for a day to 35,000 *baht* for a month.

With other car rental companies, you should check the small print on the contract for liabilities. Insurance may not be included. Obtain a copy of the vehicle registration and carry it around with you.

HIRING A CHAUFFEUR-DRIVEN CAR

H IRING AN experienced driver with a car is gaining popularity in Thailand. The cost can be surprisingly low – often less than 50 percent extra on top of the normal price of car rental. Some drivers are knowledgeable about sights and will suggest interesting itineraries. Most car rental firms can arrange drivers. **Siam Express** offers packages including a chauffeur, car, and accommodation in a wide range of hotels.

RENTING A MOPED

M OPEDS AND MOTORCYCLES are widely available for rent in the resorts, provincial capitals, and other large towns. In areas with a lot of guesthouses you can rent anything from a moped to a heavy-duty dirt-bike. Driver's licenses are rarely requested, and few firms bother with insurance. Costs are low: 200–300 *baht* is average for a day's rental.

Safety precautions are essential. Check tires, oil, and brakes before you set out. Wear a helmet (compulsory in many towns) and proper shoes. Long sleeves and trousers will minimize cuts and grazes in a minor accident. Take great care on dirt roads and avoid driving alone in rural areas. Bear in mind that medical help is not always easily available.

GASOLINE AND SERVICING

G AS STATIONS in Thailand are well manned and are located on main roads in towns and along highways. They are modern and most provide unleaded gas. Attendants will fill your tank, wash your windows, and pump up your tires. Some garages have a resident mechanic for bigger jobs, or will at least be able to recommend one. Most of them have a small general shop, and all have Asian toilet facilities. Many garages are open 24 hours, while others close at about 8pm. Gas itself is often cheaper than in the West.

Logo of PTT, a gasoline company with stations throughout Thailand

PARKING

M ULTISTORY parking lots in Bangkok are generally attached to major hotels and department stores. Parking is usually free for hotel guests, and for visitors for up to two or three hours. A ticket is issued on entry and should be stamped by a cashier; pay on the way out. Apart from these arrangements, parking can be difficult in Bangkok.

Throughout Thailand, pavements painted with red and white stripes indicate a no-parking zone. In provincial cities, many hotels and large guesthouses provide free parking facilities for guests. In quieter towns you can generally park anywhere that is not obviously going to be in the way of passing traffic.

Mopeds for rent in Naton town, Ko Samui

Traffic policeman waving vehicles through at a Bangkok intersection

ROADS AND ROAD SIGNS

MULTILANE NATIONAL highways exist mostly in and around Bangkok. A toll is charged to travel on the expressways, including the one to Bangkok airport. The fee is indicated above the booth – the exact change is required at manually operated booths. The expressways are less congested than other Bangkok roads, but they are still prone to traffic jams.

Many roads in Bangkok are one-way, though a lane may be reserved for buses traveling in the opposite direction.

National highways (in some places also known as routes), such as Highway 1 through the Central Plains, are fast and furious, and can be congested in places. Provincial highways are paved and vary in quality. Smaller roads linking villages are sometimes no more than dirt tracks. Main roads in towns are called *thanons*; numbered lanes leading off these are called *sois* and *troks*. In the rainy season, all roads can become flooded.

Destinations are often given in Roman as well as Thai script. Arabic numerals are always used for distances, and kilometer markers are placed along all main roads. Road markings and traffic symbols are easy to understand.

RULES OF THE ROAD

D RIVING is on the left. The speed limit is 60 kph (35 mph) within city limits, unless signed otherwise, and 80 kph (50 mph) on open roads. The standard international road rules apply, but are of little interest to Thai drivers. Indeed, the only consistent rule of thumb is that "size wins."

The eccentric use of indicators and headlights can be unnerving. A left signal can indicate to another driver that it is alright to pass, while a right signal can indicate hazardous oncoming traffic, and a flash of the headlights means: "I'm coming through."

Horns are used constantly, often as a warning of presence rather than obvious danger. Drivers think nothing of straddling lanes and passing on curves and up hill. Yield to larger vehicles at unmarked intersections. It is legal to turn left at red lights if there is a blue sign with a white left arrow, or occasionally if you are in the left lane. On minor roads, beware of roaming animals.

Auto Guide Company map

Traffic fines are most commonly imposed for illegal turns. If you get a ticket and your license is taken, go to the local police station, the address of which will be on the ticket, and pay the fine. Drive slowly through army checkpoints in border areas, and be prepared to stop if necessary.

Typical road scene in Thailand's notoriously busy capital city

ROAD MAPS

M OST THAIS RELY ON mental maps and see no need for the level of cartography favored in the West. Tourist maps are widely available but cover major roads only. Some provincial, foldout maps produced by the Prannok Witthaya Map Center are excellent, showing all roads and reliefs, but are sold in few outlets. The *Thailand Highways Map* by the Auto Guide Company and the *Thailand Highway Map* by the Roads Association are the best atlases, and are written in Thai and Roman scripts.

RENTING A BICYCLE

I N THE COOL SEASON, cycling in quiet areas is a pleasant way to get around. Guesthouses and small agencies often have bicycles for rent for 20–100 *baht* a day, though the bikes may be rickety. New mountain bikes may be available, but, perhaps surprisingly, costs may exceed those of mopeds. Taking plenty of water is essential and, of course, great care is always necessary on the roads.

General Index

Acknowledgments

DORLING KINDERSLEY would like to thank the following people whose contributions and assistance have made the preparation of this book possible.

MAIN CONTRIBUTORS
PHILIP CORNWEL-SMITH is a journalist focusing on entertainment, lifestyle and topical issues. After working on guides to London, in 1994 he moved to Thailand and was founding editor of the Bangkok listings magazine *Metro*.

ANDREW FORBES has studied Thai history and culture for more than 20 years and has lived in the country on and off since 1984. He writes for the *Asian Wall Street Journal* and *Far Eastern Economic Review* among other publications.

TIM FORSYTH is a writer and lecturer at the London School of Economics. He has travelled extensively throughout Northern Thailand and other parts of Southeast Asia.

RACHEL HARRISON has lectured at the School of Oriental and African Studies in London and contributed to Thai phrase books. She has a special interest in Northeast Thailand.

DAVID HENLEY is director of Crescent Press Agency's Thailand Bureau and has lived in Thailand for more than a decade. An authority on Thai cuisine, he contributes regularly to the *Bangkok Post* and *The Australian*.

JOHN HOSKIN has been based in Bangkok since 1980. He is the author of several books on travel, art and culture in Thailand and Indochina, including *The Mekong: A River and Its People*.

GAVIN PATTISON is a London-based writer who has contributed to the *Blue Guide to Thailand* among other titles. He has travelled extensively in Thailand, Indonesia. and other parts of Southeast Asia.

ADDITIONAL ILLUSTRATIONS
Robert Ashby, Graham Bell, Peter Bull, Joanna Cameron, Chris Forsey, Paul Guest, Stephen Gyapay, Ruth Lindsay, Maltings Partnership, Mel Pickering, Robbie Polley, Sally Anne Reisen, Mike Taylor, Pat Thorne, Paul Weston.

ADDITIONAL PHOTOGRAPHY
Alberto Cassio, Peter Chadwick, Crescent Press Agency, Philip Dowell, Neil Fletcher, Dave King, Alan Newnham, Harry Taylor.

ADDITIONAL CARTOGRAPHY
Christine Purcell and Gary Bowes (ERA-Maptec Ltd).

DESIGN AND EDITORIAL ASSISTANCE
Alexander Allan, Gillian Allan, Douglas Amrine, Vicky Barber, Tessa Bindloss, Vivien Crump, Catherine Day, Silvia Gaillard, Victoria Heyworth-Dunne, Paul Hines, Leanne Hogbin, Nancy Jones, Esther Labi, Helen Partington, Lee Redmond, Julian Sheather, Ellie Smith, Veronica Wood.

ADDITIONAL RESEARCH
Parita Boonyoo, Debbie Guthrie Haer, Sathorn Leelakachornjit, Elizabeth Lu, James Mahon, Pharadee Narkkarphunchiwan, Warangkana Nibhatsukit, Pimalaporn Wongchinsri, Wanee Tipchindachaikul, Somchai Worasart.

PROOFREADER
Denise Heywood.

INDEX
Hilary Bird.

SPECIAL ASSISTANCE
Dorling Kindersley would like to thank all the regional branches of the Tourism Authority of Thailand (TAT). Particular thanks also to: the Ayutthaya Historical Studies Centre (Thailand), Dr Peter Barrett (Medical Advisory Service for Travellers Abroad, London), William Booth (Jim Thompson's House, Bangkok), Alberto Cassio (Photobank, Bangkok), Crescent Press Agency (Chiang Mai), Gerald Cubitt, John Dransfield (Kew Gardens Herbarium, London), Michael Freeman, Helen Goldie (Durham University), Philip Harris (Bahn Thai Restaurant, London), Kietisak Itchayanan (National Culture Commission, Bangkok), Elizabeth Moore (London School of Oriental and African Studies), Tony Moore (British Thai Boxing Council), Phra Maha Pradit Panyatulo (Wat Buddhapadipa, London), Paisarn Piammattawat, Rattika Rhienpanish (Mai Thai Restaurant, London), Vidhisha Nayanthara Samarasekara, Philip Stott (London School of Oriental and African Studies), Dusadee Swangviboonpong (London School of Oriental and African Studies), Thai Airways (London), William Warren (Bangkok), Terri S Yamaka (TAT, London).

PHOTOGRAPHY PERMISSIONS
Dorling Kindersley would like to thank the following for their assistance and kind permission to photograph at their establishments: Ancient City, Ayutthaya Historical Park, Ban Chiang National Museum, Ban Phin (House of Opium), Chakra Bongse House, Chan Kasem National Museum, Chao Sam Phraya National Museum, Chiang Mai National Museum, In Buri National Museum, Jim Thompson's Thai Silk Shop, Kamphaeng Phet Historical Park, Khon Kaen National Museum, Khorat (Nakhon Ratchasima) National Museum, Lampang National Museum, Lamphun National Museum, Lop Buri National Museum, Muang Tam Historical Park, Nakhon Pathom National Museum, Nakhon Si Thammarat National Museum, Nan National Museum, Narai Ratchaniwet Palace, National Gallery, National Museum (Bangkok), Oriental Hotel, Pha Taem, Phimai National Museum, Phnom Rung Historical Park, Prasart Museum, Ramkamhaeng National Museum, Ratchaburi National Museum, Royal Barge Museum, Sawankha Woranayok National Museum, Siriraj Hospital, Si Satchanalai-Chalieng Historical Park, Songkhla National Museum, Sukhothai Historical Park, Surin National Museum, Ubon Ratchathani National Museum, U Thong National Museum. Also all the other temples, museums, hotels, restaurants, shops, galleries and sights too numerous to thank individually.

PICTURE CREDITS
t = top; tl = top left; tlc = top left center; tc = top center; trc = top right center; tr = top right; cla = center left above; ca = center above; cra - center right above; cl = center left; c = center; cr = center right; clb = center left below; cb = center below; crb = center right below; bl = bottom left; bc = bottom center; bcl - bottom center left; br = bottom right; (d) = detail.

The publisher would like to thank the following individuals, companies and picture libraries for kind permission to reproduce their photographs.

THE NATIONAL MUSEUM (BANGKOK): 50tl, 51cl, tc, 58tl, 58–59c, 84tl, tr, cl, 85tcb, cr, crb, 75cr.

ARDEA LONDON: Francois Gohier 201tl; Wardene Weisser 201lb; ASIA ACCESS: Jeffrey Alford 370t; Naomi Duguid 228, 370b; ASIA IMAGES: © 1988 38–39c, 42b; © 1993 Matthew Burns 43cr, 257br, 342, 471crb; © 1995 Matthew Burns 34br; © 1990 Allen W Hopkins 273b, 298tr; © 1991 Allen W Hopkins 445b; © 1995 Allen W Hopkins 83br, 431t; AUSCAPES INTERNATIONAL:Kevin Deacon 339ca; AXIOM: © 1995 Jim Holmes 292c/b.

BAN PHIN (HOUSE OF OPIUM): 223cb, 238b; CHACRIT BOONSOM: 446t; BFI STILLS POSTERS & DESIGNS: © 1974 Danjaq, LLC and United Artists Corporation Inc. All Rights Reserved 357br; THE BOWERS MUSEUM OF CULTURAL ART: 50cl/clb; ASHLEY J BOYD: 307c, 313c, 331cl/cr, 335b, 338tl/ca/cb/ bl/br, 339c/br/ bc/ bl, 347cr, 349b, 376c/bl; BY PERMISSION OF THE BRITISH

LIBRARY: Manuscript Or 14025: 26–27c; BRITISH THAI BOXING COUNCIL:Tony Moore 40tl

DEMETRIO CARRASCO: 19br, 28cla, 42tl, 43bl, 274, 290–1; JEAN-LOUP CHARMET 223cra, 254–5c, 255br; BRUCE COLEMAN LTD: © Werner Layer 201c; © J Zwaenepoel 201tr; CRESCENT PRESS AGENCY: 383tl; Joe Cummings 285b; Ron Emmons 299c; David Henley 19c, 22tr, 26tr, 34tl, 36bl/br, 37bra/br, 40clb, 47t, 49b, 57br, 59cla, 60tl/cbr, 61t/ca/b, 62tl/ca, 63t, 64b, 65b, 77cr, 87b, 95t/ bra, 116tl/cb, 117ca/br, 121t, 129t/cra/cr/clb/cb/cl/cbc/crb/bl/bc/bra/br, 130b, 152tl, 153tl/ br, 165t, 196tl/tr/cb/ br, 197tl/br, 198tr, 214tl, 215b, 216t/b, 243t, 244t, 265b, 272, 337tl/br/ bl, 366c, 367tr, 381c, 382c, 386cl, 387bl, 442cr, 432br, 449 inset, 454u, 464t, John Hobday 24bla, 209cr; Daniel Kestenholz 98ca; Rainer Krack 26tl, 345b, 355cr, 386bl, 407t, 450br; GERALD CUBITT: 20tc, 24 all except bla, 25 all except crb/bl, 51tl, 77tl, 79t, 101br, 127t, 129cla, 149t/cb, 174tl/tr/ bl, 175t all, 181t, 195b, 197bl, 200t/c/cb, 204b, 209cl/ bl, 211t, 213bl, 220tl/cb/b, 221tl/ca/cb, 223bl, 239bl, 244c, 245t, 246bc, 270ca, 276cb, 279t, 287cla, 296ca/cb, 297br, 300-1c, 302, 305b, 313b, 316c, 317, 336t, 339tl, 340tl/ca/ cb/bl/bc, 341tl/tr/c, 344bl, 345t, 346c, 360c/b, 363cdb, 371tl/cl, 375c, 385b, 433tl, 434bl, 446bl, 459tl; MICHAEL CUTHBERT: 360t,, 361c, 366br.

JAMES DAVIS TRAVEL PHOTOGRAPHY: 149b, 298ca, 334c; JEAN-LEO DUGAST: 114r, 26cl, 441tc.

JOHN EVERINGHAM: 4t,5t, 22bl, 23tl, 26br, 34cl, 35tc, 36–7c, 37cra/cr,/crb/ bl, 41cra, 44b, 75bl, 128tl, 210b, 211cr, 230b, 257cb, 299b, 326b, 327t/b, 328bl, 338tr, 341b, 344cl, 348cl, 352tr, 353t, 354cl, 356ca, 442tr, 444tc, 445cla.

FEATURE MAGAZINE: 311t, 371br; MICHAEL FREEMAN: 19tl, 22tl, 34tr, 38cla/crac, 45ca, 52–3c, 53tl, 54c/clb, 57t/ ca/crb, 59t/bl, 60bl, 65t/cl, 79b, 80b, 81b, 101t, 103b, 116bc, 132b, 150ca/cb/br/brb, 151crb/bl, 168t, 169tr, 170tl, 177b, 181b, 190b, 194t, 196ca, 197tr/ ca, 198b, 199t/bl/brb, 202, 203b, 215ca, 250–1, 253br, 254c, 255tl, 260b, 300ca, 301c, 320t, 321b, 132bl, 347tl, 407c, 434c, 439clc; TIM FORSYTH:197cb, 246bl.

GRAMMY ENTERTAINMENT PUBLIC COMPANY LTD: 441cl.

ROBERT HARDING PICTURE LIBRARY: 44t, 68cbl, 70c, 78c, 226b, 256tr, 257tl, 279cr/br, 339tr, 442clb; © Alain Evrard 16, 22cb, 43t, 45cb, 112bl; © Robert McCleod 45b; © Luca Tettoni 261t, 268b; © Ken Wilson 171b; CHRISTINE HEMMET: 27bl, 373bra; THE HUTCHISON LIBRARY: 3c, © Robert Francis 470tl; Jeremy Horner 195c.

THE IMAGE BANK: 11tr; © Peter Hendrie 76tr; © Andrea Pistolesi 126.

JEWELRY REALTY LTD, BANGKOK: 300tl, 301tr. DR OY KANCHAVANIT: 347bc; SUTHEP KRITSANAVARIN: 125cl.

FRANK LANE PICTURE AGENCY: © D Fleetham/Silvestris 25cb; © T & P Garner 340br; © David Hosking 158b; © E & D Hosking 174cb, 200b, 353c; © L Lee Rue 25bl; © T Whittaker 276tr; © De Zylva 331b.

MAGNUM: © Marc Riboud 255bl; STUART MILLER: 361b; . THE ORIENTAL BANGKOK: 108br.

PHOTOBANK (BANGKOK): 1, 8–9, 20c, 21t, 22–3c, 23tr/cra, 27tl/cra, 34–5c, 35bl, 36tr/cl, 37t, 38tl/tr/clb/br, 39 all, 42c, 49t, 50ca,/cr, 51ca/bla/bra, 52tl,/ca/c, 53ca/ cb, 54cla, 55crb, 56clb, 58c/b, 60cla, 62–3c, 63cb, 64–5c, 65cr, 68tr, 71tc, 76b, 84bl, 85tl, 95c/bl/br, 125cra/crb/b, 146–7, 148t/b, 149ca, 150–1c, 151ca, 152ca, 153c, 155b, 160b, 166tl, 172–3, 174cl, 185b, 194cl, 206b, 220ca, 223br, 239br, 245b, 253c, 254b, 284c, 294–5, 297b, 298tl, 299t, 300b, 307b, 314, 315b, 318c, 320b, 322bl/ br, 336bl/ br, 340tr, 349tl, 350b, 355t, 357tl/tr, 362b, 363tl,tr/ b, 374c, 406c, 407b, 410tr/bl, 436cla, 437c, 439cra, 440t/cla/br, 444cl, 466br, 472b; PHOTOBANK (SINGAPORE): 18t, 26bl, 35cl, 38bl, 39cra/bra, 40cra, 40–1c, 41tc, 48, 50–1c, 51ca/51cbr, 52cbc, 54tl, 55tc/cla, 56cla/cra, 59bca, 60ca/ cra, 60–1c, 61cbr, 62cb/bc, 64cr, 69ca/b, 81t, 82b, 88ca, 91t, 102b, 116tr/cl, 117t/cr, 120b, 121b, 151tl/crb, 152l, 152–3c, 154, 168b, 169tl, 170c, 176, 196bl, 196–7c, 198cla, 198–9c, 199tr/ca/cb/bra, 214ca, 215t, 216c, 231t, 243 all except t, 246tr, 247 all, 252clb/bc, 255c, 257bl/bc, 258, 337c, 373br, 434tr; PHOTO EFEO: 255tr; PICTOR INTERNATIONAL: 2–3, 4b, 47b, 66–7, 194br, 334b, 343b, 356bl, 358–9; PICTURES COLOUR LIBRARY: 65crb, 237tr, 296b; POPPERFOTO: 111b.

RIVER BOOKS (BANGKOK): 27crb, 64cl, 98clb, 151tr. SEACO PICTURE LIBRARY: 455cr, 469t;SCIENCE PHOTO LIBRARY: CNE, 1988 Distribution Spot Image 10bl; TONY STONE IMAGES: Glen Allison 44c, 324–5; Marcus Brooke 387br; David Hanson 18b; Hideo Kurihara 104–5; Ed Pritchard 473b; SUPERSTOCK LTD: 122.l, 320t.

THAI AIRWAYS INTERNATIONAL PUBLIC COMPANY LTD: 466t/cl; JIM THOMPSON'S THAI SILK COMPANY: 256cl/cr/b; TOURISM AUTHORITY OF THAILAND: 21cr, 46b, 263c/bl; TRAVEL INK: Alan Hartley 68ca, 123t, 297t, 298cb, 304b, 316b, 386cb; Pauline Thornton 17ca, 122bl.

WELLCOME INSTITUTE LIBRARY (LONDON): 223cla.

Front endpaper: All special photography except Asia Access/ Naomi Duguid tlc; Asia Images © 1993 Matthew Burns bl; CRESCENT PRESS AGENCY: Photo David Henley tr; GERALD CUBITT crc; JAMES DAVIS TRAVEL PHOTOGRAPHY blc; MICHAEL FREEMAN tl; PHOTOBANK BANGKOK cr; PHOTOBANK (SINGAPORE) cl, clc, trc.
Back endpaper: All special photography.
Jacket Front - DK Picture Library: Philip Blenkinsop cb; Stuart Isett cbr; Corbis: Danny Lehman bl; Robert Hardy Picture Library: Main image. Back - DK Picture Library: Philip Blenkinsop b; Robert Hardy Picture Library: Ellen Rooney t. Spine - Robert Hardy Picture Library.

All other pictures © Dorling Kindersley. See www.dkimages.com for more information.

SPECIAL EDITIONS OF DK TRAVEL GUIDES

Phrase Book

THAI IS A TONAL LANGUAGE and regarded by most linguists as head of a distinct language group, though it incorporates many Sanskrit words from ancient India, and some of modern English ones, too. There are five tones: mid, high, low, rising, and falling. The particular tone, or pitch, at which each syllable is pronounced determines its meaning. For instance "mâi" (falling tone) means "not," but "mǎi" (rising tone) is "silk." The Thai script, meanwhile, is one of the most elaborate in the world, running left to right and using over 80 letters. In the third column of this phrase book is a phonetic transliteration for English speakers, including guidance for tones in the form of accents. This differs from the system used elsewhere in the guide, which follows the Thai Royal Institute's recommended romanization of common names.

GUIDELINES FOR PRONUNCIATION

When reading the phonetics, pronounce syllables as if they form English words. For instance:

a	as in "**a**go"
e	as in "h**e**n"
i	as in "th**i**n"
o	as in "**o**n"
u	as in "g**u**n"
ah	as in "r**a**ther"
ai	as in "Th**ai**"
air	as in "p**air**"
ao	as in "M**ao** Zedong"
ay	as in "d**ay**"
er	as in "**e**nter"
ew	as in "f**ew**"
oh	as in "g**o**"
oo	as in "b**oo**t"
OO	as in "b**oo**k"
oy	as in "t**oy**"
g	as in "**g**ive"
ng	as in "si**ng**"

These sounds have no close equivalents in English:

eu	can be likened to a sound of disgust – the sound could be written as "**errgh**"
bp	a single sound between a "b" and a "p'
dt	a single sound between a "d" and a "t"

Note that when "p," "t," and "k" occur at the end of Thai words, the sound is "swallowed." Also note that many Thais use an "l" instead of an "r" sound.

THE FIVE TONES

Accents indicate the tone of each syllable.

no mark	The **mid tone** is voiced at the speaker's normal, even pitch.
á é í ó ú	The **high tone** is pitched slightly higher than the mid tone.
à è ì ò ù	The **low tone** is pitched slightly lower than the mid tone.
ǎ ě ǐ ǒ ǔ	The **rising tone** sounds like a questioning pitch, starting low and rising.
â ê î ô û	The **falling tone** sounds similar to an English speaker stressing a one-syllable word for emphasis.

MALE AND FEMALE POLITE FORMS

In polite speech, Thai men add the particle "**krúp**" at the end of each sentence; women add "**ká**" at the end of questions and "**kâ**" at the end of statements. These particles have been omitted from all but the most essential polite terms in this phrase book, but they should be used as much as possible. The polite forms of the word "I" are, for men, "**pǒm**" and, for women, "**dee-chún**."

IN AN EMERGENCY

Help!	ช่วยด้วย	chôo-ay dôo-ay!
Fire!	ไฟไหม้	fai mâi!
Where is the nearest hospital?	แถวนี้มีโรงพยาบาล อยู่ที่ไหน	tǎir-o née mee rohng pa-yah-bahn yòo têe-nǎi?
Call an ambulance!	เรียกรถพยาบาล ให้หน่อย	rêe-uk rót pa-yah-bahn hâi nòy!
Call the police!	เรียกตำรวจให้หน่อย	rêe-uk dtum ròo-ut hâi nòy!
Call a doctor!	เรียกหมอให้หน่อย	rêe-uk mǒr hâi nòy!

COMMUNICATION ESSENTIALS

Yes.	ใช่ or ครับ/ค่ะ	châi or krúp/kâ
No.	ไม่ใช่ or ไม่ครับ/ไม่ค่ะ	mâi châi or mâi krúp/ mâi kâ
May I have ...?	ขอ ...	kǒr ...
Please can you ...?	ช่วย ...	chôo-ay ...
Thank you.	ขอบคุณ	kòrp-kOOn
No, thank you.	ไม่เอา ขอบคุณ	mâi ao kòrp-kOOn
Excuse me/sorry.	ขอโทษ (ครับ/ค่ะ)	kǒr-tôht (krúp/kâ)
Never mind.	ไม่เป็นไร	mâi bpen rai
Hello.	สวัสดี (ครับ/ค่ะ)	sa-wùt dee (krúp/kâ)
Goodbye.	ลาก่อนนะ	lah gòrn ná
Here.	ที่นี่	têe-nêe
There.	ที่โน่น	têe-nûn
What?	อะไร	a-rai?
Why?	ทำไม	tum-mai?
Where?	ที่ไหน	têe nǎi?
How?	ยังไง	yung ngai?

USEFUL PHRASES

How are you?	คุณสบายดีหรือ (ครับ/คะ)	kOOn sa-bai dee reu (krúp/kà)?
Very well, thank you – and you?	สบายดี (ครับ/ค่ะ) แล้วคุณล่ะ	sa-bai dee (krúp/kà) – láir-o kOOn lâ?
What is your name?	คุณชื่ออะไร (ครับ/คะ)	kOOn chêu a-rai (krúp/kâ)?
My name is ...	(ผม/ดิฉัน) ชื่อ ...	(pǒm/dee-chún) chêu ....
Where is/are ...?	... อยู่ที่ไหน	.... yòo têe-nǎi?
How do I get to ...?	... ไปยังไง	.... bpai yung- ngai?
Do you speak English?	คุณพูดภาษาอังกฤษ เป็นไหม	kOOn pôot pah-sǎh ung-grìt bpen mái?
I understand.	เข้าใจ	kâo-jai
I don't understand.	ไม่เข้าใจ	mâi kâo-jai
Could you speak slowly?	ช่วยพูดช้าๆหน่อย ได้ไหม	chôo-ay pôot cháh cháh nòy dâi mái?
I can't speak Thai.	พูดภาษาไทย ไม่เป็น	pôot pah-sǎh tai mâi bpen
I don't know.	ไม่ทราบ or ไม่รู้	mâi sâhp or mâi ròo

USEFUL WORDS

wife	ภรรยา	pun-ra-yah
husband	สามี	săh-mee
daughter(s)	ลูกสาว	lôok săo
son(s)	ลูกชาย	lôok chai
woman/women	ผู้หญิง	pôo-yĭng
man/men	ผู้ชาย	pôo-chai
child/children	เด็ก	dèk
big	ใหญ่	yài
small	เล็ก	lék
hot	ร้อน	rórn
cold	เย็น or หนาว	yen or năo
good	ดี	dee
bad	ไม่ดี	mâi dee
enough	พอ	por
well	สบายดี	sa-bai dee
open	เปิด	bpèrt
closed	ปิด	bpìt
left	ซ้าย	sái
right	ขวา	kwăh
straight ahead	อยู่ตรงหน้า	yòo dtrong nâh
between	ระหว่าง	ra-wàhng
on the corner of	ตรงหัวมุม	dtrong hŏo-a mOOm
near	ใกล้	glâi
far	ไกล	glai
up	ขึ้น	kêun
down	ลง	long
early	เช้า	cháo
late	ช้า or สาย	cháh or săi
entrance	ทางเข้า	tahng kâo
exit	ทางออก	tahng òrk
toilet	ห้องน้ำ	hôrng náhm
free/no charge	ฟรี	free

TELEPHONING

Where is the nearest public telephone?	แถวนี้มีโทรศัพท์ อยู่ที่ไหน	tăir-o née mee toh-ra-sùp yòo têe-năi?
Can I call abroad from here?	จะโทรศัพท์ไปต่าง ประเทศจาก ที่นี่ได้ไหม	ja toh bpai dtàhng bpra-tâyt jàhk têe nêe dâi mái?
I'd like to reverse the charges.	ขอให้เก็บเงิน ปลายทาง	kŏr hâi gèp ngern bplai tahng
Hello, this is ... speaking.	ฮันโล (ผม/ดิฉัน) ... พูด (ครับ/ค่ะ)	hello (pŏm/dee-chún) ... pôot (krúp/kâ)
I would like to speak to ...	ขอพูดกับคุณ ... หน่อย (ครับ/ค่ะ)	kŏr pôot gùp khun ... nòy (krúp/kâ)
May I leave a message?	ขอฝากสั่งอะไร หน่อยได้ไหม	kŏr fàhk sùng a-rai nòy dâi mái?
Could you speak up a little, please?	ช่วยพูดดังๆหน่อย ได้ไหม	chôo-ay pôot dung dung nòy dâi mái?
Hold on.	รอสักครู่	ror sùk krôo
I'll call back later.	เดี๋ยวจะโทรมาใหม่	dĕe-o ja toh mah mài
local call	โทรศัพท์ภายใน ท้องถิ่น	toh-ra-sùp pai nai tórng tìn
phone booth/kiosk	ตู้โทรศัพท์	dtôo toh-ra-sùp
phone card	บัตรโทรศัพท์	but toh-ra-sùp

SHOPPING

How much does this cost?	นี่ราคาเท่าไร	nêe rah-kah tâo-rài?
I would like ...	ต้องการ ...	dtôrng-gahn ...
Do you have ...?	มี ... ไหม	mee ... mái?
I am just looking.	ชมดูเท่านั้น	chom doo tâo-nún
Do you take credit cards/travelers' checks?	รับบัตรเครดิต/เช็คเดิน ทางไหม	rub but cray-dit/ chék dern tang mái?
What time do you open/close?	เปิด/ปิดกี่โมง	bpèrt/bpìt gèe mohng?
Can you ship this overseas?	ส่งของนี้ไปต่าง ประเทศได้ไหม	sòng kŏng nee bpai dtàhng bpra-tâyt dâi mái?
Does it come in other colors?	มีสีอื่นอีกไหม	mee sĕe èun èek mái?
black	สีดำ	sĕe dum
blue	สีน้ำเงิน	sĕe núm ngern
green	สีเขียว	sĕe kĕe-o
red	สีแดง	sĕe dairng
white	สีขาว	sĕe kăo
yellow	สีเหลือง	sĕe lĕu-ung
cheap	ถูก	tòok
expensive	แพง	pairng
gold	ทอง	torng
hill-tribe handicrafts	หัตถกรรมชาวเขา	hùt-ta-gum chao kăo
ladies' wear	เสื้อผ้าสตรี	sêu-pâh sa-dtree
silver	เงิน	ngern
Thai silk	ผ้าไหมไทย	pâh-măi tai
bookstore	ร้านขายหนังสือ	ráhn kăi núng-sĕu
department store	ห้าง	hâhng
market	ตลาด	dta-làht
newsstand	ร้านขายหนังสือพิมพ์	ráhn kăi núng-sĕu pim
pharmacy	ร้านขายยา	ráhn kăi yah
shoe shop	ร้านขายรองเท้า	ráhn kăi rorng táo
supermarket	ซุปเปอร์มาเก็ต	sÓOp-bpèr-mah-gèt
tailor	ร้านตัดเสื้อ	ráhn dtùt sêu-a

SIGHTSEEING

travel agent	บริษัทนำเที่ยว	bor-ri-sùt num têe-o
tourist office	สำนักงานการ ท่องเที่ยว	sŭm-núk ngahn gahn tôrng têe-o
tourist police	ตำรวจท่องเที่ยว	dtum-ròo-ut tôrng têe-o
closed on public holidays	ปิดวันหยุดราชการ	bpit wun yÒOt râht-cha-gahn
beach	หาด or ชายหาด	hàht or chai-hàht
cave	ถ้ำ	thûm
cliff	หน้าผา	nâh păh
coral	หินปะการัง	hĭn bpa-gah-rung
elephant camp	ค่ายช้าง	kâi cháhng
festival	งานออกร้าน	ngahn òrk ráhn
hill/mountain	เขา	kăo
hill-tribe village	หมู่บ้านชาวเขา	mòo bâhn chao kăo
historical park	อุทยานประวัติศาสตร์	ÒO-ta-yahn bpra wùt sàht
island (ko)	เกาะ	gòr

lake	ทะเลสาบ	ta-lay sàhp
temple (wat)	วัด	wút
museum	พิพิธภัณฑ์	pí-pít-ta-pun
national park	อุทยานแห่งชาติ	ÒO-ta yahn hàirng châht
old town	เมืองเก่า	meu-ung gòw
palace	วัง	wang
park/garden	สวน	sǒo-un
river	แม่น้ำ	mâir náhm
ruins	โบราณสถาน	boh-rahn sa-tǎhn
Thai boxing	มวยไทย	moo-ay tai
Thai massage	นวด	nôo-ut
trekking	การเดินทางเท้า	gahn dern tahng táo
waterfall	น้ำตก	náhm dtòk
zoo	สวนสัตว์	sǒo-un sàt

TRANSPORTATION

When does the train for ... leave?	รถไฟไป ... ออกเมื่อไร	rót fai bpai ... òrk meu-rài?
How long does it take to get to ...?	ใช้เวลานาน เท่าไรไปถึงที่ ...	chái way-lah nahn tâo-rài bpai těung têe ...?
A ticket to ... please.	ขอตั๋วไป ... หน่อย (ครับ/ค่ะ)	kǒr dtǒo-a bpai ... nòy (krúp/kâ)
Do I have to change?	ต้องเปลี่ยนรถ หรือเปล่า	dtông bplèe-un rót réu bplào?
I'd like to reserve a seat, please.	ขอจองที่นั่ง	kǒr jorng têe nûng
Which platform for the ... train?	รถไฟไป ... อยู่ ชานชาลาไหน	rót fai bpai ... yòo chahn cha-lah nǎi?
What station is this?	ที่นี่สถานีอะไร	têe nêe sa-tǎhn-nee a-rai?
Where is the bus stop?	ป้ายรถเมล์อยู่ที่ไหน	bpài rót may yòo têe-nǎi?
Where is the bus station?	สถานีรถเมล์อยู่ที่ไหน	sa-tǎhn-nee rót may yòo têe-nǎi?
Which buses go to ...?	รถเมล์สายไหนไป ...	rót may sǎi nǎi bpai ...?
What time does the bus for ... leave?	รถเมล์ไป ... ออกกี่โมง	rót may bpai ... òrk gèe mohng?
Would you tell me when we get to ...?	ถึง ... แล้ว ช่วยบอกด้วย	těung ... láir-o chôo-ay bòrk dôo-ay?
Do you know... Road?	รู้จักถนน ... ไหม	róo-jùk ta-nǒn ... mái?
Is it far?	ไกลไหม	glai mái?
Turn left.	เลี้ยวซ้าย	lée-o sái
Turn right.	เลี้ยวขวา	lée-o kwǎh
Go straight.	เลยไปอีก	ler-ee bpai èek
Park over there.	จอดที่นั่น	jòrt têe-nôhn
Park right here.	จอดตรงนี้	jòrt dtrong née
air-conditioned bus	รถปรับอากาศ	rót bprùp ah-gàht
arrivals	ถึง	těung
booking office	ที่จองตั๋ว	têe jorng dtǒo-a
bus station	สถานีรถเมล์	sa-tǎhn-nee rót may
departures	ออก	òrk
baggage room	ที่ฝากของ	têe fàhk kǒrng
ordinary bus	รถธรรมดา	rót tum-ma-dah
tour bus	รถทัวร์	rót too-a

ticket	ตั๋ว	dtǒo-a
ferry	เรือข้ามฟาก	reu-a kâhm fâhk
train	รถไฟ	rót fai
railroad station	สถานีรถไฟ	sa-tǎhn-nee rót fai
moped	รถมอเตอร์ไซค์	rót mor-dter-sai
bicycle	รถจักรยานต์	rót jùk-gra-yahn
taxi	แท็กซี่	táirk-sêe
airport	สนามบิน	sa-nǎhm bin

BARGAINING

How much is this?	นี่ราคาเท่าไร	nêe rah-kah tâo-rai?
How much to go to ...?	ไป ... เท่าไร	bpai ... tâo-rài?
That's a little expensive.	แพงไปหน่อย	pairng bpai nòy
Could you lower the price a bit?	ลดราคาหน่อยได้ไหม	lót rah-kah nòy dâi mái?
How about ... baht?	... บาทได้ไหม	... bàht dâi mái?
Will you go for ... baht?	... บาทไปไหม	... bàht bpai mái?
I'll settle for ... baht.	... บาทก็แล้วกัน	... bàht gôr láir-o gun

STAYING IN A HOTEL

Do you have a vacant room?	มีห้องว่างไหม	mee hôrng wâhng mái?
double/twin room	ห้องคู่	hôrng kôo
single room	ห้องเดี่ยว	hôrng dèe-o
air-conditioned room	ห้องแอร์	hôrng air
I have a reservation.	จองห้องไว้แล้ว	jorng hôrng wái láir-o
I'd like a room for one night/three nights.	(ผม/ดิฉัน) จะพักอยู่ คืนหนึ่ง/สามคืน	(pǒm/dee-chún) ja púk yòo keun nèung / sǎhm keun
What is the charge per night?	ค่าห้องวันละเท่าไร	kâh hôrng wun la tâo-rài?
I don't know yet how long I'll stay.	ไม่ทราบว่าจะอยู่นาน เท่าไร	mâi sâhp wâh ja yòo nahn tâo-rài
May I see the room first please?	ขอดูห้องก่อนได้ไหม	kǒr doo hôrng gòrn dâi mái?
May I leave some things in the safe?	ขอฝากของไว้ในตู้เซฟ ได้ไหม	kǒr fàhk kǒrng wái nai dtôo sáyf dâi mái?
Will you spray some mosquito repellent, please?	ช่วยฉีดยากันยุงให้ หน่อยได้ไหม	chôo-ay chèet yah gun yOOng hâi nòy dâi mái?
air conditioner	เครื่องปรับอากาศ	krêu-ung bprùp ah-gàht
bedroom	ห้องนอน	hôrng norn
bill	บิล	bin
fan	พัดลม	pùt lom
hotel	โรงแรม	rohng-rairm
key	กุญแจ	gOOn-jair
manager	ผู้จัดการ	pôo-jùt-gahn
mosquito screen	มุ้งลวด	mÓOng lôo-ut
shower	ฝักบัว	fùk boo-a
swimming pool	สระว่ายน้ำ	sà wâi náhm
toilet/bathroom	ห้องน้ำ	hôrng náhm

EATING OUT

A table for two please.	ขอโต๊ะสำหรับ สองคน	kŏr dtó sŭm-rùp sŏrng kon
May I see the menu?	ขอดูเมนูหน่อย	kŏr doo may-noo nòy
Do you have ...?	มี ... ไหม	mee ... mái?
I'd like ...	ขอ	kŏr ...
Not too spicy, ok?	ไม่เอาเผ็ดมากนะ	mâi ao pèt mâhk na
Is it spicy?	เผ็ดไหม	pèt mái?
I can eat Thai food.	ทานอาหารไทยเป็น	tahn ah-hăhn tai bpen
May I have a glass of water, please.	ขอน้ำแข็งเปล่า แก้วหนึ่ง	kŏr núm kăirng bplào gâir-o nèung
I didn't order this.	นี่ไม่ได้สั่ง (ครับ/ค่ะ)	nêe mâi dâi sùng (krúp/kâ)
Waiter/waitress!	คุณ (ครับ/คะ)	kOOn (krúp/kâ)
That was an excellent meal.	อร่อยมาก (ครับ/ค่ะ)	a-ròy mâhk (krúp/kâ)
The check, please.	ขอบิลหน่อย (ครับ/ค่ะ)	kŏr bin nòy (krúp/kâ)
ashtray	ที่เขี่ยบุหรี่	têe-kèe-a bOO-rèe
bamboo shoots	หน่อไม้	nòr mái
banana	กล้วย	glôo-ay
beef	เนื้อวัว	néu-a woo-a
beer	เบียร์	bee-a
boiled	ต้ม	dtôm
bottle	ขวด	kòo-ut
bowl	ชาม	chahm
char-grilled	ย่าง	yâhng
chicken	ไก่	gài
chili	พริก	prík
chili paste	น้ำพริก	núm prík
chopsticks	ตะเกียบ	dta-gèe-up
coconut	มะพร้าว	ma-práo
coffee	กาแฟ	gah-fair
crab	ปู	bpoo
crispy noodles	หมี่กรอบ	mèe gròrp
custard apple	น้อยหน่า	nóy-nàh
deep fried	ทอด	tôrt
drink(s)	เครื่องดื่ม	krêu-ung dèum
dry noodles	ก๋วยเตี๋ยวแห้ง	gŏo-ay dtĕe-o hâirng
duck	เป็ด	bpèt
durian	ทุเรียน	tOO-ree-un
egg	ไข่	kài
egg noodles	บะหมี่	ba-mèe
fish	ปลา	bplah
fish sauce	น้ำปลา	núm bplah
fork	ส้อม	sôrm
fruit	ผลไม้	pŏn-la-mái
fruit juice	น้ำผลไม้	núm pŏn-la-mái
ginger	ขิง	kĭng
glass	แก้ว	gâir-o
iced coffee	กาแฟเย็น	ga-fair yen
iced water	น้ำแข็งเปล่า	núm kăirng bplào
jackfruit	ขนุน	ka-nŎOn
mango	มะม่วง	ma-môo-ung
Mekong whisky	แม่โขง	mâir-kŏhng
menu	เมนู	may-noo
morning glory	ผักบุ้ง	pùk bÔOng

mushroom	เห็ด	hèt
noodle soup	ก๋วยเตี๋ยวน้ำ	gŏo-ay dtĕe-o náhm
oven-cooked	อบ	òp
papaya	มะละกอ	ma-la-gor
pineapple	สับปะรด	sùp-bpa-rót
plate	จาน	jahn
pomelo	ส้มโอ	sôm oh
pork	เนื้อหมู	néu-a mŏo
rambutan	เงาะ	ngór
restaurant	ร้านอาหาร	ráhn ah-hăhn
rice	ข้าว	kâo
rice noodles	ก๋วยเตี๋ยว	gŏo-ay dtĕe-o
shrimp	กุ้ง	gÔOng
soy sauce	อาหารว่าง	ah-hăhn wâhng
snack	น้ำซีอิ๊ว	núm see éw
spoon	ช้อน	chórn
spring greens	ผักคะน้า	pùk ka-náh
squid	ปลาหมึก	bplah-mèuk
sticky rice	ข้าวเหนียว	kâo-nĕe-o
stir-fried	ผัด	pùt
sweet corn	ข้าวโพด	kâo pôht
tea	น้ำชา	núm chah
vegetables	ผัก	pùk
vinegar	น้ำส้ม	núm sôm
waiter	คนเสิร์ฟ	kon sèrp
waitress	คนเสิร์ฟหญิง	kon sèrp yĭng
water	น้ำ	náhm

HEALTH

I do not feel well.	รู้สึกไม่สบาย	róo-sèuk mâi sa-bai
I have a pain in ...	เจ็บที่ ...	jèp têe ...
It hurts here.	เจ็บตรงนี้	jèp dtrong née
It hurts all the time.	เจ็บตลอดเวลา	jèp dta-lòrt way-lah
It hurts only now and then.	เจ็บเป็นบางครั้ง บางคราว	jèp bpen bahng krúng bahng krao
I have a fever.	ตัวร้อนเป็นไข้	dtoo-a rórn bpen kâi
I'm allergic to ...	(ผม/ดิฉัน) แพ้ ...	(pŏm/dee-chún) páir ...
How many tablets do I take?	ต้องกินยากี่เม็ด ต่อครั้ง	dtông gin yah gèe mét dtòr krúng
accident	อุบัติเหตุ	OO-bùt-dti-hàyt
acupuncture	ฝังเข็ม	fŭng kĕm
ambulance	รถพยาบาล	rót pa-yah-bahn
aspirin	แอซพิริน or ยาแก้ไข้	air-sa-bprin or yah-gâir-kâi
asthma	โรคหืด	rôhk hèut
bite (by dog)	หมากัด	măh gùt
bite (by insect)	แมลงกัด	ma-lairng gùt
blood	เลือด	lêu-ut
burn	ไหม้	mâi
cholera	อหิวาต์	a-hi-wah
cough	ไอ	ai
dentist	ทันตแพทย์ or หมอฟัน	tun-dta-pâirt or mŏr fun
diabetes	โรคเบาหวาน	rôhk bao wăhn
diarrhea	ท้องเสีย	tórng sĕe-a
dizzy	เวียนหัว	wee-un hŏo-a
doctor	หมอ	mŏr
dysentery	โรคบิด	rôhk bìt

earache	ปวดหู	bpòo-ut hŏo
fever	ไข้	kâi
filling	อุดฟัน	Òot fun
hayfever	ไข้จาม	kâi jahm
headache	ปวดหัว	bpòo-ut hŏo-a
heart attack	หัวใจวาย	hŏo-a jai wai
hepatitis	ตับอักเสบ	dtùp ùk-sàyp
hospital	โรงพยาบาล	rohng pa-yah-bahn
injection	ฉีดยา	chèet yah
malaria	มาเลเรีย	mah-lay-ree-a
medicine	ยา	yah
penicillin	ยาเพนนิซีลลิน	yah pen-ní-seen-lin
prescription	ใบสั่งยา	bai sùng yah
prickly heat	ผด	pòt
rabies	โรคสุนัขบ้า	rôhk sÒO-nùk bâh
sore throat	เจ็บคอ	jèp kor
stomach ache	ปวดท้อง	bpòo-ut tórng
temperature	ตัวร้อน	dtoo-ah rórn
toothache	ปวดฟัน	boo-ut fun
traditional medicine	ยาแผนโบราณ	yah pǎirn boh-rahn
vomit	อาเจียน	ah-jee-un

Numbers

0	๐ or ศูนย์	sŏon
1	๑ or หนึ่ง	nèung
2	๒ or สอง	sŏrng
3	๓ or สาม	sǎhm
4	๔ or สี่	sèe
5	๕ or ห้า	hâh
6	๖ or หก	hòk
7	๗ or เจ็ด	jèt
8	๘ or แปด	bpàirt
9	๙ or เก้า	gâo
10	๑๐ or สิบ	sìp
11	๑๑ or สิบเอ็ด	sìp-èt
12	๑๒ or สิบสอง	sìp-sŏrng
13	๑๓ or สิบสาม	sìp-sǎhm
14	๑๔ or สิบสี่	sìp-sèe
15	๑๕ or สิบห้า	sìp-hâh
16	๑๖ or สิบหก	sìp-hòk
17	๑๗ or สิบเจ็ด	sìp-jèt
18	๑๘ or สิบแปด	sìp-bpàirt
19	๑๙ or สิบเก้า	sìp-gâo
20	๒๐ or ยี่สิบ	yêe-sìp
21	๒๑ or ยี่สิบเอ็ด	yêe-sìp-èt
22	๒๒ or ยี่สิบสอง	yêe-sìp-sŏrng
30	๓๐ or สามสิบ	sǎhm-sìp
40	๔๐ or สี่สิบ	sèe-sìp
50	๕๐ or ห้าสิบ	hâh-sìp
60	๖๐ or หกสิบ	hòk-sìp
70	๗๐ or เจ็ดสิบ	jèt-sìp
80	๘๐ or แปดสิบ	bpàirt-sìp
90	๙๐ or เก้าสิบ	gâo-sìp
100	๑๐๐ or หนึ่งร้อย	nèung róy
101	๑๐๑ or ร้อยเอ็ด	róy-èt
200	๒๐๐ or สองร้อย	sŏrng róy
1,000	๑๐๐๐ or หนึ่งพัน	nèung pun
1,001	๑๐๐๑ or หนึ่งพันหนึ่ง	nèung pun nèung
10,000	๑๐,๐๐๐ or หนึ่งหมื่น	nèung mèun
100,000	๑๐๐,๐๐๐ or หนึ่งแสน	nèung sǎirn

Time and Seasons

one minute	หนึ่งนาที	nèung nah-tee
one hour	หนึ่งชั่วโมง	nèung chôo-a mohng
half an hour	ครึ่งชั่วโมง	krêung chôo-a mohng
quarter of an hour	สิบห้านาที	sìp-hâh nah-tee
midnight	เที่ยงคืน	têe-ung keun
1am	ตีหนึ่ง	dtee nèung
2am	ตีสอง	dtee sŏrng
3am	ตีสาม	dtee sǎhm
4am	ตีสี่	dtee sèe
5am	ตีห้า	dtee hâh
6am	หกโมงเช้า	hòk mohng cháo
7am	เจ็ดโมงเช้า	jèt mohng cháo
	or โมงเช้า	or mohng cháo
8am	สองโมงเช้า	sŏrng mohng cháo
9am	สามโมงเช้า	sǎhm mohng cháo
10am	สี่โมงเช้า	sèe mohng cháo
11am	ห้าโมงเช้า	hâh mohng cháo
noon	เที่ยงวัน	têe-ung wun
1pm	บ่ายโมง	bài mohng
2pm	บ่ายสองโมง	bài sŏrng mohng
3pm	บ่ายสามโมง	bài sǎhm mohng
4pm	บ่ายสี่โมง	bài sèe mohng
5pm	ห้าโมงเย็น	hâh mohng yen
6pm	หกโมงเย็น	hòk mohng yen
7pm	ทุ่มหนึ่ง	tÔOm nèung
8pm	สองทุ่ม	sŏrng tÔOm
9pm	สามทุ่ม	sǎhm tÔOm
10pm	สี่ทุ่ม	sèe tÔOm
11pm	ห้าทุ่ม	hâh tÔOm
half past one (pm)	บ่ายโมงครึ่ง	bài mohng krêung
quarter past one (pm)	บ่ายโมงสิบห้านาที	bài mohng sìp-hâh nah-tee
quarter to two (pm)	อีกสิบห้านาทีบ่ายสองโมง	èek sìp-hâh nah-tee bài sŏrng mohng
a day	หนึ่งวัน	neung wun
a weekend	สุดสัปดาห์	sÒOt sùp-pah-dah
a week	หนึ่งอาทิตย์	nèung ah-tít
a month	หนึ่งเดือน	nèung deu-un
a year	หนึ่งปี	nèung bpee
Monday	วันจันทร์	wun jun
Tuesday	วันอังคาร	wun ung-kahn
Wednesday	วันพุธ	wun pÓOt
Thursday	วันพฤหัส	wun pa-réu-hùt
Friday	วันศุกร์	wun sÒOk
Saturday	วันเสาร์	wun sǎo
Sunday	วันอาทิตย์	wun ah-tít
cool season	หน้าหนาว	nâh nǎo
hot season	หน้าร้อน	nâh rórn
rainy season	หน้าฝน	nâh fǒn
vacation	วันหยุด	wun yÒOt
public holiday	วันหยุดประจำปี	wun yÒOt bpra-jum-bpee
Christmas	คริสต์มาส	krít-sa-maht
New Year	ปีใหม่	bpee mài
Thai New Year	สงกรานต์	sŏng-grahn
Chinese New Year	ตรุษจีน	dtrÒOt jeen

Bangkok City Centre

THON BURI
Pages 118–125
Street Finder maps 1, 5, 6

Bangkok Noi/Thon Buri Railway Station

National Museum

Wat Phra Kaeo

Grand Palace

Wat Pho

RATCHADAMNOEN KLANG

Phra Pin Klao Bridge

Memorial Bridge

Phra Pok Klao Bridge

YAOWARAT

Wongwian Yai Railway Station

OLD CITY
Pages 72–89
Street Finder maps 1, 2, 5

CHAO PHRAYA EXPRESS

Nonthaburi (Phibun 3)

Phibun 2

Wat Khian
Wat Took
Wat Khema
Phibun 1

Rama VI Bridge

This service operates daily from 6am to 6pm. Boats serve the piers shown here about every 10 minutes at peak times and about every 20 minutes otherwise.

Rama VI
Wat Soi Thong
Bang Pho

Kiek Kai

Wat Chan Samoson
Cholapatan
Phayap

Wat Thep Nari
Sang Hee

Krung Thon Bridge

Phra Pin Klao
(Wat Dao Dung)
Thewet

Rama VIII Bridge

Bangkok Noi/
Thon Buri
Railway Station
Wat Sam Phraya
Phra Athit

Phra Pin Klao Bridge

Phrannok
Maharaj
Chang
Tien
Rachinee
Saphan Phut
Ratchawong

Memorial Bridge
Phra Pok Klao Bridge
Krom Chaotha
(Harbour Dept)
Si Phraya
Wat Muang Khae
Oriental

Taksin Bridge
Wat Sawetchat
Sathorn (Central Pier)

Wat Chanyawat
Wat Ratcha Singkhon

0 kilometres 1

0 miles 1